GREEN GLORY™

Champions of the Hardwood·1998-2001

By Jack Ebling and John Lewandowski

Foreword by Tom Izzo

To thank everyone would take longer than the Parade of Champions did on April 5, 2000.

But special appreciation goes to everyone whose contribution has made Spartan Basketball what it is today.

Thanks to the players who made their dream a reality and made our jobs more enjoyable, from Mateen Cleaves to Mat Ishbia.

Thanks to the coaches who provided great access and a free flow of information, especially an open, honest Tom Izzo.

Thanks to Lanita Brown, Bob Ofoli and many other loyal fans who never lost hope when their heroes lost a game.

Thanks to the Lansing State Journal and Michigan State University, our employers, for their cooperation with this project.

Thanks to the late Ed Senyczko, a sports editor at the State Journal, and his friend Roger Valdiserri, a sports information director at Notre Dame, for giving two young men their starts many years ago.

Thanks to Earle Robinson, Larry Lage, Gordon Trowbridge, Steve Grinczel and Drew Sharp from the media and Terry Denbow, Mark Hollis, Matt Larson, Becky Olsen and Kevin Fowler of MSU for their assistance and input.

Thanks to friends Duane Vernon, Vickki Dozier, Jon Barkan and Lynn Torrico, parents Joseph and Marietta Lewandowski and associates Paul Viglianti and Gametime Sports & Entertainment for all their support.

Thanks to Lansing Printing, especially project coordinator Stacey Trzeciak and page designer Theresa Dunham, for input, understanding and patience.

Most of all, thanks to our families — our spouses, Robin Ebling and Teressa Lewandowski, and our pride-and-joy, Zach and Ali Ebling and Brock and Davis Lewandowski — for making our lives much more enjoyable.

— Jack Ebling and John Lewandowski

FOREWORD

The success of Michigan State University has been a team effort for nearly 150 years. That's especially true today for Spartan Basketball, where the whole is greater than the sum of the parts.

The day I succeeded Jud Heathcote as head coach in 1995, I said, "Don't expect me to do this all by myself. . . . If you do, it's not going to get done." And I really believe that. It takes a lot of people to build a championship program.

The things we've accomplished, especially the past three seasons, have been the result of hard work and teamwork. Without some incredible sacrifices and a sense of togetherness, this book would never have been written.

I have hundreds of people I'd like to thank. But first and foremost, I have to thank Jud. He gave me the opportunity to come here from Northern Michigan and eventually became the driving force in getting me this job.

If every successful coach has a great mentor, I'm incredibly lucky that way. Jud was my Marv Harshman. And that's saying a lot.

Second on the list would be Gordon Guyer, MSU's president at the time. When people wondered if I was right for the position, Gordon was the guy who helped push it through — and another "Yooper."

Someone who deserves more credit than he gets is George Perles. When I was talking about the Wisconsin job, he knew the A.D. and made a call to try to help me. Then, he was one of the first to say, "Have you thought about hanging on? . . . I think you can get the job here."

I also want to thank the players, the assistants, the managers, the support staff, the administration, the faculty and the fans. That covers just about everybody — and not because it's politically correct. If you want the truth, that's the truth around here.

It started with Steve Smith, my first recruit as an assistant in 1986. I can't forget the Steigenga-Peplowski-Montgomery class that gave me credibility. And I'll always love Eric Snow, who gave this program everything he had. Then, there was Antonio Smith, my first recruit as a head coach, and Jason Klein and Morris Peterson, the guys who came with him. Finally, I owe a lot to Mateen Cleaves, who wanted to win and never wavered. He took a chance and left as a champion.

Every assistant the past six years played an integral part in what we achieved: Stan Joplin with Mateen's recruitment, Stan Heath with Jason Richardson, Mike Garland with player development, Brian Gregory with scouting and preparation and Tom Crean as my right-hand man and a terrific recruiter.

Of all the programs that have gone from one level to the next, none have relied on support people more than this one. I really believe that. From the secretaries to the medical staff to everyone at the Clara Bell Smith Academic Center, they've all played a huge role.

Since we moved into Breslin Center in 1989, we've had three presidents and five athletic directors. No one knows how difficult that has been. But when Peter McPherson and I first talked about this job, we made some promises. If I've kept mine, he has kept his every bit as much as president.

The MSU Board of Trustees has been very supportive. And the faculty has been very good. We're starting to rebuild a bridge that was damaged. Professors see we're not a win-at-all-cost program. We do care about academics. We want to be successful on and off the court.

I've often said our fans are the key to a 44-game winning streak at home the past three sea-

FOREWORD

sons. We haven't had many non-sellouts since 1989. And that's a big reason why we have the best record in the Big Ten over the past 12 years.

Believe it or not, to go to The Palace last season and play Bowling Green before more than 22,000 fans, when they were expecting 14,000, was one of the highlights of the year. I loved it! But fans don't just help you win games. They help you get players by generating enthusiasm.

I still think Doug Weaver gave me the greatest compliment I've ever had when he said, "You're the ultimate program guy." I think I learned that from the people at Northern and from Jud, George and Ron Mason.

When everything was going so well, they'd meet Up North at George's place or Doug's place. Then, I'd have to hear the stories for 10 years. I remember Jud going to bat for George when things got tough. I remember Jud and Ron talking and publicly backing George as A.D. when that wasn't the popular thing to do. They said it was the right thing.

Jud used to say, "Nobody, ever, is bigger than the program." I don't think I ever could be. It takes too many people and too much cooperation. And I saw what happened when the relationship between the athletic department and the administration went from a marriage to a divorce. We're still reeling from that in some ways 11 years later.

When things have been down, we've been our own worst enemy. But when everyone pulls together as a family, we can do almost anything. And when we do well as a team, it's good for everyone at Michigan State University. When Michigan State goes to the Frozen Four or the Citrus Bowl or has a Rhodes Scholar, that's good for Spartan Basketball, too.

If we took a recruit to the football locker room or sat him near the penalty box in hockey, he always thought that was special. And if I can help Stacy Slobodnik sign a golfer or Joe Baum get a soccer player, that's what it's all about.

The joy in this job isn't just in winning. It's about building lasting relationships. That's how you bridge the past and the present. And that's how you build tradition, something the great programs have and the wannabes don't.

When we got ready for our 100-years celebration in 1999, Gus Ganakas was the one who pulled it all together. He didn't just bring the 20-year guys here. He brought the 60-year guys. And the letters I got when we hung the '57 Final Four banner made me appreciate this place even more.

To hear Johnny Green talk about doing situps in tense situations last season and saying, "If I could just give them two minutes…" or to know Morris Peterson gave Vince Carter grief in the locker room when we beat North Carolina meant almost as much as the win itself.

To think about all the guys who've worn this uniform is really something. There was "Smitty," who was great as a player and just as important as a generous supporter. There was "Magic," who talked to the guys a couple of times when it was really important. There was Gregory Kelser, who was always there for us, and Eric Snow, who called every week.

But it means a lot to the others, too — to Terry Donnelly, to "Bobo" Charles and to all the guys who've come back or followed us. When we get to another Final Four, I want to get all the basketball alumni and bring them by our hotel. I want them to meet the guys so our players can see what loyalty is all about.

We're playing for them — for every Spartan who ever lived and everyone who has ever been a part of Michigan State. The baton has been passed. But there's a long race to run. All I can promise is we'll work as hard as we can to win it.

Tom Izzo

CONTENTS

CONTENTS

THE PROGRAM

SPARTAN BASKETBALL

A priceless trophy was presented the night of Monday, April 3, 2000, in Indianapolis.

The Michigan State Spartans were kings of the college basketball world for the second time.

But that crowning achievement and the triumphs that followed didn't happen in "One Shining Moment."

They were the culmination of decades of effort by people who shared one goal, if not the same winners' platform.

The 62nd NCAA Division I Men's Basketball Championship was a tribute to all those people, not just the players and coaches in the RCA Dome.

Where did it all begin?

• With the return of point guard Mateen Cleaves on Jan. 5, 2000, after a 10-week absence with a stress fracture in his right foot?

• With lessons from a Final Four appearance in March 1999 in St. Petersburg, Fla., after the second of four straight Big Ten titles?

• With the first of seven straight wins over Michigan in 1998 and a seismic shift in public perception, thanks to cracks in Ann Arbor?

• With survival at South Florida and a shocking rout of fifth-ranked Purdue in December 1997, amid loud grumbling over a 4-3 start?

• With the arrival of Cleaves, Tom Izzo's first marquee recruit, a true coach-on-the-court and the leader of the "Flintstones" in 1996?

• With an upset of power-house Arkansas in the Great Eight in 1995, when MSU first crashed the offensive board with four players?

• With the appointment of Izzo as Jud Heathcote's hand-picked successor, when fools might have overlooked the only sane choice?

• With the the courage of President Cecil Mackey and the construction of Breslin Center when Jenison Field House was obsolete?

• With 1987's football win over Michigan that helped land a breakthough class, including Matt Steigenga, Mike Peplowski and Mark Montgomery?

• With the return of Izzo after the briefest of stops at Tulsa, thanks to a head coaching job at Siena for top MSU aide Mike Deane?

• With Izzo's persistence in persuit of Heathcote to hire him and pursuing a position that meant a $15,000 pay cut in 1983?

• With the school's first crown in 1979, a win over Indiana State in Salt Lake City that remains the highest-rated NCAA telecast?

• With the signing of Earvin "Magic" Johnson, a lightning bolt for Spartan Basketball that is still giving off sparks today?

• With the hiring of the hard-headed Heathcote, a little-known coach from Montana who mixed discipline and wit and never wavered?

• Or with the work of Gus Ganakas, who laid a firm foundation for Johnson's recruitment, then spent 25 years as a true team player?

Whatever the start, Spartan Basketball in 2001 is a product of all 15 of those things, as Izzo would be the first to tell you.

"I think it started with the '79 team — with Gus's work to get 'Magic' and the job Jud did with those guys," Izzo said. "That's considered the modern era. Nothing against the '57 (Final Four) team — I love those guys. But they don't carry any weight in recruiting. The '79 team brought national prominence. And I still use 'Magic' to this day.

"Probably the next major thing was Breslin. There were things between. You can look at some good years and bad years. But I don't think they changed the program. Breslin did. It gave credence to the program. It was finally a big-league atmosphere.

"I really believe the one thing Jud did that was big was to run a clean program. It was something no one could argue with. If we were in on a kid, people wouldn't think something was going on. That was something I fed off and tried to take to another level.

"And I still think Cleaves' signing was big. He could've gone anywhere. It was breaking through the 'Fab Five' and saying, 'Michigan's not going to get every player.' They'd have two guys at a position and somehow get a third one. That didn't mean we couldn't beat them in games. But it was always an underdog beating a favorite. We weren't on a par with them. Cleaves helped changed that."

All four of those factors were

SPARTAN BASKETBALL

"MAGIC" TOUCH *– Earvin "Magic" Johnson contributed 24 points, seven rebounds and five assists in Michigan State's 75-64 victory over Indiana State in the 1979 NCAA championship game. It marked the beginning of Johnson's rivalry with Larry Bird. More than 20 years later, MSU's recruiting pitches still feature "Magic."*

huge. But there's a major problem with Izzo's assessment — excessive modesty. Without his appointment, the maniacal work that followed and similar dedication from his staff and players, MSU Basketball would be a solid program, not a standard of excellence.

It is amazing that Izzo was anywhere near campus. He was rejected as an assistant by Heathcote once, then had to beg for an entry-level position. He could have more-than-tripled that $7,000 salary as a video coordinator for the New Jersey Nets. He would have been the head coach at Northern Michigan if not for a last-minute change-of-heart. He chose not to become the head coach at Michigan Tech a year later. And he resisted when Heathcote tried to nudge him out of the nest after each of his first two seasons at MSU.

"I'd applied to be an assistant here when I had a broken jaw in '82," Izzo said. "Mike Deane got the job that year. I don't know where I was on the list. But I'm sure I wasn't in the top three or four. And Mike wasn't Jud's first choice, either. I think he tried to hire Seth Greenberg (now the head coach at South Florida).

"When I came back a year later and asked to be the No. 3 assistant, Jud said I was overqualified. You have to remember, he came up at a time when there was one assistant. Now, he had Mike and Edgar Wilson. The third guy had been Frank Rourke. And that was more to help Frank than Jud. But Mike tried to change Jud's thinking. He

SPARTAN BASKETBALL

said, 'We've got to get more help around here!' You could have a part-timer and a grad assistant. So I became the part-time/g.a."

Just after he accepted that job, Izzo got a call from a former coach at NMU, Stan Albeck, about a leap to pro basketball. And when Albeck moved from New Jersey to the Chicago Bulls, he tried to hire his successor with the Wildcats, Glenn Brown, as an NBA assistant. That would have paved the way for Izzo, a 1977 Division II All-American, to return to the U.P.

"Stan offered me a job right away," Izzo said. "They'd just got-

ten this new computer system at the Meadowlands and needed someone to run it. They were going to pay me $25,000. But they couldn't come up with the money right away. I don't know if I'd have taken it or not — I probably would have.

"The next year, Stan got the Chicago job and was Michael Jordan's first NBA coach. Glenn was going with him. And I was getting the Northern job. I was 90-percent sure I'd take it. They were going to name me interim coach for a year. But Glenn had it all set up. The day they were supposed to

have the press conference, he called me at 9 a.m. His wife didn't want to go to Chicago. So he turned it down. Glenn would've been a good pro coach."

Maybe we never would have heard of Phil Jackson as an NBA genius. Maybe the Bulls wouldn't have won six world titles. And maybe Izzo would had been as successful at NMU or Michigan Tech as Dick Bennett was at Wisconsin-Green Bay before moving to Wisconsin.

"I was offered the Tech job my second year here," Izzo said. "That was close. After my first year, Jud

Photo Credit: Bruce Fox, University Relations

HEATHCOTE PASSES THE TORCH – *Jud Heathcote, the winningest coach in Michigan State basketball history, spent 12 years grooming Tom Izzo to become his successor. Give Heathcote credit. He knew exactly what he was doing when he handpicked Izzo to be his replacement. Over the last four seasons, Izzo has compiled a 115-25 record while leading the Spartans to four straight Big Ten regular-season titles, two Big Ten Tournament crowns and three straight Final Fours, including the 2000 NCAA championship.*

had called me in and said, 'I don't know if this is going to work.' I was a lot like him — stubborn. He used to say, 'You always think it's your way!' Of course, I had no say at all. But it was hard to adjust to the way Jud was. His favorite line was, 'I don't coach coaches.' You had to figure out what he wanted. Mike was very good at that. It was a lot harder for me.

"Again after my second year, Jud told me, 'Maybe you should look for a job.' But he wouldn't fire me. I said, 'No, I'm going to do a better job here!' And after my third year, Jud went to bat for me with Doug (Weaver, MSU's athletic director). That was when people were starting to pay the part-time guy $20,000, $30,000 or even $40,000 a year."

A job that began as a glorified go-fer could never match the chance to be a top assistant in a successful program like Tulsa's. But Izzo didn't realize how valued he was by J.D. Barnett, head coach of the Golden Hurricanes, until he tried to come home in 1986, just weeks after he had succeeded Arizona-bound "traitor" Kevin O'Neill.

"I'd just gotten J.D. to hire Flip Saunders as the part-timer — for about a grand more than I was making," Izzo said of the Minnesota Timberwolves coach. "Flip was the guy who almost got me killed. He was back in Minnesota and saw Mike had gone to Siena. Jud had just offered me the job. And not thinking anything bad, Flip called J.D. and said, 'Is Tom going back to Michigan State?'

Photo Credit: Bruce Fox, University Relations

HEATHCOTE AND HIS DISCIPLES — Jud Heathcote spent his final season on the sidelines with two of his prized pupils, Tom Izzo and Brian Gregory. The 1994-95 Spartans, led by Shawn Respert and Eric Snow, went 22-6 overall, including a second-place finish in the Big Ten at 14-4.

"It was 8 a.m., and I was already in the office when J.D. called. He said, 'Tom, what's going on?' I said, 'Nothing.' I was going to talk to him as soon as he hit the door. He said, 'Flip is looking for you.' I said, 'OK, I'll give him a call.' Then, J.D. said, "WHAT IN THE HELL IS GOING ON?" I said, 'J.D., I want to come out to your house and talk to you.' He said, 'Oh, no, you're not!'

"J.D. had just gone through the thing with Kevin, where he put

SPARTAN BASKETBALL

Photo Credit: Kevin Fowler, MSU Sports Information

EYE FOR TALENT – Tom Izzo played an integral role in signing future NBA All-Star Steve Smith, who returned to campus on Jan. 2, 1999, to have his jersey retired. Smith, a two-time All-American, ranks No. 2 on Michigan State's all-time scoring chart with 2,263 career points.

all his stuff outside. Now, the g.a. I was staying with, (ex-Georgia coach) Ron Jirsa, could hear him going on and on. He said, 'Tom, you'd better get out of here!' I said, 'OK, give me a ride back from my car dealer,' because J.D. kept screaming, 'Turn your car in!' But he'd already called Ron and told him not to talk to me. So I dropped off the car, jumped in a cab and came back. Right away, I said, 'Ron, where's my stuff?' Now, I'm really pissed."

Cooler heads prevailed when Izzo did what he has done so often in his life, talk through a tense situation with his best friend, Steve Mariucci, a football coach without

a macho mentality.

"I called Mariucci and said, 'What do I do?'" Izzo remembered. "He said, 'Do you have the job?' I said, 'Yeah, I got it at 7 this morning. Jud had to get it approved by (MSU vice president) Roger Wilkinson. . . . But I really feel bad. I wasn't looking for a job. It's just that this was a once-in-a-lifetime deal.' And Steve said, 'Tom, get the hell outta there!' I called the airport and was out on a 4:30 p.m. plane."

Homeward bound. Back with Heathcote. Time to be a sponge and a salesman. And there was no better mentor for someone who wanted to teach toughness and earn respect.

"Without Jud, I wouldn't be nearly as good a coach," Izzo said. "I thought Jud had a good way of handling the media. I used to marvel that there were people who were mad at him when he kept (arrest-plagued star) Scott Skiles, good basketball people, and he never held a grudge. He sort of understood it. He didn't like it. And he was going to fight for his guy. But Jud had the ability to forget. He'd be mad at a player on the court, walk off and tell him a joke on the way to the locker room. And it's a great quality to have when you can laugh at yourself. He made it through some tough times because of the way he dealt with people and because of his credibility."

The winningest coach in MSU history and a hero to many of his peers survived six losing seasons, the last two in 1986-87 and 1987-88. But Izzo's first recruit, a skinny kid Heathcote had spotted, Steve Smith, was a ray of hope. And after a 17-11 football win over Michigan en route to the 1988 Rose Bowl, Izzo scored huge points with Peplowski and Montgomery. Steigenga, the gem of the the class, would soon pick the Spartans over North Carolina.

"I don't think Jud thought of me as a head coach then," Izzo said. "But I think his thoughts of me started to change. He knew how much work I'd done. I must've talked to Steigenga's dad 200 straight days. That's when there were no rules on calls. And Jud would just shake his head. He gave me all the credit for that. He didn't give any to anyone else. But he didn't take any for himself, either."

Heathcote never needed to hog the spotlight. What he needed was someone who could recruit and build relationships without compromising the program's ethics or promising instant stardom. Breslin made that an easier sell. And Izzo was the perfect salesman.

The first time his name was mentioned publicly as a potential

successor to Heathcote was in 1989 in the *Lansing State Journal*, when Izzo and then-Kansas State coach Lon Kruger were suggested as eventual replacements after MSU beat the Wildcats in the Great Alaska Shootout.

But Heathcote had been watching a protege grow. From 1983 to 1995, he gradually assigned greater responsibility until he knew Izzo was ready to replace him. And Heathcote fought

hard to make that happen — on his timetable and no one else's.

"There was no specific time I first saw him as a head coach," Heathcote said. "It was a cumulative thing. Tom grew a little bit every year until he had a grasp of everything. As he grew, he earned the job. It wasn't given to him. He deserved it. And I would've felt the same way about Mike if he'd stayed."

Deane left. Izzo didn't. But if

BUILD IT AND THEY WILL COME – *The construction of the Jack Breslin Student Events Center has played a major role in the resurgence of Michigan State's basketball program. The 14,759-seat facility has helped attract some of the nation's top recruiting classes since it opened its doors in 1989.*

SPARTAN BASKETBALL

Heathcote wasn't thinking that far down the road, Izzo wasn't, either. He didn't wake up every morning and say, "That corner office will be mine some day." It became his with help from Heathcote, Interim President Gordon Guyer and some supportive members of the Board of Trustees.

"The first time I said I wanted to be the head coach at Michigan State was…a lot later than you'd think," Izzo said. "I just didn't think it was possible. I dreamed about being a head coach at a big school. I just didn't see it happening here."

He considered a Central Michigan offer and made a great impression on Athletic Director Herb Deromedi. Izzo might even have wound up at another Big Ten school. He probably should have had the Wisconsin job in 1992 and talked with Northwestern a year later.

"I was feeling a little more pressure about whether I should look at Central," Izzo said. "Then, there was the Wisconsin deal. And I did interview at Northwestern a little bit. I started thinking, 'I've got to find a job.' I knew if a new guy came in I probably wouldn't stay here. But I really didn't think I'd get this one.

"When you work for Jud, you have to be more of a realist than a dreamer. I didn't know if not having head coaching experience would hurt me. Finally, I started thinking, 'Maybe I could get this job!' And Jud started doing more and more for me. He'd say, 'You've got to learn this, and you've got to learn that.' But Jud ran his own ship.

Photo Credit: Bruce Schwartzman, Schwartzman Sports Photography

CHAIRMAN OF THE BOARDS – *Antonio Smith's blue-collar approach to the game mirrors Tom Izzo's personality. Smith made his first career start against No. 25 Arkansas in the 1995 Great Eight and responded with a 13-point, eight-rebound effort. The Spartans outrebounded Arkansas 47-23 en route to a 75-72 victory.*

SPARTAN BASKETBALL

You had to earn your keep with the guy. And I think I earned it as a recruiter faster than I did as a coach."

Heathcote's reputation was that of a teacher and master strategist, not as a pitchman to 17-year-olds. And he wasn't about to turn the program over to anyone who thought coaching was luring players to campus by any means possible, then rolling the balls out.

"That's the ultimate for Jud, whether you can teach the game," Izzo said. "But you didn't get much chance to show him. I still remember his shooting drills. He'd have 13 guys in one line and watch every guy. I break my guys into two groups to get more bang for the buck. But that wasn't the system he was brought up in. I'm sure I didn't instill enough confidence for him to feel that comfortable with me. If I had, I don't know if it would've made any difference."

The difference with a new facility was obvious and immediate. After winning five Big Ten championships and earning eight postseason berths (six NCAA, two NIT) in a half-century in Jenison Field House, MSU won five league titles and received 12 berths (nine NCAA, three NIT) in its first dozen years in Breslin.

When Izzo took over in 1995, Heathcote moved to Spokane, Wash., for family reasons and to be out of the way of a new regime. But Izzo never wanted him to leave. He wished Heathcote had been around more, the way he was at Tournament time.

"Jud has had a bigger impact on the program than he knows," Izzo said. "I was a blue-collar guy to start with. But of all the people to work for, I wind up with Jud Heathcote. I mean, you can't get a more down-to-earth, more blood-over-glamor guy than Jud."

A little blood has never bothered Izzo in football or basketball. And that attitude has carried over to the way his teams have rebounded and defended. The Spartans have led the nation in rebounding margin for three straight years, thanks in part to an adjustment after some bad news.

"It all goes back to the Arkansas game in '95 at The Palace," Izzo said of an upset in the Great Eight. "When I got back from a jog that day, (trainer Tom) Mackowiak said, 'Quinton Brooks can't play.' I said, 'What do you mean, he can't play?' He was so sick he couldn't go. That was the day I decided, 'OK, we'll put Antonio Smith in the lineup and pound the boards!' We outrebounded them by 24. Jamie Feick, Jon Garavaglia and 'Tone did a great, great job and had 32 rebounds.

"We'd just come off that incredible performance in Maui, when we beat the hell out of Chaminade by three, then got introduced to Vince Carter and Antawn Jamison for North Carolina. We also lost to Santa Clara and Steve Nash when all our guards were hurt. So beating Arkansas was our first big win."

The 1995-96 Spartans were 6-6 in preconference play, including a loss to Central Michigan in the Oldsmobile Spartan Classic. But a 6-2 start in the Big Ten, including wins at home against Indiana and Iowa and road triumphs over Illinois and Minnesota, gave everyone false hope. Finishing 9-9 in the league and 16-16 overall, including a win over Washington in the NIT, was Izzo's best coaching job.

"We went to Minnesota when we were both ranked and won," Izzo said. "So we were 6-2 when we went to Purdue, the best team in the league. We really played well and lost. Then, after we beat Ohio State, we went to Penn State and got beat by four, then came home and lost to Minnesota in overtime the week you spent with us. And you remember, we had no fans. The atmosphere in Breslin was terrible."

Before MSU won championships, it learned to play well against champions. When Minnesota raised a tainted Big Ten championship banner on Senior Day in 1997, the Spartans led much of the way and lost by seven.

But when MSU had its Senior Day ceremony two nights later, Izzo was furious. Indiana fans had purchased thousands of tickets and made Breslin almost as red as Crisler Arena in Ann Arbor has been green as the Izzone has grown.

"I remember seeing (Associate A.D.) Greg Ianni after we came off the floor for warmups," Izzo said. "I don't think I've ever been that mad. And I probably took it out on our guys. We won the game. But I thought those guys were working so hard, and to have that happen…

SPARTAN BASKETBALL

Photo Credit: Kevin Fowler, MSU Sports Information

"FLINTSTONES" PUT SPARTANS BACK ON THE MAP *– Michigan State's "Flintstones" – Morris Peterson, Mateen Cleaves, Antonio Smith and Charlie Bell – gained even more notoriety than the popular cartoon characters. From 1998-2001, the "Flintstones" helped the Spartans claim four straight Big Ten regular-season titles on the way to three Final Four appearances, including the 2000 national championship.*

"A coach does not make a program. A coach is a major part of it. But to have a good program, you still need all the pieces to the puzzle. When I look at that game and the Minnesota game, we didn't do our part. But we didn't get any help from the fans. And I felt it was a major insult to the program to have that many red sweaters in the crowd."

After a win over George Washington, the NIT sent MSU to Florida State, another insult. The Spartans weren't nearly the attraction in Cleaves' first season — a 9-9, 17-12 tease — that they would be the following four years. The record wasn't quite the same, either. MSU was 33-28 in Izzo's first two seasons, 115-25 in the next four.

Everything came together in 1997-98, as the Spartans shared the Big Ten title with Illinois at 13-3, snapped a five-game losing streak against Michigan, advanced to the Sweet 16 of the NCAA Tournament and finished 22-8.

But after losing to Detroit for the third-straight year, MSU was just 4-3. The cynics were smiling. And the *Lansing State Journal* asked fans to rate Izzo's performance, with the theory that he was the wrong man for the job — an idea the paper would soon regret and one Izzo wouldn't forget.

"I understand one thing a little

better now," Izzo said. "When you make a lot of money, you have a lot of pressure. That's just the way it is. It's never going to change. And I'm not sure it changes for anyone. The more money you make, the higher standard you're held to.

"But when we were 4-3, we were down! That was as low as it got. We beat Wright State at home, then went on the road and beat South Florida on ESPN. We put so much into that game it was almost like we'd beaten North Carolina. That game was a war. And that was the way we played. That win really propelled our program.

"Then, we went into Purdue, when no one thought we'd win, and beat them badly (74-57). We really did play well. I don't know if they were looking ahead. But it was the day of their first bowl game in a long time. They had a big party afterward and moved our game up. I know they were better than they played that night."

With the addition of guard Charlie Bell and forward Andre Hutson, the nucleus of Izzo's first Final Four teams was nearly complete. A win over Michigan, thanks largely to a 3-point shot designed and delivered by forward Jason Klein, redeemed the faith of MSU's recruits and helped reverse the fortunes of both programs.

"It all changed very quickly," Bell said. "Michigan had some guys leave early. It had a coaching change. And it had to rebuild. But I just liked Michigan State better. Coach Izzo was so genuine."

"Michigan was just coming off the 'Fab Five' years," Izzo said.

"They had a very good program with very good players. And we'd just lost a couple of great guards in Shawn Respert and Eric Snow. So it was tough recruiting against them at first. But I had great assistants and great support from our administration. Once we beat them, that meant a lot."

The Spartans never lost to the Wolverines again in Bell's career. But they lost the glow from that victory just hours after that game ended. After Cleaves and a female student had a loud disagreement at her off-campus apartment, he was charged with having an unopened can of beer in a car driven by Hutson.

"Everyone knows how fragile life is," Izzo said. "But that was my first indication of how fragile this job is and how you can go from the highest high at 11 at night to the lowest low at 6:30 in the morning. I learned a lot through that. Now that it's over, I think it helped me be a better coach and a better parent. It gave me a better understanding of the realities of the world. Everything isn't perfect.

"That was the hardest time for me. I didn't know how to handle it. And we'd won enough that it mattered. If we hadn't won, it wouldn't have mattered as much. But we were playing for a championship at Wisconsin. I remember getting calls from everybody with suggestions. But the hardest part for me was I could never get the information as fast as I needed it.

"I was trying to be fair to the player, to myself, to the team and to people I felt I was obligated to,

because I think we're all role models. I was trying to understand that what was right 20 years ago might not be right now. I have to give the president (Peter McPherson) a lot of credit. We talked about it. But he left it my hands. That was an important step. He trusted that I would make the right decision and said he'd back me."

Izzo benched Cleaves for the first half in Madison. The Spartans rallied to win and clinched at least a share of their first league title in eight seasons. But back-to-back losses to Purdue in overtime, MSU's last defeat in Breslin, and an upset by Minnesota in the first round of the Big Ten Tournament made everyone wonder, "Is Izzo's team a pretender?"

The Spartans, seeded fourth in the East Region, beat 13th-seeded Eastern Michigan by 12 on Bell's birthday, then topped fifth-seeded, eighth-ranked Princeton by seven in a classic in Hartford, Conn. If any MSU team has done a better job of preparation for a totally different scheme in less than 48 hours, no historian could remember it.

"I thought we had the worst draw in America," Izzo said. "But I didn't say anything. I mean, Eastern Michigan? With everything to play for and a helluva team? Winning that game was big. It was such a late start and seemed to take forever. I think there were six people left at the end, including you and my parents.

"Then, we had to get ready for Princeton. They were so hard to play. And our staff and players did

SPARTAN BASKETBALL

CLEAVES IS CLUTCH – *Mateen Cleaves celebrates after his 3-pointer from the top of the circle gave Michigan State a 59-54 lead over Princeton with 34 seconds left. Cleaves scored a game-high 27 points to go with nine rebounds and five assists as the Spartans knocked off Princeton in the 1998 NCAA Tournament second round in Hartford, Conn.*

an incredible job of preparing in that two-day period. I think that was when we gained some credibilty as coaches. We hardly gave up any backdoors. And we got a backdoor play on them, too."

In a Sweet 16 game with top-ranked, top-seeded North Carolina in Greensboro, N.C., Izzo learned a valuable lesson. Too much respect for an opponent is just as bad as too little, as the Spartans discovered too late.

"I broke tradition," Izzo said of a 15-point loss. "I talked to some people in the ACC. And the No. 1 thing they said was, 'How are you going to get back on defense? Jamison and Carter run so well.' So I chickened out and did what they always tell a young coach not to do: 'Don't coach differently in the Tournament. And don't change your philosophy.' I did that in the first half and got us killed on the boards. Since that day, I don't think we've ever rebounded with less than four guys."

His program rebounded from that setback and earned Big Ten titles, No. 1 seeds in the NCAA Tournament and Final Four berths the next three seasons. And in 2000, MSU became the first school to have two No. 1 finishes in the Division I-A football polls and two national titles in basketball — plus a couple of championships in hockey.

But when Izzo says, "We always talk about leaving footprints in the sand," he is much too modest. Prints in the sand are washed away. His teams' accomplishments will last forever.

THE PLAYERS

ANTONIO SMITH

Photo Credit: Kevin Fowler, MSU Sports Information

When Tom Izzo succeeded Jud Heathcote as Michigan State's 16th head basketball coach in 1995, the Spartans had just lost the Big Ten's No. 2 career scorer and leading scorer in league play in sweet-shooting guard Shawn Respert.

Perhaps more importantly, they would be without one of the best defenders, playmakers and leaders in school history, power forward-turned-point guard Eric Snow.

It was only appropriate that Snow's lucky No. 13 went to another unheralded freshman, a rock-solid rebounder and a leader of legendary proportions, Antonio Smith.

Smith wasn't the program's first player from Flint. Technically, Phillip H. Wessells was the original "Flintstone," lettering for Michigan Agricultural College in 1905.

Many others followed him to East Lansing, including single-game scoring king Terry Furlow, an explosive performer in the mid-1970s. But without the signing of Smith, MSU might not have struck the motherlode of stars less than an hour away.

"Would I have come to Michigan State if 'Tone hadn't been there?" said boyhood pal and Northern High teammate Mateen Cleaves. "I really don't know....I might have, just because of Coach Izzo. But having 'Tone there sure made the decision a lot easier."

Izzo didn't recruit Smith to get Cleaves, Morris Peterson, Charlie Bell or Kelvin Torbert. Though Smith lacked the flair and the fleeting fame of Albert White and Terrance Roberson, he was second to Robert Traylor in Michigan's Mr. Basketball voting.

Smith became the first player from Flint to score 400 points in three straight seasons. After choosing the Spartans over Minnesota and California, Smith left as the No. 3 scorer in the city's glorious history with 1,483 points.

And he saved the best for last. Smith had 21 points and 12 rebounds in the Class A quarterfinals against Grand Rapids Ottawa Hills, 21 and 12 in the semifinals against Kalamazoo Central in Breslin Center and 27 and 15 in the championship win over Detroit Pershing the following afternoon.

Not bad for a supposed non-scorer who disliked basketball for several years and wanted to become a soccer player instead of a 6-foot-8, 250-pound post player.

"I could have signed five McDonald's All-Americans, and I'd rather have had Antonio as my first recruit than any of them,"

ANTONIO SMITH

Izzo insisted. "I've said it before, and I'll say it again: Antonio Smith is what this program is all about."

Izzo inherited plenty of players who would contribute in varying degrees over the next three years — the likes of Quinton Brooks, Jamie Feick, Ray Weathers, Daimon Beathea, Jon Garavaglia, Steve Polonowski, Steve Nicodemus, David Hart and Thomas Kelley.

But the first player who showed what "Izzoball" was all about — and still is — was Smith. His initial start for MSU came as a freshman in a Great Eight upset of Arkansas. Brooks was ill on Nov. 28, 1995. And the Spartans wanted to bolster their rebounding. That, they did. On his first attempt, Smith broke an opponent's nose, Izzo said.

"How did I get this way?" said the normally soft-spoken Smith, when asked about his ferocity on the boards. "By having my brothers (NFL defensive linemen Fernando and Robaire) beat on me. Nothing can be worse than dealing with those two. I've been tossed around, slammed into walls and thrown on cement."

Yet, Smith's temper was legendary, too, as Garavaglia learned the hard way on Feb. 1, 1997, after a lackadaisical effort and a 20-point loss at Michigan. A disgusted sophomore went after a disinterested senior and sent necessary shock waves throughout the program.

Slamming his teammate against a wall and tossing him halfway across the room, according to Cleaves' version, Smith hollered, "You may not care if we win or not, but I do!...Play harder!" — give or take a few words.

Smith also gave Izzo an earful on rare occasions. And a demanding head coach always listened when he might have erupted at someone else.

"Antonio gave 110 percent every practice," Bell said. "He'd earned the right to speak his mind. I remember this meeting we had my first year. Coach was talking bad about all of us. And I saw Antonio sitting back. All of a sudden, he went off on Coach. But you know what? Coach Izzo respected that. He always respected what 'Tone had to say."

As the program's first three-time captain and first sophomore leader since Earvin "Magic" Johnson 18 years earlier, Smith didn't say a lot. But he meant every word he said. If you didn't believe him, you would soon have the bruises to prove it.

"We have four guys from Flint on this team," Polonowski said in 1997. "And there's one leader who keeps them in line. It only takes one grab from 'Tone....whatever you were doing, you're not doing it any more."

Photo Credit: Kevin Fowler, MSU Sports Information

ANTONIO SMITH

That was in striking contrast to some other behavior. Growing up, he would offer to take Robaire's punishment when his not-so-little brother would get in trouble. And whenever Izzo berated someone, Smith would try to make things better.

"He takes the blame for everything," Izzo said, shaking his head. "He's everyone's best friend. He eats with the guy who just got ripped. And if all the players are OK, he'll eat with the managers."

Bell couldn't get over the fact that Smith had a "Tickle Me, Elmo" doll in his car. But when Smith finally won in Ann Arbor as a senior and wrapped up a share of the 1999 conference title, even some media cynics were tickled.

"No net-cutting. No finger-pointing. No throat-slitting. No rubbing their butts against the block 'M' at midcourt, as a couple of the 'Fab Five' once did to the 'S' at Breslin Center," wrote Drew Sharp of the *Detroit Free Press*. "Act like you've won a championship before."

And what a champion Smith was. He was a captain of teams that won back-to-back league crowns, the school's first Big Ten Tournament title and six games in the NCAA Tournament, en route to Sweet 16 and Final Four appearances.

He was a third-team All-Big Ten pick by the media and the coaches as a senior and a member of the All-Big Ten Tournament team. And he ranks third on his school's career rebounding list with 1,016, trailing only Gregory Kelser with 1,092 and Johnny Green with 1,036.

Yet, the true measure of Smith's leadership style probably came at the annual MSU Basketball Bust in 1999, when he refused to accept the Inspiration Award and said it belonged to the Spartans' scout team.

Smith's inspiration was irrefutable a few weeks later in an Elite Eight matchup with defending national champ Kentucky.

When the Wildcats pounced and grabbed a 17-4 lead, Smith took charge in a quick timeout and did all his coach's talking for him.

"I wanted to start grabbing people," Smith said. "But I just grabbed a towel and started hollering....basically, I told them we had been through too much and come too far not to play more aggressively."

The Spartans rallied for a 73-

Photo Credit: Kevin Fowler, MSU Sports Information

66 triumph, outscoring Kentucky 69-49 the rest of the way. And when only one strand of the net remained intact, Izzo called Smith to the top of the ladder and let him deliver the kindest cut of all.

"We started this together," Izzo said. "And I wanted him to share that special moment with me. He was my first recruit as a head coach, the first one to take a chance on me."

"It was all his idea," Smith said of the net-snipping, not necessarily his recruitment. "I can't describe my emotions. We've been through so much together. We started as a .500 team. Now, we're celebrating a chance to be in the Final Four together."

Izzo did one other thing to commemorate Smith's contributions. He instituted the Antonio Smith Glue and Guts Award at MSU, with Cleaves an appropriate first winner in 2000.

Soon after the season ended, Smith got more recognition off the court than he ever did on it. He was charged with malicious destruction of property for breaking a cooler lock at an East Lansing 7-Eleven. And with Cleaves, he was accused of larceny over the disappearance of a 40-ounce bottle of beer. After 75 minutes of jury deliberation, Smith was acquitted on both counts.

"I'm really happy with the decision," he said. "I want to apologize to the university for all the bad publicity they got from this case."

Smith wasn't picked in the 1999 NBA Draft. And after being the last cut of the New York Knicks that year, he was released by the Pistons the following fall, much to Cleaves' dismay.

"When 'Tonio got let go, I was hurt," he said. "I had tears coming out of my eyes. Here, when they release you, they tell you in front of the whole team. So we're sitting in the locker room when they said, 'We released Antonio.' I'd seen 'Tonio work from Day One. And from Day One we had dreams together.

"I know how much he wanted to play in the NBA. It was tough. Mike Curry loves him to death. They didn't want to cut him here. And John Wallace was telling me Jeff Van Gundy didn't want to let him go in New York. Van Gundy used to say, 'If you guys had the heart Antonio had . . .'

"If you're not a special talent, this league is all about being in the right situation. With some guys that takes a little while. But why wouldn't you have a guy like 'Tonio on your team instead of some knucklehead who won't work hard and is one of the first guys to leave?...It's a cold, cold world."

Smith spent the past two seasons with the Grand Rapids Hoops of the defunct Continental Basketball Association and the International Basketball League. The dream of an NBA future as an undersized power forward remains alive.

"You've got to do something to catch these coaches' eyes every day," said Cleaves, the Pistons' first-round pick in 2000. "You've got to throw these players around. But 'Tonio was too concerned with not making anyone mad....Hey, no one is going to take it personally. And if someone is kicking my ass every day, I'd tell the coach, 'We need him on the team!'

"Next year, he's going to make somebody's team. I truly believe that. I hope he gets another shot here. I'll always want to play with Antonio Smith."

They did at Flint Northern and MSU and have the championships to prove it. When Smith thinks of that, the coldest days always seem a lot warmer.

13 ANTONIO SMITH

Forward—6-foot-8, 250 pounds
Flint, Mich. (Flint Northern HS)

Smith's Statistics

	G/GS	MIN/Avg.	FG/FGA	Pct.	3FG/3FGA	Pct.	FT/FTA	Pct.	REB/Avg.	PF/FO	A	BK	ST	PTS	Avg.
1995-96	32/20	622/19.4	56/120	.467	0/4	.000	26/57	.456	129/4.0	70/0	14	5	18	138	4.3
1996-97	29/28	906/31.2	92/163	.564	0/1	.000	63/127	.496	306/10.6	75/1	44	6	29	247	8.5
1997-98	30/30	888/29.6	84/199	.422	0/0	.000	69/122	.566	262/8.7	90/1	34	10	27	237	7.9
1998-99	38/37	1105/29.1	106/198	.535	0/3	.000	36/78	.462	319/8.4	104/4	41	12	56	248	6.5
	129/115	3521/27.3	338/680	.497	0/8	.000	194/384	.505	1016/7.9	339/6	133	33	130	870	6.7

JASON KLEIN

Photo Credit: Kevin Fowler, MSU Sports Information

It's tough for any player to split the double-team of expectations and potential, two of the nation's top defenders.

There were moments when Jason Klein was fine at Michigan State from 1995-99. Tom Izzo's second signee did enough good things to start for two Big Ten championship teams. And if we hadn't seen how good he could be, those contributions would have sufficed.

"Jason had a good career here," Izzo said. "We always want-

ed him to shoot the ball more. But he helped us win a lot of games. He's one of the guys who paved the way."

College basketball was never a smooth ride for the Grosse Ile native. He couldn't have been as good as his critics demanded. But he was probably better than he thought.

"If I'm not feeling comfortable and shoot and miss, that's bad," Klein said before the start of his final Big Ten season. "But if I don't shoot it, that's bad, too. I have to shoot the ball regardless."

Izzo gave Klein "the greenest of green lights." And if you saw him play on certain nights in high school, you would think: "All-conference in college for sure and probably a future pro."

Klein averaged 28.3 points and 12.5 rebounds as a high school senior. He had 35 points in a loss to Detroit Country Day in a Class B quarterfinal, dominating sophomore sensation Shane Battier.

Klein finished fifth in the Mr. Basketball voting and was ranked 77th in the nation by *Hoop Scoop*. UCLA wanted his services badly and finished a distant second. Bob Knight came from Indiana to see him. And Michigan couldn't get in the door.

But he averaged just 12.3 minutes and 3.3 points in his first two seasons at MSU, both with 9-9 league showings and second-round NIT exits — hardly a harbinger of things to come.

Klein's best game as a freshman or sophomore came against Ohio State at St. John Arena. The

6-foot-7 forward came off the bench to shoot 5-for-7 from the field and score 13 points, including a game-winning 3 with 47 seconds left after he had suffered a bloody nose and a cut forehead.

"It has been a long time," Klein said as trainer Tom Mackowiak treated the wounds. "It has been two years since I've felt like that. But Coach said if the shots were there, we should shoot them. I pretty much said, 'Just do it tonight.'"

He did it more often as a junior, averaging 27.1 minutes and 11.2 points, second only to Mateen Cleaves' 16.1 scoring average. And that was after Klein lost a month of summer training with mononucleosis and more time after practice began with a hyperextended elbow and tonsilitis.

His tip-in at the buzzer beat Dan Monson's Gonzaga team by two points in the 1997 Coca-Cola Spartan Classic final, restoring some confidence and rekindling the flame.

A month later, MSU forward Morris Peterson got a strange phone call early one morning from someone who claimed to be Klein. The message: "Hey, do you want to go shoot?"

"I thought to myself, 'This can't be Jason!'" Peterson said of a new Klein or a perfect impression. "Finally, I asked, 'OK, who is this really?'"

Izzo had never seen a long-range shooter more reluctant to take advantage of that gift. He actually had to tell Klein, "I want you to shoot it every time you're

JASON KLEIN

open....You can even shoot it if you're not!"

Shortly after that, Klein had two of his three highest-scoring games — a career-high 25 points in a win at Ohio State and 22 points in an overtime loss to Purdue in Breslin Center.

But it was what happened 12 days earlier that should stand as Klein's lasting contribution to the program. When an 18-point lead had all-but-vanished and the Spartans needed a huge shot to preserve their first win over the Wolverines in three years, guess who spoke up?

Klein insisted he could get open on the left wing, close to the corner, and would bury the shot that would guarantee a win. Izzo was thrilled by that new assertiveness and watched Klein keep his word.

His teammates couldn't have been happier for him — or for themselves. Four days later, they would lock up a share of their first Big Ten title in eight years and the first of four in a row.

Poised for a big senior season, Klein struggled to find the range. His scoring average dipped nearly two points to 9.4. And his 3-point

accuracy plunged from 41.1 percent to 33.8, the worst of his career.

"I haven't had the career I expected from an individual standpoint," Klein said. "But it has been great when you look at what the team has done the last two years. Do I still dream of making the big shot that wins the big game? Who doesn't?"

In the last four games of his MSU career, Klein was 1-for-5 against Mississippi and Oklahoma, 1-for-6 against Kentucky and 2-for-6 against Duke in the 1999 NCAA Tournament. Even a seance couldn't help.

But Klein played in 124 games for the Spartans and started 78 of them. His 870 points left him in 36th place on the school's all-time scoring list. And he can always say he was one of four captains of a Final Four team.

Klein has played professionally in Spain and Italy the last two years and hasn't been back to campus like a lot of Izzo's other players. He should try to get back for the next Michigan game. The streak he was instrumental in starting is at seven wins-and-counting.

Photo Credit: Kevin Fowler, MSU Sports Information

44 JASON KLEIN
Guard—6-foot-7, 200 pounds
Grosse Ile, Mich. (Grosse Ile HS)

Klein's Statistics

	G/GS	MIN/Avg.	FG/FGA	Pct.	3FG/3FGA	Pct.	FT/FTA	Pct.	REB/Avg.	PF/FO	A	BK	ST	PTS	Avg.
1995-96	28/10	270/9.6	22/67	.328	13/38	.342	1/5	.200	31/1.1	16/0	7	4	6	58	2.1
1996-97	29/9	432/14.9	49/119	.412	24/67	.358	7/9	.778	59/2.0	32/0	12	5	5	129	4.5
1997-98	30/23	812/27.1	118/288	.410	69/168	.411	32/44	.727	112/3.7	46/1	38	8	21	337	11.2
1998-99	37/36	854/23.1	132/320	.413	46/136	.338	36/47	.766	99/2.7	58/0	36	8	24	346	9.4
	124/78	2368/19.1	321/794	.404	152/409	.372	76/105	.724	301/2.4	152/1	93	25	56	870	7.0

MORRIS PETERSON

Clara Mae Spencer had to be proud as she watched from a front-row seat in heaven.

Her grandson, Morris Peterson Jr., became the Big Ten's Most Valuable Player, a first-team All-American, the go-to guy for an NCAA champion, a graduate of Michigan State University and a first-round pick in the NBA Draft — all in a span of less than three months.

That might have been the greatest memorial tribute any grandmother has received.

All five accomplishments were in question when "Mo Pete" arrived in East Lansing in 1995, part of Tom Izzo's first incoming class as head coach of the Spartans.

Antonio Smith from Flint Northern High and Jason Klein from Grosse Ile, a banger and a bomber, got most of the publicity that year — and rightly so for a program that needed an instant infusion of talent.

But there were two other "Flintstones" in that group, Peterson and junior-college transfer Anthony Mull, both from Northwestern High.

"Peterson can play all over — at guard, at small forward or inside," said his high school coach, the highly respected Grover Kirkland. "He only scored 2.0 points per game as a sophomore. But he came on so fast. At 6-foot-7, he's a Jalen Rose-type player — minus the swagger. I think he's the best sleeper in the state."

Peterson woke up just in time to earn a scholarship offer from Izzo and justify that faith with outstanding junior and senior seasons

for MSU, becoming the first non-starter to be first-team All-Big Ten.

He grew an astonishing seven inches from 5-6 to 6-1 in ninth grade and sprouted 13 inches by the time he left high school. The rest of Peterson's growth — the most important part — would come later.

He wasn't on the Spartans' original list of elite prospects, despite averaging 22.4 points per game as a junior. And he was ranked just 21st in Michigan in the preseason issue of *Hoop Scoop* magazine.

It wasn't terrible to be rated below the top five: Terrance Roberson, Robert Traylor, Smith, Klein and Albert White. Roberson, an amazing talent, was rejected by Michigan and MSU due to character issues and went to Fresno State. Traylor and White became Wolverines. And Smith and Klein started for the Spartans in the 1999 Final Four.

But Peterson was also listed behind Big Ten recruits Julian Bonner of Northwestern, Jason Singleton of Ohio State, Jarrett Stephens of Penn State and Guy Rucker of Iowa, plus 11 others from the state.

The analysts were right in one way. He was no White, a player Izzo pursued aggressively and thought he would sign, only to be stung by a mysterious commitment to Michigan. Peterson was better than that.

The signs of that sudden progress were all present. The media, as well as reluctant recruiters and cautious fans, just happened to ignore most of them.

When Kirkland said, "I'd put this kid up there with anyone we've had," he was talking about the likes of Wildcat greats Trent Tucker, Barry Stevens, Jeff Grayer, Andre Rison, Glen Rice and Anthony Pendleton.

Today, he compares players to Peterson, one of the all-time, feel-good stories in college basketball. And with the exception of incoming Spartan Kelvin Torbert, the best of them all in Kirkland's eyes, no one has been any better.

A few writers and broadcasters got a glimpse of Peterson's unshakable confidence in 1995 at a sold-out Saginaw Valley Conference game between Northern, with Smith and Mateen Cleaves, and Flint Southwestern Academy, with heralded 10th-grader Charlie Bell.

When Peterson spotted us in the hallway outside the gym, he walked over and introduced himself. He said he wanted to come to East Lansing and, with an endearing smile, suggested he was every bit as good as the three stars we had come to see.

Peterson finally nudged his way onto an MSU short list that included Joe Harmsen, a Northwestern signee, and Neshaun Coleman, who played at OSU. As hard as it is to believe today, he might have been the third choice initially.

The more Izzo and his assistants saw, the more they liked. And they weren't alone. Minnesota, Wisconsin, Connecticut and Missouri showed strong interest. But he committed to the Spartans before the state tournament began.

"He's an athlete," Izzo said.

MORRIS PETERSON

Photo Credit: Kevin Fowler, MSU Sports Information

"He's tall. He can run. And he led one of the toughest leagues anywhere in 3-point shooting. I don't know if he's another Steve Smith. But I know I like him."

Why wouldn't he? Peterson averaged 20.6 points and 12.8 rebounds per game as a senior and was qualified academically.

As for a lack of swagger, Peterson could turn that on and off faster than he could soar for an alley-oop. He said he didn't mind the comparisons to Rose, another left-handed matchup nightmare. He also said he could shoot and drive better than the former Michigan star.

That demeanor got Peterson in trouble almost immediately at MSU. He missed enough classes that Izzo left him home from the Maui Invitational, the first three games of his collegiate career. And his coaches did everything but send him a "Hi from Lahaina!" postcard to get his attention.

Peterson appeared in just four games for a total of 12 minutes as a freshman. A broken finger made him a medical redshirt and was the best thing that ever happened to him. Without that injury, he never would have won a national title — and neither would the 1999-2000 Spartans.

His redshirt-freshman season got off to a great start with two 19-point efforts in the first four games, in a win over East Tennessee State and a loss at Detroit. Then, Peterson took a step backward. He scored in double figures just twice in his last 25 games, despite starting 18 times.

MORRIS PETERSON

"We had a lot of battles his first two years," said MSU assistant Tom Crean. "But I remember when it all started to change. He came in one day and was sobbing uncontrollably. He flunked a test he'd really studied for. And I knew right then he was starting to care. I told Tom, 'We've got him now!'"

Crean played a major role in Peterson's development and figured out which buttons to push for maximum motivation. That extra attention was appreciated by a father who had coached basketball in Mississippi and become an assistant principal in Flint.

"I love Coach Crean," Morris Peterson Sr. said. "He's one of the best things that ever happened to Morris. Morris was a young kid when he first came to Michigan State. And Coach Crean had the patience to work with him on and off the court. If Coach hadn't taken the time with him, Morris wouldn't have become the player he is."

Izzo chose to credit Peterson's parents, especially his mother, Valarie, who was as supportive of a confrontational coach as any mom could be. She was also a good enough player in her day to have taught her son a few lessons in humility.

Peterson's sophomore season brought more frustration individually and his first Big Ten championship ring. He broke his right wrist on a rough landing after an acrobatic tip against Gonzaga and missed the next three games.

Roommate Thomas Kelley had already been sidelined for two months with a fractured foot. And

when Peterson's mom said there had to be unhealthy vibes in their house, she suggested they move.

Izzo just wanted a one-way player to move his feet. He had already said, "Morris is still going dorm-to-dorm, trying to find the

first guy he can guard…Some people think I'm kidding about that."

When Peterson returned to practice with an odd-looking cast dubbed "The Club," the Spartans were a disappointing 4-3. They finished 22-8.

Photo Credit: Kevin Fowler, MSU Sports Information

MORRIS PETERSON

"That was when I finally decided I had to play defense," Peterson said of the switch from a non-defender to a perimeter stopper. "I tried to make myself into the person and the player I knew I could be."

Photo Credit: Kevin Fowler, MSU Sports Information

When MSU played in Minneapolis in 1998, Minnesota coach Clem Haskins complained about Peterson's cast before the game. After trainer Tom Mackowiak made the necessary adjustments, Peterson came off the bench, as he did in all 27 appearances that season, and had 11 points in a 14-point victory.

That triggered an eight-game, Big Ten winning streak, when about the only complaint came from Cleaves. He still wanted Peterson to swap numbers with David Thomas to make a "Flintstone" straight — No. 11 Peterson, No. 12 Cleaves, No. 13 Smith and No. 14 Bell.

His number didn't seem to bother him in a 21-point romp at Iowa, when he ran the court for slams and hit three 3s. Peterson finished with a career-high 20 points in just 19 minutes. And asked when the game's top star would lose "The Club," Izzo answered, "Never."

Everyone figured Peterson would start as a junior. But he did the unthinkable in an age of selfishness by accepting a role as the nation's best sixth man. He started just four of 38 games and had a school-record 448 bench points.

"It's tempting to start him," Izzo said. "I discuss that with the staff nearly every night. I'll have to start asking my wife, I guess. But he can go in and help in so many different areas. He can even check a point guard."

The Spartans' point guard had a different view of the leading scorer on a 33-5 Final Four team,

MORRIS PETERSON

Photo Credit: Kevin Fowler, MSU Sports Information

one he had been waiting to see for years, as a healthy "Mo Pete" finally gained momentum.

"He's playing so much harder," Cleaves said. "He always had tools, even back in elementary school. But he put it on himself to do a lot of extra shooting. And he realized everyone feeds off his defense."

Peterson had 24 points in 28 minutes against Duke and was the MVP of the Pearl Harbor Classic. He had 23 points in a rare start against Louisville, 27 in 28 minutes against Iowa and was the Most Outstanding Player of the NCAA Tournament's Midwest Region after a 19-point, 10-rebound effort against Kentucky. But he never matched his mom's point total in her best game.

"In Picayune, Miss., she once scored 42 points in a game," said her son, explaining why he wouldn't switch numbers. "I mean, my mother was bad! When I was about 5, she was letting me score. I was sure I could beat her. And she said, 'Whoa, wait a minute!' She tied up her shoes, got this look on her face and really kicked my butt.

"Now, she'll say, 'I can tell you've missed a day or two of shooting, haven't you? You need to keep your elbow up.' But I've always been a momma's boy and don't mind if anyone knows it."

That isn't hard to see, since he wears her name on his left biceps. And Valarie, a teacher at a Flint middle school, couldn't be prouder of a son who drew raves as an intern at the Parkwood YMCA in East Lansing. Basketball wasn't all she taught him. Peterson has always cared about kids. And he plans to run his own community center.

He ran North Carolina into the ground in Chapel Hill with 31 points as a senior, as he totally dominated freshman sensation Joseph Forte. Peterson added 29 at Iowa, 32 at Michigan and 26 against Ohio State, when the final score could have be listed as: "Flintstones" 73, Buckeyes 72.

Remember the freshman who couldn't focus long enough to go to class in 1995? He was a picture of concentration and a model of consistency in the 2000 NCAA Tournament. Peterson averaged 20 points and never scored less than 18 in his last four games.

He couldn't have been higher than he was on a spectacular alley-oop slam in the closing minutes of an Elite Eight win over Iowa State, the game that should have been for the NCAA title.

But the Midwest Region's Most Outstanding Player — again — had never been lower than he plunged moments later when he learned his grandmother and lifelong fan had died that morning in Mississippi.

Peterson's family decided not to tell him the devastating truth until after the Spartans beat the Cyclones at The Palace of Auburn Hills and advanced to another Final Four.

After the game and an on-court celebration ended, Izzo pulled Peterson into a room where his family was waiting and delivered the news.

"That was really tough," Izzo

said as he boarded the bus home. "He went from the top of the top to the bottom of the bottom in a matter of seconds. But whatever Morris wants to do at this point is what we want him to do."

Peterson wanted to fly to Mississippi for the funeral, then give her a gift he knew she would treasure — a national title, a key component of his tribute to Clara Mae.

"She'd do anything for me," he said. "And I really felt her with me tonight. I didn't know she'd passed away. But I felt her with me all night long."

Peterson said his parents and Izzo did the right thing by withholding information about the passing of his grandmother, who had suffered a stroke a month earlier.

"I wanted to go see her as soon as I could," he said. "But I called down there the other day. When my sister put the phone by her ear, I told her just how much I loved her. I heard she got this big smile on her face."

Peterson wore her name on his shoes immediately after the stroke and described how much she meant to him — and always will.

"There will never be anyone like her," he said. "'Man, could she cook! She made the best gumbo in the world. And when I couldn't beat my sister at basketball or video games, my grandmother would play me and let me win....Tonight was for her."

He finished his career as MSU's No. 9 career scorer with 1,588 points. Appropriately, Peterson

ranks just ahead of No. 10 Cleaves and No. 11 Bell. And his 137 games were the most until Bell hit the 140 mark in 2001.

Peterson spent his last night as a collegian in a crowded hotel room in Minneapolis, signing Upper Deck NBA rookie cards until 2 a.m. and dining on a delivery from Pizza Hut.

Less than 20 hours later, he was the toast of Toronto and a soon-to-be-wealthy young man by any currency.

Peterson wasn't picked 16th by Sacramento, as many anticipated, or 20th by Philadelphia, as logic indicated.

Instead, the 2000 Big Ten Co-MVP and All-American went to Canada, sliding to the Raptors at 21 — the number he wanted to wear before being assigned 24, the reverse of 42.

"It means I've got to get a lot more tickets," Peterson said of playing in the second-closest NBA city to Flint. "Toronto is a great place and a team on the rise. I really couldn't be happier."

As the next-to-last player to stroll from the TNT Green Room to the podium, he had reason to worry, if not to be bitter, after a 16-city workout tour.

His agent, Arn Tellem, arranged the sessions and said Peterson lacked the two ingredients that made prospects sizzle — youth and size. Peterson insisted he had nothing to hide and went through every drill coaches asked him to perform.

He wound up being selected by one of just 13 teams that didn't

MORRIS PETERSON

have him in for private sessions, a team that tried to trade up to take him with the 13th pick.

Peterson went 16 slots later than another Tellem client, Florida sophomore forward Mike Miller. But in their head-to-head matchup in the NCAA title game, Peterson outscored Miller 21-10 and helped the Spartans spank the Gators.

"You put me to shame in the championship game," Miller told Peterson when they posed for a picture after a meeting with Tellem. "Go ahead and take the shot — the champ and the loser together again."

When Peterson returned to room 2726, he signed 2,000 Press Pass basketball cards with help from his sister, Tonda. Then, it was off to a surprisingly peaceful sleep for someone whose life was about to change dramatically.

"I didn't think I'd sleep at all," Peterson said. "But I woke up at 7 a.m., dozed off until my sister showed up by mistake at 8:30, then went back to sleep until 10."

Draft Day's first obligation was an NBA Players Association appearance, where the draftees got sound advice from ex-Minnesota star Quincy Lewis, who had just completed his first season with Utah.

"'Q' told us to be sure we're in shape," Peterson said. "He also told us to watch out for the women. And he said to be sure we bend our knees when we carry the veterans' bags. He said we'd be doing a lot of that."

After the players and their guests had lunch with NBA Commissioner David Stern, the suitbag Peterson had been fretting

Photo Credit: Kevin Fowler, MSU Sports Information

about finally arrived. He had been practicing his walk to the podium and his GQ pose in a cream Coogi stocking cap, a matching sweater and jeans.

But when Peterson tried on a hidden-button, navy suit with light-blue pinstripes, a light-blue shirt and tie and navy alligator shoes, his look matched his game.

MORRIS PETERSON

"Conservative…but eye-catching," he repeated to anyone who'd listen, as family members and friends, including Cleaves, came by for a preview.

"Image is everything," said Sandra Scott of Haj & Scott's Design, whose clients include Deion Sanders. "You have to look good. But you have to be humble. You can't wear a $1,400 suit all the time. Veterans don't like that. You can get a $700 suit and be just as clean."

Peterson's clean-up included a lining and shaping of his hair. He knew he'd only be drafted once.

"This is my prom," he said. "I didn't go to my prom in high school. I couldn't get anyone to go with me.…Actually, it was because we were on our way to Tonda's college graduation. But I was named Homecoming king."

As the movie "Superman" ended on television, Peterson gazed at a hotel bill that would seem much smaller in a matter of hours. The NBA paid for his flight and his room. But its per diem didn't cover his other room charges.

Peterson decided the once-in-a-lifetime opportunity was priceless. He was especially happy to make some new friends.

"Mike Miller is really funny," he said. "I wasn't sure I'd like him after we played in Indianapolis. But he gave me a nickname, 'Sweet Mo Pete.' I got to know Jamal Crawford here, too. He's OK, even though he went to that school down the road. But besides Mateen, I've probably spent the most time with Etan Thomas of Syracuse. He's pretty laid back, too."

Conservative…but eye-catching.

And as Peterson thought of everything and everyone in his first 22-plus years, he couldn't stop thanking his parents for their love and support.

"They've been an integral part of everything," he said with pride and emotion. "They supported me through the good times and bad times — even if my mom did miss one game when she thought it was at night. I tease her about that all the time."

He also thanks her for most of his basketball ability. And he remembers the one-on-one losses to his two older sisters as well as his first dunk in ninth grade.

Peterson wasn't sure what kind of jam he was in when the Green Room kept emptying on Draft Night. DePaul guard Quentin Richardson, the 18th pick, put a video camera on Peterson and announced, "They're saving the best for last!"

He was good enough to make the NBA's all-rookie team and star in a Game-Six playoff win over Philadelphia. He had never stopped believing.

When Peterson's name was called on June 28, 2000, he hugged his family and Izzo, then walked to the podium and began his life as a pro. As he moved from interview to interview, chants of "Flint Town!" and "Go Green!" arose in the Target Center.

But the next morning, there was another lesson in life. His flight to Toronto for a press conference was delayed several hours. Peterson knew what that meant.

He had waited four seasons to start for the Spartans. And he had waited for what seemed like forever to be picked by the Raptors. He could wait a little longer. Grandma would still be watching.

42 MORRIS PETERSON

Forward—6-foot-7, 215 pounds
Flint, Mich. (Flint Northwestern HS)

Peterson's Statistics

	G/GS	MIN/Avg.	FG/FGA	Pct.	3FG/3FGA	Pct.	FT/FTA	Pct.	REB/Avg.	PF/FO	A	BK	ST	PTS	Avg.
1995-96	4/0	12/3.0	1/1	1.000	0/0	.000	0/1	.000	3/0.8	2/0	0	0	0	2	0.5
1996-97	29/18	518/17.9	72/166	.434	16/59	.271	36/51	.706	97/3.4	60/1	18	6	19	196	6.8
1997-98	27/0	503/18.6	81/182	.445	23/69	.333	32/58	.552	94/3.5	61/2	24	3	21	217	8.0
1998-99	38/4	907/23.9	190/343	.554	22/59	.373	114/140	.814	216/5.7	97/4	36	22	33	516	13.6
1999-2000	39/38	1136/29.1	218/469	.465	85/200	.425	136/176	.773	235/6.0	79/0	49	11	46	657	16.8
	137/60	3076/22.5	562/1161	.484	146/387	.377	318/426	.746	645/4.7	299/7	127	42	119	1588	11.6

MATEEN CLEAVES

Some coaches and players are meant to be together: Bill Walsh and Joe Montana… Phil Jackson and Michael Jordan… Tom Izzo and, yes, Mateen Cleaves.

Michigan State might produce a better basketball player during Izzo's tenure, though not too much better than the school's first three-time All-American and its second Final Four MVP.

Finding a better leader than Cleaves would be a very tall order for a very short coach. It took two decades to find anyone who belonged in the same breath with Earvin Johnson as a winner. By the time that club grows to three members, Izzo won't be coaching anyone. He will be sitting in the stands, watching his son, Steven Thomas Mateen.

Cleaves was probably as close to a player/son as Izzo will have with the Spartans. Though Herb and Fran Cleaves did a fine job of parenting, Izzo and his wife, Lupe, were there as backups the past five years.

"Mateen and I hit it off right away for some reason," Izzo said of a fellow point guard. "His bedroom was all green-and-white. And his dad was a big Michigan State guy. He was very aware of the link with Flint and the commitment to minority athletes here, going back 50 years."

Cleaves never saw the likes of Spartan football greats Don Coleman and LeRoy Bolden in the 1940s and '50s. And he was born 20 months after fellow "Flintstone" Terry Furlow scored 50 points against Iowa, a single-game record that still stands.

Yet, Cleaves knew all about MSU's history. A bond was formed long before he enrolled in 1996 as the star of Northern High's '95 Class A champs, as a Mr. Basketball runner-up to collegiate dud Winfred Walton and as the first prep All-American to commit to Izzo's program.

"For a lot of years, guys have come here from Flint and gotten a fair deal," Cleaves said. "You can see them now in the NBA and the NFL. So when people say Flint has been good to Michigan State, I say Michigan State has been good to Flint. That had a lot to do with my decision."

So did Izzo's persistence in pursuing a two-sport star who loved playing quarterback and might have made a great collegiate safety. In fact, the first time Cleaves visited MSU with his parents was for a spring Green & White Game.

"I still think our love of football was big," Izzo said. "I was the only coach who went to his seven-on-seven passing scrimmages. I used to go up and sit in that weight room while he lifted. And when he broke his arm one summer, I went up there a couple of times when he couldn't do anything. I really think if he hadn't hurt his back, he would've tried playing football for Nick Saban."

If it involved fierce competition and physical contact, Cleaves had to be involved in the battle. He was beaten a few times, like everyone else. But stay beaten? No restraints were strong enough to keep him out of the fray — long

before and well after he became a Spartan.

When Cleaves was 4 years old, he vanished from his parents' sight at a friend's pool party. By the time a fully clothed father could rescue his sunken son, that rock-solid non-swimmer was lower than the lowest crossover dribble.

As soon as he coughed the chlorine from his lungs, the youngest of the Cleaves' six children threw a fit worth at least two technical fouls. He squawked non-stop to get back in the water, as if to say, "OK, pool, you won that one….Now, show me what you've got! Let's go again."

He was never "'Teen Angel'" — an impossible role for anyone to play, especially someone from a rough neighborhood in a rougher town. Still, his love of kids made Cleaves a pied piper at Flint's Berston Recreation Center, where he would wow the crowd, then preach the importance of family and education.

"He's such a caring person," said Antonio Smith, his teammate and soulmate in high school and college. "He's always bringing little kids to games and playing around with them. When I go back to Berston, Mateen will be sitting up on stage with a kid, being an older brother."

Other brothers can be incredibly special, as he learned when Herbert "Sluggo" Cleaves was killed in a drive-by shooting in 2001. But he was determined to become a teacher for many years — and still might be. He majored in elementary education at MSU

MATEEN CLEAVES

before switching to communication as a senior.

Cleaves' recruiting process was an education no money could buy. His dad wanted him to commit to the Spartans before his final year at Northern. Meanwhile, his mom insisted on an open search, one that nearly ended in tragedy.

Infatuated with Florida State and charmed by Bobby Bowden, Cleaves seriously considered an opportunity to play football and basketball, perhaps as the second coming of Heisman Trophy winner and NBA first-round pick Charlie Ward.

He also drew full-court presses from Cincinnati's Bob Huggins and Michigan's Steve Fisher. But in the blink of a tired eye, Cleaves' career and his life nearly ended. On a wild official visit to Ann Arbor, Cleaves and five Wolverines were involved in the rollover of a Ford Explorer on M-14 in Superior Township.

Star forward Maurice Taylor had fallen asleep at the wheel at 5:10 a.m. on Feb. 17, 1996, returning from a night of revelry in Detroit. That was outside the NCAA's 30-mile radius for off-campus entertainment of recruits, a secondary recruiting violation.

Freshman center Robert Traylor broke his arm but might have acted as a human airbag. Riding in the back seat, Cleaves injured his back and wasn't the same player for more than a year. And the Michigan program hasn't been the same since the crash — two head coaches ago.

That accident led to a long look at reported abuses involving booster Ed Martin, a probe that helped shift the balance of power in the state and led to FBI and IRS inquiries. It also infuriated Cleaves' dad, whose calls to the Wolverines' coaches weren't returned.

His son never spoke publicly about the details of that weekend, reconsidered a lawsuit and remained friends with the Michigan players. He also helped beat the Wolverines five straight times, a streak that grew after his departure.

It was Cleaves' arrival that sparked a resurgence of interest in MSU's program. It also triggered a run of triumphs that will last at least twice as long as the success after Earvin Johnson's signing in 1977.

"Though Michigan was one of his choices, 'Magic' was a home-grown guy," Izzo said of the Lansing native. "He was supposed to come to Michigan State. Mateen could have gone either way. Cincinnati was a hot program at the time, too. And FSU had the lure of football. But I don't think Michigan was ever really a player with him. He was one of those rare birds who grew up as a Michigan State guy."

With a flair for the dramatic, Cleaves made a stunning opening statement in his press conference in Northern's Viking Room: "I'd like to announce I'm going to forego my four years of college and enter the NBA Draft in June" — an ironic line from one of the few megastars to stay in school four years.

Cleaves followed that prank with more sleight-of-tongue and said, "I'm going to go to the University of...Michigan State," then donned a green-and-white cap that would have looked great with one of the thousands of No. 12 jerseys he would soon help to sell.

"Everybody loves Michigan, with the hype and the fame and the baggy shorts and all that," Cleaves said, denying that the accident had any impact on his choice whatsoever. "They have the horses. But State was always in my heart. And I fell in love with Coach Izzo."

A champagne toast for the staff in Breslin Center on Monday, March 25, 1996, was the first of countless celebrations Cleaves would cause. If he had waited one more day to announce, it would have been the 17th anniversary of the Spartans' NCAA title win over Indiana State.

"There were a couple of things about Mateen Cleaves that made him unique," Izzo said. "He told me during his junior year he was coming to Michigan State. And every time I talked to him about it, he said, 'I already told you what I'm doing!' That never changed."

Cleaves' game changed dramatically — and not for the better — in an injury-plagued senior year at Northern and his first year on campus. The accident cost him a spring and summer of preparation. And his rehabilitation was slowed when NCAA rules kept him from being treated by MSU's doctors and trainers until he enrolled for classes.

When he finally shed a cumbersome brace after nearly four months, Cleaves weighed close to 230 pounds, 40 more than he should have. That extra weight made him vulnerable to guards who will tell their grandkids, "Do you know I blew past Mateen Cleaves?"

Or as Izzo put it: "He thinks he's still in the Indy 500, when he's driving along in a Pinto instead of a race car."

More than a few despondent fans and some silly members of the media figured Cleaves must have been a lemon all along. The player who scored 39 points on Mike Bibby at the Nike Camp 18 months earlier had regressed to the point his No. 1 fan was worried.

"My mom is always concerned about me," Cleaves said. "But even she said, 'Mateen, you're getting no lift at all on your jumper....And is your lateral movement back where it was?' My first thought was,

'That's it! I'm going to redshirt!' Then, the more I thought about it, the more that seemed like a bailout."

Cleaves wore No. 24 in high school and No. 12 with the Spartans. Midway through his freshman year, that division by two seemed entirely appropriate. He was roughly half the dominating, dunking guard everyone remembered. His critics can call Cleaves a

lot of things — and have the past six years. But no one can call him a quitter. Stung by his mom's feedback, he decided to get back in shape, play through the discomfort and become the player he was supposed to be.

"His safety and career come first...especially since I'm not in the last year of my contract," Izzo joked with a deadpan delivery worthy of Jud Heathcote. "The

Photo Credit: Kevin Fowler, MSU Sports Information

MATEEN CLEAVES

decision to play was a family decision. Ultimately, any decision is Mateen's, except whether he should start. I made that one."

Izzo also made the comment that Cleaves would have been a great "Yooper," since no one in the Upper Peninsula could dunk, either. But Izzo never stopped believing in Cleaves in a 17-12 freshman season. It wasn't until the following year, a 22-8 breakthrough, that it appeared the kindred spirits might come to blows.

"I remember he had a miserable first half at Northwestern," Izzo said three years later. "I was telling Zach Randolph, 'See that shower over there? I had Mateen in there at halftime and did everything but turn the water on him.' He walked out and couldn't have been madder. But he came back into the locker room and said, 'Hey, guys, that was my fault.'

"That was the first time I'd heard him do that. I told him, 'Hey, the other guys can't handle it. You can!' I remember saying to myself that night, 'Here's a kid nobody understands. But he sure has a lot of character.' Then, he went out and got, what was it, 30 points in the second half?"

Actually, it was 32 of a career-high 34 as the Spartans rallied for a 72-66 overtime win — the game that made Cleaves a leader his teammates couldn't question.

"It started to get to the point where I knew who was going to have the ball at the end of the game," Izzo said. "He knew who was going to have the ball at the end of the game. And the team knew who

was going to have the ball at the end of the game. None of us knew who was going to get the shot. Mateen took a lot of them and made a lot of plays for others. He was one of the great shot-clock guys."

He was also a sophomore with rough edges. After MSU beat Michigan for the first time in three years, Cleaves and freshman Andre Hutson were arrested at 4:45 a.m. on alcohol-related misdemeanors. With a championship at stake four nights later at Wisconsin, the timing couldn't have been worse.

"I'll never forget the press conference that day," Izzo said of Cleaves' public apology. "There were more TV cameras than there were for the Michigan game the night before. I really didn't know what to do. If I'd listened to what everyone said, I either would've played him or shot him.

"I decided the night before the Wisconsin game to bench them both for a half and impose other discipline. Maybe I was harder than I should've been. But he said, 'You do what you have to do, Coach. If I have to sit out, it was my fault. I understand it.' He asked me to go to the podium with him when he gave his statement. And I did. That was the kind of solidarity that said I wasn't going to bail on the guy. Later on, I think that helped us."

Ten days later, they were headed for the NCAA Tournament. Their team was a Big Ten champ for the first time in eight years. Cleaves was the conference Player of the Year. And Izzo was the league's Coach of the Year.

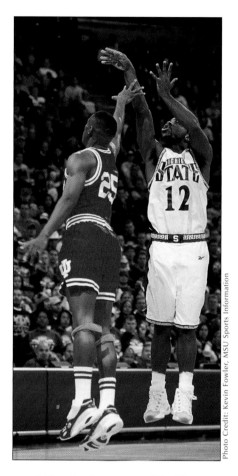

Photo Credit: Kevin Fowler, MSU Sports Information

"Coach Izzo won?" Cleaves asked that day after practice. "Yeah! That's my guy!...He's a father, a brother and a friend all in one. If I'd had a vote, I wouldn't just have put a check by his name. I'd have been campaigning and passing out fliers."

At 6-foot-2, 205 pounds, he wished he could have been passing footballs a few times in his final two seasons. Cleaves was one of the few MSU basketball players who bothered to buy football tickets. And he died a little bit every time the Spartans lost.

"One of my best memories of him was at the Penn State football game in '99," Izzo said of a 35-28

MATEEN CLEAVES

triumph. "There he is, with a stress fracture, jumping up and down on his crutches on the sideline. Pretty soon, he has the whole crowd jumping up and down. But that was Mateen. He loved Michigan State. And he loved football."

The night before Cleaves' emotion-packed return against the Nittany Lions on Jan. 5, 2000, Izzo took a calculated risk for his favorite player. Instead of watching more tape of Penn State, he said, "We're going watch the football game!" — Florida State's win over Virginia Tech in the Sugar Bowl.

It was a bonding experience in Kellogg Center. And when the Seminoles, Cleaves' second-favorite football team, rallied to win the national title, he let everyone know, "They're winning it now! And we're going to win it later!"

Mateen (pronounced "MAH-teen") is a Muslim name that means "firm and unshakable." His parents couldn't have picked a better label if they had been piped into the Psychic Friends Hotline or had swiped Miss Cleo's Tarot Readings.

Izzo said he could count on one hand the number of bad practices Cleaves had in four seasons. And no Spartan ever wanted to win more than a point guard who hammered that point home in a series of halftime attitude adjustments. Locker rooms in Cleveland and Auburn Hills might never look the same.

The postgame celebration after the final win in Indianapolis made up for everything — the abuse

from fans around the Big Ten, the injuries that slowed his development and the constant feedback from a demanding head coach, often at high decibels.

"One Shining Moment" had long been Cleaves' favorite song. On April 3, 2000, it became one of Izzo's.

"Mateen was a superstar who sacrificed for the good of the program," Izzo said. "He'll be the best recruiter Michigan State has for the next 10 years. He's loyal to this place. And he's loyal to me. As long as I'm here, people are going to know there was a great player who

knew winning was the most important thing. When other seniors played for NBA contracts, he took four or five shots. He knew defense was more important than offense and knew toughness and leadership meant more than glitz and glamor."

Cleaves meant so much to the Izzos that they borrowed "Mateen" as a second middle name. Firm and unshakable, indeed.

"I cried my eyes out when I heard that," Cleaves' mother said. "What an honor! That means we're family forever. It's like Tom Izzo is my other son. I just hope he finds

Photo Credit: Kevin Fowler, MSU Sports Information

MATEEN CLEAVES

a role for me to help his program. After what happened with Mateen, I'd tell anybody, 'If you get a chance to go to Michigan State, you'd be crazy not to.'"

When Cleaves could have gone anywhere else, he came to East Lansing. And when he could have left for the NBA, his dream of a lifetime, he chose to chase a championship — even if he had to celebrate on crutches.

The most decorated player in MSU history was the first-round pick of the Detroit Pistons, the team he wanted to join all along. After a hit-and-miss rookie season, he vowed to improve as much as he did after his freshman year with Izzo.

"The NBA is kind of set up for guys to be selfish, to be honest," Cleaves said. "It's all about the minutes you get, the points you

score, the assists and the rebounds. When you negotiate your contract, that's about it. And it's going to be hard to change that. But if everything could just be predicated on winning…"

Wrong league. But as the 14th selection, Cleaves signed a three-year contract for $4.1 million, with a fourth season worth roughly $3 million if Detroit exercises its option, according to Lansing-based agent Charles Tucker.

"He has enough other money coming in that he won't have to touch his salary," Tucker said. "He has a lot of investments. He got his mom a nice home and gave her a Chrysler 300. But he isn't wasting any money. He has told his mom, 'You don't need that now.' People won't even ask him any more. He's too tough."

He is still an unabashed sup-

porter of the Spartans, to the point of driving his teammates crazy. When MSU beat North Carolina in Breslin Center, Cleaves asked for updates at the scorer's table at The Palace, then tormented former Tar Heels Jerry Stackhouse and Eric Montross.

"The other guys hate it when State wins anything," Cleaves said with a familiar laugh. "They might see jerseys hanging from their lockers. They know if we win, I'm doing something."

He showed his loyalty to MSU by talking with Izzo at least once a week, by talking to Toronto's No. 24, fellow "Flintstone" Morris Peterson, after nearly every game and by calling Bell regularly to make sure everything was fine in Breslin.

"It feels good just to hear Coach's voice sometimes," Cleaves

Photo Credit: Kevin Fowler, MSU Sports Information

MATEEN CLEAVES

said. "Words can't express how I feel about him. He's the best person in the world. If I have a good game, he'll call and say, 'Keep doing what you're doing. Bye.' But if I have a bad game or he thinks I'm down, he'll call and talk for an hour or two."

Cleaves has almost a year left to complete his degree and promises to finish that work in less time than the decade Shaquille O'Neal needed.

His mom also returned to school to complete her degree in gerontology. And his dad's big wish has long been to finish the last 25 credits he needs for his bachelor's degree in social work and to pursue a master's and a Ph.D.

"I'm going to pay for him to go back to school," Cleaves said. "I'm going to surprise him with something else, too. But I have a great deal of respect for my father. He was at every game. I could hear him over all the other parents, hollering the whole time."

Cleaves had one other gift to give, besides a smile for anyone who needed it. He saved all his game shoes to distribute in the Flint Public Schools for outstanding students with excellent attendance.

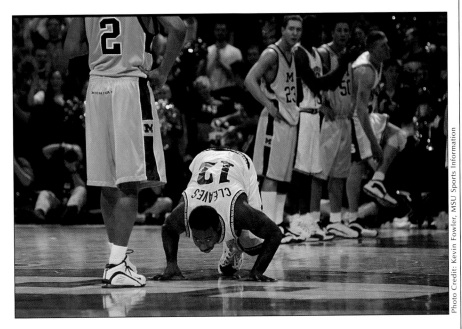
Photo Credit: Kevin Fowler, MSU Sports Information

He promised to sign each pair of Nikes. The only other writing was on the backs, just above the heels:

OTWT

Flint

"That stands for 'Only time will tell,'" Cleaves said. "I don't want to be given anything. I don't want any handouts. I've always been 10 times harder on myself than anyone else could be. I take that as a challenge. But I just want to be a leader. That means being the first guy in and one of the last to leave."

Cleaves is only going one place — back to work as a work-in-progress. And when people say he has to learn how to lose, a champ at every level has other ideas.

The Pistons were 32-50 last season. In four years at MSU, Cleaves' teams were a combined 104-32. Learn how to lose? He'd rather help another team learn how to win.

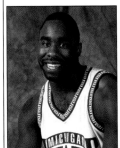

12 MATEEN CLEAVES
Guard—6-foot-2, 205 pounds
Flint, Mich. (Flint Northern HS)

Cleaves' Statistics

	G/GS	MIN/Avg.	FG/FGA	Pct.	3FG/3FGA	Pct.	FT/FTA	Pct.	REB/Avg.	PF/FO	A	BK	ST	PTS	Avg.
1996-97	29/24	750/25.9	111/277	.401	18/76	.237	57/79	.722	73/2.5	61/2	146	4	17	297	10.2
1997-98	30/29	1005/33.5	161/403	.400	51/152	.336	111/158	.703	75/2.5	80/1	217	6	73	484	16.1
1998-99	38/38	1185/31.1	159/392	.406	42/144	.292	85/108	.787	62/1.6	78/0	274	2	69	445	11.7
1999-2000	26/24	820/31.5	109/259	.421	32/85	.376	65/86	.756	46/1.8	57/0	179	4	36	315	12.1
	123/115	3760/30.6	540/1331	.406	143/457	.313	318/431	.738	256/2.1	276/3	816	16	195	1541	12.5

A.J. GRANGER

Most college basketball players think they are better than they are. A.J. Granger was better than he imagined.

When he finally figured that out, "Mr. March" used his remaining time at Michigan State wisely, helping the Spartans march to two Final Fours and capture an NCAA title.

"I wasn't really that comfortable and confident until the end of my junior year," said Granger, a two-time NCAA All-Midwest Region selection. "The biggest problem was I never gave myself credit for the things I could do. I never thought I'd get 10 rebounds in a game at Michigan State."

Granger got 10 rebounds in the first game of his junior season, eight games before his first 10-point performance. But he scored in double figures 20 times in his last 44 games and was huge when he had to be.

The 6-foot-9, 230-pounder from Findlay, Ohio, was a throwback in many ways, including his lifestyle off the court. He was married to the former Heather Wilhelm at age 22, less than four months after his final basket against Florida.

But if MSU coach Tom Izzo had thrown up his hands in frustration and given up on Granger, their team would never have won 65 games over a two-year span. And Iowa State, Wisconsin or Florida would have enjoyed "One Shining Moment."

"Every kid needs to be challenged every day," said Izzo, who rode a reluctant Granger harder than a winning jockey would in the Kentucky Derby. "I've told A.J. he's good enough to play in the NBA. I really believe that. Maybe the light finally went on."

He was a shining star at Liberty-Benton High, earning All-Ohio honors twice and Division IV Player of the Year acclaim. As a junior his school went 27-0. And he averaged 22.0 points and 9.0 rebounds as a senior, when the Eagles were 20-3.

Granger was the MVP of Ohio's North-South All-Star Game with a 19-point, 10-rebound effort. He was picked as one of the top 90 prospects in the nation by *Hoop Scoop* magazine and was a better athlete than many expected.

After lettering as one of the world's tallest cross country runners, Granger showed his versatility in track. He won a state discus crown with a throw of 180 feet, finished fourth in the shot put and set a school record for the 100-meter dash with a time of 11.3 seconds.

Granger got off to a much slower start with the Spartans. He failed to score more than four points in any of his 22 freshman appearances, shooting just 34.4 percent from the field and 45.5 percent at the line.

"Right after Christmas, the coaches were really pushing me," Granger said of a maddening moment. "I had a stretch where I couldn't do anything right. Then, they kind of laid off me for a while. And I started playing a lot better."

Granger said he didn't need coaches two inches from his eardrums to know he had made mistakes. But if that was where Izzo had to be, it wasn't the first time a coach had camped there.

"Since eighth grade, I've had coaches in my face, screaming at me all the time," Granger said. "That's the reason it wasn't as hard to take the coaches here. If I hadn't been exposed to all that, it would have been a mind-blowing experience."

Instead, Granger listened and learned. Eventually, he seized an opportunity and replaced struggling senior Jon Garavaglia. When Granger started the final seven games of 1996-97, MSU went 5-2 and reached the second round of the NIT.

After playing just 24 minutes in a 14-game span, Granger played 39 minutes against Penn State and Ohio State and contributed six points, eight rebounds and improved post defense. He also freed sophomore Antonio Smith to average nearly five more rebounds per game.

"I didn't know how hard I had to work to get things done at this level," Granger said. "But I wasn't going to get upset about anything. You have to work for everything you get around here. And it all worked out."

Or so it seemed. Granger looked like a starter for the next three seasons. But he regressed in 1997-98, partly due to illness and injury. He didn't start a single game that season and almost started to pack and leave.

"I was so close to quitting you

Photo Credit: Kevin Fowler, MSU Sports Information

wouldn't believe it," Granger said just before Senior Day two years later. "I've never told anyone that before. But I went from 229 pounds to 212 with mono. And I had a stress fracture in my left foot. It was the lowest point of my life — no joke."

Granger lost his starting job to freshman Andre Hutson and never scored in double figures as a sophomore. But he was a better player the following fall after a trip to Belgium, The Netherlands and Germany with the Big Ten's touring team.

Travel wasn't as easy or enjoyable for the Granger family early in his junior season. His mother, Dawn, was lucky to break just five ribs and her right wrist in a car-truck collison on her way to East Lansing for the Western Michigan-MSU game. And his father, Joe, barely escaped paralysis in a body-surfing accident in Hawaii.

The Spartans were staying on the north shore of Oahu and competing in the Pearl Harbor Classic when Granger's dad slammed head-first into a sandbar, fracturing his first two vertebrae three days before Christmas.

Granger wasn't aware of that when his defense helped MSU beat Bill Self's Tulsa Golden Hurricane in the tournament's semifinals. He didn't see his dad in the stands, a bit of a surprise. But he wasn't distraught or determined to win that game for his No. 1 fan.

"My dad didn't want anyone to tell me," Granger said the next morning before his second two-hour round-trip to The Queen's

A.J. Granger

Medical Center in Honolulu. "I think he's going to be all right. But he's really lucky. With that kind of injury, he could've drowned."

Instead, Granger's father was fitted for a cervical halo to stabilize his head. But discomfort and inconvenience were a lot better than death or an inability to move his limbs.

"My dad said his spine cracked from his neck to his butt, like a zipper," Granger said. "Joe Klein, Jason's dad, was with him. And when he couldn't move his mouth or turn his head, our trainers took him to a local hospital, then to Honolulu when an MRI was worse than they thought."

Granger was better than anyone imagined he could be in the championship game. With little or no preparation, he came off the bench and had his breakout game, a 16-point performance against Alabama that made a proud patient smile until he could fly home to Ohio.

"You have to take your hat off to the kid," Izzo said after Granger missed film sessions, a shootaround and the pregame meal to be with his dad. "He just showed up for the game and played....It just goes to show that coaching means nothing. Now, all our players will want to miss meetings."

The Spartans trailed the Crimson Tide 43-37 when Granger hit a 3-pointer. By the end of a 20-4 run, MSU had a 10-point lead. And Granger had new respect from at least one opponent.

"He surprised me, to be honest with you," Alabama coach Mark Gottfried said. "We didn't expect him to step up and make those shots. But he was the difference in the game."

Granger flew home with his team after the final game to be with his mom and younger brother, Tyler. When he returned to campus, friends in Findlay took over and did everything they could

to help. They brought plenty of food, plowed the driveway and delivered clippings from No. 43's games.

"I'm lucky," Granger said. "There was a chance I never would've seen my father again. But he's fine. And so is my mom. I just hope our run of bad luck is over. We've definitely had our share."

Perhaps because of the two

Photo Credit: Kevin Fowler, MSU Sports Information

near-tragedies or perhaps just because his play improved, fans began to appreciate Granger late in his junior season. As their jeers turned to cheers, he understood why and didn't hold grudges.

"I could tell the support for me was about 50-50," Granger told Steve Grinczel of Booth News Service. "I could hear some people cheer for me. And I could hear some moan when I'd go in. But that's going to happen. I didn't have a very good sophomore year. There were bound to be doubters."

Granger seemed reluctant to become the Spartans' version of Brian Cardinal, a sweet-shooting, often-annoying forward from Purdue. But as he gradually became more aggressive, other parts of his game improved, too.

Beginning with 10 points in 21 minutes at Michigan, Granger seemed to be a different player. His stats improved from 2.6 points per game as a sophomore to 6.6 as a junior and from 1.8 rebounds to 3.9. His shooting percentages also soared — from 40.5 to 53.2 from the field, from 26.3 to 50.0 past the arc and from 59.1 to 71.4 at the foul line.

"There's no doubt his game has taken the biggest jump of anyone's in the last month," Izzo said in mid-March. "He can go inside now and make some shots, then step out and hit 3s. And he has gotten tougher, which is hard to do. He's starting to have some success posting up. I think he's almost enjoying it, which wasn't the case before."

Heading into the 1999 NCAA

Tournament, no one would have picked Granger as one of the top 40 players in the Midwest Region, much like the situation with David Thomas in the South Region two years later.

But Granger was great in MSU's four Tournament wins, averaging 12.0 points and 4.3 rebounds in less than 22 minutes. He was 16-for-23 from the field, 7-for-8 on 3-point tries and 9-for-9 at the line. And when Kentucky threatened to run away and hide in an Elite Eight classic, Granger fueled an amazing comeback.

"When we had a chance to pull away, A.J. did a nice job of sticking the 3s to prevent us from doing that," said Kentucky coach Tubby Smith, whose team led 17-4 and lost 73-66. "He beat us. We switched from man-to-man to zone. And that's when Granger knocked them down."

A player who described himself as "gumpy" finished with 14 points on 4-for-5 shooting from the field and was 3-for-3 from long range and from the line. Coupled with similar accuracy and a 10-point, seven-rebound night against Oklahoma, Granger was an obvious All-Region selection.

Saddled with expectations for the first time as a senior, he had an up-and-down start, often playing to the caliber of the competition. After hitting a total of just three shots against Howard and Eastern Michigan, Granger was the second-best player on the floor against Kansas with 13 points and nine rebounds.

"Every coach has a guy he

Photo Credit: Kevin Fowler, MSU Sports Information

picks on more than others," said Izzo, who nearly removed Granger from the lineup before the Great Eight. "Unfortunately for A.J., I'm picking on him. But that's only because I think he has a lot to give, more than even he knows."

After barely being noticed in a 33-point win over Mississippi Valley State, he was one of the few Spartans who showed up in a stunning loss at Wright State. Granger led all scorers that night with 17 points, more than twice as many as any other MSU starter. He and Hutson were 9-for-15 from the

A.J. GRANGER

field, while the team's non-Ohioans were 9-for-40.

Granger scored 15 points against Penn State and contributed 13 points and eight rebounds in an overtime win against Indiana. But he had just one rebound in 33 minutes in a loss at Ohio State. Suddenly, Granger was back on the bench, partly to add some punch to a unit that was outscored 24-6 by the Buckeyes.

"A power forward can't get one rebound and play here," Izzo said. "That's illegal. Plus, we aren't getting anything offensively from our bench. So I made that change for negative and positive reasons."

Granger was a reserve for four games and had his second discussion of the season with Izzo, a give-and-take that seemed to increase understanding both ways.

"We'd never really talked that much," Granger said. "Finally, we both sat down, said what needed to be said and laid everything out on the table....Before that, I don't know if I was afraid to let him know what my goals really were."

He played like an NBA prospect the rest of the season, starting with 13 points and a game-high eight rebounds in his return as a starter against Connecticut. Granger followed with game-highs of 18 points and 12 rebounds at Purdue and 11 points and 11 rebounds at Wisconsin — back-to-back double-doubles on the road.

Those performances were a Valentine's Day present for

Wilhelm, a basketball player at Muskingum College who transferred to Bowling Green. The couple had been engaged since Christmas Day 1998, just after Granger's breakthrough in the Pearl Harbor Classic.

The next cause for celebration came on Senior Day, when Granger had 18 points and missed just one shot in a 51-point pounding of Michigan. He was 7-for-8 from the field, including 4-for-4 accuracy from long range. And why not? It was March again for a player who hit 35 of his final 38 tries at the line.

"I really don't know how I'll be remembered," Granger said the day before his final home game. "When I first got here, I didn't feel accepted. The first year, no one knew who I was. Then, I started to hear comments like, 'We see all the little things you do. There aren't any stats for what you do on the floor.'"

There were other numbers to note, beginning with his game-high 17 points in the championship game of the Big Ten Tournament against Illinois. And in the second week of the NCAA Tournament, Granger had 19 points in a comeback against Syracuse and 18 points in 37 minutes against Iowa State.

He probably saved his best game for last, however. Granger said goodbye to college basketball with 19 points and nine rebounds in the final win over Florida. At age 21, he was a national champion. A month later, he had a degree in marketing. And less than two

months after that, Granger was a husband.

If no one ever gets it all, his lone disappointment was not being picked in the second round of the 2000 NBA Draft. NBA Director of Scouting Marty Blake couldn't understand it and called Granger the best player not to be selected. And after a futile four days of watching in a Vancouver Grizzlies camp, Granger left to pursue other options.

He signed with Milon of Athens in the A1 league in Greece and faced a major adjustment — one game a week at 5 p.m. on Saturdays, 90-minute practices with no film sessions and a gym that seated just 1,200 people.

"There's no comparison," Granger told Mitch Albom of the *Detroit Free Press* as the Spartans began their title defense. "I tried at first to explain to these guys what it was like last year, to win the title, to make the friendships that we made as teammates at MSU. But I gave up. Nobody here can understand it....They think this league is the biggest thing there is."

It isn't as big as the Big Ten. And it isn't as big as the NBA. Granger knows all about the first league. Soon, he might know more about the second, with a new zone-defense rule helping players who can shoot from the perimeter.

Granger had to wait his turn once before. Maybe he just needs to find another coach who believes in him as much as his family does. Or as much as he has come to believe in himself.

A.J. GRANGER

Photo Credit: Kevin Fowler, MSU Sports Information

43 A.J. GRANGER

Forward—6-foot-9, 230 pounds

Findlay, Ohio (Liberty-Benton HS)

Granger's Statistics

	G/GS	MIN/Avg.	FG/FGA	Pct.	3FG/3FGA	Pct.	FT/FTA	Pct.	REB/Avg.	PF/FO	A	BK	ST	PTS	Avg.
1996-97	22/7	182/8.3	11/32	.344	0/1	.000	5/11	.455	29/1.3	28/0	5	1	8	27	1.2
1997-98	30/0	360/12.0	30/74	.405	5/19	.263	13/22	.591	55/1.8	57/1	14	10	13	78	2.6
1998-99	38/5	786/20.7	91/171	.532	23/46	.500	45/63	.714	147/3.9	84/0	22	17	21	250	6.6
1999-2000	39/35	1122/28.8	127/254	.500	49/109	.450	67/75	.893	205/5.3	78/1	48	21	17	370	9.5
	129/47	2450/19.0	259/531	.488	77/175	.440	130/171	.760	436/3.4	247/2	89	49	59	725	5.6

DAVID THOMAS

Some things are well worth the wait. Some people are, too.

At age 24, in the final two weeks of a five-year career at Michigan State, David Thomas delivered his two best performances — career-highs of 14 rebounds against Fresno State and 19 points against Temple in the 2001 NCAA Tournament.

Without those efforts, MSU might not have reached the Sweet 16 for a fourth-straight year and never would have made it to the Final Four for the third-straight time.

But Temple coaching legend John Chaney, normally a wise old Owl, was wrong when he stared at Thomas' stat line and insisted, "The wrong guy beat us."

Thomas was the perfect guy to do that. He represented everything positive about Spartan Basketball as the ultimate survivor.

"Patience and perseverance," Thomas said after the win over Fresno State amid three family crises. "Patience and perseverance."

Tom Izzo's most important import wasn't always a basketball player. Thomas grew up in Brampton, Ont., near Toronto, when the NBA's Raptors didn't exist.

"I used to play hockey all the time," Thomas said. "We had a field in our little complex. And some of the dads used to make an ice rink for us. We'd be out there until midnight playing hockey. Then, we'd skate home, drink some hot chocolate and go to bed.

I wish I would've played a little more and stuck with it. But things happen for a reason. I finally chose basketball."

Only a few major programs chose Thomas, a grade-13 student, as a prospect in 1996. Izzo spotted him while recruiting Kentucky-bound center Jamaal Magloire and immediately saw another Steve Smith.

After looking at Seton Hall, Villanova, Virginia Tech and Syracuse, Thomas signed late with MSU and had no idea what he was getting into as part of a big-time, Big Ten program.

"I was like some country hick coming in here," Thomas said. "I didn't know anything. I was overwhelmed by this gym and by how intense everything was. But it was a great learning experience. I definitely made the right decision."

So did Izzo in signing a player who would start at four positions, including three games as a slender — OK, downright skinny — 6-foot-7 freshman in a 17-12 season.

Thomas started the first seven games of his sophomore year at small forward, ahead of future All-American Morris Peterson. And he made the Spartan Coca-Cola Classic all-tournament team with 10 rebounds against Central Michigan and 10 points and 10 rebounds against Gonzaga, his first double-double.

But Thomas missed six games in that 22-8, Sweet 16 breakthrough season with a pair of knee sprains, then sat out 1998-99 as a redshirt.

The fun was just beginning.

Thomas started the first 11 games of 1999-2000 at point guard, replacing All-American Mateen Cleaves, who had fractured his foot. Though he could never match Cleaves' efficiency, Thomas did have seven assists against North Carolina and three steals against Kansas and Kentucky.

He missed four games late in the Big Ten season with a stress fracture of his own and scored just one point in six NCAA Tournament triumphs as a junior, hardly an indication of what was to come.

In Thomas' first four years on campus, he had never scored more than 12 points or grabbed more than 10 rebounds and had made a copy of Gray's Anatomy as valuable as the MSU media guide.

So when Izzo kept talking about a key player in the Spartans' bid for back-to-back national titles, doubting Thomas was a normal reaction — and the wrong one, teammates warned.

"David has helped me a lot the past two years," sophomore forward Jason Richardson said. "He plays the 4, the 3, the 2 and the 1. It's great that a guy can move around like that. I wish I had the ability to go from the 1 all the way to the 4."

With more arms than some octopi, Thomas was omnipresent on defense and 4-for-4 from the field in an 11-point, eight-rebound effort against Indiana, when he was the ESPN Player of the Game.

And in a gut-check win at Wisconsin, the player who had missed two tying free throws

DAVID THOMAS

against Temple in 1998 made amends. With a share of the Big Ten title at stake, Thomas hit two free throws to ice a 51-47 victory over the Badgers.

"I didn't plan on those being my only two points of the night," Thomas said. "I just tried to stay composed and deliver like a senior. I've only missed two free throws all year."

He would finish the season 28-for-31 at the line, a team-best 90.3-percent accuracy. But those Big Ten games were just the start of a memorable six-week span.

"I finally got it," Thomas said of his new confidence. "It all starts with your shot. When you knock down a couple of jumpers, you feel comfortable and bounce a little more on defense. You're more active. You're like a psycho out there."

No one was more active than the player who had gone from a pipecleaner to a sinewy 210-pounder. And when Thomas celebrated Senior Day with a title-clinching win over Michigan, no one in Breslin Center had a bigger smile.

"When you lose to the Wolverines, you don't just let yourself down," Thomas said. "You disappoint your whole school and your community. In our last home game, we couldn't let that happen."

He couldn't let the season end against Fresno State in Memphis, either, as he grabbed 14 rebounds in 27 minutes, more than the Bulldogs' top two rebounders snared in nearly triple that time.

"I just tried to bring energy," said Thomas, who supplied as much in March as Lansing's Board of Water & Light. "Our big guys did a good job against their big guys. That left a lot of rebounds for someone to grab."

There weren't many left when Thomas was done, as MSU outrebounded Fresno State 48-32 and got all the loose balls it left on the floor in a loss to Penn State in the Big Ten Tournament nine days earlier.

"'D.T.' does a great job of that," senior guard Charlie Bell said. "That's what we depend on him to do. He's not a go-to, go-to guy on offense. But he can make some noise if you leave him alone."

That's what Chaney forgot when he decided to give Thomas the open shots that usually occur against Temple's trademark 1-3-1 matchup zone. So what if Thomas was averaging just 4.9 points per game? He was shooting a respectable 47.7 percent from the field.

With a place in history at stake, Thomas was 8-for-10 against the Owls, arguably the best clutch performance by a "non-scorer" since Terry Donnelly went 5-for-5 to sink Indiana State in the 1979 NCAA title game.

"Coach called me in (after a scoreless effort against Gonzaga) and said, 'We need you to play big, 'D.T.'…He has always had my back and always been on my side," Thomas said after his 19 points, seven rebounds, two assists, two steals and zero turnovers.

"He's so long and athletic,"

senior forward Andre Hutson said of a player with pro potential in Izzo's eyes. "He flies around. And he kills us in practice. He just has a knack for the ball."

Thomas also had incredible motivation. His cousin, Wayne Thomas, had cancer and would die after the Temple game. His mother, Linda, had been diagnosed with breast cancer and was beginning radiation. And his grandmother, Martha Rolley, had experienced two heart attacks in a month and would die in May.

"It's Wayne who brings the family together," Thomas said. "They put a TV in the room for him. I don't know if he saw the Temple game. I know he didn't see

Photo Credit: Kevin Fowler, MSU Sports Information

DAVID THOMAS

Photo Credit: Kevin Fowler, MSU Sports Information

the Fresno game. But when my sister, Tracey, told him I had 14 rebounds, he gave her the thumbs-up sign. I just found out how bad it was while we were in Memphis. It has been on my mind constantly."

Maturity matters at times like these. And a player who was born before Jud Heathcote ever coached a Big Ten game — the same year Izzo was a senior at Northern Michigan and Earvin Johnson was a senior at Lansing Everett — played like "Magic" for one memorable game.

"If you're playing a lot of different positions, you never get credit for what you can do," Izzo said. "He's rebounding better. He can defend inside guys. He can defend outside guys. And he can handle the ball when we need him to help break the press. David is a player I'll always appreciate. He has sacrificed so much for the team."

His final assist came hours after his playing career ended against Arizona in Minneapolis. When an overloaded elevator became stuck between the third and fourth floors of the Spartans' Hilton Airport headquarters, 21 people were trapped in various states of distress for almost a half-hour.

Thomas, one of five MSU players on board, stripped to the waist and came to the rescue with a maneuver worthy of Spiderman. Following step-by-step instructions from an elevator repairman, he pushed his way through a ceiling panel and slithered up to shut the power off, then fix the problem.

"It was getting pretty scary," Thomas said the next afternoon. "There were so many people there. And there was…a lot of loud talking, put it that way. I had to use my long arms again. If no one on the elevator had been tall, I don't know what would've happened."

Richardson and teammates Aloysius Anagonye, Mike Chappell and Brandon Smith were among the passengers, while Hutson and Zach Randolph waited a half-floor above and offered support.

After the fourth-floor elevator door was wedged open a few inches and propped with a chair, a portable fan blew air to the jammed cabin about four feet below. Bottled water was lowered. And a flashlight was passed down to Smith, before Thomas killed the lights and completed the shutdown.

"It was close to midnight," said MSU fund-raiser and broadcaster Terry Braverman, who waited above with Hutson and Randolph. "And it was getting a little hairy. David was really the hero. He had to shut everything down before we could get them off the elevator."

Patience and perseverance — Thomas scored after the buzzer sounded.

11 DAVID THOMAS

Guard/Forward—6-foot-7, 210 pounds
Brampton, Ontario (Notre Dame HS)

Thomas's Statistics

	G/GS	MIN/Avg.	FG/FGA	Pct.	3FG/3FGA	Pct.	FT/FTA	Pct.	REB/Avg.	PF/FO	A	BK	ST	PTS	Avg.
1996-97	23/3	197/8.6	10/25	.400	0/2	.000	4/5	.800	42/1.8	37/1	7	2	12	24	1.0
1997-98	24/7	354/14.8	38/81	.469	0/4	.000	8/15	.533	91/3.8	33/1	20	4	13	84	3.5
1999-2000	34/11	459/13.5	31/76	.408	1/9	.111	20/28	.714	82/2.4	48/0	52	5	28	83	2.4
2000-01	33/25	739/22.4	73/148	.493	3/18	.167	28/31	.903	156/4.7	62/1	63	18	37	177	5.4
	114/46	1749/15.3	152/330	.461	4/33	.121	60/79	.759	371/3.3	180/3	142	29	90	368	3.2

CHARLIE BELL

He showed up in East Lansing as the No. 1 scorer in Flint's illustrious prep basketball history. He showed his coaches and teammates a lot more by transforming himself into "Championship Charlie."

If Charlie Bell III was never the prolific scorer at Michigan State that he was at Southwestern Academy, he became a much better all-around player — a guard-dog defender, a voracious rebounder and, more often than not, the most versatile backcourt talent in the nation.

Bell didn't dominate the headlines or the highlights the way Mateen Cleaves, Morris Peterson or Jason Richardson did. But he was always there: 140 appearances in 140 games. The only bells on campus that rang more often from 1997-2001 were located at the top of Beaumont Tower.

When a still-underrated MSU career was through, Bell left with as much on his resume as anyone who ever set foot on campus:

•Big Ten individual records of 115 career victories, two more than teammate Andre Hutson, and 136 starts.

•Four straight conference crowns, a pair of Big Ten Tournament titles, three straight No. 1 seeds in the NCAA Tournament, four Sweet 16s in a row, back-to-back-to-back Final Fours and NCAA supremacy in 2000.

•The No. 11 spot on the Spartans' career scoring list with 1,468 points, one of the top three rebound totals for a guard with 624, seventh place on the school's all-time assist list with 371 and the No. 7 spot in 3-point baskets with 125.

•A legitimate degree in advertising and the respect of almost everyone, from his professors to MSU non-athletes to the kids who wore his No. 14 jerseys across the state.

•And a gorgeous girlfriend who shared the spotlight, Miss Michigan USA Kenya Howard, an engineer for General Motors with bachelor's and master's degrees from MSU.

"Charlie is someone our young guys can look up to and model themselves after," Spartan assistant Brian Gregory said. "In every aspect of his life, he's squared away. He has things under control and understands what's important. Unfortunately, in this day and age, sometimes that's overlooked. I know Charlie has a very strong faith. He knows if he does the right things, good things are going to happen to him. And you're seeing that."

People who knew him saw that right away. A conversation with Bell always left you thinking he was two years older than he was. And if it seemed he was almost too perfect sometimes, it's a good thing you didn't see him do the dishes and the family's spring cleaning.

"I'm just very, very proud of him," said Belle Bell, Charlie's mom. "If I'd asked God for the perfect child, I wouldn't have gotten better than Charlie Bell. He has already exceeded all my expectations. I have to ask my husband every day, 'Is he that good?'"

He might be. But, remember, that's his mother talking. To get a more objective view, we have to check with a coach who saw his moods and mistakes every day for four years.

"He's one of the finest people I've ever been around," Southwestern coach Reggie Manville insisted in 1997. "He has never been bigger than this program or bigger than the school. Charlie has truly been a dream."

He could be. But, don't forget, that's his coach speaking. To get a less biased view, we need to fast-forward to someone who played with him or against him every day in practice.

"Playing with Charlie Bell is tremendous," MSU's David Thomas said. "Coming in here as Flint's No. 1 scorer and accepting a role as a defensive player says so much about him. It says how much he means to the program and how much the program means to him."

Maybe so. But, c'mon, we're talking with a Spartan teammate. To get a truer picture, we need to check with an opponent who has studied Bell and uncovered some weaknesses.

"Charlie Bell is the best guard in the country," said Oklahoma coach Kelvin Sampson, whose team lost to the Spartans in the 1999 Sweet 16. "A lot of people like Jason Williams of Duke. But Bell is a rock. He's not going to let you go sideways too much."

MSU began recruiting Bell in his sophomore year at Southwestern. The only question

CHARLIE BELL

worth asking was, "Why did Tom Izzo wait so long?"

Bell had 38 points against Flint Northwestern, Peterson's school, in just his third varsity game as a 14-year-old freshman. He averaged 21.5 points per game that season against players three years older and didn't turn 15 until March.

Izzo got involved soon after that, then brought in Stan Heath and Tom Crean for triple-team attention, as the 6-foot-3 Bell averaged 32.3 points per game as a junior.

Bell had 40 points against Northwestern, the school closest to his home, in the third game of his junior season. He added 42 against Ann Arbor Pioneer, a Flint-record 52 at Saginaw Arthur Hill, 43 at Flint Central and 46 against Bay City Western.

By the end of 11th grade, Bell was within 17 points of Glen Rice's city scoring record. So the Spartans had every reason to think they were chasing an explosive scorer — and no proof they were pursuing an all-around talent.

"I never thought he'd be this good in this many areas, to tell you the truth," Izzo said five years later. "He could always score. But he played inside so much you never saw the guard skills. I didn't figure he'd rebound the same way against bigger people. And I'd been programmed to think no scorer could ever guard anyone."

MSU already had early commitments from Ohio standouts Doug Davis and Andre Hutson when Bell made his official visit on Oct. 25, 1996, the same weekend

Photo Credit: Kevin Fowler, MSU Sports Information

the Spartans whipped Wisconsin 30-13 in football.

Bell had already made trips to Michigan, Connecticut, Penn State and Minnesota, where he saw MSU beat the Golden Gophers 27-9 in the Metrodome. As much as Izzo wanted Bell, Nick Saban wanted him to have season football tickets as a good-luck charm.

Izzo got his wish on Wednesday, Nov. 6, the day after Election Day. And the only ballot that mattered to Izzo that week was the one Bell punched in his mind after deciding to stay in the state.

"When I looked all around, I saw that anything any school can offer can be found right here," Bell said. "But the big reason I'm coming is Coach Izzo....And with a point guard from Flint, if I'm the two-guard, I'll probably get the ball a lot."

That point guard, Mateen Cleaves, had been a rival of Bell's at Flint Northern and had helped hold him to a 19.5-point average in their six meetings. But Cleaves always respected Bell's game and encouraged him to take Anthony Mull's spot as the team's fourth "Flintstone."

"Antonio Smith, Morris and Mateen are all from Flint," Bell said. "And I look forward to playing with them instead of against them. Together, with hard work, we want to bring a national championship to Michigan State and honor to Flint."

Missions accomplished. But not before he finished his work at Southwestern, including straight A's as a senior to finish with a 3.0 grade-point average.

Bell obliterated Rice's career record in his first game as a senior and finally settled matters with Northern, scoring 43 in a 76-72 road triumph over the seventh-ranked, defending Class A champ.

Bell averaged 30.5 points and 13.8 rebounds as a senior, finished with 2,252 points and was a Parade All-American. He also played in Magic's Roundball Classic at The Palace of Auburn Hills, where he received extra attention from an unapologetic Earvin Johnson.

"I got to get my boy out here!...That's my boy!" Johnson said when Bell made his way to

midcourt for a pregame photo, then went one-on-one with gifted guard Tracy McGrady and was outscored 13-10.

"I think I held my own," Bell said. "I wasn't great. But I didn't try to overshadow anyone. I just tried to play my game."

That attitude served him well the next four years. The former cross country runner reported for practice in excellent shape and moved into the lineup when projected starter Thomas Kelley stepped on Bell's foot in practice and suffered a season-ending fracture.

Bell started all 30 games that year and led the Spartans with 15 points in his collegiate debut against East Tennessee State, the first time a true freshman had led MSU in a season-opener since Jay Vincent had 25 points against Central Michigan in 1977.

Despite that sweet beginning, Bell had his doubters. Could he stroke the 3?...Could he check bigger guards?...Could he handle the ball?...Could he handle constant feedback from Izzo?...The fourth concern nearly ended his career before his first game.

"Coach asks an awful lot of you," Bell said after a four-year adjustment. "In high school I wasn't yelled at once. Here I didn't make it through the first hour. The first week I was here, I was ready to quit. I was convinced I wasn't good enough to play here."

Ask not for whom the Bell toils, Tom Izzo. He toils for thee. Or as Belle Bell would explain to his son's coach later, "All he wants

to do is please you." More often than not, Bell did.

His freshman highlight came on March 12, 1998, Bell's 19th birthday. When everyone kept talking about Cleaves and Eastern Michigan guards Earl Boykins and Derrick Dial, Bell shouted, "What about me!" with 22 points in an NCAA East Region first-round win in Hartford, Conn.

Bell's sophomore season started much the same way with 22 first-half points in a 30-point win at Oakland. But when his averages dropped from 9.2 points per game to 7.8, from 4.4 rebounds to 3.8 and from 1.3 assists to 1.0, the only numbers he talked about were the Spartans' 33 wins and five losses.

"Is he a throwback?...No doubt about it," Gregory said near the end of Bell's stay. "The term in basketball is old-school. He's definitely old-school. He's a great athlete. But he's more of a basketball player. He doesn't do many things flashy. He just gets the job done. The bottom line is, his stats are better than probably 90 percent of the players in the country. And his teams keep winning."

Bell cared more about championships than most people ever realized. His cool, almost-casual demeanor was misinterpreted, especially compared to Cleaves' fiery leadership. Bell was never indifferent, just in control.

When Cleaves went down with a stress fracture and missed the first 13 games of Bell's junior year, guess who stepped to the point and beat Kansas with 21

CHARLIE BELL

points, steady playmaking and stifling defense in the 1999 Great Eight? If you said, "No. 14, the guy who braided his hair that week," you just scored more points than some Jayhawks.

Bell followed with 20-point games at Arizona and against Oakland, becoming the first Spartan to reach that mark in three straight games since Shawn Respert, the Big Ten's No. 2 career scorer, in 1995.

And if MSU didn't exactly burn it up with a 9-4 preconference mark, it survived until Cleaves returned in January and became stronger as a result, with Bell speaking up for the first time.

"We've always had great leaders here, from 'Magic' to Scott Skiles to Eric (Snow) to Mateen," Bell said. "Someone has to get the guys going. That's not really my personality. But when I see something wrong, I'll get in a guy's face."

He led the Spartans with 22 points in an overtime win over Indiana, had 20 points against Illinois on Super Bowl Sunday and had 23 points — a belated Valentine's Day gift — against Ohio State, all in Breslin Center.

But Bell saved his best work for last as a junior. He poured home a career-high 31 points in a 51-point dismemberment of

Michigan on Senior Day, then was a rock in the NCAA title game with nine points, eight rebounds, five assists and great defense against Florida.

His life was just as successful academically and socially, though his relationship with Miss Michigan USA took some time to develop, much like his point guard skills.

"I met her on campus a couple of years ago," Bell said. "I'm really a shy guy. But this one, I couldn't pass up. I had to try to get her number. The bad part was she never went to games. So that didn't work."

Eventually, Howard showed up

Photo Credit: Kevin Fowler, MSU Sports Information

CHARLIE BELL

in an MSU jersey as often as she did with her Miss Michigan USA sash. And as Bell prepared for his senior season, he found the perfect way to practice his shooting and score other valuable points.

"I spent the summer working out around here and having my girlfriend rebound for me," Bell said. "She likes to work out. So I'd miss a couple every now and then, just so she could chase them."

On Sunday, Nov. 19, 2000, both had plenty to celebrate. That was the day Howard was crowned as the pageant's winner in Port Huron and Bell had 13 points, 11 rebounds and 10 assists against Oakland in East Lansing. He became just the second Spartan to post a triple-double, joining some guy named Johnson.

Through the Spartans' first six games, including wins over North Carolina and Florida, Bell averaged 17.0 points, 5.2 rebounds and 5.7 assists. He also shot 57.8 percent from the field, 54.5 beyond the arc and 80.0 at the foul line, including 12-for-13 accuracy from the floor in a 31-point night against Eastern Washington.

A popular pick as one of the nation's top backcourt defenders, Bell didn't disappoint in that area, either. He held Oakland's Jason Rozycki to three points just two days after his 32-point eruption beat Michigan. And North Carolina star Joseph Forte was limited to 11 points, less than half his average entering the game.

"I knew with Mateen and 'Mo Pete' gone, people would be watching to see who'd step up,"

Photo Credit: Kevin Fowler, MSU Sports Information

CHARLIE BELL

Bell said. "I knew we would be on TV a lot. And I wanted to show people I was one of the best players in the country. Then, there's the pride thing, being from Flint. We all have tattoos on our arms. And with all the junk those other guys talked, I had to represent."

Misrepresentation is a felony in Flint. The first signs of trouble arose in a one-point triumph over Kentucky. Bell was 1-for-11 from the field, 1-for-7 from long range. But that wasn't the reason he got

Photo Credit: Kevin Fowler, MSU Sports Information

ripped at halftime by a coach who demanded vocal leadership and all-out effort.

"He was definitely fired up," Bell said, softening his description for family newspapers. "He said we were playing like a bunch of girls. I wasn't playing like an All-American. And he let me know that. He challenged all of us. If you go out there and play hard and lose, he's all right with that. But if you're not hustling, then there's a problem."

When the game was there to win or lose, Bell delivered the critical assist for Andre Hutson's game-wining layup, then soared above the sequoias to snare and secure the critical rebound — two huge plays that eventually meant a No. 1 seed in the NCAA Tournament.

His spirits soared even more a few weeks later as an 11-0 team prepared for its Big Ten opener. On Jan. 2, 2001, the night before he had 26 points against Penn State, Bell's No. 42 was retired at Southwestern — with his MSU coaches and teammates in attendance.

"I told them, 'You don't have to come,'" Bell said. "I was amazed that they would take the time to drive over and watch me get honored. They said, 'We're here to support you.' But that was big for me, being the first one from Flint to have my jersey retired. It was something special. I'm sure there were a lot of people who deserved it and didn't have it done."

The Spartans might not have deserved a win over Wisconsin in

Breslin. But after struggling in a 3-for-12 shooting performance, Bell sent the game into overtime with an in-out-and-in 3-pointer, his first trey in six attempts. He also found Richardson with a spectacular alley-oop feed to put the game away.

"They say big-time players make big-time plays in big games," said Brad Soderberg, the Badgers' acting head coach. "Bell did that. He made a big-time play at the most crucial time in the game. You can't put a price on a guy like that. He's really a great player."

Other coaches agreed, even when Bell hit a January slump that lasted in some form through his last 20 games. Though he never danced or shrieked at the ceiling, he did what he had to do to win games — and another championship.

"Charlie Bell has made great strides as a player," said Indiana interim head coach Mike Davis. "My first year in the league as an assistant, he was just a guy who was good in transition. Now, if I had a vote for Player of the Year, he'd get my vote. They aren't nearly the same team without him. He plays great defense. His shot is really good. And he makes everyone else on the floor better."

In one 20-minute interview, Bell said the words "win," "won," "winner" or "winning" a total of 17 times. And he understood the significance of becoming the winningest player in conference history in terms of games and rings.

"Last year was Mateen's and Morris' title," Bell said. "This year,

CHARLIE BELL

it belongs to me and to Andre, David (Thomas), Brandon (Smith) and Mike (Chappell). We're the leaders of this team. And a lot of people thought we wouldn't be able to do that. But we proved them wrong. We did lead this team to a Big Ten championship."

Bell never missed a game in four seasons and shifted from shooting guard to the point whenever Izzo asked. He knew he would never be Cleaves as a point guard. But he was just enough of everything to rank with the 10 best players in MSU history.

"He has been a chameleon," Gregory said. "Whatever the situation, Charlie has been able to adapt and be successful. When people were talking about a slump and saying he wasn't playing well, he hung in there and stayed true to his colors. We've seen more-talented, more-decorated players who weren't able to bounce back."

Back at Bell's place, if you hollered, "Hey, Champ!" you had to be prepared for two responses — a smile from the player and a slurp from his pet rottweiler.

"I don't go out and party a lot," Bell said. "I just go home and sit around with my girlfriend. We

might rent a movie or order a pizza. I try to rest as much as possible. I might play with the dog a little bit. I got him right after we won the national title. So I named him Champ....I had to name him appropriately."

Bell could have named him Pro Guard or Proud Graduate, too. Before a Final Four loss to Arizona that saw him shoot 1-for-10 and commit five turnovers but still lead all rebounders with 10, Bell was praised by the Spartans' greatest player.

"What NBA guys are looking for now are winners," said Johnson, an expert in that area. "That's why Charlie Bell will help some team. He can play more than one position. And coming from the program he has, he knows what it means to put winning first."

Bell and Hutson missed their commencement ceremonies because they had job interviews at the Desert Classic, one of three NBA tryout camps. And both players seemed to help themselves, with Bell beating Penn State bomber Joe Crispin in the 3-point shooting competition.

"We'll probably have a little

gathering when we get home," Bell said. "It's very disappointing to miss commencement. You put in four years to get to this point. It was a dream of mine. And it's special. I don't think enough attention is paid to it. Maybe that's another reason so many guys leave school early."

Seeing their sons get degrees to go with their championship jewelry was a dream for the parents of all five seniors. But none was happier than Belle Bell as she fought back tears with her son three time zones away.

"I had to be here," she said. "That's the whole reason he's at Michigan State. I talked to Charlie in Arizona just before I left. He said, 'Mom, I'm sorry. I know you wanted to see me walk across that stage.' I said, 'Just so I know you're getting that degree.'...I'm just really proud of them."

With all the classes they missed in March for four straight years, the sign on the door to MSU locker room, "A Championship Effort Is The Only Effort Accepted Here," applied to academics, too. "Championship Charlie" wouldn't have it any other way.

14 CHARLIE BELL
Guard—6-foot-3, 200 pounds
Flint, Mich. (Southwestern Academy)

Bell's Statistics

	G/GS	MIN/Avg.	FG/FGA	Pct.	3FG/3FGA	Pct.	FT/FTA	Pct.	REB/Avg.	PF/FO	A	BK	ST	PTS	Avg.
1997-98	30/30	725/24.2	94/216	.435	19/56	.339	69/87	.793	133/4.4	53/0	40	1	17	276	9.2
1998-99	38/35	861/22.7	116/243	.477	16/45	.356	49/65	.754	146/3.8	85/2	39	3	27	297	7.8
1999-2000	39/38	1078/27.6	159/351	.453	38/111	.342	93/116	.802	190/4.9	94/3	123	8	47	449	11.5
2000-01	33/33	1034/31.3	150/373	.402	52/152	.342	94/122	.770	155/4.7	53/1	169	6	33	446	13.5
	140/136	3698/26.4	519/1183	.439	125/364	.343	305/390	.782	624/4.5	285/6	371	18	124	1468	10.5

ANDRE HUTSON

He claims he never had a clever nickname. He never wanted or needed one.

But long before he finally grew to 6-foot-8, 240 pounds, he could have been known as "Andre the Giant."

Andre Hutson was always that huge an influence on everyone around him, as an incident five years ago in Ohio illustrates.

It was another "Pick on the Disabled Day" for mindless jerks at Trotwood-Madison High, near Dayton, when a defenseless girl was flattened in the middle of the hall.

A towering football-basketball hero saw what happened and came to her rescue, helping her up, gathering her books and walking her to class safely.

Even then, in his quiet way, Hutson led by example.

The harassing of handicappers stopped immediately.

But for every sensitive bone in his body, Hutson has at least two strong ones. For that, Michigan State's basketball program should be eternally grateful.

His contributions to the Spartans from 1997-2001 shouldn't be overlooked by fans and can't be overestimated. We know his efforts won't be forgotten by appreciative coaches and teammates.

"There aren't many players in the nation like Andre Hutson," MSU coach Tom Izzo said with total admiration. "He's the ultimate warrior. He's one of the most underrated players around. A lot of what he does doesn't show up in a boxscore."

"The Warrior," his first nickname other than "'Dre'" in East Lansing, was the title for a promotional flier for Hutson from MSU's sports information department.

Predictably, he wasn't aware of it when writers and broadcasters received it in the mail. Yet, a lot of what Hutson did the past four seasons was the stuff of legends, individually and collectively.

Hutson credits the tutelage of Smith in his first two years — advanced courses in toughness. Judging by the results, he must have earned a couple of A's.

"I studied a lot of what Antonio did and learned a lot of his tactics," Hutson said. "I'm just trying to pass those on to the other guys. The big thing is being out there and being tough, not letting anybody get to you mentally or physically and always showing you're tougher than the next player. When the other players on the team see that you remain tough, they say, 'If he's going to play that hard and isn't going to back down, I'm not going to back down either.'"

Hutson played in 138 games for Spartans, second only to teammate Charlie Bell's 140 appearances. And he started 129 times, behind only Bell's 136.

In 102 seasons of basketball at MAC, MSC and MSU, Hutson became the first player with at least 1,200 points (12th on the school's all-time list with 1,393), 700 rebounds (fifth with 835) and 60-percent accuracy from the field (fourth at 60.8).

He outplayed stars Etan Thomas of Syracuse and Marcus Fizer of Iowa State in the 2000 NCAA Tournament. And with a severely hyperextended knee suffered the day before the game, Hutson was huge with 10 points and 10 rebounds in a Final Four win over Wisconsin.

Two nights later, he was a key ballhandler in breaking Florida's press in the NCAA title game. And he defended players from 7-0 North Carolina center Brendan Haywood to 6-3 Wisconsin guard Roy Boone with equal success.

Most importantly, Hutson was a winner, joining Bell and mid-1970s Indiana guard Quinn Buckner as the only starters for four Big Ten championship teams.

Hutson appeared in 113 victories, second to Bell's 115 wins in Big Ten history, and never looked at his stats before the Big Ten standings.

He didn't jump, shout and knock himself out the way Mateen Cleaves did to inspire his teammates. But in his own quiet way, Hutson wanted to win just as much.

No wonder Izzo correctly predicted Hutson would be the Spartans' MVP in 2000-01, an honor he shared with sophomore Jason Richardson in the players' balloting and with Bell in the media vote.

"Andre is the one guy who has been consistent all season," Bell said. "Jason and I have been up-and-down. Andre is always there. Whatever happens, we can always go to him."

For a player who was lost in the shadows all too often in East

ANDRE HUTSON

Lansing and around the league, an evening with five major team awards was an indelible mark of respect.

Hutson also shared Best Defender honors with Bell, the Chairman of the Boards rebounding prize with freshman Zach Randolph and the Antonio Smith Glue and Guts Award with sophomore Aloysius Anagonye at the annual MSU Basketball Bust.

"No doubt, this is the greatest honor I've ever received," Hutson said of the MVP sweep. "I think my teammates really respect me. I ask a lot from all of them and try to give everything back and love them like brothers. But we have so many good players. Charlie and Jason have been so dominant, I don't know why those two shouldn't get it."

When so many athletes never seem to get it, Hutson always has. Teamwork and schoolwork were valued, not ignored or viewed as necessary evils.

Hutson grasped the significance of education at an early age. And much of that credit should go to his family, especially his mother, Linda Morris, a video-teleconferencing specialist at Wright-Patterson Air Force Base.

"When Andre was in first grade, he asked me, 'How long do I have to go to school?'" she said. "I told him, 'You have to go through 12th grade, then through four years of college.' That was always a given."

Hutson was junior class president and a National Honor Society member at Trotwood-Madison. His

Photo Credit: Kevin Fowler, MSU Sports Information

ANDRE HUTSON

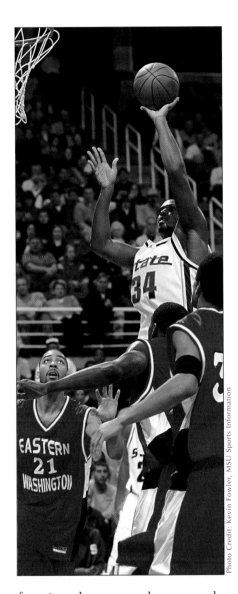

Photo Credit: Kevin Fowler, MSU Sports Information

favorite class was always math. And after a brief period as an accounting major, he received his degree in finance in May.

"I don't know any other players with that major," Hutson said. "There might be some. But I don't know them. I always wanted to be in business. And I thought if I did have the opportunity to play professionally, I could help myself instead of hiring other people. Maybe I'll be an agent some day."

Quick, someone give Izzo the Heimlich maneuver. He just choked on a pasty. But if any agent could earn Izzo's complete trust, the money here is on Hutson.

He hired an agent, Mike Harrison of Immortal Entertainment in Santa Monica, Calif., in April to help him get started. But Hutson knew, as he always has, he would get whatever he deserved in the long run — exactly what Izzo had preached all season.

After hovering just off the radar screen for most of his career, Hutson accepted an invitation to the NBA's Portsmouth (Va.) Tryout Camp in April. When he withdrew in favor of a spot in the Desert Classic in Tempe, Ariz., in May, he received some rare criticism.

"If I come out and continue to play the way I can, I should be all right," said Hutson, echoing the "Don't try to do anything you can't do" advice of NBA talent evaluators. "I plan to outwork a lot of guys and be the first big guy down the floor. But we've been on TV and in the NCAA Tournament so much, a lot of people know how we play."

They knew Hutson could do a little of everything. Entering a league of players with specialized skills, his greatest strength for the Spartans was the lack of an exploitable weakness.

Dare him to shoot? He was good for 20 points. Play him tight? He could dribble and drive as well as some shooting guards. Try to burn him on defense? Better check with the Tar Heels' Haywood first.

"I think he definitely got better

as a senior," said NBA Draft expert Chris Monter of monterdraftnews.com. "He was a focal point of their offense for the first time. He still has to show more face-to-the-basket offense to be an NBA power forward. But he should have a chance."

The question for many years was whether Hutson would be a pro in football or basketball. As a 6-foot-8, left-handed quarterback with strength and mobility, he could have gone almost anywhere.

"He was recruited more for football than basketball," his mother said. "He was the starting quarterback for the varsity as a 6-5 freshman and had 1,700 yards passing before he broke his arm late in the season. But by his junior year, it was clear he loved basketball more. A lot of the fans were heartbroken. They were sure he'd be an NFL quarterback."

Hutson decided it was better to try to improve in the sport he loved than to keep playing football and wishing his passes would lead to easy baskets.

"A lot of people back home always thought I was better in football," Hutson said. "When I first got here, I thought about football. And Coach (Bobby) Williams sort of pushed me last summer to come out and throw with the guys a little bit. They were really short of quarterbacks. But it was my senior year. As much as I love football and watch it all the time, I don't have a desire to play it any more."

That was disappointing to Williams, who thought Hutson was an outstanding prospect, even if he

ANDRE HUTSON

quit football after his junior year of high school when a coaching change meant a switch to the option.

"He was a great quarterback, not just a good one," Williams said. "(Former MSU assistant) Mark Dantonio was recruiting him for football. And when he came on his official visit for basketball, he

stopped in to talk with us. But I was serious about him helping us last year. We had a quarterback situation with some guys leaving. And I always thought he was very talented."

So did Tom Crean, the Spartans' top basketball assistant before a 1999 move to Marquette.

And with good reason. Hutson averaged 22 points and 12 rebounds per game as a high school senior, earning Ohio Player of the Year honors from the state's coaches.

Hutson didn't grow up as an MSU fan. But at least he grew up, something a lot of pampered athletes never do. And when he agreed to join Izzo's maturing program, it was a perfect fit.

Talent and tenacity became a lethal combination, as Hutson proved in developing from a role player to the No. 1 option in most of MSU's offensive sets last season.

His scoring increased each year, from 8.5 points per game as a freshman to 8.9 as a sophomore, then to 10.2 as a junior and 13.8 as a senior, thanks largely to a lot of hard work.

"I really couldn't work with the coaches in the summer, but I knew what I needed to do," Hutson said. "We have a shooting machine. And I'd take 400 to 500 jumpers a day, then work on my post moves, going over both shoulders. I'd spend 15 to 20 minutes on ballhandling drills before each workout. The big thing was getting stronger and adding more weight."

Without losing the speed to run the floor as well as any collegiate big man or the quickness to cover guards 20 feet from the basket, Hutson followed Izzo's greenprint for success.

Hutson finished his collegiate career with 17 double-doubles. And if Ohio State didn't recruit him hard enough, Izzo just wants to know where to send the thank-you note.

Photo Credit: Kevin Fowler, MSU Sports Information

ANDRE HUTSON

"Tom is a lot like I was in that he demands improvement in the off-season," said former MSU coach and long-time Hutson fan Jud Heathcote. "Andre has improved every year. He might have improved more between his junior and senior years than at any other time. The championship team, as good as it was, didn't have a strong post presence. Their last team had Hutson, plus Randolph and Anagonye."

It didn't have Cleaves, Morris Peterson or A.J. Granger, three huge contributors from a group that won its last 11 games. And leadership concerns meant more to Izzo than any talent dropoff, if there was one.

"That had to come from Charlie and me for the most part," Hutson said. "We have to push other guys to get better. Mateen had a big mouth and was really loud. But I don't think leadership is as effective from the back row. It has to come from a guy with the ball in his hands."

Hutson's quiet maturity was mistaken for a lack of leadership by Izzo, who had to learn to appreciate strong, silent types after four seasons of Cleaves' effervescence.

"It took me until February of their senior year to realize you don't have to wear your emotions on your sleeve to care — because that's me," Izzo said. "They taught me you don't always have to do it that way."

That finally sunk in when Izzo saw just how much a fourth-straight Big Ten title meant to the seniors, especially to Hutson. If

that treasured trophy meant any less than the previous year's NCAA hardware, it was hard to tell around No. 34.

The first sign came in an over-time escape against Wisconsin on Jan. 13, 2001, in Breslin Center. Hutson had 10 points, nine rebounds, two steals, a blocked shot on the perimeter and a crucial stop against the Badgers' Mark Vershaw as regulation time ended.

Still, Izzo complained that Hutson didn't have his usual energy. He was right, as he soon learned when he was summoned to the training room. There, Hutson was in intense pain for almost 90 minutes with severe cramping.

The diagnosis? "Dehydration secondary to pneumonia." And more than one doctor told Izzo not to expect Hutson to return to form for at least five weeks.

"Andre hadn't been the same for three games," Izzo said the next day. "He struggled at Indiana and wasn't the same player. And he was sluggish again Saturday. I'm relieved to know what it is."

With Hutson's availability supposedly a week-to-week decision, you can imagine everyone's surprise when he missed one game, played 17 minutes off the bench in a blowout at Northwestern and was his team's lone bright spot in a loss at OSU.

"I'll be damned," Izzo said. "I had two different doctors come up to me at Rebounders Club and say, 'I want to talk to you about Hutson.' Remember when I told you it would be five to six weeks

before he was back to normal? That's what they told me. I didn't believe that in a million years. But I didn't believe he could do this, either."

Hutson couldn't walk two weeks earlier. And as hard as he tried, he couldn't stop two huge runs by the Buckeyes in Value City Arena, where MSU has never won.

But without Hutson's 17 points and seven rebounds, the Spartans might have suffered their worst Big Ten defeat since a 36-point pasting at Iowa in 1996.

"You saw why Andre Hutson is one of the most underrated players in the Big Ten," Izzo said. "He played his heart out. When he got two fouls in the first half, we had to take him out. And we didn't get any more rebounds when we did."

When Hutson returned in the second half, he played all 20 minutes, scored 15 of his team-high 17 points and outplayed OSU shot-blocker Ken Johnson.

No one would have known that without a stat sheet. After falling a game behind Illinois, Hutson looked as if he had been held scoreless in his final game in Columbus.

"I've been taking a lot of antibiotics," he said. "And I've been drinking a lot of fluids. I've been drinking so much juice I have to use the bathroom every 15 minutes. But the tough part is taking a loss. It doesn't matter where it is. It puts us in a bad position to try to win another championship."

His 7-for-10 shooting and seven rebounds weren't nearly enough to keep the Buckeyes from

ANDRE HUTSON

beating a top-five team for the first time in eight years.

"Andre played great today," MSU forward Jason Richardson said. "He gave us a real boost. But he's the only one who did. He tried to carry us alone."

"That type of effort from Andre is what won us three straight Big Ten championships," assistant coach Brian Gregory said. "He understands that. And after what he has been through, 'super-human' would be a good word for it."

"Insufficient" would have been a better one in Hutson's mind. And

when he lashed out at those who didn't pull their weight, 6-9, 270-pound freshman Zach Randolph was first on the list.

"During the game I was begging him to pick it up," Hutson said. "I didn't get that response. So after the game I went up and told him this was my last year. I asked him to suck it up for me the rest of the year. I pretty much spoke from the heart. And I think that really touched him."

Three nights later, Hutson administered a flying bearhug after Randolph's extra-effort produced a

three-point play in a win at Michigan. It was the first sign that Randolph had learned to play Izzo's way.

"Andre has been a huge help to me," Randolph said. "I've learned a lot from watching and listening to him, on and off the court. When he talks, you have to listen."

Hutson's deep, resonant voice — a cross between James Earl Jones and Barry White — commands immediate respect. And many people have suggested he go into broadcasting.

But it was Hutson's reaction to

Photo Credit: Kevin Fowler, MSU Sports Information

ANDRE HUTSON

an ESPN broadcast of OSU's win over Illinois, the game that gave the league co-champions, that Izzo will never forget.

That near-berserk response put him flat on the floor and 11 feet in the air. It also showed how important winning was to Hutson, as the Spartans were back in control of their Big Ten destiny.

When the Buckeyes' Sean Connolly hit the 3-point shot that led to a shared championship, Hutson was hollering as loud as any Ohioan. But when his high school teammate, Tim Martin, missed two free throws that could have iced the game, including an airball, Hutson collapsed in agony.

He was smiling again seconds later when Fighting Illini guard Frank Williams missed a desperation 3 and left MSU and Illinois tied atop the conference, just the way they finished.

The finish to Hutson's career came in a Final Four meltdown against Arizona. He had 18 of his 20 points in the second half, nearly 60 percent of the Spartans' scoring after the break.

After the game in a somber locker room, many in the media were stunned to see a sobbing Hutson. That shouldn't have been

Photo Credit: Kevin Fowler, MSU Sports Information

a shock with someone who has always had his eyes on the prize, even if he was often silent while pursuing it.

"He has always been so goal-oriented," his mother said before Senior Day. "In eighth grade I went through his book bag one day and found this list. I wish I'd kept it. But it said he'd graduate on top of his class, make the Sweet 16, win a national championship and be a great husband and father."

Hutson arrived on campus as a winner. Four years, four Big Ten titles, three Final Fours and an NCAA title later, he left the same way — as the key to the winningest class the conference has ever known.

34 ANDRE HUTSON
Forward—6-foot-8, 240 pounds
Trotwood, Ohio (Trotwood-Madison HS)

Hutson's Statistics

	G/GS	MIN/Avg.	FG/FGA	Pct.	3FG/3FGA	Pct.	FT/FTA	Pct.	REB/Avg.	PF/FO	A	BK	ST	PTS	Avg.
1997-98	30/26	631/21.0	87/142	.613	0/0	.000	52/69	.754	156/5.2	73/0	25	24	22	226	7.5
1998-99	37/34	926/25.0	111/180	.617	0/0	.000	107/137	.781	192/5.2	100/1	23	22	26	329	8.9
1999-2000	39/38	1056/27.1	147/251	.586	0/1	.000	103/154	.669	243/6.2	94/0	57	12	29	397	10.2
2000-01	32/31	956/29.9	173/278	.622	0/0	.000	95/131	.725	244/7.6	79/1	61	17	27	441	13.8
	138/129	3569/25.9	518/851	.609	0/1	.000	357/491	.727	835/6.1	346/2	166	75	104	1393	10.1

JASON RICHARDSON

His greatest gift isn't an ability to jump out of any gym. It's his willingness to stay there, long after others have left, to become the best basketball player he can be.

Jason Richardson has the athletic talent and appetite for triumphs to be an NBA star as his game matures. He grew a great deal in two seasons at Michigan State. And Spartan Basketball is richer for that relationship.

But was his college career too short? That all depends on whom you ask. In the minds of Big Ten opponents, Richardson should have left a year sooner. In the eyes of his new employer, he became a pro at just the right time. In the view of his MSU coaches and teammates, he could have soared with one more season.

His mother, Elaine Richardson Cook, had serious reservations about him leaving early. But they vanished with a Sunday sermon at Victorious Believers Ministries: "The Windows of Opportunity Are Open Now."

They were wide open in East Lansing, too. Richardson would have been a preseason All-American and a possible National Player of the Year in 2001-02. Instead, he will try to be the first former Spartan to become an NBA Rookie of the Year.

"I thought about staying at Michigan State and trying to win another title," said a player with two Big Ten championships, two Final Fours and an NCAA crown to his credit. "But you have to make the best decision for yourself. I felt I was pretty much ready for it."

Some thought Richardson was destined for greatness long before he became Michigan's Mr. Basketball in 1999 and the best dunker in MSU's first 102 seasons of basketball.

When his late cousin, Marlow Prescott, and an influential uncle, Brian Bowen, first saw Richardson, they couldn't get over his enormous limbs — perfect for a budding basketball player.

"That's our 'baller there," Bowen said on first inspection in January 1981, according to Mick McCabe of the *Detroit Free Press*. "That's the one who's going to make the money."

Richardson was 4 days old. But Bowen was right. Now 6-foot-6, 220 pounds, "J-Rich" will make more in his first year of NBA play than some relatives will make in a lifetime.

"I got up for a minute and heard his cousin, Marlow, say, 'Hey, check out Jason!'" his mother said. "I thought they were talking about his huge hands and feet. But they were trying to make him hold a basketball."

Prescott had gone home to grab the ball he had just bought and was proud to be the first one to feed it to Richardson, an unrecorded assist. His mom had other ideas, however, and screamed, "What are you doing?...Leave my child alone! Get that ball out of his crib!"

His cousins used to take Richardson to Sherman Park in Carrollton and lift him up so he

could dunk at age 3. But Richardson was 5 when his mother first learned he was different from the average child.

"One day I happened to go to the park and saw Jason out there with all the older guys," Cook said. "I hollered, 'Don't let my baby in with those big guys!' But his Uncle Brian said, 'Leave him alone. He can handle it....Go back home.'"

It was at about that time that Richardson found a new and unexpected love — hockey. Eventually, he had to make a choice of nets and picked the smaller, higher one.

"A couple of friends around the corner played hockey, so I asked for ice skates for Christmas," Richardson said. "I'd never been on skates in my life. But I put them on and played hockey for a couple of years. When it interfered with basketball, I had to give it up. If I put a pair of skates on, I could still play."

He could play almost any sport with his exceptional reflexes and hand-eye coordination, according to Bowen, who was "Uncle Dad" to Richardson and the dominant male influence in his life.

"He was always an exceptional athlete, no matter what you put in his hands," Bowen said. "We've had a lot of athletes in this family. But Jason could skate right away. None of us taught him. And when he picked up a golf club, he could hit a ball further than any of the men."

Richardson's first major goal was to be able to dunk a basketball by the time he entered Nouvel

Catholic Central in Saginaw. That breakthrough still ranks as his third-favorite slam, though no one was there to see it.

"I'll never forget my first one," Richardson said. "I was 6-2 or 6-3. I'd just finished eighth grade. And they had a dunk contest every year at Nouvel. I wanted to be in that contest in the worst way. But I was all by myself when it finally happened. I ran all the way home and told my Uncle Brian, 'I can dunk! I can dunk!' He said, 'No way!' And I said, 'I'll betcha $5!' We went back to the park. And I did it again."

Richardson transferred to Arthur Hill High after his freshman year, improved as a sophomore and junior, then exploded onto the national scene with exceptional camp and AAU performances. He was the MVP of the prestigious adidas Big Time Tournament and led the Michigan Mustangs to a national title in 1998.

That led to a fierce recruiting battle between the Spartans and Wolverines, with Pittsburgh, Connecticut and Cincinnati lurking. MSU rallied to land the player ranked No. 6 by the *Recruiter's Handbook* and No. 8 by respected analyst Bob Gibbons — the highest for any signee in the program since Earvin Johnson.

"My mind was all toward Michigan," Richardson said. "My family had all been Michigan fans. One minute, I was going to Michigan. The next morning, my mind was focused on Michigan State. I committed to Michigan State that day."

JASON RICHARDSON

Not before he was late for a 7 p.m. press conference at Arthur Hill, however. Richardson couldn't get Michigan coach Brian Ellerbe off the phone in a two-hour plea to postpone the commitment.

"He wanted me to give him one more visit," Richardson said. "But there was a family atmosphere at Michigan State. The coaches were like fathers. And the players were like brothers. When I went to Michigan, it wasn't like that. Guys didn't really say much to each other. I thought their guys got along and everyone was cool with each other. Once I got there and saw what was going on, it kind of shocked me."

His choice shocked many who assumed the Wolverines were still in control of the state, even after the Spartans had landed Mr. Basketball runner-ups Mateen Cleaves and Charlie Bell from the same loaded conference in the previous two-and-a-half years.

"I think it all comes back to Tom Izzo," Arthur Hill coach Dave Slaggert said. "He's one genuine, sincere person. He hit a gold mine in the Saginaw Valley — and he's still hitting one."

Richardson averaged 25.3 points and 12.8 rebounds per game as a senior, carrying the Lumberjacks to the Class A championship game, where they lost to Ann Arbor Pioneer and friendly rival LaVell Blanchard. But Richardson edged Blanchard in the Mr. Basketball voting by Michigan prep coaches, 741 points to 631.

In an unconventional campaign for the award, Slaggert sent out 800 highlight videos, mostly to members of BCAM, the Basketball Coaches Association of Michigan. And Arthur Hill upgraded its schedule, largely to show what Richardson could do.

"We did a lot to showcase Jason," Slaggert admitted to Hugh Bernreuter of the *Saginaw News*. "But in the end he had to produce. And he did. It would've saved me a lot of money not to do those things, not to mention about a million hours of work. But Jason is the kind of kid you just want to do things for."

Photo Credit: Kevin Fowler, MSU Sports Information

JASON RICHARDSON

Richardson was also a McDonald's All-American and the West MVP in Magic's Roundball Classic at The Palace of Auburn Hills. His 23 points and nine rebounds there were overshadowed by a spectacular, postgame dunking display.

And it was there that Richardson and Blanchard refuted the notion that they couldn't play together. Though Blanchard finally signed with Michigan over Virginia, Georgetown and California, the idea of him joining Richardson at MSU wasn't as far-fetched as many imagined, based on later triumphs and attrition.

"LaVell and I have joked about playing together and how much fun that would be," Richardson said before proving to be a prophet. "We'll have to see. But if everyone sticks around, with Mateen at the point, we could win the national championship."

Blanchard, the *USA TODAY* and Gatorade National Player of the Year, would have been welcome almost anywhere else. But Izzo didn't have a spot on the wing after adding Duke transfer Mike Chappell and Richardson. And he refused to create an opening, despite Richardson's recruiting efforts.

The Spartans were almost without Richardson's services, too. A clerical error failed to properly account for a ninth-grade English class at Nouvel, leaving him a half-unit short of the required 13 in his core curriculum.

"This thing just hit us like a

slap in the face," Izzo said of the first decision by the NCAA Initial-Eligibility Clearinghouse. "He had a fine GPA and made the test score. I think he was even on the honor roll. There was nothing else he could do."

Critics ripped the NCAA, insisting those letters obviously stood for No Clue At All and Never Cares About Athletes. It was said that March Madness had given way to September Stupidity. And State Sen. Mike Goschka even introduced a joint resolution that declared Richardson eligible to compete under Michigan law.

"We just filed some new information," then-MSU Interim Director of Athletics Clarence Underwood said. "Our original case was rejected. So we filed another appeal and got partial-qualifier status. Now, we've gathered more data. I'm a little more optimistic."

The key work came from the school's compliance staff, especially Associate A.D. John Hardt and Coordinator Judy Van Horn, and the school's legal team. Privately, Richardson was receiving support from an attorney friend, Mat Ishbia's father, Jeff.

"Outwardly, he accepted it all like a champ," Bowen said. "Inside, he was like any other person. He isn't superhuman. That hurt him a lot. He'd really focused on getting his grades and making sure everything was all right. To have that almost cost him a year was like a blindside hit in football. It tore him apart."

Perhaps through his unshak-

able faith, Richardson kept practicing well and had the best mid-semester grades on the team. Finally, on Nov. 4, 1999, nearly two months after learning he was ineligible, MSU received word that the Division I Initial-Eligibility Waiver Committee had granted him full-qualifier status.

"Sometimes when you get things thrown at you, you've just got to handle them," Richardson said the day before the Spartans' exhibition opener — justice, just in time. "I'm ready to go out there and go crazy."

That crazy scene following the announcement after practice nearly gave Izzo a coronary. When Cleaves was leading the celebration with his fractured foot in a cast, the first guy who jumped on the soon-to-be three-time All-American might have been ineligible for life.

"Mateen was hugging Jason," Izzo said. "And everyone else was jumping on them. I'm telling you, I was ready to clobber someone if he landed on Mateen's foot again."

Richardson had a season-high 12 rebounds against Minnesota and nine points against Florida in the the NCAA title game — an appropriate thank you for the organization's careful, compassionate review of his case.

But the lasting memory from his freshman year was his greatest dunk, an ad-lib in a loss at Arizona that still has fans buzzing in Tucson.

"Yeah, I remember that play," Izzo said with a smile. "It took me a long time to coach it. But Jason

JASON RICHARDSON

has more ups than everyone in the U.P. put together."

"We were down by two and had a fast-break opportunity," Richardson remembered. "Charlie Bell went up for a layup and Richard Jefferson partially blocked it. I didn't know I was going to catch it. But I jumped, caught the ball, turned backward and threw it down. I was kind of in shock. They put a camera on my face. And I said, 'Whoa!' I still look at that dunk and say, 'Wow, I did that?'"

No. 23 did a lot more than that in Miami and Brazil as the No. 2 scorer for USA Basketball and Coach Jim Boeheim of Syracuse in the World Championship for Young Men (20-and-under).

"He didn't play much against us in the NCAA Tournament," Boeheim said. "Michigan State had so many veterans I hardly remember him. But from the first day of tryouts for us, he really stood out. He and Jason Williams of Duke were the two best players we had. And Richardson got us qualified for the World Championship by hitting a couple of shots."

Richardson took a few good-natured shots. He teased Boeheim about getting an NCAA ring the Orangemen have never worn. But the best part of that trip was playing well enough to be promoted to the USA Select Team, coached by Cincinnati's Bob Huggins.

That team practiced with the USA Olympians for a week, when Richardson met his basketball hero, high school-to-NBA leaper Kevin Garnett. And in an exhibition game in Hawaii, Richardson scored 19 first-half points against the half-hearted defense of Ray Allen and Allan Houston.

"I don't think they were taking us too seriously at first," Richardson said. "The first shot I took, I thought it was an airball. Somehow, it went in. I said, 'Yesss!' But they took it more seriously in the second half. Gary Payton and Jason Kidd played a lot better defense and pretty much locked me down (in a one-point period)."

Back on campus, Richardson paid the price to get better and went from being his team's sixth man to one of the top five players in the nation in Dick Vitale's eyes. He was a finalist for the Wooden Award and the Naismith Award. And that didn't happen by reading his press clippings.

"We told him he really needed to work on his shooting," MSU assistant Mike Garland said. "That shows in his statistics. And he had to learn shot selection. That's something he worked on by watching film. Then, he got hours and hours of shots in. Jason was taking 1,200 shots a night on our shooting machine."

Richardson didn't arrive with the idea he was already a pro. He was able to accept criticism and self-evaluate. And that was a key to helping him develop into his team's top scorer and a first-team All-Big Ten choice.

"I tried to get in every morning, before we lifted weights," Richardson said. "I'd come in for open gym, then come back at night. It was like that every day for me, anywhere from six or seven hours — a decent amount more than most guys."

With a work ethic like that and a polite nature toward everyone he met, Richardson would have been easy to root for if he had never scored on an alley-oop or a 360-degree jam. Instead, he sent the always-excitable Vitale into full-blown convulsions with several Jordanesque plays.

Photo Credit: Kevin Fowler, MSU Sports Information

JASON RICHARDSON

"He's a skywalker, a slam-bam-jam, dipsy-doo dunkaroo!" Vitale said before the sedative took effect. "What I love about him is that he's patient. He played on a national championship team and didn't get a ton of minutes. But he waited his turn. Now, he's our Small Forward of the Year."

Richardson was borderline-brilliant in several games from November through January. Without his 25 points against Wisconsin and 24 against Ohio State in back-to-back home games, MSU never would have won a fourth-straight Big Ten championship.

And if Richardson's success in the classroom was surprising, his mother set that example by raising six kids as a single parent, working full time and returning to school to earn her degree from Saginaw Valley State.

"I tried to instill the idea that education is very important," Cook said. "I told them, 'No matter what happens, don't ever give up on your dream.' I chose marriage over education. But once my marriage dissolved, I went back to school. I don't think the kids even knew it at first. I was working full-time on the third shift at the Saginaw Post Office. When I got home, I'd spend some time with them. Then, when they went to school, so did I."

With a bachelor's degree in social work, she became a facilitator for Saginaw Social Services. All her kids had some form of higher education. And she hoped her third child would earn a diploma before playing pro basketball.

"After the season, I hope he's looking forward to the summer and getting ready for next year," she said in February 2001. "We don't even discuss anything else. I want the (Senior Day) roses!"

Richardson wanted it all. But with a daughter, Jaela', to worry about, an early departure to the NBA was always a strong possibility.

"It's not like my family is dirt-poor," Richardson said. "We're a middle-class family. But just the fact my mom raised six kids on her own and never owned a house is something I think about. Then, there's the situation with my daughter. That'll probably be a factor. Right now, she's with her mother. And they're not doing too well. So I'd like to take care of my daughter and be a father figure in her life."

Richardson struggled in his last four games in the NCAA Tournament, going 14-for-46 from the field and 4-for-16 from 3-point range. In his final game with the Spartans, he was 2-for-11 from the field, was outplayed by Arizona's Jefferson and was outscored 17-6.

Moments later, Richardson said he was definitely returning as a junior — the same thing he told WLNS-TV in Lansing after a title-clinching romp over Michigan, his fourth-straight win over the Wolverines.

It was the same thing he stressed for 30 minutes the Tuesday before the Final Four and the same thing he told roommate Aloysius Anagonye when the team returned home. And it fit with what people like Boeheim and Earvin "Magic" Johnson, the last Spartan star to leave early, urged him to do.

Suddenly, in the time it takes for Richardson to soar and slam, that decision changed. Izzo didn't agree. But he understood. When kids grow up wanting to be like "J-Rich," it won't hurt the MSU program. And it won't hurt kids who have made a good choice for a role model.

23 JASON RICHARDSON
Guard/Forward—6-foot-6, 220 pounds
Saginaw, Mich. (Arthur Hill HS)

Richardson's Statistics

	G/GS	MIN/Avg.	FG/FGA	Pct.	3FG/3FGA	Pct.	FT/FTA	Pct.	REB/Avg.	PF/FO	A	BK	ST	PTS	Avg.
1999-2000	37/3	582/15.7	79/157	.503	8/27	.296	23/42	.548	153/4.1	56/1	23	6	20	189	5.1
2000-01	33/32	940/28.5	182/362	.503	49/122	.402	73/106	.689	195/5.9	74/1	73	28	38	486	14.7
	70/35	1522/21.7	261/519	.503	57/149	.383	96/148	.649	348/5.0	130/2	96	34	58	675	9.6

ALOYSIUS ANAGONYE

I t isn't fair to either player to call him Antonio Smith with an accent — and a better jump hook.

But as an offensive rebounder and a budding leader, Aloysius Anagonye is good enough to do what Smith did for four seasons at Michigan State.

Anagonye — and you can call him "Al" — can make Tom Izzo smile and say, "That's my guy! He's a Spartan warrior."

No wonder Anagonye won the second Antonio Smith Glue and Guts Award at the 2001 MSU Basketball Bust.

"That award was special because I know how much Antonio meant to Coach Izzo and this program," Anagonye said. "I'm trying to become that kind of leader. Coach recruits people he likes, not just players. So it means a lot to know what he thinks of me."

Izzo thinks the 6-foot-8, 255-pounder will be the linchpin of the Spartans' retooling efforts in 2001-02, after the loss of four starters and seven contributors.

"Al can be an incredible captain," Izzo said. "And I really think he will be. He's a lunch-pail guy who cares about winning. The other players all see and respect that."

Izzo saw those qualities before almost any other coach. When he was recruiting Anagonye in 1998, Izzo said there was one player he absolutely had to have. And it wasn't 1999 Mr. Basketball Jason Richardson or Gatorade National Player of the Year LaVell Blanchard.

Still, Anagonye was noncommital, if not torn, through the summer and much of that fall. It wasn't until he visited campus for Midnight Mania in October 1998 that he understood the essense of

Spartan spirit, with help from a crowd of 9,500.

"I enjoyed myself very much," the normally shy Anagonye gushed the next day from his home in Southfield, a Detroit suburb. "It

Photo Credit: Kevin Fowler, MSU Sports Information

ALOYSIUS ANAGONYE

reminded me of a giant pep rally. It was a great atmosphere. The whole environment up there is great."

The Detroit DePorres High center took his time with a huge decision and carefully weighed four major options:

• To join Izzo's emerging program, fresh from MSU's first Big Ten title in eight seasons and an NCAA Tournament Sweet 16 breakthrough.

• To stay a few minutes closer to home and try to lift the Detroit Titans, Spartan-slayers the previous three years, to another level.

• To pick Michigan, where the opportunity to play right away and take a lot of shots for a decimated team would never be greater.

• Or to make a bold, unexpected move and leave "The Wolverine State" entirely — as a Penn State recruit, for instance.

"If you let recruiting get to you, it will," Anagonye said. "You have to understand coaches. We both want something out of this. And it's the right place when we want the same thing. It's like a business decision."

He decided to come to East Lansing, where he joined Richardson and Ohioans Adam Wolfe and Jason Andreas in a heralded, four-player incoming class.

Arriving together and leaving at the same time can be very different things, as Anagonye would later discover. His immediate concern was leading DePorres to a second-straight Class C state championship in Breslin Center.

Anagonye averaged 16 points and 11 rebounds as a senior and

finished third in the Mr. Basketball voting. But he influenced games much more than numbers showed.

After spending five years in Lagos, Nigeria, Anagonye was ridiculed about his accent and appearance when he arrived in Southfield. Soon, his scowl spoke volumes and told kids, "Better not tease too much."

That same intense expression could be partly to blame for Anagonye's biggest problem in two seasons at MSU. Legend has it he once was assessed a personal foul while checking in at the scorer's table.

Anagonye averaged a foul every 4.9 minutes as a freshman backup but was a winner in the last game of the season for a third-straight year, this time in Indianapolis.

While everyone else was accepting congratulations, Anagonye was studying his greatest deficiency. Instead of blaming officials for his 94 fouls, he watched those calls transgression-by-transgression.

"He came in that summer and watched film of all the times he fouled people," Izzo said in amazement. "That's kind of sick when you think about it. Who comes in and watches how they foul? But Al did that. He really took it to heart."

Anagonye's favorite praise is any compliment that goes to someone else. He deflected almost as many positive comments as teammate David Thomas did passes as a sophomore.

That selflessness was fine — to a point. But as Izzo pointed out, a little ego can go a long way toward

maximizing individual potential and team success.

"I've asked Al and David to sacrifice a little bit for the team, to try to get other players involved and to be role players," Izzo said. "Al has accepted that with open arms. But I want them to attain individual goals, too — not just be 'team, team, team' all the time."

With a new emphasis on curtailing rough play, especially in the post, some speculated that Anagonye would have more fouls than points as a sophomore. That didn't happen, but only because his scoring increased.

He averaged a foul every 5.6 minutes, was disqualified from three games and had four fouls in 12 other contests, including a Final Four loss to Arizona, when he had zero points and two rebounds in just eight minutes.

Photo Credit: Kevin Fowler, MSU Sports Information

ALOYSIUS ANAGONYE

But when Anagonye used his chest and hips instead of his forearms and hands on defense, he was a solid contributor for the Spartans. He started 24 of 33 games and again finished with more rebounds on offense than defense.

In a 72-57 dissection of Seton Hall, Anagonye had a career-high 12 rebounds to lead his team's 60-39 dominance. He also scored in double-figures for the first time with 10 points, giving him his only double-double in just 20 minutes of action.

"Al was really big for us," guard Charlie Bell said. "He did a great job of taking open shots and rebounding. And he did a great job on the defensive end. We really need him to do that if we're going to keep winning these games. He opens it up a lot more for everybody else."

When inside force Andre Hutson was sidelined by pneumonia, Anagonye shook off his own physical problems and helped defeat Ohio State and star center Ken Johnson.

"We've got another guy who's sicker than a dog right now in Anagonye," Izzo said. "He just sucked it up and got it done. Don't ask me how. He did an incredible job for how he feels."

That was during an eight-game stretch in January and February when Anagonye and Thomas were replaced in the starting lineup by freshmen Zach Randolph and Marcus Taylor, respectively.

"If I looked at our defense the last two games, I'd say Al has done

Photo Credit: Kevin Fowler, MSU Sports Information

a better job than anybody on our team," Izzo said on Feb. 1, before a loss at Illinois. "He's constantly talking. He's providing good leadership. And I still think Al is going to be a heckuva player before he leaves. His offensive skills are going to improve."

They improved significantly

on March 18, 2001, when MSU beat Fresno State 81-65 in South Region second-round play in Memphis — arguably the Spartans' best performance all season. Anagonye was 5-for-7 from the field in scoring a career-high 13 points. And his aggression put Fresno star Melvin Ely on the

ALOYSIUS ANAGONYE

bench with foul trouble, a surprising turnabout.

"All I want to do is win and stay alive," Anagonye said after that game. "If I got zero points and zero rebounds and we won, that's what matters. I'd be satisfied."

Izzo won't be satisfied until Anagonye becomes a cross between Smith and Hutson — a ferocious rebounder and consistent scorer with irrepressible leadership skills.

"He's starting to look more comfortable and is beginning to play his best basketball," Izzo said. "He's going to the boards and is improving his reaction time to the ball. He had been a little robotic. But that's changing. He made a huge play for a basket at Wisconsin. He has a good jump hook. And he has really improved at the foul line."

Anagonye finished with 62.4-percent accuracy from the field and 71.4-percent work at the line as a sophomore. That improvement from 55.6 and 63.0 shooting as a freshman was a sign Izzo might be right.

"When you look at the great programs at Duke and North Carolina, their players grew over the years," Izzo said. "I think a lot

of our players have done that, too. And I expect Al to improve as much as anyone as a junior."

For that to happen, Anagonye will have to play more that 17.1 minutes per game. He will have to learn to set screens without fouling. And he might even have to smile on the floor so officials know he isn't the terrorist most opponents suggest.

Anagonye's best shots the past two seasons have come in collisions under the basket, not in scoring opportunities. That will have to change for a team that lost 62.7 points per game from its 2000-01 lineup.

But Anagonye's greatest contribution should be the aggressive leadership and passion Izzo seldom saw from a phenomenally successful senior class.

"Al is a different kind of Mateen (Cleaves) and Antonio," Izzo said. "I'd better have one of those guys every year. Al brings a little bit of fire and vigor that I need for me. He can give out a little. And he can take a lot."

Anagonye takes all feedback from Izzo, whatever the decibel level, and files it away with his "C.D." philosophy — "coach's decision."

"He'll sacrifice for the team," Izzo said. "You never have to worry about him off the court. He's a good student and a good recruiter. He did a good job with Alan Anderson and a good job with Kelvin Torbert. Al was one of Alan's favorite guys. Al's a lot like 'Tone that way, 'Tone was a quiet guy too. But he was one of the best recruiters we've ever had."

Anagonye wasn't quite good enough to keep Richardson and Randolph from leaving for the NBA. And when Izzo told him Richardson was leaving, Anagonye refused to believe it.

"Oh, no, Coach," he said. "You're wrong. I just talked to him a couple of days ago. He looked me in the eye and told me he's staying. He's not going anywhere."

Things change. So do people. And as mad as Anagonye was at Richardson, he has tried to channel that emotion into dramatic offseason improvement.

Anagonye has never won less than a league title. Not even Smith or Cleaves could say that. And No. 25 might be saying a lot more things in a louder voice than anyone has heard.

25 ANAGONYE'S STATISTICS

Forward—6-foot-8, 255 pounds
Southfield, Mich. (Detroit DePorres HS)

Anagonye's Statistics

	G/GS	MIN/Avg.	FG/FGA	Pct.	3FG/3FGA	Pct.	FT/FTA	Pct.	REB/Avg.	PF/FO	A	BK	ST	PTS	Avg.
1999-2000	34/5	463/13.6	35/63	.556	0/0	.000	29/46	.630	103/3.0	94/1	10	20	16	99	2.9
2000-01	33/24	584/17.7	58/93	.624	0/0	.000	40/56	.714	103/3.1	104/3	24	17	13	156	4.7
	67/29	1047/15.6	93/156	.596	0/0	.000	69/102	.676	206/3.1	198/4	34	37	29	255	3.8

ZACH RANDOLPH

W ho can know what it is like to be 6-foot-9, 270 pounds, with a troubled past and a chance for a tremendous future? Only those who have run 100 miles in Zach Randolph's size-15 shoes.

That life has included a devoted mom and an incarcerated dad, caring coaches and destructive friends, illegal acts and kindness toward ill youngsters, academic purgatory and an NCAA reprieve.

It has shown us Randolph's childlike side and has slapped him with the responsibilities of fatherhood. And after a year of tough love in Tom Izzo's program, it has sent him off to the NBA, ready or not.

When Randolph's dreams meet reality head-on, no one will call a charging foul. But if "The Good Zach" — the one we often saw at Michigan State — is in control, he is strong enough to score.

No one figured Randolph would finish his four years of eligibility at MSU. He was too big, too good and too close to friends in the pros. But one season was one fewer than his mother, Mae, and his coaches, Marion (Ind.) High's Moe Smedley and Izzo, suggested.

"A lot of people don't get this opportunity," Randolph told the *Lansing State Journal*'s Tim Martin after his press conference at St. Paul Missionary Baptist Church in Marion. "I'm not going to waste it.…But there's nothing we can take for granted. And I wanted to do this now. It's a dream of mine."

So was leading his team to the 2000 Indiana state championship. So was sweeping MVP honors in

three postseason all-star appearances. And so was helping the Spartans earn another Big Ten title and Final Four berth, after being turned on to MSU by close friend Marcus Taylor.

His toughest opponents to date have been himself, a rough envi-

ronment and test scores that nearly blocked his shot. But Randolph persevered and rebounded — his specialty at every level.

He had already had two minor brushes with the law when he received a stolen gun and sold it for $120 in 1998. Randolph pleaded

Photo Credit: Kevin Fowler, MSU Sports Information

ZACH RANDOLPH

guilty to that offense, spent 30 days in a juvenile detention center and did 60 hours of community service.

If most high school opponents had tried for 60 hours, they couldn't have found a way to defend him. After dominating Indiana Mr. Basketball Jared Jeffries with 28 points and 11 rebounds in the state final, Randolph showed the rest of the world what he could do.

He had 23 points and 15 rebounds in the McDonald's All-American Game, 24 points and eight rebounds against international competition in the Nike Hoop Summit and 39 points and 24 rebounds in the Nike Derby Festival Classic.

But when Randolph went one-on-one with test questions, he struggled to reach the 820 SAT or 17 ACT scores a 2.7 student needed for freshman eligibility.

"I'm confident I'm going to get it this time," Randolph told Larry Lage of the *Lansing State Journal* the week of his third and final attempt. "I just want to do this for myself, my coaches and my future teammates at Michigan State."

When he came up short, many wondered if Randolph should have entered the NBA Draft out of high school. Some said he would never play college basketball. Others ripped Izzo for taking a chance on an academic risk with records on and off the court.

After getting to know the person, not just the player, Izzo became even more determined to help Randolph succeed. And on July 7, 2000, they learned the NCAA Division I Initial-Eligibility

Waiver Committee had approved an institutional appeal.

Four professors on the Learning Disabilities Subcommittee ruled in MSU's favor, recognizing a .5 jump in Randolph's grade-point average as a senior. Though ineligible athletes at other schools wondered how Randolph became eligible, 561 of 1,145 eligibilty appeals, 49 percent, were granted the previous year.

"I've been celebrating all day," Randolph said that Friday night from his home in Marion. "I feel like two tons of stress just got lifted off my back. This is the best day of my life. I'm about to live my dream of playing college basketball. And it's for a team that just won the national championship."

Randolph celebrated by playing so well at the USA Basketball World Championship for Young Men Trials that he got Duke's Carlos Boozer cut. Suddenly, he became the nation's No. 1-ranked incoming freshman, according to analyst Bob Gibbons and Dick Vitale's *ESPN Magazine College Basketball Preview*.

The first indication that Randolph might have been exactly that came in a win over Florida, when he was 10-for-13 from the field and had 27 points and seven rebounds in 23 minutes. He scored in double figures in 23 games and played more than 19 minutes just 15 times. Still, Randolph was a huge factor for the NCAA's top rebounding team.

"Being outrebounded like that is something I can't imagine," said the nation's best below-the-rim rebounder after a 46-17 edge over Northwestern. "I know it wouldn't

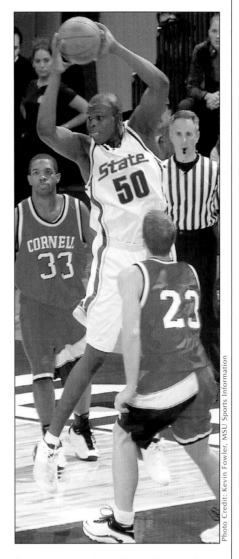

Photo Credit: Kevin Fowler, MSU Sports Information

feel good. Other than that, I don't know. And I don't really want to find out….What would I do if I had to play Michigan State? I'd tell my players not to miss."

Randolph missed having a father around in his formative years. But he grew up a lot in East Lansing, with help from friends and teammates like senior Andre Hutson, as mature an influence as any 19-year-old could want.

"We room together on the road and talk about everything, just try-

ZACH RANDOLPH

ing to get his head straight," Hutson said. "I think he has come a long way. He's definitely doing better in the classroom. And he's a little more well-mannered than he was. He's a flamboyant guy who speaks his mind with everyone. Sometimes he says the wrong thing. But he has really grown up in one year."

Those who got to know Randolph appreciated his spirit and love of people, especially kids. He was never happier than in a conversation with someone who looked up to him, even if it had to be from a hospital bed.

"My son, Jacob, was in Sparrow just after Christmas for an ear operation," Val Korrey of Lansing said. "Zach was making his rounds and stood at the side of the bed for 15 minutes, just smiling and talking. I couldn't believe how he handled himself. Now, a 6-year-old sees him on TV and says, 'Dad, there's my buddy!' And I see why Tom decided to recruit him."

Izzo decided to play him with the game on the line at Indiana. After contributing 11 points and eight rebounds, Randolph missed an insurance free throw and fell just short of a block on Kirk Haston's game-winning 3-pointer. But Izzo defended that effort after a 23-game winning streak ended.

"We questioned whether we should've played our best defensive lineup," Izzo said. "I wouldn't have had Zach in there with that lineup. But Zach felt he could guard the guy. He probably did the best job of the five we had out there....How far has Zach come? From Pluto to Earth."

He was still in orbit when an ailing Hutson got his attention after loss No. 2 at Ohio State. After Randolph loafed through his worst effort of the season, two points and one rebound in 17 defenseless minutes, Hutson let him have it in the locker room.

That was the fifth of Randolph's eight starts. He thought he should have been playing ahead of sophomore Aloysius Anagonye. And

coming off the bench was tough to explain when he talked to friends like NBA rookie Darius Miles, who skipped college and signed for millions.

"Not starting him was the right thing to do," Izzo said. "He needed to realize that you have to do more than just play. There's way more to winning than that. But it's hard for Zach because he's so outgoing. When he went to all those all-star games, he was probably the life of

Photo Credit: Kevin Fowler, MSU Sports Information

the party. Now, he sees those guys in the NBA. And they're playing."

Izzo tried to make Randolph a better player, not just a part of the puzzle. One goal was to improve his ballhandling and shooting so some day he could play like the second Karl Malone, not a sawed-off Shaquille O'Neal.

Beauty is in the eye of the beaten. One day before MSU spanked Fresno State in NCAA Tournament's second round, no less an expert on talent than Bulldogs coach Jerry Tarkanian said what Randolph's friends had been telling him.

"I think their backup center might be one of the five best centers in the country," Tarkanian said. "He doesn't even start for them. And he'll probably go straight to the NBA next year. But I know what it's like to have talent like that. I had it at UNLV."

Randolph averaged 10.8 points and 6.7 rebounds per game in just 19.8 minutes of play. If his defense had allowed him to assume full-time duty in a demanding system, he could have posted All-America numbers.

"I think I've adapted pretty well," Randolph said, noting a loss of 15 pounds of baby fat to a solid 255 pounds. "But we'll see what happens today. 'Tark' loves to play up-

tempo. And it'll be a fistfight inside. But we're not going to back down."

His best game might have come seven days later — an eight-point, 14-rebound effort against Temple that lifted the Spartans to the Final Four. Randolph played well enough that when he missed a short, showboat shot, Izzo just smiled with gritted teeth and said, "'Zebo,' next time use the backboard, OK?"

"About halfway through the season, Zach started to realize what this program is all about," Izzo said. "Our seniors talked to him. And he was a man in there today. No doubt, it was Zach's best game, even better than his 27 points against Florida."

If so, Randolph saved his best for next-to-last. He had surprised most obervers with a 2.5 GPA in his first semester, earning MSU Student-Athlete of the Month recognition. But he didn't enjoy the academic aspects and knew there were no math tests in the NBA.

For every prospective agent who said he should leave, other observers wanted him to stay, including Earvin "Magic" Johnson, who left MSU and joined the Los Angeles Lakers after his sophomore season. But on April 11, 2001, Randolph said goodbye to the college game.

"Well, they finally got to him," Smedley said. "A lot of guys want to make a quick buck off Zach. It's criminal that guys are allowed to do that. Everyone I talked to said he'd more than double his money if he waited a year. But money talks. And if you knew where he came from, $50,000 to him would be like $10 million to us."

That was roughly what Randolph tried to explain to Izzo. Having an NBA salary of any kind, as opposed to the financial constraints in college, is a far greater disparity in lifestyle than the difference between a coach making close to $4 million in the pros and $1.2 million in college — especially with a 2-year-old son, Zachariah, to consider.

"That played a big role," said Izzo, who drove to Marion to back Randolph — again. "He wanted to take care of his mother and his family. But this also gives him a chance to live out his dreams. That may be an equally big part of it. You have to support that."

Randolph is better for having been a Spartan. And the program is better for that relationship, too. If, as Izzo said, the goal is help kids grow into men, No. 50 has a good start — the only start that matters.

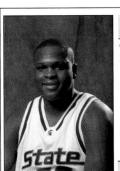

50 ZACH RANDOLPH
Center—6-foot-9, 255 pounds
Marion, Ind. (Marion HS)

Randdolph's Statistics

	G/GS	MIN/Avg.	FG/FGA	Pct.	3FG/3FGA	Pct.	FT/FTA	Pct.	REB/Avg.	PF/FO	A	BK	ST	PTS	Avg.
2000-01	33/8	654/19.8	138/235	.587	0/1	.000	80/126	.635	221/6.7	60/1	34	22	24	356	10.8

MARCUS TAYLOR

Photo Credit: Kevin Fowler, MSU Sports Information

T he comparisons to Earvin "Magic" Johnson were inevitable — and incredibly unfair, especially for a hometown hero who was five inches shorter.

Marcus Taylor doesn't have to be the second coming of the greatest point guard to play the game of basketball. He just has to be the first "T," as his father calls him with omnipresent pride. That should be plenty good enough.

After one season at Michigan State, cynics can say, "He didn't do what Earvin did." Neither did Scott Skiles, Steve Smith or Mateen

Cleaves as freshmen. The fact that Taylor has been mentioned in that company is an indication of what lies ahead.

He has the ability and, now, the opportunity to lead the Spartans as a sophomore and beyond. When underclassmen with similar credentials leaped to the NBA, Taylor was determined to make himself and MSU better.

"I'll be going to a lot of camps and working on my game," he said in May 2001, when rumors had him considering a transfer. "I'll have more responsibility next season. But I know I can get the job done."

Tom Izzo believes that, too, and has since he started picturing Taylor in green-and-white in fifth grade.

That was two years after a prodigy had to move from the third-grade group to play with the seventh- and eighth-graders at Phil Odlum's Waverly basketball camp.

It was one year after a fourth-grader began a highlight video of his workouts by dribbling up to the camera and saying, "I'm Marcus Taylor. I'm going to be the greatest basketball player who ever lived."

And it was roughly the same time he got lost inside a friend's massive house in California near the end of a week-long visit. That friend wore No. 32 for the Los Angeles Lakers.

Perhaps the best example of Taylor's impact came in a letter from Molly Peterman, a junior at Lansing Eastern High who became a basketball standout at the University of Detroit.

MARCUS TAYLOR

"I remember Marcus from a camp in the summer of '93," Peterman wrote three years later. "I recall saying, 'Gosh, Mom, I can just picture his name on the back of an NBA jersey.' I was going into eighth grade and admired that one sixth-grader all week. Though Marcus doesn't know who I am, I see him around and brag to my friends about his athletic ability. Whether they believe me or not, one day he'll really be something great."

In pickup games at age 13, Taylor had the ball stripped repeatedly — by Seattle rookie point guard Eric Snow. One year later, Taylor held his own against Snow and Spartan starters Ray Weathers and Thomas Kelley.

"Last year, Eric used to take it away from him," said James Taylor, Marcus' dad, after a workout in Jenison Field House. "Now, he can't do that....He can if he fouls and really gets rough. But he tried to get into Marc's ear and talk a lot. Marc never changed his expression."

He turned the head of an MSU incoming freshman in 1996, Mateen Cleaves, with his shooting and passing. Four years later, those players would pass the torch between Final Four appearances.

"That boy can really go far," Cleaves said before Taylor began ninth grade. "He should be a great one. The big thing is, he listens. When his father tells him something, he listens. And when I tell him a little something, he listens. Then, he goes out and does it."

His brilliance sparked a media debate about when young athletes should receive publicity. The *Lansing State Journal* waited until Taylor was in eighth grade to write columns about him, then jumped in with both feet and previewed his varsity debut with the headline, "The Phenom is finally here."

He was listed as Honorable Mention All-America by *Street & Smith's College Basketball* and was ranked as the No. 21 player in the state by the *Detroit Free Press* before he played a high school game.

Taylor's first game wasn't just a sellout. It was an event, with four newspapers represented — and not to see Lansing Catholic Central. They saw a polished performance with No. 32, of course, contributing 27 points, five rebounds, nine assists and one turnover in a 59-43 win at Waverly.

He was the nation's No. 1-ranked sophomore. And he drew 10,250 fans to Breslin Center for a battle with East Lansing and Co-Area Player of the Year Thomas Jackson, who became a solid contributor at Butler.

The best example of Taylor's competitiveness came after completing 10th grade, when he led a depleted Waverly squad against powerful River Rouge in the Tom Izzo Spartan Shootout. Though Rouge won the scrimmage, Taylor more than held his own against senior star Brent Darby, an Ohio State signee.

"He just has to be more physical and show a little more heart," Darby said after Taylor drove

through everything Rouge had except the Ford plant and got clobbered repeatedly for that courage.

"The only way he could stop me was to hold me," Taylor said after the battle nearly degenerated

Photo Credit: Kevin Fowler, MSU Sports Information

MARCUS TAYLOR

from talking to something more dangerous. "If this had been a real game, he'd have fouled out early."

Taylor didn't play AAU ball, as his family monitored his every move. That response made his father one of the few positive figures in the shoe-company expose *Sole Influence* by Dan Wetzel and Don Yeager.

Taylor's only summer showcase was the Nike All-America Camp in Indianapolis. And all he did was become the only player in the event's history to be named MVP in successive years.

His reputation spread to the point a 16-year-old from Hinsdale, Ill., bought the Internet domain MarcusTaylor.com for $70 in a speculative venture.

Speculation that Taylor would sign with the Spartans was high long before he canceled recruiting visits to Kentucky, Michigan, North Carolina, UCLA and Syracuse.

"We figured, 'Why play around with it? Why waste everyone's time and money?'" his father said. "Marc wanted to browse. But you don't do that on official visits where you only see what they want you to see. That's like me saying, 'C'mon over,' then cleaning the house."

The decision was as big a surprise as that morning's sunrise. But it didn't have to be a secret to be a success. In a packed Waverly auditorium, with three stations broadcasting live, Taylor said all the right things.

"He has always been very good in front of people," his father said.

"That goes back to the days when he used to be in spelling bees."

Taylor learned to spell success long before his commitment, then used that freedom from in-season sales pitches to lead the Warriors to a Class A championship, another thing he had in common with Johnson.

He broke Johnson's city scoring record and wound up No. 1 among Michigan Class A players with 2,448 career points, a 25.5 average. And he finished fourth in state history with 704 rebounds, third with 580 assists and first with 493 free throws.

The numbers Taylor cherished most were his 22 points, six rebounds and nine assists in the title game against Detroit Pershing, one day after a payback upset of Saginaw.

Mid-Michigan's first Mr. Basketball since Robert Henderson of Lansing Eastern in 1982 was a McDonald's All-American. Taylor also received a "Tomorrow's Winners" award as the state's top senior male athlete from the Michigan Sports Hall of Fame.

Without his friendship and influence, MSU never would have signed All-America center Zach Randolph. And after sharing the spotlight in a one-point win over an international all-star team in the Nike Hoop Summit at the Final Four in Indianapolis, Taylor said, "We'll take the 'T & Z Show' to East Lansing."

First, both players took part in the 2000 USA Basketball World Championship for Young Men Trials. But when the roster was

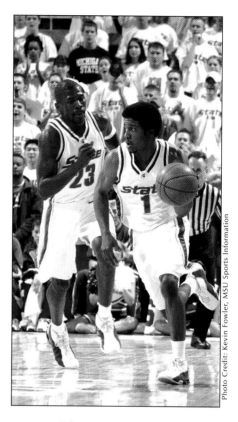

Photo Credit: Kevin Fowler, MSU Sports Information

trimmed from 16 to 12, MSU's two representatives were sophomore Jason Richardson and Randolph.

"It was very difficult to make these cuts," USA coach Jim Boeheim of Syracuse said by phone that night. "Marcus was the toughest cut of all. He was very good on defense. He did a good job at the point and really shot well. Michigan State should be very happy."

So why was Taylor cut? Boeheim couldn't say. But a glut of point guards, inexperience, politics and a reluctance to have 25 percent of the USA roster from one school were some of the popular theories.

"Marc outplayed all of them," his father said. "That's what all the other guys said, every single one of them. I don't know what's going on. I know he's disappointed."

Taylor's future MSU teammates agreed with that assessment and weren't afraid to say so with Boeheim in earshot.

"Marcus played like he was several years older," Richardson said. "I'm shocked he didn't make it. He was one of the best guys here. He gave the ball up the way he should. Some other guards didn't do that."

Taylor gave up much of his scoring to do what Izzo demanded as a freshman and earned a 2001 league championship ring, something freshmen peers Omar Cook of St. John's and Andre Barrett of Seton Hall would never wear.

"It is hard for anyone to make that adjustment, especially being the main scorer and go-to guy," said MSU senior guard Charlie Bell, who endured a similar transformation three years earlier. "You have to realize, everyone here was the main player on their high school team. You have to push that aside and do what you have to do to win. If you're a true winner, you can sacrifice that."

Taylor still managed to score 16 points against Oakland, the sec-ond-most in any Spartan freshman's debut. He had 15 points and seven assists against Florida, then 15 and nine the next game at Loyola before breaking his right ring finger in a scramble against Kentucky.

After missing three games, Taylor scored 11 points against Penn State and started nine Big Ten matchups. And in the second round of the NCAA Tournament, he handled Fresno State's pressure defense, scored 11 points in 23 minutes and outplayed standout Tito Maddox.

"I'd say I'm a sophomore now," said Taylor, who set MSU freshman records for starts and assists on a Final Four team. "Zach and I are coming off the bench right now. But we really have seven starters."

Five of those seven departed after a loss to Arizona, leaving Taylor and Aloysius Anagonye to lead MSU in 2001-02. And if Taylor still has some things to prove, his freshman numbers were comparable to Cleaves' totals for minutes played.

"He had a better year than Mateen had as a freshman," said Izzo, who was tough on Taylor to try to speed his development. "Once he gets stronger and more comfortable with the system, he's going to be a great point guard here."

Johnson also had some advice for Taylor, a protege who has barely scratched the surface.

"What Marcus is missing can only come with playing every day all summer," Johnson said. "He needs to be able to read situations. I never had an off-day at his age. I used to drive to Detroit and drive to Flint to play, not just to work on my shooting. Watch Jason Williams and see how he plays as a sophomore. There's no hesitation. He reads the situation, and he's gone."

If Taylor can improve as much as Williams did between his freshman and sophomore seasons, the Spartans might be back in business as a title contender — with No. 1 playing that way.

"I have to turn it up a notch and take advantage of this opportunity," Taylor said before heading to the 2001 USA Basketball Trials. "A lot of people are already against us. I want to prove them wrong."

And prove Peterman was right.

1 MARCUS TAYLOR
Guard—6-foot-3, 190 pounds
Lansing, Mich. (Waverly HS)

Taylor's Statistics

	G/GS	MIN/Avg.	FG/FGA	Pct.	3FG/3FGA	Pct.	FT/FTA	Pct.	REB/Avg.	PF/FO	A	BK	ST	PTS	Avg.
2000-01	30/9	661/22.0	86/217	.396	19/70	.271	32/43	.744	39/1.3	51/1	107	4	11	223	7.4

THOMAS KELLEY

Sometimes we have to go backward to move forward. Thomas Kelley did both at break-foot speed and wound up way ahead of where he started.

The 6-foot-2 guard from Grand Rapids arrived at Michigan State in 1994 with comparisons to NBA blur Kevin Johnson. By the time he left, Kelley was linked more closely with Johnson & Johnson.

He was the only one to play for Jud Heathcote, then appear in a Final Four under Tom Izzo. But MSU learned what Kelley could do after his 36 points and 10 assists as a Union High sophomore against Lansing Sexton.

He received letters from every Big Ten school except Indiana and others from Southern California to Syracuse. Kelley committed to the Spartans in September 1993, before he made any official visits.

A sensational senior season ended four months later, when Kelley suffered torn cartilage in his right knee. He was averaging 27.7 points per game.

After a full recovery, Kelley struggled as an MSU freshman, the only recruit that year. He backed up Eric Snow at point guard and tried his best to please a demanding boss, as "Tom-Tom" turned into "T.K."

"Only two guards other than 'Magic' could go to their left as well as their right in all the time I coached," Heathcote said. "Thomas Kelley was one of them and didn't even realize it. When I mentioned that in the class I taught, Thomas must have heard

about it. He came up to me a few days later and said, 'Coach, do you know why I go to my left so well?' I said, 'No, Thomas, I don't.' He said, 'Because I'm left handed.' I said, 'Then, why don't you shoot left-handed?' He said, 'No, I only eat and write left-handed.'…I never did figure that out."

With five games left in his first year with the Spartans, Kelley suffered a stress fracture in his right foot. Two surgeries cost him seven months of competition and development.

Kelley's confidence never wavered. Standing in the tunnel at Breslin Center, he watched his future competition at the point, Flint Northern junior Mateen Cleaves, score 28 points en route to a Class A title. Moving well on his crutches, Kelley responded, "Yeah, Cleaves is OK."

When Kelley was OK to play as a sophomore, his game had regressed. Some wondered which Kelley was better — Thomas or Kisha, a star of MSU women's team. And Drew Sharp of the

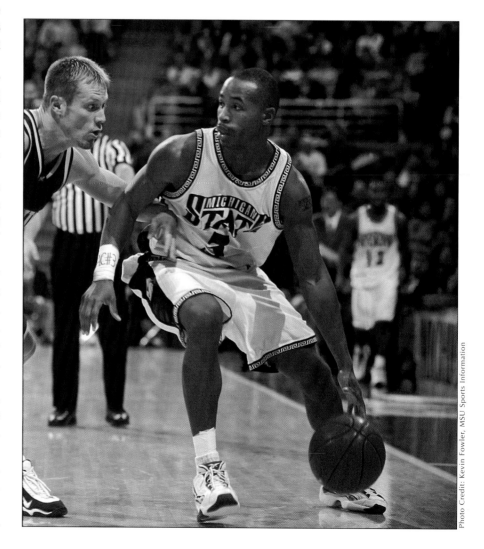

Photo Credit: Kevin Fowler, MSU Sports Information

S

THOMAS KELLEY

Detroit Free Press wrote that Kelley had created a new position, "pointless guard."

Committing more turnovers than anyone should, Kelley was booed in Breslin Center when he re-entered the game and replaced fan favorite Mike Respert in a 22-point loss to Michigan.

"That's a joke!" an irate Izzo said. "It's disappointing when hometown people don't understand what kids are going through. I'm his biggest critic, but only to make him better. I understand how much time he has missed."

When he was healthy and had some help, Kelley was very effective. He outscored former high school teammate Geno Carlisle of Northwestern 13-11 and held the Big Ten's leading scorer 9.8 points below his average.

But when he lacked his usual quickness or MSU's other players became spectators, Kelley broke the Big Ten mark for consecutive dribbles. Once, faced with trapping pressure, he dribbled backward across the timeline.

Things began to turn around for Kelley as a junior. With 27 points in a win at Evansville, the most for any Spartan in Izzo's sec-

ond season, "T.K." suddenly stood for "Tough Kid."

"It's about time I had some good times," he said in December 1996. "I've been going through some real hard ones. I hope this cuts me some slack."

Kelley averaged 8.1 points as a junior and appeared ready for a big senior year at shooting guard. He and Cleaves had meshed as well as anyone could have hoped. And Izzo predicted that No. 3 would lead his team in scoring.

After getting 18 points in a win over Athletes in Action, Kelley was struck down again. He jumped and came down on freshman Charlie Bell in practice, suffering a broken left foot. And a supposed two-month layoff turned into a redshirt season.

"It's a huge loss for us," Izzo said. "Thomas was really starting to adapt to his new role....It's really a shame. His entire career, it has been one thing after another."

Instead of eliciting cheers, Kelley was leading them again in street clothes. As the only Spartan who had played with Respert and Snow and the only one to appear in an NCAA Tournament, Kelley was gaining new respect.

"One morning 'T.K.' woke up as a different person," said his roommate, forward Morris Peterson. "He doesn't miss class any more. And he doesn't miss workouts. He's a leader to me and to everyone else."

Kelley realized how lucky he was in September 1998, when MSU cornerback Amp Campbell went down with a fractured neck at Oregon. Suddenly, a healthy sendoff meant everything to a fifth-year senior and co-captain in 1998-99.

He started just one more game but was a key reserve in a 33-5 season. In the Spartans' first Big Ten Tournament title win, Kelley took the pressure off Cleaves with four big baskets in a rout of Illinois.

"I learned to appreciate things more in life and learned how important school is, too," Kelley said before Senior Day. "I'm going to walk at graduation in May. Then, I'll have my degree this summer after taking a couple more classes."

That achievement was more impressive than his pro career in Europe and Australia. But Kelley was proof that a few broken bones don't have to lead to broken dreams.

3 THOMAS KELLEY

Guard—6-foot-2, 190 pounds
Grand Rapids, Mich. (Union HS)

Kelley's Statistics

	G/GS	MIN/Avg.	FG/FGA	Pct.	3FG/3FGA	Pct.	FT/FTA	Pct.	REB/Avg.	PF/FO	A	BK	ST	PTS	Avg.
1994-95	16/0	88/5.5	9/20	.450	0/1	.000	4/8	.500	8/0.5	13/0	8	1	0	22	1.4
1995-96	32/15	819/25.6	56/150	.373	7/32	.219	45/57	.790	70/2.2	64/1	114	12	21	164	5.1
1996-97	29/6	587/20.2	80/165	.485	12/45	.267	62/86	.721	54/1.9	47/1	62	7	18	234	8.1
1998-99	38/1	569/15.0	77/214	.360	8/28	.286	30/36	.833	46/1.2	45/1	51	5	30	192	5.1
	115/22	2063/17.9	222/549	.404	27/106	.255	141/187	.754	178/1.5	169/3	235	25	69	612	5.3

DOUG DAVIS

He didn't want to sit behind Mateen Cleaves and didn't want to redshirt. Instead, Doug Davis sat out a season and became a Miami (Ohio) RedHawk.

At Michigan State from 1997-99, the Columbus, Ohio, native started one game and averaged just 2.0 points and 1.2 assists. Yet, there were times the past two seasons when fans had to ask, "Wouldn't Davis have helped ease the loss of Cleaves?"

"Doug was definitely good enough to play here," MSU coach Tom Izzo said. "He could shoot the ball. And he could get after people on defense. I wish he would have redshirted for us. But he had to do what he had to do."

The 6-foot-3, 175-pounder had to get stronger to be a solid Big Ten point guard. But if senior Thomas Kelley hadn't broken his foot in November 1997, Davis might have sat out that season, like it or not.

That would have made him a redshirt-freshman backup in 1998-99, a sophomore fill-in when Cleaves missed 13 games the following year, an experienced junior when Cleaves was an NBA rookie last season and a fifth-year senior in 2001-02.

Davis was a two-time All-Ohioan from Westland High, where

his last three teams went 65-7. He averaged 24.2 points in 1996-97 and was one of four Mr. Basketball finalists, with winner Kenny Gregory and fellow runners-up Andre Hutson and Michael Redd.

"I wanted to come to a place where Mateen could guide me along, we could win some games and I could get some experience in college basketball," Davis told Bob Baptist of the *Columbus Dispatch* midway through his freshman year. "Then, whenever the time comes for me to do my thing, that'll be the time."

That time came 14 months later when Davis decided to move closer to home. He figured Cleaves would return for his senior year and was right about his roommate. And with prep All-American Marcus Taylor leaning to MSU, there were doubts that Davis would ever start in East Lansing.

The psychology major also had a tough time with the "constructive criticism" Izzo offered his players, especially his point guards. Though that wasn't the reason he left the program, his eardrums would have voted yes.

"First, Mateen comes at me in summer ball, doing everything to

me," Davis said. "Then, I come to practice, and Coach Izzo is screaming and getting in my face. It shook me a little bit. I don't think anybody ever yelled at me in high school, certainly not the way Coach Izzo screams."

Davis helped the Spartans beat Ohio State and Purdue as a sophomore and had a six-game stretch with 10 assists and one turnover. But when he left, Izzo did all he could to help him.

As a Miami junior last season, Davis averaged 9.8 points and 2.3 assists in 30.8 minutes. He also watched MSU reach a third-straight Final Four and rooted for his second-favorite team.

30 DOUG DAVIS

Guard—6-foot-3, 175 pounds
Columbus, Ohio (Westland HS)

Davis' Statistics

	G/GS	MIN/Avg.	FG/FGA	Pct.	3FG/3FGA	Pct.	FT/FTA	Pct.	REB/Avg.	PF/FO	A	BK	ST	PTS	Avg.
1997-98	26/1	200/7.7	20/50	.400	9/23	.391	5/10	.500	21/0.8	16/0	19	1	5	54	2.1
1998-99	38/0	281/7.4	25/64	.391	13/35	.371	10/21	.476	19/0.5	32/1	42	6	8	73	1.9
	64/1	481/7.5	45/114	.395	22/58	.379	15/31	.484	40/0.6	48/1	61	7	13	127	2.0

LORENZO GUESS

He had two full pages in the Michigan State basketball media guide and one page in the Spartans' football book... Guess which sport he didn't play as a junior or senior?

After switching back-and-forth from point guard to defensive back, Lorenzo Guess made the tough choice — and the right one — to give up basketball and focus on football in 2000-01.

Heading into his senior season, the 6-foot-1, 190-pounder from Wayne Memorial High in suburban Detroit had played in five more college football games than basketball games. And he had made 45 more tackles than points.

But Guess hadn't forgotten two seasons of MSU basketball for Tom Izzo's Big Ten champions, as seen by the black cloth-and-leather coat he wore with pride from the 1999 Big Ten Tournament.

And his coaches and teammates hadn't forgotten him, as seen by an absentee tribute in the basketball guide and an open invitation to play both sports, though football had to be his top priority.

"I love Lorenzo," Izzo said. "I loved him as a high school quarterback. And he was a very good basketball player. But as much as I enjoyed having him around, he had to make a commitment to football."

The Midwest's No. 4 football prospect in 1996 was ranked No. 60 in the nation in basketball. Guess opened a few more eyes with 10 points, a game-high seven rebounds and four steals in Magic's Roundball Classic at The Palace.

As a freshman and sophomore with the Spartans, he averaged just 2.5 minutes and 0.6 points. But after deciding to stick with football, he still helped the basketball program with some strong defensive work.

When friend Mateen Cleaves missed 13 games with a stress fracture and students asked, "What's wrong with the Spartans?" Guess turned up the pressure.

"Nothing's wrong!" he said. "You watch...They'll win it all. I know those guys, especially the seniors. When the title is on the line this time, Mateen won't let them lose."

Guess became a prophet, as MSU beat Florida to claim an NCAA basketball championship and match the football team's success against the Gators in the Citrus Bowl on Jan. 1, 2000.

He watched Cleaves' "One Shining Moment" on the big screen in Breslin Center with five football teammates. And if Guess missed celebrating in Indianapolis, he did a great job of hiding it.

Seventeen months later, Guess could make a difference for the Spartans at free safety, as a nickelback or on special teams in 2001.

"Lorenzo's in a battle with Duron Bryan for a starting position," MSU defensive coordinator Bill Miller said. "He has started games here. And we've won with him. But either way, he'll be a valuable player. It'd be a real fun deal if they were all like him."

Izzo couldn't have said it any better.

Photo Credit: Kevin Fowler, MSU Sports Information

5 LORENZO GUESS

Guard—6-foot-1, 190 pounds
Wayne, Mich. (Wayne Memorial HS)

Guess' Statistics

	G/GS	MIN/Avg.	FG/FGA	Pct.	3FG/3FGA	Pct.	FT/FTA	Pct.	REB/Avg.	PF/FO	A	BK	ST	PTS	Avg.
1997-98	15/0	37/2.5	4/9	.445	0/1	.000	0/1	.000	3/0.2	3/0	0	0	2	8	0.5
1998-99	13/0	33/2.5	5/10	.500	1/2	.500	0/0	.000	8/0.6	0/0	0	0	0	11	0.8
	28/0	70/2.5	9/19	.473	1/3	.333	0/1	.000	11/0.4	3/0	0	0	2	19	0.6

STEVE CHERRY

e was carried off the court on adoring fans' shoulders on Feb. 17, 1998, after an 80-75 win over Michigan in Breslin Center.

Steve Cherry didn't score the winning basket for Michigan State. He didn't have the key assist. He didn't even break a sweat.

But the walk-on forward was part of an MSU team that broke a five-game losing streak against the Wolverines. And he represented every student on campus — a McDonald's customer, not a McDonald's All-American.

Cherry was the Spartans' version of "Rudy," famed Notre Dame football walk-on Dan Ruettiger, with one key difference. Ruettiger played the final 27 seconds against Georgia Tech as a senior. Cherry just cheered in his first of five straight victories over Michigan.

"It was really a shock because I didn't play one second of the game," Cherry said the following day, still shaking his head about the hero's ride. "I didn't want them to do it, especially when I could smell the alcohol on their breath. But I really didn't have a choice."

The 6-foot-6, 195-pounder had several choices in 1996, when he averaged 17.0 points and 7.8

rebounds as a senior at Coldwater High and earned *Detroit Free Press* All-State recognition.

Cherry attracted interest from Oakland, Lake Superior State and Loyola but wanted to attend a big school with a highly respected business department.

That led him to East Lansing, where he imitated MSU's opponents for four years, one as a redshirted freshman and three as the last sub on Tom Izzo's list of active players.

"Preparation is the key to everything we do," assistant coach Brian Gregory said. "We need help from everyone we have that way. And guys like him are a big reason we've beaten so many different kinds of teams."

As leads would grow, the chant would go: "CHER-RY!...CHER-RY!" When Izzo emptied his bench, No. 22 appeared in 40 games and scored 19 points despite a lingering ankle problem.

After postseason ankle surgery, he pursued a master's degree in hospitality at MSU. But he saved his best basketball moment for Senior Day, a 51-point waxing of the Wolverines on March 4, 2000, in Breslin.

Cherry played a career-high 10

minutes and hit his first 3-pointer in Big Ten play. A player once known as "C-Bomb" put his team up by 57 with 7:15 to play on a pass from senior point guard Mateen Cleaves.

It was a three-time All-American's 20th and final assist of the day in a Big Ten-record performance. And when someone asks the trivia question, "Who scored the basket on Cleaves' last assist as a Spartan in Breslin?" the answer will always be Cherry.

He didn't get carried off the court again. But he was part of another scrumptious treat, a payback for the ages with a Cherry on top.

Photo Credit: Kevin Fowler, MSU Sports Information

22 STEVE CHERRY

Forward—6-foot-6, 195 pounds
Coldwater, Mich. (Coldwater HS)

Cherry's Statistics

	G/GS	MIN/Avg.	FG/FGA	Pct.	3FG/3FGA	Pct.	FT/FTA	Pct.	REB/Avg.	PF/FO	A	BK	ST	PTS	Avg.
1997-98	11/0	15/1.4	1/3	.333	0/1	.000	0/0	.000	4/0.4	0/0	0	0	0	2	0.2
1998-99	17/0	28/1.6	4/10	.400	0/4	.000	1/2	.500	7/0.4	3/0	2	0	1	9	0.5
1999-2000	12/0	31/2.6	3/11	.273	2/6	.333	0/0	.000	2/0.2	2/0	3	0	1	8	0.7
	40/0	74/1.9	8/24	.333	2/11	.182	1/2	.500	13/0.3	5/0	5	0	2	19	0.5

BRANDON SMITH

He could become the nation's first basketball coach/screenwriter/oral surgeon.

But for four years at Michigan State, Brandon Smith was just "Mookie," a backup point guard who helped write a championship script and did more in drills than in games.

The 5-foot-11, 195-pounder from Rochester, N.Y., transferred from Coastal Carolina and sat out the 1997-98 season. He never scored more than three points in a game. Coaches and teammates said he never had to.

"He drove Mateen (Cleaves) crazy in practice," said MSU coach Tom Izzo, who gave Smith a scholarship after his first year in the program. "Plus, if you asked the guys which player they'd confide in or who was the best motivator on the bench, it was him."

Smith scored just 21 points in 65 games with the Spartans — as many as his roommate, Andre Hutson, had against Purdue as a freshman in 1998. Yet, Hutson said Smith's contributions were one of the team's untold stories.

"'Mookie' was a guy who'd get in your face, no matter how many honors you had," Hutson said. "He didn't care about that. But he gave me a lot of confidence and told me I had to speak up as a senior."

It was Smith who spoke up and let everyone have it in a two-and-a-half-hour meeting last February after a dismal defensive effort at Minnesota. And he didn't hurt the team the way some feared when he had to play meaningful minutes in December.

Smith moved up in the playing group when freshman Marcus Taylor missed three games with a fractured finger. MSU was 3-0 in that span, as Smith played 39 minutes, including 19 against Bowling Green, and committed just four turnovers. He also helped on defense in a win at Penn State.

"I've tried to help every day by motivating and leading," Smith said. "It's like being a coach out there. When people get down on themselves, I tell them it's all right. And when I pressure guys in practice and they do a good job in the games, I feel good. I feel I've helped us win."

The Spartans won 115 times and lost 25 after Smith came to campus. Though he will never be known for an awkward shot that connected just once in 12 tries last season, Smith has always known his days as a player would end.

"Sooner or later, I want to get into coaching," said Smith, a noted TV basketball junkie. "I'd like to coach on the college level or maybe in the NBA some day. I have a lot of things I want to do first."

The microbiology major still plans to attend dental school. Smith also insisted he is determined to try acting school before he starts his own music company.

A lack of ambition is clearly not his problem. But if he becomes a coach and has to watch film, favorite movies like "Crouching Tiger, Hidden Dragon" and "The Matrix" won't count.

Maybe Smith can write a screenplay about a troubled coach who thinks handling a stubborn star is like pulling teeth. He is one of the few who could.

Photo Credit: Kevin Fowler, MSU Sports Information

10 BRANDON SMITH

Guard—5-foot-11, 195 pounds
Rochester, N.Y. (Pittsford Sutherland HS)

Smith's Statistics

	G/GS	MIN/Avg.	FG/FGA	Pct.	3FG/3FGA	Pct.	FT/FTA	Pct.	REB/Avg.	PF/FO	A	BK	ST	PTS	Avg.
1998-99	21/0	43/2.0	1/8	.125	0/4	.000	2/4	.500	5/0.2	2/0	8	0	2	4	0.2
1999-2000	27/0	118/4.4	3/11	.273	1/3	.333	3/9	.333	5/0.2	12/0	22	0	1	10	0.4
2000-01	18/1	113/6.3	1/12	.083	1/8	.125	4/7	.571	11/0.6	9/0	15	0	2	7	0.4
	66/1	274/4.2	5/31	.161	2/15	.133	9/20	.450	21/0.3	23/0	45	0	5	21	0.3

MIKE CHAPPELL

From Southfield-Lathrup High to Duke, then back to Michigan State, he never stopped growing. The young man got two inches taller, too.

Mike Chappell reached 6-foot-9 before he showed up in East Lansing as a re-recruited transfer in 1998. If he never reached the level of consistency everyone expected, he did more than enough to make Tom Izzo wish Chappell had signed with the Spartans two years earlier.

"It's hard to imagine the sacrifices Mike made," Izzo said. "To not have quite the career he'd hoped for and still be so positive is incredible. But you look back and say, 'Maybe we don't win the national championship against Florida without his five points in a row.'"

When Chappell looks back, he can smile about a 19-point effort at Oakland in his first MSU start, about 21 points in just 20 minutes

of a payback trouncing of Wright State and about a near-perfect, 12-point contribution in a rout at Michigan.

But he'd rather be remembered another way — as a proud graduate who gave everything he had, in good times and bad, for the most successful teams in conference history.

"I think that's the mark any athlete wants to leave," Chappell said. "I hope I can be remembered as a guy who did whatever it took to win. Any guy would sacrifice scoring 20 or 30 points if he could win championships year-in and year-out. That's what this year's group has done."

Chappell was around for the majority of those victories, as the Spartans went 93-17 while he sat out his transfer season and came off the bench the past two years.

In an unprecedented run of success, MSU earned three more Big Ten regular-season trophies and back-to-back Big Ten Tournament crowns, reached the Final Four three times as No. 1 seeds and was the NCAA champ in 2000.

And to think Chappell might have missed all that when he wavered on his plan to become a Spartan in 1996. Instead, the *Parade* All-American was "seduced" by the Blue Devils' success on college basketball's brightest stage.

"Michigan State was first for a long time when I was in high school," Chappell said of his recruitment by then-Duke assistant Tommy Amaker. "It was really nothing anyone did wrong. It was just that Duke was Duke."

Chappell started 21 of the Blue Devils' first 22 games as a sophomore. A midseason slump changed that, however, as his season averages plunged to 7.1 points and 14.4 minutes. He still led Mike Krzyzewski's team with 43.4-percent 3-point accuracy.

Once Chappell decided to transfer, the Spartans made another pitch — this time as a Big Ten champ and a Sweet 16 team. But Michigan and Detroit Mercy wanted him, too.

"I've always been partial to Michigan State," Chappell said when announcing his choice. "That's not any big secret. I loved the 'Fab Five' at Michigan. But I was a Steve Smith fan long before that.

"I really think the two big things were my familiarity with the campus up there and my relation-

MIKE CHAPPELL

ships with the coaches. Whatever choice I made, there had to be trust. My relationships with the coaches were paramount."

When the Spartans reached the Final Four in St. Petersburg, Fla., the following spring, top-ranked Duke was waiting. The Blue Devils beat MSU by six points for the second time in four months. And a sign from the touring "Cameron Crazies" told Chappell, "It's not too late to change your mind."

Instead, he changed uniforms and was seen as a perfect replacement for Jason Klein at small forward — a position that was filled in sensational fashion by Big Ten MVP and All-American Morris Peterson.

"I'm a firm believer that everything happens for a reason," Chappell said a week before MSU's 2001 Spring Commencement. "That's what happened here with the transfer and the up-and-down seasons. But it was definitely a memorable five years."

The greatest memory was his brief-but-critical performance against the Gators on April 3, 2000, in Indianapolis. At the end of a disappointing junior season with averages of 5.9 points and 2.2 rebounds, Chappell came to the rescue.

Leading just 50-44 when Mateen Cleaves suffered a severe ankle sprain, Izzo turned to a 31.0-percent 3-point shooter. When Chappell drained a 3 from the top, then added a putback in traffic, the lead was a safe 11 points again in what became a 13-point triumph.

"It seemed like he was really down-and-out," Izzo said. "But he made two of the biggest shots in that game. I know you can't live with that forever. He doesn't have to. He was great to have on this team. I wouldn't trade him."

A lot of the fans and a majority of the media had other ideas. It was suggested that Chappell was a liability his senior year, when his scoring dropped to 4.7 points per game. He shot 31.1 percent beyond the arc with a green light to launch from anywhere.

"He's someone who stayed the course, took some hits and never changed his demeanor or his life," said MSU assistant Brian Gregory, who transferred from Navy to Oakland as a player and had a little more understanding of Chappell's ordeal. "That's why I think it was special for Mike to do it in his home state for the school he has always felt a part of, with his fami-

ly and friends there to share in it."

If he hadn't transferred, Chappell's senior season at Duke would have ended with a loss to Florida in a 2000 East Region semifinal. Instead, he became a Gator-tamer with a championship ring no one can take away.

Photo Credit: Kevin Fowler, MSU Sports Information

20 MIKE CHAPPELL
Guard/Forward—6-foot-9, 220 pounds
Southfield, Mich. (Lathrup HS)

Chappell's Statistics

	G/GS	MIN/Avg.	FG/FGA	Pct.	3FG/3FGA	Pct.	FT/FTA	Pct.	REB/Avg.	PF/FO	A	BK	ST	PTS	Avg.
1999-2000	39/3	563/14.4	75/196	.383	37/117	.316	43/59	.729	85/2.2	62/1	23	4	5	230	5.9
2000-01	33/1	449/13.6	54/122	.443	19/61	.311	28/37	.757	64/1.9	50/1	23	3	10	155	4.7
	72/4	1012/14.1	129/318	.406	56/178	.315	71/96	.740	149/2.1	112/2	46	7	15	385	5.3

ADAM BALLINGER

He would have been Michigan State's only senior this season. Instead, Adam Ballinger has two years left. And he's due for a break that doesn't involve a bone.

The 6-foot-9, 250-pounder from Bluffton, Ind., played just four games in 1998-99, largely because of a fractured fibula. After helping the Spartans win an NCAA title in 2000, Ballinger's bad luck continued with a shattered thumb on his shooting hand six-and-a-half months later.

After missing the first eight games last season, Ballinger struggled to play half as well as he had in October 2000. But he did just enough to make MSU coach Tom Izzo foresee a breakthrough, not another fracture.

"I really think he's one of those guys who could raise his game a level," Izzo said. "He was playing the best basketball I've ever seen him play last fall before the injury. That really set him back. But like (A.J.) Granger his junior year, Adam could make a big leap. He brings a dimension we don't have on this team."

That ability to step to the perimeter and hit open jumpers anywhere within 20 feet could help a program that lost 11 players in a span of 13 months.

Ballinger was a 65-percent shooter in high school, averaging 26 points and 9.5 rebounds for a 22-2 team. But after a Big Ten tour of Illinois, Indiana and Northwestern, a trip to East Lansing ended his recruitment.

"When we saw the campus and fell in love with the facilities,

there was no sense stretching it out," said Ken Ballinger, Adam's dad and a high school counselor. "Coach Izzo is a blue-collar guy who knows how to get after you. As a parent, I liked the fact that the inmates don't run the asylum up there."

Ballinger could barely run at all in his first season with the Spartans, when he was perfect from the field (3-for-3) in four appearances before a medical redshirt.

His redshirt-freshman year

held promise, as he led his team with 64.4-percent accuracy from the field (29-for-45), including a 16-foot jumper against Florida in the championship game.

Just when it seemed Ballinger might emerge as a difficult matchup for opponents, MSU's annual preseason injury jinx knocked him out of action for eight weeks.

"It's the 'Tom Izzo Rule' that we've got to lose a guy the first

Photo Credit: Kevin Fowler, MSU Sports Information

ADAM BALLINGER

week of practice," Izzo said of a strange pattern, including a stress fracture that sidelined point guard Mateen Cleaves for 13 games in 1999.

"I had the ball in the post with my fingers spread," Ballinger said. "Andre Hutson came over my shoulder and slapped down on the ball. He caught my thumb in just the right place. I didn't know how bad it was. But I knew it wasn't just sprained."

Ballinger wasn't the same player as a sophomore, hitting 46.5 percent from the field (20-for-43) and looking tentative with the ball in most situations.

"Like a lot of guys who aren't egomaniacs or real cocky individuals, sometimes that works against you," Izzo said. "He kind of lost confidence after the injury. He was under fire right away. We played Seton Hall in his first game back, then jumped into the Big Ten."

Ballinger had played an entire season with back pain. But when he shredded a thumb, it was as debilitating as a shattered right foot for an NFL placekicker or a NASCAR driver.

"Not being able to shoot for two months really hurt," Ballinger said. "I was ready to go before the season. But missing eight games was like starting all over again."

His first career start came against Ohio State in Breslin Center, after four-year fixture Andre Hutson went down with pneumonia. It wasn't the way Ballinger wanted to earn a start. But it would have to do.

"You have to take what you get," Ballinger said. "This is a great chance for me. I'm excited about it. But I'd also like to have Andre back. Right now, I'm just going to try to do all I can."

Ballinger did more than anyone expected in a 71-56 triumph, scoring a career-high 10 points in 16 minutes and helping to hold OSU center Ken Johnson to 10 shots and 12 points.

"I thought Ballinger did a pretty good job," Izzo said. "I told him at halftime he was 1-for-4 on what were 4-for-4 shots. He had good looks. But he was looking to pass, then saying, 'Oh, I'm open. I'll shoot,' instead of looking to shoot and saying, 'I'm not open. I'll pass.'"

That changed in the second half. Ballinger's eight points in eight minutes helped MSU pull away. At least temporarily, that quieted teammates who wanted him to shoot more.

"Everyone was getting on me at halftime, telling me to shoot first," Ballinger said. "That's one thing I bring to the team. So in the second half, I wasn't tentative at all. I was a little nervous at the start. I think anyone would be. But it was great to hear my name announced."

Ballinger had scored just six points in his previous seven games — hardly what you would expect from an Indiana kid whose favorite player was Larry Bird.

"We know Adam has one of the better jump shots on this team," guard Charlie Bell said. "If he stops hesitating and just shoots it, we know he can knock them down."

The advertising major knows all the knocks against his game and can wage a campaign to convince his doubters. Or maybe Ballinger should just work to help his mom, Donna, sell more custom-made, 18-karat-gold Spartan jewelry (www.donnaballinger.com) by winning championships.

Nothing sells like success. And if MSU could win five Big Ten titles in five years, Ballinger's No. 55 might show up on a few more pair of distinctive earrings.

55 ADAM BALLINGER

Forward—6-foot-9, 250 pounds
Bluffton, Ind. (Bluffton HS)

Ballinger's Statistics

	G/GS	MIN/Avg.	FG/FGA	Pct.	3FG/3FGA	Pct.	FT/FTA	Pct.	REB/Avg.	PF/FO	A	BK	ST	PTS	Avg.
1998-99	4/0	22/5.5	3/3	1.000	0/0	.000	0/2	.000	5/1.3	2/0	1	3	1	6	1.5
1999-2000	37/0	382/10.3	29/45	.644	0/0	.000	15/19	.789	64/1.7	41/0	10	14	8	73	2.0
2000-01	25/1	206/8.2	20/43	.465	0/1	.000	8/11	.727	40/1.6	30/0	4	10	3	48	1.9
	66/1	610/9.2	52/91	.571	0/1	.000	23/32	.719	109/1.7	73/0	15	27	12	127	1.9

Mat Ishbia

"Don't get me wrong," a Michigan State fan said on her way into the Breslin Center. "I think Tom Izzo is a very good coach. But every time he plays Mat Ishbia, they win....Why doesn't Izzo just start him?"

Despite a slight cause-and-effect problem, that fan was right about one thing. Until a Final Four loss to Arizona, MSU was 34-0 the past two seasons when Ishbia appeared in the final few minutes.

The 5-foot-10, 165-pound walk on's greatest contribution has come in practice the past three years. Ishbia has never known the feeling of falling short of a Big Ten title or failing to reach the Final Four.

"Sure, it's tough to sit sometimes," Ishbia said. "I'd love to play every second. But I'd rather win than play. And if I can help the other guys play well enough to build a big lead, I know I'll have a chance to get in."

Ishbia averaged 23.0 points and 7.1 assists as a senior at Birmingham Seaholm High in suburban Detroit. But he needed some luck and his usual hustle in East Lansing to earn a tryout in 1998.

After Ishbia became friends with former MSU football recruit Antonio Gates through AAU play, they drove up to Breslin for a pick-up game. When Ishbia stole the ball from Mateen Cleaves and everyone else, Cleaves said Ishbia could help and might be a coach one day.

Izzo has seen the same thing, though Ishbia, an Academic All-Big Ten selection, is majoring in finance, not physical education. Maybe he'll be the first coach/agent. But when Izzo needs help reading the mood of the team, he calls for No. 15.

"Mat has tremendous respect from the other players," Izzo said. "I've called him in twice to give me the pulse of the team. He's that kind of guy — very similar to what Mike Longaker was for Jud Heathcote."

Ishbia and Jason Richardson became buddies in AAU ball. Ishbia's father, Jeff, an attorney, helped Richardson through an eligibility crisis before the 1999-2000 season. But when Jeff counseled his son to try a program with more opportunity to play, Ishbia followed his dream.

"Mat has tremendous heart and tremendous drive," his dad said with pride. "He was the typical kid-next-door, shooting 200 jumpers on the driveway before school. But his dream was to play in the Big Ten — at Michigan State, in particular."

Ishbia is doing just that. And if he never scores more than two points in a game, he just wants the Spartans to have one point more than the opposition.

"If I can help one teammate one time to get one more rebound, I've helped," Ishbia said. "It might be yelling, 'Watch the screen!' But from where I am on the bench, they probably won't hear me."

Ishbia could be the people's choice in Breslin for five seasons. He isn't leaving early for the NBA. And no one has floated his name as the next head coach of the Detroit Pistons...yet.

Photo Credit: Kevin Fowler, MSU Sports Information

15 Mat Ishbia

Guard—5-foot-10, 165 pounds
Bloomfield, Mich. (Seaholm HS)

Ishbia's Statistics

	G/GS	MIN/Avg.	FG/FGA	Pct.	3FG/3FGA	Pct.	FT/FTA	Pct.	REB/Avg.	PF/FO	A	BK	ST	PTS	Avg.
1999-2000	18/0	40/2.2	3/5	.600	0/1	.000	3/6	.500	4/0.2	3/0	3	0	2	9	0.5
2000-01	17/0	35/2.1	2/8	.250	0/2	.000	1/2	.500	6/0.4	5/0	1	0	2	5	0.3
	35/0	75/2.1	5/13	.385	0/3	.000	4/8	.500	10/0.3	8/0	4	0	4	14	0.4

ADAM WOLFE

He stepped to the microphone at a champions' lovefest with 25,000 fans and fired the first shot of his Michigan State career.

"My name is Adam Wolfe," an Ohioan said on April 5, 2000, in Spartan Stadium. "You don't know me....But you will."

Swish.

The 6-foot-9, 235-pounder from Westerville might as well have said, "Don't worry that Morris Peterson and A.J. Granger are graduating. I shoot left-handed, just like Peterson. And Granger isn't the only Buckeye who can play."

From then on, people said, "Have you seen the Wolfe kid?... You know Kentucky wanted him."

So did the Spartans. When Tom Izzo made that known, MSU had the second member of a five-player class — after fellow Ohioan Jason Andreas and before Michiganians Mike Chappell, Jason Richardson and Aloysius Anagonye.

"Kentucky was very high on his list," said his coach at South High, Ed Calo. "They said he plays a lot like Scott Padgett and wanted him to fill that forward spot in another year. But Michigan State has been there all along. He just really likes that coaching staff."

Wolfe, who stood 6-8, 215 at the time, was a logical signee for Ohio State, 15 minutes from his home. But after also visiting North Carolina and Duke and considering Kansas, he decided to join Andreas in a car pool to East Lansing.

Wolfe averaged 23.0 points, 10.1 rebounds and 3.5 blocked shots as a senior for the school that sent football stars Ki-Jana Carter and Andy Katzenmoyer to Penn State and OSU, respectively.

After a year of growth, Wolfe thought he was ready to step in and help with a national title defense in 2000-01. And it looked that way after his 21 points in the Green & White Scrimmage.

Anyone who saw him play in the summer or early fall said roughly the same thing: "Wolfe is going to be a major headache for opposing defenses."

It didn't quite happen that way, as migraines prevented him from practicing enough to stay with the playing group. Later, flu kept him out of action.

But with nine points and eight rebounds in 14 minutes against Illinois-Chicago and six points and six rebounds in seven minutes at Michigan, Wolfe showed flashes of what lies ahead.

"I still think Wolfe is going to be a player — I really, really do," Izzo said. "No. 1, he has to stay healthy and headache-free, which he has for a while. And No. 2, he has to start loving the game and getting some confidence.

"When you get in a hole early, it's hard to play your way out of it. But I put him in some situations early where he played pretty well. He played really well against Florida. He'll play more at the 3 (small forward) next year."

Wolfe should do more than play as a sophomore. He could start. Or he could be one of the team's top subs. After all, that's what Peterson and Granger were — as juniors.

Photo Credit: Kevin Fowler, MSU Sports Information

3 ADAM WOLFE

Forward—6-foot-9, 235 pounds
Westerville, Ohio (Westerville South HS)

Wolfe's Statistics

	G/GS	MIN/Avg.	FG/FGA	Pct.	3FG/3FGA	Pct.	FT/FTA	Pct.	REB/Avg.	PF/FO	A	BK	ST	PTS	Avg.
2000-01	23/0	139/6.0	15/55	.273	3/18	.167	7/8	.875	40/1.7	15/0	3	4	7	40	1.7

JASON ANDREAS

Tom Izzo trusts his eyes more than any recruiting analyst's rankings. So it didn't matter where Jason Andreas sat on anyone's list of the top 50 prospects — or the top 500. It only mattered that he was good enough to play for Michigan State.

In two seasons on campus, the 6-foot-10, 245-pounder from Sugar Creek, Ohio, has done nothing to change Izzo's mind. Andreas is still seen as a definite keeper and the Spartans' kind of player.

"He's very tough and very smart," Izzo said. "He has made incredible improvement. I've put him in for certain situations. But you can only play so many people. If you look at where he was and where he is, he has made more improvement than anyone on the team. Offensively, he's so much better. And he doesn't take anything from anybody. He's going to be one of my kind of guys."

He was supposed to be an Ohio State kind of guy in most people's minds. His father, Dan Andreas, lettered for OSU from 1968-70. And his uncle, Bill Andreas, was a three-year starter for the Buckeyes from 1973-75.

But when people asked the Garaway High standout, "Are you going to State?" he didn't have to tell them which one. Andreas didn't need his 3.9 grade-point average to figure out the wisdom there.

"It all came down to the people up there, the coaches and the commitment they've made to academics," said Andreas, who also considered OSU, Penn State, Northwestern and Nebraska. "Michigan State was on me so early. And in four trips up there, I could only be impressed."

Andreas' stats weren't as impressive as some, with averages of 14.0 points and 7.5 rebounds as a high school senior. But before undergoing knee surgery, he did more than enough to stamp himself as a future Spartan.

"Jason did an awful lot as a junior, despite battling viral bronchitis all year and only being healthy for three games," Garaway coach Bill Romine said. "I've never coached anyone quite like him. And I don't know that I ever will."

Izzo just knows he liked what he saw at practice and in brief appearances in 24 games in 2000-01. Andreas hit both his shots from the field in a three-minute stint against Penn State.

Appropriately, his best work came against the Buckeyes in Breslin Center. With senior standout Andre Hutson sidelined by pneumonia, Andreas had three rebounds in 11 minutes and helped frustrate OSU center Ken Johnson.

"My dad and my uncle were here," Andreas said after the game. "But I never felt any pressure to go to Ohio State. And they were definitely pulling for Michigan State. They're green-and-white now."

So is their favorite Big Ten player, a recruit Izzo swears he will never regret signing. If Andreas doesn't play major minutes in 2001-02, it will be as big a surprise as it was when Izzo signed him and smiled for a week.

Photo Credit: Kevin Fowler, MSU Sports Information

44 JASON ANDREAS
Center—6-foot-10, 245 pounds
Sugar Creek, Ohio (Garaway HS)

Andreas' Statistics

	G/GS	MIN/Avg.	FG/FGA	Pct.	3FG/3FGA	Pct.	FT/FTA	Pct.	REB/Avg.	PF/FO	A	BK	ST	PTS	Avg.
2000-01	24/0	115/4.8	5/11	.455	0/0	.000	3/6	.500	25/1.0	19/0	2	4	3	13	0.5

THE STAFF

TOM IZZO

The party was still going strong the night of March 3, 2001, long after Michigan State had beaten Michigan to claim a fourth-straight Big Ten basketball title. And more than one man was receiving congratulations.

"People ask what I did to raise such a great son," Carl Izzo said with Upper Peninsula pride and just a touch of wonder. "I gave him two pieces of advice: 'Never be late for work. . . . And never leave early.'"

To this day, Tom Izzo is one of the first people up-and-at-'em each morning and one of the last to say good night.

Your boy learned his lessons well, Carl and Dorothy.

All those examples of hard work from his grandfather's company, Tony Izzo & Sons & Grandsons, paid off. Any business that can make and repair shoes and install floor covering, siding, awnings or gutters has to provide quite an apprenticeship.

But that's the way it was — and, to a large degree, still is — in Iron Mountain. Maybe it's the water. Maybe it's the weather. Or maybe it's the 374 wooden steps Izzo and Steve Mariucci would run to reach the top of the world's largest man-made ski jump.

Friends forever, they knew life wasn't an endless series of ski lifts. It was lifting themselves and their teams up, over and over, until they reached the top.

Their bond began in grade school, when all Mariucci heard about was this public-school kid from the west side of town. And,

yes, with a population of 8,500, it was big enough to have sides.

"It was 'Izzo this, and Izzo that!'" said Mariucci, a Catholic-school kid from the north side. "I was really sick of it. His nickname was 'Poncho.' And from fifth grade until we got to high school, I was the one who had to cover him. I couldn't play him to his right the way I would everyone else. He could dribble behind his back. He was really good."

When they became teammates, they became inseparable. Steve would throw passes to Tom in football. Tom would hand the baton to Steve on a record-setting mile relay in track. But in basketball, where Izzo ruled, a rare mistake helped make him a hero.

In a 1972 regional final against West Iron County, Izzo was fouled with two seconds left and the Mountaineers trailing by one. He missed the front end of a one-and-one and soon collapsed in tears. Mariucci was there to pick him up. Hundreds of letters of support helped, too.

A year-and-a-half later, Izzo and Mariucci were roommates at Northern Michigan in Marquette. Dick Allen, Izzo's high school football coach, had arranged for him to walk on in basketball — "the 25th man on a 25-man team." Four games into his sophomore year, Izzo made his first career start — ironically, against Michigan State. Meanwhile, coaching futures were being shaped.

"We lived in a trailer," Mariucci said. "Don't laugh! We had three different ones. And we had a greaseboard. Forget about having pictures on the wall. We might have had Farrah Fawcett. But that was it. We had a grease-board and no erasers. We'd use our sleeves or whatever we had. And we'd talk football and basketball X's and O's. Now, that's really stupid for college students. But we had no social life."

They had a bet to see who would be the head coach at Notre Dame first — Mariucci in football or Izzo in basketball. And career goals were always on the minds of a quarterback and a point guard, both Division II All-Americans.

"When you start to realize you're not going to play at the next level, coaching becomes a reality, not just something to fall back on," said Mariucci, head coach of the San Francisco 49ers. "We knew we weren't going to be pros. Instead, we got our teaching certificates and our driver's-ed certificates, so we could make six bucks an hour in the summers."

After starring in a backcourt with current MSU assistant Mike Garland, Izzo's first coaching job was at Ishpeming High. He promptly led the Hematites to a rare league title in 1978, then lost in the U.P. championship game to, of all teams, Iron Mountain.

The next season, he was back at Northern as Glenn Brown's assistant instead of his coach-on-the-court. Before Izzo spent 12 seasons learning from often-volatile Jud Heathcote at MSU, he picked up a

Photo Credit: Northern Michigan Sports Information

few things from someone with a totally different demeanor.

"Glenn taught me you get more bees with honey than vinegar," Izzo said. "I was more like Jud. Take my personality now and

multiply it by 10. That's why I had a hard time suspending Mateen Cleaves for being in a fight. I would've been in all of them. That's true! Ask Garland.

"I wanted confrontation all the

TOM IZZO

Photo Credit: Theresa Peterson, Iron Mountain Daily News

Photo Credit: Kevin Fowler, MSU Sports Information

time when I started coaching. I'd even go after guys I'd played with for two years. Glenn would say, 'You're going to learn, young man!' I'd go at it with profs if they weren't fair to our guys. And I was always at it with the administration. I couldn't get money to drive down here and scout. I didn't even want to stay in a hotel. I'd drive right back. I just wanted gas money. So I'd get pissed. But Glenn had the perfect temperament."

Just after breaking his jaw playing softball, an obvious error in Mariucci's scorebook, Izzo was the best man in his best friend's wedding. And if he didn't deliver the greatest toast ever made, at least he kept his mouth shut.

He couldn't always do that in his first few seasons at MSU under difficult conditions. He was put on the road as a fill-in recruiter in 1983 when Edgar Wilson left the

staff and was elevated again the following year when Heathcote suffered a mild heart attack.

After taking an assistant's job at Tulsa, Izzo had a chance to return to East Lansing weeks later when Mike Deane left to become the head coach at Siena. But telling irate Tulsa boss J.D. Barnett was a traumatic experience.

"Tom was really at odds with that," Mariucci said. "He's a loyal guy. His handshake is good. And he really didn't want to do an about-face. But he had to do it. It was the right thing professionally and for all the right reasons."

Back at MSU, the recruits began coming. And after two tough seasons from 1986-88, the Spartans started a streak of 13 consecutive postseason appearances. In Izzo's six seasons as head coach, his teams have gone 148-53, .736 success. And he's 16-3, .842, in

four NCAA Tournaments, the third-best mark for anyone with 10 games or more — ahead of John Wooden (47-10, .825) and Mike Krzyzewski (56-14, .800).

"I see Tom and 'Coach K' as being very similar," said ESPN analyst Jay Bilas, who played for Krzyzewski when Duke was emerging in the mid 1980s, then coached under him. "They have the same intensity and commitment to get results. It isn't the final score that matters as much as the final product. Tom's able to really chew a guy out. That tells me he has put some serious time in with his players to have those kinds of relationships."

Izzo could holler at Cleaves and scream at everyone else without a total rebellion, something a lot of coaches couldn't do. It's called communication, the No. 1 asset for an effective leader,

TOM IZZO

ESPN/ABC analyst Dick Vitale insisted.

"Just give me six months!" Izzo told his team in October 1999. "Six months for something that will last a lifetime." When those players and coaches followed him into a basketball mineshaft, they left Indianapolis with rings of gold.

"Tom can do that because he relates to his guys," Earvin "Magic" Johnson said just after the 2000 NCAA championship game, an 89-76 win over Florida. "And his guys play just like him, with a toughness you seldom see. I love the way he prepares his team. He has shaped this program and made it the closest thing to a Duke or a North Carolina. The credit all goes to him."

Izzo prefers to praise: No. 1, his players; No. 2, his staff; No. 3, the administration; No. 4, the fans and, No. 5, just about anyone he has ever met. His tributes to opposing coaches have become almost comical when the Spartans could have beaten their teams by 60 points.

"I think what he has done has been remarkable," said new Louisville coach Rick Pitino, who reached the Final Four with Providence, then led Kentucky to three Final Fours and a title in a five-year span. "He has not only done it quickly. He has done it with all the fundamentals you look for in a program. He has also developed a family atmosphere, which is very important. One of the toughest things in this business is to stay hungry and not

Photo Credit: Mark Bell, Instructional Media Center

embrace your success. You have to stay PHD: poor, hungry and driven. Tom Izzo has obviously done that."

Maybe not the poor part. Izzo is making more than he ever thought possible but not nearly as much as he could be. The bottom line? MSU President Peter McPherson will boost Izzo's $1.2 million compensation package and re-emphasize a long-held position: MSU pays for superior performance.

Yet, Izzo realizes riches aren't always measured by W-2 forms. And the response he and his program received two days after winning the title will stay with him forever.

"Wow!" Izzo said as he peeked through the gates at Spartan Stadium, where a jammed Parade of Champions route ended with another rally of 25,000 fans who

had waited in the west lower and upper decks for hours. "Look at all the people! . . . Hey, I've always said I loved football. I finally get to run through the tunnel."

After MSU ran away with the 2000 title, winning six straight games by double-digits, Izzo thought he'd already seen everyone in Mid-Michigan at a ceremony on the Capitol steps, then stacked along the parade route.

No wonder Izzo had to fight hard to control his emotions, something his wife, Lupe, and his dad weren't quite able to do.

"From the Capitol, it looked like an ocean of people," Lupe said later. "And the parade was unbelievable. Doctors came out of Sparrow Hospital in their scrubs."

Even non-basketball fans took a break — between surgeries, we hope — to salute a team of battlers and a coach who has spent pre-

TOM IZZO

cious spare time raising money for Sparrow pediatrics.

When a tardy procession finally reached the stadium, Izzo was touched by the love and togetherness he saw wherever he looked. And he never had to look more than a few feet away.

"This is the ultimate in terms of having everyone on the same page," he said of a fairly new development for Spartan athletics and for MSU as an institution.

The best moment of all might have been a surprise visit by Bobby Williams' football team in full uniform for pre-practice handshakes and hugs among the school's two groups of Gator-tamers.

No one has done more to build a Spartan coalition — young and old, students and faculty, judges and a politically incorrect Spartan

governor — than Izzo, who still doesn't fully realize his importance.

When a bedsheet atop the stands read "Izzo 4 Prez," Al Gore and George W. Bush were lucky a self-deprecating leader wasn't on the ballot in November in Michigan.

"It's embarrassing," Izzo said. "I'm sure all the attention is fun for the players. But I'm too old to be a rock star."

As he gripped the podium and heard chants of "IZ-ZO . . . IZ-ZO . . ." he would've been excused for feeling like Jack Dawson, Leonardo DiCaprio's character in "Titanic," and screaming, "I'M THE KING OF THE WORLD!"

Long after the crowd had left, Izzo stayed behind to talk with some students and sign every piece

of paper he was handed except a blank check.

"He'll never change," Lupe said of a man who wondered why the rally hadn't been held in Breslin Center, a building half the right size. "That's what made me fall in love with him in the first place."

It took a championship for so many others, including the Atlanta Hawks, who offered to more than triple his income. On Friday, May 12, 2000, Izzo was closer to saying yes than most people knew, as much for the challenge of winning an NBA title as for any financial windfall.

"Tom would have to change a lot," pleaded Vitale, who failed in a similar shift from the Detroit Titans to the Detroit Pistons 22 years earlier. "To become a great pro coach, you have to surround yourself with great NBA players. But there's nothing wrong with being great in college. If he stays at Michigan State, he'll have it all!"

He would have a chance to build coach-player relationships he couldn't find in the NBA, win many more championships and chase the legends. But Izzo had already said there was no way he would coach as long as Jud Heathcote did — 19 years with the Spartans and to age 67.

"The very fact Tom worked 12 years for Jud says a lot about his ability to adapt," broadcaster and MSU Hall of Famer Gregory Kelser said. "Tom has prepared himself to be a success at whatever he has done. But I've been around him since 1983. And I've never heard

Photo Credit: Frank Tate, Instructional Media Center

him talk about a burning desire to coach in the NBA."

"I never even thought about the NBA thing with Tom," said Philadelphia point guard Eric Snow, one of Izzo's favorite players as a Heathcote assistant. "He meant so much to me at Michigan State that I'm sure he could do it. But I know how much he likes to teach and coach. And that happens more often in college. He's a little like (76ers) Coach (Larry) Brown that way."

Izzo talked to Brown and several others with an NBA perspective. New York Knicks coach Jeff Van Gundy told Izzo if he worked as hard as the five hardest workers in the pros, he would work half as hard as he does now — no small consideration with two adorable, young children.

"These jobs aren't always as much fun as you'd think," Izzo said of the college game a full 11 months before losing a sophomore and a freshman to the NBA. "Last year in July, the best month of the year, I was gone 27 days. And you have a lot more time in the NBA than everyone thinks. That's what the guys I checked with told me."

Yet, with the chance to trade one set of problems for a much more lucrative set, Izzo couldn't do it. Yes, he was close to leaving. His hand was on the doorknob. But he couldn't twist it and twist the knife on so many people — players, administrators and friends — who had believed in him with all their hearts.

"I talked to Tom once or twice a day when he was going through

that ordeal," Mariucci said. "I swear I didn't know what he was going to do. The night before he had to make his decision, I thought he was going to take it. And not just because it was a huge contract, but because it was another thing he hadn't accomplished.

"The next morning he called pretty early. He got me out of bed and said, 'Hey, I'm going to stay.' That doesn't happen very often. Not many people can leave a lot of money on the table and walk away from it. If there had been any conflict, any hard feelings, any regrets or anything negative, he'd be in Atlanta right now. But he thinks this place is utopia."

Proclaiming himself "a Spartan for life," Izzo sealed his image as someone people could trust. And if he ever needed anything, there were several hundred-thousand homes where he could get it.

A post on the Rivals.com message board put it best the day before the decision: "Tom — I've got $243.49 in my bank account, a blue '89 convertible Mustang and a fridge full of beer. You're welcome to all of it if you stay."

Izzo didn't want anyone's charity and didn't need a contract that alienated faculty when he had worked so hard to build bridges. No wonder Izzo was more excited about finishing a work well-in-progress than starting over with Atlanta's rubble.

"I didn't have any money when I came here," he said, thinking of the cars and a fabulous home he almost apologized for having. "I make a lot of money now. So I'll

just set my sights on helping a couple of my players become millionaires."

As he left the Clara Bell Smith Student-Athlete Academic Center, Izzo knew he had faced the toughest decision he would ever have and had done what was best for the players he had recruited, for Spartan Basketball and for Michigan State University.

"Tom is what I call a program guy," Heathcote said. "He's also a dummy when it comes to money. But if you look up 'loyalty' in the dictionary, you'll see Tom's picture. . . . He has done all right for a really short guy from Iron Mountain."

A short guy with a long memory. He'll never forget what Heathcote did to help him, just the way he couldn't forget the people he had told he would do all he could to justify their faith in him. By staying, he justified their faith in humanity.

"When I called them, the Hawks were a little surprised," Izzo said. "(Atlanta President) Stan Kasten said, 'Is there anything I can do to talk you out of the worst decision of your life?'"

Izzo's next decision? To seize the moment to defend what former MSU football coach George Perles did in saying no to the Green Bay Packers and New York Jets to stay at MSU in the late 1980s, moves that brought scorn and ridicule.

But the football coach mentioned most that day was Penn State's Joe Paterno, who has spent a half-century in Happy Valley. Another charismatic Italian, Paterno said no to other opportu-

TOM IZZO

nities and became more closely identified with the school than the Nittany Lion.

"Almost anyone I've met in athletics wants to move to the next level," MSU broadcaster and former basketball coach and administrator Gus Ganakas said. "That's true with junior high and high school, high school and college or college and the pros. But to make the decision he made, that's Tom. His loyalty emerged. He could be the Paterno of college basketball."

Izzo will never coach that long. But MSU vice president Terry Denbow, a former Penn State administrator, remembered when Paterno rejected a lucrative offer from the NFL's New England Patriots.

"Paterno said, 'My wife went to bed with a millionaire and woke up with me,'" Denbow said. "From that point on, he was seen forever as a college coach. And what Tom did was great for Michigan State and good for college basketball."

That didn't mean there wouldn't be speculation about other pro opportunities, beginning the following year with non-stop rumors about the Detroit Pistons. As flattering as that had to be, it was also maddening.

"It's going to be a continuous thing," Mariucci said. "Every year, somebody is going to say, 'Maybe we can grab him this year. Maybe he'll change his mind. Maybe he'll leave some day.' Maybe I'm wrong. But I think everyone is looking for an Izzo type. He has a great reputation. His integrity is the best. And owners are going to want those types of coaches."

The idea of Izzo coaching in the pros — in pro football — is one with strange appeal. If he could coach special teams for the 49ers and basketball for the Spartans, Izzo would be willing to work 22 hours a day instead of 19.

"He could be a head coach in the NFL," Mariucci insisted. "The things we used to do on the grease-board, the X's and O's, can be

Photo Credit: Theresa Peterson, Iron Mountain Daily News

learned. That's only a percentage of the responsibilities we have. The other things — evaluating players, motivating, being organized, hiring and firing — cross the boundary between any sports. Tom could coach football tomorrow, whether it would be running backs, defensive backs or linebackers, the position he played. And he was a good football player — a better football player than I was."

Izzo learns a lot faster than most, though he jokes: "I'm getting smarter....I'm smart enough to know when I shouldn't read the papers."

He still isn't alert enough to avoid embarrassing situations. He walked into a piece of lumber sticking out of the back of a truck — producing a shiner that actually made Lupe feel sorry for him the first time they met. And when she said she wanted a date last season, he promised her a night at the movies, just like old times. Unfortunately, he told her to leave her purse, then forgot his wallet. Somehow, they scraped together just enough change to buy a bag of popcorn.

There are some things money can't buy, like the sign that reads: "Welcome to Iron Mountain — Proud Hometown of Tom Izzo & Steve Mariucci."

Or the smile on Becky Cawood's face, when sons Johnny and Anders got to accompany the team on a trip to Indiana in 1999 after the death of their father, Izzo's friend, John.

Or the honorary doctorates Izzo received from his alma mater in April 2001, after returning home as NMU's commencement speaker,

and serving as one of MSU's convocation speakers a week later.

But Ingham County Family Court "Assistant Judge" Raquel Izzo had the final word on Friday, Dec. 22, 2000. "He's my brother," the precocious 6-year-old said of Steven Thomas Mateen Izzo.

With that, the tears and the laughter in Judge George Economy's courtroom all made sense. A 6-month-old boy's adoption became final. And a family of three was officially four — with talk of a larger number.

"I hope so," Lupe said. "Steven was Tom's Father's Day present...A brother for a brother and a sister for a sister would be nice."

With gavel in hand, Raquel made her dad and Economy joke

about the possibility of law school in 2016. And as Steven looked up with blue-gray eyes from a sharp, green jumper, his parents had a prize no trophy could match.

Economy echoed those thoughts for a small group of family and friends when he read the "Adoption Creed" by an unknown poet:

> *Not flesh of my flesh*
> *Nor bone of my bone*
> *But still miraculously*
> *My own.*
> *Never forget*
> *For a single minute*
> *You didn't grow under my heart,*
> *But in it.*

Photo Credit: Theresa Peterson, Iron Mountain Daily News

TOM IZZO

Later, Economy couldn't stop talking about the Izzos' warmth and the example they were setting.

"You're talking about one of our sports icons," Economy said. "He's a god in this town! And look at what he has done. If he can do this, a lot of other people can. We don't stop to realize how blessed we are. But Tom and Lupe know that. They want their home to be filled with the sounds of children."

The name is Steven (for Mariucci), Thomas (for the boy's new father), and Mateen (for a three-time All-American).

Yet, it was a time for children

to act like adults and for adults to share in the joy of children. Economy, a diehard maize-and-blue fan, joked, "Tommy, if you want the kid, you're going to have to go coach at Michigan!"

No one loves his family more than Izzo loves Lupe, Raquel and Steven. But let's be reasonable, Judge. Every man has his limits.

Maybe that was why Izzo donned Economy's black robe and sat in the judge's chair before he left the courtroom.

"I always wanted to do this," Izzo said. "OK, for one moment, I finally have some REAL power!"

Economy called it the power of love.

Moments later, Izzo was asked about top-ranked Duke's loss to Stanford the night before and how that might impact the Spartans' ranking.

"Do you think we'll be No. 1?" Izzo said with a smile that suggested his mind was elsewhere. "Do you think it really matters?"

It didn't matter one bit that day, not with his wife, his daughter and, yes, his son all smiling up at him. Plenty of hard work and the power of love paid off in a way no contract could.

TOM IZZO

Photo Credit: Theresa Peterson, Iron Mountain Daily News

TOM IZZO

YEAR	OVERALL	BIG TEN	BIG TEN TOURNAMENT	NIT	NCAA
1995-96	16-16	9-9	—	1-1	—
1996-97	17-12	9-9	—	1-1	—
1997-98	22-8	13-3*	0-1	—	2-1
1998-99	33-5	15-1*	3-0*	—	4-1
1999-2000	32-7	13-3*	3-0*	—	6-0*
2000-01	28-5	13-3*	0-1	—	4-1
TOTAL	148-53	72-28	6-2	2-2	16-3

* Championship

TOM CREAN

Michigan State left a lasting impression on Tom Crean in his five years on campus. Just ask his Marquette basketball players. But Crean had almost as significant an impact on MSU's program in his second stay in East Lansing — perhaps not his last one.

Recruiter? Check. . . . Teacher? Check. . . . Motivator? He could give clinics on the subject. And if Tom Izzo had gone to the Atlanta Hawks in May 2000, the first call for a possible replacement should have been to Crean in Milwaukee.

He arrived in 1989 as a graduate assistant in Jud Heathcote's program. That season, the Spartans improved from 18-15 to 28-6, captured an outright Big Ten championship and advanced to the NCAA Tournament's Sweet 16. Just a coincidence? Perhaps not entirely.

MSU's success and Crean's incredible drive immediately earned him a rare opportunity for someone just a year out of Central Michigan, where he didn't even play college basketball. He was hired as a Western Kentucky assistant in 1990 and was instrumental in helping the Hilltoppers win 67 games in his second, third and fourth seasons.

After Crean followed Ralph Willard to Pittsburgh in 1994, the players he recruited to Bowling Green, Ky., stunned Michigan in the 1995 NCAA Tournament.

"No question I had to work harder because I didn't have the same playing experience," said Crean, who helped coach at Mount Pleasant High and Alma College while a CMU undergraduate in psychology. "But I was used to that. I didn't graduate from high school with my class, either. I was really sick my freshman year with what was eventually diagnosed as Epstein-Barre virus. So I had to go to summer school to get those credits back. But I did it."

Though much has been made of Tom Izzo's first salary at MSU being just $7,000, Crean said he started at $700. Yet, the bond between the two is unmistakable. Without Izzo's encouragement, Heathcote never would have given Crean a chance. And without that opportunity, Marquette would have a different head coach in 2001-02.

"I would never accept it as a disadvantage that I didn't have the pedigree or the playing experience," Crean said. "But Tom was always a friend and a mentor. When I was a nobody at Alma, he took me on a recruiting trip to Pittsburgh, to Rensselaer, Pa., and to Detroit. He didn't have to do that."

When Izzo succeeded Heathcote in 1995, he quickly hired Crean and named him associate head coach two years later. Their styles blended perfectly as recruiters and as good-cop, bad-cop coaches with an appreciation of football. Crean's brother-in-law is 15-year NFL quarterback Jim Harbaugh and his father-in-law, Joani's dad, is long-time collegiate coach Jack Harbaugh.

"He was instrumental in helping us build the program, from the smallest things to the biggest things," Izzo said of an assistant who earned a tremendous amount of trust. "When we were trying to get the fan interest back, he was a big part of that. And he was very involved in the building of our academic center."

Photo Credit: Kevin Fowler, MSU Sports Information

TOM CREAN

Photo Credit: Kevin Fowler, MSU Sports Information

Crean was a stickler for individual workouts. But it was his use of every advantage as a recruiter that drew national attention. When Charlie Bell made his official visit, Crean put a picture of Bell's face on a life-size cutout of his hero, Michael Jordan. Just the thought that went into each presentation was impressive.

"I still think our best visit was Shane Battier, a guy we didn't get," Crean said. "But I'll never forget the Mateen Cleaves visit. Tom brought in three boxes — a foot-

ball jersey with his name on it, a basketball jersey with his name on it and a cap and gown with his name on it. No one else showed him all three."

Since Crean succeeded another ex-MSU assistant, Mike Deane, as Marquette's head coach, the Golden Eagles have heard enough about Cleaves and Morris Peterson to make them hate the Detroit Pistons and Toronto Raptors. And they have been exposed to the Izzo approach.

"We were running a loose-ball

drill one day, and Brian Wardle got popped in the nose," Crean said of the No. 2 scorer in Conference USA history. "He was bleeding like crazy. But I told him, 'You'd better hurry up! We're not going to finish this drill till you're back.' He came right back out with cotton up his nose.

"Maybe the best example was the day before the Cincinnati game. We have what we call the Eagle drill, where we start by drawing a charge. Then, a coach rolls a ball toward midcourt. The player has to get up, sprint to the ball and dive on it, then pick it up and go in for a layup, while coaches club him with pads. We never do that the day before a game. But before we left Milwaukee, Wardle said to me, 'We have to do the Eagle drill.' I said, 'Are you sure?…OK, it's all on you.'"

Marquette pulled a major upset the next night. But the team Crean's players wanted to play the most was the one they heard about all the time, the one whose national championship ring the Creans received as gifts from Izzo.

"One of our seniors, Brian Barone, asked who we were going to play in the future," assistant coach and ex-Spartan Dwayne Stephens said. "We talked about Notre Dame and maybe Michigan State. Barone said, 'Why couldn't we have played Michigan State this year? I don't care how good they are. We'd beat them! After all the stuff they put us through…'"

The Spartans gave Marquette another head coach. That should have been payment enough.

BRIAN GREGORY

Some people score a lot of points and dominate the headlines. Others make the selfless plays that make those basketball victories possible.

From his early days in Mount Prospect, Ill., Brian Gregory has been "Mr. Assister."

After a year at the U.S. Naval Academy, when the Midshipmen went 30-5 and reached the NCAA Tournament's Elite Eight with David Robinson, Gregory transferred to Oakland University. He left there in 1990 as the Grizzlies' all-time assist king with 906 in three seasons. And his average of 10.7 feeds per game as a junior was second in the country.

Those contributions should have have foreshadowed the kind of coach "B.G." would be in two stints at Michigan State that sandwiched stops at Toledo and Northwestern.

There is no one Tom Izzo trusts more and no one outside the head coach's office in Breslin Center who understands as much about the program. If Gregory doesn't get the credit he should, he is appreciated most by the man who rehired him.

After succeeding Tom Crean as the Spartans' graduate assistant in 1990, Gregory made an immediate and lasting impression with Izzo. When he quickly became a favorite of MSU head coach Jud Heathcote, it was clear the military's loss was college basketball's gain.

"Jud loves guys who played the game — and loves point guards," Izzo said. "I think he always liked Brian's background. He was an Academic All-American from a small college. Having gone to the Naval Academy, he had the discipline Jud thought was important to be a good person, not to mention a good coach."

Have we mentioned how Gregory picked up each aspect of the job like a damp sponge absorbs a small spill? He began as a factor in the Spartans' improved academic performance. He became as good as any assistant in the nation in formulating detailed scouting breakdowns. He studied the intricacies of post play and helped Andre Hutson improve offensively.

And after leaving MSU in 1996, he developed into an outstanding recruiter.

"It all starts with the head coach," Gregory said. "If he believes academics are important, there's a better chance the players will, too. With Jud and Tom, we've always put a lot of time into preparation. And when you talk to recruits or parents, Tom is an easy sell."

Gregory's relationship with Izzo was strong enough to withstand a potential strain. A new head coach had to pick two of his three assistants to recruit off-campus and brought Crean back from Pittsburgh instead of elevating Gregory.

Photo Credit: Kevin Fowler, MSU Sports Information

"Deciding about Brian was probably one of the hardest things I've ever had to do," Izzo said. "He was probably the most intelligent assistant Jud had, as hard-working as any of us and more organized than anybody. I thought Crean had the recruiting experience. And I thought I could still keep Brian. I was looking for the best of both worlds, which wasn't totally fair. But I did what I thought I had to do to develop the program. To this day, I think I did the right thing."

Gregory stayed on Izzo's staff for a year, then went to Toledo when MSU assistant Stan Joplin took the head coaching job in 1996. The following year, Izzo helped Gregory move to Northwestern, where head coach Kevin O'Neill and center Evan Eschmeyer nearly led the Wildcats to their first NCAA Tournament berth.

When Crean left to become head coach at Marquette in 1999, Izzo knew he wanted to bring Gregory home, a move O'Neill understood and accepted. By then, the Spartans were hiring a finished product as a top assistant — one of the three hardest-working aides in the country according to a Rivals.com survey of his peers two years later.

"To be honest with you, losing Brian for three years was very difficult for me," Izzo said. "But I think it was better for Brian in the long run because he got to learn other systems. I think he's a better coach for it. We use a lot of things Kevin did inside at Northwestern. So that

helped me big-time when Brian came back. Now, he's back where he belongs — with us."

Gregory could leave at any time. He is too talented and personable to be an assistant forever, as seen by his work with 32-7 and 28-5 teams the past two seasons and his recruitment of Zach Randolph and Alan Anderson. But don't expect him to grab the the first job that comes open.

"He could've had the Delaware job last year," Izzo said. "I think we all knew that. And I think he was second choice at Northwestern, I really do. I talked to the A.D. (Rick Taylor) a couple of times. They were looking for someone with a little more experience. I don't think he'll leave for an average job. It'll have to be the right one. I know his wife (Yvette) likes it here. And he really likes the job he has."

Some see enough of a physical resemblance to call him "Rick Pitino without the bank account." But Heathcote wouldn't be surprised if Gregory leads some school to a championship, too.

Izzo agreed and recommended Gregory to Wisconsin A.D. Pat Richter after acting head coach Brad Soderberg was released in March. When Richter passed on Gregory in favor of a "big-name coach," new Badger boss Bo Ryan wasn't exactly the first name that came to mind.

Izzo also made a call to Xavier on Gregory's behalf when that job came open in the spring. Gregory was representing Izzo on an MSU

Alumni Association tour when the job came open. But Izzo did what he could, though he would have hated to lose his top aide and Gregory didn't want to leave.

If Gregory has to wait another year or two, everyone at MSU benefits. With a new starting point guard for the second-straight year, Izzo will take all the assists he can get.

Photo Credit: Kevin Fowler, MSU Sports Information

STAN HEATH

He was ready to leave the coaching nest last season. Now, Stan Heath is set to soar.

After five years as a Michigan State basketball assistant, Heath was named the head coach of the Kent State Golden Flashes on April 19, 2001, replacing new Rutgers leader Gary Waters.

And if there is a better first-year situation in the nation than the one in Kent, Ohio, it's as hard to find as a hair on Heath's head.

After helping the Spartans win four consecutive Big Ten titles, Heath will inherit four senior starters, including star guard Trevor Huffman, from a Mid-American Conference champ that beat Indiana in the opening round of the NCAA Tournament and finished 24-10.

"There's no question Stan is ready for this job," MSU coach Tom Izzo said. "He helped us go from start-to-finish with three Final Four appearances and a national championship. We've built it and maintained it. And he has been a big part of that."

The former Eastern Michigan guard coached at Lincoln High in Ypsilanti, Hillsdale College, Albion College and Wayne State before serving at Bowling Green from 1994-96.

Heath finished second last year for the top job at Ball State, yet another MAC institution. If Heath had been involved with any more programs in the league, he could have applied to become commissioner.

"I look at life as the glass always being half-full," Heath said after just missing an opportunity in Muncie, Ind. "But Tom told me to do two things this season — make sure I think like a head coach and don't just take a job to be a head coach."

He followed instructions well enough to help the Spartans finish 28-5. That impressed the right people, especially Kent State Director of Athletics Laing Kennedy, who entrusted Heath with a program that was 70-25 with three straight NCAA berths.

His appointment at MSU came after Stan Joplin left Izzo's staff and began a successful run at Toledo. Izzo considered several strong candidates and nearly hired ex-Michigan assistant Mike Boyd. But Heath won out. And the Spartans won 132 of their next 169 games.

"I knew Stan a little bit when he was in Division III," said Izzo, who has always appreciated the small-college ranks. "Stan Joplin and Stan Heath were good friends. And I wanted someone who'd be loyal, hard-working and have some connections in Detroit. I thought it was critical we start doing a better job in Detroit.

"I knew Mike very well (from Northern Michigan) and felt very comfortable with him. But that was a time when the Michigan-

Michigan State thing was even crazier. Though Mike had been away a few years, I didn't want it to be a controversial hire. I wanted it to be all-positive. I have great, great respect for Mike and think he could've done a phenomenal job. But I went with Stan. I had a younger staff. I thought we could build this family atmosphere I went with a guy who was family-oriented. He had the connections I wanted in Detroit. And I thought he would spent a lot of time with the kids."

Heath was instrumental in the recruitment of Jason Richardson, winning a battle with the stunned Wolverines. And he was heavily involved in other key signings, including the addition of 2001 National Player of the Year Kelvin Torbert.

Granted, Heath has never been a head coach. But at 36 years old, he's four years younger than Izzo was when he took over at MSU and eight years younger than Jud Heathcote when he was hired at Montana.

"Stan's strengths are his character and his relationships with people," Izzo said. "He's a very honest guy. There's no B.S. to Stan. He's very up-front. And when he sells me, people know whatever he says is the truth.

"I think he did an incredible job with Jason Richardson, getting to know the family, especially his uncle (Brian Bowen). That's when he really started to make some hay. You don't just recruit a kid. You recruit a support system of people. Stan did that. And he was very

important in the Torbert recruitment."

When it was Izzo's turn to sell Heath as a prospective head coach, it took a couple of cracks to get that done. But Izzo said Heath's Kent State candidacy was one of the easier pitches he has given.

"I really appreciate that," Heath said. "I have so many great memories of Michigan State and so many people to thank. But it matters when a head coach like Tom Izzo is on the phone. If Tom called you, you'd be nuts not to listen. It'd be like E.F. Hutton talking."

The best candidates have credentials that speak for themselves. In the March 19 issue of Sports Illustrated, Heath was recognized as one of "five college coaches waiting in the wings," with Iowa

State assistant Leonard Perry (now Idaho's head coach), Florida assistant John Pelphrey, Iona head coach Jeff Ruland and Hofstra head coach Jay Wright (now at Villanova).

"Plain and simple, Kent State just hired a winner in Stan Heath," said Dan Wetzel, senior writer for cbs.sportsline.com. "This is a guy who brings great energy, integrity and skill to the job. He was instrumental in helping Michigan State become one of the nation's dominant programs. With Stan's Midwest recruiting ties and obvious bench skills, I would expect Kent State to remain a team to beat in the Mid-American Conference and a dangerous program on the national stage."

He's way out of the nest now. Fly, Stan, fly.

Photo Credit: Kevin Fowler, MSU Sports Information

MIKE GARLAND

Photo Credit: Kevin Fowler, MSU Sports Information

Tom Izzo has tough challenges in front of him as Michigan State tries to replace seven players this season. But at least he can focus straight ahead. He knows Mike Garland has his back — and always will.

That's why Izzo hired an assistant with no college coaching experience in 1996 and promoted him this season. Experience is great. Trust is better. And there is no one Izzo trusts more in battle than his former backcourt partner from Northern Michigan University.

Izzo and Garland have been through it all in 28 years, from bench-clearing brawls to false alarms for fatherhood. Each time one of them was reeling, the other came to the rescue.

"I liked Mike right away," Izzo said. "He was a guy who was recruited by big-time colleges to play football and decided he wanted to play basketball. He was a quarterback in high school. And with my love for football, Garland was my kind of guy."

Their relationship started in 1973 when Garland, a sophomore from the often-mean streets of Belleville, Mich., was approached by a pint-sized freshman from Iron Mountain and his buddy, some guy named Mariucci.

When Izzo asked for directions and said he was trying out for the basketball team, Garland nearly broke out in laughter at the last man on a 25-man team.

The joke would soon be on Izzo's opponents. When Northern lost all but three players to fouls at Michigan Tech and still won with a fiery point guard, that three-on-five matchup for roughly five minutes became part of Upper Peninsula lore.

But Garland had moments to savor, too. When an opposing center gave Izzo a cheap shot, Garland said the next foul was his. By tackling a 7-footer and slamming him into a wall, No. 23 in green-and-gold showed No. 10 why one of his references would always be ex-Belleville football coach Lloyd Carr.

"Tom and I worked well together at Northern," Garland said. "And we said we'd be together again. I always thought he'd be working for me, though. I guess that's why he was the point guard."

Showing that leadership, Izzo

said he took Garland's wife, Cynthia, to the hospital in Marquette to deliver her first baby. After a previous false alarm, Garland channeled his aggressions into protecting Izzo again when fans joined a melee of players on the floor and began throwing punches.

"Tom's a fighter and always has been," Garland said. "And he's tremendously loyal. You can't help but respect him for that."

Respect isn't just a two-way street with Izzo and Garland. It's an eight-lane expressway.

"Mike's probably the toughest of all the assistants we've had," Izzo said. "He has been in the city. He wasn't born with a silver spoon in his mouth. He came up the hard way and has a great appreciation for inner-city kids. I think he can be put in any setting and be successful, which is important to me. Other guys might have had some recruiting experience. Mike was a true coach."

Garland became nationally known as an instructor at Howard Garfinkel's Five-Star Basketball Camps but never expected the chance to work at MSU, even when Izzo said to be ready.

"I told him, 'Some day, I'm going to get a job and hire you,'" Izzo said. "Eleven years later, I did. I used to go down and speak at his banquets. And he used to come up here once in a while. I tried to get Jud to hire him. But he didn't have any college experience.

"That's when the part-time position wasn't a full-paying job. And Mike had a family. He had

MIKE GARLAND

three kids by then. So it wasn't like he could take a pay cut. With the part-time job changing, to be honest with you, Mike Garland was the guy I wanted right off the bat."

Ironically, in nine seasons at Belleville High, Garland's record was 153-49. In six seasons with the Spartans, Izzo's mark is a nearly identical 148-53. But if you reverse four Minnesota wins during a period of scandal, Izzo is an eerie 152-49. "The Odd Couple," indeed.

It was Garland who worked tirelessly with Jason Richardson to develop his skills. And it was Garland who said Richardson

would be sensational in 2001-02. Reviewing the tape, he just didn't say where.

But Izzo said Garland is more than a disciplinarian and a teacher. And as an off-campus recruiter for the first time, after a spring promotion, Garland will have a chance to sell the program and take a major step toward a head coaching opportunity.

Sometimes, however, it's enough just to remember the good ol' days and relive them, as MSU did in a nine-hour bus ride back from Penn State on Feb. 24-25, 2001.

"It was awesome!" Izzo said. "It was just like Division II. Garland and I were salivating we

were so excited. We got three times as much meal money as we used to get. And there was no brown-bag lunch. We had to stop at Mickey D's to get a gourmet meal. But the best part for me was coming back on the bus and saying, 'Welcome to Division II!...I don't think the other guys appreciated it as much as Garland and I did."

And if the Spartans had lost in Happy Valley?

"I'd have made them walk back," Izzo said.

Either that or try to win their next home game against Michigan three-against-five. After all, that's what Izzo and Garland would have done.

Photo Credit: Kevin Fowler, MSU Sports Information

DAVE OWENS

Bob Knight's influence continued in the Big Ten long after he left Indiana University.

Former IU head manager and Knight devotee Dave Owens played an essential role in the Michigan State program as the Spartans' video coordinator and assistant to the head coach.

If Owens hadn't worked with the Hoosiers, he never would have been hired by Tom Izzo in 1997 to handle MSU's complex video demands and provide detailed breakdowns of opponents.

"Tom said, 'To be honest with you, one of the reasons you're here is where you were,'" said Owens, a high school coach for four years before he begged for an opportunity as an IU graduate student. "That shows the respect Tom has for Coach Knight. To hire someone he'd never met, heading into his third and most critical year, says a lot."

For four seasons in Breslin Center, Owens saw surprising similarities between leaders whose teams won national titles in their fifth tries in Bloomington, Ind., and East Lansing.

"One of the things Tom always said was how he wanted this program to be similar to Coach Knight's in terms of being very clean and very disciplined," Owens said. "For integrity and honesty, the two programs are very much the same. But the basketball philosophies are just the opposite. Michigan State plays zone when it has to, uses a lot of set plays and runs whenever it can. Indiana was strictly man-to-man, ran the motion offense and almost always set up in the half-court."

Owens set up most days in front of an Avid computer system and gave MSU an edge in determining tendencies and devising strategy. With help from 10 student managers, he taped three or four games most nights and broke them down by players and situations within 24 hours.

The Spartans also used highlight tapes for motivation, as we saw before a win over Michigan that meant a share of a fourth-straight Big Ten title. Owens' editing for that senior salute included artistic shots, the rap song "Bombs over Baghdad," highlights of each departing player's career and the closing message: "We Can Be Heroes."

"It had something for every guy from every season," Izzo said of a tape that even had clips of Mike Chappell shredding the Wolverines as a member of the Duke Blue Devils. "You could see how far every guy had come. And it had that long pass from Mateen (Cleaves) to Andre (Hutson) against Kentucky (in the 1999 NCAA Tournament's Elite Eight). Dave did an incredible job."

Owens did enough good work to earn a job offer from new Kent State coach and former MSU aide Stan Heath in April 2001. His goal was to be a bench coach again, but Owens said no to that opportunity. Instead, he became the coach at Owosso High in late June.

If Owens couldn't work for Knight, he was happy in a program with many of the same guiding principles — and much better media relations.

Photo Credit: Mark Bell, Instructional Media Center

SPARTAN SUPPORT

LORI SODERBERG

HEAD COACH'S SECRETARY

BETH MARINEZ

RECRUITING SECRETARY

GUS GANAKAS

FORMER ADMISTRATIVE
ASSISTANT

RICHARD BADER

ADMINISTRATIVE ASSISTANT

TOM MACKOWIAK

BASKETBALL TRAINER

JEFF KOVAN

TEAM PHYSICIAN

SPARTAN SUPPORT

DAVE PRUDER

EQUIPMENT MANAGER

MIKE VORKAPICH

STRENGTH AND CONDITIONING

LIZ FRIEDMAN

ACADEMIC SUPPORT

KEVIN CARR

LIFE SKILLS DIRECTOR

MATT LARSON

SPORTS INFORMATION

DOUG HERNER

ASSISTANT CAMP COORDINATOR

1998 NON-CONFERENCE

Confidence can be a wonderful thing.

And Mateen Cleaves believed the 1998-99 Michigan State Spartans could play with any college basketball team — perhaps even the Jordan-less, Pippen-less Chicago Bulls, the decimated NBA champions.

"Hey, we're going to be really good," Cleaves said loud enough to make people listen. "Last year, we accomplished a lot. But we can do better than that this time. You watch. . . . You'll see."

The surprising part about MSU's status in mid-November 1998 was what the so-called experts saw in a program that still had plenty to prove on the scoreboard.

The fourth try under Tom Izzo's leadership began with the Spartans ranked second in *Basketball Times*, fourth in the *USA TODAY*/ESPN survey of coaches and fifth in the Associated Press media poll.

MSU had finished 22-8 the previous season, by far its best record under Izzo. But good enough to be a consensus top-five pick? . . . That required a leap of faith, even with all five starters returning.

After sharing the 1998 Big Ten regular-season title with Illinois at 13-3, the top-seeded Spartans had been stunned in their first Big Ten Tournament game by eighth-seeded Minnesota, 76-73 — still one of the four biggest upsets in the event's history.

And after beating Eastern

Photo Credit: Kevin Fowler, MSU Sports Information

Michigan and Princeton in the first two rounds of the NCAA Tournament's East Region, MSU was clubbed 73-58 by top-ranked North Carolina in Greensboro, N.C., a Sweet 16 "neutral site."

That showed the Spartans just how far the gap was between good and great. All spring, summer and fall in 1998, the leadership of Antonio Smith, a senior center, and Cleaves, a junior point guard, was felt in and out of Breslin Center.

To this day, Izzo talks about the importance of having a team's best players be its hardest workers.

And no one worked harder than Cleaves, who threatened to drag his teammates along by the earlobes.

In the opener, an 89-58 win at home over Northeast Louisiana on Nov. 13, Cleaves had to start hollering before halftime. But after a 20-7 lead dwindled to 37-30, MSU exploded with 52-28 dominance in the last 20 minutes.

Perhaps it helped that mid-1980s standout Scott Skiles returned to campus to have No. 4 retired. He also wore No. 25 as a freshman. And the then-Phoenix Suns assistant, now the team's

1998 NON-CONFERENCE

Photo Credit: Kevin Fowler, MSU Sports Information

head coach, might have scored 25 points in either half of this game — in street clothes.

Instead, Smith, a reluctant shooter throughout his career, had 14 of his game-high 16 points in the second half. Sophomore forward Andre Hutson had 12 points and nine rebounds. Senior forward Jason Klein had 12 points, including a pair of 3-pointers. And Cleaves added 10 points and 11 assists.

But the strengths of the 1998-99 team were visible immediately. The Spartans outrebounded the Indians 50-35. And the bench was huge, as

junior forward Morris Peterson, the nation's best sixth man, had 12 points and junior forward A.J. Granger added nine points and a career-high 10 rebounds.

Four days later, Izzo's players bused to Rochester to face Oakland in the first game in the Golden Grizzlies' Recreation and Athletic Center. Though Oakland began as a branch campus of MSU, the Spartans were rude guests in romping 96-66.

The lead was 52-43 at halftime. But with three 20-point scorers for the first time in five seasons, MSU shot 62.1 percent from the field after the break. And despite holding the score down, the Spartans tied the highest point total in 93 games of the Izzo era.

The star was sophomore guard Charlie Bell, who matched Oakland center Dan Champagne with game-highs of 26 points and eight rebounds. Bell was 10-for-15 from the field and 5-for-5 at the foul line, drawing raves from Detroit Pistons observers.

"Cleaves is good," said head coach Alvin Gentry, now the leader of the Los Angeles Clippers. "He's the one who gets all the publicity. But the guy I really like is Bell. He can do it all."

Bell did everything Izzo could have asked except to drive the bus. The rumor is, he apologized for that. And his scoring output was a career-high, topping a 22-point outburst on his birthday (March 12) against Eastern Michigan.

Cleaves did more than his share, too, with 21 points on 9-for-13 shooting, including 3-for-5

work beyond the arc. And Smith had the best back-to-back offensive games, scoring 20 points on 10-for-12 success from the field.

There was only one problem for a 2-0 team. Those wins did nothing to prepare the Spartans for what they would face three nights later in a 60-59 loss at the Apollo of Temple in Philadelphia.

MSU shot 55.6 percent in the first half and held the seventh-ranked Owls to 21.7-percent accuracy. But the first sign of trouble came when that disparity produced just a 33-21 cushion over a four-point favorite.

Up 56-47 with 2:19 left, the Spartans were caught off-guard by a new rule, then and caught and passed in a wild last second. Instead of alternate possessions when both teams put their hands on the ball, the briefest tie-up gave the ball to the defense. And the Owls forced five turnovers that way, including three in the final minute in the eyes of officials Phil Bova, Jody Silvester and Tim Higgins.

"Leading by nine, I thought the only way we could lose was if we really screwed it up," Klein said. "And we didn't suck it up in the last two minutes. That's not how Michigan State plays."

Fifteen second-half turnovers, including nine by Cleaves, were one too many, as Temple point guard Pepe Sanchez took control. John Chaney's choice as the nation's top floor leader scored nine of his 11 points in the last 2:07, including two free throws with :00.5 showing.

"This loss was my fault," said Cleaves, who outscored Sanchez 17-11 and had a 6-0 edge in assists, only to miss a free throw with :52 left. "It was my kind of game. . . . I should've taken over at the end."

The Spartans took the loss about as hard as any in the Izzo era. A great opportunity had been squandered. And when a raucous crowd stormed the court, it was as if the Owls knew a win over MSU was a crowning achievement.

"We couldn't be as aggressive as we wanted," Smith said of the Spartans' 27 fouls and refusal to throw an open lob to Peterson. "It was just their night. But our margin of error isn't that great against good teams."

Photo Credit: Kevin Fowler, MSU Sports Information

Why should it be? More than two years later, after a fourth-straight Big Ten title, Izzo reflected on that finish and the knowledge his team could play with anyone on the road. It just had to learn to finish.

"That was the game we had a 15-point lead," Izzo said. "After that, I knew we'd be a pretty good team. We went against that matchup zone and played very, very well. We cracked a little at the end, an unforgettable finish. But how well and how hard we played against a team that emphasized toughness, defense and rebounding was big. And to see our players in the locker room and see how hard they took the loss, I knew we were making progress."

It would soon reach the point that any win over MSU meant Mardi Gras time. But a one-point win triggered a dangerous fan surge that had Izzo concerned for one of the few times in his athletic career.

"That was the only game in my career when I was miked," he said of an NFL Films feature, a favor to best friend and 49ers head coach Steve Mariucci. "But a cop grabbed me after the game. It was as hostile a crowd as we've seen. And it was the first time I said, 'Wow! We must be something special.'"

The following Friday, his team took its frustrations out on Central Florida in the first round of the Coca-Cola Spartan Classic. MSU built a 52-33 bulge by halftime, stumbled briefly, then coasted, 87-64.

The forwards were huge, as Klein led all scorers with 19 points

and Hutson added 18. They were a combined 14-for-22 from the field and 7-for-8 at the line. And Smith snared 10 rebounds.

The greatest significance of the game? The night after Thanksgiving 1998 was the last non-sellout for the Spartans at home, a string of 42 games-and-counting.

The next evening, MSU mashed Western Michigan 90-66 for its 13th Classic title in 17 tries. The Broncos had beaten UNC Wilmington 67-61 on Friday and led the Spartans by nine points in the first half before wilting.

With MSU career scoring king Shawn Respert on hand for the draping of his No. 24 banner at halftime, the Broncos' Kylo Jones did a great impression of the Big Ten's No. 2 all-time scorer. Jones hit eight 3-pointers in 13 tries and finished with 28 points, 22 before halftime.

But Peterson, the Classic MVP, had a career-high 21 points off the bench. Hutson and Klein combined for 29 points on 13-for-18 shooting. And after allowing 18 unanswered points before the break, the defense held WMU to six points in the final 7:05.

At 4-1, with an edge of nearly 22 points per game, the Spartans appeared ready for the toughest week any team would face all season — a Great Eight matchup in Chicago with No. 4 Duke, the pre-season pick to win it all, and a visit to No. 1 Connecticut. If it wasn't exactly a suicide mission, it was a brutal test no team could pass.

"Those next two games were tough for one reason," Izzo said

Photo Credit: Kevin Fowler, MSU Sports Information

with a smile two years later. "My superstar point guard went about 4-for-150 (actually 5-for-32)."

It didn't help MSU that the Blue Devils led 13-0. And it was 21-4 after just 7:50. A measuring stick for a maturing program had landed right between the Spartans' eyes.

But Peterson came off the bench and made MSU fans wish he had played 40 minutes. They also wished he'd had a twin brother, as "Mo Pete" led a surge to within 39-30 at the break with 14 of his game-high 24 points.

The Spartans made it interesting for a friendly United Center crowd of 19,412. They drew within 58-55 with 6:08 left, even after an apparent basket and free-throw opportunity for Smith was waved off by a charging call.

Duke answered the way champions do, hitting seven free throws in the last 90 seconds to win 73-67. All-America guard Trajan Langdon was nearly as good as Peterson, saving a star-studded team with 23 points.

"We were getting killed, then cut it to three and had a good shot to tie it," Izzo said. "Morris Peterson really came to life. And Mike Krzyzewski said later we were one of the toughest teams they played. We outrebounded them (41-25) and really played well once we got going."

Playing the last 30 minutes against the Devils hadn't proven any more successful than ruling the first 35 against the Owls. And after a late trip home, MSU had a whole day-and-a-half before its trip to a basketball torture chamber in Storrs, Conn.

"We had a couple of great practices," Izzo said. "When we got there, their fans were all over me before we got in the building. But we got off to a great start that no one saw because the Army-Navy football game went long on CBS."

After a cry of "LET'S GET READY TO ROUND-BALLLLL!" by rent-a-mouth ring voice Michael Buffer, the Spartans jumped to an 11-2 lead. And they held All-America forward Richard Hamilton in check all day, as Peterson outscored him 14-11. But roly-poly point guard Khalid El-Amin was the best player on the floor — to Cleaves' dismay.

"Khalid hit some shots just before halftime," Izzo said of the

Huskies' 38-34 lead. "They came against Charlie Bell, who had switched off on him. And Mateen was so mad, because it was a personal grudge match between them. Mateen was just livid."

That emotion didn't translate to effective play. After being just 3-for-17 from the field against Duke, Cleaves was 2-for-15 at UConn. And he was outscored 20-6 by El-Amin before a tougher battle with Izzo in Gampel Pavilion.

"It was one of the rare times when Mateen got caught up in the old playground mentality — 'If you're going to do me, I'm going to do you,'" Izzo said. "He still played hard. But he didn't shoot well. And we ended up losing up by 14 (82-68)."

The Spartans outrebounded the Huskies 39-30 but were outscored 18-1 at the foul line. And, yes, that was with Big Ten officials, who couldn't be blamed for UConn's 63.6-percent accuracy from the field in the last 20 minutes.

"I remember Mateen and I really having it out," Izzo said. "We did, too! There were no ifs, ands and buts about it. That was when I went after him in the shower. And I was walking down the hall to the press conference, yelling at him. He was so mad at everyone, especially himself."

Cleaves' teammates weren't thrilled to be 4-3, either. Hutson, who didn't miss a shot in a 12-point effort, summarized the fragile state of State as well as anyone could.

"If guys aren't getting tired of losing, they've got to start getting tired of it," he said in a deep voice that commanded respect. "We haven't played a complete game yet. To become a championship team, we have to do that."

Smith, who had 10 points and a game-high 12 rebounds, added, "You have to have character when you go on the road. When you play in the NCAA Tournament, you're going to have to play back-to-back games against tough teams. We'd better get used to it."

The Spartans would have that opportunity. And they wouldn't lose again in an 11-3 non-conference run. But none of that would have happened if Cleaves hadn't turned his season around.

"Could I have lost him right there?" Izzo asked in March 2001. "Maybe. . . . I was at my worst with him. And he was at his worst with me. It was an interesting time. I think where I gained the most respect for him was seeing how much he was hurt. I was adding fuel to the fire.

"But he bounced back and realized he didn't have to be a great scorer to be a great player. I think that was a big turning point for him. I can't remember who we played next. But I do remember he was almost the exact opposite. That was a big plus in our relationship. And he became even better than before."

How did Cleaves do that? He started by facing the media and answering questions when there were toxic-waste dumps where he'd rather have been.

"I'm going to shoot with my eyes closed," Cleaves finally said when asked what he planned to do

for the umpteenth time. "It's hard because I want to win and have fun. Sometimes God works in mysterious ways. Things don't always go your way. But you have to suck it up and work through it."

Cleaves and his teammates went back to work and were a different team by the following Thursday. The new MSU won 29 of its next 31 games, with help from surprising sources.

The first was senior guard Thomas Kelley, who lifted a 14th-ranked team past East Tennessee State 86-53 on Dec. 10 in Johnson City, Tenn. Kelley had a game-high 21 points and was 10-for-15 from

Photo Credit: Kevin Fowler, MSU Sports Information

the field — not bad for a guy who came in shooting 29 percent.

The Spartans led 41-17 with 3:52 left in the first half and finished with 63.9-percent accuracy from the field, the best shooting under Izzo to that point.

Three days later, their Sunday-best was defense in a 77-33 thrashing of Illinois-Chicago in Breslin. That was the lowest total for an MSU opponent since a 43-32 win over Michigan on Feb. 17, 1951, nearly four years before Izzo was born.

In one of just five starts in 38 games, Peterson led all scorers with 18 points and grabbed nine rebounds. Kelley added 12 points. And Smith had eight points and 14 rebounds. But a balanced offense was almost embarrassing against the doused Flames, who managed just nine baskets in 41 attempts.

After final exams and an eight-day layoff, the Spartans were favored in the inaugural Pearl Harbor Classic, an eight-team, three-day bonding experience for the players and coaches.

"Hawaii was good because there was a lot of team time," Izzo said. "We played in a tournament setting together. And we played some tough teams. I mean, Tulsa was tough! But we played well enough to win grinder games, a stepping-stone for the Big Ten season."

The first was a 79-67 win over Pepperdine on Dec. 21. The Waves were strong in the first half, led 28-18 and held a 36-35 advantage at the break. But the waters calmed considerably in the second half.

Peterson had a game-high 18 points. Cleaves had all 16 of his points in the second half. And Bell was solid with 14. But the keys were a 28-14 rebounding edge and MSU's 86.4-percent success at the line in the last 20 minutes.

The next day, the Spartans tried the opposite approach and sprinted to a 20-6 lead over Tulsa, an NCAA Elite Eight program just 15 months later. Again, free throws were crucial, as MSU was 21-for-22 in the second half.

Peterson had 21 points. And Cleaves added 15 points and seven assists. But the Golden Hurricane outrebounded the Spartans 29-27, the first foe all season to hold that advantage. Perhaps that was due to the coaching of Bill Self, who would leave Tulsa for Illinois and battle MSU again in 2001.

The tournament title came after a 75-58 win over Alabama. The Spartans fell behind 13-3 and led just 37-36 at the half. But they dominated the Crimson Tide in every department in the second half.

Cleaves led the winners with 17 points. But the hero was Granger, who had 16 points after his father, Joe, was hospitalized with a serious neck injury body-surfing on the north shore of Oahu.

"You have to take your hat off to the kid," Izzo said after Granger missed all the day's preparation, then had a season-best effort. "That just shows that coaching means nothing. It was the best game of his career for sure."

MSU was home the day before

Photo Credit: Kevin Fowler, MSU Sports Information

Christmas and returned to work in plenty of time to beat UNC Asheville 64-39 on Dec. 30. Klein led a balanced attack with 12 points. Cleaves had eight assists and six steals. And the Spartans forced 21 turnovers and grabbed 22 offensive rebounds.

The final tuneup for conference play came when MSU welcomed the Louisville Cardinals of Denny Crum to Breslin on Jan. 2. Two-time All-American and NBA star Steve Smith was there to have No. 21 retired. But only about 8,000 fans — honorary "Yoopers" — showed up in one of of the worst blizzards in decades.

The Spartans grabbed a 10-0 lead and never trailed in a 69-57 triumph over a fading powerhouse that had just pounded defending NCAA champ Kentucky. Perhaps it helped MSU to try a new starting lineup, with Peterson and Granger replacing Hutson and Bell.

"I wasn't playing as hard as I should've been," Hutson said. "And that's the way Coach should've reacted. With the guys we have, if someone isn't playing well, he should be replaced."

Peterson responded as expected with 23 points. And Bell and Hutson combined for 15. But Bell had one unexpected problem — figuring out where to sit in his first collegiate game as a non-starter.

"I tried to go down near the end of the bench," Bell said. "They told me, 'What are you doing? . . . Get outta here!' They have some kind of thing going on down there. So I wound up back by the coaches."

Tongue-deep-in-cheek, Bell also said he missed a couple of shots to pad his rebound stats — "just doing what Antonio does." The 6-foot-3 Bell finished with a game-high nine rebounds, one more than Hutson.

"Charlie showed a lot of character today," Cleaves said. "He came out and played and sucked up his pride. It was the same with Andre. He could have been down in the dumps. But that's not what this team is about."

It was about ready to roll through the Big Ten in one of the most dominant performances in league history.

MSU 89, NE Louisiana 58
Nov. 13, 1998 • Breslin Center • East Lansing, Mich.

NE Louisiana	FG-FGA	FT-FTA	REB	PF	TP	A	TO	BLK	S	MIN
Matt Hogarth	1-5	2-4	8	2	4	0	4	0	1	33
Mike Smith	5-16	2-4	7	2	13	2	6	0	1	38
Wojciech Myrda	2-4	1-2	1	5	5	0	0	1	0	15
Todd Daniels	3-12	0-0	4	4	8	2	4	0	1	29
Marcus Anthony	3-11	0-0	2	1	7	0	1	0	4	31
Jimmy Walton	4-8	0-0	1	2	10	2	3	0	0	18
Marlon McCoy	2-3	4-4	3	1	8	0	0	0	2	10
David Walker	0-0	0-0	2	2	0	1	0	0	0	10
Jayde Hixon	1-4	1-3	2	3	3	2	1	2	0	16
Totals	21-63	10-17	35	22	58	9	19	3	9	200

Three-Point Field Goals: Smith 1-9, Daniels 2-5, Anthony 1-5, Walton 2-4, Team 6-23.

FG%: 1st Half 12-32 .375, 2nd Half 9-31 .290, Game 21-63 .333; 3FG%: 1st Half 5-15 .333, 2nd Half 1-8 .125, Game 6-23 .261; FT%: 1st Half 1-2 .500, 2nd Half 9-15 .600, Game 10-17 .588; Team Rebounds: 5; Deadball Rebounds: 3.

Michigan State	FG-FGA	FT-FTA	REB	PF	TP	A	TO	BLK	S	MIN
Andre Hutson	5-9	2-2	9	3	12	0	1	0	0	18
Jason Klein	5-11	0-0	4	1	12	3	0	1	2	24
Antonio Smith	6-7	4-7	6	2	16	1	1	0	2	26
Mateen Cleaves	4-7	2-3	4	0	10	11	5	0	2	28
Charlie Bell	3-9	0-0	1	2	6	0	0	1	2	22
Thomas Kelley	3-9	2-2	3	1	8	2	2	0	0	18
Brandon Smith	0-0	0-0	0	0	0	2	0	0	0	3
Steve Cherry	1-1	0-0	0	0	2	0	1	0	0	2
Doug Davis	0-0	0-0	2	2	0	1	2	0	0	8
Morris Peterson	4-9	4-4	5	1	12	1	0	0	2	18
A.J. Granger	3-7	3-5	10	4	9	2	2	0	2	25
Adam Ballinger	1-1	0-2	3	2	2	0	0	1	0	8
Totals	35-70	17-25	50	18	89	23	14	3	12	200

Three-Point Field Goals: Klein 2-5, Kelley 0-1, Peterson 0-2, Team 2-8.

FG%: 1st Half 16-39 .410, 2nd Half 19-31 .613, Game 35-70 .500; 3FG%: 1st Half 1-6 .167, 2nd Half 1-2 .500, Game 2-8 .250; FT%: 1st Half 4-6 .667, 2nd Half 13-19 .684, Game 17-25 .680; Team Rebounds: 3; Deadball Rebounds: 4.

SCORE BY PERIODS	1	2		F
NE Louisiana	30	28	--	58
Michigan State	37	52	--	89

OFFICIALS – Jody Silvester, Randy Drury, Gene Monje
TECHNICAL FOULS – None
ATTENDANCE – 14,659

Temple 60, MSU 59
Nov. 20, 1998 • The Apollo of Temple • Philadelphia, Pa.

Michigan State	FG-FGA	FT-FTA	REB	PF	TP	A	TO	BLK	S	MIN
A.J. Granger	2-2	0-0	5	4	4	2	2	0	0	26
Jason Klein	3-6	2-2	5	4	10	2	1	0	0	24
Antonio Smith	3-4	0-0	4	4	6	1	2	0	3	21
Mateen Cleaves	7-9	2-4	2	4	17	6	10	0	1	37
Charlie Bell	2-6	0-1	8	3	4	2	3	0	0	31
Morris Peterson	5-8	1-2	4	2	12	0	3	0	0	25
Andre Hutson	1-1	4-4	4	2	6	1	1	0	0	23
Thomas Kelley	0-5	0-0	3	3	0	1	0	0	0	11
Doug Davis	0-0	0-0	0	1	0	0	1	0	0	2
Totals	23-41	9-13	38	27	59	15	23	0	5	200

Three-Point Field Goals: Klein 2-4, Cleaves 1-2, Bell 0-1, Peterson 1-4, Team 4-11.

FG%: 1st Half 15-27 .556, 2nd Half 8-14 .571, Game 23-41 .561; 3FG%: 1st Half 3-6 .500, 2nd Half 1-5 .200, Game 4-11 .364; FT%: 1st Half 0-1 .000, 2nd Half 9-12 .750, Game 9-13 .692; Team Rebounds: 6; Deadball Rebounds: 2.

Temple	FG-FGA	FT-FTA	REB	PF	TP	A	TO	BLK	S	MIN
Mark Karcher	3-9	1-3	3	2	7	4	1	0	1	29
Lamont Barnes	5-10	1-5	7	3	11	0	0	0	3	34
Kevin Lyde	4-7	1-2	4	3	9	0	2	0	1	24
Pepe Sanchez	2-7	7-7	2	3	11	0	0	0	2	32
Rasheed Brokenborough	2-7	4-4	3	1	9	4	2	0	2	36
Quincy Wadley	2-7	1-4	1	3	6	0	0	0	2	27
Lynn Greer	1-6	4-6	1	2	7	1	1	0	1	16
Keaton Sanders	0-0	0-0	0	0	0	0	0	0	0	2
Totals	19-53	19-31	25	17	60	9	9	0	12	200

Three-Point Field Goals: Karcher 0-2, Barnes 0-1, Sanchez 0-2, Brokenborough 1-4, Wadley 1-5, Greer 1-4, Team 3-18.

FG%: 1st Half 5-23 .217, 2nd Half 14-30 .467, Game 19-53 .358; 3FG%: 1st Half 1-9 .111, 2nd Half 2-9 .222, Game 3-18 .167; FT%: 1st Half 10-14 .714, 2nd Half 9-17 .529, Game 19-31 .613; Team Rebounds: 4; Deadball Rebounds: 3.

SCORE BY PERIODS	1	2		F
Michigan State	33	26	--	59
Temple	21	39	--	60

OFFICIALS – Phil Bova, Jody Silvester, Tim Higgins
TECHNICAL FOULS – None
ATTENDANCE – 10,206

MSU 96, Oakland 66

Nov. 17, 1998 • Athletic Center "O"rena • Rochester, Mich.

Michigan State	FG-FGA	FT-FTA	REB	PF	TP	A	TO	BLK	S	MIN
Mateen Cleaves	9-13	0-1	3	2	21	6	2	0	1	32
Antonio Smith	10-12	0-3	6	1	20	2	1	0	0	32
Charlie Bell	10-15	5-5	8	2	26	0	1	0	0	23
A.J. Granger	2-6	4-4	6	0	8	0	1	2	0	32
Jason Klein	1-6	0-0	3	2	2	0	0	0	0	27
Thomas Kelley	2-5	0-0	1	2	5	1	2	0	1	23
Adam Ballinger	0-0	0-0	1	0	0	1	1	0	0	4
Brandon Smith	0-0	0-0	1	1	0	0	2	0	0	3
Steve Cherry	1-1	0-0	1	0	2	0	0	0	0	3
Doug Davis	1-3	0-1	1	0	3	1	0	0	0	5
Morris Peterson	4-6	0-0	4	3	9	3	1	1	0	15
Totals	40-67	9-14	38	13	96	14	11	3	2	200

Three-Point Field Goals: Cleaves 3-5, Bell 1-4, Klein 0-2, Kelley 1-1, Davis 1-2, Peterson 1-3, Team 7-17.
FG%: 1st Half 22-38 .579, 2nd Half 18-29 .621, Game 40-67 .597; 3FG%: 1st Half 3-10 .300, 2nd Half 4-7 .571, Game 7-17 .412; FT%: 1st Half 5-7 .714, 2nd Half 4-7 .571, Game 9-14 .643; Team Rebounds: 3; Deadball Rebounds: 1.

Oakland	FG-FGA	FT-FTA	REB	PF	TP	A	TO	BLK	S	MIN
Myke Thom	1-6	0-0	2	4	3	2	2	0	0	34
Sean Carlson	3-7	3-4	2	1	11	4	3	0	0	31
Dan Champagne	10-17	5-6	8	3	26	1	1	0	0	35
Brad Buddenborg	6-14	0-0	3	0	16	1	3	0	1	35
Jon Champagne	4-6	0-0	4	2	8	1	0	0	0	24
Jason Rozycki	0-1	0-0	2	2	0	1	0	0	0	13
Steve Reynolds	0-1	2-2	1	0	2	0	0	0	1	5
Ryan Hiller	0-3	0-0	3	0	0	0	0	0	0	6
Mychal Covington	0-1	0-0	0	1	0	3	1	0	0	10
Ryan Williams	0-1	0-0	1	2	0	2	2	0	0	6
Jeff Mullett	0-0	0-0	0	0	0	0	0	0	0	1
Totals	24-57	10-12	27	15	66	15	12	0	2	200

Three-Point Field Goals: Thom 1-2, Carlson 2-4, D. Champagne 1-3, Buddenborg 4-8, J. Champagne 0-1, Rozycki 0-1, Reynolds 0-1, Hiller 1-2, Team 8-22.
FG%: 1st Half 15-29 .517, 2nd Half 9-28 .321, Game 24-57 .421; 3FG%: 1st Half 7-14 .500, 2nd Half 1-8 .125, Game 8-22 .364; FT%: 1st Half 6-8 .750, 2nd Half 4-4 1.000, Game 10-12 .833; Team Rebounds: 1; Deadball Rebounds: 1.

SCORE BY PERIODS	1	2	F
Michigan State	52	44	96
Oakland	43	23	66

TECHNICAL FOULS – None
ATTENDANCE – 3,450

MSU 87, Central Florida 64

Nov. 27, 1998 • Breslin Center • East Lansing, Mich.

Central Florida	FG-FGA	FT-FTA	REB	PF	TP	A	TO	BLK	S	MIN
Mario Lovett	2-7	4-4	10	3	8	2	1	2	1	27
Brad Traina	4-7	1-2	4	0	9	1	2	1	0	21
Bucky Hodge	4-7	1-1	2	4	9	1	3	0	1	24
D'Quarius Stewart	5-8	0-1	3	2	12	2	4	1	3	34
Cory Perry	2-5	0-0	0	1	5	5	5	0	0	33
Davin Granberry	4-6	1-1	3	3	9	0	5	0	0	16
Inyo Cue	0-6	0-0	0	0	0	2	0	0	1	17
Ryan Reynolds	0-0	0-0	0	0	0	0	0	0	0	1
Jason Thornton	3-3	0-0	0	0	7	0	1	0	0	14
Beronti Simms	1-1	3-3	0	2	5	0	0	0	0	13
Totals	25-50	10-12	24	15	64	11	23	4	6	200

Three-Point Field Goals: Traina 0-2, Stewart 2-4, Perry 1-3, Cue 0-2, Thornton 1-1, Team 4-12.
FG%: 1st Half 12-27 .444, 2nd Half 13-23 .565, Game 25-50 .500; 3FG%: 1st Half 3-8 .375, 2nd Half 1-4 .250, Game 4-12 .333; FT%: 1st Half 6-6 1.000, 2nd Half 4-6 .667, Game 10-12 .833; Team Rebounds: 2; Deadball Rebounds: 1.

Michigan State	FG-FGA	FT-FTA	REB	PF	TP	A	TO	BLK	S	MIN
Andre Hutson	6-8	6-7	4	1	18	2	0	0	2	26
Jason Klein	8-14	1-1	2	1	19	1	1	0	2	24
Antonio Smith	2-3	0-1	10	1	4	2	4	0	4	27
Mateen Cleaves	1-5	0-0	2	3	3	9	5	0	2	27
Charlie Bell	6-10	2-2	1	2	14	1	1	0	1	20
Thomas Kelley	4-8	2-2	2	0	10	3	2	1	1	20
Brandon Smith	0-1	0-0	1	0	0	1	1	0	0	2
Steve Cherry	0-1	0-0	0	0	0	0	0	0	0	2
Doug Davis	0-0	0-0	0	0	0	0	0	0	0	3
Morris Peterson	3-5	2-2	6	1	8	3	0	0	2	21
A.J. Granger	4-7	0-1	3	4	9	0	1	0	0	19
Adam Ballinger	1-1	0-0	2	0	2	0	1	2	0	9
Totals	35-63	13-16	33	13	87	22	16	3	15	200

Three-Point Field Goals: Klein 2-5, Cleaves 1-2, Bell 0-1, B. Smith 0-1, Cherry 0-1, Peterson 0-1, Granger 1-1, Team 4-12.
FG%: 1st Half 21-37 .568, 2nd Half 14-26 .538, Game 35-63 .556; 3FG%: 1st Half 2-4 .500, 2nd Half 2-8 .250, Game 4-12 .333; FT%: 1st Half 8-11 .727, 2nd Half 5-5 1.000, Game 13-16 .813; Team Rebounds: 1; Deadball Rebounds: 0.

SCORE BY PERIODS	1	2	F
Central Florida	33	31	64
Michigan State	52	35	87

OFFICIALS – Steve Welmer, Randy Drury, Sid Rodeheffer
TECHNICAL FOULS – None
ATTENDANCE – 13,705

MSU 90, Western Michigan 66

Nov. 28, 1998 • Breslin Center • East Lansing, Mich.

Western Michigan	FG-FGA	FT-FTA	REB	PF	TP	A	TO	BLK	S	MIN
Tony Barksdale	3-10	4-6	3	3	10	3	3	0	1	34
Brad VanTimmeren	2-4	0-0	4	5	4	2	1	1	1	27
Emil Mulic	2-3	0-1	1	3	4	0	3	2	1	14
Rod Brown	2-6	0-2	3	0	4	6	0	0	0	33
Kylo Jones	10-17	0-0	2	4	28	2	2	0	3	38
Darren Kahl	0-0	0-0	0	0	0	0	1	0	0	1
Thadus Williams	3-6	0-0	1	2	8	1	2	1	0	22
Bronson Nichols	0-0	0-0	1	0	0	0	0	0	0	2
Isaac Bullock	1-5	5-6	9	4	8	4	1	0	1	28
Tony Collins	0-0	0-0	0	0	0	0	1	0	0	1
Totals	23-51	9-15	25	21	66	16	22	4	10	200

Three-Point Field Goals: Barksdale 0-3, VanTimmeren 0-1, Jones 8-13, Williams 2-4, Bullock 1-3, Team 11-24.
FG%: 1st Half 13-25 .520, 2nd Half 10-26 .385, Game 23-51 .451; 3FG%: 1st Half 8-13 .615, 2nd Half 3-11 .273, Game 11-24 .458; FT%: 1st Half 1-2 .500, 2nd Half 8-13 .615, Game 9-15 .600; Team Rebounds: 1; Deadball Rebounds: 3.

Michigan State	FG-FGA	FT-FTA	REB	PF	TP	A	TO	BLK	S	MIN
Andre Hutson	6-7	3-4	6	3	15	1	1	1	2	26
Jason Klein	7-11	0-0	3	1	14	1	1	0	0	24
Antonio Smith	1-8	1-4	11	3	3	2	1	0	2	27
Mateen Cleaves	4-12	3-5	2	2	12	6	2	1	2	31
Charlie Bell	2-5	2-2	4	4	6	0	0	0	1	23
Thomas Kelley	3-7	1-2	1	2	7	6	3	1	1	21
Brandon Smith	0-0	0-0	1	0	0	1	0	0	0	1
Steve Cherry	0-1	0-0	0	0	0	0	0	0	0	1
Doug Davis	1-1	0-0	0	0	2	0	0	0	1	1
Morris Peterson	8-12	5-6	6	1	21	0	4	2	2	27
A.J. Granger	3-3	2-2	7	0	8	3	1	2	0	17
Adam Ballinger	1-1	0-0	1	0	2	0	0	0	0	1
Totals	36-68	17-25	43	16	90	20	13	7	12	200

Three-Point Field Goals: Klein 0-3, A. Smith 0-1, Cleaves 1-4, Peterson 0-1, Team 1-9.
FG%: 1st Half 16-33 .485, 2nd Half 20-35 .571, Game 36-68 .529; 3FG%: 1st Half 0-3 .000, 2nd Half 1-6 .167, Game 1-9 .111; FT%: 1st Half 8-12 .667, 2nd Half 9-13 .692, Game 17-25 .680; Team Rebounds: 2; Deadball Rebounds: 3.

SCORE BY PERIODS	1	2	F
Western Michigan	35	31	66
Michigan State	40	50	90

OFFICIALS – Steve Welmer, Gene Monje, Art McDonald
TECHNICAL FOULS – None
ATTENDANCE – 14,659

Duke 73, MSU 67

Dec. 2, 1998 • United Center • Chicago, Ill.

Michigan State	FG-FGA	FT-FTA	REB	PF	TP	A	TO	BLK	S	MIN
Andre Hutson	4-6	2-3	10	2	10	2	5	0	0	30
Jason Klein	4-11	0-0	5	2	9	0	0	0	0	21
Antonio Smith	2-6	1-3	5	3	5	2	3	0	3	32
Charlie Bell	4-8	0-0	8	5	8	2	3	0	1	30
Mateen Cleaves	3-17	2-2	1	4	9	6	2	0	0	33
Thomas Kelley	0-4	0-0	0	1	0	1	1	0	0	8
Brandon Smith	0-0	0-0	0	0	0	0	0	0	0	1
Doug Davis	0-0	0-0	0	0	0	0	0	0	0	1
Morris Peterson	10-17	0-0	5	4	24	2	2	0	0	28
A.J. Granger	0-1	2-2	2	3	2	0	2	0	0	16
Totals	27-70	7-10	41	24	67	15	20	0	5	200

Three-Point Field Goals: Klein 1-5, Cleaves 1-4, Peterson 4-4, Team 6-13.
FG%: 1st Half 11-31 .355, 2nd Half 16-39 .410, Game 27-70 .386; 3FG%: 1st Half 4-6 .667, 2nd Half 2-7 .286, Game 6-13 .462; FT%: 1st Half 4-4 1.000, 2nd Half 3-6 .500, Game 7-10 .700; Team Rebounds: 5; Deadball Rebounds: 1.

Duke	FG-FGA	FT-FTA	REB	PF	TP	A	TO	BLK	S	MIN
Chris Carrawell	5-7	2-3	4	3	12	1	5	0	1	30
Elton Brand	5-9	2-2	3	3	12	0	6	1	0	29
Shane Battier	1-2	1-3	5	5	3	1	0	3	1	24
William Avery	4-8	5-8	5	3	14	5	1	0	2	38
Trajan Langdon	7-12	5-5	2	2	23	0	4	0	2	38
Nate James	0-0	0-0	0	0	0	0	0	0	0	3
Chris Burgess	2-2	4-6	3	2	8	1	1	1	2	22
Taymon Domzals	0-0	0-0	0	0	0	1	1	0	1	6
Corey Maggette	0-1	1-2	0	1	1	1	0	1	0	10
Totals	24-41	20-29	25	19	73	9	21	5	9	200

Three-Point Field Goals: Battier 0-1, Avery 1-3, Langdon 4-7, Team 5-11.
FG%: 1st Half 14-20 .700, 2nd Half 10-21 .476, Game 24-41 .585; 3FG%: 1st Half 4-6 .667, 2nd Half 1-5 .200, Game 5-11 .455; FT%: 1st Half 7-9 .778, 2nd Half 13-20 .650, Game 20-29 .690; Team Rebounds: 5; Deadball Rebounds: 5.

SCORE BY PERIODS	1	2	F
Michigan State	30	37	67
Duke	39	34	73

OFFICIALS – Don Rutledge, Kerry Sitton, Phil Robinson
TECHNICAL FOULS – None
ATTENDANCE – 19,412

Connecticut 82, MSU 68
Dec. 5, 1998 • Gampel Pavilion • Storrs, Conn.

Michigan State	FG-FGA	FT-FTA	REB	PF	TP	A	TO	BLK	S	MIN
Antonio Smith	5-7	0-0	12	3	10	3	3	0	0	33
Andre Hutson	6-6	0-0	3	4	12	0	1	0	2	22
Jason Klein	5-11	0-0	1	1	12	0	3	1	2	28
Mateen Cleaves	2-15	1-3	2	1	6	7	1	0	0	31
Charlie Bell	2-7	0-0	5	2	4	1	2	0	0	22
Thomas Kelley	2-9	0-0	3	1	5	1	1	0	0	15
Brandon Smith	0-0	0-0	0	0	0	1	0	0	0	1
Doug Davis	0-1	0-0	0	1	0	0	0	0	0	6
Morris Peterson	7-8	0-0	3	4	14	1	4	0	0	25
A.J. Granger	2-6	0-0	3	2	5	0	1	0	0	17
Totals	31-70	1-3	39	19	68	14	17	1	4	200

Three-Point Field Goals: Klein 2-4, Cleaves 1-7, Kelley 1-1, Peterson 0-1, Granger 1-1, Team 5-14.
FG%: 1st Half 16-32 .500, 2nd Half 15-38 .395, Game 31-70 .443; 3FG%: 1st Half 2-8 .250, 2nd Half 3-6 .500, Game 5-14 .357; FT%: 1st Half 0-1 .000, 2nd Half 1-2 .500, Game 1-3 .333; Team Rebounds: 7; Deadball Rebounds: 1.

Connecticut	FG-FGA	FT-FTA	REB	PF	TP	A	TO	BLK	S	MIN
Kevin Freeman	5-7	6-8	6	3	16	1	3	0	1	29
Richard Hamilton	5-14	0-0	1	0	11	3	0	0	1	36
Jake Voskuhl	7-10	3-4	5	3	17	1	1	1	0	28
Ricky Moore	1-3	5-6	2	1	7	4	0	0	1	31
Khalid El-Amin	7-12	2-4	3	2	20	6	4	0	1	31
Rashamel Jones	0-0	0-0	0	0	0	1	0	0	0	5
Antric Klaiber	0-0	0-0	0	0	0	0	0	0	0	1
Albert Mouring	4-6	2-2	5	1	11	2	2	1	0	16
E.J. Harrison	0-0	0-0	0	0	0	0	0	0	0	1
Souleymane Wane	0-3	0-0	1	1	0	0	0	1	0	6
Edmund Saunders	0-0	0-0	3	1	0	0	0	2	0	16
Totals	29-55	18-24	30	12	82	18	10	5	5	200

Three-Point Field Goals: Freeman 0-1, Hamilton 1-6, El-Amin 4-7, Mouring 1-1, Team 6-15.
FG%: 1st Half 15-33 .455, 2nd Half 14-22 .636, Game 29-55 .527; 3FG%: 1st Half 4-11 .364, 2nd Half 2-4 .500, Game 6-15 .400; FT%: 1st Half 4-6 .667, 2nd Half 14-18 .778, Game 18-24 .750; Team Rebounds: 4; Deadball Rebounds: 3.

SCORE BY PERIODS	1	2	F
Michigan State	34	34	-- 68
Connecticut	38	44	-- 82

OFFICIALS – Ed Hightower, Tom Rucker, Jim Burr
TECHNICAL FOULS – None
ATTENDANCE – 10,027

MSU 86, East Tennessee State 53
Dec. 10, 1998 • Memorial Center • Johnson City, Tenn.

Michigan State	FG-FGA	FT-FTA	REB	PF	TP	A	TO	BLK	S	MIN
Andre Hutson	4-4	1-1	4	4	9	2	0	1	0	22
Jason Klein	5-11	1-1	1	0	13	0	0	0	2	20
Antonio Smith	3-4	0-0	11	3	6	2	3	0	2	25
Mateen Cleaves	3-5	0-0	1	1	7	9	4	0	1	27
Charlie Bell	5-7	1-2	5	2	11	1	2	0	0	21
Thomas Kelley	10-15	0-0	1	1	21	3	3	0	1	24
Lorenzo Guess	0-0	0-0	0	0	0	0	0	0	0	1
Brandon Smith	0-1	0-0	0	0	0	0	0	0	2	3
Steve Cherry	0-0	0-0	0	0	0	0	0	0	0	1
Doug Davis	4-5	0-0	0	0	8	0	0	0	0	13
Morris Peterson	4-8	0-0	6	1	9	0	1	1	0	20
A.J. Granger	1-1	0-0	5	3	2	1	0	0	2	23
Totals	39-61	3-4	33	16	86	18	13	2	10	200

Three-Point Field Goals: Klein 2-5, Cleaves 1-2, Kelley 1-3, B. Smith 0-1, Peterson 1-2, Team 5-13.
FG%: 1st Half 21-31 .677, 2nd Half 18-30 .600, Game 39-61 .639; 3FG%: 1st Half 2-7 .286, 2nd Half 3-6 .500, Game 5-13 .385; FT%: 1st Half 2-3 .667, 2nd Half 1-1 1.000, Game 3-4 .750; Team Rebounds: 0; Deadball Rebounds: 1.

East Tennessee State	FG-FGA	FT-FTA	REB	PF	TP	A	TO	BLK	S	MIN
Reggie Todd	3-5	2-3	4	3	8	0	1	0	0	23
Greg Stephens	2-7	2-4	3	2	7	4	1	0	3	31
Leo Murray	5-9	0-0	4	2	10	0	0	0	1	20
Kyle Keeton	2-6	1-2	2	0	6	1	2	0	0	25
D.J. McDuffie	1-3	0-0	0	2	2	0	1	1	1	13
Dimeco Childress	0-4	0-0	1	1	0	1	1	0	0	22
Cliff Decoster	0-2	1-2	0	2	1	1	6	0	0	11
Gabe Lisicky	0-3	0-0	0	0	0	2	1	0	1	18
Adrian Meeks	4-6	2-2	2	2	10	0	1	0	1	12
Gareth Davis	2-2	1-1	2	0	5	1	0	0	1	10
Ryan Wilson	2-4	0-0	0	0	4	0	1	0	0	15
Totals	21-51	9-14	22	12	53	10	16	1	7	200

Three-Point Field Goals: Stephens 1-2, Keeton 1-2, Childress 0-1, Lisicky 0-3, Team 2-8.
FG%: 1st Half 10-27 .370, 2nd Half 11-24 .458, Game 21-51 .412; 3FG%: 1st Half 1-4 .250, 2nd Half 1-4 .250, Game 2-8 .250; FT%: 1st Half 3-4 .750, 2nd Half 6-10 .600, Game 9-14 .643; Team Rebounds: 4; Deadball Rebounds: 2.

SCORE BY PERIODS	1	2	F
Michigan State	46	40	-- 86
East Tennessee State	24	29	-- 53

OFFICIALS – Mike Wood, Ted Valentine, Carl Hess
TECHNICAL FOULS – None
ATTENDANCE – 5,335

MSU 77, Illinois-Chicago 33
Dec. 13, 1998 • Breslin Center • East Lansing, Mich.

Illinois-Chicago	FG-FGA	FT-FTA	REB	PF	TP	A	TO	BLK	S	MIN
Ian Hanavan	3-8	5-5	8	4	11	0	3	1	2	29
Vladimir Buscaglia	1-3	0-0	1	1	3	0	0	1	0	13
Thor Solverson	0-0	3-4	0	2	3	0	2	0	2	24
Jason Ayers	2-5	2-2	3	2	6	3	3	0	0	20
Bryant Notree	2-11	2-2	6	3	6	1	5	0	0	29
Leonard Walker	0-4	0-0	4	0	0	0	0	0	0	11
Jon-Pierre Mitchom	0-0	0-0	0	1	0	0	3	0	0	17
T.J. Mixson	0-2	0-1	0	0	0	1	0	0	0	3
Jordan Kardos	0-2	1-2	2	2	1	1	2	0	0	12
Tarrie Monroe	0-1	0-0	0	3	0	0	1	0	0	6
Steve Farmer	0-1	0-0	2	3	0	0	0	0	0	11
Anton Collins	0-1	0-0	0	1	0	0	0	0	0	5
Joel Bullock	1-3	1-2	0	0	3	0	3	0	0	13
Frank Wade	0-0	0-0	0	1	0	0	0	0	0	7
Totals	9-41	14-18	30	20	33	5	27	2	4	200

Three-Point Field Goals: Hanavan 0-1, Buscaglia 1-2, Notree 0-1, Kardos 0-2, Team 1-6.
FG%: 1st Half 5-15 .333, 2nd Half 4-26 .154, Game 9-41 .220; 3FG%: 1st Half 0-1 .000, 2nd Half 1-5 .200, Game 1-6 .167; FT%: 1st Half 7-9 .778, 2nd Half 7-9 .778, Game 14-18 .778; Team Rebounds: 4; Deadball Rebounds: 0.

Michigan State	FG-FGA	FT-FTA	REB	PF	TP	A	TO	BLK	S	MIN
Andre Hutson	2-5	1-2	1	4	5	1	2	2	2	19
Morris Peterson	7-15	4-4	9	1	18	5	0	2	0	30
Antonio Smith	4-9	0-0	14	2	8	1	1	0	2	30
Mateen Cleaves	3-6	0-0	0	1	6	4	4	1	3	25
Charlie Bell	4-6	0-0	4	3	8	3	0	0	2	22
Thomas Kelley	3-6	5-6	0	0	12	1	0	0	1	17
Brandon Smith	0-1	1-2	1	0	1	2	1	0	0	6
Steve Cherry	1-2	0-0	3	1	2	0	0	0	1	4
Doug Davis	2-5	1-4	2	3	7	4	1	1	1	19
A.J. Granger	4-7	2-2	5	3	10	0	2	1	0	24
Lorenzo Guess	0-1	0-0	0	0	0	0	0	0	0	4
Totals	30-63	14-20	41	18	77	21	11	7	12	200

Three-Point Field Goals: Peterson 0-1, Kelley 1-2, B. Smith 0-1, Cherry 0-1, Davis 2-4, Granger 0-1, Team 3-10.
FG%: 1st Half 13-36 .361, 2nd Half 17-27 .630, Game 30-63 .476; 3FG%: 1st Half 1-5 .200, 2nd Half 2-5 .400, Game 3-10 .300; FT%: 1st Half 5-5 1.000, 2nd Half 9-15 .600, Game 14-20 .700; Team Rebounds: 2; Deadball Rebounds: 4.

SCORE BY PERIODS	1	2	F
Illinois-Chicago	17	16	-- 33
Michigan State	32	45	-- 77

OFFICIALS – Mike Sanzere, Tom Clark, Terry Sauder
TECHNICAL FOULS – Hanavan (UIC)
ATTENDANCE – 14,659

MSU 79, Pepperdine 67
Dec. 21, 1998 • Cannon Activity Center • Laie, Hawaii

Michigan State	FG-FGA	FT-FTA	REB	PF	TP	A	TO	BLK	S	MIN
Andre Hutson	2-3	4-6	3	2	8	2	1	1	0	31
Jason Klein	2-6	2-4	1	2	6	2	0	1	0	18
Antonio Smith	4-6	1-2	4	3	9	0	1	0	2	30
Mateen Cleaves	6-10	3-3	1	2	16	3	4	0	1	29
Charlie Bell	5-9	4-4	5	1	14	1	3	0	0	28
Thomas Kelley	1-3	4-4	2	1	6	0	1	0	0	16
Lorenzo Guess	0-0	0-0	0	0	0	0	0	0	0	1
Doug Davis	0-1	0-0	0	0	0	0	0	0	0	9
Morris Peterson	5-7	8-10	7	2	18	0	0	0	0	29
A.J. Granger	1-3	0-0	2	1	2	0	0	0	0	10
Totals	26-48	26-33	28	14	79	8	10	2	3	200

Three-Point Field Goals: Cleaves 1-3, Bell 0-3, Team 1-6.
FG%: 1st Half 14-24 .583, 2nd Half 12-24 .500, Game 26-48 .542; 3FG%: 1st Half 0-4 .000, 2nd Half 1-2 .500, Game 1-6 .167; FT%: 1st Half 7-11 .636, 2nd Half 19-22 .864, Game 26-33 .788; Team Rebounds: 3; Deadball Rebounds: 8.

Pepperdine	FG-FGA	FT-FTA	REB	PF	TP	A	TO	BLK	S	MIN
David Lafazarian	4-7	4-4	1	2	12	1	1	0	0	23
Kelvin Gibbs	4-9	2-2	2	3	11	1	0	1	0	28
Nick Sheppard	1-2	0-0	0	3	2	1	1	0	0	10
Jelani Gardner	4-12	0-2	4	3	9	2	3	0	0	33
Tommie Prince	3-5	0-0	1	7	0	5	0	0	0	33
Robert Fornby	0-0	0-0	1	0	0	0	0	0	1	1
Tezale Archie	1-1	2-2	1	2	4	1	1	0	1	22
Al Minahan	2-4	0-0	0	1	6	1	1	0	0	9
Ross Varner	1-3	0-0	2	4	2	0	1	0	0	24
Marc McDowell	6-7	0-0	1	2	12	0	2	1	0	16
Cedric Suitt	1-1	0-0	1	0	2	0	0	0	0	1
Totals	27-51	8-10	14	22	67	7	14	2	1	200

Three-Point Field Goals: Lafazarian 0-1, Gibbs 1-4, Gardner 1-3, Prince 1-2, Minahan 2-3, Team 5-13.
FG%: 1st Half 14-23 .609, 2nd Half 13-28 .464, Game 27-51 .529; 3FG%: 1st Half 4-6 .667, 2nd Half 1-7 .143, Game 5-13 .385; FT%: 1st Half 4-4 1.000, 2nd Half 4-6 .667, Game 8-10 .800; Team Rebounds: 1; Deadball Rebounds: 3.

SCORE BY PERIODS	1	2	F
Michigan State	35	44	-- 79
Pepperdine	36	31	-- 67

TECHNICAL FOULS – None
ATTENDANCE – 750

MSU 68, Tulsa 58
Dec. 22, 1998 • Cannon Activity Center • Laie, Hawaii

Michigan State	FG-FGA	FT-FTA	REB	PF	TP	A	TO	BLK	S	MIN
Antonio Smith	1-2	2-2	5	5	4	1	2	0	0	28
Jason Klein	3-9	3-4	3	2	10	0	2	0	0	21
Andre Hutson	1-5	6-7	6	3	8	1	1	0	1	30
Mateen Cleaves	4-5	6-6	1	2	15	7	8	0	5	36
Charlie Bell	2-2	0-2	2	4	5	1	1	0	2	28
Thomas Kelley	1-2	0-0	1	2	2	0	1	0	0	16
Doug Davis	0-0	0-0	0	1	0	1	1	0	0	4
Morris Peterson	8-14	5-5	5	4	21	0	3	0	1	20
A.J. Granger	1-3	1-1	2	3	3	1	1	1	1	17
Totals	21-42	23-27	27	26	68	12	21	1	9	200

Three-Point Field Goals: Klein 1-4, Cleaves 1-2, Bell 1-1, Peterson 0-1, Team 3-8.

FG%: 1st Half 13-25 .520, 2nd Half 8-17 .471, Game 21-42 .500; 3FG%: 1st Half 2-6 .333, 2nd Half 1-2 .500, Game 3-8 .375; FT%: 1st Half 2-5 .400, 2nd Half 21-22 .954, Game 23-27 .852; Team Rebounds: 2; Deadball Rebounds: 3.

Tulsa	FG-FGA	FT-FTA	REB	PF	TP	A	TO	BLK	S	MIN
Eric Coley	5-11	5-7	7	4	15	5	3	3	5	31
Michael Ruffin	3-4	8-17	6	3	14	1	4	2	4	37
Brandon Kurtz	0-0	0-0	1	0	0	0	2	0	0	8
Shawn Williams	0-2	0-0	0	1	0	0	0	0	0	17
Marcus Hill	2-10	0-0	3	2	6	0	2	0	1	32
Greg Harrington	0-3	5-7	3	1	5	1	2	0	0	24
Tony Heard	5-10	2-2	2	0	15	1	3	0	1	27
Zac Bennet	0-2	0-0	0	3	0	0	2	0	0	10
John Cornwell	1-2	0-0	2	2	2	0	0	0	0	6
DeAngelo McDaniel	0-0	1-2	1	3	1	0	0	0	0	8
Totals	16-44	21-35	29	19	58	8	18	5	11	200

Three-Point Field Goals: Coley 0-1, Williams 0-2, Hill 2-5, Harrington 0-2, Heard 3-7, Team 5-17.

FG%: 1st Half 9-22 .409, 2nd Half 7-22 .318, Game 16-44 .364; 3FG%: 1st Half 3-8 .375, 2nd Half 2-9 .222, Game 5-17 .294; FT%: 1st Half 2-4 .500, 2nd Half 19-31 .613, Game 21-35 .600; Team Rebounds: 4; Deadball Rebounds: 9.

SCORE BY PERIODS	1	2	F
Michigan State	30	38	68
Tulsa	23	35	58

TECHNICAL FOULS – Tulsa bench
ATTENDANCE – 650

MSU 75, Alabama 58
Dec. 23, 1998 • Cannon Activity Center • Laie, Hawaii

Michigan State	FG-FGA	FT-FTA	REB	PF	TP	A	TO	BLK	S	MIN
Antonio Smith	3-6	3-3	10	3	9	1	1	0	2	31
Andre Hutson	3-4	2-3	2	3	8	0	1	0	1	16
Jason Klein	1-5	0-0	2	1	3	1	0	0	2	22
Mateen Cleaves	5-12	4-6	1	2	17	7	6	0	2	36
Charlie Bell	2-6	0-0	4	2	4	0	1	0	0	26
Thomas Kelley	2-5	0-0	1	1	4	2	0	0	0	14
Lorenzo Guess	0-0	0-0	0	0	0	0	0	0	0	1
Brandon Smith	0-0	0-0	0	0	0	0	0	0	0	1
Steve Cherry	0-0	0-0	1	0	0	1	0	0	0	1
Doug Davis	1-3	0-0	0	0	2	2	2	0	0	4
Morris Peterson	4-5	4-6	4	0	12	1	1	0	0	23
A.J. Granger	5-7	4-4	4	1	16	1	1	1	0	25
Totals	26-53	17-22	31	13	75	16	12	2	7	200

Three-Point Field Goals: Klein 1-2, Cleaves 3-6, Bell 0-1, Kelley 0-2, Davis 0-1, Granger 2-2, Team 6-14.

FG%: 1st Half 13-28 .464, 2nd Half 13-25 .520, Game 26-53 .491; 3FG%: 1st Half 3-9 .333, 2nd Half 3-5 .600, Game 6-14 .429; FT%: 1st Half 8-11 .727, 2nd Half 9-11 .818, Game 17-22 .773; Team Rebounds: 2; Deadball Rebounds: 4.

Alabama	FG-FGA	FT-FTA	REB	PF	TP	A	TO	BLK	S	MIN
Mcxxxx Mazique	9-12	1-1	5	5	19	0	0	0	0	28
Chris Rollins	3-5	0-0	4	1	6	1	2	0	0	32
Jeremy Hays	5-9	2-5	7	4	12	0	3	2	1	33
Brian Williams	6-16	3-4	3	1	16	3	4	0	1	38
Tarik London	1-1	0-0	2	3	2	1	3	0	0	29
Neil Ashby	0-0	0-0	0	0	0	0	0	0	0	1
Cedric Patton	1-3	0-0	1	2	2	1	0	0	0	7
Chauncey Jones	0-3	0-0	2	0	0	2	0	0	0	13
Sam Haginas	0-2	1-1	2	1	1	1	0	0	0	19
Totals	25-51	7-11	24	20	58	9	12	2	3	200

Three-Point Field Goals: Rollins 0-1, Williams 1-7, Patton 0-1, Team 1-9.

FG%: 1st Half 16-32 .500, 2nd Half 9-19 .474, Game 25-51 .490; 3FG%: 1st Half 1-5 .200, 2nd Half 0-4 .000, Game 1-9 .111; FT%: 1st Half 3-3 1.000, 2nd Half 4-8 .500, Game 7-11 .636; Team Rebounds: 2; Deadball Rebounds: 3.

SCORE BY PERIODS	1	2	F
Michigan State	37	38	75
Alabama	36	22	58

TECHNICAL FOULS – None
ATTENDANCE – 1,200

MSU 64, UNC Asheville 39
Dec. 30, 1998 • Breslin Center • East Lansing, Mich.

UNC Asheville	FG-FGA	FT-FTA	REB	PF	TP	A	TO	BLK	S	MIN
Kevin Martin	7-14	5-7	5	3	21	1	4	0	1	37
Matt Osikowicz	1-2	0-0	3	4	2	1	0	1	0	13
Adam Earnhardt	0-2	0-0	2	2	0	0	2	0	0	19
Mike Matthews	2-7	4-7	3	3	9	1	6	0	2	34
John Risinger	0-3	4-4	2	2	4	1	5	0	1	26
Nick Perkins	0-0	0-0	0	0	0	0	0	0	0	2
Nicholas McDevitt	0-0	0-0	0	0	0	0	0	0	0	1
Bryan Richerson	0-2	0-0	1	0	0	1	2	0	0	8
Juelian Flowers	0-3	1-2	2	1	1	1	1	0	0	22
Ben Ezell	0-1	0-0	3	0	0	0	0	0	0	13
Jeff Coble	0-1	0-0	0	0	0	1	1	0	0	4
Jason Horton	1-1	0-0	3	1	2	0	0	0	0	8
Remco Smits	0-3	0-0	1	3	0	0	0	0	0	13
Totals	11-39	14-20	28	19	39	6	21	3	5	200

Three-Point Field Goals: Martin 2-5, Matthews 1-5, Risinger 0-1, Coble 0-1, Team 3-12.
FG%: 1st Half 6-19 .316, 2nd Half 5-20 .250, Game 11-39 .282; 3FG%: 1st Half 2-8 .250, 2nd Half 1-4 .250, Game 3-12 .250; FT%: 1st Half 3-5 .600, 2nd Half 11-15 .733, Game 14-20 .700; Team Rebounds: 3; Deadball Rebounds: 3.

Michigan State	FG-FGA	FT-FTA	REB	PF	TP	A	TO	BLK	S	MIN
Andre Hutson	4-5	3-3	6	2	11	1	2	0	0	21
Jason Klein	5-8	1-2	5	3	12	0	1	0	1	19
Antonio Smith	1-5	3-5	5	2	5	0	1	0	1	23
Mateen Cleaves	1-6	0-0	2	2	2	8	2	0	6	25
Charlie Bell	0-2	0-0	1	1	0	2	3	0	1	17
Thomas Kelley	4-12	2-2	3	2	10	3	3	0	0	22
Brandon Smith	0-1	0-0	1	0	0	0	0	0	0	4
Steve Cherry	0-0	0-0	0	1	0	0	1	0	0	2
Doug Davis	2-3	0-1	4	5	5	2	1	1	2	18
Morris Peterson	4-10	0-1	6	1	10	2	1	1	2	23
A.J. Granger	2-5	2-5	6	1	7	0	2	0	0	23
Lorenzo Guess	0-1	0-0	5	0	2	0	0	0	0	3
Totals	24-60	11-19	45	20	64	18	17	5	13	200

Three-Point Field Goals: Klein 1-3, Cleaves 0-1, Bell 0-2, Kelley 0-2, B. Smith 0-1, Davis 1-2, Peterson 2-3, Granger 1-1, Team 5-15.
FG%: 1st Half 13-29 .448, 2nd Half 11-31 .355, Game 24-60 .400; 3FG%: 1st Half 3-7 .429, 2nd Half 2-8 .250, Game 5-15 .333; FT%: 1st Half 1-5 .200, 2nd Half 10-14 .714, Game 11-19 .579; Team Rebounds: 1; Deadball Rebounds: 2.

SCORE BY PERIODS	1	2	F
UNC Asheville	17	22	39
Michigan State	30	34	64

OFFICIALS – Donnee Gray, Glen Mayborg, Jim Jenkins
TECHNICAL FOULS – None
ATTENDANCE – 14,659

MSU 69, Louisville 57
Jan. 2, 1999 • Breslin Center • East Lansing, Mich.

Louisville	FG-FGA	FT-FTA	REB	PF	TP	A	TO	BLK	S	MIN
Tony Williams	2-8	0-1	3	1	5	4	1	0	0	32
Nate Johnson	4-10	4-6	7	4	12	0	3	0	4	34
Alex Sanders	7-13	0-0	3	4	16	2	2	0	2	31
Marques Maybin	2-3	0-0	3	1	4	1	3	0	0	17
Cameron Murray	3-9	2-5	1	4	9	2	7	0	1	38
Eric Johnson	2-5	0-0	0	2	4	0	1	0	0	22
Dion Edward	2-3	0-0	5	5	4	0	2	2	1	13
Tobiah Hopper	1-2	1-2	3	1	3	0	0	0	0	13
Totals	23-53	7-14	26	22	57	9	20	2	10	200

Three-Point Field Goals: Williams 1-5, N. Johnson 0-1, Sanders 2-5, Maybin 0-1, Murray 1-3, E. Johnson 0-1, Team 4-16.

FG%: 1st Half 10-25 .400, 2nd Half 13-28 .464, Game 23-53 .434; 3FG%: 1st Half 2-7 .286, 2nd Half 2-9 .222, Game 4-16 .250; FT%: 1st Half 2-6 .333, 2nd Half 5-8 .625, Game 7-14 .500; Team Rebounds: 1; Deadball Rebounds: 2.

Michigan State	FG-FGA	FT-FTA	REB	PF	TP	A	TO	BLK	S	MIN
Morris Peterson	8-12	4-4	5	3	23	0	4	1	1	28
A.J. Granger	2-5	1-1	4	1	5	0	3	0	1	24
Antonio Smith	1-2	0-2	6	3	3	1	1	1	1	28
Mateen Cleaves	4-12	1-2	0	1	9	7	2	0	3	35
Jason Klein	5-9	2-2	4	1	13	2	1	0	0	29
Thomas Kelley	1-5	0-0	1	1	2	0	1	0	1	6
Charlie Bell	2-4	4-6	9	3	8	0	1	0	1	25
Brandon Smith	0-0	0-0	0	1	0	0	2	0	0	2
Doug Davis	0-0	0-0	0	0	0	0	1	0	0	3
Andre Hutson	0-0	7-8	8	4	7	2	4	1	0	20
Totals	23-49	19-25	38	18	69	10	24	3	7	200

Three-Point Field Goals: Peterson 3-4, Granger 0-1, Cleaves 0-4, Klein 1-5, Team 4-14.

FG%: 1st Half 13-27 .481, 2nd Half 10-22 .455, Game 23-49 .469; 3FG%: 1st Half 3-9 .333, 2nd Half 1-5 .200, Game 4-14 .286; FT%: 1st Half 5-6 .833, 2nd Half 14-19 .737, Game 19-25 .760; Team Rebounds: 1; Deadball Rebounds: 3.

SCORE BY PERIODS	1	2	F
Louisville	24	33	57
Michigan State	34	35	69

OFFICIALS – Dan Chrisman, Sid Rodeheffer, Keith Maxwell
TECHNICAL FOULS – None
ATTENDANCE – 14,659

1999 BIG TEN

A seven-game winning streak should have meant more than it did on Jan. 6, 1999. But Michigan State's success the previous 31 days didn't matter one bit to the Wisconsin Badgers in the Spartans' Big Ten opener.

And it paled in comparison to the 22-game streak that would follow, including the greatest conference season in school history.

MSU began the defense of its 1998 co-championship with Illinois in the same building where it had locked up a share of the title less than 11 months earlier, Wisconsin's Kohl Center.

If the Spartans' 11-3 preconference record was impressive to most observers, it didn't faze Dick Bennett's Badgers in a 66-51 shocker.

Wisconsin jumped to a 9-0 lead and had a shutout for the first 7:13. But Tom Izzo's team battled back for a 27-24 halftime advantage, thanks in part to some students who were majoring in hypocrisy.

Recalling Mateen Cleaves' beer-related suspension for the first half of the 1998 game, the Badgers serenaded MSU's point guard with chants of "AL-CO-HOL-IC" — an odd taunt in a party town where the favorite baseball team is the Brewers.

Cleaves was 0-for-3 from the field in a pointless first 18:39. But when he stepped to the foul line and heard the insults, he responded with two free throws, then followed with a left-handed bank.

Wisconsin regrouped at halftime and restated its one-night

Photo Credit: Kevin Fowler, MSU Sports Information

superiority with the best 20 minutes the Spartans would see all season. A 15-6 run in the first 5:06 changed the game, as MSU was colder than a frozen Lake Mendota.

The Spartans missed their first 14 3-point shots, much to the dismay of 100 members of the Izzone, who bused over from East Lansing.

MSU had the best bench in the Big Ten in 1999, without question. But when nearly every shooter has

frostbite, even the deepest team is in deep trouble.

With the Badgers dominating the second half 42-24, it was impossible to tell which team was ranked 12th in the nation and which one was 24th.

Wisconsin point guard Ty Calderwood was 5-for-7 from the field and outscored Cleaves 12-8. And shooting guard Sean Mason and defensive specialist Mike Kelley each had 11 points, as the Badgers ruled the backcourt.

222222

22222222

The Spartans, 17-for-51 from the field, were led by forward Morris Peterson with a game-high 13 points off the bench. But the starters combined for just 23 points, including zero by guard Charlie Bell.

"I thought we played a decent first half," Izzo said. "Then, Mason and those guys started hitting their shots, coming off screens down low. We got drilled in the second half. And that wasn't a great way to start the Big Ten."

It was a great night for the natives in "Mad-town." But Wisconsin hasn't beaten the Spartans since — a streak that has stretched to eight games-and-counting.

"It has been a long time," Izzo said 26 months later. "But they did beat us. And they beat us by a lot. That was a real downer. To regroup and win 15 straight in the league, I think that's still as good an accomplishment as anything we've done."

A ridiculous concern from early December, "Can MSU ever win again?" was soon replaced by the legitimate question, "Will the Spartans lose again this season?"

"That run did get to be incredible, didn't it?" Izzo said. "We had more close games that year — Penn State . . . Minnesota . . . Northwestern — and everyone just thinks we were awesome. The last two years, when we were winning by 10, 12, 15 points, we questioned everything. That just proves the old adage: If you win, it doesn't matter a year from now if it's by one or 100."

MSU was just looking for a one-point win and an end to Cleaves' struggles when a sweet assist and some well-timed scheduling — the 1979 national champs' reunion — came to the rescue against Michigan.

Cleaves had been 8-for-29 from the field in his last three games against UNC Asheville, Louisville and Wisconsin. And the Wolverines had to feel good about their chances, having beaten the Badgers 59-55 in Ann Arbor.

But there was something about

Photo Credit: Kevin Fowler, MSU Sports Information

1999 BIG TEN

seeing that block "M" that motivated Cleaves to be a different player. It didn't hurt that he met with Earvin "Magic" Johnson that morning for a brief leadership summit.

"I just told him he had to be Mateen again," Johnson said. "He wasn't having fun out there. I said, 'What happened to that smile you had? And where's the swagger? . . . Your team needs that more than anything else.'"

It needed Cleaves' 25 points, eight assists and four steals, as well as his intangibles, in an 81-67 win over Michigan, the first of six straight double-digit wins in the series.

MSU used a 10-0 run in the final 2:23 of the first half for a 38-27 advantage and a 14-5 surge midway through the second half to put the game away.

Cleaves had 18 points in the last 20 minutes. Peterson, a surprise starter in place of Bell, had 16 points. And center Antonio Smith had 10 points and a game-high eight rebounds, as the Spartans ruled the boards 37-21.

"We were having fun again, maybe for the first time since last year," forward Jason Klein said after a 12-point, six-rebound effort, including four offensive boards. "'Magic' told us before the game that fun leads to wins and wins lead to championships."

When the Spartans handcuffed the Wolverines' high-scoring backcourt, the game was essentially over. Louis Bullock, who was averaging 21.5 points, scored just six in the first 35 minutes and finished

Photo Credit: Kevin Fowler, MSU Sports Information

3-for-14 from the field. And Izzone target Robbie Reid, a 12.6-point scorer, was held to seven with 2-for-8 accuracy.

The feel-good scene was heightened when MSU's 1978-79 team was saluted at halftime and 1977-81 center Jay Vincent, a two-time Big Ten scoring champ, had No. 31 hung from the rafters.

But the best part of the win over Michigan was its lasting effect. Instead of fading with time as even the fondest memories often do, the lessons were fresh in everyone's mind when Minnesota visited four days later.

Klein was especially active in the 71-55 win, scoring a game-high 21 points and hitting 4-of-7 3-pointers. That seemed to rub off on his teammates, who flew around the floor and treated every loose ball like a treasure.

When the Golden Gophers threatened to draw even with 13:58 left, the Spartans answered with back-to-back-to-back 3s by seldom-used point guard Lorenzo Guess, Peterson and forward A.J. Granger.

Minnesota's 7-1 freshman center Joel Przybilla blocked eight MSU shots. But he was outrebounded 11-3 by Smith. And the Spartans held forward Quincy Lewis, the Big Ten's scoring champ that winter, to 14 points.

The Gophers shot 50 percent from the field. Yet, 20 turnovers led to 23 MSU points. And in the hustle stat of the season, Izzo's team had an 18-1 edge in offensive rebounds.

At 2-1 in the league and 13-4

overall, the Spartans traveled to Champaign, Ill., to face last-place Illinois. All that did was prove to everyone there is no such thing as a breather on the road in the Big Ten.

MSU finally prevailed 51-49, but not before receiving a huge scare. Cleaves was convinced a 50-footer at the buzzer by Fighting

Illini guard Cory Bradford was good, only to see it bounce off the back of the rim.

Klein led all scorers with 15 points and had the Spartans' only 3s, as they struggled with 2-for-19 long-range accuracy against Lon Kruger's zone defense.

But Peterson added 11 points and 10 rebounds off the bench, his

1999 BIG TEN

first career double-double. And the last of his three alley-oop slams from Cleaves made it 49-45.

"We were trying to get a shot for Jason," Cleaves said. "But the play broke down. I saw 'Pete' flying down the baseline. So I just threw it up to him and let him go get it."

There were five possessions in the last 18.4 seconds, including baskets by Bradford that sandwiched free throws by forward Andre Hutson. And when Smith missed the front end of a one-and-one situation, there was still time for an Illinois outlet pass and a desperation shot, not a heave.

When Iowa came to East Lansing five nights later, the idea was still to put the ball in the hole, not to climb into one. But MSU dug a 19-4 crater in the first seven minutes against the nation's 14th-ranked team.

What followed was 19 minutes of excellence that will seldom be matched in Mid-Michigan. The Spartans went from 15 down to 20 up with an incredible 43-8 surge that showed their resiliency to be champions and more.

A 19-2 blitz to start the second half put the game away, as MSU cruised to sole possession of first place with an 80-65 win. The Spartans had 19 assists to the Hawkeyes' nine and committed just 14 turnovers to a pressing team's 21.

It was a "Flintstones" kind of night. Peterson led all scorers with 19 points off the bench. Cleaves had 15 points and 10 assists, cracking the 1,000-point barrier and passing Johnson for fourth place on the school's career assist list. Bell added 13 points. And Smith had 11 points and nine rebounds, second only to the dozen caroms for 5-11 Iowa point guard Dean Oliver.

MSU's next challenge took them to the league's other Assembly Hall, an odd-shaped, concrete shrine to basketball in Bloomington Ind. The Spartans had lost six straight at Indiana, dating back to 1991. But the scary part was almost losing two of their three best players to injury.

Izzo's team sprinted to a 30-14 advantage over Bob Knight's 18th-ranked Hoosiers. But IU guard A.J. Guyton, who nearly committed to MSU, scored 16 points in 6:46 to cut the Spartans' lead to 38-34 at halftime.

"I told our team, 'We had a run. And they had a run. Let's

make sure the last run goes our way,'" Izzo did. "Luckily, it did."

Luck had little or nothing to do with a 73-59 triumph. Up 47-45 with 16:02 to play, MSU turned up its defense and turned Knight's face redder than his sweater. An 11-0 run put the game out of reach, as the Hoosiers went 15 straight possessions without a basket.

But just when it seemed the Spartans had proven their point to a CBS national audience, they nearly lost their point guard and their spiritual leader in one violent second when Cleaves and Smith collided under the MSU basket.

1999 BIG TEN

After writhing in pain for several moments, Smith told his boyhood pal, "Get up, 'Mo!' We've got six minutes left." Both players limped off the floor with their team ahead 61-50. But they weren't on the bench long enough to get comfortable — just 31 seconds.

"Nothing would've stopped us from going back in," Cleaves said, nursing a bruised tailbone. "I didn't care if something was broken. We wanted to win this game more than anything in the world today."

Cleaves led the Spartans with 16 points and 13 assists. Klein and Peterson each had 13 points. And MSU's defense was huge, holding Guyton to 23 points and scoring 22 off 18 turnovers. IU forward Luke Recker, who had scored 52 points in his previous two games, was held to one.

"I thought last year Michigan State would move up and be really, really good this year," Knight said. "The early schedule they played hurt their record. But in the long run, it will really help them."

Tough schedules never hurt, if you survive them. And back in the top 10 for the first time since Dec. 6, the Spartans made it six straight wins by overtaking Ohio State 76-71 in Breslin Center.

Behind the backcourt tandem of Michael Redd and Scoonie Penn, the Buckeyes led 42-34 with 14:36 left. But a 22-7 run, keyed by two 3's from Klein, made all the difference. And eight free throws in the final 45 seconds iced the win.

"We weren't into the game in the first half," Klein said. "And the crowd wasn't into it, either. We needed that run to get us going and get the crowd going."

Cleaves was just 4-for-13 from the field but led his team with 16 points and nine assists. Klein and Bell each had 14 points. And in his first start since March 8, 1997, guard Thomas Kelley had seven points and a game-high three steals.

MSU closed out an 8-1 month, its best January since 1935, by smashing Northwestern 65-48 in East Lansing on Jan. 30, Izzo's 44th birthday.

With the game tied at 10, six different Spartans scored in a 16-0 blitz. Ten first-half steals produced a 39-23 halftime advantage. And the Wildcats never got closer than 11 points the rest of the way.

Hutson led the Spartans with 14 points and had eight rebounds. Peterson added 11 points and a team-high nine rebounds. And Smith added nine points and enough muscle to hold star center Evan Eschmeyer to 15 points, half his output one year earlier.

"The last time I saw that much contact was in a karate movie," Northwestern coach Kevin O'Neill said. "I'm tired of it. He's tired of it. And his mother's tired of it. . . .She told me to say that."

O'Neill, a close friend of Izzo, said MSU was the best team the Wildcats had faced. But neither coach knew how that script would change a month later when they met in the Big Ten Tournament.

All Izzo could worry about was a game at Penn State three days later. Apparently, his players didn't worry quite as much. On

Photo Credit: Kevin Fowler, MSU Sports Information

1999 BIG TEN

Groundhog Day, the Spartans saw shadows late into the night — in the shape of Nittany Lion defenders.

MSU grabbed a 22-8 advantage but led just 37-33 at the half. And radio analyst Gus Ganakas, the Spartans' head coach from 1969-76, was a prophet with his projection for the second half.

"It's all Cleaves!" Ganakas said after a two-point first half. "It's all up to him."

When Penn State drew even at 57, the fun was just beginning. Six ties and five lead changes later, it was 68-all after Cleaves' second 3 of the half with :50 left.

After a Lions miss and an MSU rebound, Izzo called time to talk things over, not to dictate the final play. And leave it to Cleaves, he came through again with a 12-foot, off-balance flip with .4-second left for a 70-68 victory.

"There was an incredible confidence Mateen had that year," Izzo said. "That was when I could really go to him and say, 'What do you think?' After I called the last play at Penn State, he said, 'Coach, I don't feel comfortable with that.' I said, 'Why not?' He said, 'I'll probably throw it away like I did the last time. And you'll be mad at me.' So I said, 'OK . . . what DO you feel comfortable with?' He said, 'I feel more comfortable with this.' And I said, 'Then, that's what we're going to run!'"

Izzo's confidence in Cleaves and himself, as seen in a willingness to defer key decisions, had a major impact on the team's psyche. Meanwhile, Penn State was emo-

tionally frail after a 98-95 loss to the Hoosiers in double-overtime on a Guyton prayer.

"I feel very fortunate, to be honest," Izzo said at Bryce Jordan Center. "I take my hat off to Jerry Dunn. I don't know if I could've gotten my team back up after what happened here Sunday."

Just two days later, the Lions let the Spartans grab 21 offensive rebounds and steal the kind of win that separates champions from good teams.

"We're a very good offensive rebounding team," Izzo said with typical self-deprication. "That's one of the few things I will brag about. But that's partly because we miss so many shots. We take the attitude that if we're going to miss that many shots, we'd better go get them."

His team outrebounded Penn State 36-27. It only seemed like a 20-rebound difference with the way MSU attacked the glass.

"It wasn't a lack of effort on our part," Dunn said. "You've got to give the other guys some credit...They've got some guys who were able to get it done."

Peterson led MSU with 17 points. Cleaves added 14 — 12 in the second half. Hutson had 13 points and nine rebounds. Klein had 12 points. And Smith snared 11 rebounds, though he couldn't stop Penn State's incredibly long Calvin Booth from scoring 18 points.

The Spartans, 8-1 and 19-4, returned to the road that weekend for a rematch with Tom Davis' Hawkeyes and played one of the best all-around games of the Izzo

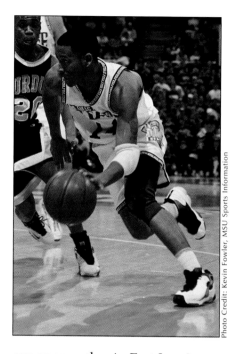

era or any other in East Lansing.

A 19-3 run late in the first half helped MSU lead 49-27 at the break, as Carver-Hawkeye Arena had seldom been as quiet. The Spartans hit 60 percent of their shots from the field in the first 20 minutes, including 6-for-10 success beyond the arc.

All week in practice, Cleaves had been draining 3 after 3 — to the point Izzo wondered if he should ease up and rest his arm for Saturday. That concern wasn't necessary, as MSU built a 31-point, second-half cushion and coasted 95-81 — its season-high point total in a Big Ten game.

"I guess Mateen saved a few 3-pointers," Izzo said of 4-for-7 work from long range in a 14-point, nine-assist, one-turnover effort. "It was great to see him get off to a great start. I think that was one of the best games I've seen him play."

Peterson's effort wasn't shabby,

1999 BIG TEN

either. He was 9-for-12 from the field and finished with a career-high 27 points. And Bell added 16 points, while missing only one shot.

"When Mateen Cleaves is on fire like that from outside and everybody is clicking, they're a scary team," said Iowa center Guy Rucker, an Inkster native. "They're the best transition team in the country. And when they're making 3-pointers, they're tough to stop. They're the best team I've faced in three years here."

The scariest part for opponents? The Spartans were getting better. When they met Illinois again in East Lansing, it wasn't going to be another two-point game — unless Kruger's team got a 15-0 head start.

Now ranked No. 4 in the nation, right where they started, the Spartans were a study in balance. Six different players scored as they raced to a 15-2 lead. And it was 33-14 at the half, as the Fighting Illini hit just 24 percent from the field and had back-to-back shot-clock violations.

In one of the strangest looking summaries you'll ever see, MSU won 61-44 and had seven players score from six to 10 points. Kelley was the only double-figure scorer with 5-for-7 accuracy. That efficiency told the story. Bradford had 13 points for Illinois, but was 4-for-17 in the process.

Maybe the Illini shouldn't have billed themselves as the defending conference co-champs. Maybe they shouldn't have scared the Spartans so much in Champaign or beaten Wisconsin the previous weekend.

Whatever the problem, Illinois got MSU's best defensive effort, when something much less would have done just fine. But Izzo sensed something special was happening. And just two nights later, he saw it close up, as the Spartans rallied in a game for the ages.

When MSU's players get together every five years for reunions, the conversation will eventually turn to Feb. 13, 1999, and a miracle in Minneapolis.

Ah, yes, Williams Arena . . . Jud Heathcote's recommended site for nuclear testing. When asked what Minnesota should do with an ancient building before its renovation, Izzo's mentor joked (we think), "Blow it up!"

Instead, four years later, the Spartans were content to ruin the Gophers' party plans, rallying from 10 points down with 7:54 left for an 84-82 triumph, an MSU-record 11th in a row in conference play.

If you like offense, you would have loved this one. Minnesota shot a torrid 65 percent in the first half, only to watch the Spartans drain nine 3s for a 43-40 halftime advantage.

The Gophers finally used an 11-3 run to take a 71-61 lead behind the brilliance of Lewis, who finished with 29 points. But MSU was far from finished. And that was all that mattered.

Another deluge of 3s began falling — first Granger, then Cleaves and finally Bell connecting from 20 feet and beyond. But with the Spartans up 80-79, they were still three great plays from victory.

The first one came on defense

— an appropriate signature for the season and for Izzo's entire tenure, but not for a night when Minnesota shot 60 percent from the field.

As Lewis made his move to the basket for what apeared to be his 30th and 31st points and the Gophers' greatest win of the year, Smith reached in, stripped the ball and alertly called timeout.

Clem Haskins' final team tried to work its Williams wizardry one more time with pressure defense. But Izzo wisely called for Bell to break long. And a catch-and-slam appeared to give MSU some daylight at 82-79.

Photo Credit: Kevin Fowler, MSU Sports Information

1999 BIG TEN

Rejecting the semi-intentional foul that makes sense in situations closer to the buzzer, the Spartans decided to play traditional defense. And they paid for that decision when guard Terrance Simmons hit a 3 with :08 left to tie the game at 82.

Everyone immediately thought "Overtime!" — everyone but Cleaves, that is. The reigning Big Ten Player of the Year weaved his way though five defenders and shook free for a short runner with a second to play.

After a 5-for-6 effort from 3-point range, Cleaves' winning shot traveled about the length of his arm. And from the reaction of MSU's players and coaches, it appeared they had won something besides another Big Ten game.

In fact, they did. The Spartans won everyone's respect that night as a group that wouldn't go away and a program that wasn't satisfied to stop halfway up the mountain.

Cleaves continued to lead that ascent with 23 points. Peterson added 20, including eight in the final 5:16. And Bell had 18 points, as he and his teammates began to think of themselves as more than a Big Ten repeat champ. National goals began to sharpen.

"Minnesota was one of those games we had no business winning," Izzo said. "But the thing that started to happen was that nobody thought we could lose — nobody. We were going to find ways to win. And we found so many different ways to do that."

Three nights later, the Spartans found a way to beat Purdue in East Lansing for the first time since 1992. MSU led 39-27 at the half, then broke the game open as Klein scored his team's next 11 points.

In an 82-69 decision that wasn't nearly that close, the Spartans got a game-high 22 points from Klein, including 5-for-7 3-point work. Bell added 13 points and Hutson 11, as the winners shot 55.6 percent from the field.

"They spoiled our victory party last year," Bell said of a season-ending, overtime loss that meant MSU had to share the 1998 title. "We wanted to see highlights of the crowd rushing the floor, the way it did before (against the Boilermakers in 1990). But it didn't happen."

The Spartans 12th conference victory happened just the way Izzo wanted — with a football mentality a respected rival appreciated.

"They were so aggressive on defense," said Purdue coach and former Steelers defensive back Gene Keady. "I really love that. The game was won in the first half with the way they got after loose balls on the floor."

Bell wasn't there to see the celebration when MSU's fans finally flooded the floor at Breslin. That's because he was busy in Ann Arbor, helping to beat the Wolverines, 73-58.

But a crowd of 2,607 showed up to watch the Spartans on four giant screens, while even more made the pilgrimmage to Ann Arbor. Neither group was disappointed, as Izzo's team moved to 13-1, 24-4 with its third-straight win over Michigan.

Nine points from Klein helped MSU take a 35-28 halftime lead.

And an 8-2 spurt after the break made it a 13-point game. The Wolverines never got closer than six the rest of the way.

The Spartans shot 60 percent from the field in the second half, while Michigan managed just 30.4-percent accuracy. In a 15-point game, MSU's bench had a 30-0 edge over the Wolverines' backups.

Cleaves was 3-for-6 from long range and led all scorers with 19 points, while Klein, Peterson and Granger combined for 31. And Smith grabbed 14 rebounds in his team's 36-24 dominance on the boards.

"This is very sweet," Smith said of his first victory in Crisler Arena. "Winning here is something we've wanted to do for a long time. It's even sweeter to get a piece of the title here."

Photo Credit: Kevin Fowler, MSU Sports Information

1999 BIG TEN

Photo Credit: Kevin Fowler, MSU Sports Information

Chants of "Let's go, State!" filled the building 45 minutes before tipoff. And a "We own Crisler!" chant capped a near-perfect evening for thousands who stayed to the end.

Winning in Ann Arbor for the first time in four seasons was another objective met for the seniors, for Izzo and for the Spartans' supporters, including President Peter McPherson, an honorary Izzone member.

"You should be ashamed of yourself!" one Michigan fan told McPherson on a night when he couldn't have been prouder.

Three days later on Feb. 21, MSU locked up an outright title with a 56-51 win over Wisconsin. That made the Spartans 14-0 in Breslin, their first perfect performance at home since 1978-79.

In throwback uniforms with an interlocking MAC logo, Izzo's players used a throwback style to thrill hundreds of basketball alumni who returned to celebrate the program's first 100 seasons.

"This team has tremendous heart and resiliency," said 1970s forward and former Heathcote assistant Edgar Wilson. "But this environment is really something. With the support they have, it's a tremendous advantage. And what Tom has really done is bring everything together and bring everyone back."

In a game with a score from an earlier era, MSU played tenacious defense and outrebounded the Badgers 39-19. Smith had 11 rebounds and Hutson 10, as that tandem outboarded Wisconsin's entire team by two.

And if the Spartans didn't punish the Badgers by a similar margin on the scoreboard, they did more than enough to deliver a payback for their only conference loss.

On a day when will meant more than skill, a working definition of "Izzoball," it was left to MSU's leader to snip the final strand of net and holler "Thank you!" to everyone in Breslin.

Seconds later, Big Ten Commissioner Jim Delany presented the league's championship trophy — the second of four in a row-and-counting.

"It's great to be here today to congratulate and honor the OUTRIGHT 1999 Big Ten Champs," Delany said. "To celebrate the last year of the century with an outright championship, what a great gift to give to your university."

Greater gifts were still being wrapped for the future. But in terms of building bridges between past and present, a major goal of Izzo's program, the afternoon of Feb. 21, 1999, was about as good as it gets.

With a week to savor their achievements and rest up before tournament play, the Spartans had one more regular-season challenge. They traveled to Purdue, won 60-46 and put a damper on the Boilermakers' Senior Day festivities.

MSU struggled through much of the first half but took a 24-21 lead at the break when sophomore guard Doug Davis scored the last five points. After Purdue tied it at 30 with 15:24 left, the Spartans blew the game open with a 26-9 surge.

Smith was the winners' lone double-figure scorer, finishing with 12 points and a game-high eight rebounds. MSU had a 39-20 edge on the boards and and a 23-2 edge in bench scoring.

The Spartans ended Big Ten play at 15-1, three games ahead of runner-up Ohio State. That was the best winning percentage in the conference since 1993. MSU also climbed to 26-4 for the first time in school history.

"I thought our guys showed a lot of grit and determination to win this game any way possible," Izzo said of a group that rose to second in the rankings. "We have no real egos on this team. And we've been able to accomplish a lot because of that."

They accomplished more than almost anyone imagined. From a frigid start in Madison to a torrid finish in West Lafayette, the Spartans had the last laugh. More than two years later, its fans are still smiling.

Wisconsin 66, MSU 51
Jan. 6, 1999 • Kohl • Madison, Wis.

Michigan State	FG-FGA	FT-FTA	REB	PF	TP	A	TO	BLK	S	MIN
Antonio Smith	3-4	2-2	5	3	8	2	4	0	1	34
A.J. Granger	1-4	0-0	0	3	3	0	1	0	0	11
Jason Klein	1-6	2-2	4	1	4	1	1	0	0	21
Mateen Cleaves	3-11	2-2	1	1	8	2	4	0	1	30
Charlie Bell	0-3	0-0	2	3	0	0	1	0	0	18
Thomas Kelley	2-7	2-3	1	3	6	0	1	0	0	21
Brandon Smith	0-0	0-0	0	0	0	0	0	0	0	1
Doug Davis	0-1	0-0	1	0	0	1	0	0	0	6
Andre Hutson	3-6	3-3	8	2	9	0	2	2	0	31
Morris Peterson	4-9	5-5	5	3	13	0	1	0	2	27
Totals	17-51	16-17	32	19	51	6	15	2	4	200

Three-Point Field Goals: Granger 1-4, Klein 0-2, Cleaves 0-5, Kelley 0-1, Davis 0-1, Peterson 0-2, Team 1-15.

FG%: 1st Half 9-24 .375, 2nd Half 8-27 .296, Game 17-51 .333; 3FG%: 1st Half 0-8 .000, 2nd Half 1-7 .143, Game 1-15 .067; FT%: 1st Half 9-9 1.000, 2nd Half 7-8 .875, Game 16-17 .941; Team Rebounds: 5; Deadball Rebounds: 0.

Wisconsin	FG-FGA	FT-FTA	REB	PF	TP	A	TO	BLK	S	MIN
Andy Kowske	4-7	2-2	6	2	10	0	2	0	1	34
Mark Vershaw	4-8	1-1	4	3	9	3	1	1	1	32
Sean Mason	4-9	0-1	3	4	11	3	3	0	0	28
Ty Calderwood	5-7	0-0	3	4	12	4	1	0	1	21
Mike Kelley	2-4	7-8	4	0	11	5	0	0	3	38
Duany Duany	0-0	0-0	0	1	0	0	0	1	0	4
Hennssy Auriantal	0-2	2-2	1	1	2	0	2	0	0	12
Jon Bryant	3-5	2-2	2	0	9	1	0	0	0	17
Maurice Linton	1-2	0-0	0	2	2	1	1	0	0	9
Charlie Wills	0-0	0-0	1	1	0	1	2	0	0	5
Totals	23-44	14-16	26	18	66	18	12	2	6	200

Three-Point Field Goals: Mason 3-7, Calderwood 2-3, Kelley 0-2, Bryant 1-3, Team 6-15.

FG%: 1st Half 8-21 .381, 2nd Half 15-23 .652, Game 23-44 .523; 3FG%: 1st Half 3-7 .429, 2nd Half 3-8 .375, Game 6-15 .400; FT%: 1st Half 5-7 .714, 2nd Half 9-9 1.000, Game 14-16 .875; Team Rebounds: 2; Deadball Rebounds: 0.

SCORE BY PERIODS	1	2	F	OFFICIALS – Ed Hightower, Gene Monje, Sid Rodeheffer
Michigan State	27	24	51	TECHNICAL FOULS – None
Wisconsin	24	42	66	ATTENDANCE – 15,504

MSU 81, Michigan 67
Jan. 9, 1999 • Breslin Center • East Lansing, Mich.

Michigan	FG-FGA	FT-FTA	REB	PF	TP	A	TO	BLK	S	MIN
Josh Asselin	6-9	5-6	4	4	17	0	1	1	0	27
Brandon Smith	4-6	1-1	2	5	10	3	5	0	2	30
Peter Vignier	3-5	3-4	5	3	9	0	4	2	2	35
Robbie Reid	2-8	2-2	2	4	7	1	3	0	3	33
Louis Bullock	3-14	8-10	2	3	15	2	2	0	1	34
Leon Jones	0-3	2-2	0	2	2	0	4	0	3	21
Darius Taylor	0-0	0-0	0	0	0	0	0	0	0	1
Ron Oliver	0-0	0-0	0	0	0	0	0	0	0	1
Chris Young	3-3	1-1	3	2	7	0	1	0	1	18
Totals	21-48	22-26	21	23	67	6	21	3	12	200

Three-Point Field Goals: Smith 1-1, Reid 1-4, Bullock 1-6, Jones 0-1, Team 3-12.

FG%: 1st Half 12-28 .429, 2nd Half 9-20 .450, Game 21-48 .438; 3FG%: 1st Half 1-5 .200, 2nd Half 2-7 .286, Game 3-12 .250; FT%: 1st Half 2-3 .667, 2nd Half 20-23 .870, Game 22-26 .846; Team Rebounds: 3; Deadball Rebounds: 0.

Michigan State	FG-FGA	FT-FTA	REB	PF	TP	A	TO	BLK	S	MIN
Andre Hutson	2-4	5-6	3	4	9	1	4	0	1	29
Morris Peterson	5-7	6-7	4	5	16	0	3	2	0	27
Antonio Smith	5-7	0-0	8	2	10	0	3	1	1	33
Mateen Cleaves	7-10	10-11	0	2	25	8	4	0	4	34
Jason Klein	6-16	0-0	6	1	12	1	2	0	0	28
Thomas Kelley	1-5	0-0	3	2	2	2	2	0	2	12
Charlie Bell	1-2	2-2	5	4	4	0	2	0	0	17
Doug Davis	0-1	0-0	0	0	0	0	1	0	0	2
A.J. Granger	1-2	0-0	5	4	3	0	0	2	1	18
Totals	28-54	23-26	37	23	81	12	22	5	9	200

Three-Point Field Goals: Peterson 0-1, Cleaves 1-2, Klein 0-5, Kelley 0-1, Bell 0-1, Granger 1-2, Team 2-12.

FG%: 1st Half 14-29 .483, 2nd Half 14-25 .560, Game 28-54 .519; 3FG%: 1st Half 1-7 .143, 2nd Half 1-5 .200, Game 2-12 .167; FT%: 1st Half 9-10 .900, 2nd Half 14-16 .875, Game 23-26 .885; Team Rebounds: 3; Deadball Rebounds: 2.

SCORE BY PERIODS	1	2	F	OFFICIALS – Jody Silvester, Dan Chrisman, Tom Clark
Michigan	27	40	67	TECHNICAL FOULS – None
Michigan State	38	43	81	ATTENDANCE – 14,659

MSU 71, Minnesota 55
Jan. 13, 1999 • Breslin Center • East Lansing, Mich.

Minnesota	FG-FGA	FT-FTA	REB	PF	TP	A	TO	BLK	S	MIN
Quincy Lewis	4-10	4-5	6	4	14	3	2	0	0	35
Miles Tarver	1-4	0-0	4	4	2	2	3	0	0	30
Joel Przybilla	4-5	3-5	3	4	11	0	5	8	1	31
Kevin Clark	1-5	4-5	4	2	7	1	2	0	1	34
Kevin Nathaniel	4-6	2-2	3	4	10	1	1	0	1	24
Nick Sinville	0-0	0-0	1	0	0	0	0	0	0	1
Mitch Ohnstad	3-5	1-3	2	2	7	2	4	0	0	19
Ryan Keating	0-0	0-0	0	1	0	0	1	0	0	2
Terrance Simmons	0-0	0-0	1	0	0	0	2	0	0	5
Antoine Broxsie	0-1	0-0	0	1	0	0	0	2	0	6
Dusty Rychart	0-0	0-0	0	0	0	0	0	0	0	1
Kyle Sanden	2-2	0-0	0	2	4	1	0	0	0	12
Totals	19-38	14-20	24	24	55	10	20	10	3	200

Three-Point Field Goals: Lewis 2-5, Tarver 0-1, Clark 1-2, Ohnstad 0-1, Team 3-9.
FG%: 1st Half 7-19 .368, 2nd Half 12-19 .632, Game 19-38 .500; 3FG%: 1st Half 1-4 .250, 2nd Half 2-5 .400, Game 3-9 .333; FT%: 1st Half 8-11 .727, 2nd Half 6-9 .667, Game 14-20 .700; Team Rebounds: 1; Deadball Rebounds: 6.

Michigan State	FG-FGA	FT-FTA	REB	PF	TP	A	TO	BLK	S	MIN
Andre Hutson	0-4	0-0	2	3	0	0	0	1	0	28
Jason Klein	7-12	3-6	3	2	21	0	0	0	0	23
Antonio Smith	2-5	2-4	11	4	6	4	3	1	1	32
Mateen Cleaves	5-13	3-5	3	2	14	6	5	0	5	33
Charlie Bell	2-6	0-1	4	1	4	1	1	0	1	21
Thomas Kelley	2-5	3-4	0	1	7	4	0	0	2	16
Lorenzo Guess	1-1	0-0	0	0	3	0	1	0	0	4
Brandon Smith	0-0	0-0	0	0	0	0	0	0	0	1
Steve Cherry	0-0	0-0	1	0	0	0	0	0	1	1
Doug Davis	0-1	0-0	0	1	0	0	0	0	0	3
Morris Peterson	5-9	0-1	5	3	11	0	0	0	0	22
A.J. Granger	2-7	0-1	5	1	5	0	1	0	0	16
Totals	26-63	11-22	37	18	71	15	11	2	9	200

Three-Point Field Goals: Klein 4-7, Cleaves 1-4, Guess 1-1, Davis 0-1, Peterson 1-3, Granger 1-2, Team 8-18.
FG%: 1st Half 12-33 .364, 2nd Half 14-30 .467, Game 26-63 .413; 3FG%: 1st Half 2-6 .333, 2nd Half 6-12 .500, Game 8-18 .444; FT%: 1st Half 4-9 .444, 2nd Half 7-13 .538, Game 11-22 .500; Team Rebounds: 3; Deadball Rebounds: 6.

SCORE BY PERIODS	1	2		F
Minnesota	23	32	--	55
Michigan State	30	41	--	71

OFFICIALS – Tom O'Neill, Phil Bova, Paul Jansson
TECHNICAL FOULS – Minnesota bench
ATTENDANCE – 14,659

MSU 51, Illinois 49
Jan. 16, 1999 • Assembly Hall • Champaign, Ill.

Michigan State	FG-FGA	FT-FTA	REB	PF	TP	A	TO	BLK	S	MIN
Andre Hutson	1-2	2-2	3	2	4	0	1	3	0	27
Jason Klein	6-15	1-2	2	1	15	0	1	0	0	27
Antonio Smith	0-2	0-1	11	0	0	0	0	1	1	32
Mateen Cleaves	3-10	1-1	3	2	7	7	2	0	0	29
Charlie Bell	1-4	2-2	3	1	4	0	2	0	0	20
Thomas Kelley	3-9	0-0	0	5	6	1	3	0	2	16
Doug Davis	0-2	2-2	0	0	2	0	2	1	0	8
Morris Peterson	5-9	1-2	10	3	11	0	5	0	0	25
A.J. Granger	1-3	0-0	3	2	2	0	0	0	1	16
Totals	20-56	9-12	37	16	51	8	16	5	4	200

Three-Point Field Goals: Klein 2-7, Cleaves 0-6, Bell 0-1, Davis 0-1, Peterson 0-2, Granger 0-2, Team 2-19.
FG%: 1st Half 10-28 .357, 2nd Half 10-28 .357, Game 20-56 .357; 3FG%: 1st Half 1-11 .091, 2nd Half 1-8 .125, Game 2-19 .105; FT%: 1st Half 6-8 .750, 2nd Half 3-4 .750, Game 9-12 .750; Team Rebounds: 2; Deadball Rebounds: 3.

Illinois	FG-FGA	FT-FTA	REB	PF	TP	A	TO	BLK	S	MIN
Victor Chukwudebe	3-6	3-4	2	3	9	0	3	0	1	25
Cleotis Brown	2-6	3-4	3	3	7	0	2	0	1	25
Fess Hawkins	1-3	1-2	4	1	3	0	0	1	0	13
Nate Mast	2-4	0-0	2	2	5	5	3	0	0	34
Cory Bradford	3-16	2-4	6	0	9	1	0	0	0	37
Arias Davis	2-4	0-0	1	0	4	1	1	0	0	10
Robert Archibald	3-6	2-2	4	4	8	0	2	1	1	13
Lucas Johnson	0-5	0-0	1	1	0	1	1	0	0	18
Damir Krupalija	2-5	0-0	9	1	4	1	2	0	1	25
Totals	18-55	11-16	36	15	49	9	15	2	4	200

Three-Point Field Goals: Brown 0-2, Mast 1-2, Bradford 1-6, Davis 0-1, Johnson 0-3, Team 2-14.
FG%: 1st Half 7-33 .212, 2nd Half 11-22 .500, Game 18-55 .327; 3FG%: 1st Half 1-8 .125, 2nd Half 1-6 .167, Game 2-14 .143; FT%: 1st Half 2-4 .500, 2nd Half 9-12 .750, Game 11-16 .688; Team Rebounds: 4; Deadball Rebounds: 5.

SCORE BY PERIODS	1	2		F
Michigan State	27	24	--	51
Illinois	17	32	--	49

OFFICIALS – Phil Bova, Steve Skiles, Lenny Memminger
TECHNICAL FOULS – None
ATTENDANCE – 15,428

MSU 80, Iowa 65
Jan. 21, 1999 • Breslin Center • East Lansing, Mich.

Iowa	FG-FGA	FT-FTA	REB	PF	TP	A	TO	BLK	S	MIN
Jess Settles	2-3	5-6	1	1	9	0	3	0	0	17
Dean Oliver	5-13	0-0	2	1	12	3	7	0	2	34
Guy Rucker	6-8	0-3	6	1	12	0	0	1	1	20
Ryan Luehrsmann	1-5	1-2	2	4	3	1	4	0	2	23
Ken McCausland	1-1	0-0	0	1	3	1	1	1	0	18
Jason Bauer	1-2	0-0	2	2	2	0	0	0	1	14
Sam Okey	2-5	2-2	2	2	6	1	2	0	0	13
Jason Price	0-1	0-0	0	1	0	0	2	0	0	7
Jacob Jaacks	2-2	5-7	2	1	10	3	1	0	0	14
Duez Henderson	1-3	4-4	8	5	6	0	1	0	0	6
Joey Range	0-2	0-0	3	1	0	0	0	0	0	18
J.R. Koch	1-5	0-2	2	2	2	0	0	0	0	16
Totals	22-50	17-26	33	21	65	9	21	2	6	200

Three-Point Field Goals: Oliver 2-6, Luehrsmann 0-3, McCausland 1-1, Jaacks 1-1, Koch 0-3, Team 4-14.
FG%: 1st Half 10-22 .455, 2nd Half 12-28 .429, Game 22-50 .440; 3FG%: 1st Half 1-6 .167, 2nd Half 3-8 .375, Game 4-14 .286; FT%: 1st Half 4-4 1.000, 2nd Half 13-22 .591, Game 17-26 .654; Team Rebounds: 3; Deadball Rebounds: 9.

Michigan State	FG-FGA	FT-FTA	REB	PF	TP	A	TO	BLK	S	MIN
Andre Hutson	1-3	2-5	8	4	4	1	0	0	2	24
Jason Klein	3-7	0-0	2	2	9	0	0	1	1	27
Antonio Smith	5-7	1-2	9	5	11	1	4	0	2	29
Mateen Cleaves	4-9	5-5	0	1	15	10	2	0	3	33
Charlie Bell	5-16	3-4	3	2	13	1	2	0	0	23
Thomas Kelley	3-8	0-0	0	0	7	1	1	0	1	12
Doug Davis	0-2	0-0	0	0	0	2	0	0	0	7
Morris Peterson	5-9	7-8	5	5	19	2	3	1	0	26
A.J. Granger	1-1	0-0	4	4	2	1	1	0	3	19
Totals	27-62	18-24	35	23	80	19	14	2	13	200

Three-Point Field Goals: Klein 3-5, Cleaves 2-6, Bell 0-1, Kelley 1-1, Davis 0-1, Peterson 2-2, Team 8-16.
FG%: 1st Half 12-31 .387, 2nd Half 15-31 .484, Game 27-62 .435; 3FG%: 1st Half 2-7 .286, 2nd Half 6-9 .667, Game 8-16 .500; FT%: 1st Half 2-2 1.000, 2nd Half 16-22 .727, Game 18-24 .750; Team Rebounds: 4; Deadball Rebounds: 1.

SCORE BY PERIODS	1	2		F
Iowa	25	40	--	65
Michigan State	28	52	--	80

OFFICIALS – Tom Rucker, Jody Silvester, Zelton Steed
TECHNICAL FOULS – None
ATTENDANCE – 14,659

Photo Credit: Kevin Fowler, MSU Sports Information

Photo Credit: Kevin Fowler, MSU Sports Information

Photo Credit: Kevin Fowler, MSU Sports Information

MSU 73, Indiana 59
Jan. 24, 1999 • Assembly Hall • Bloomington, Ind.

Michigan State	FG-FGA	FT-FTA	REB	PF	TP	A	TO	BLK	S	MIN
Antonio Smith	2-5	0-4	11	1	4	0	1	0	3	31
Jason Klein	6-12	0-0	1	1	13	1	0	0	2	25
Andre Hutson	2-4	1-2	6	3	5	0	1	1	0	25
Mateen Cleaves	6-12	3-3	3	1	16	13	4	0	1	32
Charlie Bell	3-6	3-3	3	4	9	3	0	0	1	19
Morris Peterson	6-8	0-0	4	4	13	0	3	0	2	18
Thomas Kelley	1-5	1-2	1	1	3	0	1	0	1	18
A.J. Granger	4-7	0-0	2	3	10	1	1	0	0	24
Doug Davis	0-3	0-0	2	1	0	2	1	0	0	8
Totals	30-62	8-14	37	19	73	20	12	1	10	200

Three-Point Field Goals: Klein 1-3, Cleaves 1-5, Bell 0-1, Peterson 1-2, Kelley 0-1, Granger 2-4, Davis 0-2, Team 5-18.

FG%: 1st Half 17-37 .459, 2nd Half 13-25 .520, Game 30-62 .484; 3FG%: 1st Half 1-10 .100, 2nd Half 4-8 .500, Game 5-18 .278; FT%: 1st Half 3-6 .500, 2nd Half 5-8 .625, Game 8-14 .571; Team Rebounds: 4; Deadball Rebounds: 2.

Indiana	FG-FGA	FT-FTA	REB	PF	TP	A	TO	BLK	S	MIN
Luke Recker	0-6	1-2	2	3	1	1	1	0	0	27
Lynn Washington	1-3	2-3	6	1	4	1	1	0	0	15
William Gladness	5-7	0-1	6	4	10	1	7	0	1	27
Michael Lewis	3-5	0-0	2	1	6	3	3	0	0	20
A.J. Guyton	9-16	2-3	3	3	23	4	2	0	0	36
Dane Fife	1-1	0-0	1	1	2	0	1	0	0	13
Kirk Haston	5-9	1-3	7	2	11	1	1	0	2	25
Rob Turner	1-1	0-0	0	0	2	0	1	0	0	4
Larry Richardson	0-2	0-0	2	0	0	1	0	0	1	13
Luke Jimenez	0-1	0-1	2	2	0	1	2	0	0	20
Totals	25-51	6-13	31	17	59	13	18	0	4	200

Three-Point Field Goals: Recker 0-4, Lewis 0-1, Guyton 3-7, Team 3-12.

FG%: 1st Half 14-22 .636, 2nd Half 11-29 .379, Game 25-51 .490; 3FG%: 1st Half 2-6 .333, 2nd Half 1-6 .167, Game 3-12 .250; FT%: 1st Half 4-7 .571, 2nd Half 2-6 .333, Game 6-13 .462; Team Rebounds: 0; Deadball Rebounds: 1.

SCORE BY PERIODS	1	2	F
Michigan State	38	35	73
Indiana	34	25	59

OFFICIALS – Ed Hightower, Jody Silvester, Donnee Gray
TECHNICAL FOULS – None
ATTENDANCE – 17,436

MSU 76, Ohio State 71
Jan. 27, 1999 • Breslin Center • East Lansing, Mich.

Ohio State	FG-FGA	FT-FTA	REB	PF	TP	A	TO	BLK	S	MIN
Jason Singleton	3-7	0-1	2	4	6	1	1	1	2	22
Jon Sanderson	1-2	2-2	4	1	4	2	3	0	1	12
Ken Johnson	1-6	0-0	7	2	2	1	0	3	0	31
Scoonie Penn	5-13	6-8	3	4	17	6	2	0	2	37
Michael Redd	7-12	4-7	2	3	20	3	4	0	2	38
Neshaun Coleman	2-3	0-0	1	3	6	0	0	0	1	13
Brian Brown	0-0	0-0	1	1	0	2	2	0	0	11
Slobodan Savovic	1-3	0-0	0	1	2	0	0	0	1	10
George Reese	7-9	0-0	7	1	14	0	1	0	1	26
Totals	27-55	12-18	29	20	71	15	14	4	10	200

Three-Point Field Goals: Sanderson 0-1, Penn 1-7, Redd 2-2, Coleman 2-2, Savovic 0-2, Team 5-14.

FG%: 1st Half 14-30 .467, 2nd Half 13-25 .520, Game 27-55 .491; 3FG%: 1st Half 2-4 .500, 2nd Half 3-10 .300, Game 5-14 .357; FT%: 1st Half 7-9 .778, 2nd Half 5-9 .556, Game 12-18 .667; Team Rebounds: 2; Deadball Rebounds: 2.

Michigan State	FG-FGA	FT-FTA	REB	PF	TP	A	TO	BLK	S	MIN
Andre Hutson	0-0	0-0	3	2	0	0	1	0	1	23
Jason Klein	5-11	0-0	1	3	14	0	2	0	1	24
Antonio Smith	1-3	1-4	11	2	3	0	2	1	0	26
Thomas Kelley	3-6	1-1	1	2	7	1	0	0	3	19
Mateen Cleaves	4-13	8-10	2	3	16	9	4	0	1	36
Charlie Bell	6-8	1-2	5	2	14	0	1	0	0	23
Doug Davis	2-2	0-0	0	2	6	0	0	0	0	4
Morris Peterson	2-5	5-5	5	2	10	2	3	1	1	22
A.J. Granger	3-4	0-2	2	1	6	1	2	0	0	23
Totals	26-52	16-24	33	19	76	13	15	2	7	200

Three-Point Field Goals: Klein 4-6, Cleaves 0-5, Bell 1-2, Davis 2-2, Peterson 1-3, Granger 0-1, Team 8-19.

FG%: 1st Half 13-27 .481, 2nd Half 13-25 .520, Game 26-52 .500; 3FG%: 1st Half 5-10 .500, 2nd Half 3-9 .333, Game 8-19 .421; FT%: 1st Half 2-3 .667, 2nd Half 14-21 .667, Game 16-24 .667; Team Rebounds: 3; Deadball Rebounds: 4.

SCORE BY PERIODS	1	2	F
Ohio State	37	34	71
Michigan State	33	43	76

OFFICIALS – Tom Rucker, Tom Clark, Randy Drury
TECHNICAL FOULS – None
ATTENDANCE – 14,659

MSU 65, Northwestern 48
Jan. 30, 1999 • Breslin Center • East Lansing, Mich.

Northwestern	FG-FGA	FT-FTA	REB	PF	TP	A	TO	BLK	S	MIN
Sean Wink	1-3	2-3	2	2	4	0	3	0	0	22
Tavaras Hardy	0-2	0-0	0	2	0	0	3	0	0	16
Evan Eschmeyer	3-9	9-9	9	4	15	5	4	0	1	32
Julian Bonner	3-8	0-0	6	0	8	2	4	0	1	32
David Newman	0-3	2-2	3	2	2	1	1	0	1	31
Joe Harmsen	0-0	0-0	0	0	0	1	0	0	0	3
Danny Allouche	0-2	0-0	2	1	0	1	0	0	0	15
Steve Lepore	3-7	0-0	2	1	9	0	1	0	1	27
Aron Molnar	5-9	0-0	2	3	10	1	4	1	2	22
Totals	15-43	13-14	27	15	48	11	20	1	6	200

Three-Point Field Goals: Wink 0-1, Bonner 2-4, Newman 0-3, Lepore 3-6, Team 5-14.
FG%: 1st Half 9-20 .450, 2nd Half 6-23 .261, Game 15-43 .349; 3FG%: 1st Half 3-7 .429, 2nd Half 2-7 .286, Game 5-14 .357; FT%: 1st Half 2-2 1.000, 2nd Half 11-12 .917, Game 13-14 .929; Team Rebounds: 1; Deadball Rebounds: 2.

Michigan State	FG-FGA	FT-FTA	REB	PF	TP	A	TO	BLK	S	MIN
Andre Hutson	5-9	4-4	8	3	14	0	1	1	0	24
Jason Klein	2-7	0-0	2	1	4	2	1	0	1	23
Antonio Smith	4-6	1-4	3	5	9	0	0	1	0	25
Mateen Cleaves	2-9	2-2	4	1	7	6	4	0	3	32
Charlie Bell	4-7	1-1	2	1	9	3	0	0	2	23
Thomas Kelley	1-3	2-2	1	4	4	2	2	0	1	13
Lorenzo Guess	0-0	0-0	0	0	0	0	0	0	0	2
Brandon Smith	0-0	0-0	0	0	0	0	1	0	0	1
Steve Cherry	0-0	0-0	0	0	0	0	0	0	0	1
Doug Davis	0-3	0-0	0	0	0	1	0	0	1	8
Morris Peterson	5-9	0-0	9	2	11	0	0	1	3	24
A.J. Granger	2-5	2-2	3	2	7	1	1	1	0	24
Totals	25-58	12-15	34	16	65	15	11	4	12	200

Three-Point Field Goals: Klein 0-3, Cleaves 1-2, Bell 0-1, Davis 0-2, Peterson 1-1, Granger 1-2, Team 3-11.
FG%: 1st Half 16-35 .457, 2nd Half 9-23 .391, Game 25-58 .431; 3FG%: 1st Half 3-9 .333, 2nd Half 0-2 .000, Game 3-11 .273; FT%: 1st Half 4-4 1.000, 2nd Half 8-11 .727, Game 12-15 .800; Team Rebounds: 2; Deadball Rebounds: 2.

SCORE BY PERIODS	1	2	F
Northwestern	23	25	-- 48
Michigan State	39	26	-- 65

OFFICIALS – Ron Zetcher, Jerry Petro, Glenn Mayborg
TECHNICAL FOULS – None
ATTENDANCE – 14,659

MSU 70, Penn State 68
Feb. 2, 1999 • Bryce Jordan Center • State College, Pa.

Michigan State	FG-FGA	FT-FTA	REB	PF	TP	A	TO	BLK	S	MIN
Antonio Smith	1-9	2-2	11	4	4	4	2	0	1	31
Jason Klein	4-7	2-3	2	1	12	0	0	0	0	25
Andre Hutson	6-9	1-2	9	3	13	0	2	1	4	32
Mateen Cleaves	4-12	4-4	3	1	14	5	4	0	1	32
Charlie Bell	1-5	0-0	3	3	2	1	1	0	0	18
Thomas Kelley	1-4	0-0	0	2	2	0	0	0	0	12
Doug Davis	2-2	0-0	0	1	6	3	0	0	0	8
Morris Peterson	7-11	3-3	6	1	17	2	2	0	1	25
A.J. Granger	0-1	0-1	1	1	0	1	1	1	0	17
Totals	26-60	12-15	36	19	70	16	12	2	7	200

Three-Point Field Goals: Smith 0-1, Klein 2-4, Cleaves 2-4, Kelley 0-1, Davis 2-2, Granger 0-1, Team 6-13.
FG%: 1st Half 14-29 .483, 2nd Half 12-31 .387, Game 26-60 .433; 3FG%: 1st Half 3-8 .375, 2nd Half 3-5 .600, Game 6-13 .462; FT%: 1st Half 6-7 .857, 2nd Half 6-8 .750, Game 12-15 .800; Team Rebounds: 3; Deadball Rebounds: 1.

Penn State	FG-FGA	FT-FTA	REB	PF	TP	A	TO	BLK	S	MIN
Gyasi Cline-Heard	3-6	2-2	5	3	8	0	1	0	2	29
Titus Ivory	3-5	4-4	2	3	11	2	1	0	0	28
Calvin Booth	7-16	4-5	8	2	18	2	0	2	0	36
Joe Crispin	3-9	0-0	1	3	7	5	4	0	1	31
Dan Earl	3-6	3-4	0	1	12	4	2	0	2	33
Greg Grays	0-1	3-4	5	0	3	2	1	0	1	25
Tyler Smith	1-2	0-0	1	0	3	0	2	0	0	4
Carl Jackson	2-3	2-2	1	3	6	0	1	1	0	14
Totals	22-48	18-21	27	15	68	15	12	3	6	200

Three-Point Field Goals: Ivory 1-2, Crispin 1-4, Earl 3-4, Grays 0-1, Smith 1-1, Team 6-12.
FG%: 1st Half 13-26 .500, 2nd Half 9-22 .409, Game 22-48 .458; 3FG%: 1st Half 4-7 .571, 2nd Half 2-5 .400, Game 6-12 .500; FT%: 1st Half 3-4 .750, 2nd Half 15-17 .882, Game 18-21 .857; Team Rebounds: 4; Deadball Rebounds: 2.

SCORE BY PERIODS	1	2	F
Michigan State	37	33	-- 70
Penn State	33	35	-- 68

OFFICIALS – Tom Rucker, Steve Welmer, Mike Sanzere
TECHNICAL FOULS – None
ATTENDANCE – 9,739

MSU 95, Iowa 81
Feb. 6, 1999 • Carver-Hawkeye Arena • Iowa City, Iowa

Michigan State	FG-FGA	FT-FTA	REB	PF	TP	A	TO	BLK	S	MIN
Andre Hutson	2-4	1-1	6	3	5	0	3	0	0	19
Jason Klein	2-3	2-2	1	4	7	4	1	0	2	20
Antonio Smith	3-6	0-2	6	4	6	0	1	0	0	25
Mateen Cleaves	5-12	0-0	2	2	14	9	1	0	2	29
Charlie Bell	5-6	6-6	5	3	16	2	1	0	1	19
Thomas Kelley	2-4	0-0	2	4	4	3	1	0	1	19
Lorenzo Guess	1-1	0-0	1	0	2	0	1	0	0	3
Brandon Smith	0-1	1-2	0	0	1	0	1	0	0	2
Steve Cherry	0-1	0-0	0	1	0	0	0	0	0	9
Doug Davis	1-2	1-2	0	2	4	2	0	1	0	2
Morris Peterson	9-12	7-8	5	4	27	2	0	1	0	28
A.J. Granger	3-5	3-4	3	2	9	0	1	0	2	25
Totals	33-57	21-27	32	25	95	22	11	2	9	200

Three-Point Field Goals: Klein 1-1, Cleaves 4-7, Kelley 0-1, Cherry 0-1, Davis 1-2, Peterson 2-3, Granger 0-2, Team 8-17.
FG%: 1st Half 20-33 .606, 2nd Half 13-24 .542, Game 33-57 .579; 3FG%: 1st Half 6-10 .600, 2nd Half 2-7 .286, Game 8-17 .471; FT%: 1st Half 3-3 1.000, 2nd Half 18-24 .750, Game 21-27 .778; Team Rebounds: 1; Deadball Rebounds: 2.

Iowa	FG-FGA	FT-FTA	REB	PF	TP	A	TO	BLK	S	MIN
Jess Settles	1-4	2-2	5	2	5	2	1	0	0	14
J.R. Koch	2-4	1-2	1	4	5	0	4	0	0	14
Jason Bauer	1-3	3-4	1	2	5	1	2	0	2	21
Dean Oliver	2-7	5-8	6	3	9	8	1	0	1	31
Kent McCausland	2-2	0-0	0	0	5	0	0	0	0	8
Sam Okey	3-5	4-9	4	3	10	1	1	0	0	21
Jason Price	0-1	0-0	1	0	0	1	0	0	0	3
Guy Rucker	4-7	0-0	1	0	8	0	0	0	0	13
Jacob Jaacks	2-5	2-2	2	2	6	0	1	0	0	13
Duez Henderson	1-1	2-2	1	0	4	0	1	0	1	10
Ryan Luehrsmann	3-6	0-0	3	3	8	4	1	0	1	24
Joey Range	7-11	2-5	4	2	16	0	0	1	2	23
Totals	28-56	21-34	31	21	81	18	11	0	7	200

Three-Point Field Goals: Settles 1-3, Koch 0-2, Bauer 0-1, Oliver 0-2, McCausland 1-1, Jaacks 0-2, Luehrsmann 2-4, Range 0-1, Team 4-16.
FG%: 1st Half 10-22 .455, 2nd Half 18-34 .529, Game 28-56 .500; 3FG%: 1st Half 1-5 .200, 2nd Half 3-11 .273, Game 4-16 .250; FT%: 1st Half 6-10 .600, 2nd Half 15-24 .625, Game 21-34 .618; Team Rebounds: 1; Deadball Rebounds: 6.

SCORE BY PERIODS	1	2	F
Michigan State	49	46	-- 95
Iowa	27	54	-- 81

OFFICIALS – Randy Drury, Jim Jenkins, Steve Skiles
TECHNICAL FOULS – None
ATTENDANCE – 15,500

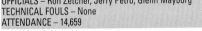

Photo Credit: Kevin Fowler, MSU Sports Information

MSU 61, Illinois 44
Feb. 11, 1999 • Breslin Center • East Lansing, Mich.

Illinois	FG-FGA	FT-FTA	REB	PF	TP	A	TO	BLK	S	MIN
Damir Krupalija	1-2	0-0	3	1	3	0	0	0	0	18
Sergio McClain	1-5	0-0	1	1	2	1	2	0	1	31
Victor Chukwudebe	2-4	0-0	3	5	4	0	0	0	1	22
Cory Bradford	4-17	1-2	2	0	13	0	3	0	0	35
Cleotis Brown	2-5	0-0	1	0	4	1	5	0	1	22
Arias Davis	0-1	0-0	0	0	0	0	0	0	0	5
Fess Hawkins	4-6	1-2	8	4	9	0	2	2	0	17
Nate Mast	2-3	0-0	0	0	5	1	0	0	0	9
Robert Archibald	0-4	4-4	3	3	4	2	1	0	1	21
Lucas Johnson	0-3	0-0	5	4	0	1	1	0	0	20
Totals	16-50	6-8	28	18	44	6	15	2	4	200

Three-Point Field Goals: Krupalija 1-1, Bradford 4-14, Brown 0-2, Mast 1-2, Johnson 0-1, Team 6-20.
FG%: 1st Half 6-25 .240, 2nd Half 10-25 .400, Game 16-50 .320; 3FG%: 1st Half 1-9 .111, 2nd Half 5-11 .455, Game 6-20 .300; FT%: 1st Half 1-2 .500, 2nd Half 5-6 .833, Game 6-8 .750; Team Rebounds: 2; Deadball Rebounds: 1.

Michigan State	FG-FGA	FT-FTA	REB	PF	TP	A	TO	BLK	S	MIN
A.J. Granger	3-4	2-3	7	0	8	1	2	0	0	27
Jason Klein	4-8	0-0	2	0	9	1	1	1	0	18
Andre Hutson	2-5	1-2	8	1	5	1	0	1	1	25
Mateen Cleaves	2-7	2-3	1	2	6	8	4	0	1	26
Charlie Bell	1-7	4-4	4	2	6	0	0	0	0	20
Thomas Kelley	5-7	0-0	1	0	10	1	1	0	1	18
Lorenzo Guess	1-1	0-0	0	0	2	0	0	0	0	4
Antonio Smith	0-2	2-2	5	2	2	0	4	1	2	23
Brandon Smith	0-1	0-0	0	0	0	0	0	0	0	2
Steve Cherry	0-0	0-0	0	0	0	1	0	0	0	2
Doug Davis	2-2	0-0	0	1	6	2	0	0	2	15
Morris Peterson	2-7	3-4	6	1	7	0	1	1	1	20
Totals	22-51	14-18	37	9	61	15	13	4	8	200

Three-Point Field Goals: Granger 0-1, Klein 1-2, Cleaves 0-4, Dell 0-2, A. Smith 0-1, Davis 2-2, Peterson 0-1, Team 3-13.
FG%: 1st Half 14-26 .538, 2nd Half 8-25 .320, Game 22-51 .431; 3FG%: 1st Half 1-7 .143, 2nd Half 2-6 .333, Game 3-13 .231; FT%: 1st Half 4-5 .800, 2nd Half 10-13 .769, Game 14-18 .778; Team Rebounds: 3; Deadball Rebounds: 3.

SCORE BY PERIODS	1	2	F
Illinois	14	30	-- 44
Michigan State	33	28	-- 61

OFFICIALS – Jim Burr, Tim Higgins, Ted Valentine
TECHNICAL FOULS – None
ATTENDANCE – 14,659

MSU 84, Minnesota 82
Feb. 13, 1999 • Williams Arena • Minneapolis, Minn.

Michigan State	FG-FGA	FT-FTA	REB	PF	TP	A	TO	BLK	S	MIN
Antonio Smith	1-2	0-0	4	3	2	1	2	0	1	26
Andre Hutson	3-3	3-6	3	4	9	0	0	0	1	32
Jason Klein	0-5	0-0	0	4	0	1	0	0	0	20
Mateen Cleaves	8-15	2-2	3	3	23	5	5	0	2	32
Charlie Bell	6-10	2-2	6	1	18	1	0	1	1	31
Thomas Kelley	0-3	0-0	1	1	0	2	1	0	0	9
Doug Davis	0-1	2-3	1	1	2	1	0	0	0	8
Morris Peterson	6-10	8-8	2	2	20	0	0	0	2	22
A.J. Granger	3-5	1-2	0	1	10	0	0	1	0	20
Totals	27-54	18-23	25	20	84	11	8	2	7	200

Three-Point Field Goals: Klein 0-3, Cleaves 5-6, Bell 4-5, Kelley 0-2, Peterson 0-2, Granger 3-4, Team 12-22.

FG%: 1st Half 12-21 .571, 2nd Half 15-33 .455, Game 27-54 .500; 3FG%: 1st Half 9-11 .818, 2nd Half 3-11 .273, Game 12-22 .545; FT%: 1st Half 10-12 .833, 2nd Half 8-11 .727, Game 18-23 .783; Team Rebounds: 5; Deadball Rebounds: 2.

Minnesota	FG-FGA	FT-FTA	REB	PF	TP	A	TO	BLK	S	MIN
Quincy Lewis	8-16	11-13	2	3	29	2	4	1	1	36
Miles Tarver	4-4	2-3	0	5	10	1	2	0	1	22
Joel Przybilla	2-4	0-0	3	1	4	3	0	3	0	27
Kevin Clark	4-6	5-7	6	1	15	2	3	0	0	39
Terrance Simmons	1-2	1-2	2	2	4	2	0	0	0	15
Mitch Ohnstad	0-0	0-0	0	0	0	0	0	0	0	4
Kevin Nathaniel	3-5	0-0	3	5	6	3	3	0	1	25
Jason Stanford	0-0	0-0	0	0	0	0	0	0	0	1
Antoine Broxsie	1-3	2-2	3	2	4	0	0	0	0	12
Dusty Rychart	4-5	2-2	6	3	10	1	2	0	0	17
Kyle Sanden	0-0	0-0	0	0	0	0	0	0	0	2
Totals	27-45	23-29	28	22	82	14	14	4	3	200

Three-Point Field Goals: Lewis 2-4, Clark 2-3, Simmons 1-2, Team 5-9.

FG%: 1st Half 13-20 .650, 2nd Half 14-25 .560, Game 27-45 .600; 3FG%: 1st Half 1-4 .250, 2nd Half 4-5 .800, Game 5-9 .556; FT%: 1st Half 13-15 .867, 2nd Half 10-14 .714, Game 23-29 .793; Team Rebounds: 3; Deadball Rebounds: 1.

SCORE BY PERIODS	1	2	F
Michigan State	43	41	-- 84
Minnesota	40	42	-- 82

OFFICIALS –Ted Hillary, Phil Bova, Randy Drury
TECHNICAL FOULS – None
ATTENDANCE – 14,887

MSU 82, Purdue 69
Feb. 16, 1999 • Breslin Center • East Lansing, Mich.

Purdue	FG-FGA	FT-FTA	REB	PF	TP	A	TO	BLK	S	MIN
Jaraan Cornell	6-12	7-11	3	3	21	0	5	0	0	31
Brian Cardinal	4-8	1-2	3	4	9	3	1	1	2	26
John Allison	1-2	0-0	3	1	2	0	0	1	0	13
Alan Eldridge	2-6	0-0	5	1	4	2	3	0	2	34
Carson Cunningham	5-9	2-2	4	0	13	2	1	0	0	24
Gary McQuay	1-2	0-0	1	1	2	2	1	0	0	11
Chad Kerkhof	0-0	0-0	0	0	0	0	0	0	0	1
Maynard Lewis	0-2	0-0	0	0	0	0	0	0	0	1
Tony Mayfield	1-1	0-0	0	3	2	0	1	0	2	12
Cameron Stephens	0-1	0-0	2	2	0	0	0	0	0	11
Mike Robinson	4-4	3-4	2	1	12	2	1	0	1	20
Rodney Smith	1-1	0-0	0	0	2	0	0	0	0	3
Greg McQuay	1-4	0-0	0	2	2	1	0	0	0	13
Totals	26-52	13-19	25	18	69	12	13	2	9	200

Three-Point Field Goals: Cornell 2-5, Cardinal 0-1, Eldridge 0-2, Cunningham 1-1, Lewis 0-2, Robinson 1-1, Team 4-12.

FG%: 1st Half 12-31 .387, 2nd Half 14-21 .667, Game 26-52 .500; 3FG%: 1st Half 1-6 .167, 2nd Half 3-6 .500, Game 4-12 .333; FT%: 1st Half 2-3 .667, 2nd Half 11-16 .688, Game 13-19 .684; Team Rebounds: 2; Deadball Rebounds: 3.

Michigan State	FG-FGA	FT-FTA	REB	PF	TP	A	TO	BLK	S	MIN
Andre Hutson	3-5	5-6	6	1	11	0	2	0	1	26
Jason Klein	7-10	3-4	1	3	22	0	0	1	0	22
Antonio Smith	1-3	0-2	6	0	2	3	2	0	4	31
Mateen Cleaves	4-6	0-0	0	2	8	11	1	0	3	28
Charlie Bell	6-12	0-0	7	1	13	1	0	0	0	24
Thomas Kelley	0-1	2-2	0	0	2	0	0	0	0	11
Lorenzo Guess	0-0	0-0	0	0	0	0	1	0	0	2
Brandon Smith	1-1	0-0	0	0	2	0	0	0	0	2
Steve Cherry	1-1	1-2	0	0	3	0	0	0	0	1
Doug Davis	2-3	2-2	1	3	6	2	1	0	0	10
Morris Peterson	4-8	1-2	1	2	9	2	1	0	1	23
A.J. Granger	1-4	2-4	3	4	4	2	2	0	0	20
Totals	30-54	16-24	29	16	82	22	13	1	10	200

Three-Point Field Goals: Klein 5-7, Bell 1-3, Davis 0-1, Peterson 0-1, Team 6-12.
FG%: 1st Half 15-29 .517, 2nd Half 15-25 .600, Game 30-54 .556; 3FG%: 1st Half 3-7 .429, 2nd Half 3-5 .600, Game 6-12 .500; FT%: 1st Half 6-7 .857, 2nd Half 10-17 .588, Game 16-24 .667; Team Rebounds: 4; Deadball Rebounds: 7.

SCORE BY PERIODS	1	2	F
Purdue	27	42	69
Michigan State	39	43	82

OFFICIALS – Ed Hightower, Tom Rucker, Phil Bova
TECHNICAL FOULS – Purdue bench
ATTENDANCE – 14,659

MSU 73, Michigan 58
Feb. 18, 1999 • Crisler Arena • Ann Arbor, Mich.

Michigan State	FG-FGA	FT-FTA	REB	PF	TP	A	TO	BLK	S	MIN
Antonio Smith	1-4	0-2	14	1	2	0	1	1	2	35
Andre Hutson	2-4	1-2	3	2	5	1	2	2	0	23
Jason Klein	5-12	0-0	7	0	11	3	0	0	0	27
Mateen Cleaves	7-11	2-2	1	4	19	8	4	1	2	31
Charlie Bell	3-5	0-0	1	5	6	0	1	0	0	16
Thomas Kelley	3-7	0-0	1	2	7	1	3	0	1	22
Doug Davis	1-2	0-1	0	0	3	2	0	0	0	9
Morris Peterson	3-5	4-5	4	4	10	0	1	0	1	16
A.J. Granger	4-7	2-2	4	4	10	1	4	0	0	21
Totals	29-57	9-14	36	22	73	12	16	3	6	200

Three-Point Field Goals: Klein 1-5, Cleaves 3-6, Bell 0-1, Kelley 1-1, Davis 1-2, Granger 0-1, Team 6-16.

FG%: 1st Half 14-32 .438, 2nd Half 15-25 .600, Game 29-57 .509; 3FG%: 1st Half 5-11 .455, 2nd Half 1-5 .200, Game 6-16 .375; FT%: 1st Half 2-4 .500, 2nd Half 7-10 .700, Game 9-14 .643; Team Rebounds: 4; Deadball Rebounds: 5.

Michigan	FG-FGA	FT-FTA	REB	PF	TP	A	TO	BLK	S	MIN
Josh Asselin	4-7	4-7	5	3	12	1	2	2	0	35
Brandon Smith	4-7	2-2	4	2	10	2	3	0	3	25
Peter Vignier	1-3	6-6	5	3	8	1	1	0	0	30
Robbie Reid	5-15	2-3	4	1	13	1	1	0	1	37
Louis Bullock	4-12	6-10	3	3	15	1	3	0	0	37
Leon Jones	0-1	0-0	1	3	0	0	1	0	0	20
Ron Oliver	0-0	0-0	0	0	0	0	0	0	0	1
Chris Young	0-1	0-0	0	2	0	0	2	0	0	15
Totals	18-46	20-28	24	17	58	6	14	2	4	200

Three-Point Field Goals: Smith 0-1, Reid 1-4, Bullock 1-3, Team 2-8.

FG%: 1st Half 11-23 .478, 2nd Half 7-23 .304, Game 18-46 .391; 3FG%: 1st Half 1-5 .200, 2nd Half 1-3 .333, Game 2-8 .250; FT%: 1st Half 5-9 .556, 2nd Half 15-19 .789, Game 20-28 .714; Team Rebounds: 2; Deadball Rebounds: 4.

SCORE BY PERIODS	1	2	F
Michigan State	35	38	73
Michigan	28	30	58

OFFICIALS – Ted Hillary, Steve Welmer, Tom O'Neill
TECHNICAL FOULS – Cleaves (MSU), Bullock (UM)
ATTENDANCE – 13,548

MSU 56, Wisconsin 51
Feb. 21, 1999 • Breslin Center • East Lansing, Mich.

Wisconsin	FG-FGA	FT-FTA	REB	PF	TP	A	TO	BLK	S	MIN
Sean Mason	4-12	3-3	7	4	13	2	2	0	1	28
Maurice Linton	0-0	0-0	0	3	0	0	0	0	0	4
Andy Kowske	3-8	0-0	3	2	6	0	1	1	0	26
Ty Calderwood	3-10	0-0	2	4	9	3	1	0	2	29
Mike Kelley	1-2	0-0	4	2	2	1	1	1	0	31
Hennssy Auriantal	1-2	0-0	0	3	2	0	0	0	1	6
Jon Bryant	2-5	0-0	1	2	5	0	0	0	0	26
Charlie Wills	1-2	2-2	2	4	4	0	1	0	1	23
Mark Vershaw	2-5	6-6	0	3	10	2	1	0	1	27
Totals	17-46	11-11	19	27	51	8	11	2	6	200

Three-Point Field Goals: Mason 2-5, Calderwood 3-8, Bryant 1-4, Team 6-17.

FG%: 1st Half 7-20 .350, 2nd Half 10-26 .385, Game 17-46 .370; 3FG%: 1st Half 1-4 .250, 2nd Half 5-13 .385, Game 6-17 .353; FT%: 1st Half 4-4 1.000, 2nd Half 7-7 1.000, Game 11-11 1.000; Team Rebounds: 0; Deadball Rebounds: 4.

Michigan State	FG-FGA	FT-FTA	REB	PF	TP	A	TO	BLK	S	MIN
Andre Hutson	2-5	4-4	10	4	8	0	2	0	0	25
Jason Klein	2-6	1-2	0	1	5	0	0	1	0	22
Antonio Smith	2-4	0-0	11	3	4	2	0	0	1	33
Mateen Cleaves	2-12	5-5	1	2	9	4	2	0	1	29
Charlie Bell	1-4	2-4	3	0	4	0	2	0	0	23
Thomas Kelley	1-4	2-2	0	2	4	2	1	0	0	13
Lorenzo Guess	0-0	0-0	0	0	0	0	0	0	0	1
Brandon Smith	0-0	0-0	0	0	0	0	0	0	0	1
Steve Cherry	0-0	0-0	0	0	0	0	0	0	0	1
Doug Davis	1-1	0-0	0	0	2	1	1	0	0	10
Morris Peterson	2-5	9-13	3	1	13	0	0	0	1	22
A.J. Granger	3-3	1-2	6	3	7	0	1	0	0	20
Totals	16-44	24-32	39	16	56	9	11	1	4	200

Three-Point Field Goals: Klein 0-1, Cleaves 0-3, Team 0-4.

FG%: 1st Half 7-20 .350, 2nd Half 9-24 .375, Game 16-44 .364; 3FG%: 1st Half 0-2 .000, 2nd Half 0-2 .000, Game 0-4 .000; FT%: 1st Half 7-10 .700, 2nd Half 17-22 .773, Game 24-32 .750; Team Rebounds: 5; Deadball Rebounds: 3.

SCORE BY PERIODS	1	2	F
Wisconsin	19	32	51
Michigan State	21	35	56

OFFICIALS – Ed Hightower, Rick Hartzell, Donnee Gray
TECHNICAL FOULS – None
ATTENDANCE – 14,659

MSU 60, Purdue 46
Feb. 28, 1999 • Mackey Arena • West Lafayette, Ind.

Michigan State	FG-FGA	FT-FTA	REB	PF	TP	A	TO	BLK	S	MIN
Antonio Smith	6-8	0-2	8	2	12	0	2	0	2	31
Andre Hutson	2-2	2-2	4	4	6	0	3	0	1	23
Jason Klein	1-8	2-2	3	0	4	1	3	0	1	24
Mateen Cleaves	3-7	1-2	2	3	8	4	3	0	0	26
Charlie Bell	2-6	3-4	5	2	7	2	1	0	0	28
Thomas Kelley	1-4	0-0	2	1	2	1	0	0	1	9
Doug Davis	3-6	0-0	3	0	7	2	0	0	0	14
Morris Peterson	3-6	2-2	6	2	8	2	2	2	0	25
A.J. Granger	3-5	0-0	5	2	6	0	2	0	1	20
Totals	24-52	10-14	39	16	60	12	16	3	8	200

Three-Point Field Goals: Klein 0-2, Cleaves 1-2, Davis 1-4, Granger 0-1, Team 2-9.

FG%: 1st Half 9-27 .333, 2nd Half 15-25 .600, Game 24-52 .462; 3FG%: 1st Half 2-6 .333, 2nd Half 0-3 .000, Game 2-9 .222; FT%: 1st Half 4-6 .667, 2nd Half 6-8 .750, Game 10-14 .714; Team Rebounds: 1; Deadball Rebounds: 3.

Purdue	FG-FGA	FT-FTA	REB	PF	TP	A	TO	BLK	S	MIN
Brian Cardinal	2-4	3-6	2	5	8	2	1	0	2	19
Greg McQuay	6-8	0-2	7	2	12	1	3	0	1	38
Alan Eldridge	5-11	0-1	3	0	11	2	4	1	3	35
Tony Mayfield	1-3	0-0	2	3	2	2	2	0	0	26
Jaraan Cornell	3-10	4-5	1	1	11	5	1	0	0	32
Gary McQuay	0-1	0-0	0	0	0	1	1	0	0	17
Maynard Lewis	1-4	0-0	1	0	2	0	0	0	0	11
Cameron Stephens	0-0	0-0	0	1	0	0	0	0	0	3
Rodney Smith	0-1	0-0	0	0	0	0	0	0	0	6
Carson Cunningham	0-3	0-0	2	0	0	1	1	0	0	10
John Allison	0-0	0-0	1	1	0	0	0	0	0	2
Totals	18-45	7-14	20	14	46	14	14	1	6	200

Three-Point Field Goals: Cardinal 1-2, Eldridge 1-5, Cornell 1-5, Cunningham 0-1, Team 3-13.

FG%: 1st Half 8-25 .320, 2nd Half 10-20 .500, Game 18-45 .400; 3FG%: 1st Half 2-7 .286, 2nd Half 1-6 .167, Game 3-13 .231; FT%: 1st Half 3-4 .750, 2nd Half 4-10 .400, Game 7-14 .500; Team Rebounds: 1; Deadball Rebounds: 4.

SCORE BY PERIODS	1	2	F
Michigan State	24	36	60
Purdue	21	25	46

OFFICIALS – Ed Hightower, Jody Silvester, Dan Christman
TECHNICAL FOULS – None
ATTENDANCE – 14,123

1999 Big Ten Tournament

Tom Izzo had always been a backer of the Big Ten Basketball Tournament, even before it was established.

When Iowa coach Tom Davis argued in favor and Indiana's Bob Knight railed against it year after year, Izzo weighed the evidence and wondered, "Why not?"

If a postseason event was as evil as Knight made it seem, why did every conference except the Big Ten, the Pac-10 and the Ivy League have one?

"Who gets hurt by it?" Izzo asked. "The exposure has to be good for recruiting. The players all seem to want it. It's a rallying point for fans and alumni. And it might help some team play its way into the NCAA Tournament."

The question was: "Which team?"

When he took over for Jud Heathcote, Izzo's program needed a break to be more than an NIT invitee. But the Big Ten Tournament didn't begin until 1998, when Michigan State was a surprise No. 1 seed. Suddenly, it could only lose the respect it had worked nine weeks to gain.

That's what happened in the league's inaugural event in Chicago's United Center. The top-seeded Spartans were spanked by eighth-seeded Minnesota 76-73, as Mateen Cleaves was embarrassed by fellow point guard Eric Harris.

Twelve months later, MSU was riding even higher with a gaudy 15-1 conference mark. That meant another Thursday bye, the second of four in a row-and-counting. And it created another 1-vs.-8 matchup, after Northwestern beat No. 9 seed Penn State 54-44 in the week's first game.

The Spartans and Wildcats had met just once in 1999, a 65-48 MSU win on Jan. 30 in Breslin Center. And with as many league victories as Northwestern's total in a 15-12 near-breakthrough season, Cleaves & Co. had to feel good about their chances.

They were right, as three more triumphs — Nos. 16, 17 and 18 in a row — and a net-snipping ceremony on Sunday proved their dominance beyond a shadow of a doubt.

First, though, there was the matter of caging the Wildcats, bet-

Photo Credit: Kevin Fowler, MSU Sports Information

ter known as "The Evan & Kevin Show" for All-America center Evan Eschmeyer and All-Adrenalin coach Kevin O'Neill.

The 6-foot-11 Eschmeyer was an All-Big Ten choice for the third-straight year and a legitimate candidate for league MVP in his sixth season. He certainly could have had Izzo's vote and those of his players.

"Eschmeyer is the best guy I've ever faced in the post," MSU forward Andre Hutson said. "He gets the ball and you get the feeling

Photo Credit: Kevin Fowler, MSU Sports Information

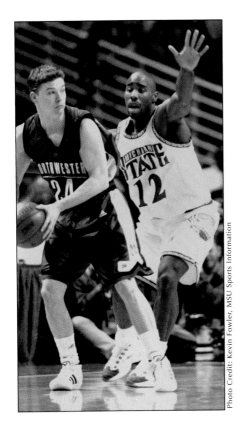

Photo Credit: Kevin Fowler, MSU Sports Information

you're really going to have to come up with something big every time to stop him."

O'Neill's players had one other potent weapon — the knowledge of assistant coach Brian Gregory, an MSU aide from 1990-96 and again starting in 1999.

Thanks largely to Gregory, the Wildcats knew exactly what the Spartans were running on offense and defense and anticipated perfectly.

"We were calling it out as they came down the floor," Gregory said. "They hadn't changed any of their calls. And our guys were really prepared. Because I'd been there before. I think that added a little bit of confidence. Eschmeyer always felt good about playing Michigan State, too."

Why shouldn't he have been confident? Northwestern had played the Spartans about as well as any Big Ten team over a two-year span and was due for another victory, just its second in the series since 1987.

"We played Michigan State three times when I was with Kevin," Gregory said in March 2001. "We lost in overtime at our place in '98. They beat us by 17 here the next year. Then, we went down to the last minute in the Tournament."

When Izzo said his fourth MSU team had a knack for winning close games, there was no greater scare than this one, with Eschmeyer 11-for-16 from the field and 8-for-8 at the line in a 30-point effort.

"They went in to Eschmeyer every time, just as they have for the past three years," Izzo said on March 5, 1999. "We didn't guard him at all. And it's not that we didn't try. He was just better than us."

Eschmeyer was good enough to make everyone in attendance think the Spartans were headed home on Friday again — everyone except some players in white jerseys.

"The thing I remember most was we had three freshmen on the court (forwards Tavaras Hardy and Steve Lepore and guard David Newman), and Eschmeyer was completely carrying us," Gregory said. "Eschmeyer always played well against them."

He did that again. But it wasn't enough. The Wildcats couldn't get the ball to him in the last

3:06. Meanwhile, MSU engineered another comeback for a 61-59 escape.

"We're up five, and Michigan State scores seven straight points on us — Mateen, Morris Peterson and Mateen again," Gregory said. "You knew right then that those guys had done it all year. That was the difference. Our two freshmen wound up taking the last two shots to tie it and win it."

Newman had a layup blocked into the band by MSU center

Photo Credit: Kevin Fowler, MSU Sports Information

1999 BIG TEN TOURNAMENT

Photo Credit: Kevin Fowler, MSU Sports Information

Antonio Smith with three seconds left. And Lepore missed a relatively open 3 at the buzzer that would have won it, after his team had gone 6-for-8 beyond the arc.

"That was the game when Eschmeyer had 100, but 'Tone had the big block late in the game," Izzo remembered. "And Brian, that jerk, nearly helped beat us! But there again, that was another close game that we won."

The Wildcats lost it as much and the Spartans won it. When Northwestern went away from an unstoppable force, it probably didn't deserve to win, especially when it was outrebounded 39-23.

"We got away from going to 'Esch' down the stretch," O'Neill said after a postgame embrace of Izzo, one of his closest friends in coaching. "Part of that was us being young. Part of that was Michigan State."

Hutson led the winners with 15 points, his highest total in nearly three-and-a-half months. Forward Jason Klein added 13. And for one of the few times in their careers, none of the "Flintstones" scored in double digits. Guard Charlie Bell had seven points, Cleaves and Smith six apiece and Peterson five.

Cleaves was 1-for-8 from the field and Peterson 1-for-6 before they combined for the Spartans' last three baskets, including the game-winner on Cleaves' 7-foot jumper with 37 ticks left.

It was much easier for MSU from there. If a team was going to get the Spartans in Chicago, it had to happen on Friday.

Saturday's game with fourth-seeded Wisconsin was another struggle for the first 20 minutes. But MSU's depth and defense made the difference in the second half of a 56-41 triumph.

"We got our running game going off our defense," Izzo said of a school-record 17th-straight win. "Maybe they got tired when we kept running fresh bodies in."

The Spartans trailed 18-8 but tied it at 22 by halftime, as they held the Badgers scoreless for the last 3:30. And that was just the start of Dick Bennett's team's problems.

MSU broke the game open wih a 12-0 run after the intermission, extending Wisconsin's scoreless period to 10:14. The Badgers never got closer than 10 points the rest of the way.

Cleaves had 14 points and 11 assists. Peterson had 10 points off

the bench. And Smith added eight points and a game-high 12 rebounds, as Flint was the basketball capital of the Midwest again.

It was the perfect payback for the Spartans' only Big Ten setback, a 15-point decision in Madison exactly two months earlier. It also showed Wisconsin's offensive ineptitude, soon reflected in a 43-32 loss to Southwest Missouri State in the opening round of the NCAA Tournament.

When MSU reached the championship game, it never expected to meet Illinois, an 11th seed that could have caused an 11th-hour shuffle of the NCAA Tournament bracket with a fourth-straight upset.

Instead, the Spartans succeeded Michigan as the Big Ten Tournament champ with a 67-50 statement, their school-record 29th victory of the season and their third tournament title.

Photo Credit: Kevin Fowler, MSU Sports Information

1999 BIG TEN TOURNAMENT

Photo Credit: Kevin Fowler, MSU Sports Information

Hutson and Peterson led the winners with 11 points apiece. Cleaves had nine points and 10 assists to earn Most Outstanding Player honors in a 29-point, 29-assist, five-turnover weekend. And Smith grabbed 13 rebounds, giving him 32 for the weekend and a spot on the All-Tournament team.

"We knew they were going to be tired in their fourth game in four days," Hutson said. "So we really wanted to dominate on the boards. As the game went on, it became easy to get rebounds."

The loss ended Illinois' season at 14-18. It also locked up a No. 1 seed in the NCAA Tournament's Midwest Region for the Spartans.

And roughly an hour after the game ended, MSU learned it would open NCAA play in Milwaukee against No. 16 seed Mount St. Mary's.

"We had a sour taste in our mouths last year after sharing the regular-season title with Illinois and losing our first game here in the Big Ten Tournament to Minnesota," Bell said. "This feels great."

Not as great as the glory ahead, as championships became much more than a dream. They became a way of life for a team and a coach who liked the Big Ten Tournament just fine on March 7, 1999.

"It's one thing to tell the world about your goals and another thing to accomplish them," Izzo said proudly. "I think (Big Ten Commissioner) Jim Delany put it best when he said, 'This is not a flash-in-the-pan team. They did it in December, January, February and March.'"

Guard Thomas Kelley scored seven quick points off the bench, as MSU grabbed a 38-25 halftime lead. And after blanking the Fighting Illini for the first 4:47 after the break, the margin ballooned to 47-25.

A 40-24 edge in rebounds, including 18 at the offensive end, led to 20 second-chance points. It also triggered another postgame celebration, despite 21 points from Illinois guard Cory Bradford.

Photo Credit: Kevin Fowler, MSU Sports Information

MSU 61, Northwestern 59
March 5, 1999 • United Center • Chicago, Ill.

Northwestern	FG-FGA	FT-FTA	REB	PF	TP	A	TO	BLK	S	MIN
Tavaras Hardy	0-1	0-0	0	3	0	1	1	0	0	19
Steve Lepore	3-8	2-2	5	0	11	9	3	0	0	33
Evan Eschmeyer	11-16	8-8	6	3	30	2	4	2	1	34
Julian Bonner	1-2	0-0	2	2	3	2	2	0	0	33
David Newman	2-6	0-0	1	2	6	3	2	0	3	32
Joe Harmsen	0-0	0-0	0	1	0	0	0	0	0	3
Sean Wink	0-1	0-0	2	3	0	1	1	0	1	23
Aron Molnar	4-7	1-2	5	2	9	0	0	0	0	20
Jeff Eschmeyer	0-0	0-0	0	1	0	0	0	0	0	3
Totals	21-41	11-12	23	17	59	18	14	2	5	200

Three-Point Field Goals: Lepore 3-5, Bonner 1-1, Newman 2-2, Wink 0-1, Team 6-9.

FG%: 1st Half 8-18 .444, 2nd Half 13-23 .565, Game 21-41 .512; 3FG%: 1st Half 3-6 .500, 2nd Half 3-3 1.000, Game 6-9 .667; FT%: 1st Half 3-4 .750, 2nd Half 8-8 1.000, Game 11-12 .917; Team Rebounds: 2; Deadball Rebounds: 0.

Michigan State	FG-FGA	FT-FTA	REB	PF	TP	A	TO	BLK	S	MIN
Jason Klein	5-11	2-2	3	1	13	0	2	0	1	26
Andre Hutson	5-6	5-6	6	3	15	1	3	0	2	27
Antonio Smith	2-5	2-2	7	3	6	2	2	2	3	26
Mateen Cleaves	3-10	0-0	0	1	6	8	1	0	1	32
Charlie Bell	3-8	0-2	5	0	7	3	0	0	0	26
Thomas Kelley	1-3	0-0	2	0	2	2	1	0	0	12
Doug Davis	0-1	0-2	1	1	0	0	0	0	0	8
Morris Peterson	2-7	0-2	6	2	5	0	2	0	0	23
A.J. Granger	3-4	0-0	2	4	7	0	0	0	2	20
Totals	24-55	9-16	34	15	61	16	11	2	9	200

Three-Point Field Goals: Klein 1-1, Cleaves 0-4, Bell 1-2, Peterson 1-1, Granger 1-1, Team 4-9.

FG%: 1st Half 12-28 .429, 2nd Half 12-27 .444, Game 24-55 .436; 3FG%: 1st Half 0-4 .000, 2nd Half 4-5 .800, Game 4-9 .444; FT%: 1st Half 0-2 .000, 2nd Half 9-14 .643, Game 9-16 .563; Team Rebounds: 2; Deadball Rebounds: 2.

SCORE BY PERIODS	1	2	F
Northwestern	22	37	-- 59
Michigan State	24	37	-- 61

OFFICIALS – Gene Monje, Tom Clark, Randy Drury
TECHNICAL FOULS – None
ATTENDANCE – 17,000

MSU 56, Wisconsin 41
March 6, 1999 • United Center • Chicago, Ill.

Wisconsin	FG-FGA	FT-FTA	REB	PF	TP	A	TO	BLK	S	MIN
Andy Kowske	6-10	3-3	6	1	15	1	1	1	0	33
Maurice Linton	0-4	0-0	3	2	0	1	3	1	0	17
Charlie Wills	2-6	0-0	6	3	4	0	1	1	1	19
Ty Calderwood	1-6	0-0	2	2	2	1	0	0	0	26
Sean Mason	3-15	1-3	9	1	9	2	2	0	0	32
Travon Davis	0-0	0-0	0	0	0	1	0	0	0	1
Jon Bryant	0-6	0-0	0	1	0	2	0	0	0	21
Mike Kelley	0-2	0-0	1	3	0	1	0	0	0	26
David Burkempe	1-1	0-0	0	1	3	0	0	0	0	1
Mark Vershaw	4-8	0-0	4	1	8	2	1	1	0	24
Totals	17-58	4-6	36	15	41	10	9	4	1	200

Three-Point Field Goals: Calderwood 0-5, Mason 2-7, Bryant 0-3, Kelley 0-1, Burkempe 1-1, Team 3-17.

FG%: 1st Half 10-29 .345, 2nd Half 7-29 .241, Game 17-58 .293; 3FG%: 1st Half 1-8 .125, 2nd Half 2-9 .222, Game 3-17 .176; FT%: 1st Half 1-1 1.000, 2nd Half 3-5 .600, Game 4-6 .667; Team Rebounds: 5; Deadball Rebounds: 0.

Michigan State	FG-FGA	FT-FTA	REB	PF	TP	A	TO	BLK	S	MIN
Jason Klein	1-6	2-2	3	0	4	0	0	0	1	23
Andre Hutson	0-4	4-4	3	0	4	1	0	0	0	27
Antonio Smith	4-5	0-0	12	3	8	1	2	0	1	33
Mateen Cleaves	5-10	4-5	3	2	14	11	1	0	1	31
Charlie Bell	3-8	0-0	3	3	8	1	0	0	0	22
Thomas Kelley	3-6	0-0	1	2	6	1	1	0	2	16
Lorenzo Guess	0-0	0-0	0	0	0	0	0	0	0	1
Brandon Smith	0-0	0-0	0	0	0	0	0	0	0	1
Steve Cherry	0-0	0-0	0	0	0	0	0	0	0	1
Doug Davis	0-1	0-1	1	0	0	1	2	0	0	8
Morris Peterson	5-6	0-0	3	5	10	0	1	1	1	18
A.J. Granger	1-5	0-0	5	0	2	0	0	1	0	19
Totals	22-51	10-12	38	15	56	16	7	2	6	200

Three-Point Field Goals: Klein 0-1, Cleaves 0-2, Bell 2-3, Davis 0-1, Team 2-7.

FG%: 1st Half 9-25 .360, 2nd Half 13-26 .500, Game 22-51 .431; 3FG%: 1st Half 0-4 .000, 2nd Half 2-3 .667, Game 2-7 .286; FT%: 1st Half 4-4 1.000, 2nd Half 6-8 .750, Game 10-12 .833; Team Rebounds: 4; Deadball Rebounds: 0.

SCORE BY PERIODS	1	2	F
Wisconsin	22	19	-- 41
Michigan State	22	34	-- 56

OFFICIALS – Ed Hightower, Ted Hillary, Gene Monje
TECHNICAL FOULS – None
ATTENDANCE – 17,000

MSU 67, Illinois 50
March 7, 1999 • United Center • Chicago, Ill.

Illinois	FG-FGA	FT-FTA	REB	PF	TP	A	TO	BLK	S	MIN
Damir Krupalija	0-1	0-0	2	0	0	2	1	0	1	27
Sergio McClain	2-5	2-5	1	0	6	2	3	0	2	30
Victor Chukwudebe	1-1	1-2	1	1	3	0	0	1	1	20
Cory Bradford	7-17	1-2	3	0	21	0	3	0	0	36
Lucas Johnson	3-7	3-5	2	4	9	1	2	0	1	27
Fess Hawkins	3-6	3-6	6	3	9	1	1	0	2	20
Nate Mast	0-0	0-0	0	0	0	0	1	0	0	4
Robert Archibald	0-1	0-0	3	1	0	2	4	0	2	13
Cleotis Brown	1-5	0-0	2	3	2	2	1	0	1	23
Totals	17-43	10-20	24	12	50	10	16	1	10	200

Three-Point Field Goals: Krupalija 0-1, McClain 0-1, Bradford 6-9, Brown 0-3, Team 6-14.

FG%: 1st Half 8-20 .400, 2nd Half 9-23 .391, Game 17-43 .395; 3FG%: 1st Half 2-4 .500, 2nd Half 4-10 .400, Game 6-14 .500; FT%: 1st Half 7-13 .538, 2nd Half 3-7 .429, Game 10-20 .500; Team Rebounds: 4; Deadball Rebounds: 5.

Michigan State	FG-FGA	FT-FTA	REB	PF	TP	A	TO	BLK	S	MIN
Jason Klein	2-9	0-0	1	2	6	3	2	0	0	21
Andre Hutson	4-7	3-4	6	1	11	1	0	1	1	25
Antonio Smith	4-6	1-2	13	3	9	2	3	1	2	33
Mateen Cleaves	4-6	0-0	0	2	9	10	4	0	1	31
Charlie Bell	3-6	0-0	1	0	6	1	1	0	3	23
Thomas Kelley	4-7	0-0	1	1	9	1	1	1	0	12
Lorenzo Guess	0-1	0-0	0	0	0	0	0	0	0	1
Brandon Smith	0-1	0-0	0	0	0	0	0	0	0	1
Steve Cherry	0-1	0-0	0	0	0	0	0	0	0	1
Doug Davis	0-2	0-0	0	2	0	1	2	1	0	9
Morris Peterson	5-10	0-0	10	3	11	0	1	0	1	22
A.J. Granger	2-3	2-4	2	2	6	1	1	0	0	21
Totals	28-59	6-10	40	16	67	20	15	4	9	200

Three-Point Field Goals: Klein 2-7, Cleaves 1-3, Bell 0-2, Kelley 1-2, Cherry 0-1, Davis 0-1, Peterson 1-2, Team 5-18.

FG%: 1st Half 16-34 .471, 2nd Half 12-25 .480, Game 28-59 .475; 3FG%: 1st Half 3-10 .300, 2nd Half 2-8 .250, Game 5-18 .278; FT%: 1st Half 3-4 .750, 2nd Half 3-6 .500, Game 6-10 .600; Team Rebounds: 5; Deadball Rebounds: 2.

SCORE BY PERIODS	1	2	F
Illinois	25	25	-- 50
Michigan State	38	29	-- 67

OFFICIALS – Ed Hightower, Tom Rucker, Ted Hillary
TECHNICAL FOULS – None
ATTENDANCE – 19,581

1999 NCAA TOURNAMENT

If respect always comes with winning, so does responsibility. And with 18 straight triumphs, the Michigan State Spartans had plenty to prove as the No. 1 seed in the NCAA Tournament's Midwest Region.

Tom Izzo's 29-4 team, the most successful group in school history, had to show up on time for a first-round tuneup with overmatched Mount St. Mary's.

It had to survive bruising battles with Mississippi in Milwaukee and Oklahoma in St. Louis. And it had to overtake defending national titlist Kentucky, a No. 3 seed that was picked to advance.

It had to demonstrate it belonged on a Final Four stage with megapowers Duke and Connecticut, plus Big Ten co-champ Ohio State. Finally, its representatives had to handle themselves with class and dignity — win or lose, at home as well as in St. Petersburg, Fla.

If that turned out to be too much to ask in MSU's longest post-season ride in two decades, it wasn't because Izzo, his staff and his players gave up under the glare of the spotlight. Instead, they were victims of events beyond their control.

"I think the pressure started to get to us, as far as how many games we'd won," Izzo remembered. "It was 16, 17, 18 . . . and now we're being talked about as a No. 1 seed. It was something we hadn't experienced before."

Izzo and top assistant Tom Crean had. The Spartans had been a No. 1 seed in the NCAA

Tournament once before — in 1990, when they came as close to losing to a 16th seed as any team has in a 75-71 overtime game against Murray State.

MSU was eliminated that year in the Sweet 16. A shot after the buzzer by Georgia Tech's Kenny Anderson mistakenly sent the game into overtime, where Jud Heathcote's 28-5 team soon became 28-6.

But instead of dwelling on disappointments when sophomore starters Charlie Bell and Andre Hutson were fifth-graders, Izzo's staff stressed the fact the 1999 Spartans were a worthy No. 1 seed.

"You know what started to happen?" Izzo said two years later. "Nobody on our team thought we could lose. Somehow, we were going to find ways to win. And we'd already found so many ways. The Minnesota game was one we had no business winning. Northwestern in the Big Ten

Tournament was the same way. I'll bet we won eight close games that year."

No one expected a close one with Mount St. Mary's, a 15-14 team that surprised nearly everyone outside the program by winning the Northeast Conference Tournament.

Still, Izzo had been victimized by the Mountaineers and legendary coach Jim Phelan, bow ties and all, in his playing days. And that memory lingered as he recalled a visit to Emmitsburg, Md., in March 1977.

"My career at Northern Michigan ended in an airplane hanger at Mount St. Mary's," Izzo said. "We got beat in the quarterfinals, when we should've been in the Division II Final Four. Jim's team won its game to get there with :01 left. It had to go the length of the court. A guy came up to set a screen, got run over and made two free throws.

"We were still supposed to play at our place. There was a rule then in Division II that your gym had to hold at least 2,500. So they put an annex onto the gym, put closed-circuit TV in there and sold tickets to meet the minimum. We went out there and got beat by a couple."

Izzo had plenty of motivation without a 22-year-old score to settle. But his players weren't convinced. Somehow, the Mountaineers led or were even with the Spartans through most of the first seven minutes at the Bradley Center.

"Let's pick it up! Let's pick it up!" MSU point guard Mateen

1999 NCAA TOURNAMENT

Cleaves hollered at his teammates after his layup and free throw gave the winners a 22-16 lead.

The rest of a 14-2 run made it 25-16. The Spartans led 38-24 at the break. And it was 48-28 early in the second half, as center Antonio Smith and backup forward A.J. Granger took control in a 76-53 victory — win No. 30.

Smith, who sat out the last 6:35 of the first half with two fouls, finished with 14 points and 12 rebounds — nearly half Mount St. Mary's total in being outboarded 46-22. And Granger led all scorers with 15 points, going 5-for-7 from the field.

MSU shot 50 percent and held the Mountaineers to 32 percent. But 19 turnovers, including back-to-back giveaways on inbounds passes, gave Izzo plenty of ammunition during the game and at Saturday's practice.

"Our goal is to win the national championship," forward Morris Peterson said after coming off the bench to grab 12 rebounds. "We didn't come close to giving a championship effort tonight. And Coach really let us have it during timeouts and at halftime."

The lead swelled to 32 points. Yet, the Spartans weren't fooled by the scoreboard. They understood their level of play had to improve dramatically against the Rebels on Sunday to avoid a second-round knockout.

"When Mateen was screaming at us, it gave us a final wakeup call," said guard Thomas Kelley, whose 3-pointer put MSU ahead to stay, 17-14, with 12:30 left in the

first half. "He said what needed to be said. Now, we need to learn from this and not let it happen again."

Pressure was suddenly a consideration. After catching conference opponents a bit off-guard with 15 straight regular-season wins and three more in the Big Ten Tournament, the Spartans were under the glare of the CBS eye.

"That's when the NCAA Tournament became more nerve-wracking," Izzo said. "The year before, anything we did was good. But the next year, we were supposed to win. We had a lot of State people there in Milwaukee. But the second game against Mississippi was a heckuva game."

The ninth-seeded Rebels, 20-12, had advanced with a 72-70 win over eighth-seeded Villanova. And Ole Miss gave MSU all it could handle before a second straight sellout crowd of 18,525 at the Bradley Center.

The Spartans trailed the Rebels through most of a sloppy first half and were down 32-29 at the break, only the second time they had

trailed after 20 minutes in 20 games.

Part of the problem was a different rotation, with Peterson starting in place of Bell, who had sprained his left ankle against Mount St. Mary's and was limited to 14 minutes off the bench.

The other part was Ole Miss's quickness, the key to a surprising 18-17 edge in first-half rebounds. But a different team emerged from the locker room and put the Rebels away with a 13-0 run late in the second half.

On a day when five of the eight higher seeds were upset, MSU appeared vulnerable, too, when 5-foot-5 point guard Jason Harrison hit a 3 over 6-2 Mateen Cleaves as the shot clock expired for a 59-56 lead.

But Cleaves answered with a 3 of his own, his only one of the day, to tie it at 59 with 4:54 left. Forward Andre Hutson blocked a shot and Cleaves converted on a drive for a two-point lead. When Smith scored on a putback, Cleaves added another layup and Peterson hit a 15-footer, the Spartans had their eight-point margin.

"I never thought about us losing the game," said Cleaves, who led the winners with 18 points. "I just knew we were going to leave everything we had on the floor, and it would turn out OK."

Izzo wasn't quite so sure. But with the ball in Cleaves' hands in the closing minutes, MSU had reason for optimism.

"People can say a lot of things about his game," Izzo said. "But they'd better always say he's a winner. He may be 2-for-12 from the field and he may do this and that. But all the kid does is win games."

Cleaves was 7-for-14 against Ole Miss, as his team outshot the Rebels 47.2 percent from the field to 42.9. The Spartans had a 19-11 lead in second-half rebounds and committed just five turnovers after the break.

Yet, no one felt safe until Peterson's jumper off a timeout made it 67-59 with 2:00 left and made Izzo leap high in the air. And why not? It all-but-assured MSU of a return trip to the Sweet 16 — a streak that has stretched to four years-and-counting.

"He's so into the game it seems like he's out on the court playing with us," Smith said. "We play through his personality. We couldn't have done what we did today or have done all season without him."

The Spartans returned home until the following Wednesday, when they left for St. Louis and a date with Kelvin Sampson's inspired Sooners, a 13th seed that had stunned fourth-seeded Arizona, 61-60, and fifth-seeded UNC Charlotte, 85-72.

"Of all teams to play, we get Oklahoma, which had just pulled two upsets," Izzo said. "They were coached by a guy who'd been at Michigan State and ran a system a lot like we did. He came from the Jud World, too. So I knew how tough they'd be. I really liked their team. And they were playing well at the time."

They were good enough to take MSU's best punch and get up for another round in a 54-46 split-decision, with the biggest split coming in OU forward Eduardo Najera's chin.

The Spartans and the Sooners

exchanged the lead 13 times and were tied five times in the first half. Thanks to Granger's 10 points and 4-for-4 shooting, MSU took a 26-25 edge to the locker room.

A 6-0 run to start the second half was huge, as OU never drew closer than three points the rest of the way. But the drama was just beginning.

With 9:04 remaining, Najera tried to set a blind pick in the backcourt on Cleaves, who was applying token defensive pressure. The sound of their collision was heard across the Mississippi River.

Najera, a sturdy 6-8, 235, was knocked out and had blood gushing from a gash that took six quick stitches on the court. Cleaves had already been ushered to the bench during a scary 10-minute stoppage.

"When you see him face-down with blood pouring out of his chin,

it makes you realize what these kids mean to you," Sampson said.

Both players were the heart-and-soul of their teams. And it shouldn't surprise anyone that Cleaves checked back into the game with a bruised forehead with 6:54 to play or that Najera returned with a concussion and a zipper on his chin at the 4:25 mark.

"The thing I remember most about that game was the big collision," Izzo said. "That was a football game, boy! It was a physical, tough game. And Kelvin's team was good. I had a lot of respect for him and his guys. That was a real big win for us."

The Spartans outshot the Sooners from the field, 40 percent to 33.3. And the winners had a 36-31 edge in rebounds in their 32nd triumph, tying a Big Ten record set by the 1975-76 Indiana Hoosiers.

MSU's forwards did most of the scoring, as Hutson had 12 points and Peterson 11. Peterson, Granger and Smith all had seven rebounds, as depth was the difference for the Spartans.

"We have a golden opportunity to get to the Final Four now," Bell said. "We've dreamed about doing that since we were kids. The Elite Eight is nice. But that's not where we want our season to finish."

To keep that from happening, MSU had to defeat a Kentucky program that had been to three straight Final Fours and gone 20-1 in the last four Tournaments, losing in overtime to Arizona between NCAA titles.

But before that Sunday afternoon classic, four things happened that Izzo will never forget.

"That was when we started doing different motivational things," he said. "We'd won 21 in a row at that point. The coaches were tight. And the players were tight. So we went out and got the 'Jerry Springer Unedited' tape. We told them we were going to watch film the night before the game. But we threw that tape on, and the players sat there for over an hour and watched it. Instead of a 20-minute film session, we watched Jerry Springer and Chris Rock. You talk about taking a chance!"

Sunday was just as exciting in a different way, as an amazing pep rally, a bus crash and a visit from Izzo's best friend set the stage for one of the greatest days in MSU basketball history.

"The pep rally at our hotel was just incredible," Izzo said. "I don't think I've ever seen anything like it. Then, on our way to the arena, we ran into the pole that held the hotel marquee in place. We had the same bus driver when we got to Florida. And he brought a piece of that light pole with him."

As the team made the short drive to the Trans World Dome, Izzo couldn't get over the stream of green-and-white fans stretched for blocks, singing the "MSU Fight Song" and hollering "Go Green! Go White!" cheers.

Once Izzo reached the football locker room, lifelong pal Steve Mariucci broke the tension with a tale about his first game as the leader of the San Francisco 49ers.

"Mariucci walked in and said, 'You see that room over there?'" Izzo remembered, rolling with laughter. "It was a room where the head coach could change. It had tinted glass and looked out into the locker room. He said, 'There's a psychologist's bench in there. . . .I laid on that thing for two hours and almost puked my guts out.'"

Nerves were a problem again when the Spartans faced Tubby Smith's 28-8 Wildcats, Southeastern Conference runners-up and winners of their first three NCAA games — 82-60 over New Mexico State, 92-88 over Kansas in overtime and 58-43 over Miami (Ohio).

MSU fell behind 17-4, as an estimated 30,000 Kentucky fans celebrated that short-lived supremacy. One popular shirt for the bluebloods read, "We don't just play college basketball. . . ." on the front and "We ARE college basketball!" on the back.

On March 21, 1999, Kentucky was just another stunned victim of the Spartans' onslaught, as Izzo's team outscored the Wildcats 69-49 over the last 32:35.

The comeback started with a timeout tirade from Smith, who said what Izzo was about to say.

"It was nothing you can print," Smith said. "I wanted to start grabbing people. But I just grabbed a towel and started hollering. Basically, I told them we'd come too far and been through too much not to play more aggressively."

Granger got MSU back in the game with three 3-pointers in a 14-point contribution. Hutson added 14 more, including the signature basket on a gutsy call, a perfect full-court pass from Cleaves against a desperate defense for his 11th assist. Pressure?...What pressure?

And Peterson was huge off the bench with game-highs of 19 points and 10 rebounds. The Midwest Region's Most Outstanding Player hit six straight free throws in the last 30 seconds. Suddenly, "Put 'Mo Pete' in St. Pete" was an itinerary, not just a slogan.

The 73-66 final score silenced the entire Commonwealth of Kentucky and gave MSU a Big Ten-record 33rd win. It also unified the Spartan family as no win had since the 1988 Rose Bowl.

If it didn't completely erase the pain of a 52-49 giveaway to the Wildcats in a Mideast Region final 21 years earlier, it came close for the likes of Jud Heathcote, Earvin Johnson and Terry Donnelly.

"We owed Kentucky!" said Donnelly, the hero of the 1979 title win over Indiana State. "But when I look at this year's team, the big thing I see is character. They all pull for one another."

Johnson's joy was obvious from across the court, as he

Photo Credit: Rod Sanford, Lansing State Journal

1999 NCAA TOURNAMENT

hollered, "I knew A.J. Granger would be a key. But Peterson was a man!...And if anyone still wonders, the streak is 22 in a row."

No one was prouder than Heathcote that day. As he waited on the court to congratulate his protege, a bond with Izzo had never been stronger.

"For Jud to be out on the floor like that made me say, 'Whoa!'" Izzo remembered. "It wasn't Jud-like. But it made me feel great. The first few years away were really hard on him. Some people would've been jealous. Instead, he really embraced our team. I think he would've liked to coach Cleaves himself."

Heathcote had to settle for preparing Cleaves' coach. And if Heathcote's finest hour was a 1979 thrashing of Notre Dame that brought a Final Four trip, Izzo's most-memorable win accomplished the same thing.

The final two highlights of the day came when Carl Izzo, a beaming dad, confronted Billy Packer at courtside and chewed him out for past slights and when Smith, the original "Flintstone," helped his coach snip the final strand of net.

"I took Antonio to Michigan State," a teary Izzo said. "Now, he's taking me to the Final Four. . . . But to do this with my family, with Jud and with 'Magic' here is a dream."

Sweet reality, too, as Izzo has come to appreciate even more as time goes by and triumphs mount.

"I think that was my favorite game of all," he said nearly two years later. "Winning the national championship was incredible. But the game that gets you to your first Final Four is huge. If you're in basketball, you dream of making the Final Four more than winning the championship. To play a program as storied as Kentucky and to see all those people in green walking to the arena, that was the first time I realized how important basketball could be."

Izzo thought back to tougher days, especially an overtime loss to

Photo Credit: Bruce Fox, University Relations

1999 NCAA TOURNAMENT

Kansas in the 1986 Sweet 16 when a clock error cost the Spartans an upset triumph.

"When we got beat by Kansas, Jud came into the locker room and hardly said anything to the guys," Izzo recalled. "He said, 'I can't tell you now what you deserve to hear. . . .I'll tell you later.' And I remember thinking how wrong that was. Those guys had played their butts off. Later on, I learned exactly what he meant. You only get so many chances to get to the Final Four. The best team doesn't always get there. You have to be a little bit lucky. Against Kentucky, Peterson hit all those free throws down the stretch. If not, we lose."

MSU hadn't lost in nearly three months when the team arrived at its Clearwater Beach, Fla., resort, a beautiful-but-remote headquarters. Even with thousands of alumni and friends nearby, it wasn't the proper Final Four environment.

"Everything was so spread out," Izzo said. "To be honest, that kind of bummed me out. I said, 'Here's my one chance to get to the Final Four, and look where we are!'"

They were an hour and 25 minutes from Tropicana Field in St. Petersburg and roughly the same distance from Tampa, where the media was based.

"I had no idea of how to deal with the media and no idea of how to deal with the practice," Izzo said. "I was scheduling things all wrong because I wanted to be there early with the traffic. Everyone else was changing hotels. And I was so dumb I didn't even know I could do that. That was the rookie trip of all rookie trips."

The highlight came the day before the national semifinals. The

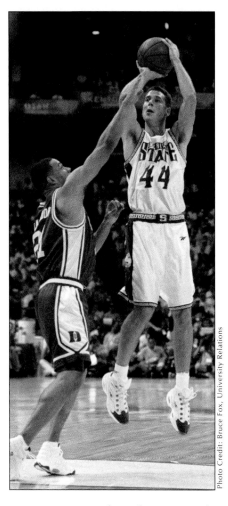

Photo Credit: Bruce Fox, University Relations

open practices drew huge crowds — but not everyone who could have been there.

"Friday had always been the day of Jud's party," Izzo said of a yearly ritual. "I always wanted to go to the practices. And when I walked out there for our scheduled hour, I swear to God, there couldn't have been a better feeling in the world. The only bad part was that Jud and those other guys weren't there. Jud said, 'Hey, we're not ruining a good party to watch your practice!'"

That was the evening when Crean, a master motivator, held a seance with slumping forward Jason Klein. The idea was to burn all of Klein's bad games. They didn't quite get them all.

The following night, exactly 20 years and one day after the Spartans won the NCAA title in Salt Lake City, they faced the 37-1 Duke Blue Devils, arguably one of best teams in history.

Mike Krzyzewski's top-ranked squad had swept through the East Region, beating Florida A&M 99-58, Tulsa 97-56, Southwest Missouri State 78-61 and Temple 85-64 — an average margin of 30 points.

If Duke was always in control against MSU, it was never completely comfortable. After leading 9-2 and 20-10, the Blue Devils took a 32-20 lead to the locker room, as center Elton Brand had 13 first-half rebounds.

"We got hurt when I decided to put Hutson on Brand," Izzo said. "That's when Andre had gotten mono. He played in that game at 213 pounds. After Brand hit his first couple of shots, I moved 'Tone onto him. But 'Tone got into foul trouble."

The Blue Devils' lead was down to 50-42 when Brand got in foul trouble, too. His fourth personal with 10:12 left was the opening the Spartans needed. And they promptly closed within three at 51-48.

But Duke point guard William Avery hit a 3 and penetrated for a basket that made it 59-50. And when Brand returned with 4:44 left, the better team polished off a 68-62 victory, the same six-point margin it had at the Great Eight in Chicago.

"If we played them 10 times, we might beat them a couple — at least once," Izzo said. "They have so many weapons. And they went right at our strengths. But they knew they were in a game."

Despite 18 points and 15 rebounds from Brand, the National Player of the Year, the Blue Devils were beatable that day, as seen by their 14-for-27 free-throw shooting.

Instead, MSU picked a bad day to have a bad first half. Duke had a

Photo Credit: Bruce Fox, University Relations

1999 NCAA TOURNAMENT

28-14 rebound advantage in the first 20 minutes, and the Spartans were 4-for-18 from long range before the break.

"I really felt they were beatable," said Peterson, who had 15 points and eight rebounds but was 6-for-17 from the field. "We got away from the things that got us here. They played harder than we did in the first half. And that's the biggest disappointment."

Not even close, as Izzo immediately discovered. Back home, Grand River Avenue was a war zone, as rioting that began before the game ended spoiled so much of what the Spartans had accomplished.

A ghost-like expression on the pasty face of President Peter McPherson was a giveaway to a much bigger story than any basketball game could be.

"I felt so cheated," Izzo said. "I got in the locker room, and it was an emotional time because 'Tone was done. The president was in there. That didn't bother me at all. But as soon as I was done talking, they scurried to get me and said there was a problem back home. We didn't even get to mourn the loss.

"The president asked if I'd get Mateen to go on TV and try to calm things down. But for us, the whole thing was really ruined. Even when we came back, there was nothing. Other teams that got beat in the Final Four had welcome-home celebrations. We had nothing. And that bothered me some."

The following day, in his final press conference at Clearwater

Beach, Izzo ripped the students and outside antagonists with a fury few had ever heard. He didn't want to fight them alone. But he and Smith would have challenged any 20.

In retrospect, though some bitterness lingers, Izzo has come to grips with that loss — a game that probably cost a tired Duke team the title two nights later against Connecticut.

"I think even Mike Krzyzewski thought that," Izzo said. "We

played such a physical game against Duke. We didn't play very well. But we did play hard. We worked our way back into it and just didn't have enough left. I still think we proved we were worthy of being in the Final Four."

They had proven they were a record-smashing team. Soon, MSU would be seen by everyone but Izzo as an elite program. The 1999 Final Four was a necessary step. And the mountaintop was clearly in reach.

Photo Credit: Bruce Fox, University Relations

MSU 76, Mount St. Mary's 53
March 12, 1999 • Bradley Center • Milwaukee, Wis.

Mount St. Mary's	FG-FGA	FT-FTA	REB	PF	TP	A	TO	BLK	S	MIN
Robert Balgac	0-1	0-0	1	1	0	1	1	0	1	13
Tony Hayden	1-5	0-0	4	1	3	2	1	0	0	29
Melvin Whitaker	5-14	3-4	4	4	13	0	1	0	0	34
Gregory Harris	4-13	3-4	2	2	12	2	3	0	4	38
Aaron Herbert	3-7	3-4	2	2	12	3	3	0	2	28
Newton Gayle	0-2	1-2	0	3	1	0	1	0	1	8
Eric Bethel	0-2	0-0	2	1	0	2	2	0	0	10
Jerry Lloyd	0-1	0-0	1	0	0	1	0	0	0	3
Stephen Moore	1-1	0-0	0	0	3	1	0	0	0	1
Terrence Wilson	1-3	3-4	1	0	6	0	2	0	0	23
Jason Grace	1-1	0-0	0	0	3	0	0	0	0	1
Todd Kessler	0-0	0-0	0	1	0	0	0	1	0	4
Konata Springer	0-0	0-0	1	2	0	0	0	0	0	8
Totals	16-50	13-18	22	17	53	12	15	2	10	200

Three-Point Field Goals: Hayden 1-3, Whitaker 0-2, Harris 1-4, Herbert 3-4, Bethel 0-1, Moore 1-1, Wilson 1-2, Grace 1-1, Team 8-18.
FG%: 1st Half 8-23 .348, 2nd Half 8-27 .296, Game 16-50 .320; 3FG%: 1st Half 2-9 .222, 2nd Half 6-9 .667, Game 8-18 .444; FT%: 1st Half 6-8 .750, 2nd Half 7-10 .700, Game 13-18 .722; Team Rebounds: 4; Deadball Rebounds: 1.

Michigan State	FG-FGA	FT-FTA	REB	PF	TP	A	TO	BLK	S	MIN
Antonio Smith	5-8	4-4	12	3	14	0	2	0	1	18
Jason Klein	4-9	0-0	8	1	9	4	1	0	1	25
Andre Hutson	3-3	5-6	2	5	11	1	2	1	2	20
Mateen Cleaves	3-8	1-1	1	3	8	8	1	0	1	25
Charlie Bell	3-6	0-0	3	1	6	0	3	0	1	19
Thomas Kelley	1-5	0-0	1	0	3	1	1	1	2	21
Lorenzo Guess	1-2	0-0	1	0	2	0	1	0	0	6
Steve Cherry	0-1	0-0	1	0	0	0	0	0	0	2
Doug Davis	0-1	0-0	0	1	0	2	2	0	0	11
Brandon Smith	0-0	0-0	0	0	0	0	1	0	0	4
Morris Peterson	4-8	0-0	12	0	8	1	4	2	1	24
A.J. Granger	5-7	4-4	5	1	15	2	1	1	1	25
Totals	29-58	14-15	46	19	76	19	19	5	10	200

Three-Point Field Goals: Klein 1-5, Cleaves 1-4, Bell 0-1, Kelley 1-2, Guess 0-1, Davis 0-1, Peterson 0-1, Granger 1-1, Team 4-16.
FG%: 1st Half 16-33 .485, 2nd Half 13-25 .520, Game 29-58 .500; 3FG%: 1st Half 3-11 .273, 2nd Half 1-5 .200, Game 4-16 .250; FT%: 1st Half 3-4 .750, 2nd Half 11-11 1.000, Game 14-15 .933; Team Rebounds: 0; Deadball Rebounds: 0.

SCORE BY PERIODS	1	2	F
Mount St. Mary's	24	29	-- 53
Michigan State	38	38	-- 76

OFFICIALS – Larry Rose, Rich Sanfillipo, Mike Wood
TECHNICAL FOULS – None
ATTENDANCE – 18,525

MSU 74, Ole Miss 66
March 14, 1999 • Bradley Center • Milwaukee, Wis.

Ole Miss	FG-FGA	FT-FTA	REB	PF	TP	A	TO	BLK	S	MIN
Jason Smith	7-13	4-4	3	3	18	0	4	1	5	36
Marcus Hicks	6-10	4-6	7	3	16	1	2	3	0	30
Jason Flanigan	0-2	2-2	2	2	2	2	0	0	0	23
Michael White	1-4	1-2	0	2	4	1	4	0	2	30
Keith Carter	4-12	1-3	8	2	10	3	1	0	0	39
Hunter Carpenter	1-3	0-0	1	0	3	0	0	0	0	1
Jason Harrison	2-4	2-2	0	2	7	4	2	0	2	20
Matt Pruitt	0-0	0-0	0	0	0	0	0	0	0	1
Darrian Brown	1-3	0-0	2	2	2	0	0	0	0	4
Lataryl Williams	0-2	0-0	1	0	0	0	0	0	0	5
Rahim Lockhart	2-3	0-0	0	4	4	0	1	0	1	10
John Engstrom	0-0	0-0	1	0	0	0	0	0	0	1
Totals	24-56	14-19	29	20	66	11	15	4	10	200

Three-Point Field Goals: Smith 0-1, White 1-3, Carter 1-8, Carpenter 1-3, Harrison 1-2, Brown 0-2, Williams 0-1, Team 4-20.
FG%: 1st Half 12-29 .414, 2nd Half 12-27 .444, Game 24-56 .429; 3FG%: 1st Half 1-9 .111, 2nd Half 3-11 .273, Game 4-20 .200; FT%: 1st Half 7-11 .636, 2nd Half 7-8 .875, Game 14-19 .737; Team Rebounds: 4; Deadball Rebounds: 4.

Michigan State	FG-FGA	FT-FTA	REB	PF	TP	A	TO	BLK	S	MIN
Antonio Smith	4-6	1-3	8	2	9	0	3	0	0	35
Morris Peterson	4-9	3-5	8	2	11	3	1	2	1	30
Andre Hutson	4-7	5-5	4	3	13	0	1	0	0	24
Mateen Cleaves	7-14	3-4	1	1	18	7	6	0	3	37
Jason Klein	1-5	4-4	5	2	6	0	1	0	0	28
Thomas Kelley	0-3	1-2	3	0	1	0	0	0	0	9
Charlie Bell	2-2	0-0	0	3	5	1	1	0	0	14
Doug Davis	0-1	2-2	0	0	2	0	0	0	0	3
A.J. Granger	3-6	2-2	3	4	9	0	2	1	2	20
Totals	25-53	21-27	36	17	74	11	15	4	6	200

Three-Point Field Goals: Cleaves 1-4, Klein 0-1, Bell 1-1, Granger 1-2, Team 3-8.
FG%: 1st Half 10-25 .400, 2nd Half 15-28 .536, Game 25-53 .472; 3FG%: 1st Half 1-5 .200, 2nd Half 2-3 .667, Game 3-8 .375; FT%: 1st Half 8-10 .800, 2nd Half 13-17 .765, Game 21-27 .778; Team Rebounds: 4; Deadball Rebounds: 2.

SCORE BY PERIODS	1	2	F
Ole Miss	32	34	-- 66
Michigan State	29	45	-- 74

OFFICIALS – Dick Paparo, Charlie Range, Stanley Reynolds
TECHNICAL FOULS – None
ATTENDANCE – 18,525

MSU 54, Oklahoma 46
March 19, 1999 • Trans World Dome • St. Louis, Mo.

Oklahoma	FG-FGA	FT-FTA	REB	PF	TP	A	TO	BLK	S	MIN
Eduardo Najera	2-8	2-2	7	2	7	0	4	2	1	31
Ryan Humphrey	4-8	2-5	10	5	10	1	1	1	2	31
Michael Johnson	4-15	3-4	2	2	12	1	0	0	2	40
Eric Martin	1-8	0-0	2	2	3	2	1	0	0	33
Alex Spaulding	3-7	1-3	4	4	7	0	1	0	0	34
Tim Heskett	1-2	0-0	2	1	3	1	0	0	0	10
Victor Avila	2-3	0-0	1	0	4	0	0	0	0	9
Renzi Stone	0-0	0-0	0	1	0	0	1	0	1	12
Totals	17-51	8-14	31	17	46	5	9	3	6	200

Three-Point Field Goals: Najera 1-4, Johnson 1-4, Martin 1-5, Spaulding 0-1, Heskett 1-1, Team 4-15.

FG%: 1st Half 9-23 .391, 2nd Half 8-28 .286, Game 17-51 .333; 3FG%: 1st Half 2-7 .286, 2nd Half 2-8 .250, Game 4-15 .267; FT%: 1st Half 5-8 .625, 2nd Half 3-6 .500, Game 8-14 .571; Team Rebounds: 3; Deadball Rebounds: 3.

Michigan State	FG-FGA	FT-FTA	REB	PF	TP	A	TO	BLK	S	MIN
Antonio Smith	0-1	0-0	7	4	0	0	1	0	1	23
Andre Hutson	3-3	6-10	5	1	12	0	3	0	0	30
Jason Klein	1-5	0-0	0	1	3	2	1	1	1	22
Mateen Cleaves	3-14	3-4	2	4	9	2	6	0	1	32
Charlie Bell	3-3	0-0	2	1	9	1	0	1	1	26
Thomas Kelley	0-4	0-0	1	0	0	1	0	1	0	11
Doug Davis	0-2	0-0	0	2	0	4	0	0	0	9
Morris Peterson	4-8	3-4	7	1	11	0	1	0	1	23
A.J. Granger	4-5	0-0	7	4	10	0	1	0	1	24
Totals	18-45	12-18	36	18	54	10	13	2	6	200

Three-Point Field Goals: Klein 1-3, Cleaves 0-4, Bell 3-3, Kelley 0-2, Peterson 0-1, Granger 2-2, Team 6-15.

FG%: 1st Half 11-30 .367, 2nd Half 7-15 .467, Game 18-45 .400; 3FG%: 1st Half 4-10 .400, 2nd Half 2-5 .400, Game 6-15 .400; FT%: 1st Half 0-2 .000, 2nd Half 12-16 .750, Game 12-18 .667; Team Rebounds: 5; Deadball Rebounds: 3.

SCORE BY PERIODS	1	2	F	
Oklahoma	25	21	--	46
Michigan State	26	28	--	54

OFFICIALS – John Cahill, Ed Corbett, Mike Kitts
TECHNICAL FOULS – None
ATTENDANCE – 42,400

MSU 73, Kentucky 66
March 21, 1999 • Trans World Dome • St. Louis, Mo.

Kentucky	FG-FGA	FT-FTA	REB	PF	TP	A	TO	BLK	S	MIN
Heshimu Evans	5-10	0-0	6	4	12	1	1	0	0	20
Scott Padgett	3-8	3-5	3	4	11	2	2	2	0	30
Michael Bradley	2-4	0-0	4	0	4	0	1	0	1	12
Wayne Turner	2-8	1-2	2	1	5	8	2	0	1	35
Desmond Allison	3-8	1-1	2	1	7	2	1	1	1	23
Saul Smith	0-1	0-0	1	1	0	1	0	1	1	13
Tayshaun Prince	3-3	4-4	2	2	12	1	0	1	0	24
Ryan Hogan	1-2	0-0	3	0	2	1	0	0	0	6
Souleymane Camara	2-4	0-0	0	0	4	0	0	0	0	11
Jamaal Magloire	3-5	3-4	6	3	9	0	1	3	1	26
Totals	24-53	12-16	29	16	66	15	9	7	5	200

Three-Point Field Goals: Evans 2-2, Padgett 2-6, Turner 0-3, Allison 0-2, Smith 0-1, Prince 2-2, Team 6-16.

FG%: 1st Half 15-29 .517, 2nd Half 9-24 .375, Game 24-53 .453; 3FG%: 1st Half 4-10 .400, 2nd Half 2-6 .333, Game 6-16 .375; FT%: 1st Half 2-2 1.000, 2nd Half 10-14 .714, Game 12-16 .750; Team Rebounds: 5; Deadball Rebounds: 1.

Michigan State	FG-FGA	FT-FTA	REB	PF	TP	A	TO	BLK	S	MIN
Antonio Smith	1-2	2-2	7	2	4	0	1	0	2	33
Andre Hutson	6-10	2-4	5	3	14	1	2	0	0	29
Jason Klein	1-6	0-0	1	3	3	0	1	0	0	18
Mateen Cleaves	4-11	0-0	4	0	10	11	3	0	0	37
Charlie Bell	3-5	0-0	3	3	7	2	1	0	2	27
Thomas Kelley	1-1	0-0	0	0	2	0	0	0	0	2
Doug Davis	0-0	0-0	0	0	0	2	0	0	0	3
Morris Peterson	6-13	7-8	10	3	19	1	1	0	0	33
A.J. Granger	4-5	3-3	2	2	14	0	2	0	0	18
Totals	26-53	14-17	33	16	73	17	11	0	4	200

Three-Point Field Goals: Klein 1-5, Cleaves 2-5, Bell 1-2, Peterson 0-2, Granger 3-3, Team 7-17.

FG%: 1st Half 13-28 .464, 2nd Half 13-25 .520, Game 26-53 .491; 3FG%: 1st Half 5-11 .455, 2nd Half 2-6 .333, Game 7-17 .412; FT%: 1st Half 4-5 .800, 2nd Half 10-12 .833, Game 14-17 .824; Team Rebounds: 1; Deadball Rebounds: 0.

SCORE BY PERIODS	1	2	F	
Kentucky	36	30	--	66
Michigan State	35	38	--	73

OFFICIALS – Jim Burr, Bob Donato, Reggie Greenwood
TECHNICAL FOULS – None
ATTENDANCE – 42,519

Duke 68, MSU 62
March 27, 1999 • Tropicana Field • St. Petersburg, Fla.

Duke	FG-FGA	FT-FTA	REB	PF	TP	A	TO	BLK	S	MIN
Chris Carrawell	3-8	6-12	4	0	13	1	3	0	0	30
Shane Battier	2-5	1-2	6	3	5	1	1	2	1	33
Elton Brand	7-10	4-5	15	4	18	1	3	1	0	29
William Avery	6-14	0-1	5	0	14	0	4	0	1	35
Trajan Langdon	3-9	0-1	6	2	7	3	1	0	0	37
Corey Maggette	3-7	3-6	4	0	9	0	0	0	0	17
Chris Burgess	0-1	0-0	4	2	0	0	0	2	0	12
Nate James	1-2	0-0	0	0	2	0	0	0	1	7
Totals	25-56	14-27	44	11	68	7	12	5	3	200

Three-Point Field Goals: Carrawell 1-1, Battier 0-3, Avery 2-4, Langdon 1-4, Maggette 0-1, Team 4-13.

FG%: 1st Half 14-33 .424, 2nd Half 11-23 .478, Game 25-56 .446; 3FG%: 1st Half 1-7 .143, 2nd Half 3-6 .500, Game 4-13 .308; FT%: 1st Half 3-4 .750, 2nd Half 11-23 .478, Game 14-27 .519; Team Rebounds: 0; Deadball Rebounds: 6.

Michigan State	FG-FGA	FT-FTA	REB	PF	TP	A	TO	BLK	S	MIN
Antonio Smith	3-7	0-0	10	5	6	0	0	0	0	34
Jason Klein	2-6	0-0	2	2	5	0	0	0	1	14
Andre Hutson	6-8	1-1	5	2	13	1	1	0	0	24
Mateen Cleaves	5-16	0-2	3	3	12	10	5	0	1	36
Charlie Bell	0-2	2-4	3	3	2	1	1	0	0	23
Morris Peterson	6-17	3-4	8	5	15	1	0	0	2	30
Thomas Kelley	2-8	0-0	4	2	4	0	0	0	1	14
A.J. Granger	2-6	0-0	4	2	5	0	1	0	0	20
Doug Davis	0-0	0-0	0	0	0	0	0	0	0	5
Totals	26-70	6-11	40	24	62	13	9	0	5	200

Three-Point Field Goals: Klein 1-3, Cleaves 2-9, Peterson 0-2, Kelley 0-1, Granger 1-3, Team 4-18.

FG%: 1st Half 9-31 .290, 2nd Half 17-39 .436, Game 26-70 .371; 3FG%: 1st Half 1-7 .143, 2nd Half 3-11 .273, Game 4-18 .222; FT%: 1st Half 1-1 1.000, 2nd Half 5-10 .500, Game 6-11 .545; Team Rebounds: 1; Deadball Rebounds: 3.

SCORE BY PERIODS	1	2	F	
Duke	32	36	--	68
Michigan State	20	42	--	62

OFFICIALS – David Libbey, Curtis Shaw, John Cahill
TECHNICAL FOULS – None
ATTENDANCE – 41,340

Photo Credit: Bruce Fox, University Relations

1999 NON-CONFERENCE

The Michigan State mission was simple. The execution was harder than any diamond in a championship ring.

From the moment then-assistant coach Tom Crean kissed the Final Four logo in St. Petersburg, Fla., and promised, "We'll be back!" there was only one goal for the Spartans in 1999-2000.

A third Big Ten title in a row was something to be collected along the way — a cup of water for a marathon runner at the 20-mile mark of a grueling race.

All that mattered was a return to the Final Four, this time in Indianapolis, and two treasured triumphs there.

That steely determination was forged in the hours after a loss to Duke in an NCAA semifinal on March 27, 1999, while the flames

of an ugly episode near campus were still burning.

That night and well into the next morning, MSU's players made pledges to each other. And point guard Mateen Cleaves, the key to those championship dreams, never wavered about finishing the job.

Cleaves could have gone to the NBA, a lifelong dream, after his junior season. But there was unfinished business with the Spartans. The megabucks of pro basketball could wait.

"After the Duke game, I said to Mateen, 'Let's sit down and talk,'" MSU coach Tom Izzo said. "He said, 'About what?' I said, 'About going to the pros. Do you want me to do some checking?' Mateen said, 'Yeah, do whatever you want.'"

Before the Spartans left Florida

and headed home to virtual silence, Izzo had to do one other thing — for himself, his program and his university.

"I've never been more angry or embarrassed about anything in my years at Michigan State," Izzo said about riots that brought the wrong kind of headlines. "If you're a season-ticket holder, I will personally buy your tickets. I don't want you in the building. And I don't want you as part of this program."

With that declaration, Izzo further endeared himself to nearly everyone associated with the school, including most Michigan taxpayers.

Once back on campus, it became even clearer that Cleaves' tax bracket would stay the same for another year. His boyhood pal, Antonio Smith, was gone. But

Photo Credit: Kevin Fowler, MSU Sports Information

Senior Morris Peterson, the best sixth man in Big Ten history, would replace Klein. And senior A.J. Granger would take Smith's spot in the lineup, though not his role as a rebounder and leader.

The Spartans were supposed to be a veteran team, one of the reasons Izzo agreed to a masochistic non-conference schedule with Cleaves' encouragement.

The only encouraging news on Oct. 25, 1999, was that Cleaves' right foot wouldn't be amputated. As rumors began to spread that day, anything less seemed possible.

It was finally announced that a stress fracture, superbly repaired by MSU orthopedic surgeon Herb Ross with a titanium screw, would keep Cleaves sidelined for 10 weeks.

Photo Credit: Kevin Fowler, MSU Sports Information

Cleaves could carry the torch for both of them.

"I'd see him every four or five days," Izzo said. "I'd say, 'Are we sitting down or what?…What are we doing here?' He'd say, 'I'm not going anywhere!' He never really did check it out. But that's another thing I respect about him. When Mateen says something, that's what he does."

Three days before Mother's Day, Cleaves made it official. His mother would get the Senior Day roses she craved. And the Spartans would get another season from the second-best leader in school history.

"People might have a hard time understanding why I would turn down the money," Cleaves said. "But I'm having fun at Michigan State. Why should I give that up when I don't have to? The NBA can wait."

His parents, Frances and Herbert, had been involved in the process. His mom even worked the phones to see if what she heard was true. But her son was true to his word.

When MSU fans finally exhaled, attention turned to a retooling process to replace Smith, starting forward Jason Klein and backup guards Thomas Kelley and Doug Davis.

1999 NON-CONFERENCE

Photo Credit: Bruce Schwartzman/John Grieshop/Jamie Sabau, Schwartzman Sports Photography

"This is a huge blow," said Izzo, more disappointed for Cleaves than for himself. "I think we're about to find out if we have a team or a program. I don't want anybody feeling sorry for us or changing the expectations."

Cleaves was remarkably upbeat, at least publicly, at a press conference in Breslin Center. But before he learned to go left with his crutches, he left an indelible message with Peterson.

"It's time for you to take over and be the All-American you know you are," Cleaves told his roommate and fellow "Flintstone" in one of his many off-court contributions.

"It has been a traumatic day," Izzo said. "I've been told that life isn't fair. And this is one of those times I believe it. But Mateen is

our leader by actions and words. He'll be a very talented assistant for 10 weeks."

After lackluster exhibition wins over the California All-Stars and the Mexican All-Stars, who could have used Lupe Izzo in the lineup, the Spartans had an easy time with Toledo in their 23rd-straight season-opening win.

A 78-33 rout of the Rockets was the second-largest margin in Breslin Center history — at least until the regular-season finale. If it was a rude way to welcome back ex-MSU assistant Stan Joplin, it was a great start with Cleaves in street clothes.

A 16-1 first-half run made it 28-7. And Toledo failed to score for the final 7:54, though no Spartan played more than 25 minutes. MSU shot 56.4 percent from the field and held the Rockets to 26.0 accuracy.

Peterson heeded Cleaves' advice and had 19 points and 10 rebounds. Junior forward Andre Hutson had 15 and 10, respectively. And junior David Thomas had five assists in his first start at point guard.

"I thought we played a lot harder tonight," Izzo said, though his team committed 22 turnovers. "We won by defending and rebounding the ball. To me, Spartan Basketball is just what you saw."

He didn't like what he saw later that week when MSU finished second in the eight-team Puerto Rico Shootout in Bayamon. Izzo wasn't sure his team could survive the challenge of playing different

styles without Cleaves. He was right, as usual.

In first-round play on Nov. 25, the Spartans were sloppy with the ball again, committing 23 turnovers against Providence. But excellent shooting from the field and balanced scoring brought an 82-58 triumph.

MSU led just 31-29 late in the first half. But 16 straight points, seven just before the break and nine immediately after intermission made it 47-29. The Friars would never draw closer than 16 points.

The Spartans shot 56.5 percent from the field and 53.8 beyond the arc. Providence hit just 34.9 and 15.0 percent, respectively, as MSU contested shots that were normally open.

Peterson led the Spartans with 18 points. Junior guard Charlie

Photo Credit: Nick Short, The State News

Photo Credit: Nick Short, The State News

Bell had 15 points and eight assists. Junior forward Mike Chappell, in his second game after transferring from Duke, added 14 points. Granger also contributed 11.

But two dangerous signs of sloppiness appeared. Bell, Thomas and freshman forward Jason Richardson had 13 of MSU's 23 turnovers. And 23-for-39 work at the foul line wouldn't have been good enough against a decent team.

The following day, the Spartans barely held on for a 59-56 win over South Carolina. It looked like another 20-plus-point victory when MSU took a 12-point lead to the locker room, thanks to 15 quick points from Peterson.

The Gamecocks refused to give in, however. Eddie Fogler's team finally went up by a point, the Spartans' first deficit of the season. After MSU went ahead 57-50, a pair of 3-pointers by guard

Herbert Lee Davis made it a one-point game again.

With Cleaves urging his teammates on from the bench, two Hutson free throws ended the scoring, though South Carolina missed two chances to tie in the final minute.

"We did just enough to win," a disgusted Izzo said. "But we're still not used to playing without Mateen. At the end of the game, he's the one we want with the ball in his hands."

MSU had 14 turnovers, the lowest number in its first three games. But it split just 52 rebounds with the Gamecocks, a total it would double three games later.

Peterson led his team again with 21 points, including 4-for-6 work from 3-point range. Bell had 13 points and Hutson 12, plus a team-high six rebounds.

In the championship game on Nov. 27, the Spartans were exposed

by superbly balanced Texas. The Longhorns shot 52.0 percent from the field and a blazing 69.2 beyond the arc, matched MSU with 36 rebounds and forced 19 turnovers.

After building a 38-23 lead, the Spartans missed Cleaves more than anyone would have imagined. It didn't help that Peterson spent much of the game in foul trouble, collecting 14 points in just 16 minutes while Izzo fumed at the officials.

"When you're ranked this high (No. 3 AP, No. 2 *USA TODAY*/ESPN), sometimes you think you're better than you are," Peterson said. "We have to realize if we don't do the little things, we'll lose a lot of games."

All five Texas starters had at least 12 points, with All-America center Chris Mihm helping his NBA Draft status. The 7-footer led everyone with 19 points, 11 rebounds and five blocked shots. When MSU let him shoot the 3, Mihm hit both attempts.

Hutson led the Spartans with 17 points on 7-for-9 shooting. He also had seven rebounds and more than held his own against Mihm in the first half. But as a ferocious, fast-paced game went on and players got tired, Mihm didn't get any shorter.

When MSU returned from its Thanksgiving trip, another loss was about to take place. Head football coach Nick Saban, a friend of Izzo's, was on the verge of bolting for a megabucks, lotsa-love deal at LSU. Suddenly, the success of Spartan Basketball was even more important.

1999 NON-CONFERENCE

Just after Saban hit the door for Baton Rouge, La., Izzo talked to a stunned football team. He asked the players to gather the following night to watch MSU play second-ranked North Carolina in the first ACC/Big Ten Challenge.

Izzo didn't tell them what kind of show they would see in a marquee matchup from Chapel Hill, N.C. That was probably a good thing for all concerned. No one in his right mind could have predicted what happened. And only a few would have believed it.

In the lobby of the Spartans' hotel on game day, ABC/ESPN analyst Dick Vitale talked with Izzo about football and basketball. Vitale had dropped MSU from No. 1 in his preseason rankings to No. 17 without Cleaves — "a Rolls-Royce without the engine," he said.

But Izzo had already dealt with one of the season's more-traumatic moments. When Cleaves hobbled into the Dean Smith Center, looked to the rafters and saw a who's-who of greatness, he finally lost it. The thought of not dressing for a game he had dreamed of playing was too much. And a player-coach sobfest that night only strengthened an already-solid bond.

Once the Spartans reached the arena on Dec. 1, the outcome was never in doubt. A stunned crowd of 21,572 saw MSU turn Carolina Blue into a headline, not just a pastel shade, in an 86-76 triumph that wasn't that close.

Izzo's team led 44-36 at halftime and built its cushion to 17 points with 11:51 remaining. When

the Tar Heels made their final surge and drew within six with four minutes left, the Spartans answered with seven straight points.

A few moments later, a note was slipped to Vitale that read: "Morris Peterson — first-team All-American." When that message was read over the air, Peterson had a new campaign manager. After scoring 31 points and holding North Carolina freshman sensation Joseph Forte to 6-for-15 shooting, his election might have been a landslide that night.

"When I think back to Scott Skiles, Steve Smith and Shawn Respert, we've had a lot of great performances in the last 15 years," Izzo said. "But what Morris did ranks up there with the best I've seen as an assistant or a head coach."

He wasn't just 12-for-18 from the field. Peterson also had six rebounds and five steals. And he had help from four other double-figure scorers: Chappell with 13, Granger with 11 and Hutson and Richardson with 10.

Hutson also outrebounded the Tar Heels' 7-foot Brendan Haywood 10-1, as MSU had a 43-28 advantage over a bigger team on the boards.

In a span of just over 20 months, Izzo's program had gone from being intimidated by North Carolina to being the Dale Earnhardt of college basketball.

"We were outcoached and outplayed," North Carolina coach Bill Guthridge said after his program's first loss in 56 non-conference home games and 71 home-open-

ers. "Tom's guys did a tremendous job. When they get Cleaves back, I can't imagine how good they'll be."

He nearly had a chance to find out in the national title game in Indianapolis. But that was more than four months away.

First, an emotional Izzo saluted the Spartan football players back home. "This one's for them!" he said after one of his five favorite games.

And a jubilant Cleaves put it all in perspective: "I'm happy we gave the football team and the university something to be proud of. It has been a tough couple of days for everyone. But these guys showed a lot of character....The way they played tonight, they probably don't even need me."

MSU didn't need him in its next three games, wins over Howard and Eastern Michigan in the Coca-Cola Spartan Classic in

East Lansing and against Kansas in the Great Eight in Chicago.

In the 75-45 trouncing of Howard, MSU trailed 7-6, then went on a 22-2 run and built its margin to 37 points. The key was a ridiculous 54-23 edge in rebounds.

Richardson thrilled the crowd with three dunks and a 16-point breakthrough. Hutson had another double-double with 14 points and 10 rebounds. Peterson added 13 points. And Bell had 11 points and nine rebounds, as no Spartan played more than 23 minutes.

MSU earned its fourth-consecutive Classic crown and its 14th in 18 years the next night with a 74-57 win over EMU. The Spartans led by 21 at halftime and coasted to a 6-1 record.

Peterson led all scorers with 16 points in 22 minutes. Hutson had 15 points and six rebounds en route to MVP honors. And with 11 points, Bell joined Hutson and Peterson on the All-Classic team.

In the Spartans' third appearance in the Great Eight, one in The Palace of Auburn Hills and two in the United Center, Izzo's team dominated the fifth-ranked Jayhawks 66-54 on Dec. 7.

MSU led 39-23 at halftime and built a 23-point lead with 14:25 to play. When a 19-2 Kansas run trimmed the margin to six, the Spartans responded with six straight points to put the game away.

The hero was clearly Bell, who went 9-for-15 from the field for a game-high 21 points. But that was only after he traded in his trademark high socks for cornrows, an uncharacteristic look.

"I'm old-school," Bell said. "But I wanted to try it. It didn't look too bad, so I thought I'd keep it. I couldn't wear the long socks with it, though. That's really old-school."

Peterson, who had 10 points and 10 rebounds, said, "I think it was all the braids tonight. I told Charlie I'm getting some next."

And Izzo, who wasn't big on the change, joked that he thought he might get strangled, saying, "When I saw him come into practice that way, I pulled up the collar on my jacket. . . . I thought Latrell Sprewell was in the building."

Granger was definitely there with 13 points and nine rebounds. And when MSU outrebounded Roy Williams' team 47-27, the game was essentially over.

"They blemish your every little pimple," said Williams, who would lead a move to reduce physical play for the following season — perhaps in part from the Spartans' dominance.

Izzo's team took a 7-1 mark to

Photo Credit: Bruce Schwartzman/John Grieshop/Jamie Sabau, Schwartzman Sports Photography

Tucson for a CBS matchup with second-ranked Arizona and got their first close look at the Wildcats' quickness in a 79-68 setback.

MSU trailed 31-12 before it knew what had happened. But an 18-2 run made it a five-point game at the break. And after Bell missed a transition layup, Richardson's flying, reverse-slam putback — arguably the best dunk in school history — tied the game at 59.

"I'll never forget that dunk and some of the plays (Arizona forward Richard) Jefferson made," Bell said of a matchup that would

happen again. "I was telling 'J.R.' that shot was a pass. . . . See, I knew he was behind me. I just put the ball in the air so he could go get it. I definitely wanted to leave it on the backboard."

Sorry, Charlie, no assist. And there was no victory for the visitors, either, when the Wildcats' 7-1 Loren Woods keyed a 12-2 run with three straight scores.

Bell finished with 20 points. And Peterson had 17. But Arizona shot 52.9 percent from the field and 87.5 at the line in a two-hour dunking drill at a raucous McKale Center.

"We didn't play defense at all," Bell said. "They got dunk after dunk after dunk and hurt us a lot in penetration. (Freshman point guard Jason) Gardner was really tough on us. And who had Gardner?…I did most of the time. He's a great player."

Gardner finished with 20 points, including four 3-pointers, plus nine assists. Jefferson added 18 points. Freshman guard Gilbert Arenas added 13. And Woods, who arrived late after a minor car accident, had 12 points on 6-for-7 shooting.

"The last thing I wrote on the chalkboard before we left the locker room was that we needed to get all the loose balls," Izzo said. "We got none. We got outshot, outworked and outhustled."

After a week off for final exams, the Spartans pounded Oakland 86-51 in Breslin. A 3 from Bell made it 43-28 at the half. And five quick points right after the break turned it into a rout.

Bell had 20 points, his third game in a row with at least that many. But the big surprises were 19 points from Chappell in a rare start and a 33-12 advantage on the boards, the lowest total for an MSU opponent since 1989.

Izzo's satisfaction level plunged in a 60-58 loss at Kentucky on Dec. 23, the program's first defeat by an unranked team in two seasons. And it never should have been close. With Cleaves in uniform, it wouldn't have been.

The Spartans seized a 26-15 lead, then struggled when Tubby Smith's team turned up the pres-

Photo Credit: Kevin Fowler, MSU Sports Information

1999 NON-CONFERENCE

sure and overplayed on defense. Still, a 28-27 halftime lead grew to seven points before another group of Wildcats rallied.

Just when a crowd of 23,318 at Rupp Arena thought a triumph was safe, MSU made a furious rally. Trailing by two in the closing seconds, Peterson passed up a shot most go-to guys would take. And when Hutson's final try was no-good, the Spartans were 8-3.

"We played scared — and you can quote me on that," Izzo said. "I guess we're not the program we thought we were. Good teams don't let opportunities slip away. And if guys are feeling good about where we are, those aren't the kind of people I want in this program."

Peterson finished with 18 points, just five in the second half. And Granger and Chappell each had 10. But MSU couldn't stop center Jamaal Magloire, who had 18 points and 11 rebounds.

Izzo couldn't help but think how close he came to signing Magloire, one of the best players ever from Toronto. And he couldn't help but wonder, "Mateen, how's the foot doing?"

If it wasn't the merriest Christmas in memory, a visit from Mississippi Valley State on Dec. 28 was the perfect stocking-stuffer. The Spartans rolled 96-63 after racing to a 28-4 advantage.

Peterson had 22 points, Hutson 19 and Chappell 18, as a 64.2-percent shooting night, the highest for an Izzo-coached team, was almost wasted.

Two nights later, MSU's players were up to their waists in humilia-

Photo Credit: Bruce Fox, University Relations

tion. With all eyes focused on Orlando, Fla., and an upcoming football matchup with Florida in the Citrus Bowl, the Spartans laid the biggest dodo egg of the decade in their final game of the 20th century.

A 53-49 loss to Wright State in Dayton, Ohio, made people assume the espn2 and CNN Headline News score crawls at the bottom of the screen were wrong.

What was wrong was 32.7-percent accuracy from the field, including 20.8 success in the second half. MSU led 32-26 at the half, as Granger had 13 of his 17

points. But after a 3 by Chappell put the Spartans up 47-46, they didn't score another basket.

"We've got a lot of work to do," Izzo said after a maddening effort. "That should fall on me. My team wasn't ready to play. That'll be remedied in the next week, one way or another."

Cleaves' return, the perfect remedy for a lot of problems, was six days away. And if anyone thought a 9-4 team was through after a brutal preconference schedule without its best player, the next three months would change that impression forever.

MSU 78, Toledo 33
Nov. 22, 1999 • Breslin Center • East Lansing, Mich.

Toledo	FG-FGA	FT-FTA	REB	PF	TP	A	TO	BLK	S	MIN
Robierre Cullars	1-6	2-4	0	1	4	0	1	0	2	32
Greg Stempin	7-20	0-0	3	2	16	0	4	1	1	40
Albert Wilson	0-1	0-0	2	5	0	1	2	0	0	10
Chad Kamstra	2-8	0-0	0	1	5	1	1	0	0	23
Justin Hall	3-12	2-5	2	4	8	1	6	0	1	32
Nick Moore	0-2	0-0	1	1	0	3	2	0	2	25
Brooks Miller	0-0	0-0	0	0	0	0	0	0	0	3
Sammy Bacino	0-0	0-1	1	0	0	0	1	0	0	7
Rory Jones	0-1	0-0	1	0	0	2	2	0	0	11
Craig Rodgers	0-0	0-0	3	1	0	0	3	0	0	17
Totals	13-50	4-10	20	15	33	8	22	1	6	200

Three-Point Field Goals: Cullars 0-1, Stempin 2-9, Kamstra 1-5, Hall 0-5, Moore 0-1, Jones 0-1, Team 3-22.
FG%: 1st Half 6-23 .261, 2nd Half 7-27 .259, Game 13-50 .260; 3FG%: 1st Half 2-9 .222, 2nd Half 1-13 .077, Game 3-22 .136; FT%: 1st Half 2-7 .286, 2nd Half 2-3 .667, Game 4-10 .400; Team Rebounds: 7; Deadball Rebounds: 4.

Michigan State	FG-FGA	FT-FTA	REB	PF	TP	A	TO	BLK	S	MIN
Andre Hutson	6-10	3-4	10	3	15	3	3	0	0	24
Morris Peterson	8-12	0-0	10	1	19	1	2	1	0	23
A.J. Granger	1-1	3-4	5	2	5	4	1	0	0	25
David Thomas	2-3	0-0	1	1	4	5	4	0	0	18
Charlie Bell	3-9	2-2	3	1	11	3	3	0	2	25
Brandon Smith	1-1	0-0	0	0	3	0	2	0	0	7
Mat Ishbia	0-0	0-0	0	0	0	1	0	0	0	2
Mike Chappell	3-8	0-0	2	3	6	4	3	0	0	24
Steve Cherry	0-1	0-0	0	0	0	0	0	0	0	1
Jason Richardson	2-4	1-4	4	3	5	1	2	0	2	21
Aloysius Anagonye	2-2	0-0	3	3	4	0	2	1	2	14
Adam Ballinger	3-4	0-0	6	0	6	1	0	2	2	16
Totals	31-55	9-14	45	17	78	23	22	4	8	200

Three-Point Field Goals: Peterson 3-4, Bell 3-6, Smith 1-1, Chappell 0-4, Richardson 0-1, Team 7-16.
FG%: 1st Half 15-30 .500, 2nd Half 16-25 .640, Game 31-55 .564; 3FG%: 1st Half 2-7 .286, 2nd Half 5-9 .556, Game 7-16 .438; FT%: 1st Half 7-12 .583, 2nd Half 2-2 1.000, Game 9-14 .643; Team Rebounds: 1; Deadball Rebounds: 3.

SCORE BY PERIODS	1	2	F
Toledo	16	17	33
Michigan State	39	39	78

OFFICIALS – Tom Rucker, Ted Hillary, Jim Jenkins
TECHNICAL FOULS – None
ATTENDANCE – 15,138

MSU 82, Providence 58
Nov. 25, 1999 • Eugenio Guerra Sports Complex • San Juan, Puerto Rico

Providence	FG-FGA	FT-FTA	REB	PF	TP	A	TO	BLK	S	MIN
Erron Maxey	10-16	1-5	7	4	22	0	3	3	1	36
Marcus Jefferson	1-5	0-0	0	4	3	0	4	0	0	12
David Murray	4-7	3-5	5	5	11	1	4	3	0	33
Jamaal Camah	2-10	3-4	4	2	7	4	1	0	1	28
Abdul Mills	3-6	0-0	1	1	6	3	0	0	2	14
Chris Rogers	0-1	0-0	1	2	0	4	1	0	0	28
Donta Wade	0-2	0-0	1	5	0	0	3	0	0	8
Romuald Augustin	3-9	1-2	4	2	8	0	2	0	3	25
Mark Jarrell-Wright	0-5	0-0	1	1	0	0	1	0	1	10
Llewellyn Cole	0-2	1-2	1	0	1	0	0	0	0	6
Totals	23-63	9-18	30	26	58	12	19	6	8	200

Three-Point Field Goals: Maxey 1-3, Jefferson 1-3, Camah 0-4, Mills 0-2, Rogers 0-1, Wade 0-2, Augustin 1-4, Jarrell-Wright 0-1, Team 3-20.
FG%: 1st Half 12-34 .353, 2nd Half 11-29 .379, Game 23-63 .365; 3FG%: 1st Half 1-9 .111, 2nd Half 2-11 .182, Game 3-20 .150; FT%: 1st Half 4-9 .444, 2nd Half 5-9 .556, Game 9-18 .500; Team Rebounds: 5; Deadball Rebounds: 5.

Michigan State	FG-FGA	FT-FTA	REB	PF	TP	A	TO	BLK	S	MIN
David Thomas	1-1	0-0	4	3	2	1	4	0	1	21
Andre Hutson	2-4	1-1	4	2	5	3	2	0	0	25
Morris Peterson	5-7	6-10	4	3	18	2	2	0	3	23
A.J. Granger	4-6	3-4	4	1	11	0	2	1	0	22
Charlie Bell	4-9	6-9	4	2	15	8	4	2	3	29
Brandon Smith	0-0	0-2	0	0	0	2	0	0	1	6
Mike Chappell	3-9	5-8	0	0	14	3	0	1	1	21
Jason Richardson	3-5	1-1	5	3	8	5	0	0	0	18
Aloysius Anagonye	3-4	1-4	4	3	7	0	2	1	0	18
Adam Ballinger	1-1	0-0	7	0	2	1	0	2	0	14
Mat Ishbia	0-0	0-0	0	0	0	0	0	0	1	3
Totals	26-46	23-39	40	17	82	18	23	6	10	200

Three-Point Field Goals: Peterson 2-2, Granger 0-1, Bell 1-3, Chappell 3-6, Richardson 1-1, Team 7-13.
FG%: 1st Half 11-20 .550, 2nd Half 15-26 .577, Game 26-46 .565; 3FG%: 1st Half 3-6 .500, 2nd Half 4-7 .571, Game 7-13 .538; FT%: 1st Half 13-24 .542, 2nd Half 10-15 .667, Game 23-39 .590; Team Rebounds: 4; Deadball Rebounds: 10.

SCORE BY PERIODS	1	2	F
Providence	29	29	58
Michigan State	38	44	82

OFFICIALS – Phil Bova, J.D. Collins, Carlos Tarrats
TECHNICAL FOULS – None
ATTENDANCE – 875

MSU 59, South Carolina 56
Nov. 26, 1999 • Eugenio Guerra Sports Complex • San Juan, Puerto Rico

South Carolina	FG-FGA	FT-FTA	REB	PF	TP	A	TO	BLK	S	MIN
Damien Kinloch	5-5	3-4	7	3	13	0	3	0	0	27
Antonio Grant	2-6	0-3	2	0	5	0	2	0	0	32
Marius Petravicius	0-1	0-0	2	4	0	1	0	0	0	16
Aaron Licas	3-11	2-2	4	2	10	4	4	0	0	36
Herbert Lee Davis	4-10	1-2	0	0	11	1	0	2	2	24
David Ross	0-0	0-0	0	2	0	1	0	0	0	3
Ivan Howell	0-1	0-0	1	0	0	0	0	0	0	1
Travis Kraft	2-4	0-0	3	1	4	0	1	0	0	10
Chuck Eidson	2-5	0-0	0	3	5	2	4	0	0	26
Tony Kitchings	3-3	2-3	5	3	8	0	1	0	1	25
Totals	21-46	8-14	26	18	56	8	15	3	3	200

Three-Point Field Goals: Grant 1-3, Licas 2-5, Davis 2-3, Kraft 0-2, Eidson 1-2, Team 6-15.
FG%: 1st Half 8-21 .381, 2nd Half 13-25 .520, Game 21-46 .457; 3FG%: 1st Half 2-7 .286, 2nd Half 4-8 .500, Game 6-15 .400; FT%: 1st Half 3-6 .500, 2nd Half 5-8 .625, Game 8-14 .571; Team Rebounds: 2; Deadball Rebounds: 4.

Michigan State	FG-FGA	FT-FTA	REB	PF	TP	A	TO	BLK	S	MIN
Andre Hutson	3-4	6-6	6	2	12	3	4	0	1	28
Morris Peterson	7-12	3-5	5	1	21	1	0	0	1	33
A.J. Granger	1-4	0-0	1	5	2	3	1	0	0	26
David Thomas	2-5	1-2	2	1	5	2	2	1	1	27
Charlie Bell	5-9	2-5	4	1	13	2	2	0	1	31
Mike Chappell	0-4	0-0	2	0	0	1	2	0	0	13
Jason Richardson	1-2	0-0	2	0	2	0	1	0	0	19
Aloysius Anagonye	0-1	2-2	0	1	2	0	1	0	0	11
Adam Ballinger	1-1	0-0	1	1	2	1	1	1	0	12
Totals	20-42	14-20	26	14	59	13	14	2	4	200

Three-Point Field Goals: Peterson 4-6, Granger 0-1, Thomas 0-2, Bell 1-3, Chappell 0-3, Richardson 0-1, Team 5-16.
FG%: 1st Half 12-25 .480, 2nd Half 8-17 .471, Game 20-42 .476; 3FG%: 1st Half 4-10 .400, 2nd Half 1-6 .167, Game 5-16 .313; FT%: 1st Half 5-7 .714, 2nd Half 9-13 .692, Game 14-20 .700; Team Rebounds: 5; Deadball Rebounds: 3.

SCORE BY PERIODS	1	2	F
South Carolina	21	35	56
Michigan State	33	26	59

OFFICIALS – Steve Skyles, Mark Massoius, Anibal Garcia
TECHNICAL FOULS – None
ATTENDANCE – 897

Texas 81, MSU 74
Nov. 27, 1999 • Eugenio Guerra Sports Complex • San Juan, Puerto Rico

Texas	FG-FGA	FT-FTA	REB	PF	TP	A	TO	BLK	S	MIN
Gabe Muoneke	6-14	3-6	4	4	16	2	3	0	1	28
Chris Owens	3-5	6-7	5	3	12	0	0	0	1	33
Chris Mihm	7-12	3-8	11	2	19	0	5	5	0	37
Ivan Wagner	5-6	5-7	2	2	17	8	5	0	3	38
William Clay	4-8	2-2	3	2	13	2	3	0	2	33
Chris McColpin	0-0	0-0	2	0	0	1	1	0	0	3
Darren Kelly	1-3	1-2	2	2	4	0	3	0	1	17
Chris Ogden	0-2	0-0	0	0	0	0	1	0	1	11
Totals	26-50	20-32	36	15	81	13	19	5	9	200

Three-Point Field Goals: Muoneke 1-1, Mihm 2-2, Wagner 2-2, Clay 3-6, Kelly 1-1, Ogden 0-1, Team 9-13.
FG%: 1st Half 10-22 .455, 2nd Half 16-28 .571, Game 26-50 .520; 3FG%: 1st Half 2-4 .500, 2nd Half 7-9 .778, Game 9-13 .692; FT%: 1st Half 9-14 .643, 2nd Half 11-18 .611, Game 20-32 .625; Team Rebounds: 7; Deadball Rebounds: 1.

Michigan State	FG-FGA	FT-FTA	REB	PF	TP	A	TO	BLK	S	MIN
Andre Hutson	7-9	3-5	7	4	17	0	3	0	1	30
Morris Peterson	5-10	0-0	1	4	14	1	2	0	0	16
A.J. Granger	3-9	0-0	6	3	6	5	4	0	0	30
David Thomas	0-4	2-2	1	3	2	4	1	0	2	27
Charlie Bell	5-12	2-2	4	5	12	0	4	0	1	35
Brandon Smith	0-0	0-0	0	0	0	0	0	0	0	4
Mike Chappell	4-10	2-2	3	2	12	2	0	0	0	24
Jason Richardson	3-8	0-0	5	2	7	1	2	1	1	14
Aloysius Anagonye	0-1	2-2	1	3	2	0	0	0	0	7
Adam Ballinger	1-1	0-0	3	3	2	2	3	0	0	13
Totals	28-64	11-13	36	29	74	13	19	1	6	200

Three-Point Field Goals: Peterson 4-7, Granger 0-1, Thomas 0-1, Bell 0-3, Chappell 2-6, Richardson 1-2, Team 7-20.
FG%: 1st Half 13-33 .394, 2nd Half 15-31 .484, Game 28-64 .438; 3FG%: 1st Half 3-7 .429, 2nd Half 4-13 .308, Game 7-20 .350; FT%: 1st Half 9-9 1.000, 2nd Half 2-4 .500, Game 11-13 .846; Team Rebounds: 5; Deadball Rebounds: 1.

SCORE BY PERIODS	1	2	F
Texas	31	50	81
Michigan State	38	36	74

OFFICIALS – Carlos Tarrats, Steve Skyles, Phil Bova
TECHNICAL FOULS – Michigan State bench
ATTENDANCE – 830

MSU 86, North Carolina 76
Dec. 1, 1999 • Smith Center • Chapel Hill, N.C.

Michigan State	FG-FGA	FT-FTA	REB	PF	TP	A	TO	BLK	S	MIN
Andre Hutson	5-11	0-1	10	2	10	0	2	0	2	35
Morris Peterson	12-18	3-5	6	3	31	2	4	1	5	30
A.J. Granger	4-8	0-0	2	2	11	1	2	1	0	25
David Thomas	1-5	0-0	6	1	2	7	4	0	2	25
Charlie Bell	1-7	5-6	6	2	7	5	1	0	2	27
Mike Chappell	4-9	3-4	1	2	13	1	1	0	0	21
Aloysius Anagonye	1-2	0-0	2	2	2	1	1	0	1	11
Jason Richardson	5-9	0-0	7	5	10	1	2	1	2	18
Adam Ballinger	0-0	0-0	1	1	0	0	0	0	1	8
Totals	33-69	11-16	43	20	86	18	17	3	15	200

Three-Point Field Goals: Peterson 4-6, Granger 3-4, Bell 0-1, Chappell 2-5, Richardson 0-1, Team 9-17.

FG%: 1st Half 19-35 .543, 2nd Half 14-34 .412, Game 33-69 .478; 3FG%: 1st Half 5-8 .625, 2nd Half 4-9 .444, Game 9-17 .529; FT%: 1st Half 1-2 .500, 2nd Half 10-14 .714, Game 11-16 .688; Team Rebounds: 2; Deadball Rebounds: 2.

North Carolina	FG-FGA	FT-FTA	REB	PF	TP	A	TO	BLK	S	MIN
Max Owens	5-9	6-6	5	3	18	0	5	0	0	25
Jason Capel	4-12	4-5	9	4	14	1	1	1	3	34
Brendan Haywood	2-3	0-2	1	2	4	0	2	1	1	25
Joseph Forte	6-15	4-6	5	2	19	2	2	0	2	33
Ed Cota	3-6	3-4	2	2	11	11	5	0	2	34
Terrence Newby	0-0	0-0	0	1	0	0	1	0	1	12
Kris Lang	1-2	2-2	2	2	4	0	2	0	0	17
Brian Bersticker	0-1	0-0	0	0	0	0	0	0	0	8
Orlando Melendez	0-0	0-0	0	1	0	0	1	0	0	2
Jonathan Holmes	0-0	0-0	1	0	0	0	0	0	0	2
Michael Brooker	2-4	0-0	1	2	6	0	0	0	0	6
Totals	23-52	19-25	28	19	76	14	17	3	9	200

Three-Point Field Goals: Owens 2-3, Capel 2-5, Forte 3-7, Cota 2-4, Brooker 2-4, Team 11-23.

FG%: 1st Half 14-25 .560, 2nd Half 9-27 .333, Game 23-52 .442; 3FG%: 1st Half 6-11 .545, 2nd Half 5-12 .417, Game 11-23 .478; FT%: 1st Half 2-6 .333, 2nd Half 17-19 .895, Game 19-25 .760; Team Rebounds: 2; Deadball Rebounds: 3.

SCORE BY PERIODS	1	2	F
Michigan State	44	42	86
North Carolina	36	40	76

OFFICIALS – Larry Rose, Duke Edsall, Bryan Kersey
TECHNICAL FOULS – Michigan State bench
ATTENDANCE – 21,572

Photo Credit: Kevin Fowler, MSU Sports Information

MSU 75, Howard 45
Dec. 3, 1999 • Breslin Center • East Lansing, Mich.

Howard	FG-FGA	FT-FTA	REB	PF	TP	A	TO	BLK	S	MIN
Jermaine Holliway	5-14	0-0	6	2	10	0	3	0	1	34
Jonathan Stokes	6-16	1-2	1	1	16	1	4	0	1	30
Bryen Alvin	4-12	0-2	4	4	8	0	2	0	0	34
Antonio Michell	0-4	0-0	0	0	0	0	0	0	0	28
Ron Williamson	1-5	3-6	3	0	5	3	1	0	3	34
Lungi Okoko	1-1	0-0	1	0	3	0	1	0	0	14
Aquil Bayyan	1-1	0-0	1	0	2	0	0	0	1	10
Nick Dodson	0-0	1-2	2	5	1	1	1	0	0	16
Totals	18-53	5-12	23	12	45	5	13	0	6	200

Three-Point Field Goals: Stokes 3-7, Michell 0-1, Okoko 1-1, Team 4-9.

FG%: 1st Half 8-27 .296, 2nd Half 10-26 .385, Game 18-53 .340; 3FG%: 1st Half 2-5 .400, 2nd Half 2-4 .500, Game 4-9 .444; FT%: 1st Half 1-2 .500, 2nd Half 4-10 .400, Game 5-12 .417; Team Rebounds: 5; Deadball Rebounds: 5.

Michigan State	FG-FGA	FT-FTA	REB	PF	TP	A	TO	BLK	S	MIN
Andre Hutson	6-7	2-4	10	1	14	1	1	2	1	20
Morris Peterson	5-13	1-2	4	0	13	1	2	1	1	23
A.J. Granger	2-7	0-0	7	1	4	1	0	2	0	21
David Thomas	1-3	0-0	1	1	2	4	1	0	0	17
Charlie Bell	5-9	0-0	9	3	11	4	1	0	1	23
Brandon Smith	1-3	0-0	2	2	2	3	3	0	0	13
Mat Ishbia	1-1	0-0	0	1	2	0	2	0	0	4
Mike Chappell	2-7	1-2	6	2	5	2	0	0	1	16
Steve Cherry	0-2	0-0	0	0	0	0	0	0	3	3
Jason Richardson	7-12	2-4	7	1	16	2	2	0	1	21
Aloysius Anagonye	1-3	0-0	4	2	2	0	1	1	4	20
Adam Ballinger	2-3	0-0	4	0	4	1	0	0	1	19
Totals	33-70	6-12	54	14	75	19	13	6	10	200

Three-Point Field Goals: Peterson 2-5, Granger 0-1, Bell 1-4, Smith 0-1, Chappell 0-4, Richardson 0-1, Team 3-16.

FG%: 1st Half 15-32 .469, 2nd Half 18-38 .474, Game 33-70 .471; 3FG%: 1st Half 2-10 .200, 2nd Half 1-6 .167, Game 3-16 .188; FT%: 1st Half 4-8 .500, 2nd Half 2-4 .500, Game 6-12 .500; Team Rebounds: 0; Deadball Rebounds: 3.

SCORE BY PERIODS	1	2	F
Howard	19	26	45
Michigan State	36	39	75

OFFICIALS – Steve Welmer, Mike Sanzere, Sid Rodeheffer
TECHNICAL FOULS – None
ATTENDANCE – 15,138

MSU 74, Eastern Michigan 57
Dec. 4, 1999 • Breslin Center • East Lansing, Mich.

Eastern Michigan	FG-FGA	FT-FTA	REB	PF	TP	A	TO	BLK	S	MIN
Adam Hess	1-7	4-6	3	3	6	1	2	0	2	25
Tyson Radney	0-0	0-0	2	5	0	0	1	1	0	7
Calvin Warner	5-9	2-4	4	1	12	0	3	0	0	29
Avin Howard	1-2	0-0	1	2	2	0	3	0	0	12
Corey Tarrant	4-6	6-9	2	2	14	3	3	0	1	25
C.J. Grantham	2-4	0-0	1	1	5	2	1	0	2	22
DeSean Hadley	2-10	0-0	2	3	6	0	0	1	0	19
Mosi Barnes	1-2	0-1	2	0	3	1	0	0	0	9
Larry Fisher	2-6	0-0	1	0	6	1	0	0	0	11
Ryan Prillman	0-0	0-0	0	0	0	0	0	0	0	1
Dante Darling	0-0	0-0	2	0	0	0	0	0	0	7
Craig Erquhart	1-6	0-0	2	5	3	3	0	1	0	19
Melvin Hicks	0-1	0-0	0	0	0	0	0	0	1	1
Rod Wells	0-0	0-0	0	0	0	1	0	1	1	1
Solomon McGee	0-1	0-0	5	5	0	4	0	1	0	12
Totals	19-54	12-20	27	27	57	11	11	5	7	200

Three-Point Field Goals: Hess 0-5, Howard 0-1, Tarrant 0-1, Grantham 1-3, Hadley 2-8, Barnes 1-2, Fisher 2-5, Erquhart 1-4, Team 7-29.

FG%: 1st Half 10-30 .333, 2nd Half 9-24 .375, Game 19-54 .352; 3FG%: 1st Half 3-15 .200, 2nd Half 4-14 .286, Game 7-29 .241; FT%: 1st Half 1-3 .333, 2nd Half 11-17 .647, Game 12-20 .600; Team Rebounds: 4; Deadball Rebounds: 6.

Michigan State	FG-FGA	FT-FTA	REB	PF	TP	A	TO	BLK	S	MIN
Andre Hutson	3-7	9-9	6	3	15	1	2	1	0	24
Morris Peterson	4-9	6-6	5	3	16	1	1	1	1	22
A.J. Granger	1-2	2-2	4	1	5	0	2	0	1	19
David Thomas	0-3	2-4	5	1	2	6	1	0	0	24
Charlie Bell	3-9	4-6	4	2	11	4	0	0	0	28
Brandon Smith	0-0	0-0	1	0	0	0	0	0	0	4
Mat Ishbia	0-0	0-0	1	0	0	0	1	0	0	1
Mike Chappell	2-7	3-6	5	3	9	2	1	0	0	20
Steve Cherry	0-0	0-0	0	1	0	0	0	0	0	1
Jason Richardson	4-10	0-1	7	3	8	1	1	0	2	20
Aloysius Anagonye	2-6	0-2	4	2	4	0	2	3	1	21
Adam Ballinger	1-1	2-2	2	2	4	1	1	0	0	16
Totals	20-54	28-38	47	21	74	16	12	5	5	200

Three-Point Field Goals: Peterson 2-5, Granger 1-1, Thomas 0-1, Bell 1-2, Chappell 2-3, Richardson 0-1, Team 6-13.

FG%: 1st Half 14-32 .438, 2nd Half 6-22 .273, Game 20-54 .370; 3FG%: 1st Half 5-11 .455, 2nd Half 1-2 .500, Game 6-13 .462; FT%: 1st Half 12-14 .857, 2nd Half 16-24 .667, Game 28-38 .737; Team Rebounds: 4; Deadball Rebounds: 7.

SCORE BY PERIODS	1	2	F
Eastern Michigan	24	33	57
Michigan State	45	29	74

OFFICIALS – Steve Welmer, Mike Sanzere, Tom Clark
TECHNICAL FOULS – Eastern Michigan bench
ATTENDANCE – 15,138

MSU 66, Kansas 54
Dec. 7, 1999 • United Center • Chicago, Ill.

Kansas	FG-FGA	FT-FTA	REB	PF	TP	A	TO	BLK	S	MIN
Nick Collison	1-7	0-0	4	5	2	1	1	0	0	15
Nick Bradford	1-5	1-4	1	2	3	3	3	0	2	24
Eric Chenowith	2-6	2-2	10	4	6	1	4	2	0	27
Kenny Gregory	6-10	1-4	2	0	14	0	0	0	1	21
Jeff Boschee	1-3	0-0	3	3	3	2	2	0	1	23
Drew Gooden	4-8	0-0	4	3	8	1	1	1	1	18
Kirk Hinrich	0-2	0-0	2	4	0	7	1	0	2	21
Jeff Carey	0-0	0-0	1	0	0	0	1	1	0	4
Marlon London	1-2	2-2	1	0	4	0	1	0	0	19
Ashante Johnson	1-3	0-0	0	0	2	0	0	0	0	9
Luke Axtell	4-7	2-4	2	1	12	1	2	0	0	19
Totals	21-53	8-16	35	22	54	16	17	4	7	200

Three-Point Field Goals: Bradford 0-2, Gregory 1-2, Boschee 1-3, Hinrich 0-2, Axtell 2-3, Team 4-12.

FG%: 1st Half 10-31 .323, 2nd Half 11-22 .500, Game 21-53 .396; 3FG%: 1st Half 1-4 .250, 2nd Half 3-8 .375, Game 4-12 .333; FT%: 1st Half 2-7 .286, 2nd Half 6-9 .667, Game 8-16 .500; Team Rebounds: 5; Deadball Rebounds: 2.

Michigan State	FG-FGA	FT-FTA	REB	PF	TP	A	TO	BLK	S	MIN
Morris Peterson	3-14	4-4	10	1	10	3	3	0	2	33
A.J. Granger	4-8	2-2	9	3	13	0	1	3	0	26
Andre Hutson	4-9	2-4	6	3	10	1	2	0	3	30
Charlie Bell	9-15	2-4	2	0	21	4	1	0	0	33
David Thomas	1-2	1-2	4	4	3	4	4	0	3	23
Mike Chappell	0-6	0-0	2	2	0	0	1	0	0	18
Jason Richardson	3-5	1-4	6	1	7	1	0	0	1	17
Aloysius Anagonye	1-4	0-0	4	3	2	1	0	0	0	9
Adam Ballinger	0-1	0-0	0	1	0	0	0	0	0	11
Totals	25-64	12-20	47	18	66	14	14	3	9	200

Three-Point Field Goals: Peterson 0-4, Granger 3-5, Bell 1-3, Chappell 0-1, Team 4-13.

FG%: 1st Half 14-34 .412, 2nd Half 11-30 .367, Game 25-64 .391; 3FG%: 1st Half 4-11 .364, 2nd Half 0-2 .000, Game 4-13 .308; FT%: 1st Half 7-7 1.000, 2nd Half 5-13 .385, Game 12-20 .600; Team Rebounds: 4; Deadball Rebounds: 3.

SCORE BY PERIODS	1	2	F
Kansas	23	31	54
Michigan State	39	27	66

OFFICIALS – Karl Hess, Bob Donato, Leslie Jones
TECHNICAL FOULS – None
ATTENDANCE – 13,127

MSU 86, Oakland 51
Dec. 18, 1999 • Breslin Center • East Lansing, Mich.

Oakland	FG-FGA	FT-FTA	REB	PF	TP	A	TO	BLK	S	MIN
Myke Thom	5-10	6-7	1	4	20	1	3	0	2	39
Jason Rozycki	2-5	0-0	1	5	6	3	2	0	0	25
Sebastien Bellin	1-2	1-2	4	3	3	0	2	0	0	33
Mychal Covington	2-7	4-5	4	3	8	0	7	0	1	35
Steve Houston	2-6	0-0	2	0	6	1	2	0	0	28
Steve Reynolds	0-0	0-0	1	0	0	1	1	0	0	11
Ryan Williams	1-1	6-6	1	2	8	1	1	1	3	16
Jeff Mullett	0-0	0-0	0	1	0	0	1	0	1	3
Jon Champagne	0-0	0-0	0	5	0	0	1	0	0	10
Totals	13-31	17-20	12	24	51	7	21	1	7	200

Three-Point Field Goals: Thom 4-8, Rozycki 2-5, Covington 0-1, Houston 2-2, Team 8-16.

FG%: 1st Half 6-15 .400, 2nd Half 7-16 .438, Game 13-31 .419; 3FG%: 1st Half 5-9 .556, 2nd Half 3-7 .429, Game 8-16 .500; FT%: 1st Half 11-12 .917, 2nd Half 6-8 .750, Game 17-20 .850; Team Rebounds: 1; Deadball Rebounds: 1.

Michigan State	FG-FGA	FT-FTA	REB	PF	TP	A	TO	BLK	S	MIN
Mike Chappell	5-10	6-7	6	3	19	1	3	0	0	20
Andre Hutson	2-4	5-6	7	1	9	1	1	1	1	28
A.J. Granger	3-7	2-2	2	1	9	1	1	0	0	26
David Thomas	3-6	0-0	0	2	7	4	2	0	2	22
Jason Richardson	3-5	0-0	5	0	6	2	1	0	1	24
Brandon Smith	0-0	0-0	0	1	0	2	0	0	1	5
Charlie Bell	7-9	5-5	4	1	20	2	1	0	0	21
Mat Ishbia	0-0	2-2	0	0	2	0	0	0	0	3
Steve Cherry	2-2	0-0	0	0	5	0	0	0	1	2
Aloysius Anagonye	1-1	3-4	4	2	5	1	2	0	0	13
Morris Peterson	1-6	2-2	4	1	4	1	3	0	1	24
Adam Ballinger	0-0	0-0	1	2	0	1	0	0	0	12
Totals	27-50	25-28	33	14	86	16	14	1	8	200

Three-Point Field Goals: Chappell 3-7, Granger 1-2, Thomas 1-2, Richardson 0-1, Bell 1-1, Cherry 1-1, Peterson 0-2, Team 7-16.

FG%: 1st Half 16-26 .615, 2nd Half 11-24 .458, Game 27-50 .540; 3FG%: 1st Half 5-9 .556, 2nd Half 2-7 .286, Game 7-16 .438; FT%: 1st Half 6-6 1.000, 2nd Half 19-22 .864, Game 25-28 .893; Team Rebounds: 0; Deadball Rebounds: 1.

SCORE BY PERIODS	1	2	F
Oakland	28	23	51
Michigan State	43	43	86

OFFICIALS – Sid Rodeheffer, Sam Lickliter, Jerry Sauder
TECHNICAL FOULS – None
ATTENDANCE – 15,138

Arizona 79, MSU 68
Dec. 11, 1999 • McKale Center • Tucson, Ariz.

Michigan State	FG-FGA	FT-FTA	REB	PF	TP	A	TO	BLK	S	MIN
Andre Hutson	2-6	4-5	3	1	8	1	2	1	1	30
Morris Peterson	5-15	6-8	3	3	17	4	6	0	1	32
A.J. Granger	3-4	0-0	4	1	6	2	2	1	1	32
David Thomas	2-5	0-0	6	4	4	1	2	1	0	20
Charlie Bell	8-20	2-3	4	5	20	3	2	0	1	29
Brandon Smith	0-0	0-0	0	0	0	0	0	0	0	3
Mike Chappell	1-5	1-2	2	1	4	0	0	0	0	17
Jason Richardson	4-6	0-0	4	0	9	1	2	0	0	19
Aloysius Anagonye	0-1	0-0	3	3	0	1	0	1	1	13
Adam Ballinger	0-0	0-0	0	0	0	0	0	0	0	5
Totals	25-62	13-18	33	18	68	13	16	4	7	200

Three-Point Field Goals: Peterson 1-3, Bell 2-4, Chappell 1-5, Richardson 1-1, Team 5-13.

FG%: 1st Half 11-28 .393, 2nd Half 14-34 .412, Game 25-62 .403; 3FG%: 1st Half 2-5 .400, 2nd Half 3-8 .375, Game 5-13 .385; FT%: 1st Half 8-9 .889, 2nd Half 5-9 .556, Game 13-18 .722; Team Rebounds: 4; Deadball Rebounds: 4.

Arizona	FG-FGA	FT-FTA	REB	PF	TP	A	TO	BLK	S	MIN
Justin Wessel	2-4	1-2	3	0	5	2	0	0	2	24
Richard Jefferson	5-10	8-9	6	2	18	6	5	2	0	37
Michael Wright	4-6	1-1	3	2	9	1	1	0	0	20
Jason Gardner	5-11	6-7	6	1	20	9	5	0	2	40
Rick Anderson	1-3	0-0	2	1	2	1	0	1	0	13
Gilbert Arenas	4-8	5-5	2	4	13	0	1	0	0	24
Loren Woods	6-7	0-0	4	2	12	2	1	1	1	29
Luke Walton	0-2	0-0	1	1	0	0	2	0	1	11
Robertas Javtokas	0-0	0-0	0	0	0	0	0	0	0	2
Totals	27-51	21-24	30	13	79	21	15	4	6	200

Three-Point Field Goals: Wessel 0-1, Jefferson 0-1, Gardner 4-10, Anderson 0-1, Arenas 0-2, Team 4-15.

FG%: 1st Half 15-31 .484, 2nd Half 12-20 .600, Game 27-51 .529; 3FG%: 1st Half 2-10 .200, 2nd Half 2-5 .400, Game 4-15 .267; FT%: 1st Half 5-7 .714, 2nd Half 16-17 .941, Game 21-24 .875; Team Rebounds: 3; Deadball Rebounds: 2.

SCORE BY PERIODS	1	2	F
Michigan State	32	36	68
Arizona	37	42	79

OFFICIALS – Ed Hightower, Art McDonald, Ron Zetcher
TECHNICAL FOULS – None
ATTENDANCE – 14,441

Kentucky 60, MSU 58
Dec. 23, 1999 • Rupp Arena • Lexington, Ky.

Michigan State	FG-FGA	FT-FTA	REB	PF	TP	A	TO	BLK	S	MIN
Morris Peterson	5-12	5-6	4	1	18	1	2	0	1	36
A.J. Granger	4-8	0-1	1	2	10	1	1	0	0	36
Andre Hutson	0-3	0-0	6	4	0	2	2	0	1	27
David Thomas	2-5	0-0	3	2	4	2	3	0	3	16
Charlie Bell	4-8	0-0	4	3	8	3	5	0	0	32
Brandon Smith	0-0	0-0	0	1	0	0	0	0	0	2
Mike Chappell	4-7	0-0	1	3	10	1	0	0	0	19
Jason Richardson	2-6	0-2	9	2	4	0	1	0	0	17
Aloysius Anagonye	1-2	0-0	1	4	2	0	1	0	0	8
Adam Ballinger	1-1	0-0	1	0	2	0	0	0	0	7
Totals	23-52	5-9	34	22	58	10	16	0	5	200

Three-Point Field Goals: Peterson 3-5, Granger 2-3, Thomas 0-1, Bell 0-1, Chappell 2-4, Richardson 0-1, Team 7-15.

FG%: 1st Half 10-24 .417, 2nd Half 13-28 .464, Game 23-52 .442; 3FG%: 1st Half 3-8 .375, 2nd Half 4-7 .571, Game 7-15 .467; FT%: 1st Half 5-7 .714, 2nd Half 0-2 .000, Game 5-9 .556; Team Rebounds: 4; Deadball Rebounds: 2.

Kentucky	FG-FGA	FT-FTA	REB	PF	TP	A	TO	BLK	S	MIN
Tayshaun Prince	5-11	4-4	5	3	17	0	1	1	0	37
Desmond Allison	1-4	0-0	1	4	2	3	2	0	0	22
Jamaal Magloire	5-10	8-10	11	3	18	0	3	1	0	37
Keith Bogans	2-8	2-2	2	2	6	3	2	0	1	31
Saul Smith	1-5	3-4	2	0	6	1	4	0	2	31
J.P. Blevins	3-6	0-1	4	0	9	0	1	0	2	25
Todd Tackett	0-1	0-0	0	0	0	0	0	0	0	2
Marvin Stone	0-0	0-0	0	0	0	0	0	0	0	3
Jules Camara	1-2	0-0	1	3	2	0	2	0	0	12
Totals	18-47	17-21	28	15	60	7	15	2	5	200

Three-Point Field Goals: Prince 3-5, Bogans 0-2, Smith 1-3, Blevins 3-4, Team 7-14.

FG%: 1st Half 8-23 .348, 2nd Half 10-24 .417, Game 18-47 .383; 3FG%: 1st Half 2-6 .333, 2nd Half 5-8 .625, Game 7-14 .500; FT%: 1st Half 9-13 .692, 2nd Half 8-8 1.000, Game 17-21 .810; Team Rebounds: 2; Deadball Rebounds: 3.

SCORE BY PERIODS	1	2	F
Michigan State	28	30	58
Kentucky	27	33	60

OFFICIALS – Jim Burr, Tom Clark, Mike Sanzere
TECHNICAL FOULS – Magloire (UK)
ATTENDANCE – 23,318

MSU 96, Mississippi Valley State 63
Dec. 28, 1999 • Breslin Center • East Lansing, Mich.

MVSU	FG-FGA	FT-FTA	REB	PF	TP	A	TO	BLK	S	MIN
James Nelson	2-2	0-0	2	1	4	0	0	0	0	13
D'Jamal Jackson	0-5	0-0	2	2	0	0	2	0	0	15
Henry Jordan	4-13	2-4	6	4	10	0	3	1	1	37
Marcus Metcalf	0-1	0-0	0	0	0	0	0	0	0	8
Dewayne Jefferson	11-21	0-1	4	2	24	1	5	0	2	29
Ashley Robinson	0-0	0-0	2	0	0	1	0	0	0	5
Mario Edwards	1-4	0-0	1	2	2	0	0	0	0	18
Dante Thornton	0-2	0-0	0	0	0	2	1	0	0	17
Johnny Dotson	4-6	2-3	0	2	12	5	3	0	6	27
Jamar Blackmon	5-7	0-0	1	1	11	2	0	0	0	16
Keith Williams	0-0	0-0	0	0	0	0	0	0	0	3
Derrick McInnis	0-1	0-0	2	3	0	0	1	1	0	12
Totals	27-62	4-8	21	18	63	11	13	4	9	200

Three-Point Field Goals: Metcalf 0-1, Jefferson 2-10, Edwards 0-1, Thornton 0-1, Dotson 2-3, Blackmon 1-2, Team 5-18.

FG%: 1st Half 9-30 .300, 2nd Half 18-32 .563, Game 27-62 .435; 3FG%: 1st Half 2-10 .200, 2nd Half 3-8 .375, Game 5-18 .278; FT%: 1st Half 0-0 .000, 2nd Half 4-8 .500, Game 4-8 .500; Team Rebounds: 3; Deadball Rebounds: 1.

Michigan State	FG-FGA	FT-FTA	REB	PF	TP	A	TO	BLK	S	MIN
Andre Hutson	8-10	3-3	2	2	19	2	0	0	2	19
Morris Peterson	8-11	2-2	8	1	22	0	2	0	1	24
A.J. Granger	2-4	0-0	2	1	5	2	1	1	0	17
Charlie Bell	3-4	1-1	2	1	7	11	0	1	2	21
Jason Richardson	4-5	2-3	7	1	11	1	4	1	1	23
Brandon Smith	0-2	0-0	2	1	0	5	3	0	0	19
Mat Ishbia	0-0	1-4	1	1	1	0	1	0	1	5
Mike Chappell	6-9	2-2	2	1	18	2	1	0	0	26
Steve Cherry	0-1	0-0	1	0	0	0	0	0	0	2
Aloysius Anagonye	1-4	5-6	7	3	7	3	3	0	0	23
Adam Ballinger	2-3	2-2	1	1	6	1	0	2	0	21
Totals	34-53	18-23	37	13	96	27	15	5	7	200

Three-Point Field Goals: Peterson 4-7, Granger 1-2, Richardson 1-1, Chappell 4-7, Team 10-17.

FG%: 1st Half 19-28 .679, 2nd Half 15-25 .600, Game 34-53 .642; 3FG%: 1st Half 8-12 .667, 2nd Half 2-5 .400, Game 10-17 .588; FT%: 1st Half 4-5 .800, 2nd Half 14-18 .778, Game 18-23 .783; Team Rebounds: 1; Deadball Rebounds: 4.

SCORE BY PERIODS	1	2	F
MVSU	20	43	63
Michigan State	50	46	96

OFFICIALS – Phil Bova, Art McDonald, Glenn Mayborg
TECHNICAL FOULS – None
ATTENDANCE – 15,138

Wright State 53, MSU 49
Dec. 30, 1999 • Ervin J. Nutter Center • Dayton, Ohio

Michigan State	FG-FGA	FT-FTA	REB	PF	TP	A	TO	BLK	S	MIN
Morris Peterson	2-15	0-1	5	3	4	1	1	1	2	34
A.J. Granger	6-10	2-2	6	2	17	2	1	2	1	32
Andre Hutson	3-5	2-3	2	2	8	2	2	1	0	29
Charlie Bell	3-9	2-2	7	2	8	2	3	0	2	36
Jason Richardson	1-4	0-0	2	1	2	2	1	0	0	18
Brandon Smith	0-0	0-0	0	0	0	0	0	0	0	1
David Thomas	0-2	0-0	2	2	0	0	0	0	0	7
Mike Chappell	3-9	2-2	4	3	10	0	2	0	0	23
Aloysius Anagonye	0-1	0-1	4	3	0	0	2	0	0	15
Adam Ballinger	0-0	0-0	1	0	0	0	0	0	0	5
Totals	18-55	8-11	34	18	49	9	12	4	5	200

Three-Point Field Goals: Peterson 0-5, Granger 3-6, Bell 0-1, Chappell 2-7, Team 5-19.

FG%: 1st Half 13-31 .419, 2nd Half 5-24 .208, Game 18-55 .327; 3FG%: 1st Half 4-12 .333, 2nd Half 1-7 .143, Game 5-19 .263; FT%: 1st Half 2-3 .667, 2nd Half 6-8 .750, Game 8-11 .727; Team Rebounds: 1; Deadball Rebounds: 0.

Wright State	FG-FGA	FT-FTA	REB	PF	TP	A	TO	BLK	S	MIN
Kevin Melson	5-15	5-6	8	3	16	4	4	2	1	35
Thomas Hope	1-3	1-2	10	5	3	2	3	0	0	40
Bruno Petersons	2-2	0-2	6	4	4	0	1	1	0	16
Tyson Freeman	1-3	0-0	2	1	3	0	3	0	1	13
Joe Bills	2-4	1-2	0	1	6	1	1	0	0	40
Israel Sheinfeld	2-6	2-2	4	2	7	1	2	1	1	24
Marcus May	3-6	6-6	0	2	14	0	2	0	0	31
Louis Holmes	0-0	0-0	0	0	0	0	0	0	0	1
Totals	16-39	15-20	31	18	53	8	17	4	3	200

Three-Point Field Goals: Melson 1-2, Hope 0-1, Freeman 1-2, Bills 1-3, Sheinfeld 1-1, May 2-4, Team 6-13.

FG%: 1st Half 10-24 .417, 2nd Half 6-15 .400, Game 16-39 .410; 3FG%: 1st Half 3-8 .375, 2nd Half 3-5 .600, Game 6-13 .462; FT%: 1st Half 3-4 .750, 2nd Half 12-16 .750, Game 15-20 .750; Team Rebounds: 1; Deadball Rebounds: 3.

SCORE BY PERIODS	1	2	F
Michigan State	32	17	49
Wright State	26	27	53

OFFICIALS – Jerry Petro, Mike Sanzere, Tom Clark
TECHNICAL FOULS – None
ATTENDANCE – 9,413

2000 BIG TEN AND UCONN

I n its first five decades of Big Ten basketball, Michigan State had never won back-to-back-to-back conference championships.

But then, it hadn't had a player like point guard Mateen Cleaves come back from an injury just in time for the league opener.

That's what happened on Jan. 5, 2000, when a soon-to-be three-time All-American returned to a leaderless 9-4 team.

Tom Izzo's players had shown flashes of greatness in wins at North Carolina and against Kansas. They had also blown big leads against Texas and at Kentucky. And they had failed to show up on time at Arizona and Wright State.

That baffling loss to the Raiders dropped the Spartans out of the top 10 for the first time in 11 months. They were No. 11 in the first Associated Press media poll of the 21st century.

So when Cleaves returned after a 10-week absence with a surgically repaired stress fracture in his right foot, the question was simple: Would MSU suddenly be the team it was supposed to be or would it take a month — three weeks too long — for everything to click?

"You can count the teams that have won three straight Big Ten titles," Izzo said of a feat that had been performed just seven times, twice in the previous 33 years. "I don't think we'll be 15-1 again. But when Mateen's OK, we should be, too. First, we have to survive January to be where we want to be in March."

Photo Credit: Kevin Fowler, MSU Sports Information

The first indication was a positive one, as the Spartans pulled away from Penn State for a 76-63 triumph in Breslin Center, their 19th win in a row against Big Ten teams.

With 16:53 left in the first half, Cleaves got a tap from assistant Stan Heath and reported to the scorer's table, as an Izzone-less crowd of 14,659 roared its approval. Cleaves entered the game at the 15:08 mark to the first of four standing ovations.

Twenty-nine seconds later, he had his first points of the season

on a mid-range jumper. Cleaves hit his first two shots of the year. And his first blind pass for a layup helped MSU grab a 20-9 lead.

After the Nittany Lions closed to within 33-31 at the half, Cleaves showed everyone what MSU had missed. He pulled his teammates together and told them what they needed to do, then showed them how to do it with a fast-break alley-oop to streaking forward Morris Peterson.

"It was just like old times," said Cleaves, who pranced his way to eight points and five assists in

21 minutes, 37 seconds. "I'd been preaching to Morris for more than two months that we'd hook up again. You have no idea how long I've been waiting for this."

The toughest part of Cleaves' day was convincing his mother, Frances, that he was ready to play and wouldn't risk reinjuring his foot. Instead, the only pain that night was felt by Penn State.

"He played just the way I taught him," Cleaves' father, Herbert, said. "But I liked the way they ran him in and out to get the chemistry going. He was dying the whole time he couldn't play."

Suddenly, life was good again. A 13-2 run gave the Spartans a 54-40 lead. They protected it with 15 points from forward A.J. Granger,

Photo Credit: Kevin Fowler, MSU Sports Information

14 from guard Charlie Bell, 12 from Peterson and 10 points and eight rebounds from sore-shouldered forward Andre Hutson, who yielded his starting spot for one game to freshman Aloysius Anagonye.

MSU held backcourt brothers Joe and Jon Crispin to 12 points on 3-for-18 shooting from the field, including 0-for-8 accuracy beyond the arc. Forward Jarrett Stephens and guard Titus Ivory each had 16 points. But that wasn't nearly enough when the Spartans shot 50.9 percent from the field and had a 39-27 edge in rebounds.

"It was a good start," Izzo said. "We ran the court a lot better. Mateen was a little rusty. But you would be, too, in your first game back. Now, some guys have to make some adjustments. I really think we can do that."

The next opportunity came three days later in Iowa City. And the Spartans took full advantage with a 75-53 win over the Hawkeyes and new head coach Steve Alford, despite a season-high 26 turnovers.

MSU led 11-0, 19-2 and 34-14 in Carver-Hawkeye Arena, as Peterson scored 20 of his game-high 29 points in the first half. Iowa never got closer than 14 points in a physical — almost dirty — second half and shot just 28.1 percent from the field, 11.1 from 3-point range.

Peterson was 8-for-13 and 4-for-7, respectively, and grabbed a game-high eight rebounds in just 28 minutes. Hutson added 14 points. And Cleaves' three assists tied him with Scott Skiles for the school's career record of 645.

Photo Credit: Kevin Fowler, MSU Sports Information

At the end of the game, Izzo glared at Alford, grabbed his hand and said he didn't appreciate the roughhouse play of Iowa center Jacob Jaacks, who fouled out before he could hurt someone — likely himself.

"It was…a typical Big Ten battle," Hutson said diplomatically after the Hawkeyes had done more hitting than they did in a 49-3 loss in Spartan Stadium three months earlier.

Three nights later, ninth-ranked Indiana came to Breslin for a Super Tuesday ESPN matchup, Bob Knight's last visit with the Hoosiers. After 45 minutes of spine-tingling play, no one who saw the finish will ever forget it.

2000 BIG TEN AND UCONN

MSU finally prevailed 77-71 in overtime to take sole possession of the Big Ten lead. But after leading 31-28 at the break, thanks to Bell's 15 first-half points, the Spartans saw a seven-point lead become a seven-point deficit with 2:45 left.

Cleaves fed Granger for a 3 with 1:21 left in regulation. And after a low-post basket by Hutson, Peterson rose over Indiana guard A.J. Guyton and hit an NBA 3 near the MSU bench with 11.3 seconds left to tie it at 62.

"That was a great shot that Peterson hit," Knight said of a 21-foot leaner. "We didn't want to foul. Someone was going to get a shot. And he made it. Obviously, that gave them new life."

The first of two overtime games with the Hoosiers was all Spartans in the final five minutes. MSU scored the first five points of the extra period and never looked back in Izzo's 100th career win.

Photo Credit: Kevin Fowler, MSU Sports Information

Photo Credit: Kevin Fowler, MSU Sports Information

"If there was ever a way to have a storybook finish to a 100th win, this would be the way," said Izzo, who couldn't turn off the tears when the game ended and fans chanted his name, waving a blizzard of "100" signs.

He wasn't as happy earlier that day, calling Izzone co-director Kevin Udy at 8:30 a.m. and quashing students' plans to wear camouflage gear to mock Knight for a hunting accident. He also ordered a ban on a "Hoosier daddy" chant that infuriated Knight at Northwestern.

Knight was relatively calm in Breslin. Perhaps he was like everyone else — caught up in a brilliant duel between Bell and Guyton, who would go on to share Big Ten Player of the Year honors with Peterson.

Bell won the battle with 22 points and deceptively strong defense. Though Guyton finished with 28 on 9-for-22 shooting from

2000 BIG TEN AND UCONN

the field, 11 of those points came in transition and six came against a slow-shifting zone. None of his baskets came in overtime.

"It's hard when someone scores 28 and you're proud of the guy who guarded him," Izzo said. "But when a guy goes through 8,913 picks . . . I know, because I counted every one of them."

Peterson added 17 points and Granger 13. And Bell wasn't the only hero in the backcourt. Cleaves had 10 points, eight assists, two steals and two turnovers in his first start of 2000.

Sounding a little like Jesse Ventura's "I don't have time to bleed" speech in "Predator," Cleaves said, "I don't have time to be tired," and played 37 minutes a week after his return.

It was the Spartans' 21st win in a row at home and 21st straight over a Big Ten opponent. That effort exemplified the Spartans' slogan for their 101st season: "Players play, tough players win," better known at Breslin as "PP-TPW."

One week later, Izzo was beaming over the decision of three-sport Saginaw High star Charles Rogers, the No. 1 football recruit in the nation, to sign with the Spartans and Bobby Williams' program.

But after a nine-day layoff from Tuesday to Thursday, Izzo's basketball team lost its football mentality — for one night only — in a 78-67 defeat at 13th-ranked Ohio State.

The Buckeyes had waited for this chance for 12 months. Jim O'Brien's team had lost 76-71 the previous year in East Lansing and hadn't had a chance to get even.

The 1999 co-champs never met in Columbus, at the Big Ten Tournament in Chicago or as half the Final Four in St. Petersburg.

When a crowd of 19,100 at Value City Arena enjoyed a convincing victory, it was no surprise the "Jim Rats" stormed the floor. Their team had just moved into a tie for the Big Ten lead with Indiana, while the 3-1, 12-5 Spartans slipped to a tie for third with Purdue and Michigan.

Neither team led by more than five points in the first 17 minutes. But with 4:10 left in the half, Cleaves drew his second foul and went to the bench. OSU promptly produced an 11-4 run and took a 42-33 lead to the locker room, thanks to 10 offensive rebounds.

That margin quickly grew to 13, as MSU had just eight assists with its 18 turnovers and shot 38.5 percent from the field. The Buckeyes had 49.1-percent accuracy and a 24-6 edge in bench points.

Peterson had game-highs of 20 points and 11 rebounds. Ohio natives Hutson and Granger had 14 and 11 points, respectively. And Cleaves had 10 points and seven assists. But reserve forward George Reese had 19 points for OSU. And the three-guard set of Scoonie Penn, Michael Redd and Brian Brown combined for 44.

"It doesn't get much better than this," O'Brien said in his familiar rasp. "It was a big-time atmosphere and a big-time game against a great team."

The Spartans didn't see it that way, as Peterson explained in a somber locker room: "They played

Photo Credit: Bruce Schwartzman/John Grieshop/John Grieshop/Jamie Sabau, Schwartzman Sports Photography

tougher than we did tonight. They outhustled us and just flat-out outplayed us."

A furious Izzo went two steps further, saying, "We need to get rid of that pretty-boy attitude and get back to playing with a meat-and-potatoes attitude."

Back in East Lansing, MSU did that with one of the strangest practices in Big Ten history — and one of the most effective. Returning to his football roots, Izzo had the Spartans work in helmets and shoulder pads the day before they hosted Northwestern.

"That might have been one of the best things we did," Izzo said. "Some of the guys really got into it. You should've seen Mateen. He always wanted to play college football. After I told him he should probably sit out, he told me he was practicing — no ifs, ands or buts."

It was a natural offshoot of War, Izzo's favorite practice drill. As MSU's rebound margins grew to amazing levels, coaches all across the country wanted to know, "What's this War drill? How do they do it?"

The answer was simple: "With will more than sheer size or skill." And the mysterious War drill? It was nothing but a "no-fatality, no-foul" battle for rebounds of coaches' intentionally missed shots.

"When I first saw the drill, I wasn't too sure," said power forward Aloysius Anagonye, a 6-foot-8, 250-pound freshman. "I thought it was a little crazy. I said, 'Someone could get hurt here.'"

Someone did — MSU's opponents. The Spartans led the nation with an average of 11.7 more rebounds than their foes, 2.0 better than runner-up Stanford. And after their lack of toughness in Columbus, the next team on the schedule was in trouble.

Enter Northwestern, a perfect team to pound into submission, 69-45. With Anagonye starting in place of Granger, MSU had one of the greatest rebounding efforts in Big Ten history, a 45-13 advantage. Though no player had more than eight, the Spartans grabbed 42 of the first 51 caroms and had an amazing 19-0 edge in offensive rebounds.

MSU led 14-0, then 33-17 at the break, as the Wildcats had more airballs than points in the first 9:32. And before the bulge grew to 28 in the second half, Izzo

Photo Credit: Bruce Schwartzman/John Grieshop/Jamie Sabau, Schwartzman Sports Photography

was deep into his bench. No Spartan played more than Cleaves' 27 minutes.

After failing to score for more than 33 minutes against the Buckeyes, Bell bounced back with 14 points on 5-for-7 shooting from the field. Peterson and Hutson each had 11 and matched Anagonye with eight rebounds. Cleaves had seven points and seven assists, while holding freshman guard Ben Johnson to three points, 9.8 below his average.

The win lifted MSU back into a tie for the league lead with OSU and Purdue. It was also the Spartans' 22nd win in a row at home, one shy of their school record from 1965-68 in Jenison Field House.

"They have a better chance of beating us 10 in a row than we have of beating them one out of

10," said Northwestern coach Kevin O'Neill, acknowledging the winners could play a lot better. "They'll be back here for a lot more dead bodies."

In a bizarre bit of scheduling, MSU met the Wildcats again five nights later in Evanston, Ill., with more than half the 5,907 in Welsh-Ryan Arena wearing green-and-white. And the second outcome was more lopsided for Northwestern's all-teenage lineup.

A 59-29 whipping could have been worse if Izzo had kept his foot to the pedal. When the Wildcats led 5-2, someone should have taken a picture. That was as close to a win over the Spartans as Northwestern is liable to get in any of their current players' careers.

The Spartans led 27-6 with 3:45 left in the half, as the Wildcats failed to score for 14:02. For the game, Northwestern shot just 17.9 percent from the field and 13.6 percent beyond the arc, while losing the battle on the boards 42-22.

It was the lowest point total for an MSU opponent since 1948 and the lowest in 50 years of conference membership, replacing Michigan's 32 points in an 11-point loss in 1951. And seven field goals were the fewest against the Spartans in 49 years.

"Defensively, we played about as well as we can play," Izzo said, brightening the day for future opponents. "But we only shot 44.9 percent and scored 59 points. That's a credit to them."

Peterson led all scorers with 19 points, more than any three

2000 BIG TEN AND UCONN

Wildcats. Hutson had 10 rebounds, more than triple Northwestern's top individual. And Cleaves had nine assists, two more than O'Neill's entire team.

Three days later on Super Bowl Sunday, MSU gave Izzo a perfect present for his 45th birthday by blasting Illinois 91-66 in Breslin. It was the Spartans' best performance all season and another example of what rebounding can do.

"It was a step in the right direction," Izzo said after runs of 13-0 late in the first half and 18-1 early in the second. "It was only one step....It was a big step, though."

MSU stepped on the Fighting Illini at every opportunity, leading 49-30 at halftime and building its cushion to 36 points with 2:40 left. The Spartans shot 54.0 percent from the field, with 23 assists and just 10 turnovers.

But the key was outrebounding the taller visitors 41-16. Hutson had a 10-9 edge by himself midway through the second half. The Spartans led 17-0 in second-chance points in the first period and finished with 17 offensive rebounds, one more than Illinois had at both ends.

"We were whipped very badly on the offensive boards," Illini coach Lon Kruger said. "We were a little awed and intimidated by how physical they were."

That was one of the nicest things anyone could say about an Izzo-coached team, especially when Bell and Cleaves did everything else. Bell had a game-high 20 points and seven rebounds. He also shadowed gunner Cory Bradford

and held him to 13 points. And Cleaves had 13 points, 12 often-spectacular assists and four steals.

"The better Mateen gets, the better we get," Bell said. "He made a couple of passes today that made me say, 'Wow!' and look at the scoreboard for replays."

With Peterson's 18 points, the three remaining "Flintstones" outscored Illinois' "Played in Peoria" group 51-11. Hutson overcame lower-back problems to produce 14 points and 11 rebounds. And Granger added nine points, six rebounds and a scrambling tie-up that summarized the day.

"I've got to watch you guys," Izzo said to the media, "We have two good years and you're ready to make us a dynasty. We have one good game and you're ready to say we're back....It was ONE good game."

Wrong. It was one great one — arguably the best all-around show in his first five seasons. And if Izzo had a problem with writers' and broadcasters' excessive praise, he had to wonder when he read Cleaves' comments. He also had to smile.

"We're not going to let down until we cut the nets in the Big Ten Tournament and cut them again the last Monday night (at the Final Four in Indianapolis)," Cleaves said prophetically.

That didn't stop Izzo from worrying about a matchup between his 6-1, 15-5 league-leaders and the 3-3, 12-5 Wolverines just two nights later. It didn't matter that MSU had won the previous three meetings by a total of 34 points. Izzo pointed to the five

games before that — Michigan victories by 22, 29, 13, 20 and 10 points.

"I remember a time not too long ago when it was the other way around," he insisted. "There are no guarantees. And nothing is forever."

The Spartans' longest streaks in the series had been five games under Pete Newell and Forddy Anderson from 1954-56 and four wins under Jud Heathcote with second-division Big Ten teams from 1981-83, just before Izzo arrived.

Even when MSU had been at its best, it had struggled with the Wolverines. It was 7-7 against Michigan en route to its first eight conference titles, including two losses in the Final Four year of 1957 and 2-2 with Earvin Johnson in 1978-79, Magical years in East Lansing.

Those disappointments all disappeared on Feb. 1 with an 82-62

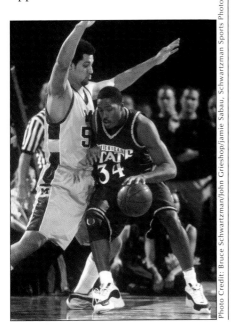

Photo Credit: Bruce Schwartzman/John Grieshop/Jamie Sabau, Schwartzman Sports Photography

triumph, the Spartans' largest victory margin in 77 visits to Ann Arbor. At least they vanished for everyone but a coaching perfectionist.

"I'm either going crazy or I know what it takes to get to the next level," Izzo said. "I'm not happy with how we played. And I let my guys know about it."

Let's see…MSU shot 50.9 percent from the field and 50.0 from 3-point range, held the Wolverines to 41.2 and 20.0 accuracy, respectively, and had a 39-29 rebound advantage… in Crisler Arena, where the Spartans had won two of the last seven. How disappointing can life get?

"It's special any time you beat Michigan," Peterson said. "I grew up watching Glen Rice and Steve Smith go at it. To win my last two games here is great."

So was Peterson, who had a career-high 32 points and 10 rebounds in 28 minutes, hitting 11-for-15 from the field and 5-for-8 from long range. His transition dunk over guard Kevin Gaines was one of the season's signature baskets.

"I'm just glad he did it on national TV," Cleaves said of an ESPN telecast. "Now, everyone should realize how good he is. I've seen him shoot that way since last summer. It's great to see his hard work pay off."

Cleaves did OK himself. He answered chants of "Al-co-hol-ic!" and "CBA!" with an NBA first-round performance. He was 5-for-9 from the field and 3-for-5 beyond the arc for a season-high 19 points, six assists and two steals.

"The last time I heard those things, I believe we won the Big Ten title here," Frances Cleaves said. "He always plays better when people make him mad. So we appreciate their fans for that."

Izzo appreciated a 10-point, 10-rebound contribution from Hutson and tremendous fan support. For every Michigan sign that read, "Save a couch, burn a Spartan," MSU had an appropriate answer on and off the court.

The Wolverines' problems began when freshman guard Jamal Crawford was yanked from the lineup over an eligibility question. When the school declined to declare him ineligible until a ruling came down, that stealth approach backfired at 5:45 p.m. when the NCAA said, "No decision."

Suddenly, a "Maize Rage" sign that spelled ESPN vertically with the taunt, "Every Spartan Pleads Not-guilty," was a boomerang to the back of the head. MSU fans didn't even have to mention Ed Martin to make Michigan fans squirm.

When Spartans hollered, "We own Crisler!" and Wolverines answered, "You own trailers!" MSU fired the final shot — the unkindest cut of all for a school with Michigan's proud tradition and omnipresent arrogance.

"Just like football!" fans in green-and-white bellowed, referring a 34-31 win over the Wolverines in Spartan Stadium. And MSU hadn't needed shoulder pads to pad its lead in the Big Ten standings.

Four days later, the Spartans welcomed defending national champ Connecticut to Breslin for a long-awaited rematch. But there were other special guests in the house for an afternoon worth remembering.

With the broadcast crew of Dick Enberg, Billy Packer and Al McGuire reunited for the first time in 19 years, the Spartans played a better first half than they had since a 50-17 pounding of Penn in the 1979 Final Four.

MSU led 46-17 at the break and coasted to an 85-66 win before a crowd that included three-time heavyweight boxing king/social icon Muhammad Ali and his son, Asaad, a huge Spartan fan.

Izzo's players met with "The Champ," then won every round against Jim Calhoun's struggling team. MSU outshot UConn 49.2 percent to 43.3, outrebounded the Huskies 40-26 and outhustled them at every opportunity.

Peterson led the winners with 16 points in their 24th win in a row at home. He also drew rave reviews from the coach of former All-America swingmen Ray Allen and Richard Hamilton.

"If his team wasn't so balanced and deep, he'd be scoring 25 a game, and we'd all be talking about how he's the best player in the country," Calhoun said of Peterson, who had more help than Habitat for Humanity.

Forward Jason Richardson, in his second game back from a chest injury, had 14 points, as the

Photo Credit: Kevin Fowler, MSU Sports Information

Spartans had a 34-13 edge in bench scoring. Granger had 13 points and a game-high eight rebounds. Bell, who nearly attended UConn, had 11 points, five assists and four steals. And though Cleaves was burned on defense by rival Khalid El-Amin, he had eight assists.

"I was surprised the way things went," Cleaves said. "I thought we'd win. But to win like that was really unbelievable."

Three nights later, in another Tuesday ESPN game, MSU met Purdue in Mackey Arena, where Bell and Hutson had never lost and where Peterson had made a memorable first visit three years earlier.

"I looked up at the ceiling and saw a '3-peat' sign, because they'd won the last three years," Peterson said of outright Big Ten titles from 1994-96. "I remember thinking, 'I hope we can win one championship before I graduate. In my wildest dreams, I didn't think we'd be in the position we're in now.'"

The Spartans were in great position to win their third in a row and back-to-back outright crowns after five straight wins by an average of 23.8 points. But they blew a 10-point lead to Brian Cardinal & Co. and stumbled 70-67 in their seventh game in 20 days.

"The difference was we ran out of gas — I hate to say that," Izzo said. "We didn't have the zip we usually have. And I'm going to take the blame for that. My heart always tells me we should go 100 miles an hour in practice. My head tells me I'm pushing them too hard."

Granger had 17 points and 12 rebounds but faded after playing 37 minutes. Cleaves had 11 points and nine assists. But Peterson was held to five points and Bell to four. And a 42-24 edge in rebounds was negated by sloppy ballhandling. MSU had 18 turnovers, including three in the final 2:18, to the Boilermakers' nine giveaways.

Back in a first-place tie with

OSU, the Spartans regrouped four days later at Wisconsin. Behind 18 points and 10 rebounds from Peterson and 11 of each from Granger, MSU pounded the Badgers 61-44 in the first of four meetings in seven weeks.

"This was a real emotional game for me because my heart is in a hospital in Mississippi," Peterson said after his grandmother, Clara Mae Spencer, had suffered a stroke three days earlier. "My whole family watched the game with her in her hotel room. So I'm glad it turned out this way."

The Spartans led 35-20 at halftime. And the Badgers never got closer than 14 points the rest of the way. The only question in the last 20 minutes was whether Wisconsin would score more points than it did in a 40-10 football win over MSU four months earlier in Camp Randall Stadium, a game that determined the Rose Bowl representative.

"We just got whipped pretty good," Dick Bennett said of his 4-7, 12-11 Badgers. "That's about the gist of it. The Spartans were as good as I can remember them being tonight....They were pretty much able to do whatever they wanted."

MSU shot 38.8 percent from the field and turned the ball over 16 times, twice as often as Wisconsin. But the Badgers were even colder, hitting 34.0 percent from the field and 21.1 percent beyond the arc. And when the Spartans had edges of 18-4 in free throws and 50-23 on the boards, they moved to 8-2, 18-6.

"We felt kind of helpless at one

point," Wisconsin forward Maurice Linton said. "Their talent was such a factor. They're loaded."

Two loaded teams met three nights later in Breslin for sole possession of first place. It was MSU's turn to get even with the Buckeyes. And it needed three "Flintstones" to do that in an 83-72 triumph.

Peterson had 26 points, Cleaves 24 and Bell 23 to account for 88.0 percent of the Spartans' output. Together, they outscored OSU by a point.

Peterson also had a thunderous jam over OSU shot-blocker Ken Johnson and a game-high 11 rebounds. And Cleaves had seven assists and his 176th career steal, moving ahead of Skiles for the top spot at MSU. But Bell was clearly the difference.

"Tonight, the stars were all good," said Izzo, whose team broke the game open with a 17-2 run midway through the first half. "But you still need that X-factor. Charlie really stepped up and answered the bell."

Photo Credit: Bruce Schwartzman/John Grieshop/Jamie Sabau, Schwartzman Sports Photography

He chimed in at just the right time and hit three straight fast-break layups to give the Spartans a 54-37 lead. The final two of those points came when O'Brien was whistled for his second technical and was forced to leave the arena floor.

"Nobody was looking for me," Bell said after 9-for-14 shooting from the field and 4-for-4 work at the line. "And when everyone forgets about me, that's when I'm going to hurt you."

Bell also had six rebounds, two steals and a loose-ball recovery that prevented a layup. Apparently, he was tired of hearing how he belonged on the side of a milk carton after his disappearance at Purdue. So he decided to assert himself, as he had in starring roles against Kansas and Indiana.

MSU also had a 23-14 advantage in free throws and a 43-30 edge in rebounds. Those numbers helped the 9-2, 19-6 Spartans climb a full game ahead of OSU, Indiana and Purdue in the Big Ten standings with five games to play.

The next challenge was a rematch with the Badgers, who made tremendous improvement in a week. Bennett's team gave MSU all it could handle in Breslin after sowing the seeds of self-doubt in Kohl Center.

"They're everything you'd want in a basketball team," Wisconsin forward Andy Kowske said. "I don't know if there's a whole lot we can do. They're better than us in every category. We'd have to play a perfect game — the best game of our lives."

The Badgers almost did that in a 59-54 squeaker. They trailed just 31-29 at the break and began the second half with a three-point play by Kowske to claim their first lead. By boxing out on every shot, they became the first team all season to outrebound the Spartans, 29-26.

But MSU snapped a tie at 39 with a 14-5 run. Cleaves' 3 with 5:35 left made it 53-44, a seemingly safe lead in some minds. Instead, the Wisconsin team that hit a Big Ten-record 11 straight 3s against Michigan showed up a minute too late.

The Spartans needed six free throws in the final 46.7 seconds to earn a 20th win for the 10th time, as Peterson and Bell each scored 15 points and Cleaves had 12.

"We're on a mission to be Big Ten champs — alone," Peterson said before MSU left for a game with Penn State. "We know the only way we can guarantee that is to win the rest of our games."

Easier said than done in a week with two road games. But the Spartans handled the first challenge in a 79-63 win over the Nittany Lions on Wednesday, Feb. 23. That lifted MSU to 11-3, 21-6 and made it 8-0 against teams with losing Big Ten records.

"Hey, that's what we're supposed to do," a smiling Izzo said after his team's fifth conference road win, thanks largely to 55.9-percent accuracy from the field and 42-22 edge in rebounds.

Peterson had 17 points, Granger 15 and Bell and Cleaves 11 apiece. Cleaves also had 10 assists to pass Michigan's Gary

2000 BIG TEN AND UCONN

Grant for second place on the Big Ten's all-time list. But the key was sore-footed guard David Thomas, who provided eight points, a game-high 10 rebounds and tight defense on Penn State's Joe Crispin in the second half.

Three days later, with a probable outright title and Big Ten Player of the Year honors at stake, the Spartans stumbled for the seventh and final time. An 81-79 overtime loss at Indiana dropped them into a first place tie with Purdue at 11-3, a half-game ahead ahead of OSU.

The Hoosiers got 34 points, including five in the last minute of regulation, from Guyton, who would soon be the media's pick as the Big Ten MVP. But after a bizarre MSU turnover, it was Guyton's airball that set off a wild celebration in Assembly Hall.

"It seemed to be our day," Guyton said. "But we earned it against the best team in the Big Ten."

Cleaves was the second-best player on the floor with 22 points, including 19 in the second half, and five steals. But he also had nine of the Spartans' 22 turnovers, nearly triple Indiana's eight giveaways.

The violation that drove Izzo crazy came on an inbounds play in front of the MSU bench with 17.4 seconds left in regulation and the score tied at 72. Granger told veteran official Jody Silvester he wanted a timeout if the five-second count reached four. But when he turned to get that, it was already too late.

Silvester, a respected ref who had worked three Final Fours since 1979, was making his final visit to Assembly Hall before retiring and had his own cheering section among Indiana fans. Though no one would ever challenge his integrity, the Spartans had to wonder what happened.

They are still wondering how they could shoot 53.1 percent from the field and 40.0 beyond the arc, hold the Hoosiers to 42.6 percent from the field, have edges of 19-17 in free throws and 39-30 in rebounds . . . and lose.

That is what happens when an opponent banks a 3 home unintentionally, gets another one to drop after it bounces to the top of the backboard and scores the game-winner on an accident. To put it another way, all the breaks MSU got in its overtime win in Breslin evened out.

Guyton joked that he deserved

Photo Credit: Kevin Fowler, MSU Sports Information

2000 BIG TEN AND UCONN

an assist on the airball putback by forward Lynn Washington, who grabbed the ball on the far side of the basket and dropped it in at the buzzer for his only points of the day.

"In a lot of ways, this was one of the better college basketball games I've been involved in," Izzo said. "Unfortunately for me, the wrong team won. There were lots of plays both ways and some big-time players who made them. But if we play that well, we're going to go a long way."

With a 1-4 record in games decided by four points or less, compared to a 4-1 mark the previous year, the Spartans decided to eliminate all suspense the following Thursday against Minnesota.

Thanks to first-half surges of 16-0 and 28-6, MSU built a 44-15 halftime lead and cruised 79-43. Forward Mike Chappell led a balanced attack with 18 points, including four 3s in seven tries. And Richardson came off the bench to grab a game-high 12 rebounds in a 45-29 domination.

After Indiana's win over Purdue and OSU's win at Penn State, that meant the Spartans and Buckeyes would share the title at 13-3 if MSU won at home against Michigan and OSU prevailed at Minnesota.

But there was no way to predict what the Spartans would do to the Wolverines in a record-obliterating 114-63 mismatch on Senior Day — Cleaves' farewell party for 14,659 of his closest friends.

Following the final introductions for Cleaves, Peterson, Granger and Steve Cherry, MSU performed a

basketball autopsy on the Michigan program. The Spartans led 51-24 at halftime, then poured home 63 more against an opponent that refused to play defense.

"It was an incredible day," Izzo said. "I don't think I can downplay it. And I don't think I can change anything. It just seemed like every guy who took a shot made the shot."

Though some said Izzo poured it on against his least-favorite foe, that wasn't the case. No one played more than 29 minutes. And the only reason Cleaves was in the game until he kissed the floor with 4:12 left was to get two assist records he richly deserved.

Izzo told him at halftime, "You've got seven assists. Make it a special day and go for 20! You've been good. . . . But I didn't bring you in to be good."

Proving he was coachable, Cleaves got 20 to break the Big Ten single-game mark of Purdue's Bruce Parkinson. And with 769-and-counting for his career, he passed Illinois point guard Bruce Douglas.

Most of his feeds seemed to benefit Bell, who blitzed and bombed the Wolverines for a career-high 31 points. But Granger had 18, Hutson 15 — plus 10 rebounds — and Peterson 12.

"I told the team in the huddle with about three minutes left, 'Hey, seniors, this was your day, but Charlie said, 'The hell with you guys, I'm taking over!'" Izzo said. "And Charlie agreed with me."

Everyone except Michigan's players, coaches and small group of fans agreed it was a perfect

Photo Credit: Kevin Fowler, MSU Sports Information

sendoff. But before a championship banner was unfurled, before a confetti drop, a fireworks show and a wild dance to Kool & The Gang's "Celebration," there were tears, too.

"At first, I tried to hold in all my emotions," Cleaves said. "But Coach is a very emotional guy. He hugged me and said, 'I love you man!' Then, I started crying, too."

A few minutes later, Cleaves was laughing again — and making a pledge no future opponent would find humorous: "Just think, they said (a three-peat) it couldn't be done. . . . But I want to thank everybody here and ask you to stay behind us because we WILL win a national championship!"

Izzo always said Cleaves was a man of his word. And the word was out: MSU had nine more games to win and the will to do whatever that took.

MSU 76, Penn State 63
Jan. 5, 2000 • Breslin Center • East Lansing, Mich.

Penn State	FG-FGA	FT-FTA	REB	PF	TP	A	TO	BLK	S	MIN
Jarrett Stephens	7-19	2-2	5	3	16	0	1	0	3	37
Titus Ivory	4-8	6-7	2	3	16	4	1	0	1	37
Carl Jackson	2-2	0-0	2	4	4	0	1	0	0	10
Joe Crispin	1-8	5-6	2	1	7	5	4	0	2	38
Jon Crispin	2-10	1-2	5	3	5	2	3	0	0	32
Brandon Watkins	0-0	0-0	1	0	0	0	1	0	0	5
Gyasi Cline-Heard	5-8	0-2	5	4	10	0	2	3	0	28
Tyler Smith	1-1	0-0	1	2	3	1	1	0	0	10
Marcus Banta	1-1	0-0	1	2	2	0	0	0	0	3
Totals	23-57	14-19	27	22	63	12	16	3	7	200

Three-Point Field Goals: Stephens 0-2, Ivory 2-4, Joe Crispin 0-3, Jon Crispin 0-5, Smith 1-1, Team 3-15.

FG%: 1st Half 11-23 .478, 2nd Half 12-34 .353, Game 23-57 .404; 3FG%: 1st Half 0-3 .000, 2nd Half 3-12 .250, Game 3-15 .200; FT%: 1st Half 9-13 .692, 2nd Half 5-6 .833, Game 14-19 .737; Team Rebounds: 3; Deadball Rebounds: 4.

Michigan State	FG-FGA	FT-FTA	REB	PF	TP	A	TO	BLK	S	MIN
Aloysius Anagonye	2-4	4-4	5	1	8	0	1	2	0	19
Morris Peterson	6-7	0-0	7	2	12	1	0	0	2	28
A.J. Granger	4-7	7-8	3	1	15	1	3	0	1	28
Charlie Bell	5-12	4-6	5	3	14	3	7	0	0	29
Mike Chappell	1-3	0-0	2	2	3	0	0	0	0	19
David Thomas	1-2	0-0	2	0	2	2	0	1	1	13
Mateen Cleaves	3-6	2-4	1	4	8	5	3	0	0	21
Jason Richardson	1-3	2-2	1	4	4	0	2	0	0	10
Andre Hutson	5-10	0-1	8	2	10	2	1	1	0	23
Adam Ballinger	0-1	0-1	2	0	0	0	0	0	0	10
Totals	28-55	19-26	39	19	76	14	17	4	4	200

Three-Point Field Goals: Peterson 0-1, Granger 0-1, Chappell 1-2, Cleaves 0-2, Richardson 0-1, Team 1-7.

FG%: 1st Half 13-29 .448, 2nd Half 15-26 .577, Game 28-55 .509; 3FG%: 1st Half 0-4 .000, 2nd Half 1-3 .333, Game 1-7 .143; FT%: 1st Half 7-9 .778, 2nd Half 12-17 .706, Game 19-26 .731; Team Rebounds: 3; Deadball Rebounds: 3.

SCORE BY PERIODS	1	2		F
Penn State	31	32	--	63
Michigan State	33	43	--	76

OFFICIALS – Ed Hightower, Phil Bova, Tom Clark
TECHNICAL FOULS – None
ATTENDANCE – 15,138

MSU 75, Iowa 53
Jan. 8, 2000 • Carver-Hawkeye Arena • Iowa City, Iowa

Michigan State	FG-FGA	FT-FTA	REB	PF	TP	A	TO	BLK	S	MIN
Andre Hutson	6-8	2-5	2	3	14	2	2	0	1	25
Morris Peterson	8-13	9-12	8	3	29	4	3	0	2	28
A.J. Granger	1-4	2-2	7	4	4	1	3	0	1	26
Charlie Bell	1-6	2-2	5	2	4	7	5	1	2	28
Mike Chappell	2-5	0-0	3	3	5	1	1	0	0	20
Brandon Smith	0-0	0-0	0	0	0	1	0	0	0	1
David Thomas	3-4	1-2	4	0	7	1	3	0	3	13
Mateen Cleaves	1-3	0-0	2	4	3	3	3	0	1	20
Mat Ishbia	1-1	0-0	0	0	2	0	0	0	0	1
Jason Richardson	0-2	5-7	3	5	5	0	2	1	0	14
Aloysius Anagonye	0-1	0-0	0	2	0	0	2	1	0	14
Adam Ballinger	0-0	2-2	3	2	2	0	0	0	0	10
Totals	23-47	23-32	45	27	75	20	26	3	10	200

Three-Point Field Goals: Peterson 4-7, Granger 0-1, Bell 0-1, Chappell 1-3, Cleaves 1-2, Richardson 0-1, Team 6-15.

FG%: 1st Half 12-28 .429, 2nd Half 11-19 .579, Game 23-47 .489; 3FG%: 1st Half 5-10 .500, 2nd Half 1-5 .200, Game 6-15 .400; FT%: 1st Half 8-10 .800, 2nd Half 15-22 .682, Game 23-32 .719; Team Rebounds: 4; Deadball Rebounds: 4.

Iowa	FG-FGA	FT-FTA	REB	PF	TP	A	TO	BLK	S	MIN
Rob Griffin	0-11	1-4	5	3	1	0	1	0	0	25
Duez Henderson	1-2	2-2	5	5	4	0	0	1	0	15
Jacob Jaacks	5-9	6-12	7	5	16	0	3	0	0	30
Dean Oliver	6-16	7-9	3	2	21	4	2	0	4	37
Kyle Galloway	0-5	0-0	0	1	0	2	2	0	2	17
Jason Price	1-2	1-2	1	1	3	0	2	0	0	11
Joe Fermino	0-0	1-4	4	1	0	0	1	0	0	20
Marcelo Gomes	0-0	0-0	0	1	0	0	1	0	0	4
Ryan Luehrsmann	3-10	0-0	2	4	7	2	3	0	1	30
Rod Thompson	0-1	0-0	1	3	0	0	0	0	1	9
Jason Smith	0-1	0-0	0	0	0	0	0	0	0	1
John Carl Williams	0-0	0-0	0	1	0	0	0	0	0	1
Totals	16-57	18-33	32	28	53	7	14	1	8	200

Three-Point Field Goals: Griffin 0-6, Jaacks 0-1, Oliver 2-7, Galloway 0-3, Price 0-1, Luehrsmann 1-7, Thompson 0-1, Smith 0-1, Team 3-27.

FG%: 1st Half 5-24 .208, 2nd Half 11-33 .333, Game 16-57 .281; 3FG%: 1st Half 2-12 .167, 2nd Half 1-15 .067, Game 3-27 .111; FT%: 1st Half 8-18 .444, 2nd Half 10-15 .667, Game 18-33 .545; Team Rebounds: 3; Deadball Rebounds: 8.

SCORE BY PERIODS	1	2		F
Michigan State	37	38	--	75
Iowa	20	33	--	53

OFFICIALS – Gene Monje, Mike Sanzere, Paul Janssen
TECHNICAL FOULS – Oliver (UI)
ATTENDANCE – 15,500

Photo Credit: Bruce Schwartzman/John Grieshop/Jamie Sabau, Schwartzman Sports Photography

Photo Credit: Kevin Fowler, MSU Sports Information

MSU 77, Indiana 71
Jan. 11, 2000 • Breslin Center • East Lansing, Mich.

Indiana	FG-FGA	FT-FTA	REB	PF	TP	A	TO	BLK	S	MIN
Dane Fife	4-4	1-2	4	5	10	1	0	1	3	36
Jeffrey Newton	1-6	0-0	3	4	2	0	2	2	0	23
Kirk Haston	3-14	5-7	8	1	11	1	6	0	0	32
Michael Lewis	3-5	2-3	5	4	10	5	2	1	2	40
A.J. Guyton	9-22	6-7	2	2	28	2	3	0	1	42
Luke Jimenez	0-0	0-0	0	0	0	0	1	0	0	1
Kyle Hornsby	0-0	0-0	0	1	0	1	0	0	0	4
Larry Richardson	0-0	0-0	0	1	0	0	1	0	0	7
Jarrad Odle	3-8	1-1	7	3	7	2	2	0	0	25
Lynn Washington	1-3	1-2	5	2	3	0	0	0	0	15
Totals	24-62	16-22	37	23	71	12	17	3	6	225

Three-Point Field Goals: Fife 1-1, Lewis 2-3, Guyton 4-9, Team 7-13.

FG%: 1st Half 11-27 .407, 2nd Half 12-28 .429, OT 1-7 .143, Game 24-62 .387; 3FG%: 1st Half 3-5 .600, 2nd Half 3-5 .600, OT 1-3 .333, Game 7-13 .538; FT%: 1st Half 3-4 .750, 2nd Half 7-11 .636, OT 6-7 .857, Game 16-22 .727; Team Rebounds: 3; Deadball Rebounds: 1.

Michigan State	FG-FGA	FT-FTA	REB	PF	TP	A	TO	BLK	S	MIN
Andre Hutson	2-5	3-5	6	2	7	1	5	0	1	28
Morris Peterson	5-13	5-9	5	4	17	0	5	0	0	28
A.J. Granger	4-10	3-4	8	1	13	0	1	2	2	39
Mateen Cleaves	3-9	4-4	4	3	10	8	2	1	2	37
Charlie Bell	7-15	7-8	4	4	22	1	3	0	4	39
Brandon Smith	0-0	0-0	0	0	0	0	0	0	0	1
David Thomas	0-1	2-2	2	4	2	1	1	0	0	16
Mat Ishbia	0-0	0-0	0	0	0	0	0	0	0	1
Mike Chappell	0-2	0-0	2	0	0	1	1	0	0	8
Jason Richardson	1-2	0-0	1	0	2	0	0	0	1	9
Aloysius Anagonye	2-3	0-0	8	1	4	0	1	1	3	18
Adam Ballinger	0-0	0-0	2	1	0	0	1	0	0	1
Totals	24-60	24-32	46	20	77	11	17	6	13	225

Three-Point Field Goals: Peterson 2-6, Granger 2-6, Cleaves 0-2, Bell 1-4, Chappell 0-2, Team 5-20.

FG%: 1st Half 11-31 .355, 2nd Half 10-24 .417, OT 3-5 .600, Game 24-60 .400; 3FG%: 1st Half 2-9 .222, 2nd Half 3-10 .300, OT 0-1 .000, Game 5-20 .250; FT%: 1st Half 7-9 .778, 2nd Half 8-11 .727, OT 9-12 .750, Game 24-32 .750; Team Rebounds: 6; Deadball Rebounds: 4.

SCORE BY PERIODS	1	2	OT	F
Indiana	28	34	9	71
Michigan State	31	31	15	77

OFFICIALS – Tom Rucker, Steve Welmer, Jody Silvester
TECHNICAL FOULS – None
ATTENDANCE – 15,138

Ohio State 78, MSU 67
Jan. 20, 2000 • Value City Arena • Columbus, Ohio

Michigan State	FG-FGA	FT-FTA	REB	PF	TP	A	TO	BLK	S	MIN
Andre Hutson	5-11	4-6	9	4	14	0	0	0	0	32
Morris Peterson	6-12	6-6	11	4	20	0	5	0	0	34
A.J. Granger	3-8	2-2	1	1	11	0	1	0	0	33
Mateen Cleaves	4-12	2-3	1	4	10	7	5	0	1	31
Charlie Bell	1-6	4-5	6	2	6	1	3	1	0	31
Brandon Smith	0-0	0-0	0	1	0	0	0	0	0	1
David Thomas	0-2	0-0	1	0	0	1	0	0	0	8
Mike Chappell	0-0	0-0	3	3	0	0	1	0	0	13
Jason Richardson	0-0	0-0	0	1	0	0	0	0	0	1
Aloysius Anagonye	1-1	4-4	1	3	6	0	2	0	0	14
Adam Ballinger	0-0	0-0	0	0	0	0	0	0	0	2
Totals	20-52	22-26	34	23	67	8	18	1	1	200

Three-Point Field Goals: Peterson 2-7, Granger 3-5, Cleaves 0-4, Bell 0-1, Team 5-17.

FG%: 1st Half 13-27 .481, 2nd Half 7-25 .280, Game 20-52 .385; 3FG%: 1st Half 3-8 .375, 2nd Half 2-9 .222, Game 5-17 .294; FT%: 1st Half 4-5 .800, 2nd Half 18-21 .857, Game 22-26 .846; Team Rebounds: 1; Deadball Rebounds: 4.

Ohio State	FG-FGA	FT-FTA	REB	PF	TP	A	TO	BLK	S	MIN
Cobe Ocokoljic	1-3	0-1	2	3	2	0	0	0	0	10
Ken Johnson	3-4	2-2	5	5	8	0	0	4	1	22
Scoonie Penn	3-11	8-10	3	2	16	4	2	0	2	36
Brian Brown	6-8	2-2	2	2	14	1	3	0	0	31
Michael Redd	6-14	2-5	5	1	14	3	3	0	1	37
Brent Darby	0-0	0-0	0	1	0	1	0	0	0	2
Boban Savovic	0-2	3-3	3	0	3	1	1	0	0	14
George Reese	8-13	3-4	5	4	19	0	0	0	0	30
Will Dudley	1-2	0-0	4	4	2	2	0	0	1	18
Totals	28-57	20-27	31	22	78	12	9	4	6	200

Three-Point Field Goals: Penn 2-8, Brown 0-1, Redd 0-2, Savovic 0-2, Team 2-13.

FG%: 1st Half 15-29 .517, 2nd Half 13-28 .464, Game 28-57 .491; 3FG%: 1st Half 2-6 .333, 2nd Half 0-7 .000, Game 2-13 .154; FT%: 1st Half 10-13 .769, 2nd Half 10-14 .714, Game 20-27 .741; Team Rebounds: 2; Deadball Rebounds: 3.

SCORE BY PERIODS	1	2		F
Michigan State	33	34	--	67
Ohio State	42	36	--	78

OFFICIALS – Ed Hightower, Tom O'Neill, Jody Silvester
TECHNICAL FOULS – None
ATTENDANCE – 19,100

MSU 69, Northwestern 45
Jan. 22, 2000 • Breslin Center • East Lansing, Mich.

Northwestern	FG-FGA	FT-FTA	REB	PF	TP	A	TO	BLK	S	MIN
Steve Lepore	3-9	2-2	1	3	11	2	1	1	1	27
Jason Burke	2-9	0-0	3	0	5	0	1	1	1	30
Brody Deren	3-4	1-2	1	2	7	0	2	0	2	22
Ben Johnson	1-5	0-1	1	1	3	2	1	1	1	35
Collier Drayton	0-0	0-0	2	3	0	0	1	0	0	13
Winston Blake	1-3	0-0	1	1	3	1	1	0	0	14
David Newman	1-3	0-0	0	0	3	1	1	0	0	19
Tavaras Hardy	2-3	0-0	1	0	4	0	2	0	0	22
Aaron Jennings	3-5	3-4	1	3	9	1	1	1	0	18
Totals	16-41	6-9	13	13	45	7	11	5	5	200

Three-Point Field Goals: Lepore 3-8, Burke 1-2, Johnson 1-3, Blake 1-1, Newman 1-3, Hardy 0-1, Team 7-18.

FG%: 1st Half 6-20 .300, 2nd Half 10-21 .476, Game 16-41 .390; 3FG%: 1st Half 2-9 .222, 2nd Half 5-9 .556, Game 7-18 .389; FT%: 1st Half 3-5 .600, 2nd Half 3-4 .750, Game 6-9 .667; Team Rebounds: 2; Deadball Rebounds: 3.

Michigan State	FG-FGA	FT-FTA	REB	PF	TP	A	TO	BLK	S	MIN
Aloysius Anagonye	3-4	1-3	8	5	7	0	2	0	0	22
Morris Peterson	4-14	2-2	8	1	11	1	3	0	0	26
Andre Hutson	3-5	5-6	8	1	11	2	1	0	0	26
Mateen Cleaves	3-9	0-0	0	1	7	7	3	0	1	27
Charlie Bell	5-7	2-3	6	0	14	3	0	0	0	24
Brandon Smith	0-1	0-0	0	0	0	0	0	0	0	4
David Thomas	4-4	0-0	2	1	8	0	0	1	2	15
Mat Ishbia	0-0	0-0	1	0	0	0	0	0	0	2
Mike Chappell	2-8	0-2	6	2	4	0	1	0	0	13
Steve Cherry	0-0	0-0	0	0	0	0	0	0	0	2
Jason Richardson	0-0	0-0	1	0	0	0	1	0	1	7
A.J. Granger	2-2	0-0	3	2	5	0	1	0	0	19
Adam Ballinger	1-3	0-0	1	1	2	0	0	0	0	13
Totals	27-57	10-16	45	14	69	13	13	1	5	200

Three-Point Field Goals: Peterson 1-4, Cleaves 1-3, Bell 2-3, Chappell 0-3, Granger 1-1, Team 5-14.

FG%: 1st Half 14-26 .538, 2nd Half 13-31 .419, Game 27-57 .474; 3FG%: 1st Half 4-9 .444, 2nd Half 1-5 .200, Game 5-14 .357; FT%: 1st Half 1-4 .250, 2nd Half 9-12 .750, Game 10-16 .625; Team Rebounds: 1; Deadball Rebounds: 3.

SCORE BY PERIODS	1	2	F
Northwestern	17	28	--	45
Michigan State	33	36	--	69

OFFICIALS – Rick Hartzell, Sid Rodeheffer, Terry Anderson
TECHNICAL FOULS – None
ATTENDANCE – 14,659

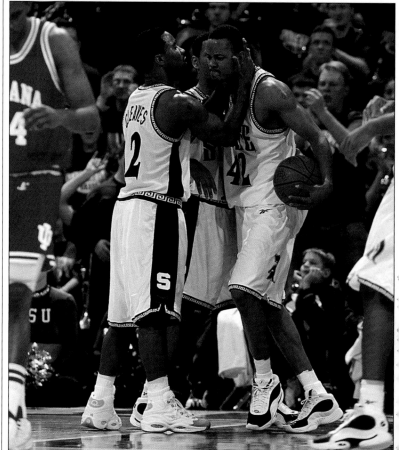

MSU 59, Northwestern 29
Jan. 27, 2000 • Welsh-Ryan Arena • Evanston, Ill.

Michigan State	FG-FGA	FT-FTA	REB	PF	TP	A	TO	BLK	S	MIN
Aloysius Anagonye	2-2	0-0	1	3	4	0	4	3	1	21
Andre Hutson	2-2	1-2	10	1	5	1	1	0	1	22
Morris Peterson	6-12	5-6	6	2	19	0	0	0	2	30
Mateen Cleaves	2-5	3-3	2	1	7	9	4	0	2	27
Charlie Bell	2-4	0-0	5	3	4	2	4	0	1	25
Brandon Smith	1-1	1-2	0	3	3	2	0	0	0	7
David Thomas	1-4	0-0	7	2	2	2	2	0	1	22
Mat Ishbia	0-0	0-0	0	0	0	0	1	0	0	2
Mike Chappell	4-11	0-0	3	1	9	0	0	0	0	20
A.J. Granger	2-8	2-2	7	2	6	0	0	1	1	24
Totals	22-49	12-15	42	18	59	16	14	5	9	200

Three-Point Field Goals: Peterson 2-4, Bell 0-2, Thomas 0-1, Chappell 1-7, Granger 0-2, Team 3-16.
FG%: 1st Half 14-29 .483, 2nd Half 8-20 .400, Game 22-49 .449; 3FG%: 1st Half 1-7 .143, 2nd Half 2-9 .222, Game 3-16 .188; FT%: 1st Half 3-4 .750, 2nd Half 9-11 .818, Game 12-15 .800; Team Rebounds: 1; Deadball Rebounds: 1.

Northwestern	FG-FGA	FT-FTA	REB	PF	TP	A	TO	BLK	S	MIN
Steve Lepore	1-7	1-1	1	3	4	1	1	0	0	25
Jason Burke	0-6	1-3	3	2	1	1	1	0	0	32
Brody Deren	0-1	0-0	1	2	0	1	2	0	0	20
Winston Blake	2-6	3-3	1	1	8	0	4	0	0	32
Ben Johnson	1-7	0-0	2	3	3	0	2	0	1	27
David Newman	0-3	3-4	2	3	3	3	2	0	1	22
Collier Drayton	0-0	0-0	1	0	0	0	0	0	0	6
Tavaras Hardy	2-5	2-3	3	1	6	1	0	0	0	17
Adam Robinson	0-0	0-2	0	0	0	1	0	0	0	2
Aaron Jennings	1-4	2-2	2	2	4	0	1	0	0	17
Totals	7-39	12-18	22	17	29	7	17	0	2	200

Three-Point Field Goals: Lepore 1-6, Burke 0-3, Blake 1-5, Johnson 1-4, Newman 0-3, Hardy 0-1, Team 3-22.
FG%: 1st Half 3-16 .188, 2nd Half 4-23 .174, Game 7-39 .179; 3FG%: 1st Half 0-7 .000, 2nd Half 3-15 .200, Game 3-22 .136; FT%: 1st Half 6-8 .750, 2nd Half 6-10 .600, Game 12-18 .667; Team Rebounds: 7; Deadball Rebounds: 3.

SCORE BY PERIODS	1	2	F
Michigan State	32	27	59
Northwestern	12	17	29

OFFICIALS – Tom Rucker, Donnee Gray, Dan Chrisman
TECHNICAL FOULS – None
ATTENDANCE – 5,907

MSU 91, Illinois 66
Jan. 30, 2000 • Breslin Center • East Lansing, Mich.

Illinois	FG-FGA	FT-FTA	REB	PF	TP	A	TO	BLK	S	MIN
Brian Cook	5-9	2-3	6	3	12	0	0	0	0	24
Sergio McClain	0-1	0-0	0	2	0	2	0	1	1	13
Robert Archibald	0-1	1-3	3	1	1	0	1	0	0	22
Cory Bradford	5-11	2-2	0	1	13	2	1	0	2	30
Frank Williams	3-8	3-3	1	2	11	4	2	0	0	33
Victor Chukwudebe	1-2	0-2	4	2	2	0	1	0	1	13
Nate Mast	0-0	0-0	0	2	0	0	0	0	0	2
Joe Cross	1-1	0-0	0	3	3	0	0	0	0	5
Lucas Johnson	1-1	4-4	0	0	7	0	1	0	1	9
Sean Harrington	3-5	0-0	3	1	8	1	0	0	0	15
Cleotis Brown	1-4	1-2	2	0	3	2	3	0	0	17
Damir Krupalija	3-5	0-0	2	1	6	0	0	0	0	21
Totals	23-48	13-19	16	17	66	12	11	1	5	200

Three-Point Field Goals: Cook 0-2, Bradford 1-5, Williams 2-4, Cross 1-1, Johnson 1-1, Harrington 2-3, Brown 0-2, Team 7-18.
FG%: 1st Half 11-25 .440, 2nd Half 12-23 .522, Game 23-48 .479; 3FG%: 1st Half 3-10 .300, 2nd Half 4-8 .500, Game 7-18 .389; FT%: 1st Half 5-6 .833, 2nd Half 8-13 .615, Game 13-19 .684; Team Rebounds: 1; Deadball Rebounds: 4.

Michigan State	FG-FGA	FT-FTA	REB	PF	TP	A	TO	BLK	S	MIN
Aloysius Anagonye	0-0	1-2	3	4	1	0	1	0	0	17
Morris Peterson	6-9	1-2	1	2	18	4	3	0	1	21
Andre Hutson	6-9	2-3	11	1	14	1	0	0	0	24
Mateen Cleaves	6-13	1-2	3	2	13	12	2	0	4	30
Charlie Bell	8-13	1-1	7	1	20	2	1	0	1	25
Brandon Smith	0-0	0-0	0	0	0	1	0	0	0	5
David Thomas	2-3	3-4	3	3	7	1	1	0	0	20
Mat Ishbia	0-0	0-0	1	0	0	0	1	0	0	2
Mike Chappell	2-9	0-0	1	0	5	0	1	0	0	17
Steve Cherry	0-1	0-0	0	1	0	0	0	0	0	2
A.J. Granger	3-5	2-2	6	2	9	1	0	1	0	24
Adam Ballinger	1-1	2-2	0	2	4	0	1	0	1	13
Totals	34-63	13-18	41	17	91	23	10	1	7	200

Three-Point Field Goals: Peterson 5-7, Cleaves 0-1, Bell 3-4, Chappell 1-6, Cherry 0-1, Granger 1-3, Team 10-22.
FG%: 1st Half 20-35 .571, 2nd Half 14-28 .500, Game 34-63 .540; 3FG%: 1st Half 6-10 .600, 2nd Half 4-12 .333, Game 10-22 .455; FT%: 1st Half 3-5 .600, 2nd Half 10-13 .769, Game 13-18 .722; Team Rebounds: 5; Deadball Rebounds: 4.

SCORE BY PERIODS	1	2	F
Illinois	30	36	66
Michigan State	49	42	91

OFFICIALS – Ed Hightower, Ted Hillary, Gene Monje
TECHNICAL FOULS – None
ATTENDANCE – 14,659

MSU 82, Michigan 62
Feb. 1, 2000 • Crisler Arena • Ann Arbor, Mich.

Michigan State	FG-FGA	FT-FTA	REB	PF	TP	A	TO	BLK	S	MIN
Aloysius Anagonye	1-1	0-0	1	3	2	0	2	1	1	17
Morris Peterson	11-15	5-8	10	1	32	2	1	0	1	28
Andre Hutson	4-9	2-3	10	3	10	4	3	2	2	30
Mateen Cleaves	5-9	6-8	2	3	19	6	5	0	2	28
Charlie Bell	1-5	4-4	4	3	7	2	2	0	0	28
Brandon Smith	0-0	0-2	0	0	0	0	0	0	0	2
David Thomas	1-1	0-0	3	2	2	0	0	0	1	11
Mike Chappell	0-2	0-0	0	0	0	0	0	0	0	11
Jason Richardson	1-3	0-0	2	2	2	1	0	0	0	12
A.J. Granger	3-8	0-0	3	4	8	1	2	0	2	22
Adam Ballinger	0-0	0-0	2	3	0	0	1	0	0	10
Totals	27-53	17-25	39	24	82	16	16	3	9	200

Three-Point Field Goals: Peterson 5-8, Cleaves 3-5, Bell 1-3, Richardson 0-1, Granger 2-5, Team 11-22.
FG%: 1st Half 15-30 .500, 2nd Half 12-23 .522, Game 27-53 .509; 3FG%: 1st Half 7-12 .583, 2nd Half 4-10 .400, Game 11-22 .500; FT%: 1st Half 1-2 .500, 2nd Half 16-23 .696, Game 17-25 .680; Team Rebounds: 2; Deadball Rebounds: 2.

Michigan	FG-FGA	FT-FTA	REB	PF	TP	A	TO	BLK	S	MIN
LaVell Blanchard	6-13	4-5	7	2	16	2	1	0	0	38
Brandon Smith	3-6	2-4	2	2	8	2	1	0	1	33
Josh Asselin	4-5	2-4	3	5	10	1	1	1	1	16
Leon Jones	3-11	3-7	3	4	11	0	4	0	0	34
Kevin Gaines	2-7	3-4	3	3	8	3	6	0	4	40
Gavin Groninger	0-3	0-0	0	0	0	0	0	0	0	12
Chris Young	2-3	1-1	3	2	5	0	1	2	0	14
Leland Anderson	1-3	2-2	1	2	4	0	2	0	0	10
Peter Vignier	0-0	0-0	1	0	0	0	2	0	0	3
Totals	21-51	17-27	29	20	62	8	18	3	6	200

Three-Point Field Goals: Blanchard 0-2, Smith 0-1, Jones 2-5, Gaines 1-5, Groninger 0-2, Team 3-15.
FG%: 1st Half 13-27 .481, 2nd Half 8-24 .333, Game 21-51 .412; 3FG%: 1st Half 1-6 .167, 2nd Half 2-9 .222, Game 3-15 .200; FT%: 1st Half 5-11 .455, 2nd Half 12-16 .750, Game 17-27 .630; Team Rebounds: 6; Deadball Rebounds: 4.

SCORE BY PERIODS	1	2	F
Michigan State	38	44	82
Michigan	32	30	62

OFFICIALS – Jim Burr, Donnee Gray, Tim Higgins
TECHNICAL FOULS – None
ATTENDANCE – 13,562

MSU 85, Connecticut 66
Feb. 5, 2000 • Breslin Center • East Lansing, Mich.

Connecticut	FG-FGA	FT-FTA	REB	PF	TP	A	TO	BLK	S	MIN
Kevin Freeman	2-8	2-2	5	3	6	0	3	0	2	32
Edmund Saunders	3-6	0-0	2	2	6	1	0	0	0	21
Jake Voskuhl	3-5	1-3	6	2	7	1	2	1	0	27
Albert Mouring	5-12	0-0	3	2	13	2	2	0	0	39
Khalid El-Amin	8-19	3-4	3	2	21	4	6	0	0	36
Ajou Deng	1-1	0-0	2	1	2	1	1	0	0	5
Beau Archibald	0-2	0-0	0	4	0	2	0	0	0	14
Souleymane Wane	3-5	1-2	3	0	7	0	2	1	1	18
Marcus Cox	1-2	2-2	0	3	4	2	0	0	0	8
Totals	26-60	9-13	26	19	66	13	15	3	6	200

Three-Point Field Goals: Freeman 0-2, Mouring 3-7, El-Amin 2-9, Archibald 0-2, Team 5-20.
FG%: 1st Half 8-28 .286, 2nd Half 18-32 .563, Game 26-60 .433; 3FG%: 1st Half 1-11 .091, 2nd Half 4-9 .444, Game 5-20 .250; FT%: 1st Half 0-0 .000, 2nd Half 9-13 .692, Game 9-13 .692; Team Rebounds: 2; Deadball Rebounds: 3.

Michigan State	FG-FGA	FT-FTA	REB	PF	TP	A	TO	BLK	S	MIN
Morris Peterson	6-15	2-2	4	1	16	2	1	0	2	29
A.J. Granger	3-9	6-7	8	2	13	0	1	0	0	30
Andre Hutson	2-3	0-0	2	3	4	0	2	1	1	22
Mateen Cleaves	3-8	1-2	2	3	7	8	7	0	1	31
Charlie Bell	4-8	0-0	4	3	11	5	2	0	4	27
Brandon Smith	0-0	2-3	0	0	2	1	0	0	0	3
David Thomas	0-1	0-0	1	0	0	1	0	0	0	7
Mat Ishbia	0-0	0-0	0	1	0	0	0	0	0	1
Mike Chappell	1-3	2-2	2	1	5	0	1	0	0	7
Steve Cherry	0-0	0-0	0	0	0	0	1	0	0	1
Jason Richardson	7-9	0-0	7	0	14	0	0	4	2	18
Aloysius Anagonye	3-4	3-3	5	3	9	0	1	0	3	18
Adam Ballinger	1-1	2-2	1	2	4	1	0	0	1	6
Totals	30-61	18-21	40	19	85	16	16	5	10	200

Three-Point Field Goals: Peterson 2-7, Granger 1-5, Cleaves 0-2, Bell 3-5, Thomas 0-1, Chappell 1-2, Team 7-22.
FG%: 1st Half 18-34 .529, 2nd Half 12-27 .444, Game 30-61 .492; 3FG%: 1st Half 3-11 .273, 2nd Half 4-11 .364, Game 7-22 .318; FT%: 1st Half 7-7 1.000, 2nd Half 11-14 .786, Game 18-21 .857; Team Rebounds: 5; Deadball Rebounds: 3.

SCORE BY PERIODS	1	2	F
Connecticut	17	49	66
Michigan State	46	39	85

OFFICIALS – Tim Higgins, Ed Colbert, Donnee Gray
TECHNICAL FOULS – None
ATTENDANCE – 14,659

Purdue 70, MSU 67

Feb. 8, 2000 • Mackey Arena • West Lafayette, Ind.

Michigan State	FG-FGA	FT-FTA	REB	PF	TP	A	TO	BLK	S	MIN
Andre Hutson	4-6	1-3	5	4	9	2	3	0	0	25
Morris Peterson	2-9	1-4	6	4	5	0	5	0	3	32
A.J. Granger	5-10	5-5	12	2	17	0	2	0	1	37
Mateen Cleaves	5-13	0-0	2	1	11	9	5	0	0	35
Charlie Bell	2-8	0-0	3	4	4	0	1	0	0	23
Brandon Smith	0-0	0-0	0	0	0	0	0	0	0	1
David Thomas	1-1	0-0	0	0	2	0	0	0	0	4
Mike Chappell	2-5	0-0	2	5	4	0	1	0	0	10
Jason Richardson	3-5	1-2	3	2	7	0	0	0	0	15
Aloysius Anagonye	3-4	0-0	7	4	6	0	1	0	0	12
Adam Ballinger	0-0	2-2	0	0	2	0	0	0	0	6
Totals	27-61	10-16	42	26	67	11	18	0	4	200

Three-Point Field Goals: Peterson 0-3, Granger 2-6, Cleaves 1-3, Bell 0-2, Chappell 0-3, Richardson 0-2, Team 3-19.

FG%: 1st Half 16-28 .571, 2nd Half 11-33 .333, Game 27-61 .443; 3FG%: 1st Half 2-8 .250, 2nd Half 1-11 .091, Game 3-19 .158; FT%: 1st Half 7-11 .636, 2nd Half 3-5 .600, Game 10-16 .625; Team Rebounds: 2; Deadball Rebounds: 4.

Purdue	FG-FGA	FT-FTA	REB	PF	TP	A	TO	BLK	S	MIN
Mike Robinson	4-8	8-12	5	3	16	2	0	1	2	37
Rodney Smith	2-3	0-0	3	4	4	2	0	0	0	15
Brian Cardinal	6-13	4-4	2	3	17	4	1	0	2	32
Jaraan Cornell	5-10	1-5	1	1	12	1	2	1	1	29
Carson Cunningham	2-8	2-4	2	0	8	4	4	0	0	35
Chad Kerkhof	1-1	0-0	0	1	2	1	0	0	1	6
Maynard Lewis	2-5	2-2	0	2	6	0	0	0	1	12
Kenny Lowe	0-0	0-0	1	0	0	0	0	0	0	1
Adam Wetzel	0-0	0-0	0	1	0	0	1	0	0	1
Greg McQuay	0-1	1-4	5	1	1	0	1	1	0	23
John Allison	1-1	2-2	3	0	4	0	0	0	0	9
Totals	23-50	20-33	24	16	70	14	9	3	7	200

Three-Point Field Goals: Cardinal 1-5, Cornell 1-4, Cunningham 2-5, Lewis 0-2, Team 4-16.

FG%: 1st Half 13-27 .481, 2nd Half 10-23 .435, Game 23-50 .460; 3FG%: 1st Half 1-7 .143, 2nd Half 3-9 .333, Game 4-16 .250; FT%: 1st Half 8-14 .571, 2nd Half 12-19 .632, Game 20-33 .606; Team Rebounds: 2; Deadball Rebounds: 10.

SCORE BY PERIODS	1	2		F
Michigan State	41	26	--	67
Purdue	35	35	--	70

OFFICIALS – Ed Hightower, Art McDonald, Tom Clark
TECHNICAL FOULS – None
ATTENDANCE – 14,123

MSU 61, Wisconsin 44

Feb. 12, 2000 • Kohl Center • Madison, Wis.

Michigan State	FG-FGA	FT-FTA	REB	PF	TP	A	TO	BLK	S	MIN
Andre Hutson	3-4	1-3	4	1	7	0	6	0	0	27
Morris Peterson	5-15	6-6	10	2	18	2	1	0	0	30
A.J. Granger	4-8	0-0	11	2	11	0	0	0	0	31
Mateen Cleaves	7-10	3-4	2	1	7	4	4	0	2	30
Charlie Bell	2-6	1-2	6	3	5	3	2	0	0	23
Brandon Smith	0-0	0-0	0	0	0	0	0	0	0	2
David Thomas	0-0	0-0	2	2	0	0	0	0	0	7
Mat Ishbia	0-0	0-0	0	0	0	0	0	0	0	1
Mike Chappell	1-3	7-7	1	1	9	1	0	0	0	8
Jason Richardson	2-3	0-0	4	1	4	0	0	1	0	20
Aloysius Anagonye	0-0	0-1	4	2	0	1	3	0	0	15
Adam Ballinger	0-0	0-0	0	1	0	0	0	0	0	6
Totals	19-49	18-23	50	16	61	11	16	1	2	200

Three-Point Field Goals: Peterson 2-3, Granger 3-5, Cleaves 0-2, Bell 0-3, Chappell 0-1, Team 5-14.

FG%: 1st Half 11-27 .407, 2nd Half 8-22 .364, Game 19-49 .388; 3FG%: 1st Half 2-9 .222, 2nd Half 3-5 .600, Game 5-14 .357; FT%: 1st Half 11-13 .846, 2nd Half 7-10 .700, Game 18-23 .783; Team Rebounds: 6; Deadball Rebounds: 1.

Wisconsin	FG-FGA	FT-FTA	REB	PF	TP	A	TO	BLK	S	MIN
Andy Kowske	3-8	0-0	7	3	6	0	0	0	0	27
Mark Vershaw	1-10	2-2	3	2	4	0	1	0	0	32
Jon Bryant	2-6	1-2	2	1	6	0	0	0	1	29
Mike Kelley	0-0	0-0	1	4	0	2	0	0	2	16
Roy Boone	2-7	0-2	2	1	4	3	3	0	0	27
Travon Davis	0-1	0-0	1	1	0	0	0	0	0	3
Maurice Linton	5-8	0-2	1	0	10	0	1	0	1	19
Duany Duany	3-5	0-0	0	2	8	0	0	0	1	18
Kirk Penney	1-6	0-0	1	0	2	0	2	0	0	12
Robert Smith	0-0	0-0	0	0	0	0	1	0	0	1
Charlie Wills	1-2	0-0	4	5	3	2	1	0	0	14
Julian Swartz	0-0	1-2	0	0	1	0	0	0	0	1
Erik Faust	0-0	0-0	0	0	0	0	0	0	0	1
Totals	18-53	4-10	23	19	44	7	8	0	5	200

Three-Point Field Goals: Vershaw 0-1, Bryant 1-3, Boone 0-4, Davis 0-1, Linton 0-1, Duany 2-4, Penney 0-3, Wills 1-2, Team 4-19.

FG%: 1st Half 9-30 .300, 2nd Half 9-23 .391, Game 18-53 .340; 3FG%: 1st Half 2-11 .182, 2nd Half 2-8 .250, Game 4-19 .211; FT%: 1st Half 0-2 .000, 2nd Half 4-8 .500, Game 4-10 .400; Team Rebounds: 1; Deadball Rebounds: 2.

SCORE BY PERIODS	1	2		F
Michigan State	35	26	--	61
Wisconsin	20	24	--	44

OFFICIALS – Jody Silvester, Art McDonald, J.D. Collins
TECHNICAL FOULS – None
ATTENDANCE – 17,142

MSU 83, Ohio State 72
Feb. 15, 2000 • Breslin Center • East Lansing, Mich.

Ohio State	FG-FGA	FT-FTA	REB	PF	TP	A	TO	BLK	S	MIN
Michael Redd	7-18	3-3	5	0	18	3	3	0	1	36
George Reese	5-10	0-0	3	4	10	0	0	0	3	34
Ken Johnson	2-6	1-1	8	4	5	0	1	3	0	34
Scoonie Penn	8-17	9-10	3	2	30	7	5	0	2	38
Brian Brown	4-6	1-1	1	4	9	1	3	0	4	27
Brent Darby	0-1	0-1	0	4	0	0	0	0	0	14
Doylan Robinson	0-0	0-0	3	2	0	0	0	0	0	9
Boban Savovic	0-0	0-0	2	1	0	0	1	0	0	1
Cobe Ocokoljic	0-0	0-0	0	0	0	0	0	0	0	2
Will Dudley	0-1	0-2	2	1	0	0	1	0	0	5
Totals	26-59	14-18	30	24	72	11	14	3	10	200

Three-Point Field Goals: Redd 1-6, Penn 5-10, Brown 0-1, Team 6-17.
FG%: 1st Half 12-27 .444, 2nd Half 14-32 .438, Game 26-59 .441; 3FG%: 1st Half 3-7 .429, 2nd Half 3-10 .300, Game 6-17 .353; FT%: 1st Half 6-8 .750, 2nd Half 8-10 .800, Game 14-18 .778; Team Rebounds: 3; Deadball Rebounds: 2.

Michigan State	FG-FGA	FT-FTA	REB	PF	TP	A	TO	BLK	S	MIN
Morris Peterson	7-18	9-12	11	2	26	1	3	1	2	33
A.J. Granger	0-4	0-0	9	2	0	2	0	1	2	31
Andre Hutson	2-7	1-5	6	4	5	1	1	0	0	26
Mateen Cleaves	6-10	9-12	0	3	24	7	6	0	1	36
Charlie Bell	9-14	4-4	6	2	23	0	2	0	2	30
David Thomas	0-0	0-0	1	0	0	1	0	0	0	5
Mike Chappell	1-2	0-0	2	1	3	0	1	0	0	5
Jason Richardson	0-1	0-0	1	2	0	0	1	0	0	11
Aloysius Anagonye	1-1	0-2	5	2	2	0	1	1	1	20
Adam Ballinger	0-0	0-0	0	0	0	0	0	0	1	3
Totals	26-57	23-35	43	19	83	12	15	3	8	200

Three-Point Field Goals: Peterson 3-9, Granger 0-2, Cleaves 3-4, Bell 1-4, Chappell 1-1, Team 8-20.
FG%: 1st Half 15-27 .556, 2nd Half 11-30 .367, Game 26-57 .456; 3FG%: 1st Half 7-9 .778, 2nd Half 1-11 .091, Game 8-20 .400; FT%: 1st Half 7-12 .583, 2nd Half 16-23 .696, Game 23-35 .657; Team Rebounds: 2; Deadball Rebounds: 5.

SCORE BY PERIODS	1	2	F
Ohio State	33	39	-- 72
Michigan State	44	39	-- 83

OFFICIALS – Jim Burr, Tom O'Neill, Gene Monje
TECHNICAL FOULS – Ohio State bench (2), Michigan State (hanging on rim)
ATTENDANCE – 14,659

MSU 59, Wisconsin 54
Feb. 19, 2000 • Breslin Center • East Lansing, Mich.

Wisconsin	FG-FGA	FT-FTA	REB	PF	TP	A	TO	BLK	S	MIN
Maurice Linton	2-6	0-0	0	2	5	2	2	0	0	24
Duany Duany	1-4	3-4	2	3	6	0	0	0	0	16
Andy Kowske	2-7	7-8	7	2	11	2	3	1	0	29
Mike Kelley	1-3	0-1	5	2	2	1	1	0	0	33
Roy Boone	3-7	2-2	6	5	8	1	4	0	1	23
Travon Davis	1-2	0-0	4	1	2	0	0	0	0	7
Jon Bryant	3-5	0-0	1	3	9	1	1	0	2	25
Kirk Penney	0-0	0-0	0	0	0	0	0	0	0	4
Charlie Wills	1-2	0-0	0	2	3	0	3	0	0	16
Mark Vershaw	2-5	3-3	3	4	8	1	3	0	1	23
Totals	16-41	15-18	29	24	54	8	17	1	4	200

Three-Point Field Goals: Linton 1-1, Duany 1-4, Kelley 0-1, Boone 0-2, Bryant 3-5, Wills 1-1, Vershaw 1-1, Team 7-15.
FG%: 1st Half 9-21 .429, 2nd Half 7-20 .350, Game 16-41 .390; 3FG%: 1st Half 5-7 .714, 2nd Half 2-8 .250, Game 7-15 .467; FT%: 1st Half 6-6 1.000, 2nd Half 9-12 .750, Game 15-18 .833; Team Rebounds: 1; Deadball Rebounds: 4.

Michigan State	FG-FGA	FT-FTA	REB	PF	TP	A	TO	BLK	S	MIN
Morris Peterson	5-13	4-5	4	2	15	0	1	0	0	32
A.J. Granger	2-4	2-2	5	2	7	2	2	0	1	33
Andre Hutson	0-4	2-3	3	4	2	1	1	1	1	32
Mateen Cleaves	3-11	5-6	1	1	12	6	2	0	2	34
Charlie Bell	4-10	6-6	3	4	15	0	0	0	1	26
David Thomas	0-0	3-4	2	2	3	0	0	0	0	7
Mike Chappell	0-0	0-0	0	1	0	1	0	0	0	5
Jason Richardson	1-4	0-0	6	0	2	0	1	0	0	16
Aloysius Anagonye	1-1	1-2	1	3	3	0	1	0	0	10
Adam Ballinger	0-0	0-0	1	0	0	0	0	0	0	5
Totals	16-47	23-28	26	19	59	10	8	1	5	200

Three-Point Field Goals: Peterson 1-5, Granger 1-1, Cleaves 1-3, Bell 1-3, Team 4-12.
FG%: 1st Half 9-23 .391, 2nd Half 7-24 .292, Game 16-47 .340; 3FG%: 1st Half 3-7 .429, 2nd Half 1-5 .200, Game 4-12 .333; FT%: 1st Half 10-11 .909, 2nd Half 13-17 .765, Game 23-28 .821; Team Rebounds: 0; Deadball Rebounds: 5.

SCORE BY PERIODS	1	2	F
Wisconsin	29	25	-- 54
Michigan State	31	28	-- 59

OFFICIALS – Art McDonald, Sid Rodeheffer, Tim Hutchenson
TECHNICAL FOULS – None
ATTENDANCE – 14,659

MSU 79, Penn State 63
Feb. 23, 2000 • Bryce Jordan Center • State College, Pa.

Michigan State	FG-FGA	FT-FTA	REB	PF	TP	A	TO	BLK	S	MIN
Andre Hutson	4-4	0-0	5	3	8	2	1	0	2	30
Morris Peterson	7-12	1-2	6	1	17	1	2	0	2	31
A.J. Granger	6-10	2-2	8	3	15	0	2	0	1	34
Mateen Cleaves	5-10	0-2	2	4	11	10	5	0	1	30
Charlie Bell	4-9	1-2	3	4	11	2	2	0	0	21
Brandon Smith	0-0	0-0	0	0	0	2	0	0	0	2
David Thomas	3-4	2-2	10	1	8	0	1	0	2	20
Mat Ishbia	0-0	0-0	0	0	0	0	0	0	1	1
Mike Chappell	1-4	1-2	3	1	3	0	0	0	0	7
Jason Richardson	0-0	0-1	0	2	0	0	1	1	0	8
Aloysius Anagonye	1-3	0-0	4	3	2	0	1	0	0	8
Adam Ballinger	2-3	0-0	1	1	4	0	0	0	0	8
Totals	33-59	7-13	42	23	79	15	18	1	8	200

Three-Point Field Goals: Peterson 2-5, Granger 1-4, Cleaves 1-3, Bell 2-4, Chappell 0-2, Team 6-18.
FG%: 1st Half 17-30 .567, 2nd Half 16-29 .552, Game 33-59 .559; 3FG%: 1st Half 3-11 .273, 2nd Half 3-7 .429, Game 6-18 .333; FT%: 1st Half 4-6 .667, 2nd Half 3-7 .429, Game 7-13 .538; Team Rebounds: 0; Deadball Rebounds: 2.

Penn State	FG-FGA	FT-FTA	REB	PF	TP	A	TO	BLK	S	MIN
Jarrett Stephens	6-15	6-6	8	2	18	3	2	0	0	35
Tyler Smith	0-0	0-0	1	0	0	1	0	0	0	23
Carl Jackson	1-1	0-0	2	2	2	0	1	0	0	10
Joe Crispin	6-16	3-4	6	1	18	4	3	0	0	33
Titus Ivory	2-9	1-3	0	2	6	6	2	0	3	33
Ken Krimmel	1-1	0-0	0	0	2	0	0	0	0	1
Jon Crispin	2-4	1-2	0	3	5	1	1	0	3	26
Brandon Watkins	1-2	0-0	1	1	2	0	0	0	1	9
Gyasi Cline-Heard	3-4	4-7	3	2	10	1	2	1	1	28
Marcus Banta	0-0	0-2	0	0	0	0	1	0	0	2
Totals	22-52	15-24	22	13	63	15	12	1	8	200

Three-Point Field Goals: Stephens 0-1, Joe Crispin 3-6, Ivory 1-4, Jon Crispin 0-1, Watkins 0-1, Team 4-13.
FG%: 1st Half 12-26 .462, 2nd Half 10-26 .385, Game 22-52 .423; 3FG%: 1st Half 4-10 .400, 2nd Half 0-3 .000, Game 4-13 .308; FT%: 1st Half 7-11 .636, 2nd Half 8-13 .615, Game 15-24 .625; Team Rebounds: 1; Deadball Rebounds: 5.

SCORE BY PERIODS	1	2	F
Michigan State	41	38	-- 79
Penn State	35	28	-- 63

OFFICIALS – Mike Sanzere, Donnee Gray, Steve Olson
TECHNICAL FOULS – Penn State bench
ATTENDANCE – 11,954

Photo Credit: Kevin Fowler, MSU Sports Information

Indiana 81, MSU 79
Feb. 26, 2000 • Assembly Hall • Bloomington, Ind.

Michigan State	FG-FGA	FT-FTA	REB	PF	TP	A	TO	BLK	S	MIN
Andre Hutson	6-7	5-10	5	3	17	2	3	0	1	36
Morris Peterson	3-10	4-5	10	3	11	0	3	1	0	36
A.J. Granger	1-2	0-0	6	3	3	1	3	0	0	35
Mateen Cleaves	7-10	5-5	1	2	22	2	9	0	5	37
Charlie Bell	4-10	3-4	7	5	13	4	2	0	0	28
David Thomas	0-2	0-0	1	2	0	1	0	0	1	10
Mike Chappell	1-1	2-2	1	1	5	0	1	0	0	4
Jason Richardson	3-5	0-0	3	1	6	1	1	0	0	20
Aloysius Anagonye	0-0	0-0	2	4	0	1	0	0	0	10
Adam Ballinger	1-2	0-0	1	0	2	0	0	1	0	9
Totals	26-49	19-26	39	24	79	12	22	2	7	225

Three-Point Field Goals: Peterson 1-4, Granger 1-2, Cleaves 3-5, Bell 2-6, Chappell 1-1, Richardson 0-2, Team 8-20.

FG%: 1st Half 12-20 .600, 2nd Half 12-23 .522, OT 2-6 .333, Game 26-49 .531; 3FG%: 1st Half 5-8 .625, 2nd Half 2-9 .222, OT 1-3 .333, Game 8-20 .400; FT%: 1st Half 4-6 .667, 2nd Half 13-18 .722, OT 2-2 1.000, Game 19-26 .731; Team Rebounds: 2; Deadball Rebounds: 3.

Indiana	FG-FGA	FT-FTA	REB	PF	TP	A	TO	BLK	S	MIN
Kirk Haston	6-13	1-2	6	3	13	1	1	4	1	31
Lynn Washington	1-5	0-1	3	2	2	0	1	0	2	25
Dane Fife	1-5	2-2	3	2	4	1	0	0	0	27
Michael Lewis	3-6	0-0	1	5	9	6	2	0	0	28
A.J. Guyton	13-24	5-5	3	0	34	1	3	0	0	38
Luke Jimenez	0-1	0-0	0	2	0	2	0	0	1	17
Kyle Hornsby	2-6	6-7	5	2	10	2	0	0	2	26
Larry Richardson	2-5	3-4	4	3	7	0	0	0	0	18
Jeffrey Newton	1-3	0-2	3	1	2	1	1	0	0	15
Totals	29-68	17-23	30	20	81	14	8	4	6	225

Three-Point Field Goals: Lewis 3-5, Guyton 3-7, Jimenez 0-1, Hornsby 0-1, Team 6-14.

FG%: 1st Half 16-37 .432, 2nd Half 9-24 .375, OT 4-7 .571, Game 29-68 .426; 3FG%: 1st Half 4-5 .800, 2nd Half 2-7 .286, OT 0-2 .000, Game 6-14 .429; FT%: 1st Half 2-4 .500, 2nd Half 14-17 .824, OT 1-2 .500, Game 17-23 .739; Team Rebounds: 2; Deadball Rebounds: 3.

SCORE BY PERIODS	1	2	OT	F
Michigan State	33	39	7	79
Indiana	38	34	9	81

OFFICIALS – Jody Silvester, Steve Welmer, Jim Jenkins
TECHNICAL FOULS – None
ATTENDANCE – 17,412

MSU 79, Minnesota 43
March 2, 2000 • Breslin Center • East Lansing, Mich.

Minnesota	FG-FGA	FT-FTA	REB	PF	TP	A	TO	BLK	S	MIN
Shane Schilling	4-14	1-1	4	2	9	0	1	0	0	29
Dusty Rychart	4-6	2-2	2	3	10	0	1	0	0	21
Ryan Wildenborg	2-4	2-2	1	3	6	0	2	0	1	18
Mitch Ohnstad	2-7	0-0	4	1	5	1	2	0	0	28
Terrance Simmons	1-11	1-2	3	0	4	3	4	0	1	30
Nick Sinville	1-2	0-2	5	0	2	0	1	0	1	19
Kevin Burleson	1-5	0-0	2	1	3	3	0	1	1	22
Ryan Keating	0-2	0-0	1	0	0	3	1	0	1	11
Kyle Sanden	2-5	0-0	3	1	4	0	0	0	0	14
John Aune	0-0	0-0	2	1	0	1	0	0	0	8
Totals	17-56	6-9	29	12	43	11	13	1	5	200

Three-Point Field Goals: Schilling 0-4, Ohnstad 1-2, Simmons 1-5, Burleson 1-4, Team 3-15.
FG%: 1st Half 6-27 .222, 2nd Half 11-29 .379, Game 17-56 .304; 3FG%: 1st Half 0-10 .000, 2nd Half 3-5 .600, Game 3-15 .200; FT%: 1st Half 3-4 .750, 2nd Half 3-5 .600, Game 6-9 .667; Team Rebounds: 2; Deadball Rebounds: 3.

Michigan State	FG-FGA	FT-FTA	REB	PF	TP	A	TO	BLK	S	MIN
Morris Peterson	6-10	1-1	7	0	13	1	1	0	2	21
A.J. Granger	4-6	0-0	6	2	9	3	1	0	0	25
Andre Hutson	0-2	3-4	3	1	3	1	2	0	1	22
Mateen Cleaves	5-10	1-2	3	1	12	9	1	0	0	24
Charlie Bell	4-7	2-2	5	1	11	1	0	0	0	18
Brandon Smith	0-2	0-0	0	1	0	3	1	0	0	12
Mat Ishbia	1-2	0-0	0	0	2	1	0	0	0	5
Mike Chappell	7-11	0-0	3	3	18	0	2	0	0	22
Steve Cherry	0-1	0-0	0	0	0	0	1	0	0	4
Jason Richardson	3-9	0-1	12	0	6	2	0	0	1	24
Adam Ballinger	2-3	1-2	3	2	5	0	1	0	2	23
Totals	32-63	8-12	45	11	79	21	10	0	8	200

Three-Point Field Goals: Peterson 0-3, Granger 1-1, Cleaves 1-3, Bell 1-2, Smith 0-1, Ishbia 0-1, Chappell 4-7, Cherry 0-1, Richardson 0-1, Team 7-20.
FG%: 1st Half 19-34 .559, 2nd Half 13-29 .448, Game 32-63 .508; 3FG%: 1st Half 5-12 .417, 2nd Half 2-8 .250, Game 7-20 .350; FT%: 1st Half 1-1 1.000, 2nd Half 7-11 .636, Game 8-12 .667; Team Rebounds: 3; Deadball Rebounds: 0.

SCORE BY PERIODS	1	2		F
Minnesota	15	28	--	43
Michigan State	44	35	--	79

OFFICIALS – Jim Burr, Steve Welmer, Tom O'Neill
TECHNICAL FOULS – None
ATTENDANCE – 14,659

MSU 114, Michigan 63
March 4, 2000 • Breslin Center • East Lansing, Mich.

Michigan	FG-FGA	FT-FTA	REB	PF	TP	A	TO	BLK	S	MIN
Gavin Groninger	3-10	0-0	3	0	7	2	4	0	0	34
Brandon Smith	2-3	2-2	3	2	6	1	2	0	0	21
Josh Asselin	5-7	3-4	3	1	13	0	0	3	0	21
Kevin Gaines	2-10	4-4	2	1	9	8	4	0	2	37
LaVell Blanchard	3-17	2-2	6	1	9	1	1	0	0	33
Leon Jones	3-7	1-2	1	4	9	1	1	0	0	20
Chris Young	0-1	0-0	0	3	0	0	1	0	0	11
Leland Anderson	3-5	0-0	5	2	6	0	1	0	0	14
Peter Vignier	2-4	0-0	3	1	4	0	1	0	0	9
Totals	23-64	12-14	32	15	63	13	15	3	2	200

Three-Point Field Goals: Groninger 1-6, Gaines 1-5, Blanchard 1-5, Jones 2-4, Team 5-20.

FG%: 1st Half 8-24 .333, 2nd Half 15-40 .375, Game 23-64 .359; 3FG%: 1st Half 3-10 .300, 2nd Half 2-10 .200, Game 5-20 .250; FT%: 1st Half 5-6 .833, 2nd Half 7-8 .875, Game 12-14 .857; Team Rebounds: 6; Deadball Rebounds: 1.

Michigan State	FG-FGA	FT-FTA	REB	PF	TP	A	TO	BLK	S	MIN
Morris Peterson	3-15	5-7	9	1	12	1	1	1	1	28
A.J. Granger	7-8	0-0	4	0	18	1	0	0	1	28
Andre Hutson	6-9	3-4	10	1	15	2	1	0	3	23
Mateen Cleaves	3-7	1-1	2	4	8	20	3	1	0	29
Charlie Bell	13-19	1-1	2	1	31	4	0	0	4	25
Brandon Smith	0-0	0-0	0	0	0	4	0	0	0	6
Mat Ishbia	0-0	0-0	0	0	0	0	0	0	0	4
Mike Chappell	3-5	0-0	4	1	8	1	1	0	0	15
Steve Cherry	1-3	0-0	1	2	3	1	0	0	0	10
Jason Richardson	5-7	0-0	4	1	13	2	0	1	1	17
Adam Ballinger	3-4	0-0	4	3	6	0	0	2	0	15
Totals	44-77	10-13	43	14	114	36	6	5	10	200

Three-Point Field Goals: Peterson 1-7, Granger 4-4, Cleaves 1-4, Bell 4-6, Chappell 2-3, Cherry 1-3, Richardson 3-5, Team 16-32.

FG%: 1st Half 20-37 .541, 2nd Half 24-40 .600, Game 44-77 .571; 3FG%: 1st Half 4-10 .400, 2nd Half 12-22 .545, Game 16-32 .500; FT%: 1st Half 7-10 .700, 2nd Half 3-3 1.000, Game 10-13 .769; Team Rebounds: 3; Deadball Rebounds: 3.

Score By Periods	1	2		F
Michigan	24	39	--	63
Michigan State	51	63	--	114

Officials – Rick Hartzell, Randy Drury, Sid Rodeheffer
Technical Fouls – None
Attendance – 14,659

With a 41-7 record in Big Ten regular-season play from 1998-2000, Michigan State had proven it could win a lot of basketball games.

But had it shown it could seal the deal and win every championship it should? Not yet. Certainly not in Tom Izzo's eyes. And not in Mateen Cleaves' or Morris Peterson's.

The Spartans had been stunned by Minnesota as a No. 1 seed in the 1998 Big Ten Tournament. And they had fallen to Duke in the Final Four as a No. 1 seed in the 1999 NCAA Tournament.

So Izzo's normal apprehension, occasionally bordering on paranoia, was well-founded on Thursday, March 9, when MSU left for Chicago to defend its title in the league's third postseason tournament.

"The easy thing is to look at outside sources and blame them for the pressure," Izzo said. "But I definitely think it's more self-inflicted. And if I'm an addict that way, you feed it."

Media coverage of MSU basketball had never been greater, not even in the "Magic" years. The same was true for fan interest, especially outside Mid-Michigan.

"We were a shocking surprise two years ago," Izzo said. "Then, we went from being everyone's darlings last season to a team that's supposed to win. We're villains now. But the other day, Mateen said, 'I like it when people pick up the paper and are mad we won.'"

Welcome to the world of Duke, the standard of excellence in college basketball and a growing fascination for the Spartans.

If they were to reach that elite level in 2000, or even approach it, they would have to play with bull's-eyes below the Michigan State bridge logos in their final nine games in Reebok jerseys.

And they would have to start in the United Center, where the Chicago Bulls had shown the way by draping banners for a pair of NBA three-peats.

The challenge for MSU's seniors? To leave with five of the last six available Big Ten regular-season and tourney titles, then carry that momentum to the NCAA Tournament as a popular pick to win it all.

"We want to leave our footprints with championships,"

Photo Credit: Kevin Fowler, MSU Sports Information

2000 BIG TEN TOURNAMENT

Peterson said of a team ranked fifth in the Associated Press media poll and fourth in the *USA TODAY*/ESPN survey of coaches. "We have to take advantage of this opportunity. There IS no next year for us."

That meant the Spartans had to avoid the kind of first-game performance as a No. 2 seed that nearly caused two upsets as a No. 1. Besides a 79-76 loss to the Golden Gophers in 1998, they barely beat eighth-seeded Northwestern 61-59 a year later en route to the trophy.

This time, the first opponent was seventh-seeded Iowa, a 14-15 team that needed two wins to qualify for the NIT and three triumphs to crash the NCAA party with the tourney champion's automatic berth.

Izzo preferred to view the Hawkeyes as the dangerous team that had beaten defending national titlist Connecticut and Big Ten co-champ Ohio State, the week's No. 1 seed in Chicago.

But just as it did in Iowa City, MSU started strong. It grabbed an 11-point advantage in the first five minutes, then withstood five Iowa surges for a deceptively tight 75-65 victory.

"We get a 15-4 lead, bring guys in and check absolutely nobody," Izzo said. "After that, it was a dog-fight the rest of the way."

Point guard Dean Oliver gave the Hawkeyes a chance with 30 points and was 11-for-17 from the field, 4-for-8 beyond the arc. His teammates were drinking different water and finished with 13-for-43 accuracy.

Photo Credit: Kevin Fowler, MSU Sports Information

Who guarded Oliver? No one, if you listened to Izzo. But Charlie Bell eventually had some success in the last six minutes, forcing Oliver to miss a key 3 and refusing to let him shoot in the next few possessions, as Iowa went 5:17 without scoring.

The balanced Spartans, who led for all but 30 seconds, hit six

straight points to take a 65-57 lead with 3:10 left, then iced the game at the foul line. They finished with a 20-10 edge in free throws, exactly the difference on the scoreboard.

Peterson finished with 22 points and nine rebounds from his forward spot. Bell had 16 points, six assists and three steals from the backcourt. And Cleaves had 14 points and seven assists at the point, as the "Flintstones" combined for 52 points.

MSU forward A.J. Granger had 10 points and nine rebounds, though his team had only a 37-35 edge in that department. And that might have been reversed if forward Andre Hutson hadn't goaded the Hawkeyes' Jacob Jaacks into fouling out in just 23 minutes.

"We have a chance," Izzo said after surviving Friday's upsets. "But the Tournament isn't 'ours to win.' I know one thing. We'll have to play better than we did in this game or we won't see Sunday in Chicago."

Iowa coach Steve Alford disagreed, saying the Spartans had an excellent chance to be watching the NCAA Tournament Selection Show from the United Center's restaurant as a No. 1 seed.

"MSU is the best team we've played this year," said Alford, whose season ended at 14-16. "Stanford can match up with them physically and can shoot it. But Stanford isn't as deep."

Neither was top-ranked Cincinnati, which had just lost National Player of the Year Kenyon Martin with a broken leg. When the Bearcats lost to Saint Louis in their first game of the Conference USA Tournament, the No. 1 seed in the NCAA's Midwest Region was suddenly in question.

It didn't hurt the Spartans that OSU was stunned by ninth seed Penn State, 71-66, or that third seed Purdue was shocked by sixth seed Wisconsin, 78-66. The basketball gods were all wearing green.

"I think we're still in control of our destiny," Granger said. "And that's all we've ever wanted to be. The motivation is there to stay close to home."

With NCAA Midwest sites in Cleveland and Auburn Hills, MSU had to beat the Badgers Saturday and the Illinois-Penn State winner Sunday. But the Spartans got another break. If Dick Bennett's team was brutal to play, it wasn't the toughest overnight assignment mentally.

"Wisconsin isn't tremendously hard to prepare for that way," Izzo said later. "They don't run 20 or 30 plays like we do or like Illinois or Purdue does. But they might be the hardest team to play. They set two or three screens. And it looks like a rugby scrum out there."

The NCAA Rules Committee thought roughly the same thing after watching the Badgers body-bump with MSU three weeks later. In its last 13 games with the Spartans, Wisconsin has scored more than 59 points just once.

On March 11, 2000, Bennett's team might have needed two over-times to reach that total, as it fell to MSU again 55-46. The Spartans scored the first eight points and

used an 11-2 run to lead 34-21 at the break.

Trailing 44-25 with 15:46 to play, the Badgers nearly drew even with a bewildering 15-2 surge before Peterson hit a 3 and put the earth back on its axis, before a Big Ten-record crowd of 22,011.

In his MSU-record 130th game, Peterson led all scorers with 18 points. Cleaves added 13, plus seven assists. And Hutson had 10 points and a game-high eight rebounds, a category the Spartans led 35-30.

MSU shot 47.6 percent from the field, Wisconsin 30.9. And the Spartans hit 50.0 percent from long range to the Badgers' 26.3 accuracy in a sumo match with just 21 free throws.

"Fatigue was a big factor that hurt them at the end," Hutson said. "They started missing their shots. And you could tell that playing three days in a row took a toll on them."

Bennett had a different perspective: "Michigan State is the type of team that can make you look tired after a full week's rest."

The 25-7 Spartans returned

Photo Credit: Kevin Fowler, MSU Sports Information

2000 BIG TEN TOURNAMENT

less than 24 hours later to face 21-8 Illinois for the championship. And if Izzo's players weren't thrilled about facing a crowd favorite that had won 10 of its last 11, they had only themselves to blame.

After a 91-66 pounding in East Lansing on Super Bowl Sunday, the Fighting Illini learned the importance of physical play — a lesson that would produce co-champions a year later and a rivalry for the next decade.

"They really showed us how far we were from being a contender," Illinois coach Lon Kruger said. "They beat us in every phase and showed us what it meant to play hard on every possession."

Illini guard Frank Williams put it another way, saying his team wouldn't roll over this time. If it did, CBS might want to re-examine its programming decisions.

"I don't know if we have a score to settle," Williams said. "But I don't think there's a team that can do what they did to us last time."

MSU didn't expect to. It had too much respect for a program that had shared the regular-season title in 1998 and advanced to the tournament final the next two seasons — with brighter days just ahead.

"Our two programs have emerged as the best in the league over the past three years," Hutson said. "And I know they're making a big deal out of playing us again."

That anticipation of a payback win was a year premature. The Spartans recovered from a sluggish start, built their lead to 63-43 and cruised 76-61 before a crowd of 19,663.

Photo Credit: Kevin Fowler, MSU Sports Information

To do that, they needed a lift from Peterson, who was benched momentarily in the first three minutes, when he was more like the player who was 9-for-35 from the field in his last three regular-season games than the one who was 17-for-31 in Chicago.

"Coach said, 'You sit here until you decide you want to go back in and play,'" Peterson said. "I said, 'I'm ready right now.' So I just went back over and checked myself in."

Granger led the winners with 17 points and six rebounds. Peterson, the Tournament's Most Outstanding Player, and Hutson each added 14 points. And Cleaves had 12, one more than Williams, Illinois' leading scorer despite 4-for-14 shooting.

MSU shot 50.0 percent from the field, the Illini just 31.1. There was a reason for that and for guard Cory Bradford's 4-for-15 afternoon, as a gushing Kruger explained after his team was outrebounded 39-32.

"They absolutely deserve a No. 1 seed," said the soon-to-be coach of the Atlanta Hawks after Izzo said no. "And they deserved that seed before today. On almost half our possessions, we wound up with no chance to score. That's the way they break you down."

A skirmish broke out with 1:35 left when Cleaves swung his elbows in the direction of Illinois agitator Lucas Johnson. When guard David Thomas innocently stepped on the floor, Izzo overreacted and grabbed him by the neck to prevent him from joining the fracas.

But the only damage was to the Illini's pride, as the Spartans would discover 11 months later. On March 12, 2000, a 26-7 team was as together as it could possibly be. And after a subdued net-snipping ceremony, Cleaves spoke louder than he had in a trash-talking day.

"We're happy....But we're not satisfied," he said after helping Peterson cut the final strand. "Winning here was a goal of ours. But we want the national championship."

An hour later, Kruger was right. The Spartans were a No. 1 seed in the Midwest for the second-straight year and would face Valparaiso the following Thursday in Cleveland.

"This championship was something we've all done before," Bell said of a modest celebration on his 21st birthday. "And this team has bigger goals. Win or lose, everyone remembers what you do in the NCAA Tournament. That's where great teams are made."

Including this one.

Photo Credit: Kevin Fowler, MSU Sports Information

MSU 75, Iowa 65
March 10, 2000 • United Center • Chicago, Ill.

Iowa	FG-FGA	FT-FTA	REB	PF	TP	A	TO	BLK	S	MIN
Rod Griffin	4-13	3-4	6	4	12	4	1	0	0	32
Duez Henderson	2-7	1-2	9	2	5	1	1	0	0	29
Jacob Jaacks	4-9	0-2	8	5	9	0	2	0	0	23
Jason Price	1-1	0-0	0	2	2	2	1	0	0	15
Dean Oliver	11-17	4-5	1	1	30	4	3	0	1	38
Joe Fermino	0-0	0-0	0	0	0	0	0	0	0	3
Marcelo Gomes	0-0	0-0	0	0	0	0	0	0	1	1
Rod Thompson	1-7	0-0	4	2	2	1	0	0	1	24
Kyle Galloway	1-6	0-0	2	3	3	3	1	0	0	27
Jason Smith	0-0	2-4	1	3	2	0	0	0	2	7
John Carl Williams	0-0	0-0	0	0	0	0	0	0	1	1
Totals	24-60	10-17	35	22	65	15	9	0	4	200

Three-Point Field Goals: Griffin 1-5, Jaacks 1-2, Oliver 4-8, Thompson 0-2, Galloway 1-4, Team 7-21.
FG%: 1st Half 12-27 .444, 2nd Half 12-33 .364, Game 24-60 .400; 3FG%: 1st Half 3-8 .375, 2nd Half 4-13 .308, Game 7-21 .333; FT%: 1st Half 5-10 .500, 2nd Half 5-7 .714, Game 10-17 .588; Team Rebounds: 4; Deadball Rebounds: 3.

Michigan State	FG-FGA	FT-FTA	REB	PF	TP	A	TO	BLK	S	MIN
Morris Peterson	7-16	4-6	9	1	22	2	0	0	0	34
A.J. Granger	2-5	5-6	9	3	10	0	2	1	0	26
Andre Hutson	4-6	1-2	5	2	9	1	2	0	1	30
Mateen Cleaves	5-11	3-4	2	2	14	7	4	0	1	36
Charlie Bell	6-10	3-3	3	4	16	6	2	1	3	30
Brandon Smith	0-0	0-0	0	0	0	0	0	0	0	1
Mike Chappell	0-0	0-0	1	2	0	0	1	0	0	9
Jason Richardson	0-1	4-4	2	2	4	1	1	0	0	17
Adam Ballinger	0-1	0-1	4	2	0	1	0	0	0	17
Totals	24-50	20-26	37	18	75	18	12	2	5	200

Three-Point Field Goals: Peterson 4-6, Granger 1-3, Cleaves 1-3, Bell 1-4, Team 7-16.
FG%: 1st Half 11-22 .500, 2nd Half 13-28 .464, Game 24-50 .480; 3FG%: 1st Half 4-6 .667, 2nd Half 3-10 .300, Game 7-16 .438; FT%: 1st Half 10-13 .769, 2nd Half 10-13 .769, Game 20-26 .769; Team Rebounds: 2; Deadball Rebounds: 0.

SCORE BY PERIODS	1	2	F	
Iowa	32	33	--	65
Michigan State	36	39	--	75

OFFICIALS – Ted Hillary, Gene Monje, Dan Chrisman
TECHNICAL FOULS – None
ATTENDANCE – 19,627

MSU 55, Wisconsin 46
March 11, 2000 • United Center • Chicago, Ill.

Wisconsin	FG-FGA	FT-FTA	REB	PF	TP	A	TO	BLK	S	MIN
Maurice Linton	1-4	0-1	2	4	2	2	1	0	0	23
Duany Duany	3-10	2-2	2	1	10	0	1	1	0	18
Andy Kowske	3-8	0-0	4	4	6	0	0	1	1	21
Mike Kelley	2-5	0-0	3	3	4	6	0	0	2	35
Mark Vershaw	4-14	2-2	7	0	11	5	0	0	1	34
Travon Davis	0-0	0-0	0	0	0	1	0	0	0	4
Jon Bryant	1-3	0-0	1	0	3	0	0	0	0	17
Kirk Penney	1-2	0-0	1	0	3	0	1	0	0	9
Roy Boone	0-4	2-2	2	1	2	0	0	0	1	14
Charlie Wills	2-5	1-2	4	3	5	0	0	0	0	25
Totals	17-55	7-9	30	16	46	14	4	2	5	200

Three-Point Field Goals: Linton 0-1, Duany 2-5, Kelley 0-2, Vershaw 1-3, Bryant 1-3, Penney 1-2, Boone 0-1, Wills 0-2, Team 5-19.

FG%: 1st Half 9-28 .321, 2nd Half 8-27 .296, Game 17-55 .309; 3FG%: 1st Half 2-7 .286, 2nd Half 3-12 .250, Game 5-19 .263; FT%: 1st Half 1-2 .500, 2nd Half 6-7 .857, Game 7-9 .778; Team Rebounds: 4; Deadball Rebounds: 0.

Michigan State	FG-FGA	FT-FTA	REB	PF	TP	A	TO	BLK	S	MIN
Mateen Cleaves	5-13	2-3	1	1	13	7	2	0	1	36
Charlie Bell	1-3	0-1	6	2	3	4	2	0	1	30
Andre Hutson	4-5	2-2	8	1	10	0	1	0	0	32
Morris Peterson	5-9	5-5	4	1	18	0	4	1	0	31
A.J. Granger	2-6	0-0	4	3	4	1	0	0	0	29
Mike Chappell	2-2	0-0	2	1	5	0	1	1	0	14
Jason Richardson	0-2	0-0	4	2	0	1	1	0	0	14
Adam Ballinger	1-2	0-1	3	1	2	0	0	0	0	14
Totals	20-42	9-12	35	12	55	13	11	2	2	200

Three-Point Field Goals: Cleaves 1-2, Bell 1-1, Peterson 3-6, Granger 0-2, Chappell 1-1, Team 6-12.

FG%: 1st Half 13-21 .619, 2nd Half 7-21 .333, Game 20-42 .476; 3FG%: 1st Half 5-8 .625, 2nd Half 1-4 .250, Game 6-12 .500; FT%: 1st Half 3-4 .750, 2nd Half 6-8 .750, Game 9-12 .750; Team Rebounds: 3; Deadball Rebounds: 0.

SCORE BY PERIODS	1	2	F	
Wisconsin	21	25	--	46
Michigan State	34	21	--	55

OFFICIALS – Ed Hightower, Ted Hillary, Gene Monje
TECHNICAL FOULS – None
ATTENDANCE – 22,011

MSU 76, Illinois 61
March 12, 2000 • United Center • Chicago, Ill.

Illinois	FG-FGA	FT-FTA	REB	PF	TP	A	TO	BLK	S	MIN
Cory Bradford	4-15	0-0	1	0	10	4	0	0	1	28
Lucas Johnson	2-8	1-2	7	3	6	1	3	0	1	25
Frank Williams	4-14	2-2	3	1	11	1	1	1	2	36
Brian Cook	3-5	1-2	5	4	7	0	1	1	0	26
Sergio McClain	1-3	3-3	5	4	5	3	3	1	0	22
Nate Mast	0-0	0-0	0	0	0	0	0	0	1	1
Victor Chukwudebe	0-1	0-0	1	1	0	0	0	0	0	4
Joe Cross	0-0	0-0	1	0	0	0	0	0	0	1
Robert Archibald	0-0	0-0	0	0	0	0	0	0	2	2
Sean Harrington	1-3	3-3	0	1	6	1	0	0	1	14
Cleotis Brown	3-11	3-4	3	1	10	1	1	0	1	19
Damir Krupalija	1-1	2-2	3	2	4	1	1	0	0	14
Marcus Griffin	0-0	2-2	1	2	2	1	0	0	0	8
Totals	19-61	17-20	32	19	61	13	10	3	6	200

Three-Point Field Goals: Bradford 2-11, Johnson 1-5, Williams 1-5, Cook 0-2, Harrington 1-3, Brown 1-3, Team 6-29.

FG%: 1st Half 9-29 .310, 2nd Half 10-32 .313, Game 19-61 .311; 3FG%: 1st Half 1-10 .100, 2nd Half 5-19 .263, Game 6-29 .207; FT%: 1st Half 8-9 .889, 2nd Half 9-11 .818, Game 17-20 .850; Team Rebounds: 2; Deadball Rebounds: 2.

Michigan State	FG-FGA	FT-FTA	REB	PF	TP	A	TO	BLK	S	MIN
Mateen Cleaves	5-13	0-0	3	2	12	6	2	0	0	32
Charlie Bell	3-9	2-2	6	3	8	6	3	0	0	32
Andre Hutson	4-7	6-8	5	3	14	2	3	1	0	28
Morris Peterson	5-6	3-3	4	4	14	1	3	0	3	28
A.J. Granger	6-9	3-3	6	0	17	2	1	1	0	34
David Thomas	0-2	2-2	2	1	2	1	0	0	0	7
Mike Chappell	1-4	0-0	1	0	2	0	1	0	0	12
Jason Richardson	2-3	1-1	4	4	5	2	0	0	2	13
Adam Ballinger	1-1	0-0	4	2	2	1	0	0	0	14
Totals	27-54	17-19	39	19	76	21	13	2	5	200

Three-Point Field Goals: Cleaves 2-5, Bell 0-3, Hutson 0-1, Peterson 1-2, Granger 2-4, Chappell 0-2, Team 5-17.

FG%: 1st Half 14-30 .467, 2nd Half 13-24 .542, Game 27-54 .500; 3FG%: 1st Half 2-9 .222, 2nd Half 3-8 .375, Game 5-17 .294; FT%: 1st Half 5-6 .833, 2nd Half 12-13 .923, Game 17-19 .895; Team Rebounds: 4; Deadball Rebounds: 1.

SCORE BY PERIODS	1	2	F	
Illinois	27	34	--	61
Michigan State	35	41	--	76

OFFICIALS – Ed Hightower, Ted Hillary, Tom Rucker
TECHNICAL FOULS – Johnson (UI), Cleaves (MSU)
ATTENDANCE – 19,663

2000 NCAA TOURNAMENT

If it's often better to be lucky than brilliant, it's best to be both in college basketball. Good fortune and great play form a lethal combination — especially in an NCAA Tournament.

The Michigan State Spartans proved that again in 2000 with a 19-day march to glory from March 16-April 3. After a 9,000-mile pre-conference odyssey, they stayed close to home, winning two games in Cleveland, two in Auburn Hills and two more — for immortality — in Indianapolis.

MSU got a huge break when Cincinnati star Kenyon Martin broke his leg in the Conference USA Tournament. Though no one wanted to see another player hurt, especially someone as impressive as Martin, one freak injury and a subsequent loss to Saint Louis changed everything.

Suddenly, the 26-7 Spartans replaced the 28-3 Bearcats as the No. 1 seed in the Midwest Region. That controversial decision was the best way for the NCAA Selection Committee to balance the brackets and account for two irrefutable facts: MSU was 17-3 with Mateen Cleaves in uniform; Cincinnati was 0-1 without Martin.

Could the Spartans have overtaken Syracuse in the Sweet 16 or beaten Iowa State in the Elite Eight on a neutral court? We'll never know. Izzo's players did what they had to do when and where they had to do it. If that isn't the dictionary definition of "champions," it's close enough.

"We could've been beaten by

Syracuse and coulda-shoulda been beaten by Iowa State," Izzo said of the first No. 1 seed with more than six losses. "So we got lucky twice. And keeping guys healthy was a big, big part of it."

By the third week in March, Mateen Cleaves was close to 100 percent with a titanium screw in

his right foot. If his stress fracture had happened when Martin's injury did, another team would have hoisted the trophy.

And by the time MSU reached the CSU Convocation Center, Jason Richardson's mysterious chest problem had vanished. David Thomas and Aloysius

Photo Credit: Bruce Schwartzman/John Grieshop/Jamie Sabau, Schwartzman Sports Photography

2000 NCAA TOURNAMENT

Anagonye were available, too, after missing a total of nine games with stress fractures.

Though Andre Hutson would hyperextend a knee two days before the Final Four and Cleaves would hobble off on one leg before a heroic return in the title game, the Spartans were healthy enough to win.

At anything close to full strength, MSU was more than good enough with supportive crowds and incredible seniors. The biggest problems were a Midwest bracket that couldn't have been tougher for a No. 1 seed and constant pressure, often self-imposed.

"Everybody just expects, expects, expects," Izzo said. "Believe it or not, I guess I do, too. But championships are forever. No one can take them away from you. And nobody remembers who's in second place."

No No. 1 seed had ever lost to a No. 16 when the Spartans met 19-12 Valparaiso, the Mid-Continent Conference champ from Northern Indiana. Two NCAA Tournaments later, the top seeds' opening-round record stands at 68-0.

MSU made sure it wouldn't spoil that mark, sprinting to a 20-3 lead over the outmanned Crusaders in the first 12:53. Homer Drew's teams had been in the field of 64 five straight years and had advanced to the Sweet 16 with an improbable run in 1998. But they never knew what hit them in a 65-38 thrashing in Cleveland.

"It was Murphy's Law," Drew said after calling a timeout just 44 seconds into the game. "Everything that could go wrong for us did."

The first thing that hurt Valpo was that the Spartans' bus wasn't hijacked. Once Izzo's players reached the arena, the outcome was never in doubt. With scalped tickets going for $300 in a building that seated just 13,374, fans got a show, not a squeaker.

The pre-Tournament pick of ESPN's Dick Vitale and Jay Bilas looked like a team that could go all the way, as it padlocked the basket and turned Valpo into Alpo.

The Crusaders' 38 points tied the second-lowest output in first- or second-round history. And their 25.0-percent field-goal shooting tied the third-lowest accuracy for the opening week.

"Michigan State is so good at attacking the ball," said Drew, a mild-mannered, neighborly type who reminded the media of Mr. Rogers. "We tried to penetrate and couldn't. They've got really long arms. And they're very quick."

Cleaves, the Spartans' shortest starter, was the dominant player with 15 points, eight assists and the kind of defense that triggered transition opportunities against a team with five European players.

"Our defense got our offense going," Cleaves said. "We were a tad timid on offense. We weren't looking to take the ball to the basket. But once we picked up our defense, that got our fast break going."

After trailing 29-15 at the break, Valpo scored the first basket of the second half to cut the deficit to 12. But MSU scored the next six

Photo Credit: Kevin Fowler, MSU Sports Information

points and never led by less than 15 the rest of the way. The reserves played 75 of a possible 200 minutes and produced 27 points and 20 rebounds.

"Getting the bench in there was a plus," Izzo said. "I thought Jason Richardson played pretty well. And I thought Mike Chappell and Adam Ballinger played well in the second half."

Richardson had nine points, including a spectacular, alley-oop dunk, and a game-high 10 rebounds in 25 minutes. His team shot 44.0 percent from the field and had a modest 39-31 edge on the boards. But defense was clearly the difference, as the Crusaders managed just six assisted baskets.

"You think you've finally got one of them beat, and you run right into another one," said Valpo sixth man Milo Stovall, a Kalamazoo Central High product and a friend of Cleaves' who had dreamed of playing for MSU.

No one dreamed of playing against the Spartans at that point, unless he suffered from a sleep disorder and was subject to nightmares. And their second-round opponent, 23-8 Utah, knew exactly how tough it would be to score against MSU in Saturday's second Midwest quarterfinal.

The eighth-seeded Runnin' Utes had just edged ninth-seeded Saint Louis 48-46 in Thursday night's late game. And Utah coach Rick Majerus knew his team would have to play as well as it had all season if it planned to stun the Spartans.

"They were my pick to win it all," said Majerus, who coaches as well as he eats. "I've got a little pool going — nothing big, just a couple of pizzas. But Michigan State is a special basketball team. There's no soft underbelly."

That self-deprecation didn't fool Izzo for a second. He had watched the Utes end Steve Smith's college career in a double-overtime, second-round struggle in 1991 in Tucson, Ariz. And he had seen Utah senior forwards Hanno Möttölä and Alex Jensen nearly

Photo Credit: Kevin Fowler, MSU Sports Information

stun Kentucky in the 1998 championship game. Most of all, he had seen Majerus work.

"There's nobody I'd like to face less," Izzo said. "He's as good as it gets. He has maintained that level of performance over time. And there's no one in college basketball who prepares a team better than Rick Majerus."

Majerus had stunned top-seeded Arizona in the 1998 West Region final with a triangle-and-two defense his team had practiced for only 15 minutes. And Izzo was certain the Utes would have some sort of surprise for the Spartans.

Utah's plan was to show Peterson more attention than a prophet in the Mormon Church

and make someone else hit outside shots. Someone did, but not before MSU suffered through a sluggish start against a team it knew and respected.

The Utes shot 56.6 percent in the first half and went to their locker room with a 35-32 lead. Just down the hall, the Spartans got a tongue-lashing like few Izzo had ever delivered.

"He got in our faces," Cleaves said. "He got in the faces of everybody there. Thank God we were able to answer the bell."

That didn't happen until after Utah led 43-37. Faced with a character check, MSU's seniors responded. And Cleaves picked up where Izzo left off, firing threats and 3-point shots with equal determination.

He challenged Peterson, grabbing his pal by the shorts and telling him he wasn't worthy of his "Flint" tattoo, the way he was playing. Eventually, that message got through in a 73-61 triumph.

"Mateen has been vocal before," Peterson said. "But it was like a demon came out of him."

After a devil of a time getting through to his team, Izzo was happy for any motivational help he could get, especially when it was backed by a stellar performance.

"Without Mateen, we'd probably be going home disappointed," Izzo said. "He grabbed us by the you-know-what and told us to follow him. I've always said he might be the best leader we've had at Michigan State, including 'Magic' Johnson. And you saw what the will to win is all about today."

Anyone can talk a good game. Cleaves went out and played one when his career was 17 minutes from a premature ending. With an assist on a Hutson layup and one of his four 3-pointers, the Spartans took a 44-43 lead with 15:25 left. As the lead swelled to 64-50, Cleaves had six more points and passes for 3s by Granger and Peterson.

Cleaves had a game-high 21 points, five assists and just one turnover in 36 minutes, more time than Izzo usually allows. But with 4-for-7 accuracy beyond the arc, precisely the margin of victory, he showed at least one skeptic he could shoot.

"Cleaves really stung us tonight," Majerus said. "We picked our poison and wanted Cleaves to shoot it. He did. And he beat us."

Hutson offered plenty of support with 19 points and a game-high eight rebounds. And Peterson finished with 13 points in a city now known as Cleavesland, Ohio.

MSU finished with 55.3-percent success from the field and 55.3 accuracy from long range. It also held a 30-21 edge in rebounds over a taller team, enough to make Majerus gush.

"If I could pick one team, I'd be the jockey for that horse," he said prophetically. "We've played

the national champion four times in the Tournament. These guys have the look of a champ. They're awful damn good."

The following week, they would have to be to beat fourth-seeded Syracuse and second-seeded Iowa State before wild crowds of 21,214 fans at The Palace — as close to a home-court advantage in Breslin-East as the NCAA allows.

Tickets for the Midwest's three remaining games, including ISU's semifinal with sixth-seeded UCLA, were going for as much as $1,200 a pair. If anyone had known what kind of basketball was in store Thursday and Saturday evenings, that price might have risen 35 miles from Flint.

The 26-5 Orangemen couldn't have taken a more-diverse path to the Sweet 16 than the Spartans did. Instead of taking on all comers,

Photo Credit: Kevin Fowler, MSU Sports Information

Photo Credit: Kevin Fowler, MSU Sports Information

Jim Boeheim stuck with a tried-and-almost-true philosophy of staying in the Carrier Dome as much as possible and scheduling teams he knew he could beat.

"A schedule doesn't make you better or worse," said the coach of the 1987 and 1996 NCAA runners-up. "It doesn't matter one bit. If you play more tough games, you might have another loss or two. But it's a myth that you become better if you play tougher teams. I don't agree with that."

MSU became better as Izzo exposed his players to top-echelon programs and all sorts of styles in November and December. If the idea was to be prepared for everything in March, that seemed like a wise decision.

"Does that mean we'll win? . . . No," Izzo said. "But we haven't backed down from anything all season. Why should we start doing that now?"

By facing Texas, North Carolina, Kansas, Arizona, Kentucky and Connecticut, the first five of those tests without Cleaves, the Spartans had gained unshakable confidence. And the program had received invaluable exposure.

"If you talked to Tommy in December, he might have said, 'What in the hell did I do?'" CBS analyst Bill Raftery said. "But his teams hadn't been on television that much. He had to play those games to get to the next level. Plus, that's his personality."

The same was true strategically, with MSU running at every opportunity, playing snug, man-to-man defense and rebounding like every missed shot was a treasure — a basic description of "Izzoball."

Syracuse preferred its patented 2-3 zone and liked to pound the ball inside to 6-foot-9, 256-pound pivot Etan Thomas whenever possible. And why not, with a player who averaged 13.9 points, 9.4 rebounds and 3.8 blocked shots?

Photo Credit: Kevin Fowler, MSU Sports Information

Photo Credit: Kevin Fowler, MSU Sports Information

Boeheim's ways seemed better in a bizarre first half — "A Clockwork Orange." Trailing 8-1, Syracuse drew even at 11 and built a 13-point cushion before Granger's three-point play with 1.2 seconds left made it 34-24.

Before Izzo could reach the locker room, a scoreless Cleaves immediately took charge, challenging himself and his teammates and rearranging some furniture. It was Izzo's favorite halftime of his first six seasons.

"I'm a church-going guy," Cleaves said later. "And I'm going to have to ask forgiveness for some of the things I was saying. I can't tell you what I told them. It's too hot for TV. I'm sure I hurt some people's pride. But I won't apologize. The second half is my apology."

Eight seconds into the period, Hutson's layup made it an eight-point game. But the Orangemen re-established control and went up 40-26, as Izzo worked the sideline without a suitcoat for the first time in more than 14 months.

Suddenly, Peterson gave Cleaves "The Look." And Cleaves gave Peterson the ball enough to produce a 75-58 victory. "Mo Pete" — or "Man" — was exactly that, scoring 16 of his game-high 21 points, including five 3s, in an amazing surge. The Spartans outscored Syracuse 49-18 in the last 19 minutes and 17-0 over the last 5:55.

"We were passing up shots and getting outrebounded," Peterson said of an 18-12 halftime deficit on the boards. "They had a 12-0 lead in fast-break points and were really taking the fight to us. So I told Mateen, 'Give me the ball!' And I meant it."

"It was a game face you don't often see," Cleaves said. "I've seen it a few times before. And when I do, I know enough to give him the ball and just get out of the way."

As the final buzzer sounded, Peterson was overcome with emotion. He pulled a sweat drenched

jersey over his head and remembered five years of early-morning workouts and late-night study sessions. They hadn't been in vain.

And he hadn't been alone. Granger finished with a career-high 19 points. Bell had 12, including the go-ahead 3, plus six rebounds. Hutson added 11 points and held a foul-plagued Thomas to seven points and three shots from the field. And Cleaves had 10 second-half points, seven assists and a possible case of laryngitis.

"I have to do something different," Cleaves said. "It's going to wear me out if I have to keep giving these halftime speeches."

MSU wore the Orangemen down and out and finally gained a 30-27 rebounding edge. The Spartans were also superior shooters. They hit 51.0 percent from the field and 47.8 beyond the arc, where they outscored Syracuse 33-12.

"And to think some people were actually scared," Izzo's father, Carl, said with a smile seconds after the buzzer, not referring to Peterson's healthy fear of losing.

There was every reason to be afraid two nights later. When 29-7 MSU met the 32-4 Cyclones, it was a matchup of the nation's two best teams. Too bad it had to happen in the Elite Eight instead of being for the NCAA title.

The day before the Midwest final, ISU coach Larry Eustachy was asked about having to play the Spartans in Auburn Hills, a task about the same as MSU having to win in Des Moines. But Eustachy, who would soon lose control of his

emotions, said the site didn't bother him at all.

"Michigan State has earned the right to be here," he said of a floor trimmed in green with an MAC logo — for the hosting Mid-American Conference, not the former Michigan Agricultural College. "There has to be some reward for what they accomplished. And I totally agree with the format."

Eustachy also agreed the game's key matchup would be

Photo Credit: Kevin Fowler, MSU Sports Information

Photo Credit: Kevin Fowler, MSU Sports Information

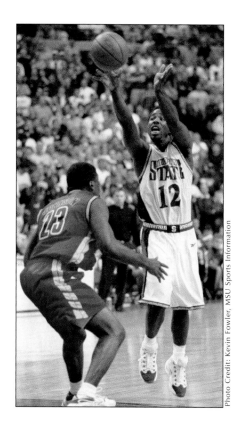

Photo Credit: Kevin Fowler, MSU Sports Information

Cleaves and junior standout Jamaal Tinsley, though much of the attention focused on the Cyclones' All-America center Marcus Fizer, a rare blend of strength and agility at 6-8, 265.

"They're both scoreboard guys," Oklahoma coach and former MSU assistant Kelvin Sampson said of the two point guards. "People like to point out the flaws in their games. Those same people would probably find a bunion on Miss America's foot."

Neither team could get more than a toe in front in the first half, as the Spartans took a 34-31 lead to the locker room, despite losing 17 of the first 20 rebounds and getting just five first-half points from Peterson.

When ISU grabbed its biggest lead, 48-40, with 11:46 left, roughly 16,000 MSU fans in the building began to squirm. And when Izzo was slapped with a technical foul, the Cyclones' two free throws put them up by seven with 5:49 to play.

But the Spartans hadn't battled all season to cancel their trip to Indianapolis without a fight. Threes from Granger and Peterson trimmed the deficit to 61-58. And Bell soon made it a one-point game with two free throws.

"Coach always says, 'Tough players win,'" said Peterson, the Midwest Region's Most Outstanding Player. "I thought down the stretch we showed how tough we were."

When official Lonnie Dixon refused to be overruled by his partners on a shaky block-charge call, a rare double foul was called on

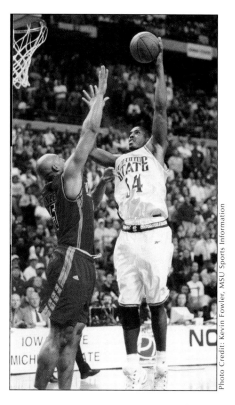

Photo Credit: Kevin Fowler, MSU Sports Information

Bell and the Cyclones' Paul Shirley. That critical call worked in MSU's favor, as Bell promptly put his team in front 62-61 with a mid-range jumper.

After another defensive stop, the Spartans scored their biggest basket of the season, even bigger than Peterson's 3 against Indiana that ultimately brought a share of the Big Ten title.

With 2:12 to play, MSU called timeout and set up the back-door lob Peterson had requested — "Screen and Re-screen." With a quick shake of Tinsley, Peterson bolted to the basket, soared high above the rim and slammed home a perfect alley-oop from Cleaves.

"We wanted to get a for-sure basket," Granger said. "I think that's as for-sure as you can get. It was a big momentum-changer. We wanted to get the crowd on its feet. And that did the job."

Indeed, ISU was just about finished. After another controversial call in the closing seconds, Eustachy charged the officials and was slapped with two technicals and an ejection. But Izzo grabbed him before he left the floor, congratulated the Cyclones and commiserated about the refs in a game with 24 fouls for each team.

If the 75-64 final seemed familiar, it was the same score as the 1979 NCAA title game against Indiana State — another ISU.

The Spartans outscored the Cyclones 23-5 over the last 5:17, including 11-for-12 work at the foul line in the final 1:07. They needed those points while being outrebounded 38-27, just the sec-

ond time all season MSU lost the battle of the boards.

Though Peterson and Granger each had 18 points, the star of the game was Hutson. He outscored Fizer 17-15 and outrebounded him 11-4. Both players had six baskets. But Hutson took six fewer shots in joining Peterson, Granger and Cleaves as All-Midwest Region selections.

"I don't want to put too much pressure on Izzo," Eustachy said. "But that's the best team in the country. I'm real impressed with the way that program is run."

Seconds after the final buzzer, Peterson danced for the CBS cameras with a *Lansing State Journal* instant section: "FINAL FOUR: ON TO INDY." And Cleaves

Photo Credit: Kevin Fowler, MSU Sports Information

2000 NCAA TOURNAMENT

Photo Credit: Kevin Fowler, MSU Sports Information

time since Tournament seeding began in, you guessed it, 1979.

And in the same city where the Spartans had upset Notre Dame to reach the Final Four that year, who should the Spartans meet but the 22-13 Wisconsin Badgers, a sixth-place team in the Big Ten and the West Region's No. 8 seed.

"The big dream was, of course, the Final Four," said Wisconsin coach Dick Bennett, who would retire early the following season. "Getting close to the end of my career, it appeared it might not ever happen. But as I told the players, if I were to die right now, I'd go to heaven with a smile on my face."

That matchup didn't cause many other smiles around the country. Instead, it made a lot of

launched his favorite assist — a toss of the game ball to former roommate and star tailback Sedrick Irvin eight rows up in the stands.

"I LOVE YOU!" Izzo screamed to one side of the arena, as the celebration began in earnest. Seconds later, his players poured into the opposite stands to find their families for some of the tightest hugs they'll ever receive.

Soon, Izzo was ready to snip another set of nets. Double-foul? What double-foul?

"I don't know," Izzo said, hugging his wife, Lupe, and crying a winner's tears. "And right now, I really don't care!"

His players cared about a lot of things, including a chance to be the first school to win two NCAA basketball titles and two national

championships in football.

But those concerns were pushed to the background moments after the game. Wearing his Final Four cap and T-shirt, Peterson learned his beloved grandmother, Clara Mae Spencer, had died that morning at age 72.

"My grandmother was right there with me," Peterson said. "It seemed like somebody was guiding those shots in. I didn't know she passed away. But I really felt her."

The Spartans felt compassion for Peterson and did what they could to ease his pain. But after returning from a mid-week funeral in Mississippi, he took care of that himself with a Final Four performance that made her smile again.

Without MSU's arrival in Indy, the Final Four would have been without a No. 1 seed for the first

Photo Credit: Kevin Fowler, MSU Sports Information

Photo Credit: Kevin Fowler, MSU Sports Information

people say, "MSU has a free pass to the championship game, if not all the way to the winners' platform." With that ludicrous level of expectation, one slip would have made the Spartans a huge disappointment nationally.

"If we do all we can and lose, I'll be able to live with it and appreciate all we've accomplished," Izzo said. "But would it bother me for the rest of my life — or at least until we win one? Yeah."

His seniors knew their legacy would be sealed or shattered by 80 minutes of basketball on the sport's biggest stage. And they insisted they could seize that opportunity without risking their career accomplishments.

"We haven't completed anything yet," Granger said of the first back-to-back Final Four berths in MSU history. "But it would be stupid to say we're not a success if we lose this week after all we've accomplished."

North Carolina State wasn't a better team than Houston in 1983. Villanova wasn't mightier than Georgetown in 1985. And Duke wasn't superior to UNLV in 1991. But proving anything can happen in one game, those major upsets ruined the favorites' reputations — something the Spartans couldn't allow.

And like the Hoyas 15 years earlier, they faced the difficult challenge of beating an opponent

four times in seven weeks — a grand slam they had never attempted.

"Playing a team you've already played three times this year almost takes the fun out of it," Izzo said. "But you can see how they've advanced with the matchups they've had. They're such a hard team to play, even if you're ready for them."

The Badgers hadn't lost to any team but MSU since Feb. 2 and had beaten ninth-seeded Fresno State, top-seeded Arizona, fourth-seeded LSU and sixth-seeded Purdue to reach the national semifinals for the first time since 1941.

Some insisted the first half of Saturday's first semifinal was pre-

World War II basketball — a cruel April Fool's joke on CBS and the nation's fans. Others like Kansas coach Roy Williams wanted to legislate against future scrums.

But if the Spartans' 53-41 win was a different sport, it was also a perfect example of their ability to adapt. Want to run? Izzo will supply the starting blocks. Want to wrestle? Just be prepared to be pinned.

MSU was prepared for this day. But after grabbing a 17-8 lead, it couldn't find the basket from the field for the final 11:37 of the half. It shot just 25.0 percent from the field in the first 20 minutes, missing all seven of its 3-point attempts.

Just when everyone expected smoke to pour from the Spartans' locker room, Izzo read the mood of the team and became a kinder, gentler coach.

"Our players were actually a little down," Izzo said of a fourth disappointing first half in a row. "That's why we didn't have our normal halftime. We kind of had a little kiss-and-hug time. We didn't feel it was time to get after them."

The most-experienced starting five in Final Four history, with 604 games played at that point, knew how to respond. Peterson, Cleaves, Granger, Bell and Hutson had heard enough fiery speeches. It was time to play some basketball.

Peterson led the way with 20

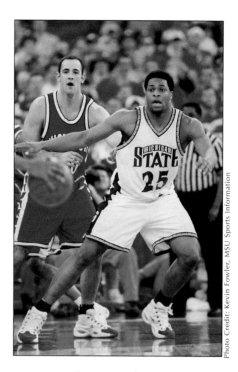

points and seven of his team's 42 rebounds — a fitting tribute to his late grandmother after attending her funeral in Mississippi.

"Morris was on a mission," Hutson said after collecting 10 points and a game-high 10 rebounds, exactly half the Badgers' total. "He wanted to play for his grandmother and made some big plays in the second half."

That was nothing new. Peterson had scored just 19 points in his last four first halves. But he had scored 53 after the break against Utah, Syracuse, Iowa State and the Badgers. Suddenly, Vitale's top "P-T-P'er" was none other than "Prime-Time Pete."

Bell received his props for brilliant defense on guard Jon Bryant, the West Region's Most Outstanding Player. With help from Cleaves, Bryant was held to five shots and two points. The Badgers' other pri-

mary threat, forward Mark Vershaw, was 2-for-11 from the field with Granger as a second skin.

"We just didn't get it done," Bennett said. "They're better than us. And we knew that."

After hearing so much about Wisconsin's defense, MSU proved what Izzo had said privately all year. Regardless of the stats, with their obvious slant toward slow-paced teams, the top defense in the league, if not in the country, belonged to the Spartans.

"Who's the best defensive team in the Big Ten? I think we are," said Bell, who also contributed eight rebounds, one more than any Badger. "We take great pride in that. And we took it as kind of a

Photo Credit: Kevin Fowler, MSU Sports Information

Photo Credit: Kevin Fowler, MSU Sports Information

slap in the face that people focused so much on Wisconsin's defense."

The nation would learn exactly how good MSU was in all areas on Monday, April 3, 2000. When the 31-7 Spartans met 29-7 Florida, a capacity crowd of 43,116 at the RCA Dome and a CBS audience saw the tougher team win.

In the hours before tipoff, a lot of respected basketball people had wondered how MSU would fare against the Gators' ferocious, full-court pressure. The Spartans hadn't faced a defense quite like Florida's. And we were about to see why.

Billy Donovan's team, the East Region champ as a No. 5 seed, had used an up-tempo game with plenty of 3-point shots to reach the Final Four for the second time in seven seasons. The Gators needed a last-second drive by forward Mike Miller to edge Butler in over-

time. But they were solid in spanking Illinois, shocking Duke and stopping Oklahoma State.

In the second NCAA semifinal, Florida grabbed an 18-3 lead over North Carolina, then squandered that margin and more. The Gators trailed 48-42 when foul trouble struck the Tar Heels, especially point guard Ed Cota. Behind the shooting and passing of Brett Nelson, Donovan's team took full advantage and roared to a 71-59 triumph.

"We're not going to change for anybody," Florida guard Justin Hamilton said. "We feel we're the best-conditioned team in college basketball. If they want to run, we're all for that. We don't feel anyone can run with us."

Those who had watched MSU knew better, including "The Magic Man," who predicted the outcome within a few points. And a sign in one of the green-and-white sec-

2000 NCAA TOURNAMENT

Photo Credit: Kevin Fowler, MSU Sports Information

With 11:03 left in the first half, MSU led 19-17 — the same score it had at halftime against Wisconsin. But a 14-3 run broke the game open. When Cleaves found the range for three 3s, he turned to the MSU faithful and let them know the fun was just beginning.

"I listened to that talk all year: 'He can't shoot!'" said Cleaves, the Final Four's Most Outstanding Player. "It was my last game as a Spartan. And I was going to take those shots. Thank God they went in."

Cleaves had 13 of his 18 points against the Gators in the first 20 minutes. And Granger added nine, as MSU raced to a 43-32 advantage

Photo Credit: Kevin Fowler, MSU Sports Information

tions of the stands said it best: "Tonight We Party Like 1979."

Just before tipoff, Izzo paused to enjoy the moment. Then, he made it shine. He was confident his team could sprint past the Gators, not just run with them. The Spartans used all five players as ballhandlers, with Hutson hitting a streaking Cleaves for easy baskets.

MSU broke the press the way it had won for three years — as a team. Eventually, Florida had to draw back on defense and gamble the Spartans couldn't hit from outside, another erroneous assumption.

"There was no doubt we could run with them," Bell said. "We're one of the best-conditioned teams in the country. We were a little insulted when we heard people say we couldn't run with Florida. But we showed that's our game, too."

Photo Credit: Kevin Fowler, MSU Sports Information

Photo Credit: Kevin Fowler, MSU Sports Information

did twist it! . . . We're looking at 16:18 to go in this game, only a six-point lead, and their leader is down. . . . He is tough! But can he come back from that?"

Can you spell "F-L-I-N-T" or begin to appreciate what that tattoo on his right shoulder meant?

"When they said they didn't think it was broken, I told Mateen he had a couple of minutes to get back," Izzo said. "Then, I told the team, 'We have a war on our hands.'"

The first goal in any war is to survive. After living without Cleaves for 13 games, the Spartans weren't about to die in less than five minutes.

It was time for someone to step forward. And that someone was Chappell, who missed his chance to play in the previous year's Final Four when he decided to transfer from Duke to MSU.

On a play known as "One," Chappell came off a double-screen and promptly knocked down a 3 near the top of the key. But his put-back basket after a miss by Richardson might have meant even more in terms of the Spartans' toughness.

Like all teams worthy of a title shot, Florida refused to quit. And with one more surge, keyed by the brilliance of center Udonis Haslem, the Gators drew within six again.

MSU made a conscious decision to deny the 3-point shot and outscored Florida 33-18 beyond the arc. By doing that, the Spartans chose to check Haslem in the post with little or no help. Haslem

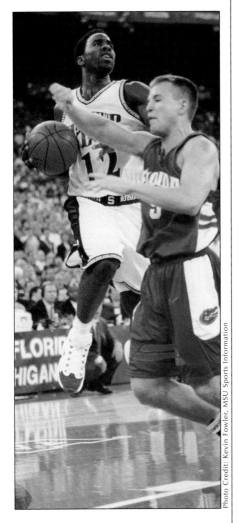

Photo Credit: Kevin Fowler, MSU Sports Information

and never became timid. But that aggressive style cost the Spartans their floor general and emotional leader early in the second half.

As Cleaves went in for a transition layup, he was fouled by Florida guard Teddy Dupay. And as both players landed, a sweep of Dupay's foot turned Cleaves' right ankle outward and turned the game inside-out.

As Cleaves crawled toward the bench and screamed, "It's broke! I know it's broke!" to trainer Tom Mackowiak, Izzo gave referee Jim Burr an earful of unprintable comments.

"Tom Izzo is really upset," CBS analyst Billy Packer said. "Here's Mateen . . . coming down . . . and he twists that ankle. Boy, he really

made Izzo pay for that move with 10-for-12 shooting from the field and 27 points.

But just when everyone started to wonder, the crowd started rising. Even Izzo took a peek toward the tunnel to see if Cleaves was returning.

"I was definitely going to try to come back," Cleaves said. "I told the trainer they were going to have to amputate my leg to keep me out of this one."

It was the closest thing MSU had experienced to the season-saving night of Feb. 1, 1979, when

2000 NCAA TOURNAMENT

Photo Credit: Kevin Fowler, MSU Sports Information

Photo Credit: Kevin Fowler, MSU Sports Information

Johnson hobbled back from a severe ankle sprain to help beat Ohio State in overtime — the loudest any MSU athletic facility has ever been.

This time was much the same. A quest that began with one shared mission had to end with "One Shining Moment." From the disappointment in St. Petersburg to the delirium of Indy, Cleaves' team made good on its promise and made enough great plays at just the right times.

He wasn't full-strength when he checked back in with 11:51 to play. Luckily for the Spartans, Cleaves didn't have to be. All he had to do was inspire the team and get the ball to Peterson, who would hit 15 of his 21 points in the last 10 minutes.

Photo Credit: Kevin Fowler, MSU Sports Information

2000 NCAA TOURNAMENT

Photo Credit: Rod Sanford, Lansing State Journal

Photo Credit: Rod Sanford, Lansing State Journal

Granger, who contributed 19 points and nine rebounds, had a critical assist without touching the ball. When he grabbed No. 42 and said, "It's time for you to go, baby!" Peterson went off in the second half for the fifth game in a row.

With the message, "R.I.P. Clara Mae Spencer," inscribed on his shoes, Peterson said his fatigue suddenly vanished. MSU had fans everywhere.

By the time Cleaves did his "Jubilation Jump" in front of the MSU cheering section, an 89-76 victory was secure.

CBS play-by-play man Jim Nantz focused on Cleaves in the closing seconds: "One of the greatest leaders the game of college basketball has ever seen. . . . And you can leave it to Cleaves! He has reinstated the Magic at Michigan State."

When the buzzer sounded for

Photo Credit: Kevin Fowler, MSU Sports Information

2000 NCAA TOURNAMENT

Photo Credit: Kevin Fowler, MSU Sports Information

the final time in Peterson's 137th and final game with the Spartans, he collapsed to his knees and wept in joy.

And when he climbed a ladder to snip his strand of the championship net, Peterson held a sign to the heavens: "This one's for you Grandma!"

A few feet away, a point guard with more rings than J.B. Robinson Jewelers found Cleaves for a warm embrace and a few special words.

"You're a champion, baby!" Johnson said in Cleaves' ear. "You're a champion! NOBODY can ever take that away from you."

It had been 21 seasons since Johnson could say that to another Spartan. And for 13 of those years, Cleaves had watched the NCAA championship game for more than just basketball. Whatever the hour, he had to hear his favorite song, "One Shining Moment."

That CBS college basketball anthem was written by David Barrett while he lived in Haslett, Mich., just a few long jumpers from campus.

If you close your eyes, you can see Izzo's arm stretched across his star's shoulder. You can hear the strains of a trumpet intro to a tune better known that night as "Mateen's Song." And you can almost taste the sweetest tears Cleaves will ever know:

The ball is tipped,
There you are.
You're running for your life.
You're a shooting star.
And all the years,
No one knows
Just how hard you worked,
But now it shows…

In One Shining Moment
You reached deep inside.
One Shining Moment
You knew…you were alive.

Feel the beat of your heart.
Feel the wind in your face.
It's more than a contest.
It's more…than a race.

And when it's done,
Win or lose,
You always did your best,
'Cause inside you knew…

That One Shining Moment,
You reached for the sky.
One Shining Moment, you knew.
One Shining Moment,
You were willing to try.
One Shining Moment, you knew…
One Shining Moment…

Forgive Cleaves if he is a frequent visitor to http://www.oneshiningmoment.com. After all, he is part of that history. For one night, it was truly "Mo's Moment."

A few feet away, Cleaves' former Flint Northern and MSU teammate Antonio Smith was

Photo Credit: Kevin Fowler, MSU Sports Information

overjoyed for the three remaining "Flintstones." But he was a little sad he hadn't had a fifth year of eligibility to share in the triumph as a player.

When Izzo finally saw his mentor, Jud Heathcote, they shared more than memories of good and bad times in Jenison and Breslin. They had a national championship bond and a glow of accomplishment.

"I really did see it in his face," Izzo said with a smile. "He gave me a little hug out there on the court. And I could see the pride."

On a floor MSU would purchase for $75,000, repaint and install in Breslin, Johnson couldn't stop beaming. In that way, he was just like everyone else who had been a part of Spartan Basketball

Photo Credit: Rod Sanford, Lansing State Journal

— as a player, coach, staff member, administrator or fan.

"I love the way they play as a team," Johnson said, wearing a green Michigan State Basketball sweatshirt. "They broke that Florida trap like it was nothing. If Mateen hadn't been hurt…"

Photo Credit: Kevin Fowler, MSU Sports Information

2000 NCAA TOURNAMENT

The Spartans might have won by more than 13. But it was better this way. A team that overcame adversity at the beginning of the season did the same in the final game.

They finished 32-7, with six NCAA Tournament wins — all by double-digits. No team had done that before. But what better way to ring in a new century?

When Izzo was handed a phone with the message, "It's the President," he made one of his few mistakes on the trip.

"I thought it must have been Peter McPherson," he said of MSU's leader. "I had no idea it was President Clinton."

Clinton, a diehard Arkansas Razorbacks fan was calling to congratulate the Spartans on winning the title — and beating a team from his beloved Southeastern Conference.

It wouldn't be Izzo's last encounter with Clinton, though a scheduled trip to the White House never materialized and became a brief meeting in Breslin in January 2001.

"This is as storybook as it gets," Izzo said of promises made and fulfilled. "These seniors have done so much for the program. To have them go out as champions means more than I can possibly say."

He didn't have to say anything that night. But Izzo did. Remembering a pledge to appear at a remote location with Vitale and ESPN's Chris Fowler and Digger Phelps, he arrived there after 1 a.m.

Then, it was back to the team hotel for a party that never official-

ly ended. Izzo was happy to spend time with his family and to share stories with best friend Steve Mariucci and other coaches.

But on the streets of Indianapolis that morning, MSU fans were impossible to miss. At a downtown Steak & Shake, one frustrated Florida fan had to leave the restaurant before being served.

Three months and three days after the Spartans had edged the Gators 37-34 in the Florida Citrus Bowl, a chant of "Just like football!" was too much for anyone in orange-and-blue to bear. The capper came when someone stopped by his table to ask about the Gators' hockey team.

The celebration back in East Lansing was peaceful, just as Izzo had hoped. If MSU's basketball program had learned how to win, its students and others in search of a good party had learned a few things, too.

Tuesday morning, Izzo accepted the Sears/NABC National Championship trophy from a trusted friend, Purdue coach and NABC President Gene Keady. That Waterford Crystal basketball was valued at $30,000, more than four times as much as his first salary at MSU in 1983-84.

Roughly 600 fans met the Spartans' charter flight at Capital City Airport that afternoon, despite strong winds and temperatures in the low 30s. As the Spartans moved toward a chain-link fence to greet their fans, Cleaves was moving well on his crutches, finishing the season the same way he started.

The following day under ideal conditions, roughly 400,000 people from across the state turned out to salute the champs at one or more of the three venues to celebrate Green Glory.

A prolonged rally at the Capitol gave every politician outside of Ann Arbor an excellent photo opportunity. And Gov. John Engler, an unabashed MSU booster, created a stir when he suggested it was time to rename Michigan "The Spartan State."

A Parade of Champions down Michigan Avenue was a tremendous success and smashed all attendance records. And when more than 25,000 fans showed up in Spartan Stadium, the conversation centered on two topics: NCAA triumphs in 2000 and the chance to repeat in 2001.

"I know the folks up there have already taken Michigan State's success for granted," ESPN's

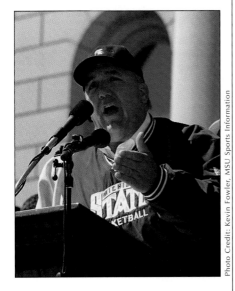

Bilas said. "But I think what Tom and his program did was one of the greatest accomplishments in the last two decades. To start the season No. 1, lose his best player to injury, then bring him back and finish No. 1 is really amazing."

Or as Izzo would have amended the team's slogan, "Players Played, Tough Players Won."

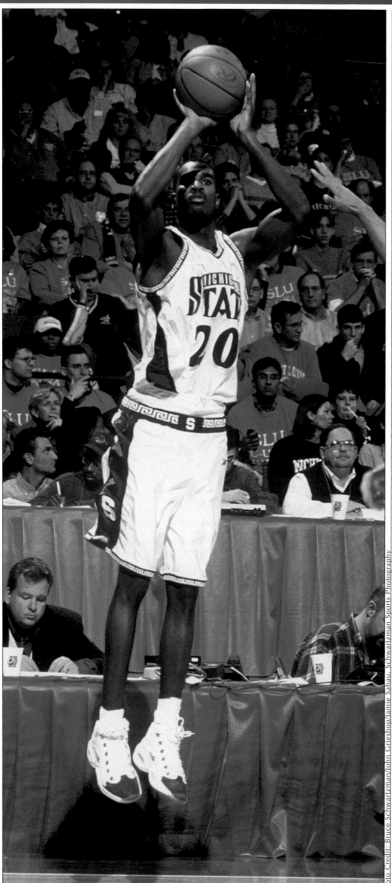

MSU 65, Valparaiso 38

March 16, 2000 • CSU Convocation Center • Cleveland, Ohio

Valparaiso	FG-FGA	FT-FTA	REB	PF	TP	A	TO	BLK	S	MIN
Lubos Barton	4-12	2-2	7	4	13	1	1	0	1	31
Jason Jenkins	0-5	0-0	3	1	0	0	0	0	0	22
Raitis Grafs	2-6	3-4	8	3	7	2	1	0	1	27
Dwayne Toatley	1-7	0-0	3	3	2	1	2	0	2	26
Jared Nuness	1-3	0-0	2	1	3	0	0	0	0	22
Milo Stovall	1-8	1-2	1	1	4	1	2	0	0	31
Ivan Vujic	3-8	0-0	4	3	6	1	5	2	0	23
Tarrance Price	1-3	1-2	1	1	3	0	1	0	0	11
Aaron Thomason	0-0	0-0	0	1	0	0	1	0	0	5
Antti Nikkila	0-0	0-0	0	0	0	0	0	0	0	2
Totals	13-52	7-10	31	18	38	6	13	2	4	200

Three-Point Field Goals: Barton 3-7, Jenkins 0-4, Toatley 0-2, Nuness 1-3, Stovall 1-5, Price 0-2, Team 5-23.
FG%: 1st Half 6-26 .231, 2nd Half 7-26 .269, Game 13-52 .250; 3FG%: 1st Half 2-11 .182, 2nd Half 3-12 .250, Game 5-23 .217; FT%: 1st Half 1-1 1.000, 2nd Half 6-9 .667, Game 7-10 .700; Team Rebounds: 2; Deadball Rebounds: 3.

Michigan State	FG-FGA	FT-FTA	REB	PF	TP	A	TO	BLK	S	MIN
Morris Peterson	5-9	1-1	4	0	12	0	1	0	0	27
A.J. Granger	3-5	0-0	3	1	7	1	0	1	0	29
Andre Hutson	1-3	2-2	4	4	4	2	0	0	0	21
Mateen Cleaves	5-11	3-3	2	0	15	8	3	0	1	32
Charlie Bell	0-3	0-0	4	3	0	1	1	0	1	16
Brandon Smith	0-1	0-0	1	0	0	0	1	0	0	4
David Thomas	0-1	1-2	2	0	1	1	2	0	2	7
Mike Chappell	2-5	4-6	4	3	9	0	2	0	0	14
Steve Cherry	0-0	0-0	0	0	0	1	0	0	0	2
Jason Richardson	3-6	2-3	10	0	9	0	0	0	1	25
Aloysius Anagonye	0-0	0-0	0	1	0	0	0	0	0	3
Adam Ballinger	3-6	2-2	3	3	8	0	0	1	0	20
Totals	22-50	15-19	39	15	65	14	10	2	5	200

Three-Point Field Goals: Peterson 1-3, Granger 1-2, Cleaves 2-6, Bell 0-2, Chappell 1-3, Richardson 1-1, Team 6-17.
FG%: 1st Half 11-26 .423, 2nd Half 11-24 .458, Game 22-50 .440; 3FG%: 1st Half 3-9 .333, 2nd Half 3-8 .375, Game 6-17 .353; FT%: 1st Half 4-4 1.000, 2nd Half 11-15 .733, Game 15-19 .789; Team Rebounds: 2; Deadball Rebounds: 1.

SCORE BY PERIODS	1	2	F
Valparaiso	15	23	-- 38
Michigan State	29	36	-- 65

OFFICIALS – Curtis Shaw, Tom Lopes, Orlandis Pool
TECHNICAL FOULS – None
ATTENDANCE – 13,374

MSU 73, Utah 61

March 18, 2000 • CSU Convocation Center • Cleveland, Ohio

Utah	FG-FGA	FT-FTA	REB	PF	TP	A	TO	BLK	S	MIN
Hanno Mottola	5-10	6-6	5	4	16	1	3	1	0	34
Alex Jensen	5-7	1-5	5	4	13	1	1	0	0	36
Phil Cullen	3-7	0-0	2	2	8	3	1	0	1	25
Tony Harvey	7-16	0-1	3	2	15	6	1	0	2	38
Jeff Johnsen	2-3	0-0	3	2	5	2	3	0	1	33
Gary Colbert	0-0	0-0	1	0	0	2	0	0	0	13
Mike Puzey	0-1	0-0	3	3	0	1	0	0	0	6
Nate Althoff	2-2	0-0	2	1	4	0	0	0	0	15
Totals	24-46	7-12	21	18	61	16	9	1	4	200

Three-Point Field Goals: Mottola 0-2, Jensen 2-4, Cullen 2-6, Harvey 1-6, Johnsen 1-2, Team 6-20.
FG%: 1st Half 13-23 .565, 2nd Half 11-23 .478, Game 24-46 .522; 3FG%: 1st Half 4-9 .444, 2nd Half 2-11 .182, Game 6-20 .300; FT%: 1st Half 5-6 .833, 2nd Half 2-6 .333, Game 7-12 .583; Team Rebounds: 0; Deadball Rebounds: 2.

Michigan State	FG-FGA	FT-FTA	REB	PF	TP	A	TO	BLK	S	MIN
Andre Hutson	7-9	5-10	8	1	19	2	1	0	0	30
Morris Peterson	5-11	0-0	3	2	13	0	2	0	1	33
A.J. Granger	3-5	0-0	3	2	7	2	3	0	1	33
Mateen Cleaves	7-14	3-4	2	1	21	5	1	0	1	36
Charlie Bell	2-5	5-6	5	1	9	3	1	0	0	31
David Thomas	0-0	0-0	1	1	0	0	0	1	0	8
Mike Chappell	0-0	0-0	0	0	0	0	0	0	0	2
Jason Richardson	1-2	0-0	4	4	2	0	0	0	0	13
Aloysius Anagonye	1-1	0-0	0	2	2	1	1	0	0	6
Adam Ballinger	0-0	0-0	0	1	0	0	1	0	0	8
Totals	26-47	13-20	30	15	73	13	10	1	3	200

Three-Point Field Goals: Peterson 3-4, Granger 1-3, Cleaves 4-7, Bell 0-1, Team 8-15.
FG%: 1st Half 13-26 .500, 2nd Half 13-21 .619, Game 26-47 .553; 3FG%: 1st Half 3-8 .375, 2nd Half 5-7 .714, Game 8-15 .533; FT%: 1st Half 3-4 .750, 2nd Half 10-16 .625, Game 13-20 .650; Team Rebounds: 4; Deadball Rebounds: 2.

SCORE BY PERIODS	1	2	F
Utah	35	26	-- 61
Michigan State	32	41	-- 73

OFFICIALS – Gerald Boudreaux, Mike Thibodeaux, Tom Lopes
TECHNICAL FOULS – None
ATTENDANCE – 13,374

MSU 75, Syracuse 58
March 23, 2000 • The Palace of Auburn Hills • Auburn Hills, Mich.

Syracuse	FG-FGA	FT-FTA	REB	PF	TP	A	TO	BLK	S	MIN
Damone Brown	4-8	0-0	5	2	8	0	0	0	0	26
Ryan Blackwell	4-13	1-3	6	3	9	4	1	0	0	37
Etan Thomas	3-3	1-2	6	4	7	0	3	2	0	37
Tony Bland	1-1	0-0	0	0	3	0	0	0	0	8
Jason Hart	5-11	0-0	3	4	11	10	4	0	3	40
Preston Shumpert	2-6	0-0	2	2	6	0	1	0	1	20
Allen Griffin	5-10	4-4	1	3	14	1	2	0	1	32
Totals	24-52	6-9	27	19	58	15	11	2	5	200

Three-Point Field Goals: Blackwell 0-1, Bland 1-1, Hart 1-4, Shumpert 2-5, Griffin 0-1, Team 4-12.
FG%: 1st Half 14-26 .538, 2nd Half 10-26 .385, Game 24-52 .462; 3FG%: 1st Half 3-7 .429, 2nd Half 1-5 .200, Game 4-12 .333; FT%: 1st Half 3-4 .750, 2nd Half 3-5 .600, Game 6-9 .667; Team Rebounds: 4; Deadball Rebounds: 2.

Michigan State	FG-FGA	FT-FTA	REB	PF	TP	A	TO	BLK	S	MIN
Andre Hutson	5-7	1-4	5	2	11	1	3	0	1	34
Morris Peterson	6-10	4-4	3	2	21	2	1	1	0	34
A.J. Granger	7-11	3-3	4	1	19	3	0	2	0	33
Mateen Cleaves	4-12	0-0	1	1	10	7	3	0	1	38
Charlie Bell	3-7	4-4	6	4	12	4	2	0	1	29
David Thomas	0-0	0-0	1	0	0	0	1	0	0	2
Mike Chappell	0-1	1-2	4	2	1	0	0	0	0	15
Jason Richardson	0-1	0-0	3	0	0	0	0	0	0	11
Aloysius Anagonye	0-0	1-2	1	1	1	0	0	0	0	4
Totals	25-49	14-19	30	13	75	17	10	3	3	200

Three-Point Field Goals: Peterson 5-9, Granger 2-4, Cleaves 2-6, Bell 2-4, Team 11-23.
FG%: 1st Half 8-24 .333, 2nd Half 17-25 .680, Game 25-49 .510; 3FG%: 1st Half 2-8 .250, 2nd Half 9-15 .600, Game 11-23 .478; FT%: 1st Half 6-9 .667, 2nd Half 8-10 .800, Game 14-19 .737; Team Rebounds: 2; Deadball Rebounds: 1.

SCORE BY PERIODS	1	2	F
Syracuse	34	24	58
Michigan State	24	51	75

OFFICIALS – Scott Thornley, Bob Sitov, Rick Hartzell
TECHNICAL FOULS – None
ATTENDANCE – 21,214

MSU 75, Iowa State 64
March 25, 2000 • The Palace of Auburn Hills • Auburn Hills, Mich.

Iowa State	FG-FGA	FT-FTA	REB	PF	TP	A	TO	BLK	S	MIN
Kantrail Horton	1-5	4-4	6	2	6	2	3	0	0	32
Stevie Johnson	1-1	0-1	5	0	2	0	2	0	0	29
Marcus Fizer	6-15	2-2	4	4	15	1	3	0	0	36
Jamaal Tinsley	5-13	5-7	3	4	18	2	5	3	0	34
Michael Nurse	5-11	2-2	4	5	17	1	3	0	0	40
Brandon Hawkins	1-2	0-0	7	2	2	0	1	0	1	13
Paul Shirley	1-3	2-2	4	5	4	2	2	0	0	16
Totals	20-50	15-18	38	24	64	8	19	3	1	200

Three-Point Field Goals: Horton 0-3, Fizer 1-6, Tinsley 3-8, Nurse 5-9, Team 9-26.
FG%: 1st Half 9-19 .474, 2nd Half 11-31 .355, Game 20-50 .400; 3FG%: 1st Half 4-11 .364, 2nd Half 5-15 .333, Game 9-26 .346; FT%: 1st Half 9-11 .818, 2nd Half 6-7 .857, Game 15-18 .833; Team Rebounds: 5; Deadball Rebounds: 0.

Michigan State	FG-FGA	FT-FTA	REB	PF	TP	A	TO	BLK	S	MIN
Andre Hutson	6-9	5-5	11	4	17	2	1	0	0	24
Morris Peterson	5-13	7-7	7	3	18	0	1	1	1	36
A.J. Granger	5-8	6-6	0	2	18	2	0	0	0	37
Mateen Cleaves	4-12	1-2	1	4	10	2	5	2	2	35
Charlie Bell	3-11	2-2	5	4	9	2	1	0	3	27
Brandon Smith	0-0	0-0	0	0	0	0	0	0	0	1
David Thomas	0-0	0-0	0	0	0	0	0	0	0	3
Mat Ishbia	0-0	0-0	0	0	0	0	0	0	0	1
Mike Chappell	1-2	0-0	0	0	2	1	0	0	0	15
Jason Richardson	0-1	0-0	2	1	0	0	0	0	0	13
Aloysius Anagonye	0-0	1-2	1	4	1	0	0	0	0	8
Adam Ballinger	0-0	0-0	0	0	0	0	0	0	0	1
Totals	24-56	22-24	27	24	75	9	8	3	6	200

Three-Point Field Goals: Peterson 1-3, Granger 2-4, Cleaves 1-4, Bell 1-6, Chappell 0-1, Richardson 0-1, Team 5-19.
FG%: 1st Half 14-29 .483, 2nd Half 10-27 .370, Game 24-56 .429; 3FG%: 1st Half 3-11 .273, 2nd Half 2-8 .250, Game 5-19 .263; FT%: 1st Half 3-3 1.000, 2nd Half 19-21 .905, Game 22-24 .917; Team Rebounds: 0; Deadball Rebounds: 2.

SCORE BY PERIODS	1	2	F
Iowa State	31	33	64
Michigan State	34	41	75

OFFICIALS – Curtis Shaw, Frank Basone, Lonnie Dixon
TECHNICAL FOULS – Iowa State bench (2), Michigan State bench
ATTENDANCE – 21,214

MSU 53, Wisconsin 41
April 1, 2000 • RCA Dome • Indianapolis, Ind.

Wisconsin	FG-FGA	FT-FTA	REB	PF	TP	A	TO	BLK	S	MIN
Andy Kowske	1-2	0-2	0	4	2	0	0	4	0	20
Mike Kelley	1-2	0-0	7	3	2	3	0	0	2	30
Mark Vershaw	2-11	1-1	2	3	5	3	1	0	0	31
Jon Bryant	1-5	0-0	1	3	2	1	2	0	0	27
Roy Boone	6-9	5-6	3	2	18	0	5	0	0	25
Charlie Wills	1-4	0-0	1	2	2	0	0	0	0	19
Duany Duany	0-2	0-0	0	0	0	0	1	0	0	11
Maurice Linton	0-4	0-0	1	0	0	0	2	0	0	10
Travon Davis	1-1	1-2	2	2	4	1	0	0	0	10
Kirk Penney	2-3	0-0	2	0	6	0	0	0	0	14
Erik Faust	0-0	0-0	0	0	0	0	0	0	0	1
Robert Smith	0-0	0-0	0	0	0	0	0	0	0	1
Julian Swartz	0-0	0-0	0	0	0	0	0	0	0	1
Totals	15-43	7-11	20	19	41	8	11	4	2	200

Three-Point Field Goals: Kelley 0-1, Vershaw 0-1, Bryant 0-3, Boone 1-1, Wills 0-1, Duany 0-1, Linton 0-1, Davis 1-1, Penney 2-3, Team 4-13.
FG%: 1st Half 6-21 .286, 2nd Half 9-22 .409, Game 15-43 .349; 3FG%: 1st Half 2-5 .400, 2nd Half 2-8 .250, Game 4-13 .308; FT%: 1st Half 3-4 .750, 2nd Half 4-7 .571, Game 7-11 .636; Team Rebounds: 1; Deadball Rebounds: 2.

Michigan State	FG-FGA	FT-FTA	REB	PF	TP	A	TO	BLK	S	MIN
Andre Hutson	3-7	4-5	10	2	10	0	3	0	0	32
Morris Peterson	7-15	4-4	7	3	20	0	1	0	1	33
A.J. Granger	0-3	1-2	7	4	1	1	3	0	0	32
Mateen Cleaves	1-7	9-11	4	3	11	1	4	0	2	36
Charlie Bell	2-9	0-0	8	2	4	2	2	0	0	30
Jason Richardson	0-0	0-0	0	1	0	0	0	0	0	10
Aloysius Anagonye	1-1	0-0	2	2	2	0	1	0	0	12
Mike Chappell	2-4	1-1	0	1	5	0	0	2	0	9
Adam Ballinger	0-0	0-0	1	0	0	0	0	1	0	3
David Thomas	0-0	0-0	0	0	0	0	0	0	0	3
Totals	16-46	19-23	42	18	53	4	14	3	3	200

Three-Point Field Goals: Peterson 2-8, Granger 0-1, Bell 0-3, Chappell 0-2, Team 2-14.
FG%: 1st Half 6-24 .250, 2nd Half 10-22 .455, Game 16-46 .348; 3FG%: 1st Half 0-7 .000, 2nd Half 2-7 .286, Game 2-14 .143; FT%: 1st Half 7-9 .778, 2nd Half 12-14 .857, Game 19-23 .826; Team Rebounds: 3; Deadball Rebounds: 2.

SCORE BY PERIODS	1	2	F
Wisconsin	17	24	41
Michigan State	19	34	53

OFFICIALS – John Clougherty, Andre Patillo, Tim Higgins
TECHNICAL FOULS – None
ATTENDANCE – 43,116

MSU 89, Florida 76
April 3, 2000 • RCA Dome • Indianapolis, Ind.

Florida	FG-FGA	FT-FTA	REB	PF	TP	A	TO	BLK	S	MIN
Brent Wright	5-8	3-5	10	4	13	4	1	0	1	29
Mike Miller	2-5	5-6	3	0	10	2	2	0	0	31
Udonis Haslem	10-12	7-7	2	4	27	0	3	1	0	28
Teddy Dupay	0-4	0-0	0	2	0	1	0	0	0	15
Justin Hamilton	0-1	0-0	0	1	0	0	0	0	0	14
Brett Nelson	4-10	0-0	4	1	11	3	3	0	0	26
Matt Bonner	0-0	0-0	3	1	0	0	0	0	0	7
Kenyan Weaks	1-3	0-0	1	2	3	1	1	0	0	22
Donnell Harvey	3-11	3-4	6	2	9	0	2	1	2	16
Major Parker	1-3	0-0	1	2	3	2	1	0	0	12
Totals	26-60	18-22	30	19	76	13	13	2	5	200

Three-Point Field Goals: Wright 0-1, Miller 1-2, Dupay 0-2, Hamilton 0-1, Nelson 3-6, Bonner 0-2, Weaks 1-1, Parker 1-3, Team 6-18.
FG%: 1st Half 11-27 .407, 2nd Half 15-33 .455, Game 26-60 .433; 3FG%: 1st Half 2-7 .286, 2nd Half 4-11 .364, Game 6-18 .333; FT%: 1st Half 8-11 .727, 2nd Half 10-11 .909, Game 18-22 .818; Team Rebounds: 1; Deadball Rebounds: 4.

Michigan State	FG-FGA	FT-FTA	REB	PF	TP	A	TO	BLK	S	MIN
Andre Hutson	2-4	2-2	1	4	6	3	1	0	0	22
Morris Peterson	7-14	4-6	2	3	21	5	3	0	1	31
A.J. Granger	7-11	2-2	9	2	19	1	2	0	0	33
Mateen Cleaves	7-11	1-1	2	1	18	4	2	0	0	31
Charlie Bell	3-6	2-3	8	2	9	5	2	0	2	33
Jason Richardson	4-7	1-2	2	1	9	0	0	0	1	16
Aloysius Anagonye	0-0	0-0	3	4	0	0	2	1	0	12
Mike Chappell	2-4	0-0	1	0	5	0	1	0	1	7
Adam Ballinger	1-1	0-0	2	0	2	0	0	0	0	7
David Thomas	0-0	0-0	1	1	0	1	1	0	0	5
Brandon Smith	0-0	0-0	0	0	0	0	0	0	0	1
Steve Cherry	0-0	0-0	0	0	0	0	0	0	0	1
Mat Ishbia	0-1	0-0	0	0	0	0	0	0	0	1
Totals	33-59	12-16	32	20	89	19	14	1	5	200

Three-Point Field Goals: Peterson 3-8, Granger 3-5, Cleaves 3-4, Bell 1-2, Chappell 1-3, Team 11-22.
FG%: 1st Half 18-34 .529, 2nd Half 15-25 .600, Game 33-59 .559; 3FG%: 1st Half 5-12 .417, 2nd Half 6-10 .600, Game 11-22 .500; FT%: 1st Half 2-3 .667, 2nd Half 10-13 .769, Game 12-16 .750; Team Rebounds: 3; Deadball Rebounds: 2.

SCORE BY PERIODS	1	2	F
Florida	32	44	76
Michigan State	43	46	89

OFFICIALS – Jim Burr, Gerald Boudreaux, David Hall
TECHNICAL FOULS – None
ATTENDANCE – 43,116

The cheering for a national champion hadn't stopped when a lot of hearts did in May 2000.

The NBA's Atlanta Hawks came after Michigan State coach Tom Izzo the way CNN covers politicians — with a press that never quits.

"If you can't be the best, buy the best" was Atlanta's logic. And it nearly paid off. After five increasingly successful seasons as Michigan State's head coach and 17 years with the program, Izzo came a lot closer to leaving than most Spartans would ever know.

Little more than a week after snipping the net in Indy, Izzo got a call from Hawks General Manager Pete Babcock. Babcock had watched MSU crush Kansas four months earlier in the Great Eight in Chicago without Mateen Cleaves. And the Hawks needed someone to replace Lenny Wilkins and reverse their fortunes after a 28-54 season.

The first face-to-face meeting of any consequence came in April at the Desert Classic, an NBA Pre-Draft Camp in Phoenix where Izzo had gone to watch A.J. Granger. Little did he know where that meeting would lead.

"For the next two weeks, I never gave it a minute's thought," Izzo said on the rear deck of his home the day before he made his decision. "They were talking to six people. I thought I was the token college guy. When they called and said they wanted to talk seriously, I asked, 'Why me?'"

Perhaps because Izzo had just

Photo Credit: Kevin Fowler, MSU Sports Information

won an NCAA title and Atlanta had never reached the NBA Finals. Perhaps because the Spartans had just won four more games than the Hawks in 43 fewer chances. Perhaps because MSU wouldn't lose 54 games in a span of six seasons. Or perhaps because Babcock and President Stan Kasten finally knew a keeper when they saw him.

The franchise that had just traded Steve Smith for Isaiah Rider made another gross miscalculation by offering Izzo $1.8 million per year, compared to an unsigned $1.2 million-a-year extension waiting in East Lansing.

Izzo wasn't interested in that. But Atlanta persisted and upped its bid to five years for a guaranteed $14.75 million, with a chance to make roughly $5 million more — enough to grab anyone's attention. Another little-known clause would have meant a $1 million payment to MSU as compensation. Plans for a Disney cruise with his family would just have to wait.

"I was flabbergasted," Izzo said after flying home on a private jet provided by the Hawks. "I'd be lying if I said the money wasn't a major part of the decision. But to be honest, it really is a lot more than that."

It was the challenge of trying to become the first coach to lead teams to NCAA and NBA crowns, an escape from some of the maddening rules and sleaze factors in the college game and a different lifestyle that had to be weighed.

"These jobs aren't always as much fun as you'd think," Izzo said of college basketball and con-

stant recruiting. "Last year in July, the best month of the year, I was on the road for 27 days. And you have a lot more time in the NBA than everyone thinks. That's what a lot of guys I checked with told me."

He spoke at length with best friend and San Francisco 49ers head coach Steve Mariucci and talked every day with Grand Rapids-area business mogul and MSU diehard Peter Secchia.

Izzo also checked with the Philadelphia 76ers' Larry Brown, the only coach to leave a defending NCAA champ for the NBA. And he picked the brains of four ex-Spartans with pro experience: Earvin Johnson, Scott Skiles, Steve Smith and Eric Snow.

"I talked to Tom for a few minutes, and he said he's intrigued with the job," said Smith, who didn't give Izzo the hard sell on Atlanta but didn't rip his former employer. "He doesn't know where he's going with it. His loyalty and his heart are at Michigan State. But it would be a dream-come-true for any coach to be at the ultimate level."

When Izzo left for a press conference on campus and a private meeting with his players, including outgoing leader Mateen Cleaves and incoming heir-apparent Marcus Taylor, nothing was certain. After a two-and-a-half-hour talk, a friend for 17 years thought he was leaning toward leaving.

But emotions played an essential role. When 5-year-old Raquel Izzo joined her parents for a tour of Atlanta's new Philips Arena, she

softly sang her version of the "MSU Fight Song" — "Pull right through for MSU..." And when asked an innocent question, Raquel snapped, "I don't want to be a Hawk. I want to be a Spartan!"

At the Izzos' home, just prior to a long-planned move to their dream house across Park Lake Road, Tom's wife talked about the difficulty of severing intense relationships with their university and community.

"It's my school and my town," said a teary-eyed Lupe, an East Lansing native, on that fateful Friday. "I love it here. . . . That's what makes it so hard."

A few hours later at assistant coach Brian Gregory's house, a team meeting tipped the scales toward staying. As usual, Cleaves led and assisted.

"I knew he would stay if he listened to his heart," Cleaves said. "So I told him, 'Just listen to what your heart tells you.' The main thing I wanted to say was that he can influence so many more lives in college than he'd be able to if he went to the pros."

Izzo jokingly blamed his players for putting him in such a tough position. If only the Spartans hadn't won so many games . . .

Yet, it was the opportunity to win a lot more and to finish what he started in 1995 that put Atlanta down for the count. It was good enough to host the Olympic Games but not to steal the most-popular man in Mid-Michigan.

"We have a chance to win more championships here," Izzo said at a packed Saturday press

2000 NON-CONFERENCE

conference in the Clara Bell Smith Student-Athlete Academic Center. "I'd like to take a shot at it. . . . My own players might be the biggest reason I decided to be a Spartan forever."

That decision surprised a lot of people, including popular websites that assumed the worst for MSU — and as it would have turned out, the worst for Izzo.

Instead, he got down to the business of trying to win another national title without players who scored 58 points against Florida. It would have been the biggest retooling on the run since UCLA repeated as champ in 1972, Bill Walton's first varsity season.

The first bonding experience for the 2000-01 Spartans was a belated ninth birthday party for Asaad Ali and dozens of pals on Saturday, May 20, Berrien Springs.

When Asaad saw the bus from East Lansing arrive at his family's 88-acre estate, he didn't stop to thank his parents, Muhammad and Lonnie. He was too busy racing toward his basketball heroes, hollering, "I've got Charlie Bell on my team!"

For the next three hours, it was hard to tell who was having more fun — Asaad or Charlie, Muhammad or Izzo — before "The Champ" quit shadow-boxing and waved goodbye to the champs.

"Asaad didn't know they were coming," Lonnie said, despite having decorations and cakes with an MSU theme. "But this is what it's all about — the looks on everyone's faces."

The winner, by a unanimous decision, was anyone lucky enough to be there. And five months later, after enough 6 a.m. workouts to suit any heavyweight titlist, the Spartans began sparring with history.

They began with "The Main Event," a fight-themed introduction of the men's and women's teams at midnight on Oct. 14 in Breslin. With help from MSU loyalist Bob Every, the Crown Boxing Club and ring announcer David "The Mad Dog" DeMarco, the players made grand entrances in green, silk robes.

Charlie "Boom-Boom" Bell, Andre "Hurricane" Hutson, David "Golden Boy" Thomas, Brandon "The Hitman" Smith, "Iron Mike" Chappell, Jason "Thunder" Richardson, Adam "Bam-Bam" Ballinger, Jason "Sugar Ray" Andreas, Aloysius "Rocky" Anagonye, Adam "White Fang" Wolfe, Zach "The Attack" Randolph, Mat "The Motor City Madman" Ishbia, "Marvelous" Marcus Taylor and Tim "The Greek" Bograkos drew huge ovations.

"This is unbelievable....You're the reason we've won 28 games in

a row here," a tuxedoed Izzo told an estimated 11,000 fans before roaring, "LET'S GET READY TO RUMMMBLE!"

It wasn't the perfect preconference schedule, with the only serious road test coming against Seton Hall, the top-rated team in *Basketball Times*. But with home games against North Carolina, Florida and Kentucky, the Spartans had never treated their fans to a better lineup.

While Izzo began an exhaustive search for new leadership on the court and in the locker room, MSU's players and coaches vowed to remain the hunters, instead of becoming the hunted.

The Spartans were ranked No. 3 in the nation by the Associated Press and *The Sporting News*, No. 4 in *Street & Smith's College Basketball* and No. 5 in the *USA TODAY*/ESPN survey of coaches and the *Blue Ribbon College Basketball Yearbook*.

Izzo was most curious about the *Lansing State Journal's* picks, since they had predicted every title and nearly every outcome in 1999-

2000. Jack Ebling's call for 2000-01? A share of the Big Ten title with Illinois at 13-3, a third-straight trip to the Final Four and a loss to Duke or Arizona in Minneapolis.

Before those picks hit the presses, sophomore forward Adam Ballinger shattered his right thumb and was lost for eight games. But he wasn't needed in the first exhibition against Northern Michigan, the alma mater of Izzo and MSU assistant Mike Garland.

"It's a great opportunity to be able to help them," said a 1977 Division II All-American who arrived at NMU as a walk-on. "Their president is coming down, Their board is coming down. And a couple of snowmen are coming here, too."

They melted quickly as the Spartans turned up the heat in a 93-40 win. Six players scored in double figures for MSU, while senior forward Andre Hutson and freshman center Zach Randolph combined for 27 rebounds.

Boxing analogies hit home like Ali's jabs in the Spartans' second tuneup, a serious game against the Harlem Globetrotters, who hadn't lost in five years and 1,270 bouts.

Trailing 35-29 at the half in its green jerseys, MSU rallied for a 72-68 triumph that was trumpeted on ABC's "Monday Night Football." Senior guard Charlie Bell had 21 points, including a driving layup and two free throws in the last 11 seconds. And Randolph added 17 points and eight rebounds, hitting all six of his shots from the field.

"We like to think of ourselves as the heavyweight champs,"

Photo Credit: Kevin Fowler, MSU Sports Information

owner Mannie Jackson said after the Trotters' first loss to collegians since April 15, 1962. "The heavyweight champs don't like to lose. But I'm not sure Michigan State's team is as good as its individuals right now. That's a great collection of athletes. And we know athletes when we see them."

One play in particular made Izzo's blood pressure rise. When a lazy pass from Hutson was stolen by ex-Louisville forward Alex Sanders, no Spartans bothered to chase him. So when Sanders blew the breakaway, he casually gathered the rebound for a layup.

"You saw a missed dunk, and not one of our guys was even on that side of midcourt," Izzo said, remembering a pair of NBA rookies. "(Mateen) Cleaves and (Morris) Peterson would be turning over in their respective cities over that trash."

On Sunday, Nov. 19, MSU opened the regular season against Oakland and unfurled its second NCAA championship banner in

Breslin. It also cruised to a 97-61 win over the Golden Grizzlies, who had beaten Michigan 97-90 just 43 hours earlier in Rochester.

With four minutes left in the first half, sophomore forward Jason Richardson had outscored Oakland 17-13. But the highlight of a breakout, 25-point effort was Richardson's basket that went through the rim twice.

"I went in — I know it did," he said of a reverse slam that bounced to the top of the backboard before he grabbed the ball for a layup. "The ball hit my head and went back through the basket."

Those shots passed through the rim more often than all the attempts of the Grizzlies' Jason Rozycki. After scoring 32 points against the Wolverines, Rozycki managed just three against Bell's airtight defense.

"Charlie actually deserves a quadruple-double," Izzo said after Bell had 13 points, a career-high 11 rebounds and 10 assists to join Earvin "Magic" Johnson in the

2000 NON-CONFERENCE

Photo Credit: Kevin Fowler, MSU Sports Information

Spartans' triple-double club. "The defense he played in the first half might have been what won the game."

After MSU's 24th-straight win in a home-opener, Izzo railed against an NCAA point-of-emphasis to eliminate rough play. Inconsistent interpretations had led to 113 fouls in Oakland's first two games and made a joke of post defense.

"A bump here or a touch there is not physical play," Izzo said. "Maybe we'll get used to it. . . . But I hope it doesn't lead to free-throw contests. That's not what people want to see. In fact, one of the reasons they did it was to open the game up more and have more scoring opportunities. The problem is we'll be doing it with our managers."

His managers could have played in an 89-56 win over Cornell in the first game of the Spartan Coca-Cola Classic the following Friday. MSU launched a ridiculous 75 shots, largely due to a 20-5 edge in offensive rebounds, and hit 37 of them.

The Spartans had 22 assists and just five turnovers, despite playing without Randolph and freshman point guard Marcus Taylor for the first 15:46. The pair had been late for a pregame meeting. And Izzo wanted to put an end to that.

"Coach was pretty upset," Hutson said. "But I pulled the guys aside and told them they can't be doing that. It lets the whole team down when your rotation is different. They both apologized to the team. And we have to make sure that doesn't happen again."

Eastern Washington moved to 2-1 with an 62-56 win over Bradley in the second semifinal. But the Eagles were grounded 83-61 Saturday, as MSU claimed its 15th title in 19 Classics. And Izzo couldn't say enough good things about Bell, who matched his career-high of 31 points with 12-for-13 accuracy from the field.

"We can get on him for not getting a rebound," said Izzo, ever the perfectionist, with a mischievous grin. "Other than that, he did everything but sell popcorn."

At No. 3 in the media poll and No. 2 on the coaches' list, the Spartans were ready to host No. 6 North Carolina on Nov. 29 in the second ACC/Big Ten Challenge. The Tar Heels were the highest-

ranked non-conference team to play in East Lansing since No. 3 Notre Dame on Feb. 4, 1974.

The last time North Carolina had visited, just 4,797 battled a snowstorm to show up in Jenison Field House in 1976 — or 1 B.E. (before Earvin), as historians prefer. Twenty-four years later, a sell-out of 14,759 was guaranteed in Breslin.

Only a few in Carolina Blue went home disappointed. MSU dominated 77-64, grabbing a 13-

Photo Credit: Kevin Fowler, MSU Sports Information

point halftime lead with a closing 16-4 run. And the Spartans outre-bounded a much-taller team, 43-29.

Richardson led the winners with 16 points. But Bell added 15 and held All-America guard Joseph Forte to 11 points on 5-for-16 shooting. And Hutson got the best of 7-foot center Brendan Haywood, with edges of 14-10 in scoring and 9-5 in rebounds.

"I'm really proud of our per-formance," Izzo said. "We played an awfully good team and got a lot of play from a lot of people. We had moments when we looked real good and moments when they made us look ugly. But it was a great win for us in a great atmos-phere."

MSU's freshmen weren't fazed by the Tar Heels' mystique, as Randolph contributed nine points and eight rebounds and Taylor added eight points and five assists — enough to eliminate any doubt about the outcome.

"They're a great basketball team and a well-coached team," first-year North Carolina coach Matt Doherty said. "When I was at Notre Dame last year, Tom called and wanted to play. I didn't want to play them. They're too good."

Many of the nation's top writ-ers agreed with that verdict when they gathered at the Roadhouse Pub for a postgame . . . discussion. They had just seen the Spartans win their 32nd-straight game in Breslin and their sixth in a row on a floor first used for the 2000 Final Four. The Tar Heels dropped to 0-2 on that unfriendly surface.

Photo Credit: Kevin Fowler, MSU Sports Information

"That place was wild the other night," Izzo said the following afternoon. "Even Dick Vitale told me afterward we might have the best environment in the country. I can't believe how many calls we've had from people asking how we do it. But it's how a program reacts after a big win that sets it apart."

MSU reacted by demolishing Illinois-Chicago 97-53 to tie its second-longest win streak, 16 games. The Spartans led by 52 and doubled the Flames' rebound total, 54-27. When Randolph had 19 points and 10 rebounds and Hutson added 11 and 12, respec-tively, Izzo had two players with double-doubles.

"Of course, our kids were intimidated," UIC coach and for-mer Illinois assistant Jimmy

Collins said. "But that's no reason why we couldn't have played with them. I would've liked to think we could've stayed within 30 points."

The Spartans' next opponent, 2000 NCAA runner-up Florida, arrived with a different objective. Though each team had lost three key players from their matchup in Indianapolis, Billy Donovan's players had a score to settle and a streak to spoil.

The Gators weren't sure if they would have fiery sharpshooter Teddy Dupay in uniform. And Donovan said that had nothing to do with a questionable leg sweep that left Cleaves limping with a severely sprained ankle in Indy.

"It was unfair to make that accusation," Donovan said of dirty-play charges across the country and a payback mentality in East Lansing. "They were two competitive kids jockeying for position. The last thing Teddy would do is take Mateen out."

Eight months after Cleaves crawled toward the sideline, Izzo was in a mellower mood. After sticking up for his star and challenging Dupay's motivation in April, Izzo hoped Florida's leading scorer would play after a one-game suspension for violating team rules.

"I'd be lying to you if I said anything other than I hope he plays," Izzo said. "A couple of years ago, I would've hoped he didn't play and nobody else played, either. But I want to see the best and see where we are. Just when you start to feel good about that, North Carolina gets clobbered at home by Kentucky."

Photo Credit: Kevin Fowler, MSU Sports Information

MSU didn't feel great about facing center Udonis Haslem again. He had led the Gators with 27 points in the championship game. And he was a better player as a junior, nearly everyone said. If he could punish the Spartans again, it might be time for an upset.

Wrong town, wrong team. MSU moved to 6-0 and dropped Florida to 3-1 with a 99-83 thumping. And no one was better than Randolph, who had a game-high 27 points and seven rebounds in only 23 minutes.

"They're not nearly as good as they were in April," Donovan said of a team that scored 10 more points in the rematch. "But they have the potential to be better. When Taylor and Randolph get more consistent, they can be better than they were."

Taylor played his best game, too, with 15 points, seven assists and two turnovers in 28 minutes against Florida's pressure. The Spartans' heralded freshmen scored 19 straight points for their team in a tight second half, when the Gators trailed 76-72.

"Did I envision that in their sixth game? No... Am I happy to see it? Yes," Izzo said of the rookies. "Zach has the greatest hands. And Marcus made some incredible passes. They deserved what they got tonight."

One huge difference this time was the foul trouble for Haslem instead of Hutson, as occurred in the title game. The Gators' best weapon finally fouled out with 13 points in just 13 minutes. Meanwhile, Bell

Photo Credit: Kevin Fowler, MSU Sports Information

had 20 points for the winners, Richardson 13 and Hutson 12.

MSU shot 55.4 percent from the field, 43.8 beyond the arc and 80.0 at the foul line. The Spartans also had a 37-26 edge in rebounds and a mere 12 turnovers, three less than Florida.

No one could fault Dupay for a lack of courage. After being reinstated the day before the game, the 5-11 junior came off the bench, battled constant taunts and scored 17 points, one less than forward Brent Wright. Greeted with signs in the Izzone like "It's time Dupay the price," his roughest moment came when he was knocked out by a Randolph elbow.

Before the Pistons' game in Seattle, Cleaves had to smile just a little. And when Izzo surveyed the scene near the end of the game, his sense of satisfaction and pride in the Breslin atmosphere was unmistakable.

"The fans were awesome," Izzo said. "I thought they were pretty classy. I didn't hear anything too bad. A couple of times, from floor to ceiling, I had to sit back and take a look. I just sat there like a proud whatever and watched 80-year-old people rise up in (section) 224."

Three days later, MSU played its first road game at Loyola and made it nine straight wins in Greater Chicago. With roughly two-thirds of a record crowd of 5,513 in green-and-white, including Gov. John Engler, the Spartans sprinted to a 29-4 lead, ruled 56-27 at the half and coasted to a 103-71 win.

2000 NON-CONFERENCE

Photo Credit: Kevin Fowler, MSU Sports Information

Bell had 19 points and seven assists. And Taylor added 15 and nine, respectively, as the point guards averaged 17 points, eight assists and two turnovers. But they had plenty of help from Richardson's 17 points and Hutson's 16.

Despite 65.2-percent shooting from the field, the second-best accuracy in the Izzo era, defensive breakdowns in the backcourt were viewed as a dangerous sign. Point guard David Bailey, a 5-8 blur, burned MSU for 25 points and even scored in the post.

"There is zero comparison defensively between this year and last year's team," a smoldering Izzo said. "Don't even put us in the same league. We've got a couple of guys who need to work on guarding this table. Our No. 1 goal was to stop penetration. What would you grade us?… I'd say a D or an E. And a D or an E isn't going to win any championships."

One week after cracking triple-digits, the Spartans proved they could win with less than 50 points. A 46-45 escape against Kentucky in Breslin was a better win than anyone imagined at the time. When the Wildcats fell to 3-5, no one knew they would be the Southeastern Conference champ,

not to mention a No. 2 seed in the NCAA Tournament.

"I guess Kentucky won the battle, and we won the score," Izzo said before an impassioned defense of beleaguered UK coach Tubby Smith. "I was very pleased with our second half after being out-worked, outplayed and outhustled in every effort stat."

Outscored in the first 20 minutes, too, after an 11-0 run made it 27-18 at the break. But the Wildcats should have had a bigger lead, shooting 52.4 percent to MSU's 21.4 and holding a 19-14 advantage over the nation's No. 1 rebounding team. With the Alis and their guests in attendance, a second-ranked team was thoroughly embarrassed.

Scorched by an Izzo tirade, the Spartans scored the first 13 points in the second half but never led by more than five. And six straight points from forward Tayshaun Prince put the visitors ahead 45-44 with 2:56 left in an ugly game.

"Kentucky made it hard for us," said Bell, who overcame 1-for-11 shooting to contribute seven rebounds and eight assists. "But Coach got our attention at half-time. It was language we'd all pay attention to. He was animated. And he was right."

With a CBS audience sensing an upset, Hutson took control. MSU's only double-figure scorer with 16 points hit a critical layup on a dropoff from Bell. The two seniors teamed to stop guard Keith Bogans' driving 10-footer. And after the 6-3 Bell soared for the rebound, Hutson had to inbound the ball four times while the Wildcats kept fouling.

"Coach has been stressing that we have to win with heart," Hutson said of a team that had been averaging 92.1 points. "We take tremendous pride in the streak here in Breslin. We couldn't let that slip away."

Just as Ballinger was due back from his thumb injury, Taylor went down with a fractured tip of his right index finger. And he did it in a diving scramble, exactly what Izzo had been asking him to do.

The 6-1 Seton Hall Pirates were supposed to provide the stiffest challenge in the preconfer-ence games. Tommy Amaker's talent-rich team had been ranked from first to 12th in 15 polls or publications. And their only loss had come in overtime at Illinois after they blew a 21-point lead.

Thus, what happened on Tuesday, Dec. 19, in the second game of a Jimmy V Classic double-header was as impressive as any-thing the Spartans did all season. A 72-57 thrashing wasn't as close as the final score, as MSU led 33-23 at the break and held an 18-point lead through much of the second half.

Before a disappointing draw of 14,667 at Continental Airlines Arena in East Rutherford, N.J., the Spartans gave their state a 3-0 record that fall in the Meadowlands Sports Complex. A few punts away, the Detroit Lions had already beaten the geographi-cally challenged New York Giants and Jets in Giants Stadium.

When the crowd was treated to an evangelical speech by Vitale on behalf of cancer research and a viewing of Valvano's famous "Don't give up. . . .Don't ever give up!" speech from the ESPY Awards, Seton Hall wasn't paying attention. If it didn't give up in the second half, it must have been terribly conditioned.

MSU played smothering defense from the opening tip and tattooed its "Tough Players Win" mantra on the Pirates' foreheads with an obscene 60 rebounds. That might have ruined Seton Hall's season — or at least started a team in turmoil on a slippery slide.

"You know what they are?" Amaker said of the winners with admiration. "They're very deter-mined. Certainly, they have a great coach on the sideline. And cer-tainly, they have a lot of good players. But their fight, their aggressiveness and their tough-ness can carry them a long way."

The former Duke point guard and assistant coach would soon take over an undisciplined pro-gram at Michigan. And for one night, he got an eyeful of what life has been like the past four years in the Big Ten.

Bell led the Spartans with 17 points, despite 4-for-15 shooting. He also had 11 rebounds and five assists. But the key player might have been sophomore forward Aloysius Anagonye, who had 10 points and 12 rebounds — as many points and one more board than freshman sensation Eddie Griffin, the nation's leading rebounder.

Randolph added 14 points. And Hutson chipped in with nine points and a career-high 13 rebounds, as MSU shot just 36.8 percent from the field and had 19 turnovers. But the Pirates were colder, hitting 32.8 percent from the field and 16.0 percent of their 25 3-point tries.

Eight days later, the Spartans survived a scare and beat Bowling Green 85-69 at The Palace of Auburn Hills, the site of their last two triumphs in the 2000 NCAA Tournament's Midwest Region. A capacity crowd of 22,076 was as much of a tribute to MSU's pro-gram as its 10-0 start.

2000 NON-CONFERENCE

The Spartans led just 47-43 with 15:19 left before building a 21-point cushion. Again, rebounding made all the difference. MSU won the battle of the boards 50-22, including a 23-4 edge on the offensive glass.

Richardson led all scorers with 21 points. Bell had 18. And fifth-year guard David Thomas added 12 points. He also matched Richardson's nine rebounds for the nation's new No. 1 team.

"I'm not sure what I'm more disappointed about — the way we played or the new rule and the way it's being called," Izzo said after his team was whistled for 18 fouls, five fewer than the Falcons. "What they're doing to the game is a shame."

That only fueled Izzo's passion at practice the next two days. Clearly, Wright State was in the wrong state the week after Christmas. Three nights after a loss to Oakland at The Palace, the Raiders faced an impossible task — beating an MSU team with a mission and a memory in Breslin.

The Spartans led 51-24 at half-time, as Bell had 18 of his 26 points and six of his 11 assists. The lead never slipped below 24 in the second half, as fifth-year forward Mike Chapell had a career-high 21.

"Last year was in the back of our heads," Bell said of a baffling 53-49 loss to Wright State in MSU's final game of the 20th century. "But we knew this was a new year. We can't get caught up in last year with all the goals we have to accomplish."

That win gave the Spartans an 11-0 start for the first time in 102 seasons and stretched its win streak to 22 games. The streak that mattered much more was the chance to claim four straight Big Ten titles, a noble New Year's resolution.

MSU 97, Oakland 61
Nov. 19, 2000 • Breslin Center • East Lansing, Mich.

Oakland	FG-FGA	FT-FTA	REB	PF	TP	A	TO	BLK	S	MIN
Kelly Williams	3-9	2-2	5	5	10	2	3	2	1	29
Brad Buddenborg	5-10	8-11	2	0	21	2	3	1	2	36
Dan Champagne	1-3	0-0	1	5	2	0	5	0	0	10
Mychal Covington	1-7	3-4	5	0	5	2	3	0	2	23
Jason Rozycki	1-5	0-0	0	2	3	2	2	0	1	32
Charles Ford	0-2	0-0	0	0	0	1	0	0	1	2
Tim Fralick	1-5	0-0	1	1	2	1	0	0	0	13
Ryan Williams	0-1	0-0	0	0	0	0	1	1	1	6
Mike Helms	2-7	3-3	3	4	7	1	4	1	2	14
Alex Miller	0-0	0-0	0	0	0	0	0	0	0	2
Jordan Sabourin	1-2	1-2	2	4	3	0	0	1	0	14
Jon Champagne	4-6	0-0	4	3	8	1	3	1	1	19
Totals	19-57	17-22	26	24	61	12	23	6	11	200

Three-Point Field Goals: K. Williams 2-4, Buddenborg 3-5, Covington 0-3, Rozycki 1-4, Ford 0-1, Fralick 0-3, Team 6-20.
FG%: 1st Half 6-26 .231, 2nd Half 13-31 .419, Game 19-57 .333; 3FG%: 1st Half 1-9 .111, 2nd Half 5-11 .455, Game 6-20 .300; FT%: 1st Half 9-12 .750, 2nd Half 8-10 .800, Game 17-22 .773; Team Rebounds: 3; Deadball Rebounds: 2.

Michigan State	FG-FGA	FT-FTA	REB	PF	TP	A	TO	BLK	S	MIN
Jason Richardson	9-14	4-4	8	0	25	1	1	0	0	29
Andre Hutson	4-7	3-5	4	3	11	0	1	0	1	20
Aloysius Anagonye	2-2	4-5	2	4	8	0	4	0	1	12
David Thomas	1-6	2-2	9	2	4	2	2	2	3	24
Charlie Bell	4-12	4-4	11	1	13	10	3	0	3	28
Marcus Taylor	6-12	2-3	2	4	16	5	4	0	1	20
Adam Wolfe	2-5	0-0	2	1	5	0	1	0	0	10
Mat Ishbia	0-0	0-0	0	1	0	0	0	0	0	3
Mike Chappell	4-10	0-0	7	5	9	1	2	1	0	23
Jason Andreas	0-0	0-0	1	0	0	0	0	0	0	9
Zach Randolph	2-6	2-2	5	1	6	2	2	1	1	22
Totals	34-74	21-25	56	22	97	24	20	4	10	200

Three-Point Field Goals: Richardson 3-5, Bell 1-2, Taylor 2-4, Wolfe 1-1, Chappell 1-4, Team 8-16.
FG%: 1st Half 17-33 .515, 2nd Half 17-41 .415, Game 34-74 .459; 3FG%: 1st Half 6-13 .462, 2nd Half 2-3 .667, Game 8-16 .500; FT%: 1st Half 11-13 .846, 2nd Half 10-12 .833, Game 21-25 .840; Team Rebounds: 5; Deadball Rebounds: 3.

SCORE BY PERIODS	1	2	F
Oakland	22	39	-- 61
Michigan State	51	46	-- 97

OFFICIALS – Donnee Gray, Randy Drury, Lenny Memminger
TECHNICAL FOULS – None
ATTENDANCE – 14,759

MSU 89, Cornell 56
Nov. 24, 2000 • Breslin Center • East Lansing, Mich.

Cornell	FG-FGA	FT-FTA	REB	PF	TP	A	TO	BLK	S	MIN
Ray Mercedes	3-9	2-2	4	2	9	0	2	0	0	31
Jake Rohe	0-4	0-0	0	0	0	1	1	0	1	20
Greg Barratt	4-10	0-1	7	2	8	1	2	1	0	27
Wallace Prather	2-7	3-4	6	0	8	4	2	0	2	28
Kevin Cuttica	0-4	0-0	2	1	0	3	0	0	0	20
Jacques Vigneault	0-0	0-0	0	1	0	1	0	0	0	2
Pete Carroll	1-1	0-0	0	0	3	0	0	0	0	3
Luke Vernon	2-3	2-2	1	1	7	0	2	0	0	6
Garn Smith	0-0	0-0	2	2	0	0	1	0	0	16
Ka-Ron Barnes	4-7	6-6	2	2	15	1	5	0	0	25
Randy Gabler	0-0	0-0	1	0	0	0	0	0	0	6
Ryan Cheesman	0-0	0-0	0	1	0	0	0	0	0	3
David Muller	2-3	0-0	1	2	6	0	0	0	0	13
Totals	18-48	13-15	26	14	56	11	15	1	3	200

Three-Point Field Goals: Mercedes 1-5, Rohe 0-2, Barratt 0-1, Prather 1-5, Cuttica 0-4, Carroll 1-1, Vernon 1-2, Barnes 1-2, Muller 2-3, Team 7-25.

FG%: 1st Half 6-23 .261, 2nd Half 12-25 .480, Game 18-48 .375; 3FG%: 1st Half 3-14 .214, 2nd Half 4-11 .364, Game 7-25 .280; FT%: 1st Half 3-5 .600, 2nd Half 10-10 1.000, Game 13-15 .867; Team Rebounds: 2; Deadball Rebounds: 1.

Michigan State	FG-FGA	FT-FTA	REB	PF	TP	A	TO	BLK	S	MIN
Jason Richardson	5-11	1-2	9	2	12	4	0	0	2	19
Aloysius Anagonye	3-5	2-2	4	4	8	0	0	0	0	18
Andre Hutson	6-11	3-3	8	0	15	3	0	1	0	23
David Thomas	4-8	0-0	3	2	8	1	1	0	0	25
Charlie Bell	6-10	0-0	4	1	14	6	1	0	1	27
Marcus Taylor	2-8	1-2	1	3	6	1	1	0	0	18
Adam Wolfe	3-4	0-0	1	2	7	0	0	0	1	13
Brandon Smith	0-2	0-0	1	0	0	3	0	0	0	7
Mat Ishbia	0-0	0-0	1	1	0	1	0	0	0	3
Mike Chappell	4-8	0-1	2	2	9	0	1	0	0	21
Jason Andreas	0-1	0-0	1	1	0	0	0	0	1	9
Zach Randolph	4-7	2-3	9	0	10	3	1	1	1	17
Totals	37-75	9-13	47	18	89	22	5	2	6	200

Three-Point Field Goals: Richardson 1-3, Bell 2-4, Taylor 1-2, Wolfe 1-2, Smith 0-1, Chappell 1-2, Team 6-14.

FG%: 1st Half 16-33 .485, 2nd Half 21-42 .500, Game 37-75 .493; 3FG%: 1st Half 3-9 .333, 2nd Half 3-5 .600, Game 6-14 .429; FT%: 1st Half 3-4 .750, 2nd Half 6-9 .667, Game 9-13 .692; Team Rebounds: 3; Deadball Rebounds: 0.

SCORE BY PERIODS	1	2	F
Cornell	18	38	-- 56
Michigan State	38	51	-- 89

OFFICIALS – Jim Burr, Mike Sanzere, Randy Drury
TECHNICAL FOULS – None
ATTENDANCE – 14,759

Photo Credit: Kevin Fowler, MSU Sports Information

MSU 83, Eastern Washington 61
Nov. 25, 2000 • Breslin Center • East Lansing, Mich.

Eastern Washington	FG-FGA	FT-FTA	REB	PF	TP	A	TO	BLK	S	MIN
Jamal Jones	6-12	0-0	2	3	13	2	0	0	2	25
Kareem Hunter	5-11	4-4	3	2	14	0	1	0	3	25
Chris White	2-6	0-0	3	2	4	0	2	0	0	18
Jason Lewis	1-1	0-0	0	0	3	5	3	0	1	30
Alvin Snow	1-4	2-2	0	1	4	2	3	0	0	23
Eddie Lincoln	0-0	2-2	0	1	2	1	0	0	0	10
Clint Hull	1-3	0-0	2	0	3	1	0	0	0	8
Marco Quinto	1-3	4-4	2	4	7	0	1	0	0	15
Marquis Poole	1-9	0-1	2	3	2	1	3	0	2	24
Jason Humbert	4-6	1-2	2	3	9	0	0	2	2	21
Chris Johnson	0-0	0-0	1	0	0	0	0	0	0	1
Totals	22-55	13-15	19	20	61	12	13	2	10	200

Three-Point Field Goals: Jones 1-6, Lewis 1-1, Hull 1-3, Quinto 1-2, Poole 0-2, Team 4-14.

FG%: 1st Half 10-23 .435, 2nd Half 12-32 .375, Game 22-55 .400; 3FG%: 1st Half 1-3 .333, 2nd Half 3-11 .273, Game 4-14 .286; FT%: 1st Half 10-11 .909, 2nd Half 3-4 .750, Game 13-15 .867; Team Rebounds: 2; Deadball Rebounds: 1.

Michigan State	FG-FGA	FT-FTA	REB	PF	TP	A	TO	BLK	S	MIN
Jason Richardson	6-9	1-2	3	2	16	0	2	1	1	26
Aloysius Anagonye	3-3	1-1	4	2	7	2	2	0	0	19
Andre Hutson	2-3	7-9	9	2	11	3	3	1	0	26
David Thomas	1-3	0-0	4	3	2	2	0	0	2	22
Charlie Bell	12-13	4-5	0	0	31	5	3	0	2	29
Marcus Taylor	1-8	2-2	1	3	4	3	5	0	1	20
Adam Wolfe	0-2	0-0	1	1	0	0	0	0	0	11
Brandon Smith	0-0	0-0	1	0	0	0	1	0	0	5
Mat Ishbia	0-0	0-0	0	1	0	0	0	0	0	3
Mike Chappell	1-3	1-2	1	1	3	2	0	0	0	16
Jason Andreas	1-1	0-0	0	0	2	0	1	1	1	6
Zach Randolph	3-3	1-2	8	1	7	2	2	1	1	17
Totals	30-48	17-23	36	16	83	19	19	4	8	200

Three-Point Field Goals: Richardson 3-4, Bell 3-3, Chappell 0-1, Team 6-8.

FG%: 1st Half 17-23 .739, 2nd Half 13-25 .520, Game 30-48 .625; 3FG%: 1st Half 2-3 .667, 2nd Half 4-5 .800, Game 6-8 .750; FT%: 1st Half 9-12 .750, 2nd Half 8-11 .727, Game 17-23 .739; Team Rebounds: 4; Deadball Rebounds: 3.

SCORE BY PERIODS	1	2	F	OFFICIALS – Mike Sanzere, Sid Rodeheffer, Steve Olson
Eastern Washington	31	30	-- 61	TECHNICAL FOULS – Eastern Washington bench
Michigan State	45	38	-- 83	ATTENDANCE – 14,759

MSU 97, Illinois-Chicago 53
Dec. 2, 2000 • Breslin Center • East Lansing, Mich.

Illinois-Chicago	FG-FGA	FT-FTA	REB	PF	TP	A	TO	BLK	S	MIN
Aaron Carr	4-10	1-2	3	1	11	2	1	0	0	30
Joe Scott	3-3	1-3	1	3	7	0	3	2	0	22
Maurice Brown	3-11	3-3	4	2	9	0	3	0	0	20
Joel Bullock	1-6	0-0	2	2	2	5	3	0	1	21
Jordan Kardos	2-4	0-0	1	3	4	0	4	1	0	15
Taurus Cook	1-4	0-0	0	0	3	1	0	0	0	9
Claude Murrell	0-0	0-0	1	0	0	1	2	0	1	6
Jon-Pierre Mitchom	5-7	0-1	1	3	12	0	1	0	0	17
Jonathon Schneiderman	1-3	0-1	1	0	2	3	2	0	1	13
Corry Tibbs	0-3	1-2	3	0	1	0	0	1	0	5
Cory Little	1-6	0-0	4	2	2	0	1	0	0	20
Tyrone Moten	0-1	0-0	0	0	0	0	0	0	0	4
Jabari Harris	0-3	0-0	2	2	0	0	2	0	0	14
Terry Muse	0-0	0-2	1	0	0	0	1	0	1	4
Totals	21-61	6-14	27	18	53	12	22	4	4	200

Three-Point Field Goals: Carr 2-5, Bullock 0-2, Cook 1-3, Mitchom 2-2, Schneiderman 0-1, Tibbs 0-3, Team 5-16.
FG%: 1st Half 11-26 .423, 2nd Half 10-35 .286, Game 21-61 .344; 3FG%: 1st Half 1-5 .200, 2nd Half 4-11 .364, Game 5-16 .313; FT%: 1st Half 1-2 .500, 2nd Half 5-12 .417, Game 6-14 .429; Team Rebounds: 3; Deadball Rebounds: 4.

Michigan State	FG-FGA	FT-FTA	REB	PF	TP	A	TO	BLK	S	MIN
Jason Richardson	7-11	1-5	6	3	17	4	0	0	0	20
Andre Hutson	4-6	3-4	12	2	11	2	3	0	0	27
Aloysius Anagonye	3-5	0-0	1	2	6	0	1	0	1	18
David Thomas	2-7	0-0	6	0	4	4	1	0	1	18
Charlie Bell	4-7	0-0	3	3	9	6	3	0	0	20
Marcus Taylor	4-8	0-1	1	0	10	5	1	0	0	21
Adam Wolfe	2-5	4-4	8	2	9	0	0	0	2	14
Brandon Smith	0-1	0-1	2	0	0	0	2	0	1	11
Mat Ishbia	1-1	0-0	0	0	2	1	1	0	0	4
Mike Chappell	2-5	4-4	1	3	10	2	3	0	3	20
Jason Andreas	0-0	0-0	2	0	0	0	0	0	0	5
Zach Randolph	7-13	5-5	10	1	19	2	5	0	3	22
Totals	36-69	17-24	54	16	97	26	20	1	10	200

Three-Point Field Goals: Richardson 2-2, Thomas 0-1, Bell 1-4, Taylor 2-4, Wolfe 1-2, Smith 0-1, Chappell 2-5, Randolph 0-1, Team 8-20.
FG%: 1st Half 17-37 .459, 2nd Half 19-32 .594, Game 36-69 .522; 3FG%: 1st Half 4-11 .364, 2nd Half 4-9 .444, Game 8-20 .400; FT%: 1st Half 4-7 .571, 2nd Half 13-17 .765, Game 17-24 .708; Team Rebounds: 2; Deadball Rebounds: 3.

SCORE BY PERIODS	1	2	F	OFFICIALS – Tom Clark, Eugene Crawford, J.D. Collins
Illinois-Chicago	24	29	-- 53	TECHNICAL FOULS – None
Michigan State	42	55	-- 97	ATTENDANCE – 14,759

MSU 99, Florida 83
Dec. 6, 2000 • Breslin Center • East Lansing, Mich.

Florida	FG-FGA	FT-FTA	REB	PF	TP	A	TO	BLK	S	MIN
Brent Wright	5-10	7-8	8	5	18	0	4	0	2	30
Major Parker	1-1	1-5	1	1	3	4	1	0	0	22
Udonis Haslem	4-8	5-6	3	5	13	0	2	0	0	13
Brent Nelson	1-10	4-4	1	3	7	4	2	0	1	28
Justin Hamilton	2-3	0-1	2	3	5	1	2	1	0	20
Orien Greene	1-2	0-0	1	0	3	3	0	0	1	19
Teddy Dupay	5-9	4-4	1	3	17	1	3	0	1	30
Matt Bonner	6-8	4-5	8	3	17	3	0	0	0	34
LaDarius Halton	0-1	0-0	0	0	0	0	1	0	0	4
Totals	25-52	25-33	26	23	83	16	15	1	5	200

Three-Point Field Goals: Wright 1-1, Nelson 1-6, Hamilton 1-1, Greene 1-2, Dupay 3-5, Bonner 1-2, Halton 0-1, Team 8-18.

FG%: 1st Half 13-24 .542, 2nd Half 12-28 .429, Game 25-52 .481; 3FG%: 1st Half 5-8 .625, 2nd Half 3-10 .300, Game 8-18 .444; FT%: 1st Half 9-12 .750, 2nd Half 16-21 .762, Game 25-33 .758; Team Rebounds: 1; Deadball Rebounds: 4.

Michigan State	FG-FGA	FT-FTA	REB	PF	TP	A	TO	BLK	S	MIN
Jason Richardson	5-10	3-4	3	2	13	1	2	1	1	33
Andre Hutson	4-6	4-4	6	3	12	4	2	0	2	30
Aloysius Anagonye	0-0	1-2	2	5	1	1	0	0	0	14
David Thomas	3-4	3-3	6	3	9	3	2	2	4	23
Charlie Bell	7-15	2-3	6	3	20	2	2	0	1	31
Marcus Taylor	6-12	0-0	1	1	15	7	2	0	0	28
Adam Wolfe	1-2	0-0	2	2	2	0	1	0	0	7
Mike Chappell	0-3	0-0	0	2	0	0	0	0	0	7
Jason Andreas	0-0	0-0	2	1	0	0	0	0	1	4
Zach Randolph	10-13	7-9	7	3	27	1	0	1	3	23
Totals	36-65	20-25	37	25	99	20	12	4	12	200

Three-Point Field Goals: Richardson 0-3, Thomas 0-1, Bell 4-6, Taylor 3-5, Chappell 0-1, Team 7-16.

FG%: 1st Half 18-35 .514, 2nd Half 18-30 .600, Game 36-65 .554; 3FG%: 1st Half 5-12 .417, 2nd Half 2-4 .500, Game 7-16 .438; FT%: 1st Half 7-8 .875, 2nd Half 13-17 .765, Game 20-25 .800; Team Rebounds: 2; Deadball Rebounds: 2.

SCORE BY PERIODS	1	2	F	OFFICIALS – Ted Hillary, Gene Monje, Ed Corbett
Florida	40	43	-- 83	TECHNICAL FOULS – None
Michigan State	48	51	-- 99	ATTENDANCE – 14,759

MSU 77, North Carolina 64
Nov. 29, 2000 • Breslin Center • East Lansing, Mich.

North Carolina	FG-FGA	FT-FTA	REB	PF	TP	A	TO	BLK	S	MIN
Jason Capel	3-6	1-2	5	5	9	5	3	0	0	30
Kris Lang	11-16	0-4	3	3	22	2	1	0	4	38
Brendan Haywood	5-8	0-0	5	4	10	1	0	3	1	27
Adam Boone	0-3	2-2	1	0	2	1	1	0	2	18
Joseph Forte	5-16	0-1	4	2	11	3	5	0	1	40
Brian Morrison	2-7	3-4	5	5	8	4	2	0	0	22
Michael Booker	0-2	0-2	2	1	0	2	0	0	2	12
Max Owens	0-0	0-0	0	0	0	0	0	0	0	1
Will Johnson	0-0	0-0	0	0	0	0	0	0	0	4
Brian Bersticker	0-3	2-4	2	2	2	1	1	0	0	8
Totals	26-61	8-19	29	22	64	19	14	3	10	200

Three-Point Field Goals: Capel 2-3, Boone 0-2, Forte 1-7, Morrison 1-4, Booker 0-2, Bersticker 0-2, Team 4-20.

FG%: 1st Half 12-28 .429, 2nd Half 14-33 .424, Game 26-61 .426; 3FG%: 1st Half 2-5 .400, 2nd Half 2-15 .133, Game 4-20 .200; FT%: 1st Half 3-5 .600, 2nd Half 5-14 .357, Game 8-19 .421; Team Rebounds: 4; Deadball Rebounds: 6.

Michigan State	FG-FGA	FT-FTA	REB	PF	TP	A	TO	BLK	S	MIN
Jason Richardson	6-11	4-4	4	2	16	1	0	1	2	32
Aloysius Anagonye	2-4	2-2	6	4	6	0	3	0	0	19
Andre Hutson	5-11	4-7	9	2	14	1	2	1	0	35
David Thomas	2-5	2-2	2	1	6	1	1	1	1	19
Charlie Bell	4-7	6-8	7	1	15	5	5	0	0	34
Marcus Taylor	3-10	2-2	0	2	8	5	1	0	1	22
Adam Wolfe	0-2	0-0	2	1	0	0	1	1	1	8
Mike Chappell	1-4	0-0	2	3	3	0	2	0	0	13
Zach Randolph	4-4	1-4	8	1	9	0	2	0	1	18
Totals	27-58	21-29	43	17	77	13	17	4	6	200

Three-Point Field Goals: Richardson 0-3, Thomas 0-1, Bell 1-3, Taylor 0-3, Wolfe 0-2, Chappell 1-3, Team 2-15.

FG%: 1st Half 18-34 .529, 2nd Half 9-24 .375, Game 27-58 .466; 3FG%: 1st Half 1-7 .143, 2nd Half 1-8 .125, Game 2-15 .133; FT%: 1st Half 5-6 .833, 2nd Half 16-23 .696, Game 21-29 .724; Team Rebounds: 3; Deadball Rebounds: 7.

SCORE BY PERIODS	1	2	F
North Carolina	29	35	64
Michigan State	42	35	77

OFFICIALS – Ed Hightower, Gene Monje, Donnee Gray
TECHNICAL FOULS – None
ATTENDANCE – 14,759

MSU 103, Loyola (Chicago) 71
Dec. 9, 2000 • Gentile Center • Chicago, Ill.

Michigan State	FG-FGA	FT-FTA	REB	PF	TP	A	TO	BLK	S	MIN
Jason Richardson	6-8	3-4	4	2	17	3	1	0	1	23
Aloysius Anagonye	4-5	1-2	1	2	9	3	0	0	0	21
Andre Hutson	8-11	0-0	6	2	16	2	1	1	1	24
David Thomas	1-2	0-0	4	2	4	1	1	1	1	21
Charlie Bell	8-13	1-1	3	0	19	7	2	0	1	25
Marcus Taylor	6-10	2-2	3	4	15	9	2	0	1	21
Adam Wolfe	1-2	0-0	1	3	2	1	0	0	0	8
Brandon Smith	0-1	0-0	1	2	0	2	0	0	0	8
Mat Ishbia	0-0	0-0	0	0	0	0	0	0	0	2
Mike Chappell	2-5	1-1	4	0	5	0	0	0	1	20
Jason Andreas	1-1	0-0	1	1	2	1	0	1	0	5
Zach Randolph	8-11	0-0	9	2	16	0	6	0	2	22
Totals	45-69	8-10	41	20	103	32	13	3	8	200

Three-Point Field Goals: Richardson 2-3, Bell 2-4, Taylor 1-3, Chappell 0-2, Team 5-12.

FG%: 1st Half 23-33 .697, 2nd Half 22-36 .611, Game 45-69 .652; 3FG%: 1st Half 4-6 .667, 2nd Half 1-6 .167, Game 5-12 .417; FT%: 1st Half 6-8 .750, 2nd Half 2-2 1.000, Game 8-10 .800; Team Rebounds: 4; Deadball Rebounds: 3.

Loyola (Chicago)	FG-FGA	FT-FTA	REB	PF	TP	A	TO	BLK	S	MIN
Ryan Blankson	1-5	1-3	2	2	3	0	1	0	0	23
Schin Kerr	3-10	0-2	4	4	8	1	3	0	2	28
Hubert Radke	2-5	0-0	2	3	5	0	1	0	0	29
David Bailey	9-14	6-7	2	0	25	5	6	0	1	30
Terry Grant	2-6	0-0	3	2	5	4	1	0	1	19
Jonathan Freeman	1-1	0-0	1	1	2	0	3	0	0	10
Jason Telford	0-0	0-0	0	1	0	0	1	0	0	8
Louis Smith	0-0	0-0	0	0	0	1	0	0	0	7
Corey Minnifield	6-8	2-4	2	2	16	2	0	3	1	22
Jerell Parker	3-7	0-4	3	1	7	0	1	0	0	21
Wayne Plowman	0-2	0-0	1	0	0	0	0	0	0	3
Totals	27-58	9-20	24	14	71	15	17	3	4	200

Three-Point Field Goals: Kerr 2-5, Radke 1-2, Bailey 1-4, Grant 1-2, Minnifield 2-3, Parker 1-2, Team 8-18.

FG%: 1st Half 11-30 .367, 2nd Half 16-28 .571, Game 27-58 .466; 3FG%: 1st Half 1-5 .200, 2nd Half 7-13 .538, Game 8-18 .444; FT%: 1st Half 4-6 .667, 2nd Half 5-14 .357, Game 9-20 .450; Team Rebounds: 3; Deadball Rebounds: 0.

SCORE BY PERIODS	1	2	F
Michigan State	56	47	103
Loyola (Chicago)	27	44	71

OFFICIALS – Tom Clark, Mike Sanzere, Jerry Sauder
TECHNICAL FOULS – None
ATTENDANCE – 5,513

Photo Credit: Kevin Fowler, MSU Sports Information

Photo Credit: Kevin Fowler, MSU Sports Information

MSU 46, Kentucky 45
Dec. 16, 2000 • Breslin Center • East Lansing, Mich.

Kentucky	FG-FGA	FT-FTA	REB	PF	TP	A	TO	BLK	S	MIN
Tayshaun Prince	5-11	1-1	3	0	13	3	2	3	0	34
Jason Parker	3-5	0-1	3	2	6	0	3	0	0	17
Marvin Stone	2-3	0-0	5	2	4	0	1	0	2	30
Keith Bogans	6-14	0-0	1	3	15	1	2	1	0	33
Saul Smith	1-7	0-0	4	1	3	10	2	0	1	38
J.P. Blevins	1-3	0-0	0	0	2	0	0	0	0	13
Gerald Fitch	0-1	2-2	9	2	2	2	2	1	3	21
Erik Daniels	0-2	0-0	1	0	0	0	0	0	0	8
Marquis Estill	0-0	0-0	1	1	0	0	1	0	0	6
Totals	18-46	3-4	28	11	45	16	13	5	6	200

Three-Point Field Goals: Prince 2-6, Bogans 3-6, Smith 1-5, Blevins 0-1, Team 6-18.

FG%: 1st Half 11-21 .524, 2nd Half 7-25 .280, Game 18-46 .391; 3FG%: 1st Half 3-9 .333, 2nd Half 3-9 .333, Game 6-18 .333; FT%: 1st Half 2-3 .667, 2nd Half 1-1 1.000, Game 3-4 .750; Team Rebounds: 2; Deadball Rebounds: 2.

Michigan State	FG-FGA	FT-FTA	REB	PF	TP	A	TO	BLK	S	MIN
Jason Richardson	3-5	1-2	5	2	8	3	1	1	0	32
Andre Hutson	7-13	2-4	5	3	16	1	3	0	2	36
Aloysius Anagonye	1-2	0-0	3	3	2	1	1	1	0	25
David Thomas	2-6	2-2	5	1	6	2	1	0	1	30
Charlie Bell	1-11	2-2	7	2	5	8	1	1	2	36
Marcus Taylor	2-4	0-0	0	0	4	1	1	0	0	12
Mike Chappell	1-4	1-2	1	2	3	0	0	0	0	10
Zach Randolph	1-6	0-0	3	1	2	0	1	1	1	19
Totals	18-51	8-12	34	14	46	16	10	4	6	200

Three-Point Field Goals: Richardson 1-1, Thomas 0-1, Bell 1-7, Taylor 0-2, Chappell 0-3, Team 2-14.

FG%: 1st Half 6-28 .214, 2nd Half 12-23 .522, Game 18-51 .353; 3FG%: 1st Half 1-8 .125, 2nd Half 1-6 .167, Game 2-14 .143; FT%: 1st Half 5-8 .625, 2nd Half 3-4 .750, Game 8-12 .667; Team Rebounds: 5; Deadball Rebounds: 2.

SCORE BY PERIODS	1	2		F
Kentucky	27	18	--	45
Michigan State	18	28	--	46

OFFICIALS – Jim Burr, Ted Valentine, Rick Hartzell
TECHNICAL FOULS – None
ATTENDANCE – 14,759

MSU 72, Seton Hall 57
Dec. 19, 2000 • Continental Airlines Arena • East Rutherford, N.J.

Michigan State	FG-FGA	FT-FTA	REB	PF	TP	A	TO	BLK	S	MIN
David Thomas	0-5	0-0	9	4	0	3	1	0	1	29
Andre Hutson	4-8	1-3	13	4	9	2	1	0	1	24
Aloysius Anagonye	4-8	2-2	12	4	10	0	4	0	0	20
Charlie Bell	4-15	7-8	11	2	17	5	6	0	2	36
Jason Richardson	7-17	2-2	5	3	16	2	5	1	0	28
Adam Wolfe	0-1	0-0	2	0	0	0	0	0	0	8
Brandon Smith	0-0	0-1	0	0	0	0	0	0	0	7
Mike Chappell	2-6	2-3	2	4	6	1	0	0	0	19
Zach Randolph	7-15	0-0	4	3	14	1	1	0	0	24
Adam Ballinger	0-1	0-0	0	0	0	0	1	0	0	5
Totals	28-76	14-19	60	24	72	14	19	1	4	200

Three-Point Field Goals: Bell 2-6, Richardson 0-3, Chappell 0-2, Team 2-11.

FG%: 1st Half 15-40 .375, 2nd Half 13-36 .361, Game 28-76 .368; 3FG%: 1st Half 1-6 .167, 2nd Half 1-5 .200, Game 2-11 .182; FT%: 1st Half 2-2 1.000, 2nd Half 12-17 .706, Game 14-19 .737; Team Rebounds: 2; Deadball Rebounds: 0.

Seton Hall	FG-FGA	FT-FTA	REB	PF	TP	A	TO	BLK	S	MIN
Marcus Toney-El	1-4	0-0	4	2	3	2	0	0	1	25
Eddie Griffin	4-17	2-2	11	4	10	2	3	3	0	30
Samuel Dalembert	3-5	1-2	3	2	7	0	5	1	0	18
Andre Barrett	5-16	1-3	5	2	12	4	1	0	4	38
Darius Lane	5-12	6-7	1	2	17	2	1	0	2	33
Ty Shine	2-6	1-5	2	2	6	0	3	0	1	22
Charles Manga	0-1	2-2	3	3	2	0	1	0	0	16
Reggie Garrett	0-0	0-0	0	0	0	0	0	0	0	2
Greg Morton	0-0	0-0	3	0	0	0	1	0	0	16
Totals	20-61	13-21	39	18	57	10	15	5	8	200

Three-Point Field Goals: Toney-El 1-2, Griffin 0-7, Barrett 1-6, Lane 1-8, Shine 1-2, Team 4-25.

FG%: 1st Half 9-25 .360, 2nd Half 11-36 .306, Game 20-61 .328; 3FG%: 1st Half 2-10 .200, 2nd Half 2-15 .133, Game 4-25 .160; FT%: 1st Half 3-5 .600, 2nd Half 10-16 .625, Game 13-21 .619; Team Rebounds: 7; Deadball Rebounds: 3.

SCORE BY PERIODS	1	2		F
Michigan State	33	39	--	72
Seton Hall	23	34	--	57

OFFICIALS – Mike Wood, Duke Edsall, Kerry Sitton
TECHNICAL FOULS – Seton Hall bench
ATTENDANCE – 14,667

MSU 85, Bowling Green 69
Dec. 27, 2000 • The Palace of Auburn Hills • Auburn Hills, Mich.

Bowling Green	FG-FGA	FT-FTA	REB	PF	TP	A	TO	BLK	S	MIN
Trent Jackson	4-7	8-10	2	4	16	1	2	0	1	26
Kevin Netter	0-3	0-0	0	5	0	0	2	0	0	11
Len Matela	4-7	2-4	5	4	10	0	2	0	1	29
Keith McLeod	4-13	0-0	2	2	9	1	1	0	2	36
Brandon Pardon	7-10	2-4	4	3	19	7	4	0	0	37
Josh Almanson	3-4	0-0	1	1	6	1	0	0	0	16
Brent Klassen	3-7	0-0	2	4	6	1	4	0	0	24
Cory Ryan	1-3	0-0	0	3	3	1	0	0	0	17
Jabari Mattox	0-0	0-0	0	0	0	0	1	0	0	2
Kris Gerken	0-0	0-0	0	0	0	0	0	0	0	2
Totals	26-54	12-18	22	23	69	12	12	0	4	200

Three-Point Field Goals: McLeod 1-3, Pardon 3-3, Ryan 1-3, Team 5-9.

FG%: 1st Half 14-25 .560, 2nd Half 12-29 .414, Game 26-54 .481; 3FG%: 1st Half 2-4 .500, 2nd Half 3-5 .600, Game 5-9 .556; FT%: 1st Half 5-8 .625, 2nd Half 7-10 .700, Game 12-18 .667; Team Rebounds: 4; Deadball Rebounds: 2.

Michigan State	FG-FGA	FT-FTA	REB	PF	TP	A	TO	BLK	S	MIN
David Thomas	5-12	2-2	9	1	12	2	0	0	0	29
Andre Hutson	4-8	3-4	6	3	11	0	1	0	3	27
Aloysius Anagonye	1-4	3-4	5	2	5	1	1	3	0	22
Jason Richardson	8-13	4-6	9	4	21	1	3	1	1	27
Charlie Bell	6-13	4-6	3	2	18	5	3	1	0	28
Brandon Smith	0-1	2-2	2	0	2	4	2	0	1	19
Zach Randolph	5-7	0-2	4	1	10	1	2	2	1	17
Mike Chappell	1-4	0-0	1	4	3	2	1	0	0	15
Adam Ballinger	1-2	0-0	0	0	2	0	0	0	0	8
Jason Andreas	0-0	1-2	2	1	1	0	0	0	0	3
Adam Wolfe	0-2	0-0	0	0	0	0	0	0	0	3
Mat Ishbia	0-1	0-0	0	0	0	0	0	0	1	2
Totals	31-67	19-28	49	18	85	16	13	7	7	200

Three-Point Field Goals: Thomas 0-2, Richardson 1-3, Bell 2-5, Chappell 1-3, Wolfe 0-2, Ishbia 0-1, Team 4-16.

FG%: 1st Half 13-31 .419, 2nd Half 18-36 .500, Game 31-67 .463; 3FG%: 1st Half 2-8 .250, 2nd Half 2-8 .250, Game 4-16 .250; FT%: 1st Half 12-16 .750, 2nd Half 7-12 .583, Game 19-28 .679; Team Rebounds: 9; Deadball Rebounds: 5.

SCORE BY PERIODS	1	2		F
Bowling Green	35	34	--	69
Michigan State	40	45	--	85

OFFICIALS – Donnee Gray, Tim Higgins, Bill Kennedy
TECHNICAL FOULS – None
ATTENDANCE – 22,076

MSU 88, Wright State 61
Dec. 30, 2000 • Breslin Center • East Lansing, Mich.

Wright State	FG-FGA	FT-FTA	REB	PF	TP	A	TO	BLK	S	MIN
Kevin Melson	6-9	1-1	3	0	14	3	4	1	2	36
Thomas Hope	3-6	0-0	4	5	6	0	0	0	0	13
Israel Sheinfeld	4-11	5-6	2	3	13	0	4	0	2	23
Vernard Hollins	1-5	1-2	2	2	4	3	4	0	0	32
Jesse Deister	2-10	3-4	3	2	8	3	0	0	0	30
Braden Bushman	0-2	0-0	0	0	0	0	0	0	0	3
Tyson Freeman	1-2	0-0	5	3	3	1	1	0	0	15
Joe Bills	0-2	0-0	1	0	0	0	1	0	1	22
Marcus May	3-5	0-0	1	0	6	0	0	0	1	6
Michael Doles	1-1	0-0	0	0	2	0	0	0	0	3
Bruno Petersons	2-7	2-2	7	1	6	1	1	1	1	17
Totals	23-60	12-15	32	16	61	14	14	2	7	200

Three-Point Field Goals: Melson 1-3, Hope 0-1, Hollins 0-1, Deister 1-7, Bushman 0-1, Freeman 1-1, Bills 0-1, May 0-2, Team 3-17.

FG%: 1st Half 8-27 .296, 2nd Half 15-33 .455, Game 23-60 .383; 3FG%: 1st Half 0-7 .000, 2nd Half 3-10 .300, Game 3-17 .176; FT%: 1st Half 8-11 .727, 2nd Half 4-4 1.000, Game 12-15 .800; Team Rebounds: 4; Deadball Rebounds: 0.

Michigan State	FG-FGA	FT-FTA	REB	PF	TP	A	TO	BLK	S	MIN
Jason Richardson	4-11	0-0	5	1	8	5	0	1	1	26
Andre Hutson	6-9	2-2	3	2	14	1	0	0	2	27
Aloysius Anagonye	3-3	0-0	4	4	6	1	2	1	2	16
David Thomas	1-2	0-0	1	3	2	3	1	0	0	22
Charlie Bell	9-17	3-4	5	0	26	11	2	0	2	34
Adam Wolfe	1-6	0-0	2	0	2	0	1	0	0	6
Brandon Smith	0-0	2-3	0	2	2	2	2	0	0	13
Mat Ishbia	0-1	0-0	0	0	0	0	0	0	0	2
Mike Chappell	8-10	1-1	2	1	21	0	0	0	1	20
Jason Andreas	0-0	0-0	1	1	0	1	0	0	0	6
Zach Randolph	3-5	1-1	9	1	7	3	1	0	0	21
Adam Ballinger	0-2	0-0	5	3	0	0	1	1	0	7
Totals	35-66	9-11	40	16	88	26	14	4	7	200

Three-Point Field Goals: Richardson 0-2, Thomas 0-1, Bell 5-8, Wolfe 0-1, Chappell 4-5, Team 9-17.

FG%: 1st Half 20-33 .606, 2nd Half 15-33 .455, Game 35-66 .530; 3FG%: 1st Half 6-10 .600, 2nd Half 3-7 .429, Game 9-17 .529; FT%: 1st Half 5-5 1.000, 2nd Half 4-6 .667, Game 9-11 .818; Team Rebounds: 2; Deadball Rebounds: 1.

SCORE BY PERIODS	1	2		F
Wright State	24	37	--	61
Michigan State	51	37	--	88

OFFICIALS – Tom Clark, Jerry Petro, Lenny Memminger
TECHNICAL FOULS – None
ATTENDANCE – 14,759

No one knows more about winning championships than former UCLA basketball coach John Wooden. His Bruins won seven straight NCAA titles and 10 in 12 tries from 1964-75, a record that will never be matched.

But before Michigan State began its quest for a fourth-straight Big Ten crown, Wooden, a former Purdue All-American, said he knew enough about the Spartans and Tom Izzo to like their chances in 2001.

"I think it's great to be a defending champ," Wooden said by phone from his home in California. "People say your opponents all get up for you. Gracious sakes, I hope so! Why do they do that? Because you're good. When people say it's tougher to stay on top than it is to get there, I disagree 100 percent. It's much tougher to get there. And Michigan State is there right now."

If staying on top is easier, why had only three teams in Big Ten history — Chicago from 1907-10, Ohio State from 1960-64 and Indiana from 1973-76 — won more than three league titles in a row? And what could MSU do to make it a four-peat foursome?

"They just have to forget the past and make every day their masterpiece," said "The Wizard of Westwood," who still follows the sport closely. "What they did last season doesn't matter any more. But I'd love to be in Coach Izzo's position. He knows that defense wins championships."

Izzo refused to let the Spartans

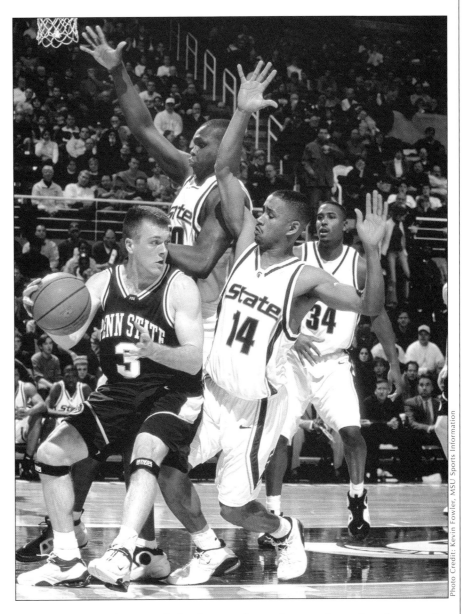

Photo Credit: Kevin Fowler, MSU Sports Information

think of themselves as defending NCAA kings. Instead, he demanded the same commitment that made MSU 13-3, 15-1 and 13-3 in league play the previous three years. The motto for 2001 was simple: "A Championship Effort Is The Only Effort Accepted Here."

"We know what it takes to win a championship," Izzo said. "And that's the effort we're demanding

from the coaches, the players, the secretaries and the fans. We're not defending or holding onto a championship in any way, shape or form. Coming from where I do, guess what? We're back hunting for another one."

That was fine with MSU's seniors, who had been overshadowed by Mateen Cleaves, Morris Peterson and occasionally A.J.

2001 BIG TEN

Granger from 1997-2000. This was the chance for Charlie Bell, Andre Hutson, David Thomas, Mike Chappell and Brandon Smith to brand themselves as champs.

"That's very big," Hutson said with a healthy degree of selfishness. "I want to put my name in the record book for winning four Big Ten championships. I think that's a big deal. It definitely is to me."

Bell and Hutson had a shot to become just the second and third players to start for four Big Ten titlists, joining former Indiana floor leader Quinn Buckner. The list of letterwinners for four-time champs wasn't much longer, with ex-Hoosiers Tom Abernethy and Jim Crews.

As conference play began, the Spartans' overall mark the past three-and-a-third seasons was a glittering 98-20, only 10 wins shy of the Hoosiers' work from 1972-76 and 1990-94. And their 41-7 Big Ten effort from 1998-2000 was 10 wins better than runner-up Purdue.

"We just have to try to win games and let the other stuff take care of itself," sophomore Jason Richardson said. "The records are nice. But it's the record at the end of the season that matters."

With an 11-0 preconference mark and MSU's first No. 1 ranking in 22 seasons, it was strange to hear all the talk of deficiencies. But the Spartans were well aware of their potential and knew they wouldn't reach it by taking premature bows on Jan. 3.

"It's kind of scary how good we could actually be when we're all on the same page," Thomas said. "We could be tremendous. We're not even clicking on all cylinders yet. There are a lot of things we have to do defensively. Offensively, we have to execute better and be a little sharper. When that happens…"

It didn't happen in the first half of the Big Ten opener against Penn State, a 98-73 win in Breslin Center and arguably the strangest 25-point decison in MSU history. The Spartans had a 42-24 edge in rebounds and shot 59.6 percent from the field. But without a 61-25 second half, all their streaks could have ended.

Photo Credit: Kevin Fowler, MSU Sports Information

The 9-1 Nittany Lions led 48-37 at the break behind 55.2-percent shooting from the field and 60.0 accuracy beyond the arc. But MSU exploded in the last 20 minutes, shot 78.6 percent from the field and held Jerry Dunn's team to 21.4 success.

Two plays demonstated the difference. Before the break, Bell loafed on an errant pass into the backcourt by point guard Marcus Taylor, then watched Penn State's Joe Crispin catch up to the ball and hit a 3 from the corner. But in a 25-4 run early in the second half, a lunging Thomas kept the ball inbounds and whipped a blind, wraparound pass to a streaking Bell for a three-point play.

"It was an incredible game," Izzo said. "They killed us in the first half. And we reciprocated. But you don't win championships by playing 20 minutes. We have a lot of work to do."

Bell worked hard enough to collect 26 points, eight assists and six steals in 36 minutes. He also held Crispin, the league's top scorer, to 1-for-7 accuracy and six of his 21 points in the second half.

Hutson had 20 points, 13 rebounds and four assists. But his biggest contribution came on defense, shifting to the perimeter to shut off 6-foot-4 Titus Ivory, who was 2-for-6 in the second half of a 22-point day.

And after missing three games with a fractured ring finger, Taylor came off the bench, shook off the rust and had 11 points in 24 minutes, the third-highest total for any Spartan.

"We're not as good as we think we are," Izzo said after a school-record, 23rd-straight win, the longest streak in the nation. "And we're not as good as you probably think we are. But we played a helluva second half. For that, I'm very proud of this team."

Three days later at Indiana, Izzo's reactions were quite different, beginning with a new pregame routine. As he looked to his left in Assembly Hall, where Bob Knight had held court for 29 seasons, there stood interim coach Mike Davis.

"The strangest part was always the introductions, when you were waiting for Bob to come over and shake your hand," Izzo said. "You'd wait and wait and wait. I think one time the referees held the game up so he could come over and say hello."

Izzo was 5-3 against Knight and shared the distinction of winning a national title in his fifth year as a Big Ten head coach. But no one will ever have the edge on Knight in terms of volatility and gamesmanship.

"The first time there was the craziest," Izzo said. "The three officials were standing right in front of me. And Bob said, 'Don't trust this guy, because he'll never call traveling. And don't trust this guy....' They all heard him and were laughing with him. I thought he was serious."

Izzo, who praises almost every coach publicly, was serious in his admiration for what Knight did for basketball and college athletics. If Izzo didn't agree with all of Knight's methods, he appreciated a

lot of his values and hoped he would return to coaching.

When the Spartans returned to Bloomington, the scene of their last loss 10-and-a-half months earlier, they were received only slightly better than ex-Indiana guard and Knight nemesis Neil Reed would have been. The Hoosiers hadn't won a Big Ten title in eight years. Three-time champ MSU was what IU used to be, minus the war zone.

But Izzo's recurring pessimism in the face of constant adulation was well-founded. And when the Spartans gave Indiana a shot at an upset, center Kirk Haston gave the Hoosiers the shot they needed, a contested 3-pointer at the buzzer for a 59-58 triumph.

After thousands of crimson-and-cream loyalists flooded the floor and Davis dropped to his knees to say thanks, Izzo said the winners deserved an impromptu party after their first win over a No. 1 team in the 30-year history of Assembly Hall.

"You can take this any way you want, but I'm happy we lost," Izzo said after his team slipped to 12-1. "I've lived my life the last three years saying you get what you deserve. We got what we deserved today. We didn't play Spartan Basketball."

The 10-6 Hoosiers played inspired ball for 40 minutes and didn't want to play 45. Haston, who had been recruited briefly by MSU, understood that and finished with a game-high 27 points, including 3-for-4 work from long range.

"I didn't want to go to over-

2001 BIG TEN

time," Davis said after diagramming a play for his go-to guy with 8.3 seconds left. "If we'd lost, we still would've felt good about ourselves. We'd have lost to the No. 1 team by two points. If we'd gone to overtime, maybe we'd have celebrated and lost by 10 or 15."

The Spartans led 46-40 with 12:06 left but went without a basket for the next 7:02. They took a 57-55 lead when Thomas rattled home a 10-footer. But after Indiana freshman Jared Jeffries hit one of two free throws, MSU missed three of four foul shots, including the front ends of two one-and-ones.

Richardson, who led the Spartans with 15 points and 15 rebounds, missed two tries and left four points at the line. Randolph, who added 11 points and eight rebounds in just 21 minutes, split a pair, then couldn't quite get to Haston's game-winning prayer.

"It's too bad we weren't able to finish the game at the free-throw line," Izzo said. "We've had a problem with that lately. But there was just something missing today. I don't think we were fat-and-sassy. People just think we're better than we are."

Despite a 42-28 edge in rebounds, MSU struggled for much of the day. It was outshot 43.4 percent to 38.9 from the field and had 19 turnovers and just seven assists. Its first-half totals of 14 turnovers and one assist were reflective of the outcome, beginning with a travel off the opening tip.

The Hoosiers were still celebrating when they lost at Michigan

two nights later. But the Spartans drew a bigger crowd in Breslin that Tuesday afternoon without launching a single shot. When outgoing President Bill Clinton stopped in East Lansing on his farewell tour, the topic quickly turned to comebacks and overcoming adversity.

"I know you had a tough game last week," Clinton told a crowd of roughly 14,000. "But you play this game long enough and a guy is going to make a 3-point shot, falling back with a hand in his face. It's not fatal. The only thing that's fatal is quitting. And you've got no quit in that team back there."

Clinton was given a No. 1 jersey with his name on the back. He said he would wear it to the dinner table at the White House that night to tease his daughter, Chelsea, a

senior at Stanford. But she could always point to the Cardinal's new No. 1 ranking.

MSU made Northwestern pay for that with an 84-53 romp the next night in Breslin, bringing the four-season win total to an even 100. With Randolph and Taylor making their first career starts, MSU shot 54.2 percent from the field and had 17 offensive rebounds, as many as the Wildcats grabbed at both ends. The Spartans' 29-rebound advantage was their second-largest of the season.

Hutson had 19 points, nine rebounds, five assists and two blocks. Bell added 14 points and Richardson 13. And with forward Aloysius Anagonye and Thomas coming off the bench, Randolph and Taylor responded. Randolph had 11 points and seven rebounds

Photo Credit: Kevin Fowler, MSU Sports Information

Photo Credit: Kevin Fowler, MSU Sports Information

in 16 minutes, while Taylor had seven assists and one turnover in 22.

"They had relentless pressure on the boards," said new Northwestern coach Bill Carmody, whose 1998 Princeton team had lost to MSU in the second round of the NCAA Tournament. "It seemed like they had more than a 30-rebound advantage. But the most-impressive thing was the way they passed the ball. Their depth wasn't really a factor. If they'd played five guys, we'd have been at a disadvantage."

The nation's shortest winning streak was one game. And three days later against Wisconsin, it appeared the string of triumphs in Breslin would stop at 38. The Badgers hit seven of their first eight shots and led 17-9 after just 5:26, matching their output in the first half of a 2000 Final Four defeat.

MSU rallied and led 36-31 at the break behind 16 points from Richardson, then built that bulge to a seemingly safe 50-40 with 7:57 left. But a 17-2 surge, including an 11-0 run, the longest against the Spartans in the season's first 32 games, gave Wisconsin a 57-52 lead and three chances to seal the upset in the final 1:47.

After a defensive stop, Richardson cut the deficit to three with a 17-footer, as critical as any of his 25 points. And when senior point guard Mike Kelley, a 74.1-percent foul shooter, missed the front end of a one-and-one for the Badgers with 48.5 seconds left, MSU had a final possession.

"When Mike stepped up to the

foul line, I said, 'This is real good,'" Wisconsin acting head coach Brad Soderberg said. "He has made a ton of those in his career. He's very hurt in that locker room right now."

One of the Big Ten's top three defensive players didn't make the stop on defense, either. Instead, Bell, who had hit just two of his first 11, came open on the right wing and rattled home an in-out-and-in-again, 21-footer with 28.5 seconds left, arguably the Spartans' biggest basket all year.

Photo Credit: Kevin Fowler, MSU Sports Information

The 17th-ranked Badgers still had a great opportunity to win. The question was whether to go to senior guard Roy Boone, who already had 22 points, including a bizarre, four-point play, or to senior forward Mark Vershaw, who was 7-for-7 from the field at that point. Vershaw got the ball, couldn't shake Hutson and missed a tough 10-footer.

The overtime was all MSU. Using "Screen and Re-screen," the alley-oop feed that finished Iowa State in the 2000 Elite Eight, Bell found Richardson with a gravity-defying pass for a slam and a free throw that made it 65-59 and made every network's highlight reel.

"They were starting to over-play him a little bit," Izzo said of a risky maneuver for most teams and a high-percentage pass for MSU. "I've got a guy who can go up to a different atmosphere to get the ball. So it's a little safer play than you'd think. But it's easier to diagram than it is to run."

The 69-59 final was the Spartans' fifth win over the Badgers in 11 months and Wisconsin's second loss on the 2000 Final Four floor. But before Izzo left the locker room, he was summoned to the MSU training room where Hutson was in severe pain for an hour-and-a-half.

After playing 38 minutes with flu-like symptoms, Hutson began to cramp up after contributing 10 points, nine rebounds, a steal and two blocked shots. He received four pints of fluids and was kept overnight at Sparrow Hospital with "dehydration secondary to pneumonia."

Photo Credit: Kevin Fowler, MSU Sports Information

With Hutson's full recovery expected to take up to five weeks, Izzo faced a tough decision for the first Ohio State game. Should he start Anagonye and Randolph inside and reduce the bench strength significantly? Or should he promote sophomore Adam Ballinger and keep Anagonye in reserve?

After eight days of preparation, Izzo started Ballinger, who responded with 10 points in 16 minutes of a 71-56 victory. With Anagonye and Buckeye-bred, red-shirt-freshman Jason Andreas, Ballinger helped to hold OSU star Ken Johnson to 12 points and six rebounds.

"I thought he did a doggone good job when you consider the position we put him in," Izzo said. "First, we throw him in there as a starter. Then, we make him guard Ken Johnson. With a friend like me, you don't need enemies."

The Spartans needed 24 points from Richardson, including 4-for-5 3-point accuracy, and 14 points and 10 rebounds from Randolph. They led just 37-35 with less than 15 minutes left, then pulled away with a pair of Richardson 3s and excellent perimeter defense.

MSU held the league's top 3-point shooters to 2-for-11 accuracy and grabbed most of those misses. The nation's best rebounding team also ruled the offensive glass with 20 second opportunities in its new Nike Shox.

"We talked about two issues that we thought were critical — rebounding on defense and getting back in transition," OSU coach Jim O'Brien said. "They ended up with 47 points on second chances or off turnovers. They just manhandled us underneath the basket."

Manhandled? Did someone say "Northwestern" again? When the 15-1 Spartans visited the 7-11 Wildcats on Jan. 24, the game was over before some fans finished parking. MSU scored the first 10 points and 17 of the first 20 in a 41-22 first half.

Izzo's players shot 64.6 percent from the field and cruised 74-58, despite being whistled for 23 fouls to just 12 for Northwestern. Richardson was 5-for-6 from the field and had 16 points in 22 min-

Photo Credit: Kevin Fowler, MSU Sports Information

utes. Randolph was 7-for-7 and added 15 points in 19 minutes. And in a surprise return, Hutson came off the bench to play 17 minutes.

"I don't know if they have a clear path to the title," Carmody said after the Spartans moved into a first-place tie with Illinois at 5-1. "But they're the defending champs. Until someone knocks them off, you have to like their chances. Tom's team runs great stuff. And the ball goes in the basket."

MSU was knocked off three days later. In the second meeting with the Buckeyes in six days, the third-ranked Spartans had a sluggish first half, then turned down

their intensity. Meanwhile, OSU outworked and outplayed its guests for a 64-55 triumph in raucous Value City Arena.

After gaining an 11-6 lead, MSU went scoreless for 7:59. When the Buckeyes built on a 26-22 halftime advantage with a 17-5 spurt, the Spartans could never get closer than seven points. A sick Bell went 2-for-13 from the field and was outscored 25-5 by OSU's Brian Brown.

The good news? Hutson returned to the lineup and had 17 points and seven rebounds in 27 minutes. But his biggest contribution, one of the best by any player all season, was a post-game eruption when he ripped Randolph for a lackadaisical, two-point, one-rebound effort.

"Don't you know that I'd do anything for you?" Hutson hollered. "I'd give you the shirt off my back if you needed it. So how can you do this to me? How could you not be there for me? How could you not show up to play? You can have other chances. This is my last one!"

An MSU team that had won 17 of its first 19 games without forceful leadership suddenly had a common bond. The underclassmen didn't need Hutson's shirt. They just needed to know what winning meant to the most-successful seniors in Big Ten history.

If the Spartans needed a reminder of how fortunate they were, they got it that weekend when travel problems paled in comparison to those of Oklahoma State. When a twin-engine propeller plane crashed and 10 people died on Jan. 27, the Cowboys' losses barely included a game that afternoon at Colorado.

"I got a chill when I heard the news," said Izzo, who occasionally uses a private plane for recruiting trips but takes the team on chartered jets. "I couldn't believe it. It really made me stop and think about things."

The Spartans' trip to Columbus had taken six-and-a-half hours in wintery weather. The de-icing truck broke down in Lansing. When the plane reached Columbus, the landing gear was down, but the pilot had to pull up due to poor visibility. So the team wound up in Cincinnati, where it sat on the runway for two hours waiting for a bus. A tough trip? Not nearly as tough as it could have been.

"I was 200-percent sure I made a mistake by flying," Izzo said. "We should've bused it. And I think we're going to start doing that more. We use a 50-passenger plane — a pretty nice jet. But when you fly to Chicago and stay 45 minutes from the airport, it isn't worth it. I won't take those turboprops."

Life's highs and lows were seen, albeit on a much-different scale, in the reaction to wins and losses. *The Detroit News* tipped off its coverage of the Big Ten race on Jan. 3 with the ridiculous headline, "Can MSU be perfect?" Twenty-six days later, after a 5-2 start and one day before the Spartans mauled Michigan, the same paper asked the question: "Does MSU lack heart?"

"I take that to heart," Izzo said

of a column that was used as motivation. "That's one of the ultimate insults, and understandably so. I've questioned our toughness a little bit, too. But to say an athlete doesn't have heart is a bit much."

The fifth-ranked Spartans had hearts as large as Secretariat's in a 91-64 victory that silenced "The Victors" in Crisler Arena. With 66.7-percent shooting from the field, MSU had a 24-0 surge in the first half and a 56-27 bulge at the break. The lead reached 44 before Izzo drew back on the reins with 11:58 left. After beating the Wolverines by 51 the previous March, this one could have reached 60.

"It's hard to know what to say after a win like that," Izzo said after a dousing to celebrate his 46th birthday. "I've been on the other end here. But I thought we

played a great game. We shot so well and got back to the defense we're capable of playing."

It was the Spartans' biggest margin of victory in Ann Arbor, as they ruled the boards 42-24 and had a 19-6 edge in assists. Richardson led the winners with 17 points. Hutson had 15 points and 10 rebounds. Bell and Randolph had 13 points apiece. And fifth-year forward Mike Chappell had 12.

MSU's old emotion was back, as Randolph discovered after a three-point play when Hutson nearly knocked him over with a flying bearhug. Meanwhile, the Wolverines' pulse was undetectable.

"It's incredibly disappointing," Michigan junior Chris Young said before accusing his team of quitting. "I can hardly show my face in here in front of all these cameras. I

want to go hide under my bed."

In an arena with as much green as blue, several visitors infiltrated Michigan's "Maize Rage" student section. But Lakeland High sophomore Tim McGorisk, a future Spartan, put it best: "I really thought it would be closer than this."

A 72-55 win over Purdue five days later in Breslin was closer at the outset. Trailing 15-14, MSU scored 22 straight points over a span of 7:10. Gene Keady's team went 7:12 without a rebound and shot 28.3 percent from the field.

Hutson led a balanced attack with 14 points. And Richardson, Randolph and Thomas each had nine rebounds in a 53-29 disparity. But the Boilermakers' 10-for-24 3-point success was a legitimate concern for the 18-2 Spartans, as future opponents saw Willie Deane's six 3s.

"We have to play better than we did, especially on the road," Bell said prophetically. "We had one stretch where we opened a lead. Other than that, Purdue was right there. We can't allow that to happen Tuesday."

He was referring to the Feb. 6 "Showdown in Champaign," with MSU and Illinois both 7-2 in the league. *The Champaign News-Gazette* gave the game blowout coverage, including a page of series history from Mike Pearson, a former sports publicist for both schools. And the angle of the paper's lead story — that the winner would likely get a No. 1 seed in the NCAA Tournament — was a swish.

"Well, it's here," Izzo said the day before the game. "Contrary to

what the Internet says, we are going to show up. And if there are 4 million orange-and-blue people around the airport, we're still going to land."

When the Spartans reached Assembly Hall, they scored the first seven points and used a 10-0 spurt at the start of the second half to reverse a five-point deficit. But MSU couldn't survive six 3s and 22 points from gunner Cory Bradford in a 77-66 setback.

"It means more because they're the national champs and three-time defending conference champs," said first-year Fighting Illini coach Bill Self, who took over when Lon Kruger got the Atlanta job Izzo rejected. "To win the conference, you have to go through Michigan State."

After five straight losses to the Spartans, including two for Big Ten Tournament titles, Illinois vowed to get as tough as Izzo's team and more than held its own inside. Meanwhile, the Illini outscored MSU 30-9 beyond the arc and took full advantage of defensive breakdowns.

"At the beginning of the year, (Bradford) was picked to be the Big Ten MVP," Bell said of an honor that would go to Illinois' clutch-shooting point guard Frank Williams. "He looked just like it tonight. You can't leave him open. You might as well count it."

Before MSU's only meeting with Minnesota, Izzo went back to his original lineup with Anagonye and Thomas starting and Randolph and Taylor coming off the bench. Though the freshmen never fully accepted it, the

Spartans went 22-3 that way.

"We should've won the Indiana game," Bell said of a late giveaway. "I was under the weather at Ohio State. And we made so many mental mistakes at Illinois. But we're not down-and-out. We know the race isn't over. We still have some laps to run."

MSU knew it had to be perfect in its last six conference games to catch the 8-2 Illini. And there was no truer test of title-worthiness than a trip to Williams Arena. The Spartans were 8-0 there in championship seasons, 7-32 in other years.

If they wanted to be in Minneapolis again seven weeks later, they would have to start playing like a Final Four team. But that didn't happen in a 94-83 escape

Photo Credit: Kevin Fowler, MSU Sports Information

against the Golden Gophers, who had just six healthy scholarship players due to NCAA sanctions and injuries.

Minnesota guard Terrance Simmons scorched MSU with a career-high 34 points, including seven 3s. And the Gophers' 16-for-30 long-range accuracy had Izzo fuming about defensive lapses nearly blowing a 35-15 lead.

"That's the kind of team I've got right now — score, score, score," he said of a problem a lot of coaches would like to have. "When you've got to do that, you're going to lose....It's hard to feel very good about this game."

Minnesota coach Dan Monson wasn't smiling, either. Without the services of three key players, his team had more 3s than two-point baskets (10) or free throws (15). But after the Gophers clawed within two at 78-76, Hutson and Richardson sparked a 9-0 run to ice the win.

MSU outrebounded Minnesota 41-23 and had six players score at least 11 points. Bell was the statistical star with 17 points, nine rebounds and six assists. The problem was stopping someone, as the Gophers tied Florida for the highest point total against the Spartans.

In MSU's last two games, both on the road, it had surrendered 160 points, about 40 more than normal. And in the Spartans' last three games, they had allowed 36 3-pointers for 108 points. Meanwhile, they had hit just nine 3s for 27 points.

But when MSU got back from the Twin Cities, three important things occurred. In a two-and-a-half-hour team meeting, the players ranked each other from 1-to-14 in several categories, opening some eyes. Senior guard Brandon Smith spoke up and said while Izzo hadn't been as hard in practice, the players weren't having as much fun, either. And Izzo admitted he was wrong about some of the criticism.

"I watched that film twice when we got home, and I'm not sure God could've covered them on some of those shots," Izzo said. "The Illinois game made me irate. When guys have ready-ready-ready-ready-ready-shoot shots and can check the wind velocity, that's ridiculous. But when guys are banking them in the way they did at Minnesota, that's not ridiculous, just frustrating."

With eight days until Iowa's visit to Breslin, MSU worked on its own weaknesses, then stunned the Hawkeyes with a 20-4 start in a 94-70 win on CBS. The fourth-ranked Spartans blanketed the perimeter and swarmed inside for their 42nd-straight home triumph.

"All week long, we emphasized being active on defense," Thomas said after MSU climbed to 20-3 and stayed a game-and-a-half behind Illinois. "We must've had at least 50 deflections. They said we had 34 at halftime."

Richardson had 21 points, Hutson 17, Bell 16 and Randolph 14, as the Spartans shot 53.6 percent and held Steve Alford's Hawkeyes to 33.8 accuracy. Point guard Dean Oliver led Iowa with

14 points but was 3-for-14 from the field. And forward Reggie Evans managed just two points.

The Hawkeyes did outrebound MSU, 40-36, the only time that happened all season. Thus, Monday's practice had a special urgency as the Spartans prepared for another quick-turnaround test. Izzo dusted off the War drill, a rare event the day before a game, and chose intensity over injury avoidance.

"We worked on rebounding double-time," Thomas said. "What happened there Sunday wasn't Michigan State Basketball. But whatever this team focuses on, we fix."

The following night, the Spartans delivered a 66-57 payback to Indiana in Breslin and tied the Hoosiers' record with 108 wins in four seasons. Appropriately, Buckner

Photo Credit: Kevin Fowler, MSU Sports Information

was on hand for the next three games as an ESPN commentator.

"Our team and this team both played great defense," he said of Bob Knight's best squads in the mid-1970s. "The biggest difference is our team was more senior-laden. This team has played more games."

It would have to play four more good ones to have a chance at four straight titles, a goal that would set MSU's seniors apart from their predecessors

"That would be the biggest thing I've ever accomplished," Hutson said, putting that achievement ahead of winning a national championship. "Last year was big. But that was Mateen Cleaves' and Morris Peterson's team. To win a fourth title in Charlie's and my senior year would be great."

Another great start gave the Spartans a 21-9 advantage. And when Indiana drew within four early in the second half and again midway through the period, MSU answered with 9-0 and 11-2 surges to climb to 21-3 for the first time.

Though Hutson led the Spartans with 15 points and Randolph added 14 points and nine rebounds, the key was Thomas' play at both ends. He was 4-for-4 from the field and had 11 points, eight rebounds and more long arms in the Hoosiers' passing lanes than stats could ever show.

Haston, the Big Ten's scoring champ at 20.3 points per game was held to 18, nine less than he had in Bloomington. Only three of those points came in the second half. Just as Thomas had predicted, MSU had a 44-31 edge in rebounds.

In the locker room after the game, Hutson said he thought he would give a couple of friends on the Buckeyes a call. Two nights later, it would be OSU's turn to try to hand the Illini a third league loss, after Wisconsin nearly did that.

First, the Spartans wanted to pay their respects as a team to the Cleaves family after the death of Mateen's brother, Herbert — or "Sluggo," as he was often known. At age 27, Herbert was killed in a drive-by shooting the previous Sunday, an innocent victim of a prior dispute.

Izzo, his staff and all the players attended a visitation Thursday evening at the Lawrence R. Moon Funeral Home in Flint. Then, the Spartans hurried back to watch the

Photo Credit: Kevin Fowler, MSU Sports Information

Illinois-OSU game. They will never experience a lower low and a higher high in such a short span.

Just when it appeared the Illini would win and virtually lock up an outright crown, the Buckeyes rallied. When a 3 from the left wing by Providence transfer Sean Connolly gave OSU a 63-61 win, MSU's players erupted in joy.

"You should've seen Andre," Izzo said. "He was jumping up and high-fiving everyone. It was really the first time I've seen that from this team. It was one of those nights that bring teams together — and a moment I know I'll never forget."

At 10-3 in Big Ten play, the Spartans' work was far from finished with trips to Penn State and Madison and a matchup with Michigan ahead. Illinois was 11-3 and would whip Iowa in Champaign, then win at Minnesota to finish 13-3.

When MSU went to Happy Valley, the Nittany Lions had their only sellout of the season, with help from nearly 200 members of the Izzone. And with injured football player Adam Taliaferro on campus for the team the first time since his spinal-cord damage five months earlier in Columbus, Penn State had emotion, too.

The Nittany Lions had already beaten the Illini in overtime, after Jon Crispin hit a 3 in the final seconds of the first half when the visitors had just four players on the floor — an innovative box-and-none defense.

As Penn State would prove to MSU and other teams in March, it was capable of beating any opponent when its 3-point shots started dropping. But after leading 47-46 with 9:58 left, Jerry Dunn's team discovered how stingy the Spartans could be in a 19-2 drought.

"When you miss shots, they get it and go," said Dunn, whose team hit just 32.4 percent to 49.2 for MSU. "Before you know it, you're up and down the floor. You don't want to be in a track meet. But you really don't have a choice."

Not when Bell and Richardson each have 16 points and play lockdown defense on Joe Crispin and Titus Ivory, a combined 8-for-34 from the field. Not when Hutson adds 11 points and 16 rebounds. And not when Randolph contributes 10 points and eight rebounds in 14 minutes.

The tricky part came when the Spartans couldn't get a flight home on Saturday night and weren't sure they could Sunday morning. So Izzo flashed back to his Division II days and told the bus driver to keep going.

After stopping at a McDonald's that was just about to close and giving that franchise its biggest order of the month, it was time to get rolling. Some players slept, when Bell the prankster would let them. Others watched videos like "Tommy Boy" — not the story of Izzo's youth.

"I would've gone to Indiana Wesleyan if I wanted to do this," Randolph cracked. Izzo's retort, "Yeah? Well, there were times when I wish you had," was funnier at the time than it is today.

Izzo and Garland reminisced about their days at NMU, a long

Photo Credit: Bruce Fox, University Relations

bus ride from anywhere. They used to climb up over the seats and sleep in the baggage shelves. But when the team arrived back at Breslin at 6:30 a.m. Sunday, the players knew even more about each other.

Izzo knew one important thing about Tuesday's game with the Badgers in Madison, Senior Night at the Kohl Center: "If they play well and we play well, we win."

MSU played just well enough to beat Wisconsin 51-47, with Hutson, Richardson and Bell teaming for 34 points and Thomas sinking the last two free throws.... So much for the notion that the Spartans couldn't win a brutal road game.

"That's probably the most excited we've been all year," Hutson said. "Wins against these guys should count as two. I sort of feel sorry for some of their sen-

iors. But we have a bigger goal. And we're almost there."

The Spartans just needed to beat Michigan a seventh-straight time to lock up a share of the Big Ten title. They also needed to do that to salute the winningest senior class in league history — with all five receiving legitimate degrees in May.

"If a championship happens, this is the right way to do it," Izzo said. "To go on the road for back-to-back wins where it's Christmas and the Fourth of July rolled into one, whatever happens now, we earned it."

They earned the right to celebrate with a 78-57 win over the Wolverines, a Senior Day lovefest against a favorite victim. The sign above each locker in Breslin said it all: "If you're going to be a CHAMPION, you must be willing to pay a greater price than your opponent every play — BEAT MICHIGAN."

Izzo started all five seniors and told Bell to commit a traveling violation so they could exit together before another net-cutting and banner-raising. And when all four Big Ten trophies were displayed, MSU had as many of those mounted basketballs as their guests had conference wins for the season.

"This is definitely the sweetest one," Hutson said after his 44th-straight win in Breslin. "We heard a lot of criticism this year. And this is the one I'll cherish."

A title for a senior class with class, one whose academic and athletic accomplishments will stand the test of time.

MSU 98, Penn State 73

Jan. 3, 2001 • Breslin Center • East Lansing, Mich.

Penn State	FG-FGA	FT-FTA	REB	PF	TP	A	TO	BLK	S	MIN
Titus Ivory	6-13	6-6	2	4	22	4	4	0	1	28
Tyler Smith	2-5	2-4	3	2	6	1	4	1	2	29
Gyasi Cline-Heard	5-10	6-9	6	3	16	3	2	1	0	33
Joe Crispin	6-16	6-7	1	5	21	4	7	0	4	35
Jon Crispin	1-5	2-2	1	4	4	1	0	0	1	34
Jamaal Tate	0-1	0-0	0	2	0	0	0	0	0	5
Ken Krimmel	0-1	0-0	1	0	0	1	1	0	0	3
Brandon Watkins	0-2	0-0	0	0	0	0	0	0	0	3
Sharif Chambliss	0-0	0-0	0	0	0	0	0	0	0	6
Stephan Bekale	0-0	0-0	0	2	0	0	0	0	0	3
B.J. Vossekuil	0-0	0-0	1	2	0	0	0	0	0	8
Ndu Egekeze	2-3	0-1	2	3	4	1	0	0	0	5
Scott Witkowsky	0-1	0-0	2	3	0	0	1	0	0	8
Totals	22-57	22-29	24	30	73	15	19	2	9	200

Three-Point Field Goals: Ivory 4-9, Joe Crispin 3-8, Jon Crispin 0-3, Tate 0-1, Watkins 0-2, Team 7-23.
FG%: 1st Half 16-29 .552, 2nd Half 6-28 .214, Game 22-57 .386; 3FG%: 1st Half 6-10 .600, 2nd Half 1-13 .077, Game 7-23 .304; FT%: 1st Half 10-14 .714, 2nd Half 12-15 .800, Game 22-29 .759; Team Rebounds: 5; Deadball Rebounds: 5.

Michigan State	FG-FGA	FT-FTA	REB	PF	TP	A	TO	BLK	S	MIN
Jason Richardson	4-6	2-4	6	3	10	3	1	0	0	21
Andre Hutson	9-12	2-5	13	3	20	4	2	0	1	35
Aloysius Anagonye	2-3	1-3	1	4	5	1	1	0	1	19
David Thomas	1-2	0-0	0	3	2	3	0	1	3	15
Charlie Bell	8-15	7-8	4	2	26	8	2	0	6	36
Marcus Taylor	2-5	6-7	1	1	11	3	3	0	0	24
Adam Wolfe	0-3	1-2	3	0	1	2	0	0	0	5
Brandon Smith	0-0	0-0	0	0	0	0	0	0	0	2
Mat Ishbia	0-0	1-2	1	0	1	0	0	0	0	1
Mike Chappell	1-2	2-4	2	1	4	1	2	0	0	16
Jason Andreas	2-2	0-0	2	3	4	0	0	0	0	3
Zach Randolph	3-5	4-7	7	1	10	0	1	0	1	17
Adam Ballinger	2-2	0-0	1	0	4	0	1	1	0	6
Totals	34-57	26-42	42	22	98	25	13	3	12	200

Three-Point Field Goals: Richardson 0-2, Bell 3-6, Taylor 1-2, Wolfe 0-2, Team 4-12.
FG%: 1st Half 12-29 .414, 2nd Half 22-28 .786, Game 34-57 .596; 3FG%: 1st Half 2-7 .286, 2nd Half 2-5 .400, Game 4-12 .333; FT%: 1st Half 11-22 .500, 2nd Half 15-20 .750, Game 26-42 .619; Team Rebounds: 1; Deadball Rebounds: 10.

SCORE BY PERIODS	1	2	F
Penn State	48	25	73
Michigan State	37	61	98

OFFICIALS – Ed Hightower, Tom Clark, Steve Welmer
TECHNICAL FOULS – Michigan State bench
ATTENDANCE – 14,759

Indiana 59, MSU 58

Jan. 7, 2001 • Assembly Hall • Bloomington, Ind.

Michigan State	FG-FGA	FT-FTA	REB	PF	TP	A	TO	BLK	S	MIN
David Thomas	2-2	0-0	0	2	4	0	2	1	1	19
Aloysius Anagonye	2-3	0-0	2	5	4	0	2	0	0	10
Andre Hutson	3-10	3-4	4	4	9	1	2	0	2	37
Charlie Bell	3-9	4-4	2	2	11	2	2	0	1	36
Jason Richardson	6-13	0-2	15	2	15	1	2	2	0	27
Marcus Taylor	1-3	0-0	1	1	2	2	4	0	1	24
Adam Wolfe	0-3	0-0	2	0	0	0	0	0	0	5
Mike Chappell	0-1	2-2	2	0	2	0	2	0	0	15
Jason Andreas	0-0	0-0	0	0	0	0	0	0	0	2
Zach Randolph	4-9	3-4	8	2	11	1	3	0	1	21
Adam Ballinger	0-1	0-0	1	0	0	0	0	0	1	6
Totals	21-54	12-16	42	18	58	7	19	3	7	200

Three-Point Field Goals: Bell 1-3, Richardson 3-6, Taylor 0-1, Team 4-10.

FG%: 1st Half 10-25 .400, 2nd Half 11-29 .379, Game 21-54 .389; 3FG%: 1st Half 1-6 .167, 2nd Half 3-4 .750, Game 4-10 .400; FT%: 1st Half 6-6 1.000, 2nd Half 6-10 .600, Game 12-16 .750; Team Rebounds: 5; Deadball Rebounds: 1.

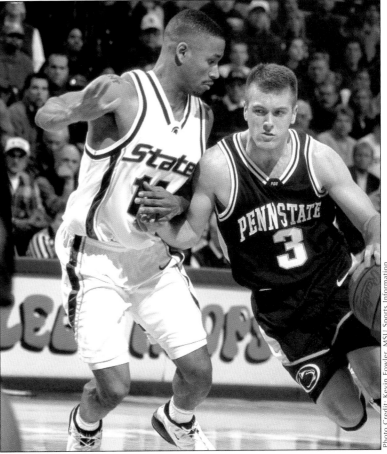

Indiana	FG-FGA	FT-FTA	REB	PF	TP	A	TO	BLK	S	MIN
Jared Jeffries	5-15	6-9	8	1	16	4	0	1	1	39
Kirk Haston	11-21	2-4	5	4	27	2	5	1	2	33
Jeff Newton	1-2	2-2	3	4	4	1	2	0	0	23
Tom Coverdale	2-4	0-0	3	0	4	5	5	0	3	37
Dane Fife	0-1	0-1	0	4	0	1	0	0	0	30
A.J. Moye	0-0	0-0	0	1	0	0	0	0	0	2
Andre Owens	1-3	0-0	2	2	2	1	0	0	0	12
Kyle Hornsby	1-4	0-0	3	0	2	0	1	0	1	13
Jarrad Odle	2-3	0-0	2	2	4	0	0	0	0	11
Totals	23-53	10-16	28	18	59	13	13	2	7	200

Three-Point Field Goals: Jeffries 0-2, Haston 3-4, Owens 0-1, Hornsby 0-2, Odle 0-1, Team 3-10.

FG%: 1st Half 13-30 .433, 2nd Half 10-23 .435, Game 23-53 .434; 3FG%: 1st Half 1-3 .333, 2nd Half 2-7 .286, Game 3-10 .300; FT%: 1st Half 1-4 .250, 2nd Half 9-12 .750, Game 10-16 .625; Team Rebounds: 2; Deadball Rebounds: 2.

SCORE BY PERIODS	1	2	F
Michigan State	27	31	58
Indiana	28	31	59

OFFICIALS – Tom Rucker, Donnee Gray, Rick Hartzell
TECHNICAL FOULS – None
ATTENDANCE – 17,128

MSU 84, Northwestern 53
Jan. 10, 2001 • Breslin Center • East Lansing, Mich.

Northwestern	FG-FGA	FT-FTA	REB	PF	TP	A	TO	BLK	S	MIN
Winston Blake	4-12	1-2	1	4	13	1	1	0	1	36
Ben Johnson	2-4	1-1	1	1	6	1	2	0	0	16
Tavaras Hardy	1-6	6-6	6	3	8	4	1	1	3	33
Jitim Young	2-5	0-1	0	1	4	0	1	0	2	22
Collier Drayton	1-3	2-4	3	2	5	4	0	0	0	37
Langston Hughes	0-0	0-0	0	0	0	0	0	0	0	3
Jason Burke	1-2	0-0	0	1	3	1	0	0	0	10
Ed McCants	2-4	0-1	1	1	5	2	1	0	0	17
Aaron Jennings	3-8	1-2	3	3	9	0	2	2	0	26
Totals	16-44	11-17	17	16	53	13	10	3	6	200

Three-Point Field Goals: Blake 4-9, Johnson 1-2, Hardy 0-1, Young 0-2, Drayton 1-2, Burke 1-1, McCants 1-3, Jennings 2-3, Team 10-23.
FG%: 1st Half 8-24 .333, 2nd Half 8-20 .400, Game 16-44 .364; 3FG%: 1st Half 5-14 .357, 2nd Half 5-9 .556, Game 10-23 .435; FT%: 1st Half 3-3 1.000, 2nd Half 8-14 .571, Game 11-17 .647; Team Rebounds: 2; Deadball Rebounds: 2.

Michigan State	FG-FGA	FT-FTA	REB	PF	TP	A	TO	BLK	S	MIN
Jason Richardson	4-8	3-4	9	3	13	2	2	1	0	25
Andre Hutson	8-9	3-4	9	1	19	5	0	2	1	28
Zach Randolph	5-8	1-2	7	2	11	0	1	0	0	16
Marcus Taylor	2-4	0-0	1	2	4	7	1	0	0	22
Charlie Bell	5-11	2-3	5	0	14	2	3	0	0	31
Adam Wolfe	1-3	0-0	1	0	2	0	1	0	1	6
Brandon Smith	1-2	0-0	0	1	3	1	0	0	0	4
David Thomas	1-2	0-0	2	2	3	1	0	0	0	20
Mat Ishbia	0-0	0-0	0	0	0	0	0	0	0	1
Mike Chappell	3-7	0-0	2	1	8	0	0	0	0	14
Aloysius Anagonye	2-3	3-4	2	3	7	1	1	0	1	16
Jason Andreas	0-0	0-0	3	1	0	1	1	0	0	5
Adam Ballinger	0-2	0-0	4	2	0	1	0	0	0	12
Totals	32-59	12-17	46	19	84	21	10	3	3	200

Three-Point Field Goals: Richardson 2-4, Taylor 0-1, Bell 2-5, Wolfe 0-1, Smith 1-2, Thomas 1-1, Chappell 2-6, Team 8-20.
FG%: 1st Half 16-29 .552, 2nd Half 16-30 .533, Game 32-59 .542; 3FG%: 1st Half 1-8 .125, 2nd Half 7-12 .583, Game 8-20 .400; FT%: 1st Half 8-12 .667, 2nd Half 4-5 .800, Game 12-17 .706; Team Rebounds: 1; Deadball Rebounds: 1.

SCORE BY PERIODS	1	2		F
Northwestern	24	29	--	53
Michigan State	41	43	--	84

OFFICIALS – Randy Drury, Jerry Petro, Winston Stith
TECHNICAL FOULS – Michigan State bench
ATTENDANCE – 14,759

MSU 69, Wisconsin 59
Jan. 13, 2001 • Breslin Center • East Lansing, Mich.

Wisconsin	FG-FGA	FT-FTA	REB	PF	TP	A	TO	BLK	S	MIN
Maurice Linton	2-9	2-2	5	3	7	2	0	0	0	29
Andy Kowske	1-2	0-1	5	2	2	0	0	1	0	35
Mark Vershaw	8-11	0-0	3	3	18	4	3	1	0	40
Mike Kelley	1-4	0-1	1	2	2	5	1	0	1	38
Roy Boone	8-17	3-3	6	2	22	1	2	1	0	39
Travon Davis	0-0	0-0	0	0	0	1	1	0	1	8
Kirk Penney	2-5	0-1	1	1	6	0	1	0	0	19
Freddie Owens	0-1	0-0	0	0	0	0	0	0	0	2
Dave Mader	0-0	0-0	0	1	0	0	1	0	0	4
Charlie Wills	0-1	2-2	0	4	2	0	0	0	0	11
Totals	22-50	7-10	22	18	59	13	10	3	2	225

Three-Point Field Goals: Linton 1-3, Vershaw 2-3, Kelley 0-1, Boone 3-7, Penney 2-3, Owens 0-1, Team 8-18.
FG%: 1st Half 12-23 .522, 2nd Half 9-22 .409, OT 1-5 .200, Game 22-50 .440; 3FG%: 1st Half 3-8 .375, 2nd Half 5-7 .714, OT 0-3 .000, Game 8-18 .444; FT%: 1st Half 4-4 1.000, 2nd Half 3-4 .750, OT 0-2 .000, Game 7-10 .700; Team Rebounds: 1; Deadball Rebounds: 3.

Michigan State	FG-FGA	FT-FTA	REB	PF	TP	A	TO	BLK	S	MIN
Jason Richardson	9-15	3-3	3	4	25	4	0	2	0	42
Andre Hutson	4-8	2-2	9	2	10	0	1	2	1	38
Zach Randolph	3-6	4-8	9	0	10	2	0	0	0	23
Marcus Taylor	2-7	2-2	1	1	6	6	1	0	0	31
Charlie Bell	3-12	3-4	2	1	10	4	3	1	0	39
David Thomas	0-3	0-0	6	4	0	1	0	0	0	16
Mike Chappell	1-1	0-0	1	0	2	0	1	0	0	7
Aloysius Anagonye	2-2	2-2	4	2	6	0	1	0	2	23
Adam Ballinger	0-0	0-0	0	0	0	0	1	0	0	6
Totals	24-54	16-21	39	14	69	17	8	5	3	225

Three-Point Field Goals: Richardson 4-7, Taylor 0-2, Bell 1-6, Thomas 0-1, Team 5-16.
FG%: 1st Half 13-25 .520, 2nd Half 8-25 .320, OT 3-4 .750, Game 24-54 .444; 3FG%: 1st Half 4-8 .500, 2nd Half 1-8 .125, OT 0-0 .000, Game 5-16 .313; FT%: 1st Half 6-8 .750, 2nd Half 4-6 .667, OT 6-7 .857, Game 16-25 .762; Team Rebounds: 4; Deadball Rebounds: 2.

SCORE BY PERIODS	1	2	OT	F
Wisconsin	31	26	2	59
Michigan State	36	21	12	69

OFFICIALS – Ted Hillary, Art McDonald, Jerry Petro
TECHNICAL FOULS – None
ATTENDANCE – 14,759

MSU 71, Ohio State 56
Jan. 21, 2001 • Breslin Center • East Lansing, Mich.

Ohio State	FG-FGA	FT-FTA	REB	PF	TP	A	TO	BLK	S	MIN
Boban Savovic	4-12	5-6	6	3	13	5	2	0	1	37
Zach Williams	3-4	0-0	4	1	6	0	3	0	0	25
Ken Johnson	6-10	0-0	6	5	12	1	3	6	1	39
Brent Darby	0-4	0-0	0	2	0	2	3	0	0	28
Brian Brown	6-12	1-2	2	3	14	3	5	0	0	32
Sean Connolly	2-5	0-0	0	2	5	3	0	0	1	24
Will Dudley	3-3	0-0	1	1	6	0	1	1	0	9
Tim Martin	0-1	0-0	2	0	0	0	0	0	0	6
Totals	24-51	6-8	27	17	56	14	17	7	4	200

Three-Point Field Goals: Savovic 0-2, Darby 0-4, Brown 1-1, Connolly 1-4, Team 2-11.
FG%: 1st Half 11-21 .524, 2nd Half 13-30 .433, Game 24-51 .471; 3FG%: 1st Half 1-7 .143, 2nd Half 1-4 .250, Game 2-11 .182; FT%: 1st Half 2-2 1.000, 2nd Half 4-6 .667, Game 6-8 .750; Team Rebounds: 6; Deadball Rebounds: 1.

Michigan State	FG-FGA	FT-FTA	REB	PF	TP	A	TO	BLK	S	MIN
Jason Richardson	9-13	2-4	4	2	24	3	0	1	3	34
Adam Ballinger	4-8	2-2	2	4	10	1	0	0	1	16
Zach Randolph	6-10	2-5	10	0	14	0	2	2	1	28
Marcus Taylor	3-10	0-0	5	3	7	3	2	0	0	28
Charlie Bell	3-9	4-4	2	0	10	6	2	0	1	33
Adam Wolfe	0-1	0-0	2	0	0	0	0	0	0	2
David Thomas	0-1	0-0	0	2	0	0	1	2	0	16
Mike Chappell	0-2	2-2	1	1	2	0	1	0	0	10
Aloysius Anagonye	1-2	2-2	2	3	4	1	1	1	0	22
Jason Andreas	0-2	0-0	3	0	0	1	0	0	0	11
Totals	26-58	14-19	36	15	71	14	10	6	6	200

Three-Point Field Goals: Richardson 4-5, Taylor 1-3, Bell 0-1, Thomas 0-1, Team 5-10.
FG%: 1st Half 13-29 .448, 2nd Half 13-29 .448, Game 26-58 .448; 3FG%: 1st Half 3-7 .429, 2nd Half 2-3 .667, Game 5-10 .500; FT%: 1st Half 0-4 .000, 2nd Half 14-15 .933, Game 14-19 .737; Team Rebounds: 5; Deadball Rebounds: 2.

SCORE BY PERIODS	1	2		F
Ohio State	25	31	--	56
Michigan State	29	42	--	71

OFFICIALS – Ed Hightower, Steve Welmer, Rick Hartzell
TECHNICAL FOULS – None
ATTENDANCE – 14,759

MSU 74, Northwestern 58
Jan. 24, 2001 • Welsh-Ryan Arena • Evanston, Ill.

Michigan State	FG-FGA	FT-FTA	REB	PF	TP	A	TO	BLK	S	MIN
David Thomas	3-5	0-0	4	2	6	1	1	1	2	23
Jason Richardson	5-6	5-7	3	3	16	2	0	0	0	22
Zach Randolph	7-7	1-2	6	1	15	2	1	2	0	19
Marcus Taylor	2-6	1-1	0	1	6	5	6	1	0	24
Charlie Bell	5-11	0-0	5	3	12	6	1	0	0	29
Adam Wolfe	0-2	0-0	2	1	0	0	1	0	1	7
Brandon Smith	0-0	0-0	0	1	0	1	3	0	0	6
Mat Ishbia	0-0	0-0	1	0	0	0	0	0	0	1
Mike Chappell	3-4	0-0	1	2	6	5	0	1	1	20
Aloysius Anagonye	2-2	0-0	2	3	4	1	1	0	0	17
Andre Hutson	3-4	0-1	3	3	6	3	4	1	1	17
Jason Andreas	1-1	1-2	1	1	3	0	1	0	0	6
Adam Ballinger	0-0	0-0	3	2	0	0	0	0	1	9
Totals	31-48	8-13	32	23	74	26	19	6	6	200

Three-Point Field Goals: Richardson 1-2, Taylor 1-2, Bell 2-5, Wolfe 0-1, Chappell 0-1, Team 4-11.
FG%: 1st Half 17-25 .680, 2nd Half 14-23 .609, Game 31-48 .646; 3FG%: 1st Half 3-6 .500, 2nd Half 1-5 .200, Game 4-11 .364; FT%: 1st Half 4-6 .667, 2nd Half 4-7 .571, Game 8-13 .615; Team Rebounds: 1; Deadball Rebounds: 2.

Northwestern	FG-FGA	FT-FTA	REB	PF	TP	A	TO	BLK	S	MIN
Winston Blake	2-11	0-2	1	1	5	1	1	0	0	28
Ben Johnson	2-4	1-1	3	0	5	1	1	0	0	26
Tavaras Hardy	5-7	7-12	4	1	17	2	1	0	1	33
Jitim Young	4-12	2-3	2	3	10	5	7	0	2	38
Collier Drayton	1-3	0-0	2	3	3	2	0	0	0	29
Langston Hughes	0-0	0-0	1	0	0	0	1	0	0	2
Jason Burke	1-2	4-4	1	0	7	2	1	0	0	7
Ed McCants	1-3	1-1	1	0	3	0	0	0	1	13
Aaron Jennings	3-5	0-0	1	4	8	3	4	0	1	24
Totals	19-47	15-23	22	12	58	16	16	0	5	200

Three-Point Field Goals: Blake 1-4, Johnson 0-1, Young 0-4, Drayton 1-2, Burke 1-1, McCants 0-2, Jennings 2-3, Team 5-17.
FG%: 1st Half 8-24 .333, 2nd Half 11-23 .478, Game 19-47 .404; 3FG%: 1st Half 2-9 .222, 2nd Half 3-8 .375, Game 5-17 .294; FT%: 1st Half 4-5 .800, 2nd Half 11-18 .611, Game 15-23 .652; Team Rebounds: 6; Deadball Rebounds: 2.

SCORE BY PERIODS	1	2	F
Michigan State	41	33	-- 74
Northwestern	22	36	-- 58

OFFICIALS – Mike Sanzere, Sid Rodeheffer, Zelton Steed
TECHNICAL FOULS – None
ATTENDANCE – 6,525

Ohio State 64, MSU 55
Jan. 27, 2001 • Value City Arena • Columbus, Ohio

Michigan State	FG-FGA	FT-FTA	REB	PF	TP	A	TO	BLK	S	MIN
Jason Richardson	4-8	2-3	8	5	11	1	2	0	2	31
Andre Hutson	7-10	3-4	7	2	17	0	1	0	1	27
Zach Randolph	1-4	0-1	1	2	2	1	2	0	0	17
Marcus Taylor	3-8	2-2	1	0	9	4	2	0	0	26
Charlie Bell	2-13	0-0	1	4	5	4	0	0	1	27
Adam Wolfe	0-1	0-0	0	0	0	0	0	0	1	4
David Thomas	2-3	1-2	2	4	5	2	1	0	0	25
Mike Chappell	2-4	0-0	3	2	4	0	2	0	0	12
Aloysius Anagonye	0-1	2-2	3	4	2	0	2	0	0	21
Jason Andreas	0-0	0-0	0	0	0	0	0	0	0	7
Adam Ballinger	0-1	0-0	2	1	0	1	0	0	0	3
Totals	21-53	10-14	31	24	55	12	13	0	4	200

Three-Point Field Goals: Richardson 1-4, Taylor 1-3, Bell 1-8, Thomas 0-1, Chappell 0-1, Team 3-17.
FG%: 1st Half 9-25 .360, 2nd Half 12-28 .429, Game 21-53 .396; 3FG%: 1st Half 1-7 .143, 2nd Half 2-10 .200, Game 3-17 .176; FT%: 1st Half 3-5 .600, 2nd Half 7-9 .778, Game 10-14 .714; Team Rebounds: 3; Deadball Rebounds: 5.

Ohio State	FG-FGA	FT-FTA	REB	PF	TP	A	TO	BLK	S	MIN
Zach Williams	4-8	1-2	3	3	9	0	1	0	0	25
Ken Johnson	3-6	0-0	7	2	6	2	1	5	1	33
Sean Connolly	0-4	0-0	1	0	0	1	1	0	0	20
Brian Brown	8-13	7-9	5	3	25	6	3	0	1	40
Boban Savovic	1-2	2-2	3	4	4	0	0	0	2	18
Brent Darby	2-7	5-6	1	1	11	4	1	0	1	32
Velimir Radinovic	0-0	0-0	0	0	0	0	0	0	0	2
Cobe Ocokoljic	1-3	2-2	2	0	4	0	1	0	0	10
Will Dudley	1-1	1-5	2	3	3	0	1	0	0	11
Tim Martin	0-0	2-2	3	0	2	0	1	0	0	9
Totals	20-44	20-28	28	16	64	13	10	5	5	200

Three-Point Field Goals: Connolly 0-3, Brown 2-4, Darby 2-6, Ocokoljic 0-1, Team 4-14.
FG%: 1st Half 8-23 .348, 2nd Half 12-21 .571, Game 20-44 .455; 3FG%: 1st Half 1-8 .125, 2nd Half 3-6 .500, Game 4-14 .286; FT%: 1st Half 9-11 .818, 2nd Half 11-17 .647, Game 20-28 .714; Team Rebounds: 1; Deadball Rebounds: 4.

SCORE BY PERIODS	1	2	F
Michigan State	22	33	-- 55
Ohio State	26	38	-- 64

OFFICIALS – Tom Rucker, Art McDonald, Steve Olson
TECHNICAL FOULS – None
ATTENDANCE – 19,200

MSU 91, Michigan 64
Jan. 30, 2001 • Crisler Arena • Ann Arbor, Mich.

Michigan State	FG-FGA	FT-FTA	REB	PF	TP	A	TO	BLK	S	MIN
Jason Richardson	6-9	2-2	5	2	17	3	1	0	1	23
Andre Hutson	5-8	5-5	10	2	15	3	1	0	1	28
Zach Randolph	6-7	1-1	6	1	13	1	1	0	0	15
Marcus Taylor	2-5	0-0	1	2	4	3	2	0	0	20
Charlie Bell	4-9	4-4	5	1	13	2	2	0	0	28
Adam Wolfe	3-5	0-0	6	1	6	0	3	0	0	7
Brandon Smith	0-2	0-0	1	0	0	2	2	0	0	9
David Thomas	1-1	2-2	2	1	5	2	1	1	1	13
Mat Ishbia	0-0	0-0	0	0	0	0	0	0	0	2
Mike Chappell	5-6	0-0	1	4	12	0	2	0	0	18
Aloysius Anagonye	1-2	4-4	3	0	6	2	0	0	1	16
Jason Andreas	0-1	0-0	0	2	0	0	0	1	0	10
Adam Ballinger	0-2	0-0	1	4	0	1	1	1	0	11
Totals	33-57	18-18	42	20	91	19	16	3	4	200

Three-Point Field Goals: Richardson 3-4, Taylor 0-1, Bell 1-3, Wolfe 0-1, Smith 0-2, Thomas 1-1, Chappell 2-3, Ballinger 0-1, Team 7-16.
FG%: 1st Half 18-27 .667, 2nd Half 15-30 .500, Game 33-57 .579; 3FG%: 1st Half 5-9 .556, 2nd Half 2-7 .286, Game 7-16 .438; FT%: 1st Half 15-15 1.000, 2nd Half 3-3 1.000, Game 18-18 1.000; Team Rebounds: 1; Deadball Rebounds: 1.

Michigan	FG-FGA	FT-FTA	REB	PF	TP	A	TO	BLK	S	MIN
Josh Asselin	1-4	0-0	1	4	2	0	0	0	1	22
LaVell Blanchard	7-19	10-12	7	1	27	1	2	1	0	35
Chris Young	2-5	7-8	7	2	11	0	0	0	1	24
Avery Queen	2-5	0-0	1	0	5	1	3	0	0	20
Bernard Robinson Jr.	4-13	1-1	3	3	10	1	0	0	1	33
Leon Jones	0-0	0-0	0	0	0	0	0	0	0	2
Maurice Searight	0-2	0-0	0	1	0	1	2	0	2	19
Jermaine Gonzales	0-0	0-0	0	0	0	0	0	0	0	1
Herb Gibson	0-0	0-2	2	0	0	0	0	0	0	2
Mike Gotfredson	0-0	0-0	0	0	0	1	0	0	0	2
Gavin Groninger	0-2	0-0	1	0	0	1	1	0	0	17
Josh Moore	4-9	1-1	1	4	9	0	1	1	0	22
Rotolu Adebiyi	0-0	0-0	0	0	0	0	0	0	0	1
Totals	20-59	19-24	24	15	64	6	9	2	5	200

Three-Point Field Goals: Blanchard 3-8, Queen 1-2, Robinson 1-4, Groninger 0-1, Team 5-15.
FG%: 1st Half 6-28 .214, 2nd Half 14-31 .452, Game 20-59 .339; 3FG%: 1st Half 2-6 .333, 2nd Half 3-9 .333, Game 5-15 .333; FT%: 1st Half 13-14 .929, 2nd Half 6-10 .600, Game 19-24 .792; Team Rebounds: 1; Deadball Rebounds: 1.

SCORE BY PERIODS	1	2	F
Michigan State	56	35	-- 91
Michigan	27	37	-- 64

OFFICIALS – Jim Burr, Tom O'Neill, Ted Valentine
TECHNICAL FOULS – Michigan bench
ATTENDANCE – 13,562

Photo Credit: Kevin Fowler, MSU Sports Information

MSU 72, Purdue 55
Feb. 4, 2001 • Breslin Center • East Lansing, Mich.

Purdue	FG-FGA	FT-FTA	REB	PF	TP	A	TO	BLK	S	MIN
Kenneth Lowe	1-5	3-4	2	3	6	2	2	0	0	29
Rodney Smith	4-13	0-0	4	4	9	1	2	0	1	29
John Allison	1-8	1-2	3	2	3	2	1	4	0	21
Maynard Lewis	2-6	0-0	2	1	5	0	1	0	2	20
Carson Cunningham	1-9	0-0	0	3	2	6	0	0	2	24
Willie Deane	6-12	2-2	5	0	20	2	0	0	0	23
Brett Buscher	1-1	1-2	1	2	3	0	0	1	0	11
Austin Parkinson	0-1	0-0	2	0	0	1	1	0	0	9
Joe Marshall	1-5	2-4	4	0	5	0	0	0	0	10
Adam Wetzel	0-0	0-0	1	2	0	1	1	0	0	13
Travis Best	0-0	2-2	1	0	2	0	1	0	0	2
Kevin Garrity	0-0	0-0	0	0	0	0	0	0	0	9
Totals	17-60	11-16	29	17	55	15	10	5	5	200

Three-Point Field Goals: Lowe 1-2, Smith 1-5, Lewis 1-2, Cunningham 0-4, Deane 6-8, Marshall 1-3, Team 10-24.
FG%: 1st Half 7-32 .219, 2nd Half 10-28 .357, Game 17-60 .283; 3FG%: 1st Half 3-11 .273, 2nd Half 7-13 .538, Game 10-24 .417; FT%: 1st Half 0-0 .000, 2nd Half 11-16 .688, Game 11-16 .688; Team Rebounds: 3; Deadball Rebounds: 4.

Michigan State	FG-FGA	FT-FTA	REB	PF	TP	A	TO	BLK	S	MIN
Jason Richardson	4-11	0-0	9	1	9	1	1	2	0	30
Andre Hutson	6-6	2-2	5	1	14	4	1	0	0	30
Zach Randolph	5-9	2-6	9	3	12	1	1	2	1	25
Marcus Taylor	4-11	2-2	2	0	10	1	2	0	1	21
Charlie Bell	3-14	0-0	6	3	7	7	2	2	0	26
Adam Wolfe	0-1	0-0	1	0	0	0	0	1	0	3
Brandon Smith	0-1	0-0	0	0	0	0	1	0	0	2
David Thomas	4-6	0-0	9	0	8	4	1	0	2	23
Mat Ishbia	1-1	0-0	0	1	2	0	0	0	1	1
Mike Chappell	0-2	4-4	3	1	4	0	0	0	1	14
Aloysius Anagonye	1-2	0-0	2	4	2	0	1	2	0	12
Jason Andreas	0-0	0-0	1	1	0	0	0	0	0	4
Adam Ballinger	1-1	2-2	4	1	4	0	1	0	0	9
Totals	29-65	12-16	53	16	72	18	12	9	6	200

Three-Point Field Goals: Richardson 1-4, Taylor 0-3, Bell 1-4, Wolfe 0-1, Thomas 0-1, Chappell 0-2, Team 2-15.
FG%: 1st Half 15-30 .500, 2nd Half 14-35 .400, Game 29-65 .446; 3FG%: 1st Half 1-8 .125, 2nd Half 1-7 .143, Game 2-15 .133; FT%: 1st Half 7-10 .700, 2nd Half 5-6 .833, Game 12-16 .750; Team Rebounds: 2; Deadball Rebounds: 2.

SCORE BY PERIODS	1	2		F
Purdue	17	38	--	55
Michigan State	38	34	--	72

OFFICIALS – Ed Hightower, Tom Rucker, Donnee Gray
TECHNICAL FOULS – None
ATTENDANCE – 14,759

Illinois 77, MSU 66
Feb. 6, 2001 • Assembly Hall • Champaign, Ill.

Michigan State	FG-FGA	FT-FTA	REB	PF	TP	A	TO	BLK	S	MIN
Jason Richardson	8-17	2-2	4	4	19	2	0	3	0	31
Andre Hutson	4-9	0-0	2	5	8	1	1	0	0	32
Zach Randolph	1-4	4-4	8	4	6	0	2	2	1	23
Marcus Taylor	5-11	0-0	5	4	11	2	4	0	0	27
Charlie Bell	5-14	3-5	3	4	14	6	1	0	0	35
David Thomas	3-5	0-0	5	1	6	0	1	1	1	19
Mike Chappell	0-2	0-0	1	0	0	0	0	0	0	7
Aloysius Anagonye	0-0	0-0	1	3	0	0	1	0	0	18
Jason Andreas	0-0	0-0	0	1	0	0	0	0	0	2
Adam Ballinger	1-1	0-0	2	0	2	0	0	0	0	6
Totals	27-63	9-11	35	27	66	11	11	6	2	200

Three-Point Field Goals: Richardson 1-6, Taylor 1-6, Bell 1-4, Thomas 0-1, Chappell 0-1, Team 3-18.
FG%: 1st Half 13-27 .481, 2nd Half 14-36 .389, Game 27-63 .429; 3FG%: 1st Half 0-6 .000, 2nd Half 3-12 .250, Game 3-18 .167; FT%: 1st Half 3-5 .600, 2nd Half 6-6 1.000, Game 9-11 .818; Team Rebounds: 4; Deadball Rebounds: 3.

Illinois	FG-FGA	FT-FTA	REB	PF	TP	A	TO	BLK	S	MIN
Brian Cook	3-6	5-5	5	1	12	1	0	2	1	33
Sergio McClain	4-6	1-3	4	3	9	5	4	0	0	31
Marcus Griffin	0-3	2-2	4	3	2	1	2	0	0	19
Cory Bradford	6-12	4-4	3	2	22	1	2	0	0	31
Frank Williams	3-13	7-8	4	0	14	1	2	0	0	34
Robert Archibald	3-4	1-4	4	3	7	2	0	0	0	20
Lucas Johnson	1-2	0-0	2	3	3	0	0	0	1	9
Sean Harrington	1-2	1-2	0	0	4	1	0	0	0	16
Damir Krupalija	1-1	2-2	2	1	4	0	0	0	0	7
Totals	22-49	23-30	29	16	77	12	10	2	2	200

Three-Point Field Goals: Cook 1-4, Bradford 6-11, Williams 1-6, Johnson 1-1, Harrington 1-2, Team 10-24.
FG%: 1st Half 12-26 .462, 2nd Half 10-23 .435, Game 22-49 .449; 3FG%: 1st Half 6-15 .400, 2nd Half 4-9 .444, Game 10-24 .417; FT%: 1st Half 4-7 .571, 2nd Half 19-23 .826, Game 23-30 .767; Team Rebounds: 1; Deadball Rebounds: 5.

SCORE BY PERIODS	1	2		F
Michigan State	29	37	--	66
Illinois	34	43	--	77

OFFICIALS – Ted Hillary, Steve Welmer, Tom O'Neill
TECHNICAL FOULS – None
ATTENDANCE – 16,683

Photo Credit: Kevin Fowler, MSU Sports Information

MSU 94, Minnesota 83
Feb. 10, 2001 • Williams Arena • Minneapolis, Minn.

Michigan State	FG-FGA	FT-FTA	REB	PF	TP	A	TO	BLK	S	MIN
Andre Hutson	6-10	2-4	7	3	14	1	3	2	1	31
Jason Richardson	5-9	5-6	6	4	16	1	3	0	0	29
Aloysius Anagonye	3-3	0-0	3	2	6	2	2	2	1	27
David Thomas	5-6	2-2	7	1	12	3	1	0	2	25
Charlie Bell	5-9	6-10	9	0	17	6	4	0	1	36
Marcus Taylor	4-9	1-2	0	5	11	3	2	0	1	20
Zach Randolph	3-7	6-7	6	3	12	2	1	0	1	16
Mike Chappell	1-2	2-2	0	1	4	0	1	0	0	13
Adam Ballinger	1-2	0-0	1	1	2	0	0	0	0	3
Totals	33-57	24-33	41	20	94	18	17	4	7	200

Three-Point Field Goals: Richardson 1-4, Bell 1-2, Taylor 2-5, Chappell 0-1, Team 4-12.

FG%: 1st Half 20-30 .667, 2nd Half 13-27 .481, Game 33-57 .579; 3FG%: 1st Half 2-5 .400, 2nd Half 2-7 .286, Game 4-12 .333; FT%: 1st Half 6-11 .545, 2nd Half 18-22 .818, Game 24-33 .727; Team Rebounds: 2; Deadball Rebounds: 2.

Minnesota	FG-FGA	FT-FTA	REB	PF	TP	A	TO	BLK	S	MIN
Shane Schilling	3-10	2-2	3	4	11	1	4	0	0	35
Dusty Rychart	4-10	1-1	2	5	10	1	0	1	1	36
Jeff Hagen	2-4	0-0	4	1	4	1	0	0	0	17
Terrance Simmons	11-18	5-8	6	2	34	5	5	0	4	39
Kevin Burleson	4-7	5-7	2	5	16	4	1	0	2	37
Ryan Wildenborg	0-2	0-0	1	4	0	0	0	0	0	8
Kerwin Fleming	2-6	2-2	0	4	8	3	4	0	1	28
Tyree Bolden	0-0	0-0	0	0	0	0	0	0	0	1
Totals	26-57	15-20	23	25	83	14	15	0	8	200

Three-Point Field Goals: Schilling 3-7, Rychart 1-2, Simmons 7-12, Burleson 3-5, Fleming 2-4, Team 16-30.

FG%: 1st Half 14-29 .483, 2nd Half 12-28 .429, Game 26-57 .456; 3FG%: 1st Half 9-16 .563, 2nd Half 7-14 .500, Game 16-30 .533; FT%: 1st Half 3-3 1.000, 2nd Half 12-17 .706, Game 15-20 .750; Team Rebounds: 5; Deadball Rebounds: 3.

SCORE BY PERIODS	1	2	F
Michigan State	48	46	94
Minnesota	40	43	83

OFFICIALS – Tom Rucker, Rick Hartzell, Art McDonald
TECHNICAL FOULS – Richardson (MSU)
ATTENDANCE – 14,210

MSU 94, Iowa 70
Feb. 18, 2001 • Breslin Center • East Lansing, Mich.

Iowa	FG-FGA	FT-FTA	REB	PF	TP	A	TO	BLK	S	MIN
Glen Worley	2-11	2-2	2	4	6	1	5	1	1	27
Reggie Evans	1-6	0-2	9	3	2	1	8	0	1	22
Sean Sonderleiter	1-1	2-2	2	4	4	1	0	0	0	20
Brody Boyd	4-11	0-0	5	0	11	0	3	0	2	24
Dean Oliver	3-14	6-7	2	2	14	3	1	0	1	33
Ryan Hogan	0-2	2-4	2	3	2	2	0	0	0	14
Jared Reiner	3-4	0-0	3	5	6	0	0	0	0	12
Duez Henderson	4-6	3-3	3	4	11	0	0	0	0	15
Rod Thompson	2-3	0-0	0	3	5	1	0	0	0	6
Kyle Galloway	0-1	0-0	1	0	0	0	1	0	0	2
Jason Smith	0-0	2-2	2	0	2	0	0	0	0	8
Cortney Scott	2-6	3-4	6	3	7	1	1	0	1	17
Totals	22-65	20-26	40	32	70	9	19	1	6	200

Three-Point Field Goals: Worley 0-2, Boyd 3-9, Oliver 2-8, Hogan 0-1, Henderson 0-1, Thompson 1-2, Galloway 0-1, Team 6-24.

FG%: 1st Half 10-30 .333, 2nd Half 12-35 .343, Game 22-65 .338; 3FG%: 1st Half 1-6 .167, 2nd Half 5-18 .278, Game 6-24 .250; FT%: 1st Half 7-11 .636, 2nd Half 13-15 .867, Game 20-26 .769; Team Rebounds: 0; Deadball Rebounds: 3.

Michigan State	FG-FGA	FT-FTA	REB	PF	TP	A	TO	BLK	S	MIN
Jason Richardson	7-11	5-6	1	3	21	2	0	0	7	26
Andre Hutson	6-8	5-10	6	2	17	0	2	0	0	30
Aloysius Anagonye	1-2	0-0	2	4	2	0	1	0	1	13
David Thomas	2-5	3-3	6	1	7	2	1	0	3	22
Charlie Bell	5-9	4-4	2	3	16	5	4	0	1	28
Marcus Taylor	4-6	0-0	4	2	8	8	1	1	0	24
Adam Wolfe	0-1	2-2	0	2	2	0	0	0	0	5
Brandon Smith	0-1	0-0	0	0	0	1	1	0	0	3
Mat Ishbia	0-1	0-0	0	0	0	0	0	0	2	2
Mike Chappell	1-1	2-3	1	0	4	1	0	0	0	12
Jason Andreas	0-0	1-2	2	3	1	0	1	0	0	5
Zach Randolph	3-7	8-11	3	5	14	1	1	0	0	14
Adam Ballinger	1-4	0-0	3	1	2	1	0	1	0	16
Totals	29-65	12-16	53	16	72	18	12	9	6	200

Three-Point Field Goals: Richardson 2-3, Bell 2-4, Taylor 0-1, Wolfe 0-1, Smith 0-1, Team 4-10.

FG%: 1st Half 12-27 .444, 2nd Half 18-29 .621, Game 30-56 .536; 3FG%: 1st Half 1-4 .250, 2nd Half 3-6 .500, Game 4-10 .400; FT%: 1st Half 13-19 .684, 2nd Half 17-22 .773, Game 30-41 .732; Team Rebounds: 4; Deadball Rebounds: 7.

SCORE BY PERIODS	1	2	F
Iowa	28	42	70
Michigan State	38	56	94

OFFICIALS – Ed Hightower, Mike Sanzere, Ted Valentine
TECHNICAL FOULS – None
ATTENDANCE – 14,759

MSU 66, Indiana 57
Feb. 20, 2001 • Breslin Center • East Lansing, Mich.

Indiana	FG-FGA	FT-FTA	REB	PF	TP	A	TO	BLK	S	MIN
Jared Jeffries	4-15	1-2	5	4	9	3	3	0	1	39
Jeffrey Newton	0-0	0-0	1	1	0	1	0	0	1	15
Kirk Haston	8-16	0-0	3	5	18	0	2	2	0	30
Tom Coverdale	2-7	0-0	3	4	6	6	2	0	1	31
Dane Fife	2-5	1-2	4	3	7	1	1	0	0	23
A.J. Moye	0-2	0-0	2	1	0	0	1	0	1	2
George Leach	0-2	0-0	1	0	0	0	0	1	0	2
Andre Owens	1-4	1-1	3	1	3	1	2	0	1	24
Kyle Hornsby	3-8	0-0	2	1	8	1	2	1	0	22
Jarrad Odle	1-1	3-4	5	2	6	0	0	0	0	12
Totals	21-60	6-9	31	22	57	13	13	3	6	200

Three-Point Field Goals: Jeffries 0-2, Haston 2-3, Coverdale 2-4, Fife 2-2, Owens 0-2, Hornsby 2-4, Odle 1-1, Team 9-18.

FG%: 1st Half 10-28 .357, 2nd Half 11-32 .344, Game 21-60 .350; 3FG%: 1st Half 2-7 .286, 2nd Half 7-11 .636, Game 9-18 .500; FT%: 1st Half 1-1 1.000, 2nd Half 5-8 .625, Game 6-9 .667; Team Rebounds: 2; Deadball Rebounds: 1.

Michigan State	FG-FGA	FT-FTA	REB	PF	TP	A	TO	BLK	S	MIN
Jason Richardson	2-10	4-6	6	0	8	0	2	2	2	31
Andre Hutson	5-10	5-6	5	4	15	0	1	1	0	31
Aloysius Anagonye	2-4	0-0	4	3	4	1	1	1	0	17
David Thomas	4-4	3-4	8	1	11	1	1	1	1	26
Charlie Bell	2-7	3-4	4	1	8	5	6	0	1	32
Marcus Taylor	1-5	0-0	1	0	2	3	1	0	0	25
Mike Chappell	0-1	0-0	2	0	0	1	1	0	0	8
Zach Randolph	4-5	6-9	9	3	14	0	0	1	1	24
Adam Ballinger	1-3	2-2	1	2	4	0	0	0	0	6
Totals	21-49	23-31	44	14	66	11	13	6	5	200

Three-Point Field Goals: Richardson 0-3, Bell 1-3, Team 1-6.

FG%: 1st Half 12-31 .387, 2nd Half 9-18 .500, Game 21-49 .429; 3FG%: 1st Half 1-5 .200, 2nd Half 0-1 .000, Game 1-6 .167; FT%: 1st Half 8-10 .800, 2nd Half 15-21 .714, Game 23-31 .742; Team Rebounds: 4; Deadball Rebounds: 2.

SCORE BY PERIODS	1	2	F
Indiana	23	34	57
Michigan State	33	33	66

OFFICIALS – Jim Burr, Steve Welmer, Donnee Gray
TECHNICAL FOULS – None
ATTENDANCE – 14,759

Photo Credit: Kevin Fowler, MSU Sports Information

MSU 76, Penn State 57
Feb. 24, 2001 • Bryce Jordan Center • State College, Pa.

Michigan State	FG-FGA	FT-FTA	REB	PF	TP	A	TO	BLK	S	MIN
Jason Richardson	7-14	2-2	7	2	16	3	2	1	1	32
Andre Hutson	5-7	1-2	16	4	11	4	4	1	3	34
Aloysius Anagonye	3-6	2-3	3	2	8	1	1	0	1	20
Marcus Taylor	2-6	1-2	2	1	5	3	1	1	1	20
Charlie Bell	5-12	5-7	2	2	16	3	3	0	2	33
Adam Wolfe	0-0	0-0	0	1	0	0	0	1	0	1
Brandon Smith	0-0	0-0	0	1	0	0	0	0	0	3
David Thomas	0-3	0-0	5	1	0	1	0	1	1	23
Mat Ishbia	0-0	0-0	0	0	0	0	0	0	0	1
Mike Chappell	2-3	0-0	0	1	5	0	0	0	0	7
Jason Andreas	0-0	0-0	0	0	0	0	0	0	0	1
Zach Randolph	5-9	0-2	8	2	10	1	1	1	0	14
Adam Ballinger	2-3	1-2	2	1	5	0	0	0	0	11
Totals	31-63	12-20	48	18	76	16	12	6	9	200

Three-Point Field Goals: Richardson 0-3, Taylor 0-2, Bell 1-4, Thomas 0-1, Chappell 1-1, Team 2-11.
FG%: 1st Half 17-38 .447, 2nd Half 14-25 .560, Game 31-63 .492; 3FG%: 1st Half 2-8 .250, 2nd Half 0-3 .000, Game 2-11 .182; FT%: 1st Half 2-3 .667, 2nd Half 10-17 .588, Game 12-20 .600; Team Rebounds: 3; Deadball Rebounds: 4.

Penn State	FG-FGA	FT-FTA	REB	PF	TP	A	TO	BLK	S	MIN
Gyasi Cline-Heard	6-12	4-9	10	3	16	1	2	1	1	34
Tyler Smith	2-6	2-2	1	3	7	2	0	1	2	27
Joe Crispin	6-23	2-2	4	3	16	1	2	1	2	37
Jon Crispin	1-4	0-0	3	1	2	3	2	0	1	23
Titus Ivory	2-11	0-0	6	4	5	3	4	0	2	31
Jamaal Tate	1-1	0-0	0	1	2	0	1	0	0	9
Ken Krimmel	0-0	0-0	0	0	0	0	0	0	0	1
Brandon Watkins	1-3	0-0	2	0	3	1	2	0	0	16
Sharif Chambliss	0-2	0-0	1	0	0	0	0	0	0	1
Stephan Bekale	0-0	0-0	1	1	0	0	0	0	0	1
B.J. Vossekuil	0-0	0-0	0	0	0	0	0	0	0	2
Marcus Banta	2-5	0-0	4	1	4	0	0	0	0	13
Ndu Egekeze	1-1	0-0	1	1	2	0	0	0	0	3
Scott Witkowsky	0-0	0-0	0	0	0	0	0	0	0	2
Totals	22-68	8-13	35	18	24	11	13	3	8	200

Three-Point Field Goals: Smith 1-2, Joe Crispin 2-10, Jon Crispin 0-1, Ivory 1-6, Watkins 1-2, Chambliss 0-2, Team 5-23.
FG%: 1st Half 12-28 .429, 2nd Half 10-40 .250, Game 22-68 .324; 3FG%: 1st Half 2-9 .222, 2nd Half 3-14 .214, Game 5-23 .217; FT%: 1st Half 4-6 .667, 2nd Half 4-7 .571, Game 8-13 .615; Team Rebounds: 2; Deadball Rebounds: 4.

SCORE BY PERIODS	1	2		F
Michigan State	38	38	--	76
Penn State	30	27	--	57

OFFICIALS – Ted Hillary, Tom Clark, Randy Drury
TECHNICAL FOULS – None
ATTENDANCE – 15,377

MSU 51, Wisconsin 47
Feb. 27, 2001 • Kohl Center • Madison, Wis.

Michigan State	FG-FGA	FT-FTA	REB	PF	TP	A	TO	BLK	S	MIN
David Thomas	0-1	2-2	3	0	2	1	1	1	1	29
Aloysius Anagonye	0-0	0-0	3	3	0	0	1	0	1	20
Andre Hutson	5-10	3-3	5	2	13	0	5	0	0	36
Charlie Bell	2-9	5-7	1	2	10	3	2	0	0	32
Jason Richardson	4-11	1-2	9	2	11	3	0	2	0	36
Marcus Taylor	3-4	0-0	2	2	7	1	0	0	0	16
Mike Chappell	0-0	0-0	3	0	0	0	0	0	0	7
Zach Randolph	3-4	0-0	4	1	6	1	4	0	2	16
Adam Ballinger	1-2	0-0	0	1	2	0	0	1	0	8
Totals	18-41	11-14	31	13	51	9	13	4	3	200

Three-Point Field Goals: Bell 1-3, Richardson 2-4, Taylor 1-2, Team 4-9.
FG%: 1st Half 11-21 .524, 2nd Half 7-20 .350, Game 18-41 .439; 3FG%: 1st Half 2-4 .500, 2nd Half 2-5 .400, Game 4-9 .444; FT%: 1st Half 4-4 1.000, 2nd Half 7-10 .700, Game 11-14 .786; Team Rebounds: 3; Deadball Rebounds: 0.

Wisconsin	FG-FGA	FT-FTA	REB	PF	TP	A	TO	BLK	S	MIN
Maurice Linton	2-4	0-0	0	0	5	1	1	0	0	16
Andy Kowske	6-8	0-0	5	3	12	0	2	1	0	30
Mark Vershaw	0-3	1-2	1	0	1	2	1	0	0	24
Mike Kelley	1-3	1-2	2	2	4	3	1	0	3	38
Roy Boone	3-10	0-0	4	3	6	6	3	0	1	30
Travon Davis	0-0	0-0	0	1	0	0	1	0	0	2
Kirk Penney	4-8	2-3	2	2	13	0	0	1	0	35
Charlie Wills	2-6	0-0	4	2	6	0	1	0	0	25
Totals	18-42	4-7	22	13	47	12	10	2	4	200

Three-Point Field Goals: Linton 1-1, Vershaw 0-1, Kelley 1-3, Boone 0-4, Penney 3-6, Wills 2-2, Team 7-17.
FG%: 1st Half 8-23 .348, 2nd Half 10-19 .526, Game 18-42 .429; 3FG%: 1st Half 3-10 .300, 2nd Half 4-7 .571, Game 7-17 .412; FT%: 1st Half 1-2 .500, 2nd Half 3-5 .600, Game 4-7 .571; Team Rebounds: 4; Deadball Rebounds: 0.

SCORE BY PERIODS	1	2		F
Michigan State	28	23	--	51
Wisconsin	20	27	--	47

OFFICIALS – Ed Hightower, Ted Hillary, Tom O'Neill
TECHNICAL FOULS – None
ATTENDANCE – 17,142

MSU 78, Michigan 57
March 3, 2001 • Breslin Center • East Lansing, Mich.

Michigan	FG-FGA	FT-FTA	REB	PF	TP	A	TO	BLK	S	MIN
Bernard Robinson Jr.	8-13	2-3	1	0	19	3	1	0	0	37
Josh Asselin	1-2	6-6	0	5	8	1	1	1	1	24
Chris Young	3-3	0-1	3	4	6	1	0	1	0	25
Avery Queen	5-10	0-0	1	0	11	8	3	0	1	37
LaVell Blanchard	2-11	0-0	9	3	5	3	2	1	0	34
Leon Jones	1-2	0-0	2	0	2	0	0	0	0	7
Colin Dill	0-1	0-0	0	0	0	0	0	0	1	2
Jermaine Gonzales	0-0	0-0	0	0	0	0	0	0	1	1
Herb Gibson	0-0	0-0	0	0	0	0	0	0	0	3
Mike Gotfredson	0-1	0-0	0	0	0	0	0	0	0	3
Gavin Groninger	0-1	0-0	4	2	0	0	0	0	0	11
Josh Moore	3-5	0-0	2	5	6	0	4	0	0	16
Totals	23-49	8-10	23	19	57	16	11	3	2	200

Three-Point Field Goals: Robinson 1-3, Queen 1-4, Blanchard 1-3, Groninger 0-1, Team 3-11.
FG%: 1st Half 10-20 .500, 2nd Half 13-29 .448, Game 23-49 .469; 3FG%: 1st Half 1-5 .200, 2nd Half 2-6 .333, Game 3-11 .273; FT%: 1st Half 6-7 .857, 2nd Half 2-3 .667, Game 8-10 .800; Team Rebounds: 1; Deadball Rebounds: 0.

Michigan State	FG-FGA	FT-FTA	REB	PF	TP	A	TO	BLK	S	MIN
David Thomas	2-4	2-2	3	1	6	3	1	0	1	24
Mike Chappell	1-5	0-0	2	2	3	1	0	0	1	16
Andre Hutson	7-12	5-6	9	1	19	3	0	0	0	28
Brandon Smith	0-0	0-0	1	3	0	0	0	0	0	7
Charlie Bell	2-11	0-0	7	1	6	7	3	0	1	28
Marcus Taylor	2-6	2-3	1	0	6	3	1	1	0	23
Adam Wolfe	1-2	0-0	0	0	2	0	0	0	0	3
Mat Ishbia	0-0	0-0	1	1	0	0	1	0	0	3
Jason Richardson	6-10	1-2	4	1	15	2	0	1	0	25
Aloysius Anagonye	3-3	3-5	5	0	9	1	0	0	1	15
Jason Andreas	0-0	0-0	1	1	0	0	1	0	0	3
Zach Randolph	3-5	5-6	3	3	11	0	1	0	1	16
Adam Ballinger	0-0	1-2	2	2	1	0	0	1	0	9
Totals	27-58	19-26	41	15	78	20	9	3	5	200

Three-Point Field Goals: Chappell 1-4, Bell 2-8, Taylor 0-2, Richardson 2-4, Team 5-18.
FG%: 1st Half 14-29 .483, 2nd Half 13-29 .448, Game 27-58 .466; 3FG%: 1st Half 4-10 .400, 2nd Half 1-8 .125, Game 5-18 .278; FT%: 1st Half 10-15 .667, 2nd Half 9-11 .818, Game 19-26 .731; Team Rebounds: 2; Deadball Rebounds: 2.

Score By Periods	1	2		F
Michigan	27	30	--	57
Michigan State	42	36	--	78

Officials – Phil Bova, Tom Clark, Mike Spanier
Technical Fouls – None
Attendance – 14,759

2001 BIG TEN TOURNAMENT

Tom Izzo is a firm believer that nothing good ever comes from defeat. Champions don't need to learn how to lose. And it's a feeling that doesn't require much practice.

But every so often, it isn't the worst thing in the world to come to grips with your shortcomings. When that happens the way it did to Michigan State on March 9 in Chicago, it can be a blessing in disguise.

After winning the previous two Big Ten Tournaments, the Spartans arrived at the United Center with a 6-1 record in the event's three-year history, by far the best for any participant.

And they remain the only program in the league that has never had to play on Thursday, when the bottom six seeds meet in 8-vs.-9, 7-vs.-10 and 6-vs.-11, first-round games.

If MSU could play on Thursday and skip Friday, it might be a lot better off, since it has always struggled on Friday and won convincingly on Saturday and Sunday.

This time, the Spartans were a No. 2 seed after losing at Illinois in the conference co-champions' only meeting. That meant a second-round date with seventh-seeded Penn State, an 82-80 winner over Michigan on a last-second putback from forward Gyasi Cline-Heard.

Before MSU knew its assignment, Izzo was asked about a projected rematch with the Fighting Illini for bragging rights and a certain No. 1 seed in the NCAA Tournament's Midwest Region.

"I think that would settle some things," he said. "But one good thing about our guys is they haven't looked ahead very much. That's a pretty good quality to have. Yet, we're all human. We've been beaten by teams we'd like another shot at. We just have to make sure we don't stumble in the meantime."

With a No. 3 national ranking, a 24-3 mark with wins over North Carolina, Florida and Kentucky and a six-game winning streak, the Spartans thought they needed two more triumphs to be the No. 1 seed in the Midwest or the South.

That seemed like a reasonable expectation for a team that entered the week No. 1 in the league in scoring (79.0), margin of victory (17.1), field-goal percentage (49.4), rebound margin (15.4) and assist/turnover ratio (1.33/1) and No. 2 in scoring defense (61.9) and free-throw accuracy (73.4).

"We have to get through the first game first," Izzo said. "So many things can happen there. As for being a No. 1 seed, from what I've been told, a lot of times that's determined by Saturday. If we get that far, should we be a No. 1?...I know I'd vote for us."

Izzo didn't have a vote in the *USA TODAY*/ESPN coaches poll, let alone the NCAA Selection Committee. His only power that week was the ability to shape his players' attitudes.

"If we do play Illinois, it'll be a great opportunity and a good championship game," senior forward Andre Hutson said. "But

Penn State is definitely a tough team to play. The last couple of years, they've knocked off some top teams. They have some great shooters and run the floor well. If you catch them on the wrong night, they can really shoot the lights out."

Photo Credit: Kevin Fowler, MSU Sports Information

2001 BIG TEN TOURNAMENT

As a No. 9 seed in 2000, the Nittany Lions stunned No. 1 Ohio State in Chicago. Jerry Dunn's latest team had already beaten Kentucky in November and the Fighting Illini in January, besides leading MSU in the second half of both matchups. And Penn State's best was yet to come in the NCAA Tournament's South Region.

"I'm excited about playing them again," Penn State guard Titus Ivory said of the Spartans after ending the Wolverines' season. "We hung in there with them in the previous games. But they're a very deep team that's very well-coached. We just ran out of gas."

Most teams' tanks have been full when they have played MSU. And if the Spartans weren't Duke yet, as Izzo insisted they weren't, they were beginning to get a taste of what the Blue Devils faced in every game. A win over either team was reason for fans to flood the floor.

"It seems like we're always the conference champions," senior guard David Thomas said. "There's a tendency to think, 'This will be a breeze.' But it's not like that. Other teams are determined to play well. They're trying to get into the NCAA Tournament. So we always get their A-game. We realize that by the second day and usually play better."

Not this time. A 65-63 loss to the Nittany Lions snapped a 10-game win string for MSU in Greater Chicago — six victories in the Big Ten Tournament, two at Northwestern, one in the Great Eight and one at Loyola.

The Spartans grabbed a 19-7 lead, outshot Penn State 47.7 percent to 40.0 from the field and had a 39-26 edge in rebounds. But they lost for three reasons: 16-for-30 work at the foul line, including three misses on the front ends of one-and-ones; 17 turnovers that led to 21 points and huge plays by Ivory and point guard Joe Crispin.

"There were a lot of pivotal moments," Izzo said. "I thought the difference was that one team looked better-coached than the other. We didn't look very organized. And they looked very organized."

Back-to-back bombs by Crispin, ESPN's 3-point champ at the Final Four, gave the Nittany Lions a 52-49 lead. And after MSU forward Jason Richardson's 3 put his team up 57-55, Ivory answered from deep in the left corner to give his team a one-point advantage.

With Penn State on top 60-59, Crispin split Hutson and guard Charlie Bell and hit a leaping leaner from 21 feet with 21.9 seconds left. Richardson countered with a tough, 20-footer to cut the deficit to 63-62 with 7.4 seconds showing.

After Crispin made it a three-point game from the line, Dunn wisely fouled point guard Marcus Taylor with 1.5 seconds left, before the Spartans could launch a tying try. After Taylor hit the first shot, an intentional miss was grabbed by the Nittany Lions. MSU had missed too many free throws to expect a miracle off a planned clanger.

Crispin finished with 22 points and finally played under control against the Spartans. And Ivory added 17 points, four assists and three steals. Richardson led MSU with 19 points, while Hutson had 17, plus nine rebounds.

"These guys have accomplished a lot," Izzo said of four Big Ten regular-season titles and two Tournament crowns since 1998. "But I said last week I thought maybe they taught me another way to win. . . . I like my way better."

Questions about the team's quiet personality and play against Penn State didn't faze the Selection Committee. A rash of surprises, including sixth-seeded Iowa over fourth-seeded Indiana for the Big Ten title, helped the Spartans earn a No. 1 seed in the South. The only outcome that could have changed that might have been a North Carolina win, instead of a blowout by Duke, in the ACC final.

By the time the pairings were announced Sunday evening, MSU had already had two excellent practices in Breslin. Back home and back to work, Izzo's team had used the weekend to refocus for another march to the Final Four.

If the Spartans had won three games in Chicago, they would have been No. 1 in the Midwest and would have played Kansas and Arizona in San Antonio, instead of Gonzaga and Temple in Atlanta.

Some late-season losses don't hurt much at all.

Penn State 65, MSU 63
March 9, 2001 • United Center • Chicago, Ill.

Penn State	FG-FGA	FT-FTA	REB	PF	TP	A	TO	BLK	S	MIN
Tyler Smith	1-3	4-5	6	3	6	3	2	1	1	34
Gyasi Cline-Heard	4-8	2-2	3	3	10	1	1	0	0	28
Titus Ivory	7-14	0-0	4	2	17	4	0	1	3	34
Jon Crispin	2-3	2-3	1	1	7	4	0	0	1	29
Joe Crispin	6-15	6-6	1	3	22	4	4	0	1	35
Jamaal Tate	0-2	3-4	2	3	3	0	0	0	0	10
Brandon Watkins	0-2	0-1	1	1	0	0	1	0	1	9
Sharif Chambliss	0-0	0-0	0	1	0	0	0	0	0	2
Stephan Bekale	0-1	0-1	0	1	0	0	1	0	0	4
Marcus Banta	0-1	0-0	0	4	0	0	0	0	0	6
Ndu Egekeze	0-1	0-0	2	2	0	0	1	0	0	6
Scott Witkowsky	0-0	0-0	1	1	0	0	0	0	0	3
Totals	20-50	17-22	26	25	65	16	10	2	7	200

Three-Point Field Goals: Smith 0-1, Ivory 3-5, Jon Crispin 1-1, Joe Crispin 4-11, Tate 0-2, Team 8-20.
FG%: 1st Half 10-26 .385, 2nd Half 10-24 .417, Game 20-50 .400; 3FG%: 1st Half 3-10 .300, 2nd Half 5-10 .500, Game 8-20 .400; FT%: 1st Half 8-11 .727, 2nd Half 9-11 .818, Game 17-22 .773; Team Rebounds: 5; Deadball Rebounds: 2.

Michigan State	FG-FGA	FT-FTA	REB	PF	TP	A	TO	BLK	S	MIN
Andre Hutson	5-8	7-8	9	3	17	1	3	0	0	35
Aloysius Anagonye	0-1	1-3	1	4	1	2	1	2	0	17
David Thomas	1-1	0-0	3	5	2	1	3	1	1	25
Jason Richardson	6-15	4-7	6	1	19	1	0	0	4	36
Charlie Bell	2-6	1-4	2	5	6	6	1	0	0	29
Marcus Taylor	0-3	1-4	0	1	1	0	2	0	0	18
Brandon Smith	0-0	0-0	0	0	0	0	0	0	0	1
Mike Chappell	2-2	2-4	2	1	7	0	2	0	0	11
Jason Andreas	0-0	0-0	0	0	0	0	0	0	0	1
Zach Randolph	5-8	0-0	9	2	10	1	2	1	0	19
Adam Ballinger	0-0	0-0	1	1	0	0	2	1	0	8
Totals	21-44	16-30	39	23	63	12	17	5	6	200

Three-Point Field Goals: Richardson 3-5, Bell 1-2, Taylor 0-1, Chappell 1-1, Team 5-9.
FG%: 1st Half 11-24 .458, 2nd Half 10-20 .500, Game 21-44 .477; 3FG%: 1st Half 1-5 .200, 2nd Half 4-4 1.000, Game 5-9 .556; FT%: 1st Half 7-12 .583, 2nd Half 9-18 .500, Game 16-30 .533; Team Rebounds: 6; Deadball Rebounds: 5.

SCORE BY PERIODS	1	2	F
Penn State	31	34	-- 65
Michigan State	30	33	-- 63

OFFICIALS – Donnee Gray, Phil Bova, Jerry Petro
TECHNICAL FOULS – None
ATTENDANCE – 21,739

Photo Credit: Kevin Fowler, MSU Sports Information

Photo Credit: Kevin Fowler, MSU Sports Information

Photo Credit: Kevin Fowler, MSU Sports Information

2001 NCAA TOURNAMENT

In Tom Izzo's first season as Michigan State's head coach, the Spartans just hoped to qualify for a tournament — the NIT. Five years later, the reigning national champs would have been ridiculed for anything less than a third-straight Final Four appearance.

That was the minimum expectation for MSU as an NCAA No. 1 seed for the third year in a row, a feat surpassed only by Duke (1998-2001) and matched by DePaul (1980-82), Virginia (1981-83), Oklahoma (1988-90) and Kentucky (1995-97).

CBS analyst Clark Kellogg was the only expert who insisted 24-7 Illinois would be No. 1 in the Midwest and the 24-4 Spartans No. 1 in the South, regardless of what North Carolina did against Duke in the ACC Tournament's title game.

ESPN'S Jay Bilas was on the right track, however. He put both Big Ten co-champs ahead of the 25-6 Tar Heels, who lost 77-64 in November in East Lansing but were the nation's top-ranked team in both polls until a late swoon.

"I think the No. 1 seed in the South will go to Michigan State or Illinois," Bilas said. "I'd put Michigan State ahead of North Carolina. Michigan State won head-to-head, has more Top 25 wins and finished stronger. The NCAA Selection Committee looks at what you've done on the road and in big games on neutral courts. The fact that Illinois didn't have to go to Michigan State and Wisconsin is meaningful."

The Selection Committee Chairman, Big East Commissioner Mike Tranghese, said the toughest decision wasn't whether the Spartans should be a No. 1, but where that first-round assignment should be — in Dayton, Ohio, or Memphis, Tenn.

"Trying to evaluate Illinois and Michigan State was brutally hard," Tranghese said after the pairings were announced. "They tied for the Big Ten championship. But Illinois won the one game they played — at Illinois. It went one

game further in the conference tournament. And its non-conference schedule was a little tougher than Michigan State's."

Thus, the Spartans were the No. 4 overall seed — behind Stanford, Duke and the Fighting Illini. That meant MSU forward Andre Hutson, a native of Trotwood, Ohio, near Dayton, would head to Memphis, while Illinois guard Cory Bradford, a Memphis product, would go to Dayton.

"Being in the South is fine with me," Izzo said. "I thought we had a shot being a Midwest No. 1, a South No. 1 or a South No. 2. But Illinois had a heckuva season. Those guys probably deserved to be in Dayton. I think they did it right. And I'm going to be pulling for Illinois until the Final Four."

The Illini didn't get there, losing for the second time in three games with Arizona. But before the Spartans would get their crack at Lute Olson's Wildcats, they would have to navigate a South Region minefield that saw six upsets in its first 12 games.

As Izzo's team tried to make history and become just the second repeat champ in 28 years, it would have to do that without three starters and two NBA first-round picks from the 2000 team. When Duke repeated in 1992, the only starter gone was role player Greg Koubek.

But MSU's first goal was to avoid being the first No. 1 seed to lose to a No. 16. That meant it had to beat 22-8 Alabama State Friday night at The Pyramid in the state

where it nearly lost to No. 16 Murray State 11 years earlier.

"If you don't think that haunts you at night . . . " Izzo said, recalling a 75-71 overtime escape against Popeye Jones and the

Racers. "That's pressure in its own way. It really is. I don't know if there have been any other overtime games with a No. 16. But I was involved in one. I have experience in that area."

2001 NCAA TOURNAMENT

The Spartans' last break in concentration came Monday night, when Hutson was the co-recipient of five awards at a jammed MSU Basketball Bust. He shared the players-vote MVP award with forward Jason Richardson and the media-vote honor with guard Charlie Bell.

"Sometimes this team is too serious," Izzo said. "Maybe that's the expectations of perfection. We could use a little more swagger. We need a jerk. . . . That's why I'm here. But there's a fine line between cocky and confident. You have to have confidence in your own ability. Sometimes we lack that."

That didn't mean the Spartans would relax in preparation — far from it. While MSU fans enjoyed plenty of barbecue and saw tourist attractions like Graceland, the former home of Elvis Presley, the players and coaches were all-business in Tennessee.

"I don't think there will be many social events on this trip, for me or my players," Izzo said, before being asked if that was because Elvis lacked appeal in Iron Mountain. "He got there about 20 years late. . . . But he was big when he got there."

No conference was as big as the Big Ten when it came to NCAA Tournament invitations. Seven teams from the league received bids, just the fifth time any conference could say that. But by Thursday night, fourth-seeded Indiana, fifth-seeded Ohio State and sixth-seeded Wisconsin had been stunned, turning the pressure higher.

The Spartans were accustomed to that. And coming off a loss, they had proven to be more focused. After their last 11 losses over a two-year span, they had won the following games by an average of 26.7 points.

So when Izzo answered questions the day before the first-round games and insisted MSU still wasn't an elite program, despite one of the best four-year runs in NCAA history, the stupified responses were understandable.

"If Tom hasn't built an elite program, he has built the closest thing to it," said *Sports Illustrated's* Seth Davis, a 1992 Duke graduate who was there for the Blue Devils' run of five straight Final Fours. "If you look at where Michigan State is now, until someone beats them, they're it. And compared to Duke, people forget how close 'Coach K' came to getting fired."

Krzyzewski survived 10-17 and 11-17 records in his second and third seasons in Durham, N.C. Izzo has never had a losing record in league play or overall, though his protestations of woe would suggest otherwise.

"Is he crazy?" said Virginia coach Pete Gillen, who picked MSU to beat Kentucky for the title and couldn't believe Izzo was resisting elite status. "Tell him he better stop drinking. His team is unbelievable. I saw them close up at the Jimmy V Classic. They play great defense. They rebound everything. And they have the best pair of freshmen in the country. What do I know? The last time I picked a winner, Moby Dick was a

minnow. But Michigan State is Noah's Ark. It has two of everything."

It also had a growing preoccupation with the biggest fish in the college basketball sea — Moby Duke. Consistency and killer-instinct have set the Blue Devils apart. But the Spartans were closer to the five-time ACC champs than Izzo was willing to admit.

"Every year I try to set a new goal," he said of catching Duke, his season-long pick to win the title. "This one is totally out of respect. I'm amazed at how they never beat themselves. Injuries and this and that, it just doesn't seem to matter. They find a way to get it done. It's like they're playing for every guy who ever played at Duke. That's my ultimate dream here."

The Spartans had received calls from Mateen Cleaves and Morris Peterson soon after the brackets were unveiled. But they didn't need a lot of outside assistance to handle the Hornets of the Southwestern Athletic Conference.

All MSU needed for a 69-35 triumph was a 40-10 second half, including 26 straight points near the end of the game. Bob Chappell, Mike's dad, and Noreese Underwood, Clarence's wife, had attended Alabama State roughly 40 years earlier. And both could have helped the Hornets in the last 10 minutes.

Though the Spartans sputtered through much of the first half and led just 29-25 at the break, they pitched a shutout for 13:56 until Alabama State finally scored with 14 seconds left. That 3-pointer kept MSU from matching the lowest yield for an NCAA first- or second-round game.

"It wasn't our normal get-after-it, get-after-it halftime," Izzo said, recalling the charged atmosphere for three straight comebacks a year earlier in the NCAA's Midwest Region. "I didn't think it was time to do that. The necktie gets tighter as the game goes on."

Whatever happened at half-time worked, as MSU shook off the rust of playing just once in 13 days and renewed its commitment to defense and running.

"The difference was mostly attitude," guard David Thomas said. "A couple of guys said a few words — Andre, 'J-Rich' and myself. But it wasn't like last year when Mateen would go off. We didn't have to do that this time."

Not when Hutson was 7-for-7 from the field in a 15-point, 11-rebound performance. Richardson added 14 points and center Zach Randolph 12 in his first NCAA Tournament game, as the Spartans outshot the Hornets 48.2 percent to 25.0 from the field and outrebounded them 48-26.

That set up a second-round matchup with 26-6 Fresno State, the regular-season champ in the Western Athletic Conference and a ninth seed that advanced to Sunday's play with an 82-70 win over eighth-seeded California.

The Bulldogs knew their bench would be tested as it hadn't been all season. As Jerry Tarkanian, the NCAA's winningest coach and No. 1 enemy over the years, said Saturday afternoon,

"We've got guys who were All-Neighborhood. They bring in guys who were All-Americans."

Fresno State needed to bring in Larry Johnson and Greg

Anthony from Tarkanian's 1990 champs at UNLV to stay with MSU in an 81-65 decision. The Spartans led 22-11, then 34-20 before sloppy ballhandling and the Bulldogs'

Photo Credit: Kevin Fowler, MSU Sports Information

2001 NCAA Tournament

pressure made it 37-30 at the half. But up 61-54 with 9:37 left, a 12-2 run blew it open before a sparse gathering of 10,719, including ex-MSU football coach Nick Saban.

As he fought back the tears before a courtside interview, Izzo didn't care that the South Region bracket looked like a bomb scene. He didn't even know second-seeded North Carolina had lost to Penn State, joining third-seeded Florida, fourth-seeded Oklahoma, fifth-seeded Virginia and sixth-seeded Texas as first-week rubble.

"I don't want to like my team too much," Izzo said after it earned a fourth-straight trip to the Sweet 16. "It's illegal for a coach to do that when a team still has games to play. But I'm damn proud of this team. All the spokes came together today."

Thomas had 10 points and a career-high 14 rebounds in 27 minutes, more than any two Fresno State players snared in nearly triple that time. Sophomore forward Aloysius Anagonye played his best game all season — the best of his life, Izzo joked — with a career-high 13 points. And Hutson had 12 points, eight rebounds and five assists, many after returning to the game with a brace on his sprained right shoulder.

"You can't even dream about something like this," said Thomas, whose six offensive rebounds matched any Bulldog's total at both ends. "Growing up, you heard so much about the Sweet 16 and the Final Four. To be in the Sweet 16 four times says so much about the people in this program."

2001 NCAA TOURNAMENT

Photo Credit: Kevin Fowler, MSU Sports Information

Bell had nine of his 13 points in the second half and contributed six rebounds to a 48-32 disparity. Freshman point guard Marcus Taylor played like a senior with 11 points and just one turnover against Fresno State's frenetic half-court defense. And Randolph had six points, three rebounds, two assists and a blocked shot, while drawing key fouls on center Melvin Ely, who had 17 points in just 27 minutes.

That all-out, all-for-one effort sent 26-4 MSU to Atlanta. There, it would face 26-6 Gonzaga, a 12th seed that had proven itself to everyone except the Selection Committee with a third-straight

Sweet 16 appearance.

"Like they said on TV, 'Why not just make Gonzaga a fourth or fifth seed since it plays that way every year?'" Izzo said. "But I'm going to take a few hours and enjoy this one first. We're a No. 1 seed that isn't being talked about like Duke and Stanford. And maybe we haven't earned that. But we laid it all on the line today."

At least Izzo and his staff knew a lot about their next opponent. They knew the name was pronounced "gone-ZAG-uh," not "gon-ZAH-gah." They knew the Jesuit school of roughly 4,000 students had produced more quality players than just John Stockton. And they knew its monogram logo, GU, stood for Grossly Underrated, not just Guard University.

Izzo knew all those things after working 12 seasons for Jud Heathcote, a long-time Gonzaga follower who relocated near its campus in Spokane, Wash., when he retired in 1995. Heathcote still had lunch each week with second-year head coach Mark Few — "Tuesdays with Jud," Few called them. But Izzo's mentor left zero doubt he wanted the Spartans to win in the Georgia Dome.

To do that, MSU had to respect the Bulldogs' surprising athleticism. And it had to contain a terrific tandem of quick, clever point guard Dan Dickau and strong, savvy center Casey Calvary, who were averaging a combined 38.0 points.

"Dickau kind of reminds me of Scott Skiles," Izzo said of

Basketball Times' 1986 National Player of the Year, a supreme complement from an assistant coach on that team. "He can go to his left, go to his right, penetrate and shoot from way out. He can beat you in a lot of different ways."

As Few said, Gonzaga didn't have to win a best four-of-seven series. It only had to beat the Spartans on Friday, March 23. The headline writers were ready with: "A Few Good Men." But during Thursday's one-hour, open practices, a veteran of NCAA Tournament play insisted that

Photo Credit: Kevin Fowler, MSU Sports Information

Photo Credit: Kevin Fowler, MSU Sports Information

would never happen.

"The thing that's so impressive about this year's team is it doesn't rely on any one player," said Ron "Bobo" Charles, a key role player for MSU's 1979 champs and an Atlanta resident who followed the Spartans religiously. "But the guy I really like on this team is David Thomas. He has always been the unsung hero. Now that he has his confidence, watch out."

His prediction for stardom would have to wait a couple of days, as Thomas was held scoreless in 18 minutes. But trailing 44-41 with 14:53 to play, his team took control with a 28-9 surge over the next 11 minutes and won 77-62 — a record, ninth-straight win by at least 11 points in NCAA Tournament play.

For Gonzaga, it was like wrestling pythons. Eventually, the Bulldogs were squeezed to death, with Bell scoring a game-high 21 points, grabbing 10 rebounds and smothering Dickau until the outcome was decided.

"They were getting a little fatigued," Bell said after the Spartans had won the rebounding battle, 49-29. "We were a little tired, also. But we knew it was Winning Time. We've been in that situation before. That's when you have to suck it up."

The Spartans did that with depth. Though Hutson had 19 points and 10 rebounds, it took contributions from Richardson, who overcame food poisoning early in the week, plus Taylor, Randolph, Chappell and Adam Ballinger to give MSU its seventh Elite Eight opportunity.

"I can't say enough about Gonzaga," Izzo said. "But I was really disappointed by our play in the first half, to be blunt about it. We emphasized transition defense. And they hurt us with the fast break. Then, we said we weren't going to jack up 3's . . . and we took 13. That's not very good coaching."

After beating "America's Team," the Spartans' next assignment was "America's Coach," John Chaney, and the 24-12 Temple Owls. After five futile trips to the regional finals, the 69-year-old Chaney was the people's choice — just not in the MSU locker room.

The problems against Temple were preparing for a 1-3-1 matchup zone unlike any in the country and controlling the tan-

Photo Credit: Kevin Fowler, MSU Sports Information

2001 NCAA Tournament

dem of point guard Lynn Greer and center Kevin Lyde. Eventually, the Spartans did both those things just enough for 69-62 triumph.

The key was superior preparation, with all the different styles MSU had faced and all the two-day turnarounds working in its favor. And with Heathcote, a master of the matchup, helping out once until 3 a.m., the Spartans had an excellent scheme they practiced the night before the game in their hotel ballroom.

"John does a lot of the same things we did," Heathcote said. "We used to skew our zone to the shooters, too. When we played Indiana, Mike Woodson hardly ever scored more than 25 against us. . . . But when you say the zone has been so successful, there's a limitation. It's so hard to rebound from the zone. And I say a pure-zone team will never win another NCAA Tournament. Over six games, someone will get hot from 3-point range and beat you."

MSU didn't do that. It did out-rebound the Owls 43-27 and tired out Lyde, who finished with 21 points, eight rebounds and the belief he could play in the NBA. It also held Greer to 7-for-21 shooting, thanks largely to Bell's work, and limited backcourt mate Quincy Wadley to 2-for-12 accuracy.

Hutson had 11 points, 10 rebounds and four assists from the critical high-post position in a 2-1-2 set. And Randolph was huge with eight points and 14 rebounds. But the day belonged to Thomas with a career-high 19 points on 8-

for-10 shooting.

"I've been overlooked before," Thomas said with a winner's smile after starring for the second-straight Sunday. "For some reason, they chose to play off me again. And I just so happened to make the shots."

He had room because Chaney stayed with a philosophy he had espoused the day before: "You have to deal with the known and leave the unknown alone. Don't let the known beat you!" Apparently, the Owls didn't know Thomas was hitting 47.7 percent from the field and 92.9 at the line in his fifth season.

Almost no one in Atlanta knew what was happening in Grand Rapids. Sixteen minutes after the final buzzer in the Georgia Dome, the nation's top-ranked hockey team polished off Wisconsin 5-1 in Van Andel Arena. For just the third

Photo Credit: Kevin Fowler, MSU Sports Information

Photo Credit: Kevin Fowler, MSU Sports Information

2001 NCAA Tournament

time, a school would be represented in the Final Four and the Frozen Four in the same season.

After another joyous net-snipping ceremony, the players dashed off to their locker room. There, a playful Richardson carried guard Mat Ishbia on his shoulder, danced around, then grabbed two water bottles to spray his teammates.

When Izzo entered about three minutes later, Richardson was a waterboy-wannabe again and doused Izzo with two cups of liquid. Only two this time? There must have been more games to play.

A beaming Izzo realized that fact as he grabbed a towel to wipe his face and back. Soon, he began to address the team — his team — that had gathered around him.

"I thought last year was something special," Izzo said, staring at the floor to keep the tears from flowing. "But after the way we pushed, pulled, prodded and handled adversity and pressure, I can't tell you how pleased I am. We are not going to forget this experience. This is a time to be happy. There aren't many times I can look out at a group like this and be so proud.

"I'll never forget what Charlie Bell's mother said to me once, 'All Charlie wants to do is to please you.' Well, there are a lot of guys who wanted to please a lot of people in this room. For that, I am

Photo Credit: Kevin Fowler, MSU Sports Information

eternally grateful. We have something special here. Your legacy will be remembered as long as I coach."

As Izzo paused, Hutson teased, "You might have to call us a dynasty, Coach."

After some laughs, Izzo said, "I'll put dynasty on there after we finish our job next week." Then, he resumed pacing.

"We're going to have some incredible reunions," he said. "We're going to remember this day for the rest of our lives. But I want to tell you, we're not done yet.

"You freshmen, you hung in there when I know it wasn't easy. For the sophomores, it hasn't been easy on 'J.R.' It hasn't been easy on Al — I'm on Al all the time. And it hasn't been easy on 'Balls' (Ballinger). You gave us a lot. You gave us a championship. And you gave us great friendships.

"For the seniors. . . .'Mookie' (Brandon Smith), what you did year-in and year-out I couldn't have done. I want to thank you. But that won't be enough. Mike, 'D.T.', Charlie and Andre, what you did for our staff, our program and our university is second-to-none. They can talk about whomever they want at the university, but your names will be remembered. I appreciate what you've done. I want you to remember that.

"You can start talking about our program being special now, because I'm ready to admit we've done something special. But make sure they know we're not done yet, right?"

"Right!" the players responded as one.

"We're going to Minnesota," Izzo said. "And whether we play Illinois or Arizona, we're on a mission."

Emotions forced him to stop again. But he kept pacing and finally continued.

"This hit me a little different than last year, and I want you to know and remember that," Izzo said. "Put this moment in the back of your head. No matter what happens the rest of your life, no one can take this moment from you. You're only going to know it when you come back. But I'm going to make sure we still have some games to play and some winning to do. Right, 'C.B.'?"

"Right," Bell said, ever eager-to-please.

Izzo had time for one more tribute: "Andre, Charlie, Mike, 'D.T.' and 'Mookie,' thanks for leading by example and helping to get this program where it's at."

It was time for the team to stand together. As each player raised his right hand and pointed his index finger toward the sky, Bell said, "1-2-3," and the Spartans shouted in unison, "Champs!"

With that proclamation, MSU became just the second Big Ten program and ninth overall to reach three straight Final Fours, joining Ohio State (1944-46 and 1960-62), San Francisco (1955-57), Cincinnati (1959-63), North Carolina (1967-69), UCLA (1967-76), Houston (1982-84), Duke

Photo Credit: Kevin Fowler, MSU Sports Information

(1988-92) and Kentucky (1996-98).

The Spartans were two wins from becoming just the eighth repeat NCAA titlist. The others were Oklahoma A&M in 1945-46, Kentucky in 1948-49, San Francisco in 1955-56, Cincinnati in 1961-62, UCLA in 1964-65 and from 1967-73 and Duke in 1991-92.

"I can't tell you how excited we are to get back to the Final Four," Izzo said to the media. "That's an incredible feat for this team. It's something we dreamed of and set a goal for. Yet, how realistic that was at the beginning of the year, I don't know. But it's here. We're going back. And I think we have as good a chance as anyone to win it, to be honest with you."

MSU became only the third defending NCAA champ in eight years to return to the Final Four, joining Arkansas in 1995 and Kentucky in 1997.

To put in perspective how difficult that is, the previous five national titlists from the Big Ten averaged 17.8 wins and 10.8 losses the following year, with none faring better than 23-8. When the Spartans boarded a plane for Minnesota on March 28, they were 28-4.

"At the beginning of the year, I was expecting perfection," Izzo said of a wilder ride than he ever imagined. "That's something you strive for and never attain. I probably didn't help that cause any."

He couldn't help the Spartans in the first Final Four semifinal in the Metrodome, either. The 27-7 Arizona Wildcats were dominant in almost every way, outshooting MSU 50.0 percent to 41.0 from the field and 50.0 to 14.3 beyond the arc. The Spartans were much too charitable, handing Arizona 12 steals and 21 rim-rattling points off turnovers.

MSU trailed just 32-30 at halftime, despite missing five free throws and committing a month's worth of errors. But the next 20 minutes were much worse, as the Spartans were outscored 14-0, the longest run they allowed all season, and 21-3 in the first 5:50.

All five Wildcats scored in double-figures, led by point guard Jason Gardner's 21 and forward Richard Jefferson's 17. Meanwhile, Bell and Richardson were a combined 3-for 21 from the field. And if Hutson hadn't scored 18 of his 20 points after the break, the margin would have been bigger than 80-61.

When Izzo entered the locker room, the only sounds were sobs and sniffles. By the time he reached the back of the room and stood in front of a greaseboard, his players had come together in a semi-circle — the last one some of them would ever form.

"I want to apologize to you

Photo Credit: Kevin Fowler, MSU Sports Information

guys because I don't know what happened today," Izzo said in a conversational tone, never raising his voice. "It started from the beginning of the game and never changed. We didn't play in any way, shape or form like we're capable of playing.

"Maybe you guys were tired. But you must find a way not to let today ruin this year. This might be the worst game we've played in the last four years.

"Remember the keys I put on the board before the game? No. 1 was turnovers. We picked a bad day to play our worst game. You guys fought back valiantly. Give Andre credit, because he took over in the second half. But from the

very first play, we didn't run things right. Everyone is allowed to have a bad game. Unfortunately, we picked the nation's biggest stage to play that way. . . .

"Seniors, I appreciate what you've done for this program. The focus wasn't there for some reason today. But let's talk about all the good things that happened this season and over the last four years. I wish I could give you one more chance to play, because you guys have done a lot for college basketball. You've been first-class all the way. I'm proud of the way you've conducted yourselves, on and off the court."

Before he left the locker room for a required press conference,

Izzo stopped at each locker and shook every player's hand. The assistant coaches did the same. Their reign — or at least this one — was over. It would soon be Duke's moment to shine.

But the love kept flowing. The following evening, Spartans were everywhere at the National Association of Basketball Coaches get-together at, of course, the State Theatre. The NABC Golden Anniversary Award for distinguished service went to Heathcote. The National Coach of the Year was Izzo.

And guess who got the evening's only two standing ovations?...Two MSU coaches with national titles and, win or lose, the respect of everyone around them.

Photo Credit: Kevin Fowler, MSU Sports Information

MSU 69, Alabama State 35
March 16, 2001 • The Pyramid • Memphis, Tenn.

Alabama State	FG-FGA	FT-FTA	REB	PF	TP	A	TO	BLK	S	MIN
Tobaire Burton	1-9	0-0	2	4	2	5	2	0	0	34
Keith Gamble	3-10	0-0	5	2	7	0	0	0	2	29
Alvin Pettway	3-4	0-2	3	5	6	1	3	1	0	18
Joey Ball	0-5	0-0	3	0	0	0	2	1	1	34
Tyrone Levett	6-13	3-3	2	2	17	0	4	0	0	32
Malcolm Campbell	1-5	0-0	0	3	0	0	0	0	0	10
Dupree McKenzie	0-1	0-0	1	0	0	0	0	0	0	7
Leonard Hooks	0-1	0-0	2	0	0	0	1	0	0	6
Xavier Oliver	0-3	0-0	3	1	0	0	0	0	0	8
Angel Branch	0-1	0-0	1	1	0	0	2	0	1	9
Michael Green	0-4	0-0	2	2	0	0	2	0	0	13
Totals	14-56	3-5	26	17	35	6	16	2	4	200

Three-Point Field Goals: Burton 0-5, Gamble 1-6, Ball 0-2, Levett 2-6, Campbell 1-4, Team 4-23.
FG%: 1st Half 10-26 .385, 2nd Half 4-30 .133, Game 14-56 .250; 3FG%: 1st Half 2-7 .286, 2nd Half 2-16 .125, Game 4-23 .174; FT%: 1st Half 3-5 .600, 2nd Half 0-0 .000, Game 3-5 .600; Team Rebounds: 2; Deadball Rebounds: 1.

Michigan State	FG-FGA	FT-FTA	REB	PF	TP	A	TO	BLK	S	MIN
David Thomas	3-6	0-0	2	2	6	1	0	0	0	19
Charlie Bell	3-8	1-2	3	0	7	5	3	0	3	27
Jason Richardson	6-10	0-0	7	1	14	3	3	0	2	25
Aloysius Anagonye	1-2	1-4	4	3	3	0	2	1	0	13
Andre Hutson	7-7	1-1	11	2	15	0	0	0	2	27
Marcus Taylor	2-5	2-2	1	0	6	3	4	0	0	23
Adam Wolfe	0-2	0-0	0	0	0	0	0	0	0	3
Brandon Smith	0-1	0-0	1	0	0	0	0	0	0	3
Mat Ishbia	0-2	0-0	2	0	0	0	0	0	0	3
Mike Chappell	1-5	0-0	7	0	2	0	1	1	2	17
Jason Andreas	0-1	0-0	1	1	0	0	0	0	0	3
Zach Randolph	2-4	8-8	5	2	12	0	1	1	0	23
Adam Ballinger	2-3	0-0	3	2	4	0	0	0	0	14
Totals	27-56	13-17	48	13	69	12	14	3	9	200

Three-Point Field Goals: Thomas 0-1, Bell 0-4, Richardson 2-4, Wolfe 0-1, Smith 0-1, Ishbia 0-1, Chappell 0-3, Team 2-15.
FG%: 1st Half 13-29 .448, 2nd Half 14-27 .519, Game 27-56 .482; 3FG%: 1st Half 1-6 .167, 2nd Half 1-9 .111, Game 2-15 .133; FT%: 1st Half 2-4 .500, 2nd Half 11-13 .846, Game 13-17 .765; Team Rebounds: 1; Deadball Rebounds: 2.

SCORE BY PERIODS	1	2	F
Alabama State	25	10	35
Michigan State	29	40	69

OFFICIALS – John Hughes, Karl Hess, Rich Sanfillipo
TECHNICAL FOULS – None
ATTENDANCE – 8,602

MSU 81, Fresno State 65
March 18, 2001 • The Pyramid • Memphis, Tenn.

Fresno State	FG-FGA	FT-FTA	REB	PF	TP	A	TO	BLK	S	MIN
Chris Jeffries	4-13	4-6	5	1	13	2	0	1	1	34
Tito Maddox	4-16	3-4	6	1	11	6	3	0	1	37
Shannon Swillis	3-8	1-2	6	2	7	0	0	2	2	35
Demetrius Porter	1-8	4-5	3	4	6	1	2	0	1	29
Melvin Ely	8-13	1-2	6	4	17	1	2	0	0	27
Damon Jackson	2-4	0-0	2	1	5	0	0	0	0	7
Noel Felix	1-2	2-2	0	1	4	0	0	0	0	9
Travis Demanby	0-2	0-0	0	0	0	1	0	0	0	13
Mustafa Al-Sayyad	1-2	0-0	3	2	2	0	0	0	0	9
Totals	24-68	15-21	32	16	65	11	7	3	5	200

Three-Point Field Goals: Jeffries 1-3, Maddox 0-2, Swillis 0-1, Porter 0-5, Jackson 1-2, Felix 0-1, Demanby 0-2, Team 2-16.

FG%: 1st Half 10-34 .294, 2nd Half 14-34 .412, Game 24-68 .353; 3FG%: 1st Half 0-9 .000, 2nd Half 2-7 .286, Game 2-16 .125; FT%: 1st Half 10-14 .714, 2nd Half 5-7 .714, Game 15-21 .714; Team Rebounds: 1; Deadball Rebounds: 4.

Michigan State	FG-FGA	FT-FTA	REB	PF	TP	A	TO	BLK	S	MIN
David Thomas	5-8	0-0	14	2	10	2	3	1	0	27
Charlie Bell	6-16	0-0	6	1	13	3	7	0	0	34
Jason Richardson	3-11	3-3	6	3	9	1	2	2	2	26
Aloysius Anagonye	5-7	3-4	6	3	13	1	1	1	0	20
Andre Hutson	5-7	2-3	8	2	12	5	1	0	0	33
Marcus Taylor	4-8	2-2	1	3	11	1	1	0	0	23
Mike Chappell	3-4	0-0	1	3	7	0	0	0	0	12
Zach Randolph	3-6	0-1	3	2	6	2	1	1	0	19
Adam Ballinger	0-0	0-0	0	0	0	0	0	0	0	6
Totals	34-67	10-13	48	19	81	15	16	5	2	200

Three-Point Field Goals: Bell 1-4, Richardson 0-3, Taylor 1-2, Chappell 1-1, Team 3-10.

FG%: 1st Half 14-32 .438, 2nd Half 20-35 .571, Game 34-67 .507; 3FG%: 1st Half 1-5 .200, 2nd Half 2-5 .400, Game 3-10 .300; FT%: 1st Half 8-11 .727, 2nd Half 2-2 1.000, Game 10-13 .769; Team Rebounds: 3; Deadball Rebounds: 2.

SCORE BY PERIODS	1	2	F
Fresno State	30	35	65
Michigan State	37	44	81

OFFICIALS – Tom Lopes, Karl Hess, Rick Hartzell
TECHNICAL FOULS – None
ATTENDANCE – 10,719

MSU 77, Gonzaga 62
March 23, 2001 • Georgia Dome • Atlanta, Ga.

Gonzaga	FG-FGA	FT-FTA	REB	PF	TP	A	TO	BLK	S	MIN
Mark Spink	4-7	2-2	5	2	10	1	1	0	1	24
Casey Calvary	6-15	3-5	11	1	17	3	1	2	0	38
Zach Gourde	1-2	2-2	2	4	4	0	1	0	1	18
Blake Stepp	3-11	0-0	3	2	8	2	0	0	2	37
Dan Dickau	06-17	2-3	4	4	19	2	5	0	0	40
Germayne Forbes	0-0	0-0	0	0	0	0	0	0	0	5
Alex Hernandez	0-1	0-0	0	3	0	0	1	0	0	13
Jimmy Tricco	0-0	0-0	0	0	0	0	0	0	0	1
Kyle Bankhead	0-0	0-0	0	0	0	0	0	0	0	3
Anthony Reason	1-3	0-1	0	2	2	5	0	0	1	12
Cory Violette	1-2	0-0	2	2	2	0	1	0	0	8
Jay Sherrell	0-0	0-0	1	0	0	0	0	0	0	1
Totals	22-58	9-13	29	20	62	13	10	2	5	200

Three-Point Field Goals: Calvary 2-2, Stepp 2-10, Dickau 5-9, Reason 0-1, Team 9-22.

FG%: 1st Half 12-27 .444, 2nd Half 10-31 .323, Game 22-58 .379; 3FG%: 1st Half 4-8 .500, 2nd Half 5-14 .357, Game 9-22 .409; FT%: 1st Half 4-6 .667, 2nd Half 5-7 .714, Game 9-13 .692; Team Rebounds: 1; Deadball Rebounds: 2.

Michigan State	FG-FGA	FT-FTA	REB	PF	TP	A	TO	BLK	S	MIN
Jason Richardson	5-13	0-1	7	2	12	3	1	2	4	34
Aloysius Anagonye	0-2	0-0	3	4	0	0	0	1	0	17
Andre Hutson	8-11	3-4	10	2	19	3	1	1	1	29
David Thomas	0-4	0-0	5	3	0	3	1	0	0	18
Charlie Bell	5-12	8-10	10	1	21	3	2	1	1	35
Marcus Taylor	3-9	0-0	0	1	6	5	2	0	1	23
Mike Chappell	2-3	0-0	6	2	5	2	1	0	0	11
Jason Andreas	0-1	0-0	1	0	0	0	0	0	0	4
Zach Randolph	4-8	2-4	5	1	10	0	1	1	0	19
Adam Ballinger	2-2	0-0	0	1	4	0	0	2	0	10
Totals	29-65	13-19	49	17	77	19	9	8	7	200

Three-Point Field Goals: Richardson 2-6, Bell 3-8, Taylor 0-4, Chappell 1-2, Team 6-20.

FG%: 1st Half 15-37 .405, 2nd Half 14-28 .500, Game 29-65 .446; 3FG%: 1st Half 4-13 .308, 2nd Half 2-7 .286, Game 6-20 .300; FT%: 1st Half 3-5 .600, 2nd Half 10-14 .714, Game 13-19 .684; Team Rebounds: 2; Deadball Rebounds: 2.

SCORE BY PERIODS	1	2	F
Gonzaga	32	30	62
Michigan State	37	40	77

OFFICIALS – Tom Lopes, Larry Rose, Olandis Poole
TECHNICAL FOULS – None
ATTENDANCE – 26,873

MSU 69, Temple 62
March 25, 2001 • Georgia Dome • Atlanta, Ga.

Temple	FG-FGA	FT-FTA	REB	PF	TP	A	TO	BLK	S	MIN
Alex Wesby	3-6	1-1	6	5	9	0	0	0	0	34
David Hawkins	1-7	2-2	2	3	4	0	1	0	1	29
Kevin Lyde	10-15	1-3	8	4	21	1	0	1	1	40
Lynn Greer	7-21	6-7	0	2	22	3	1	0	2	40
Quincy Wadley	2-12	0-0	4	3	4	2	2	0	1	40
Greg Jefferson	0-0	0-0	0	1	0	0	0	0	1	7
Ron Rollerson	1-2	0-0	5	0	2	0	0	0	0	10
Roulda Thomas	0-0	0-0	0	0	0	0	0	0	0	0+
Totals	24-63	10-13	27	18	62	6	4	1	5	200

Three-Point Field Goals: Wesby 2-5, Hawkins 0-4, Greer 2-7, Wadley 0-7, Team 4-23.

FG%: 1st Half 13-30 .433, 2nd Half 11-33 .333, Game 24-63 .381; 3FG%: 1st Half 1-10 .100, 2nd Half 3-13 .231, Game 4-23 .174; FT%: 1st Half 0-1 .000, 2nd Half 10-12 .833, Game 10-13 .769; Team Rebounds: 2; Deadball Rebounds: 1.

Michigan State	FG-FGA	FT-FTA	REB	PF	TP	A	TO	BLK	S	MIN
David Thomas	8-10	2-3	7	1	19	2	0	0	2	30
Aloysius Anagonye	1-1	0-0	1	5	2	2	1	1	0	19
Andre Hutson	2-5	7-10	10	3	11	4	0	1	0	34
Charlie Bell	6-14	0-0	4	2	14	3	3	0	1	36
Jason Richardson	4-11	2-3	2	1	11	2	3	0	0	31
Marcus Taylor	2-5	0-0	1	4	4	3	0	0	0	17
Mike Chappell	0-3	0-0	0	0	0	0	1	0	0	7
Zach Randolph	3-5	2-6	14	2	8	3	2	0	0	24
Adam Ballinger	0-0	0-0	0	0	0	0	0	0	0	2
Totals	26-54	13-22	43	15	69	19	11	2	3	200

Three-Point Field Goals: Thomas 1-2, Bell 2-7, Richardson 1-3, Chappell 0-3, Team 4-15.

FG%: 1st Half 13-29 .448, 2nd Half 13-25 .520, Game 26-54 .481; 3FG%: 1st Half 2-9 .222, 2nd Half 2-6 .333, Game 4-15 .267; FT%: 1st Half 2-2 1.000, 2nd Half 11-20 .550, Game 13-22 .591; Team Rebounds: 4; Deadball Rebounds: 8.

SCORE BY PERIODS	1	2	F
Temple	27	35	62
Michigan State	30	39	69

OFFICIALS – Jim Burr, Andre Pattillo, Mark Whitehead
TECHNICAL FOULS – None
ATTENDANCE – 25,995

Arizona 80, MSU 61
March 31, 2001 • Metrodome • Minneapolis, Minn.

Arizona	FG-FGA	FT-FTA	REB	PF	TP	A	TO	BLK	S	MIN
Michael Wright	6-10	1-1	3	2	13	0	1	1	0	23
Richard Jefferson	6-13	2-4	8	1	17	2	2	2	2	34
Loren Woods	5-13	1-1	8	2	11	2	1	3	0	37
Gilbert Arenas	4-7	3-4	2	2	12	7	1	0	6	27
Jason Gardner	6-11	6-6	1	1	21	1	1	1	3	38
Eugene Edgerson	3-4	0-0	6	1	6	1	0	0	0	17
Luke Walton	0-1	0-0	1	0	0	2	2	0	0	16
Justin Wessel	0-0	0-0	0	1	0	0	0	0	1	3
Lamont Frazier	0-1	0-0	0	1	0	0	0	0	0	4
Travis Hanour	0-0	0-0	0	0	0	0	0	0	0	1
Totals	30-60	13-16	33	11	80	15	8	7	12	200

Three-Point Field Goals: Jefferson 3-5, Arenas 1-2, Gardner 3-7, Team 7-14.
FG%: 1st Half 12-25 .480, 2nd Half 18-35 .514, Game 30-60 .500; 3FG%: 1st Half 4-7 .571, 2nd Half 3-7 .429, Game 7-14 .500; FT%: 1st Half 4-5 .800, 2nd Half 9-11 .818, Game 13-16 .813; Team Rebounds: 4; Deadball Rebounds: 1.

Michigan State	FG-FGA	FT-FTA	REB	PF	TP	A	TO	BLK	S	MIN
David Thomas	4-6	0-0	5	1	8	2	3	0	1	20
Aloysius Anagonye	0-1	0-0	2	4	0	0	0	0	0	8
Andre Hutson	9-14	2-2	5	2	20	0	2	2	0	37
Charlie Bell	1-10	1-1	10	1	3	3	5	0	0	36
Jason Richardson	2-11	1-2	7	2	6	2	2	0	0	28
Marcus Taylor	3-9	1-2	1	3	8	2	2	0	1	20
Adam Ballinger	1-1	0-1	2	0	2	0	0	1	0	9
Zach Randolph	5-8	2-4	5	3	12	0	1	0	0	24
Mike Chappell	0-0	2-2	0	1	2	2	0	0	0	12
Brandon Smith	0-0	0-0	0	1	0	0	0	0	0	3
Adam Wolfe	0-0	0-0	0	0	0	0	0	0	0	1
Jason Andreas	0-0	0-0	0	0	0	0	0	0	0	1
Mat Ishbia	0-1	0-0	0	0	0	0	0	0	0	1
Totals	25-61	9-14	40	18	61	11	15	3	2	200

Three-Point Field Goals: Bell 0-6, Richardson 1-4, Taylor 1-4, Team 2-14.
FG%: 1st Half 12-29 .414, 2nd Half 13-32 .406, Game 25-61 .410; 3FG%: 1st Half 1-6 .167, 2nd Half 1-8 .125, Game 2-14 .143; FT%: 1st Half 5-10 .500, 2nd Half 4-4 1.000, Game 9-14 .643; Team Rebounds: 3; Deadball Rebounds: 0.

SCORE BY PERIODS	1	2	F
Arizona	32	48	-- 80
Michigan State	30	31	-- 61

OFFICIALS – Tim Higgins, Tony Greene, Bob Donato
TECHNICAL FOULS – Jefferson (UA)
ATTENDANCE – 45,406

Photo Credit: Kevin Fowler, MSU Sports Information

THE PROMISE

SPARTAN BASKETBALL

As Tom Izzo traipsed from an awkward press conference to a somber Michigan State locker room the night of March 31, 2001, another media horde awaited. Its questions were roughly the same. And the answers were just as elusive.

"What happened?" was the general theme of the inquiry. If Izzo could have explained that, an 80-61 no-show against Arizona on the sport's biggest stage wouldn't have been so maddening for the days, weeks and months to follow.

The Spartan players fans had watched all season were abducted just before tipoff of the first NCAA semifinal in the Metrodome. What other explanation could there be for the Wildcats' 21 points off 12 steals, often in self-defense?

"Part of it was Arizona's speed," Izzo said after the defending champs' worst game of a young century. "But a lot of it was the lack of direction on our passes. They made a couple of great steals. They also had a couple of plays where they had to protect themselves from getting hurt by the ball."

The hurt was unmistakable as MSU's players sat in front of their lockers. A bid to become only the second back-to-back titlists in 28 years had ended with an avalanche of errors and an uncharacteristic whimper.

Numb as he was, it didn't take long for Izzo to feel his players' intense pain. Before he opened the door and re-entered the room, he realized he couldn't let one game destroy four seasons of grand accomplishments.

With 115 wins, four Big Ten titles, two conference tournament crowns, three No. 1 seeds in the

SCHOOL IS IN SESSION – *Tom Izzo, the teacher, drives home a point to point guard Marcus Taylor, a willing student, in Taylor's freshman season.*

BIG TEN PERFORMANCE CHART — 1989-2001
(since the opening of Breslin Center)

School	Big 10 Record	Overall Record	Big 10 Titles (solo/co)	Big 10 Tourns	+.500 Marks	-.500 Marks	NCAA Bids	NIT Bids	Sweet 16s	Final Fours	NCAA Titles
MSU	140-68	264-109	5 (2/3)	2	11	0	9	3	5	3	1
Indiana	136-72	270-116	2 (1/1)	0	12	0	12	0	4	1	0
Purdue	132-76	263-118	3 (3/0)	0	12	0	10	2	4	0	0
Illinois	118-90	235-138	2 (0/2)	0	10	2	7	1	1	0	0
Michigan	114-94	240-142	0	1	9	3	7	3	3	2	0
Iowa	102-106	227-143	0	1	9	3	7	1	1	0	0
Ohio State	101-107	202-157	3 (1/2)	0	7	5	6	1	3	1	0
*Minnesota	42-62	104-81	0	0	2	3	1	3	1	0	0
Wisconsin	86-122	196-168	0	0	6	4	5	3	1	1	0
Penn State	57-97	192-152	0	0	8	4	3	5	1	0	0
Northwestern	29-179	106-233	0	0	2	10	0	2	0	0	0

* Numbers reduced for NCAA sanctions

NCAA Tournament, three Final Four berths and a national championship, no group had done more in that span.

And the question of whether MSU had reached elite status seemed as ridiculous to most observers as it was real to Izzo.

"If Tom doesn't think he has an elite program yet, he's nuts," Jud Heathcote said of his Spartan protege with appropriate pride.

"When you talk about the top teams in the country, Michigan State's name comes up very, very quickly," Arizona coach Lute Olson said. "No question, they've achieved elite status. I remember when I was coaching in the Big Ten, other than getting guys in their immediate area, it was tough for them to recruit against Michigan. The tide has turned."

When a program becomes a model of consistency instead of a one-year wonder, it has arrived. And when Izzo begins to acknowledge that fact, it must be at or near the summit of a steep college basketball mountain.

"I grew up in a period where you had to earn respect over time," Izzo said. "Today, we're more of a quick-fix society. But to have won four Big Ten titles in a row shows pretty good consistency and continuity."

The 2000-01 Spartans were never ranked lower than fifth in the nation and finished No. 3 in both polls, after spending two weeks in the No. 1 spot. To get more consistency than that, you would have to hire Tony Izzo & Sons & Grandsons.

Among teams in the Big Ten, a league with five of the last 12 Final Four berths, MSU had dominated in nearly every department. It had the most overall wins (28), the fewest losses (five), the best percentage (.849) and the furthest postseason advancement. It also led the conference in field-goal shooting (48.9 percent) and scoring margin (15.6) and paced the nation in rebound margin (15.4).

Best of all, it wasn't just one season of brilliance. Since the Spartans moved into Breslin Center in 1989-90, they have had the highest winning percentages and the most championships in the conference.

After a fourth-straight regular-season crown, the Spartans have a chance to match Ohio State's mark of five conference titles in a row from 1960-64 — a standard few figured the program would ever approach.

"Four in a row? . . . I would've liked to win one in a row!" said MSU radio analyst Gus Ganakas, the school's head coach from 1969-76.

SPARTAN BASKETBALL

If the Central Collegiate Hockey Association can present the Ron Mason Cup to the winner of its playoffs, the Big Ten might want to consider a basketball version — the Tom Izzo Trophy — if the Spartans can somehow stretch their streak to six or seven regular-season championships.

Immediately after the Final Four, another crown was like a strong possibility. Yes, MSU was losing a senior class with more triumphs than any group in league history. But with a projected starting lineup of Zach Randolph at center, Jason Richardson and Aloysius Anagonye at forward and Marcus Taylor and Kelvin Torbert at guard, it made sense to think about 2002 Final Four tickets in Atlanta.

"I still think we could be really good — really, really good — because Zach and Marcus are going to be a lot better next year," Izzo said prematurely. "With Zach, Marcus, 'J.R.' and Al, that's a helluva nucleus."

The first red flag came from CBS analyst Rick Pitino, who had won a national title at Kentucky and was ready to try to resurrect the program at Louisville.

When asked about Izzo's chances to build a dynasty, Pitino said, "It's difficult, because you're going to lose players early to the NBA Draft. That hurt me. It hasn't hurt him yet."

It seemed as though that trend toward early departures might skip the Spartans again. After the South Region final, Randolph said he thought he would be back as a sophomore. And after the title-clinching win over Michigan, in a one-on-one interview before leaving for the Final Four and after a performance against Arizona he would rather forget, Richardson restated his plan to stay.

"I know I have a long way to go," Richardson said. "I had a chance to get us to the championship game and didn't respond. I have to learn to answer that challenge. But when I said I was coming back after the Michigan game, I meant it. There are a lot of things I have to get better at — way better. I talked with (Duke All-American) Jason Williams about that. His parents want him to come back, just like mine do."

One Jason left. One Jason stayed. But the day after MSU's season ended, Izzo wasn't thinking about Williams. He was preoccupied with the consistency of a Blue Devil program that would soon win its third NCAA title in 11 years.

"Duke is still my model," Izzo said. "It almost never has a letdown. And excellence isn't expected. It's demanded. A few weeks ago when they played in Chapel Hill, I asked our guys who would win, Duke or North Carolina. Most of them said, 'Carolina.' But I said, 'Don't ever count a Duke team out!' Their guys were playing for everyone who'd ever played at Duke. Shorthanded, they won that game."

Izzo's fascination with the Blue Devils stopped just short of changing the lyrics of Michael Jordan's old Gatorade jingle to: "Like Duke — if I could be like Duke. . . . I wannabe, I wannabe like Duke."

He failed to realize the Spartan program had been to more Final Fours in the last three years than the Blue Devils had in the past seven. And as revered as Mike Krzyzewski had become, his first six seasons as head coach in Durham, N.C., were nothing like Izzo's first six in East Lansing.

A building block for the Blue Devils, 1980s forward Jay Bilas, put it best between in-depth analyses for ESPN's "College Hoops Tonight" telecasts.

"To win four straight Big Ten titles is almost obscene," Bilas said. "I'm sure a lot of Michigan State fans think it's their birthright to win every year. But I hope the peo-

STARTS FOR MIKE KRZYZEWSKI AT DUKE AND TOM IZZO AT MSU							
Coach, Years	League Record	Overall Record	NCAA Record	League Titles	League Tournaments	Final Fours	NCAA Titles
Krzyzewski, 1980-86	40-44	122-68	6-3	1	1	1	0
Izzo, 1995-2001	72-28	148-53	16-3	4	2	3	1

ple up there realize what they have. There aren't many coaches or many people like Tom Izzo.

"He has only been a head coach for six years. Already, I'd put him up there with Mike Krzyzewski, Lute Olson and Roy Williams. There's a reason Bob Knight said the last team he ever wanted to play at Indiana was Michigan State."

Knight is at Texas Tech these days. But an impressive collection of new Big Ten head coaches in the past four years — including Jim O'Brien of Ohio State, Steve Alford of Iowa, Dan Monson of Minnesota, Bill Self of Illinois, Mike Davis of Indiana, Bill Carmody of Northwestern and Tommy Amaker of Michigan — hasn't made Izzo's life any easier.

"I still say we have the best conference," said Izzo, second only to Purdue's Gene Keady in conference seniority among the current coaches. "And when you say that, how do you stay up there? I guarantee you Tommy is going to come in and do a very good job at Michigan. They're going to get that thing rolling. Mike could have everyone back at Indiana. They're going to be good. And Danny had a great recruiting class at Minnesota. They're going to be better."

That isn't counting the top two choices to win the league in 2002: Illinois, last year's co-champ and a Midwest Region finalist, and Iowa, the Big Ten Tournament titlist.

But the greatest challenge to the Spartans will come from within. Can they use the disappoint-ment of the Metrodome as motiva-tion? Duke did with that a 1990 blowout by UNLV en route to its first NCAA title — in Krzyzewski's 11th season in Durham. And can they overcome some of the most devastating departures any pro-gram has endured?

TAKING THE LEAD – *Junior power forward Aloysius Anagonye and sophomore point guard Marcus Taylor should be the leaders of the Spartans in 2001-02 and 2002-03. Tom Izzo thinks Anagonye can be another Antonio Smith and Taylor can be a better scorer than Mateen Cleaves.*

Photo Credit: Kevin Fowler, MSU Sports Information

SPARTAN BASKETBALL

TOWER OF STRENGTH – *Junior power forward Aloysius Anagonye (25) can be a strong defender for two more seasons if he learns to stay out of foul trouble.*

Photo Credit: Kevin Fowler, MSU Sports Information

"I want to improve our offense next year," Izzo said before he realized the extent of the personnel losses. "We've lived with being a defense-and-rebounding team. I set that image because I wanted to set that image. It's what we do. Yet, we scored 70 points a game, and people say we can't score enough. . . . Maybe we proved them right against Arizona."

MSU proved a lot of people wrong who said, "Goodbye, Cleaves. Goodbye, Peterson. Goodbye, Final Four." Instead they came within two victories of a third-straight 30-win season — a feat achieved only by Kentucky.

"I lose perspective of that," Izzo said. "I lose perspective of a lot of things. But I'd like to take a week and say, 'Where am I?' It has been a melee and a little bit hard on my family. I want to get a little perspective in my life again. I don't know if I need a break. But I'm pretty good at chewing other people out. I need to chew myself out and figure out, 'Where's the next step we take?'"

A lot of people assumed his next step would be to the NBA, specifically to the Detroit Pistons, where George Irvine was stomping on quarter-inch ice.

Before the Spartans left the Twin Cities, Izzo tried to end growing speculation that he would coach Cleaves again next season. Reaching the Final Four would prove to be easier than quashing that rumor.

"I don't know if I'd be a very good pro coach, to be honest with you," Izzo said at the team's Hilton

Airport headquarters. "I think I've still got some work to do here. I think I'm still a college guy. I still want to coach Zach and Marcus. And I want a shot at Torbert."

He would have to settle for two out of three. But the suspicion lingered that Izzo wouldn't say no if a team like the Pistons and a respected basketball person like President Joe Dumars made an offer of close to $20 million.

Many people in the media insisted that Izzo could help to right a stumbling franchise. Izzo answered that he wasn't going anywhere. Both sides were right.

Yet, some part of "No" was hard to understand. Because Izzo hadn't said "Never," a stupid answer to almost any question, some assumed he really meant "Maybe." Closing the door wasn't enough. It had to be soldered shut.

On April 4, 2001, Izzo tried his best to do that, though skeptics continued to look for loopholes. In his office in Breslin, he told the *Lansing State Journal* and Booth News Service that the only place he was going was back to work for MSU and a program that was "upper-echelon — but not elite yet."

"I'm not going to wait until anything is open," Izzo said emphatically. "I have no interest in anything else. . . . Period. . . . The End. The only thing I have an interest in doing is cleaning up college basketball, which is a bigger job than I can handle."

Long before Izzo knew who was leaving, he was sure one person was staying — the one he saw in the mirror each morning. If the press and the public couldn't accept that answer, that was their problem.

"I'm embarrassed by what has been reported," Izzo said. "I saw Joe (Dumars) on TV, denying this and denying that — which he should, because nothing has happened. If it does come open, I have no interest. If it doesn't come open, and I hope it doesn't, I have no interest in any other place."

Izzo didn't have an interest in the Atlanta job until the Hawks tried to recruit him in a way no Northern Michigan player had

Photo Credit: Kevin Fowler, MSU Sports Information

TAYLOR-MADE – *Sophomore point guard Marcus Taylor has been around the Michigan State coaches since he was in fifth grade. He could make a quantum leap as a sophomore.*

Spartan Basketball

ever been courted. His near-acceptance of that position was seen as evidence Izzo would leave if something better — or closer to home — came along.

"I think last year I was human," Izzo said of nearly accepting Atlanta's five-year, megabucks deal. "I said, 'God, you have to look at something when you can set your family up for life.' But when I got married, I was making 50 grand a year. I lived just fine. When we had our first kid, I was making 75 grand a year and living just fine. Now that we have a second one, as long as I can make 100 grand at whatever I do, I guess I can live just fine."

When it was noted that Butch Davis had said, "No. . . . No. . . . Where do I sign?" when he left the University of Miami to coach the NFL's Cleveland Browns, there were two important differences.

As much as he loved football, Izzo wasn't Davis. And his word to MSU was his bond when he told President Peter McPherson and others in high places that he would be back.

McPherson had lived up to his end of the bargain and then some for six years. A series of non-requested, non-negotiated raises had lifted Izzo's compensation to roughly $1.2 million, counting $100,000 in deferred income but not including all his incentives.

"This university does pay for performance," MSU vice president Terry Denbow said. "He has both worth and value. People always say it isn't about the dollars. But it really isn't with Tom."

McPherson approached Izzo about another significant raise and contract revisions before the 2000-01 season ended. Sensitive to faculty perceptions and uneasy about annual increases, even to market levels, Izzo balked.

But McPherson, a banker with a politician's instincts, wouldn't be deterred. A new package worth roughly $1.6 million per year, with more of that money coming from outside sources, was a near-certainty. Rewarding Izzo for excellence and encouraging him to stay at MSU as long as possible was a smart business decision, emotions aside.

"Tell Tom to stay right where he is," said ESPN/ABC analyst Dick Vitale, who moved from the Detroit Titans to the Detroit Pistons in 1978 and went 34-60. "There's nothing like being happy. He can make a call to Rick Pitino about that. All Tom's strengths would be negated at the pro level. He's the perfect fit for college basketball. And he's building a program just like the one at Duke under Michael Krzyzewski."

Indeed, the value of Spartan Basketball to the institution the past three seasons was incalculable. Increased contributions and applications for admission were just the start. MSU couldn't have purchased the same television time on CBS or bought the same newspaper space for ads if it had sold Brody Complex.

Best of all, Spartan Pride — among students, faculty, alumni and fans — soared to new heights throughout the state, across the

country and around the world. And that wasn't just because MSU won.

Izzo's teams became the standard for excellence in other areas, too. When Charlie Bell, Andre Hutson, David Thomas, Mike Chappell and Brandon Smith all earned degrees the first weekend in May, the Spartans were 5-for-5 in that department — more graduates than some programs had in the past decade.

No wonder the addition of the Alfred Berkowitz Basketball Complex, a privately funded, $7.5 million addition to Breslin Center, met with such little resistance. The Berkowitz Foundation pledged $2 million toward the project, scheduled for completion in late 2001.

A second auxiliary practice facility, to be known as "Jud's Gym" in Heathcote's honor, is probably the most important aspect of the construction. But new basketball offices for the men's and women's programs, video review rooms and workrooms and expanded conference rooms could make Breslin the equal of any facility in the nation.

Izzo was well on his way to doing the same for MSU's program. He won't coach nearly as long as Heathcote did before retiring at age 67. But after six emotion-packed seasons, the 46-year-old Izzo should have plenty of motivation this season.

"I'm going to worry about trying to win another national title and get us into a more-elite group," Izzo said. "I think the NBA has problems. I think the college game has problems. But I also think everyone is built for a certain place. Maybe I'm built for college. . . . Maybe I'm built for high school."

He has built a program that's the envy of more than 300 other Division I coaches. Yet, Izzo refuses to let that go to his head or to snub people who can't help him.

"I hate to say it, but admiration is short-lived," Izzo said. "There were people who wanted me gone (in December 1997). And what'll happen if the president leaves or we don't do quite as well next year? But I think I've realized, for all the problems, this is where I want to be. No matter what you're making and where you're working, the grass is going to seem greener somewhere else."

That's true for players, too. And the greater green for Richardson and Randolph was the color of money. When they left for the NBA after two years and one season, respectively, they weren't finished products. But they were finished with college basketball, for better or worse.

With Cleaves and Morris Peterson taken 14th and 21st in 2000, Richardson and Randolph made MSU the only program to have two first-round picks in each of the last two summers. They also made life a lot tougher for a team that would have been picked in most Final Four projections.

On the way back from Randolph's announcement in Marion, Ind., Izzo called on his cell phone and showed he still had a sense of humor: "I'm just about

Photo Credit: Kevin Fowler, MSU Sports Information

READY TO BLOSSOM? *– Junior forward Adam Ballinger is entering his fourth season in the program. He could provide the mid-range shooting that MSU needs the next two seasons.*

SPARTAN BASKETBALL

ready to go into a team meeting. . . . We'll have more coaches than players!"

He and a revamped staff will have their share of good ones — not to the level of the past two seasons, but good enough to shock a lot of teams that think, "OK, it's time to get back at the Spartans."

The biggest problems in 2001-02 will be MSU's lack of depth and experience, not ability and enthusiasm, on a team with eight scholarship recruits and zero seniors.

"I asked our walk-ons if any of them are declaring for the NBA Draft," Izzo told Skip Myslenski of the *Chicago Tribune*. "Do you know we've decided to change our uniforms next year? We're going to wear diapers with an 'S' on the back. We'll be Dick Vitale's true 'Diaper Dandies.' I don't know if we'll be dandy, but we'll belong in diapers."

The Spartans lost 62.7 points, 31.7 rebounds and 13.3 assists with their seven departures — more points and rebounds than Wisconsin and Northwestern had as teams last season.

But Izzo is a firm believer that Anagonye, a mature junior, can be the second-best leader he has had. Just mentioning him in the same sentence as Cleaves is as good a compliment as any MSU player will receive.

And Taylor should be much better in his second collegiate season. The ball should be in his hands more than anyone had it last season. After a summer of USA Basketball play and more group activity, Taylor could blossom to

be the best shooting point guard since Scott Skiles 16 years ago.

Adam Ballinger, a fourth-year junior with a soft mid-range shot, could see plenty of action at power forward or center. So could third-year sophomores Adam Wolfe and

Jason Andreas at forward and center, respectively.

Those five are the only MSU veterans to arrive with scholarships. That creates opportunities for fourth-year junior guard Mat Ishbia and redshirt-freshman

Photo Credit: Kevin Fowler, MSU Sports Information

NO CRYING WOLFE – *Sophomore forward Adam Wolfe should provide offense for the Spartans in 2001-02, his third season in the program, provided he stays healthy.*

SPARTAN BASKETBALL

Photo Credit: Kevin Fowler, MSU Sports Information

ANOTHER MSU OHIOAN – *The Spartans have had great success with players from Ohio, from Johnny Green to A.J. Granger. But sophomore center Jason Andreas could be another contributor who said no to Ohio State.*

"If there's one guy I would pay whatever the price of admission is to go watch, it's Kelvin Torbert," Dave Telep of BlueChipHoops.com said in a round-table recruiting discussion in *The Sporting News*. "I think he's an amazing, complete basketball player at both ends — just a dynamic offensive player who can do things that other guys can't. There is no one in the class of 2001 who can do what Kelvin Torbert does through the course of a basketball game. This guy kind of has a fadeaway jumper where he hangs in the air like Michael Jordan. It's one thing to say it. It's another to see it."

Torbert's commitment on Oct. 25, 2000, gave the Spartans a huge infusion of talent and disappointed runner-up Connecticut, plus Cincinnati and Michigan. But he had been on campus so often and played so many pickup games there, he made his announcement before an official visit to MSU.

"The most important factors were how I hit it off with Coach Izzo, being able to stay close to home and being part of the family atmosphere at Michigan State," Torbert said. "I saw the other guys there, heard how great Michigan State was and knew how much fun they had. I also heard how Coach Izzo was really dedicated to making them better."

The Spartans also added 6-5 swingman Alan Anderson from Minneapolis De La Salle, a slasher and an outstanding defender, and 6-3 combo guard Chris Hill, an outstanding shooter from Indianapolis Lawrence North.

guard Tim Bograkos, the son of the ex-Spartan basketball and baseball letterman with the same name.

Most of the excitement centers on the arrival of Torbert, Michigan's Mr. Basketball and *The Sporting News* and Gatorade National Player of the Year from among roughly 540,000 candidates. The latest "Flintstone" from Northwestern-Edison High broke Glen Rice's school scoring record by 324 points, finished with 1,978 and averaged 27.2 as a senior.

SPARTAN BASKETBALL

Anderson has often been compared with ex-Duke forward Chris Carrawell, while Hill has reminded some of MSU career scoring king Shawn Respert.

"I play with a lot of energy and bring a lot of excitement to the floor," Anderson said. "Some poeple say I play like Vince Carter. But I see myself more as a young Ray Allen. I like to play defense. And I can blow past a defender at any time."

Torbert and Anderson were solid B students in high school and quickly qualified to play as freshmen. Hill had B+ grades in pre-calculus and chemistry as a junior to spoil a 4.0 GPA. His coach, Jack Kiefer, said the only question about his intelligence was his interest in possibly becoming a sportswriter.

"A lot of people liken my game to Allen Houston's," Hill said. "I'm known for my shooting ability. But I've worked hard on getting to the basket and shooting off the dribble. And I'm looking forward to helping Marcus at the point, if that's what Coach Izzo wants."

Hill also passed for more than 300 yards in back-to-back football games in 2000. But he will be strictly a basketball player for the Spartans after saying no to Marquette and first-love Notre Dame.

"His range is amazing," Kiefer said. "Teams defend him by trying to push him out of bounds. He had eight 3-pointers in one game in Las Vegas. There's no doubt that he's a Big Ten player. He'll be better in college than he has been in high school."

Anderson's choice was a major disappointment to Minnesota and runner-up Kansas. But MSU did the best job of recruiting him and got a major out-of-state commitment.

"Alan was just so comfortable with Tom Izzo and Brian Gregory," De La Salle coach and former Minnesota assistant Dave Thorson said. "Brian was the only one who flew from Las Vegas to Murfreesboro, Tenn., to watch him the summer before his junior year. Kids have a long memory sometimes. And Brian deserves all the credit. Plus, the head coach is such an Everyman. It's hard not to like Tom Izzo."

Photo Credit: Flint Journal

THE NEXT SUPERSTAR? – *Flint Northwestern-Edison standout Kelvin Torbert is the Spartans' highest-ranked recruit in history — higher than even Earvin Johnson.*

SPARTAN BASKETBALL

Before anyone had committed for the incoming class of 2001, the Spartans had a treasured commitment from 6-10 junior center Paul Davis of Rochester, a terrific shooter for someone that big and a second-team All-American for 2002 on several lists.

"He's a player who can score inside or outside," Rochester coach Hal Commerson told the *Lansing State Journal* in June 2000. "He's a very coordinated athlete, which is unbelievable for a kid his size and age."

Izzo wanted to sign a top point guard. If early attention mattered, it didn't hurt that he had been following Saginaw star Anthony Roberson, a first-team All-American, since his football games in ninth grade, months before he made a basket in high school.

Despite those efforts, some prospects still prefer Duke. And some like Michigan, especially with Amaker in charge. But Izzo's new status as one of the sport's giants hasn't escaped anyone's attention.

"I saw him walk in," Detroit Redford phenom Dion Harris told Mick McCabe of the *Detroit Free Press* last February, late in his sophomore season. "I was pretty excited. . . . I don't know if I want to commit early, but I'm a big State fan. I don't know if he was here to see me. But it feels good to know he's here watching us."

Izzo's program still has the squeaky image in recruiting that Heathcote's had. And that isn't by accident.

"It feels good to know when someone sees me or one of my assistants, you hear, 'There's a good, clean program.' The players don't big-time you. And the coaches don't big-time you. We're developing an image. When I go to Detroit or Flint now, people want to talk about our players. I see people taking pride in what we've done. Those things mean the world to me."

When Izzo helped Stan Heath become head coach at Kent State, he elevated trusted aide and for-

Photo Credit: Minneapolis Star Tribune

ALL-AROUND TALENT – *Minneapolis De La Salle's Alan Anderson is expected to make an immediate contribution at both ends of the floor as a freshman swingman in 2001-02.*

SPARTAN BASKETBALL

GREEN LIGHT – *Freshman guard Chris Hill should provide perimeter shooting for several seasons.*

Photo Credit: The Indianapolis Star-News

mer NMU teammate Mike Garland to the No. 2 assistant's spot and spent the latter part of May and early June interviewing candidates.

"No one can sell me, the program and the university better than Mike," Izzo said of his backcourt partner in the mid-1970s. "I think he'll be our next great recruiter. But Mike hasn't been given anything. He has earned everything he has gotten."

Garland was hired by Izzo in 1996 to run the office while others traveled and was assigned to work on players' individual improvement. The third assistant is prohibited from recruiting off campus. But Garland made the most of that assignment and stamped himself as another possible head coach.

"If I've been in Tom's shadow, that's been a great shadow to be in," Garland said. "A lot of times,

I say things just before he says them or say them at the same time. We're 'Ebony and Ivory.' It's an unbelievable relationship that goes beyond the basketball court."

Garland and Gregory helped with the hiring process for the No. 3 position, involving Detroit Redford High coach Derrick McDowell, Western Michigan assistant Lorenzo Neely, ex-Spartan point guards Benny White of Detroit King and Mark Montgomery of Central Michigan, Robert Murphy of Detroit Crockett, Ernie Ziegler of Bowling Green and former MSU forward Dwayne Stephens of Marquette.

"I'm looking for somebody with college experience or someone who has dealt with colleges extensively," Izzo said. "The big thing is he has to be able to coach. And we have some great candidates that way. Finally, he has to be good at individual development and with individual relationships."

Izzo finally chose Montgomery in early June and went back to work on recruiting, scheduling and new duties as a freshman board member for the National Association of Basketball Coaches. If that organization can't make all the necessary changes concerning agents, early departures and NCAA foolishness, it won't be because Izzo didn't try.

Scheduling for 2001-02 was almost as difficult, with uncertainty about the Spartans' opponents and sites for the Preseason NIT, the third ACC/Big Ten Challenge and the Pete Newell Challenge

with Stanford and San Francisco in Oakland, Calif.

"It could be the toughest schedule of any we've played," Izzo said. "We'll be at Florida. We get Arizona and Seton Hall here. If we add, say, Maryland and Stanford, plus at least two real good teams in New York, that's incredible. But I still want to play Kentucky again. I'd like to get Duke home-and-home. I think we're going to keep Florida. I still want to go to Kansas. I'd like to get UCLA for a home-and-home. And I'd love to get Notre Dame."

Fifty-game seasons aren't possible. But success similar to the past few years isn't out of the question, Izzo insisted.

"I'm on a mission," he said. "Don't feel sorry for us. And don't change your expectations one bit. I told the staff to saddle up, because we're going to go after it even harder."

In CBS SportsLine's "Pre-preseason Top 25" on April 16, 2001, MSU was ranked a surprising 11th with the comment: "Six of the top nine players gone . . . can Izzo work yet another miracle?"

It's not about miracles. It's all about work.

"The most important thing in life is to get up one more time than we're knocked down," Izzo said with Iron Mountain wisdom.

His program has been to the mountaintop. And he has been as low as he ever wants to go. But stay down? . . . Not Tom Izzo. Not Michigan State. Not when hard work and teamwork count.

That's the greatest glory of all.